WENDELL WILLKIE

Fighter for Freedom

WENDELL WILLKIE .

Fighter for Freedom

ELLSWORTH BARNARD

NORTHERN MICHIGAN UNIVERSITY PRESS
MARQUETTE, MICHIGAN

Library of Congress Catalog Card Number 66-19668

Printed in U.S.A.

THE BOOK CONCERN, *Printers*, Inc.
HANCOCK, MICHIGAN

FOR MARY

Acknowledgments

Many persons have helped, during many years, in the making of this book. Specific debts are acknowledged in the notes; here I offer a general statement of my gratitude—not least to those who have passed beyond the reach of words. That I do not fill a page with names does not mean that I have forgotten the heart-warming friendliness with which many people responded to the questions of an obscure seeker for information about an almost forgotten man.

Some individuals, however, it is proper to name. First, I am grateful to Mrs. Wendell Willkie and Philip H. Willkie for their encouragement and cooperation, especially in making available to me Willkie's private correspondence and permitting me to quote from it without restriction. No less generous was Robert T. Willkie, who shared unstintingly his rich store of recollections of his brother, their parents, and the family background—often in words that it would have been impertinent to change. And before their deaths the other brothers, Fred and Edward, added vivid details and illuminating insights.

In putting together the complicated story of Willkie's years with Commonwealth & Southern, I have been particularly indebted to Granville Bourne, who was helpful in many ways. Concerning Willkie's last years, his most intimate associate, Lem Jones, spoke to me without reserve. And another personal friend, Joseph Barnes—the author, also, of an unjustly neglected biography—has been an unfailing source of encouragement and information.

Equally great is my debt to a number of libraries and their staffs. Individual persons have in a few instances ignored or brushed off my requests for information, but I have met unfailing courtesy and helpfulness at every library in which I have needed to work: the Elwood Public Library, the Akron Public Library, the New York Public Library, the Library of Congress, the Roosevelt Memorial Library, and the Libraries of Amherst College, Bowdoin College, the University of Chicago, Indiana University, and the University of Massachusetts. I ought also to include the Reference Department of the Akron *Beacon Journal.*

In addition, I am grateful to the Director of the Roosevelt Library, Herman Kahn, for permission to quote without restriction from unpublished letters of Franklin D. Roosevelt and other documents, as well as from Roosevelt letters previously published.

Letters written by other persons are used by permission of the writers, or their executors, when they could be reached with a reasonable effort.

In other instances, I can only hope that the writers or their heirs, should they ever read this book, will approve the use to which the quotations have been put.

My thanks are also due to the following publishers for permission to use somewhat extensive quotations from the books named: Harper and Row, Samuel Rosenman's *Working with Roosevelt* and Robert E. Sherwood's *Roosevelt and Hopkins;* Simon and Schuster, Joseph Barnes's *Willkie* and Wendell Willkie's *One World* and *An American Program;* Viking Press, Walter White's *A Man Called White.*

I am similarly indebted to the editors or publishers of the following periodicals for permission to quote at some length from the articles named, all but one of which are by Willkie: *The Atlantic Monthly,* "Brace Up, America!"; *Fortune,* "We the People"; *The New Republic,* "Fair Trial"; *Reader's Digest,* "The Faith That Is America"; *The Saturday Evening Post,* "Idle Money, Idle Men" and "The Case for the Minorities" (Copyright 1937 and 1942, Curtis Publishing Company); *Harper's Magazine,* "Wendell Willkie, Man of Words" by Fred Rodell.

Brief quotations from many sources have been introduced without specific permission under the doctrine of "fair use"; and it is only fair in return to acknowledge that these have been indispensable to the realization—as far as it has been realized—of the aim of this work.

Various editorial chores have been performed by friends and colleagues, and for their aid, also, I am grateful. Among them I ought to name Roy Heath, Director of the Northern Michigan University Press, who has been unflagging in his enthusiasm for the book and in his efforts to get it into print.

For many years it seemed that I might involuntarily achieve what must now be almost a unique distinction—the completion of a major research project without the financial blessing of some foundation. But President Edgar L. Harden of Northern Michigan University offered me a modest grant which it would have been ungrateful not to accept. It was also through his good offices that the Northern Michigan University Foundation assumed the risk of financing publication of a work on which many commercial publishers and several prestigious university presses had cast a cold eye.

My greatest debt is acknowledged in the dedication.

Table of Contents

Introduction

In this book my primary aim has been to record, once and for all, the essential facts in the life of Wendell Willkie. Granting that there is a place for the kind of biography in which the facts are embroidered by imagination, my own preference is for what can be documented. Moreover, the facts need at this point to be documented, as they have not been in previous biographies. I have therefore been free with notes. With the exception of one small group of items, I have put no words into any person's mouth without telling who heard him say them; I have related no episode or anecdote without telling where I heard or read it; I have quoted no printed statement by or about Willkie without telling where the reader can find it. The very few exceptions are things told me by persons who (as the notes will indicate) did not wish to be named as the source, but which seem to me too important to omit.

Those who would find the notes tedious do not have to read them.

Allied to this distaste for undocumented assertions is a prejudice against unproved and unprovable suppositions as to causes and motives. The fact is that we know next to nothing about why people are what they are or do what they do. Heredity and environment of course count for something; moralists insist—rightly, in my judgment—that within limits human beings are free to shape their own lives; and there is also an argument for Divine Grace, as the only means of coping with the mystery of the uniqueness of each human being. My own notion is that the two great forces in human affairs, collectively and individually, are personalities and ideas; but the effect of these also is imponderable.

So I will stick to the facts and let the reader interpret them as he wishes, for the facts themselves are elusive enough. When we try to get *behind* the great events that were visible to all the world—Willkie's nomination at Philadelphia, his defeat in the election, his world tour, his crushing loss in the Wisconsin primary— we move in a world of shadows, where the "facts" are not the things that happened but people's *statements about* what happened. Willkie's own memory, it should be said, was far from infallible in recalling the events of his early life.

A responsible biographer therefore believes nothing without reserve—

nothing that he hears, nothing that he reads, until it is validated by other sources or in other ways.

Such validation is mainly of two sorts. First, one may simply consult all the sources possible, accepting what is agreed on by the majority and rejecting what is not. But in treating a contemporary subject it is impossible to go to *all* the sources; and many will feel, besides, that there ought to be some criterion of truth besides mere quantity of testimony. This second criterion is consistency. As a biographer reads and listens and reflects, the image of his subject becomes more substantial and sharply defined, acquires more and more a seemingly independent identity. The time comes when any detail can be referred to this image and accepted or rejected according to whether or not it fits.

It is true, of course, that no person is totally consistent in his behavior—that in particular situations he may rise above or fall below his usual level. But the very notion of *character* involves a permanent pattern of life—the knowledge that what a person did yesterday will not be contradicted by what he does today, and that what he is today, he will be tomorrow.

And now, why is it worth while to tell the story of Wendell Willkie and get it straight? "Who *was* Wendell Willkie?" has been the common question of college students to whom I have mentioned the writing of this book.

The answer is that he was the man who, during the last four years of his life, in a decisive period of American history, had a greater influence on the mind of the American people and the policy of the American government than any other person except Franklin Roosevelt. And he exercised this influence despite the fact that he held no office and spoke for no organization—except, briefly, the Republican party. He exercised it by sheer ability and force of character.

For one thing, he embodied, as the story will show, the nation's legendary virtues: a carefree superiority to mean and petty motives; an unaffected sympathy for the underdog; reckless courage linked with ebullient energy; eagerness to enter, and unwillingness to quit, a fight in a good cause. His appeal also lay in his almost infallible sense of the dramatic moment, his unerring gift for the symbolic act that clarified the issue for millions of confused but well meaning fellow Americans.

And this was reinforced simply by the rightness of his judgments, which time after time were confirmed by the course of events, until all his utterances took on the character of prophecy. And finally, there was the homage paid—in part through hatred—to an integrity that, inevitably tarnished in the campaign of 1940, was thereafter all but absolute.

Why, then, has he been forgotten? Here, too, there are several answers. One is that he was betrayed by the course of history. As during the first years of his fame events worked for him, so at the end of his life and since his death they have turned against him. The cold war with Russia and China has made his vision of "one world," which he taught millions of Americans to believe in, seem impossibly remote; and men of little faith, trapped in a nightmare which for the moment seems the only reality, prefer to forget their former dream.

Another answer is that his achievement was to a large extent intangible. No memorable legislative act or military victory, no historic "plan" or "doctrine," is associated with his name. The revolution in Republican ideas on foreign policy that he initiated almost single-handed is credited to Senator Vandenberg (once a vehement critic of Willkie's internationalist philosophy) and President Eisenhower (whose allegiance the Republicans could never have gained without this revolution). Those who still fight for the causes he espoused are often unaware of the continuing impetus of his advocacy.

And finally, there has been a tacit conspiracy on the part of both major parties (against whom, as Roscoe Drummond rightly says, he was "perpetually campaigning") to have his name forgotten. The Democrats naturally do not wish it remembered that the Republican party was ever led by a genuine liberal, who in some aspects of his social philosophy was bolder than Roosevelt himself; and the Republican Old Guard (whose continued dominance in the party was dramatically demonstrated by the nomination of Senator Goldwater) are still more eager to have this fact forgotten.

Nevertheless, Willkie's story is a great story; and though it has been partly told before, sometimes well and sometimes badly, no retelling can fail to appeal to those who are more concerned with America's past and future than with their immediate personal affairs.

The appeal of the story is perhaps three-fold. First, it must interest all who are students, whether amateur or professional, of the great game of American politics—especially the politics of Presidential elections. Second, the story throws light on two crucial issues, not yet settled, in American history: the relation between private and governmental activity in the economic sphere; and, more important, the relation between the United States and the other nations of the world (a relation whose extremes were dramatized for the American people by the phrases "America First" and "One World"). And third, it is a human story: the drama of a unique individual who asserted his right to free thought in the full sense of the phrase, who was not afraid to change his mind, and who at all costs defended his convictions against the unreflective followers of habit, tradition, or the main chance. In such a struggle, the issues may fade, but the drama remains undimmed.

Let me add, to conclude this introduction, a personal comment.

In a fruitless application for a foundation fellowship, many years ago, I wrote: "I am asked to state my 'ultimate purpose as a scholar or artist.' In the first place, the writing of this book is an act of personal devotion to a man whom I admired more than I have admired any other person in American public life during our time. . . . In the second place, I should like to advance the ideas that Willkie fought for, in whatever small way I can. They were, on the whole, the *right* ideas."

This statement stands.

I

Background and Beginnings

1

Wendell Willkie was born in Elwood, Indiana on February 18, 1892. Elwood today is a pleasant town of 12,000 in central Indiana, in the midst of level fields of rich black soil, on which corn, soy beans, truck crops, and alfalfa thrive. Here and there the straight horizon is broken by groups of farm buildings or by rectangular upthrusts of trees: oaks, maples, hickories, locusts—the foliage lush and green in early June, drooping and dusty in August. In spring and early summer, from the open fields, come the prolonged, piercingly sweet notes of meadowlarks and the husky trills of red-winged blackbirds; from the hedges and thickets, the ringing calls—cheery or plaintive according to one's mood—of bob-whites; from the trees along the streets and the shrubbery about the well kept houses, the liquid whistles of cardinals. Life is unhurried, peaceful; more responsive to the cycle of the seasons than to the unpredictable activities of Wall Street or Washington, or the revolutions in human affairs in other lands, though news of these is brought almost instantaneously to the television screens that, like the rest of America, the inhabitants of Elwood watch.

But in 1892 the picture was different. Fewer years then separated Elwood from the time when its site was untouched wilderness than separate that date from this. The first settler in the township is thought to have arrived about 1830. The opening of a crossroads store in 1852 marked the birth of Elwood. In 1856 the arrival of the first railroad, known as the Panhandle (now a part of the Pennsylvania system) spurred the growth of the settlement—but not much, for when the village was incorporated in 1872 (the year a second railroad—now the Nickel Plate—passed through it), the population was less than 400. Fifteen years later it was still well under 1,000.

The year 1887, however, brought a change as radical and rapid as it had been unforeseen. The discovery of natural gas in the area began a boom that for a dozen years filled the minds of many citizens with dreams of illimitable greatness. Factories sprang up. Workers flocked in. When Elwood was incorporated as a city in 1891, the population was past the 3,000 mark.[1] In 1893, on April 14, the Elwood *Free Press* announced the official population as 9,029.

Local industries mentioned in the May 26 issue include the Tin Plate

Works, then employing 300 workers (of which more later), the Window Glass Works, the Bottle Works, the McCloy Lamp Flue Works (the McBeth Lamp Flue Works, employing 500, had burned on January 21, but were immediately rebuilt), and the "immense [Akron Steel] Forge Works," which were to be in operation within ninety days. There was also the Diamond Plate Glass Works, which had been closed indefinitely the week before, after being taken over by the Pittsburgh Plate Glass Company.

One result of this industrial boom was a semi-frontier culture, ebullient and unrestrained. The statement in a *Life* story on Willkie that Elwood at this time "boasted forty saloons and forty bawdy houses" may be exaggerated but a random sampling of the local press during the nineties brings to light stories of frequent raids on various "resorts." For instance, the *Daily Record* of January 6, 1896 records that "seven shameless women" from the resort of Alice Shaffer "near the Post Office" spent the night in jail. The next day fines were imposed, which were paid by the madam, after which, presumably, all returned to business as usual.

Saloon keepers were even more leniently treated. The weekly *Free Press* complained on September 25, 1896, that "the liquor license seems to have received but little attention. Several saloon keepers are behind in their payments and one man has not paid for a license he took out almost a year ago." Gambling also flourished; and many people thought it did so with the sanction of the police. On January 15, 1900, the *Daily Record* reported a fruitless raid on three gambling rooms; obviously the proprietors had been tipped off.

In general, what strikes the present day reader most forcibly, despite our own worries about crime and juvenile delinquency, is the commonness of violence. Hardly a day passed when someone was not shot or stabbed in Elwood or a neighboring community. Robberies and burglaries, likewise, were of almost nightly occurrence. Rape and seduction were nearly as common (paternity suits were frequent), as well as sex crimes against young girls. If Dr. Kinsey had done his research fifty years earlier, his conclusions might have been even more sensational.

As one might expect, something of this violence carried over into religion. The harvest looked plenteous and the laborers were not few. Revivalist preachers were even more popular then than now. The *Daily Record* announced on March 11, 1893: "As soon as the weather becomes settled, Brother Bushong with a full corps of attendants will set up a tent meeting here in Elwood. It will be a regular pentecostal service, saint and sinner will get his dues. Elwood will be shaken up from center to circumference. Brother Bushong is a real dynamite striker. He brings them."

The established churches offered milder exercises in piety, which were possibly less popular. The *Daily Press* on January 23, 1893, informed its readers: "The Epworth League at the M. E. church was fairly well attended and was led by Mr. Duggins, who recounted the trials and pleasures of a Christian's life as exemplified in himself."

The dominant cultural crudity was matched in many respects by the physical conditions. The streets were mostly unpaved, and in spring or during a heavy rain (as on the day in 1892 when the Tin Plate Works were dedicated, in the presence of Eastern financiers and industrialists, with a speech by Governor William McKinley of Ohio), they turned into sloughs of black muck. It was Herman Willkie, Wendell's father, who in early 1893 circulated a petition calling for the paving of Anderson Street between the Panhandle and the L. E. and W. railroads (the main north-south street in the center of town). The *Free Press* on March 30 announced, "The petition is being largely signed and the street will be paved." Similarly, flush toilets and bathtubs were almost unheard of until after 1900. The backyard privy was nearly universal (and tempted boisterous youths to overturn it or carry it off).

The general rawness of this society was not mitigated or balanced by a class, or even a group, of relatively wealthy families desirous of emulating the manners and taste of the elite of New York or Boston or Philadelphia. The rapidity of the city's industrial expansion made it necessary for the larger factories to be financed almost wholly by outside capital. Elwood profited from the wages of the workers, which were relatively high, but the profits of the owners went elsewhere.. There were no "first families."

Elwood's cultural crudity *was* mitigated, however, by the efforts of a group of middle class citizens who had an eagerness for learning, an urge to self-improvement, and a desire to diffuse culture throughout the community. In this group were Willkie's father and mother.

This desire for uplift found a nation-wide expression in the Chatauqua movement, of which one phase was the organization of "Chatauqua Literary and Scientific Circles." According to the Elwood *Free Press* of April 28, 1893, the local group, known as the "Hyperion Circle," met every Wednesday afternoon at the home of one of the members, of whom there were about twenty. All subscribed to the *Chatauquan,* a periodical published especially for such groups, and each week a particular topic was chosen for discussion, with some member designated as leader. Sometimes this office was filled by the president, Rev. T. M. Gould; but "another educated, well-informed gentleman, Herman F. Willkie, often leads." (He was also vice president.)

A similar opportunity was offered by the University of Chicago through its extension courses. In a letter to Willkie after the 1940 election, a Mrs. Jamison of St. Louis recalled: "In the nineties I knew your father and mother very well. My husband at that time was pastor of the Elwood Presbyterian Church. A group of kindred spirits—the Willkies, Jamisons,

Mrs. Taylor [?—name illegible]—took a course in Chicago University extension work. We would attend the class early and stay late to enjoy the conversation."[2]

2

Wendell Willkie was the son of Herman Francis Willkie and Henrietta Trisch Willkie.

Both of Willkie's parents were persons of extraordinary ability and character, who typified the strength that America has always received from those who have sought a better life within its borders. The grandparents were all born in Germany, and all left mainly because they desired a freer life.

The first to arrive in America was Lewis Treusch (later Trisch), who was brought by his parents in 1830, when he was a year old.[3] The journey seems to have been connected with the first wave of political liberalism in Europe which broke against the barriers of "legitimacy" set up at the Congress of Vienna by the reactionary victors over Napoleon, and which resulted in the overthrow of the Bourbon King of France in 1830 and the passage of the Reform Bill of 1832 in England. The family settled first at York, Pennsylvania, and five years later moved to Bucyrus, Ohio, where the father was first a blacksmith and wagon-maker and later a farmer.[4]

Next, as a result of the second revolutionary wave, in 1848, came Julia von Hessen-Lois, whose father, Jacob, a member of the minor aristocracy, had been dangerously active in politics.[5] The family went first to England. Later Julia made her way to America as a lady's maid.[6] A few years later, in Warsaw, Indiana, she met and married Lewis Trisch, who had moved there in 1852.[7] Thence the young couple moved to Fort Dodge, Kansas. But living in constant contact with slavery (this was the time when "bleeding Kansas" was the stage for a rehearsal of the Civil War) and with the fanaticism that it engendered, was intolerable, if not actually perilous, and they returned to Warsaw.[8] Here the husband earned a comfortable living at his father's trade of blacksmithing (he made many wagons for the Union Army during the Civil War),[9] besides editing the local newspaper on the side,[10] until his death in 1873.[11] He left two sons, who do not figure in the Willkie story; a daughter Jennie, who became a physician (in those days an almost unheard-of achievement for a woman); and another daughter, Henrietta, who married Herman Willkie.

The Willkie branch of the family had also come from Germany. (The name had been spelled "Willcke" or "Willeke.") In fact, Willkie's father, Herman Francis Willkie, had been born there, in Aschersleben, Saxony in 1857, the son of Joseph William and Minna Mathilda (Breitschuh)

Willkie. The father first went to America in 1858 and returned to get his wife and three children, of whom Herman was the second, in 1861.[12] Herman later used to tell his sons that his earliest memory was of Union soldiers marching through the streets of New York and of being told by his parents—to allay fears associated with some vague earlier episode in which he had toddled in front of drilling German soldiers and been threatened—that these "were 'good' soldiers who were going to fight for people and not for kings."[13]

William Willkie had been a coppersmith, but in Indiana he settled on a farm near Fort Worth. "He was not a good farmer"; his wife bore him five more children and died soon after; and altogether, the family seems to have lived for a time a rather harsh and bare existence. Later, William Willkie let a son-in-law run the farm, and make money, while he entertained himself with reading, writing, and playing the accordion. Nevertheless, he seems to have been widely respected. His nine-year-old grandson Robert was impressed by the mile-long procession of carriages at his funeral.[14]

Herman Willkie shared his father's love of reading and his independence, but his restless energy would never have let him indulge in so leisurely a life. By hard work and self-denial he managed a year at Valparaiso College (at a total cost of $111.50), some time at Taylor College, and enough more at Fort Wayne College (alternating teaching and study) to get his degree in 1884. He then became Superintendent of Schools in Milford, Indiana. Here he met Henrietta Trisch, who was teaching there after completing a short course at Terre Haute Normal School, and married her early in 1885.[15] The wedding took place at Fort Wayne "in the parlor of the College and the ceremony was performed by Dr. Yokum, the President of the school."[16]

After three years of teaching at Lagro, Indiana, Herman Willkie secured a position as Superintendent of Schools in Elwood, and moved there with his family in 1888, the year after the discovery of natural gas. Until that time the schools of the community had been rather haphazardly organized: as the new superintendent commented, "pupils were not classified into grades, but classified themselves more as to size and age than as to ability."[17] He set up a system of grades and also inaugurated a two-year high school course. In this he taught algebra, arithmetic, and Latin; an assistant taught the other courses.

Herman Willkie was evidently a successful organizer and teacher. The respect in which he was held by his students is shown by his successful institution of a kind of honor system, by which the students of the high school were left alone one hour a day so that he might supervise the teaching in the lower grades, and were put on their honor not to misbehave.

The law, however, was more attractive than teaching. While carrying on his work in the schools, he studied law, and was admitted to the bar September 25, 1890.[19] He resigned as Superintendent of Schools, and henceforth his law practice was the most important of the many activities which made him, from the time of his arrival until his death in 1930, one of Elwood's most prominent citizens.

Herman Willkie was a great lawyer, and had he been more single-minded in his ambitions, he could have gained a fortune and perhaps a national reputation. (Until his father's death, Wendell always consulted him about an important case.)[20] As his son Fred saw it, there were three main factors in his mastery of his profession. The first was that he knew the law; he was a genuine student of it, read widely, and remembered what he read. (Robert adds: "I never knew him to get caught on procedure.") The second was that, although he held strong convictions, he always was objective in the analysis of a case; he could see how it would look to other people, and therefore seldom went wrong in choosing his line of attack or defense or in making an appeal to the jury.[21] Finally, he worked hard preparing his cases. When Fred, as a small boy, asked, "Why do you win all your cases?" his father answered, "I don't win them *all.* But I win *many,* because I prepare them, and if I don't think a client has a good case, I try to persuade him to withdraw it."[22] Here is obviously a fourth quality, namely, his honesty with his clients.

His courtroom technique was also skillful. When cross-examining a witness, he would seem casual and easy-going until he had him where he wanted him.[23] And in addressing the jury, he not only spoke eloquently and with conviction, but he could toss in appropriate quotations from Shakespeare, the Bible, or *McGuffey's Reader* in a way that ordinary people (who perhaps thought almost all of them to be Biblical) found tremendously impressive.[24] Possibly it was this eloquence and aggressiveness that caused him to be referred to sometimes as "Hell-Fire Willkie."[25]

One naturally asks why, with these great abilities, he remained a small-town lawyer. One answer is that he was an inveterate crusader. "I do not think he was ever really happy," his oldest son has written, "without a cause."[26] And his causes were often unpopular. In a town where drunkenness, gambling, and prostitution were prevalent, while the municipal government and most of the town's respectable citizens looked the other way, Herman Willkie spoke out persistently and vigorously, defending temperance and denouncing sin. (In the Willkie home there was no drinking, smoking, dancing, or card-playing.[27] Wendell once told an Akron audience: "I was brought up in a home so strict about dancing that I never learned to dance a step," and added that he still thought it was "wrong to dance on Sunday.")[28]

This activity gained him many enemies, few friends, and no financial reward. Typical is a story of his complying with the request of the city attorney for aid in prosecuting a saloon-keeper who, although a chronic violator of the law, had always escaped punishment. This time the offender was convicted; but Herman Willkie refused the offered payment—as he had refused an offer of $200 to defend the saloon-keeper.[29] On another occasion, during a fight over "local option," the leader of the "wet" faction, Pat Bradley, first tried to buy his support, and then his neutrality, but Herman Willkie declined; and pointing to his four sons, who were present, he declared, "There is the reason."[30]

There was, however, nothing fanatical or self-righteous in his crusading. He had the saving ability to see and judge people as individuals. There was even one saloon-keeper, a German named Schaefer, for whom he acted as attorney because he liked him personally, and believed him to be honest; and he performed a similar service for a former "hired girl" in the Willkie household who became a successful madam of a house in Anderson and insisted that he handle the legal details involved in her investments in real estate. (He defended himself to his wife by saying that "he appreciated her confidence, it was good clean business, and if he started to turn down business because of the person, he was not living up to professional standards.")[31]

Again, unlike many crusaders against "Vice," he was fundamentally kind-hearted. Soon after being admitted to the bar he was made a justice of the peace; and a local "columnist" told how a woman named Bertha Budson, having been fined $19.50 in "'Squire Willkie's court" for assault and battery, and having failed to pay, was ordered to jail. "Constable Trabue . . . had his prisoner at the depot . . . waiting for the train, when the 'Squire came along, noticed the pitiful look of the woman and the tears flowing down her cheeks." So he ordered her released and gave her another day to raise the money.[32] The sequel is not recorded.

Another little episode also reveals his character in a kindly light. Calvin Sizelove, the small son of a neighbor, had a customer on his paper route who got behind in his payments to the extent of about seventy cents, and always found some excuse for not paying. Calvin had only vague ideas about the function of a lawyer, but he was friends with the Willkie children and shared their admiration for their father, so he asked Herman Willkie for advice. The latter listened gravely and said he would write the man a letter. Calvin got his money.[33]

This fundamental kindness was naturally associated with sympathy for the underdog, and as a rule his clients were the poor rather than the rich, and the unions (when labor was only beginning to organize) rather than the corporations. Another source of business which did not always bring big fees was the damage suits brought by workers in factories or on the railroads. In the days before workmen's compensation laws, such suits were the workers' only recourse, and Herman Willkie always accepted them, although the cards were stacked against the plaintiff, in that if there had been any "contributory negligence" on his part, no matter how slight, he could get no damages.

But what really kept him from professional eminence was the diversity of his interests: in politics, in religion, in business ventures, and above all in his family.

Herman Willkie was of course a Democrat, "and there never was a time when he did not help with the organization, contribute money and . . . go out to the rural schoolhouses in the evening to 'carry the gospel' and help organize for the party. He often made as many as fifteen or twenty such speeches."[34] (The *Free Press* on October 9, 1896 reported that at a meeting for Bryan in Orestes, "Perry Behymer and 'Squire Willkie both made strong speeches, which were received with enthusiastic applause.")[35] But he was too much of an individualist to be a party "regular"; once, for instance, "when he was satisfied that both the Republicans and Democrats were permitting gambling and women he supported the Socialist ticket"—which won. This "did not endear him to the organization."[36]

Another preoccupation was religion, both as an intellectual pursuit and as a force in community affairs. His father had been a Catholic, and although his mother had been Protestant, Herman had been brought up in his father's faith. He broke away, however, at some time before reaching manhood; probably in large part because of a local priest's intolerance of other faiths. He "once confided that he had joined the Methodist Church to see if all those tales [about Protestant depravity] were really true of some of the nice people he knew."[37] Probably, also, his intellectual independence was too great to accept the Church's claim to authority over its members in matters of faith and morals. At any rate, "he couldn't resist [buying] books on religion and theology."[38] He had the reputation of knowing more about the Bible than anyone else in Elwood, including the ministers,[39] and he would bring armfuls of books to the adult Sunday School class that he taught.[40]

This class eventually became a source of dissension, for "he seems to have offered more of Shakespeare and ethics than of the Bible at times."[41] Furthermore, "he did not adhere strictly to the Methodist doctrines and the class became definitely interdenominational to the extent that there was greater attendance at his class than at the sermon delivered by the parson."

There were other difficulties, also. Besides being superintendent of the Sunday School, and teaching in it, he was a trustee of the church and active in all its affairs. As elsewhere, he was often on the minority side in an argument; and no arguments can be more bitter than those between factions in a church. For instance, he clashed with other members of the church on the issue of "bringing 'evangelists' into town because he always claimed that the 'converts' were the same every year and the expense of the special campaign put the church in the hole."[42] Another controversy concerned the building of a new church, larger and more expensive than Herman Willkie thought the group could afford. Having been overruled, he still "contributed at least twice what he should have and really paid it while the greater number of the others fell far short." He also signed a $500 note for the church, which in the end he had to pay.[43]

Under these circumstances, when appealed to by the holder of the mortgage on the church, who had "not been able to secure payment nor satisfactory assurances in regard to it," Herman Willkie felt justified in making vigorous representations to the other church leaders. Rebuffed, he agreed to file suit. "This brought the desired result. The church aroused itself and paid off the mortgage." Another result was that Mr. and Mrs. Willkie left the Methodist church and joined the Presbyterian, to which Mrs. Willkie had originally belonged.[44]

Herman Willkie remained a Presbyterian, though an increasingly liberal one. His Christianity was less a matter of doctrine than of an attitude toward life—never more clearly revealed, perhaps, than in this picture of him in his last illness, given by Paul Harmon, who had been almost a member of the family. He was dying of cancer, slowly and painfully, and "usually one doesn't like to visit a close friend who is dying when both of you know it. This wasn't the case with Mr. Willkie. When I visited Elwood I could hardly wait to see him . . . he would say, 'I've been waiting to see you. I've been reading this book and I want to know what you think about the conclusions of the author.' Then would ensue a spirited discussion, with Julia, who was taking care of him, maybe chiming in from the kitchen where she was working and a great time was had by all of us. Never a word about his illness or how bad he felt . . . he didn't have the time to discuss such an unprofitable and uninteresting matter."[45]

It is a little odd that, along with being an altruistic crusader and a sincere Christian, he should have aspired to be a successful business man and make a fortune. Soon after coming to Elwood he began investing in real estate. The workers in the new factories needed homes, and Herman Willkie built at least two hundred houses,[46] "sold [them] on payments and endorsed the notes to the banks."[47] (He had a taste for carpentry himself, "doing the actual carpenter work on the house at 16th and North B Streets, where he lived until 1891,"[48] as well as much of the work on the large house at 19th and North A Streets, which the family moved into in June, 1900.) He also built the "Willkie Block" in the business section, plans for which were described in enthusiastic detail by the Elwood *Free Press* of March 10, 1893. The cost of the lot was given as $4400 (the present equivalent would be many times greater) and the estimated cost of the building as $11,000. In addition, he invested in "a brick yard where the clay ran out, a sawmill, a canning factory," and other enterprises.[49]

None of his projects panned out. The panic of 1893, the gradual failure of the gas supply after 1900, the policies of the great corporations that owned the larger factories and opened or closed them without regard to local conditions, not only prevented Herman Willkie from getting rich, but on occasion left him deeply in debt. When the workers were unable to pay for their houses, he became responsible to the banks. "For four or five years he kept a set of bankruptcy papers prepared and when the banks pressed him too hard he would ask for time to work out the situation, warning them that if they refused, he would have to file. He was at least $25,000 in the hole, but he finally did work it out, although it took five or six of his top earning years."[50] (Part of his losses he retrieved by moving some of the houses out of town and selling them to farmers for use as barns or small tool sheds.)[51]

Despite these losses, he was able to raise a large family in what was then regarded as moderate comfort. But at his death in 1930 he was, financially, where he had been forty-two years earlier, when he moved to Elwood.

Herman Willkie's character and activities were bound to arouse adverse criticism, and even enmity, so that during much of his life in Elwood he was a controversial figure. (His youngest son, Edward, remembered being involved more than once in fights on his father's behalf,[52] and doubtless this was also true of the older sons.) For one thing, the large Catholic population was inclined to view him with hostility as an apostate, although during his campaign against the Ku Klux Klan in the twenties, "he and Father Biegel were almost intimate friends."[53] On the other hand, his unorthodoxy and outspokenness offended many Methodists, some of whom took revenge by accusing him (though not openly) of misappropriating church funds.[54] Similarly, his political independence, his crusades against "vice," and his activity in behalf of organized labor aroused the distrust, if not the enmity, of many "solid citizens."

Finally, his aggressive tactics in many legal cases where he was on the unpopular side gave rise to the charge that he was a "crooked lawyer."[55] The exact basis for this charge remains vague, but some light may be shed on it by the account of a lecture that he gave to an Indiana University Law School class. It was the professor's custom in this class to have a series of weekly lectures by practicing lawyers, and on January 8, 1912, Herman Willkie was invited to speak. His subject was "Practice vs. Ethics," and he warned his hearers that "ideas of ethics acquired in the classroom" would lead a young lawyer "into many close places where the good of his cause must be furthered by a departure from the ethical standpoint. He advised the 'Laws' not to let a small point of ethics stand in the way of their cases. ('When you're fighting the devil, you have to use his own methods. If you're fighting the railroad, don't be afraid to go out and get perjured evidence, because you can be sure *they* will.')[56] His address was one of the most humorous ever given to the 'Laws.' His energetic method of presenting his argument caused them to believe that he had always practiced his advice which was, 'Be a scrapper. Do not be a sissy. Go in to win and do it.'"

After all, however, his enemies seem to have been a minority, for in 1922 his fellow citizens entrusted to him the office of City Attorney, in which he served two terms. Their evident judgment was that the dislike and distrust with which he was regarded by some of the people of Elwood, though understandable, were undeserved, and that he was a man of exceptional integrity and good will.

His wife, Henrietta Trisch Willkie, was perhaps his equal in intellect, energy, and force of character. She shared his desire for intellectual betterment, approved his crusades against vice, and ultimately became his law partner.

Together, Herman and Henrietta Willkie, besides pursuing the cultural "do-it-yourself" program outlined by Chatauqua and availing themselves of the University of Chicago's extension courses, accumulated a private library of between five and six thousand volumes[57]—a fabulous number for the time and place. In addition, wishing to extend to the community the opportunities that they enjoyed, they took the lead, at the beginning of 1899, in setting up a public library. Herman Willkie drafted the articles of incorporation of the Elwood Library Association; both of them solicited subscriptions at ten dollars a share; both were among the first trustees and retained this office for many years; and Mrs. Willkie was the first permanent secretary of the library board.[58]

Her legal career began in 1897, after the birth of her fifth child, Edward, when she applied for admission to the bar, and was admitted over the strong objections of some members[59] who evidently believed that woman's place was in the home. It has been suggested that she was the first woman admitted to the bar in Indiana, although apparently nobody has checked the records. Although Robert intimates that her determination to practice law was due less to an interest in it than to a desire to outdo other members of her sex, she appears to have been moderately active. The *Daily Record* for January 23, 1900 mentions that "Mr. and Mrs. H. F. Willkie . . . were among the Elwood contingent at Anderson today." (Anderson was the county seat.) Edward recalled that some persons chose his mother rather than his father to handle their business.[60] And it is said that on one occasion she opposed her husband in court and won the case.[61]

This triumph must have given her great satisfaction, for if she had one dominant trait, it was her competitive spirit. At her death her sons chose as her epitaph "She was driven by an indomitable will"—and they felt that to be strictly accurate they should have added "to conquer."[62] Robert gives a brilliant thumbnail sketch of this aspect of her character. "She was smart and able and possessed of unbelievable energy"—although never in good health during the years when she was bearing children. (Yet, "in a day when infant mortality and the rate of miscarriage were high, it was her boast that *she* had never lost any.") "She had absolute belief in herself. She liked to conquer anything from crocheting to law, then she lost interest for there was always something else to conquer. For instance she read 'Chatauqua' until she had a string of buttons; she learned to paint china; she did half a dozen of the thread games and did top work—quilting, drawn thread work, flowers on doilies, knitting and tatting, cutting the patterns and making her own dresses. . . . She could also do a master stroke of cooking when the notion hit her. She was a perfectionist." She also insisted that other people be perfectionists: "it even became hard for us to get a plumber. We boys often mowed other lawns and paid some one else to do our own in order to escape her meticulous supervision."

It is evident, therefore, that Henrietta Willkie was a no less remarkable person than her husband. She lacked, however, his fundamental kind-heartedness. She could, when she chose, be brilliantly witty and entertaining,[63] but as a rule she neither sought nor received the affection of her associates or her family. On the other hand, she was neither possessive nor repressive in her attitude toward her children; in many ways she was tolerant—more than most mothers—of the activities of a "rambunctious lot"[64] of offspring, and she was hospitable to the neighborhood youngsters who made the Willkie home their own.[65]

3

Such parents would hardly provide a conventional upbringing for their children, of whom there were six: Julia, born December 25, 1885; Robert, October 9, 1887; Fred, September 30, 1890; Wendell (named Lewis Wendell), February 18, 1892; Edward, December 25, 1896; and Charlotte, October 24, 1899.

Unconventional, even in that age, was the utter freedom given the children in playtime activities—a freedom that was fully appreciated. "We had," says Robert, "the great thrill of working out things for ourselves. . . . We played marbles—at least twenty different games. There were tops to spin, home-made kites to fly; go-sheepy-go to be played in the evening, and tag in the day. We had a wagon we had assembled from parts we obtained through trading. . . . In the winter we skated and in the summer we went to the swimming hole. . . . We built wigwams and huts. There were always plenty of wooden boxes and barrels at groceries to be had for carrying away. . . . The things you could contrive with them are unbelievable."

The boys' natural ingenuity was aided by the writings of Dan Beard, Boy Scout leader and author of books and magazine articles outlining innumerable do-it-yourself projects. Besides stilts and wagons, they made their own sleds ("the boy who tried to join the gang with a 'boughten' sled was likely to find himself most uncomfortable"); Robert was inspired by a Dan Beard blueprint to take the lead in the classic feat of building a boat in the basement that was too big to get out (a surprising performance by so keen-witted a family) and too well built to take apart; and once—utilizing a windfall provided when the City Council ordered the board sidewalks taken up, following Dan Beard's instructions, and aided by the neighboring McCarels—they built a 125-foot-long roller coaster on which they sold rides at two for a penny.

At other times, inspired by a youthful wanderlust, they would spend a summer day hiking or hitching rides around the countryside. One of these adventures, when Wendell was a small boy, almost had serious consequences. He and Bob, along with Earl McCarel, had walked to "Mudsock" (Dundee), and had caught a ride back on a wagon carrying gas pipe, which had the front and rear axles connected by a long wooden tongue, on which the boys could sit. Ordinarily, the slow pace of the horses made this safe enough; but this time, as they jumped off on nearing home, Wendell tripped and fell, and the rear wheel went over his leg. Robert carried him home, where a doctor found that the bone was not broken; but he carried the scar for the rest of his life.[66]

A more ambitious undertaking, which Bob's boat was to have been the means of carrying out, was to emulate La Salle in his exploration of the Mississippi. On the maps in their geography books they could see that Duck Creek emptied into the White River, the White into the Wabash, the Wabash into the Ohio, and the Ohio into the Mississippi. In the expanding world of boyhood, the desire seems almost instinctive to follow a stream to its source or to its mouth. And even after the fiasco of Bob's boat, Wendell still entertained the dream and tried twice to realize it, on vacation visits to Northern Indiana; once with Ed on the Tippecanoe River and once with Earl McCarel on the Chain O' Lakes. But in each case sandbars and mudbanks weakened their resolution after a few miles and they made an inglorious return on foot.[67]

Such were the pursuits of ordinary days. But though these days were never dull—were far too short, in fact, for all the plans that clamored to be carried out—there were certain holidays that stood out with a special, recurrent brilliance. "There was Decoration Day—not Memorial Day. Everybody went to the cemetery. I was almost sorry that we had nobody in it. The bands, the Elwood Band and the Tin Plate Band, marched and played. The Grand Army of the Republic marched in parades. . . .

"The bands played again on the Fourth of July. Sometimes we had to listen to the oration, but that was not bad. The speaker would make the old eagle scream. He tore apart emperors and potentates of 'decadent' Europe. . . . Then in the evening there were fireworks. Not supervised, professional fireworks from some safely distant spot, but in your own front yard. In this matter Father was always generous. . . . We went to bed without a doubt that we were the chosen people.

"Christmas was not so different except that we used candles instead of the electric lights. There was a disadvantage, however; we all had to go to a Sunday School entertainment and speak a little piece. They always gave us a bag of candy and an orange as a Christmas 'treat.' If you were good you might make two such Sunday School programs and get two bags. We practically always had snow."[68]

This free and easy quality of life encountered relatively few restraints from the parents. The many activities of Mrs. Willkie especially, who under other circumstances might have regimented her household to the last detail, made the dressing and feeding of the family (from the children's point of view) adequate but delightfully casual. From the first of May to the last of September, for instance, they enjoyed the luxury of going barefoot—the delicious feeling of crisp spring grass against the soles of feet imprisoned through the winter, of hot dust or cool mud between wriggling toes. Only on Sundays and at school was this freedom curtailed (most children went barefoot to school, but Mrs. Willkie's pride forbade); only during the nightly foot-washing did its desirability seem doubtful. And above the boys' bare feet, in hot weather, were only knee pants and a shirt buttoned to their top.

The feeding of the family, in those days before advertising had made America vitamin-conscious, was also a relatively simple matter. "When the tribe was all at home Father would go on a buying spree and lay in about thirty bushels of potatoes, twenty bushels of apples, five bushels of Kiefer pears, a hundred pounds of maple syrup, another hundred or so of 'white clover' honey, and fifty pounds or more of sorghum molasses. Not only that—but when fruits such as berries, peaches, cherries, or grapes were ripe Mother canned a standard two hundred quarts and made about fifty pints of jellies and jams. Father bought the fruit. There were also the three and six gallon crocks of mince meat. We children hated to chop that meat, but loved the finished product! Meat was often bought by the side or quarter; otherwise Father brought meat when he came home for a meal." Cured meats were absent because of Herman Willkie's unpleasant memories of his childhood; and vegetables were rare because it was another minor eccentricity that he thought "they made children pot-bellied."[69]

With all this the children were more than satisfied. Nor did they object, after Mrs. Willkie's law practice began to take her away from home (though there was usually a housekeeper), at having to find for themselves an occasional meal,[70] not to mention between-meal snacks. In the latter their friends often shared, since the "new" house with its ample basement was a kind of clubhouse for all the boys and girls in the neighborhood, who trooped in and out at will, casually snatching a banana from the bunch that was always hanging in the basement.

The children, however, did not always escape parental supervision, as Mrs. Willkie herself (who obviously did not lack a sense of humor) later recalled: "One Sunday afternoon, at home, everything suddenly seemed too quiet. . . . Diligent search yielded no children but she thought she heard a noise in the attic. She climbed up the ladder and stuck her head through the hole in the attic floor and there were Bob, Julia, Fred, and Wen playing cards, and about that time Julia said, 'Well, I guess that's my trick,' and Wen replied, 'No it isn't, I'll just take that with my little Jesus.' They had made a deck of playing cards by using the cards they had gotten at Sunday School and of course, Jesus was the joker, he took everything."[71]

Altogether, the Willkie children in their outdoor games and play seem to have followed happily what was then the normal pattern, only with more than common energy and ingenuity. The story, widespread during the 1940 campaign, that they had been the terror of the town made good newspaper copy, but it was untrue.

The story also overlooks their religious upbringing. They went to Sunday School faithfully and took it seriously (despite the card game just described). "Each evening we got down on our knees and said our prayers before going to bed. We may have skipped washing our feet now and then, but not the prayers—kneeling, no matter how cold or sleepy."[72]

The really remarkable part of the young Willkies' upbringing was the emphasis on intellect. Both parents had been teachers; both continued, after entering other careers, to read widely and eagerly, seeking knowledge and ideas for their own sake; and both were ambitious for their children.

Often they would take evenings off from their own activities to help the children with their school work;[73] not taking the easy way of doing the problems themselves, or simply telling the children the answers, but by suggestion and encouragement helping them to find the answers for themselves. The father, especially, was a master of this technique;[74] and he had a gift, in other ways, for making learning fun. He would wake the children in the morning—when this was necessary, for they were a lively lot, and Wendell, especially, "fought the bed,"[75] reluctant to yield to it at night, eager to leave it in the morning—with some ringing quotation from Shakespeare or other classics, especially those in *McGuffey's Reader,* which he "knew by heart."[76] Often the quotation would contain a moral (Ben Franklin was a frequent source) not too subtly worded to impress itself on youthful minds. One favorite was

> Should I let ants and bees be wise
> While I my moments waste?[77]

And in the evening—"every evening when he was home"—he would read to them "from the *Book of Saints,* from *Pickwick Papers,* from *The Sea Wolf,* etc., etc. We would all voluntarily leave the most exciting game of 'Go, Sheepy, Go' to hear him read."[78] And without urging, the children would be eager on their own to read further in the authors to whom they thus were introduced, or to act out dramatic scenes from their works.

At mealtimes the father would encourage them to argue, taking part himself, pointing out fallacies, but always urging them to defend their particular points of view. In this Mrs. Willkie joined (she had perhaps less taste for literature than did her husband, but not for argument, and even when he was teaching the Sunday School class for adults, was always interrupting him),[79] and the whole family would engage with gusto in an intellectual free-for-all. Economics and politics, history and literature, all supplied subjects for furious debate, with contemporary events and persons often taken as the starting point. Bryan vs. McKinley, free silver vs. the gold standard, free trade vs. protective tariffs; Theodore Roosevelt, the Spanish-American War, and American imperialism; big business vs. small, and management vs. labor, as these topics were made vital by the way the great corporations manipulated the local factories—such were the themes on which the young Willkies were encouraged to sharpen their wits. The only recorded occasion when they were awed into silence was when William Jennings Bryan, a personal friend of their father, paid a visit to their home during the 1900 campaign.[80]

Herman Willkie likewise gave his sons lessons in practical economics, which were also exercises in "character building," by encouraging them, even as children, to get vacation jobs and earn money. He did so in part because the money was needed, for, as noted, there were financial ups and downs, and especially when the children were in college, the going was hard and they were naturally expected to earn as much of their expenses as they could.

Wendell's first job, at an early but uncertain age, was driving a cow owned by Mrs. De Hority (a member of one of the town's more prominent families) from a barn near the center of town to a pasture on the outskirts. (An Elwood family friend in 1940 commented on "the Romance of going back to that same woods where you had driven Mrs. De Hority's cows to pasture to make the acceptance speech for the biggest office in the world.")[81] This job he had inherited from Fred.[82] Later the two of them took over from Bob the business of "peddling bills" for a Cleveland advertising agency. "They received two dollars a thousand for delivering matter to the front door of every house in Elwood and three dollars a thousand when delivery was made to the back door. In their moments of idleness the two amused themselves by describing the front and back doors of any house one might mention to the other." One of Wendell's temporary jobs was sorting out the good potatoes from the bad in a lot bought by a local wholesale house. Still another was separating nails from trash in the junk shop of Abe Levi. (Later, when he returned to Elwood briefly to practice law, he straightened out some minor legal matter for Mr. Levi; and still later, when the latter was on a visit to New York, Wendell invited him to the office of Commonwealth & Southern and introduced him to an applauding office force as "my first client.")[83]

But whatever job Wendell or his brothers might undertake, in boyhood or later, they never forgot the lesson of thrift and industry, of the dignity and satisfaction of honest work, which their father had inculcated.

Herman Willkie's greatest lesson to his children, however, the source of his great and lasting influence, lay simply in his being the kind of man he was. The tenderness that Mrs. Willkie could not give her sons and daughters was supplied in double measure by the father. When the children were small, he was sometimes seen pushing one of them in a go-cart along the street, at the same time reading a book.[84] When illness or some less serious childish trouble led the children to waken their parents during the night, it was always the father who went to care for and comfort them. ("I have them during the day; you can have them at night," Henrietta told her husband.)[85] The mother was often impatient —probably not without reason—but the father never lost his temper. When a child had been guilty of some misconduct, he never preached or scolded, but preferred to wait for an occasion when he could point out to the offender quietly and privately why his act was wrong.[86] Or perhaps, when some of the boys would be in a fault-finding mood, criticizing some one or complaining about some alleged unfairness, he would remark: "You boys better get yourselves out on a stump and look at yourselves for a while."[87] At the same time, he was always willing to make allowance for boyish pranks. Once Bob, playing hooky from high school, saw his father coming down the street and ducked into the nearest door, which happened to be a saloon. His father had seen him, however, and that night, in private, he asked for an explanation. It was given and accepted; nothing was said about the absence from school.[88]

His interest in their welfare did not lessen as they grew up. Typical, once more, was the matter of vacation jobs. Shortly before school was out for the summer, he would begin talking unobtrusively about what the boys were going to do during the vacation. When they had decided what they wanted to do, he would (if it involved leaving home) buy each of them a one-way ticket to his destination, along with a pair of new shoes. After that, the boy was on his own. His father simply advised him, "Don't get too friendly with everybody you meet," and asked him to provide an address. To this address he would send long letters which made the recipient feel as if his father had actually been along with him and was commenting on what they had seen and done.[89]

All the boys worshipped their father. "I think most of the important things we did as boys and young men," Robert told a reporter in 1940, "were done with the idea in mind of not letting father down."[90] In the previous year Wendell had written to an Elwood friend, "My father's memory is a religion to me."[91] Often Paul Harmon would tell Wendell, after the latter had become famous: "Don't get too cocky. Your father was twice as big a man as you are." And Wendell would answer soberly, "I know it."[92] Fred and Edward felt much the same.[93] When Herman Willkie died in 1930, the epitaph that his sons had inscribed on his gravestone was: "He devoted his life to his children."

II

Youth

1

It is during his first year in high school, beginning January 29, 1906,[1] that Wendell Willkie emerges as a distinct person. The picture is of a more or less normal adolescent, eager for pranks, loyal to a small group of friends, rebellious against constituted authority. These qualities are evident in his organizing, along with Earl McCarel, Walter Jacobs, and Leonard Spach, a club called "L. T. O. M."—the letters standing for what the members doubtless considered to be a hilarious invention, "Little Turds of Misery."[2]

Beneath a rather aggressive exterior, however, there was a high degree of sensitivity, along with a keen mind—although one not yet awakened. Possessed of a "photographic memory"[3] and (thanks to his upbringing) a measure of intellectual sophistication far greater than that of most of his schoolmates, he nevertheless, during the first year and a half, made a record that was completely undistinguished. The school's marking system included five grades: "E, excellent; G, good; P, passed; C, conditioned; F, failed." There were two marking periods each year. The first year Wendell got two P's in Beginning Latin, a G and a P in Algebra, two P's in Botany and a G and a P in American Literature and Composition. The first semester of his second year showed a P in Caesar, a G in Algebra and Geometry, a P in Ancient History, and a P in Literature and Composition.

The seeming need for discipline may have been one reason why, after half a year, his parents sent him to Culver Military Academy Summer Camp. He had also developed a tendency to stoop, which they hoped a military school would correct.[4] Still another reason was to get out of his mind the project—reminiscent of his plans to float down the Mississippi—of joining his friend George De Hority in a bicycle trip to Washington along the National Road. At Culver, the parents of both boys hoped, "they would settle down."[5]

For Wendell, however, this proved a sorry substitute. He was desperately homesick; he hated the military discipline (which his friend liked); and he suffered from the customary hazing, which he refused to submit to voluntarily but was too weak to resist with success. Night after night he would lie on his bed and cry.

In retrospect, however, the experience apparently did not seem so grim. Certainly Willkie's letter to the officer who was then commandant goes farther than politeness requires: "I enjoyed the time I spent at Culver very much. . . . I have always thought it was the best secondary school in America."[6] But the next summer he refused to go back.

No doubt the experience toughened him, physically and morally. In the fall he played on the class football team—his only recorded participation in organized sport. The team picture shows him with the unruly lock of hair that was to be so famous, above a rather square impassive face that was later to lengthen and become more sensitive, before acquiring the familiar fullness of the last years. The solemnity of his expression, however, is belied by tales of his school pranks. Once he appeared at school with pants legs rolled up to reveal one red stocking and one green one and with his shirtsleeves held up by women's garters of different colors.[7] On other occasions he joined his classmates in such extracurricular activities as hanging the school's skeleton from a nearby tree[8] and painting "E. H. S. '10" in mammoth letters on a towering gas tank.[9]

Proud of this achievement, some of the group joined in putting the class numerals on the sidewalk in front of the school. The principal, an irascible character known as "Mickey" Owens, called together the likely culprits and demanded of each in turn whether he had taken part in the painting. Each of them admitted it until Wendell's turn came; he answered with a firm denial. Owens, furious, challenged the statement; whereupon Wendell retorted, "It wasn't paint; it was shoe polish."[10]

This normal boyish ebullience was accompanied, during his second year in high school, by a normal interest in the opposite sex. Parental religion forbade dancing but not other kinds of parties. Hayrides in the winter, on a large sled drawn by a pair of work horses and covered with a foot or so of hay into which couples could burrow for warmth and a measure of privacy, were especially popular. And not all teen-age girls in Elwood had mothers who, like Ethel Kohlmorgan's, were shocked at the thought of their dating one of the Willkie boys.[11] Eunice Carter, for instance,[12] had Wendell for a partner on her first date (on a hayride) and found him pleasant and well behaved.

Later Wendell "went steady" for a time with Hazel Smith, and this friend too remembers him as an attractive companion, awkward physically, but possessed of an engaging combination of mental alertness and love of fun. She belonged to the Delta sorority, whose members sometimes joined the Betas in parties, often held in the Willkie basement, where someone would play the piano and there would be ice cream.[13]

During the summer vacation, he would spend the evening with Hazel and then be up at four in the morning to drive a bakery wagon on a lengthy route through the city and the surrounding territory, generally bartering part of his employer's products for those of the farmers.[14]

2

This adolescent attachment was accompanied by another and far deeper friendship. During Wendell's second year, Elwood High School acquired a new English teacher, Philip Carleton Bing, known affectionately among his students as "Pat." Young, red-headed, slightly built but bubbling over with intellectual energy that seemed as inexhaustible as his humor, he perceived at once the keenness of the boy's mind and made him aware, as even his parents had not been able to do, of the pleasure of using it.

"He encouraged discussion on all sorts of subjects, not just English." And he was not interested in mere memorization. "He wanted to teach his students to think for themselves."[15] So he was delighted when, for instance, Paul Harmon slyly inquired whether "lawyer" and "liar" were not synonymous, and Wendell delivered an impassioned speech in defense of his father's profession.[16]

This was what Wendell needed, and the new interest in English carried over into his other subjects. During his last two and a half years in high school he received two E's and two G's in Latin, three E's in mathematics, E's in zoology and physics respectively, five E's in English, and five E's in history.[17]

Wendell's enthusiasm for Bing was unbounded and vocal, and the teacher himself could not discourage it. When on one occasion he told the boy flatly that he thought the latter's admiration was too great, Wendell simply reaffirmed his unqualified devotion. "Well, then," returned Bing, "I'll just have to call you my obsequious satellite." Thereafter some of the students referred to Wendell as "O. S."—but without chilling his ardor.[18]

Wendell's hero-worship, however, was not much greater than that of many others of Bing's students. Writing to Willkie after his "Report to the People" following his round-the-world trip in 1942, one of them recalled "our old teacher, 'Pat' Bing.

"How happy, how proud he would have been if he could have heard your timely and to the point address of the evening.

"Two remarks I remember Mr. Bing for were, 'I believe in calling an ace an ace.' . . . 'Make something of yourself.' You certainly have. . . .

"I believe we owe our courage, ability to take it on the chin, our ability to rebound after a beating to the teaching and inspiration given us by our dear teacher, Mr. Bing."[19]

Despite Wendell's brilliance after being aroused by Bing, one or two episodes are remembered that placed him temporarily at the mercy of his classmates, even the least brilliant. Once the English class was discussing *As You Like It,* and Mr. Bing asked if anyone could recite Jacques' speech on "The Seven Ages of Man." Wendell seized the chance to shine. From hearing his father read Shakespeare and from acting out the plays with his brothers and sisters, he knew long passages by heart, and this was one. He started in confidently, "All the world's a stage" and continued easily until he reached the lines, "And first the infant/ Muling and puking in [he meant to say] the nurse's arms," but somehow it came out "in the nurse's eye." The class exploded. Too late he realized what he had said and tried to correct himself. Wave after wave of laughter swept the classroom, until he himself had to join.[20]

His pride had another fall when a debating team of three boys, of which he was captain, met a team composed of two girls, Katherine Henze (the captain) and Eunice Carter, and one boy, Earl Whiteman. The topic was "Resolved: that immigration should be restricted in the United States." Wendell's team upheld the negative, and anticipated an easy victory. The other team, however, buckled down to work—and won. The only person more surprised than they was Wendell. His mouth dropped open, and for a moment almost unique in his career, he was speechless. Then his natural generosity triumphed, and he hastened to offer congratulations.[21]

There were perhaps some students who at times resented Wendell's assurance and aggressiveness, but his sponstaneous friendliness and openheartedness were generally irresistible. When his class, as juniors, gave a banquet in honor of the seniors, it was Wendell who was chosen as toastmaster. And this time he quoted Shakespeare to better effect than before: "Now good digestion wait on appetite, / And health on both."[22]

Mr. Bing's influence did not end in the schoolroom. One evening each week he would invite the boys in his class to join him in his room, where he would light his large curve-stemmed pipe and start them talking about some serious subject.[23] His influence on his students in such extracurricular activities was perhaps hardly less than in the classroom.

3

It was natural for Bing, who took such a personal interest in his students, to wish to bring together the two most brilliant of them. The other was Gwyneth Harry. Gwyneth was two years younger than Wendell, but only half a year behind him in school, and with beauty to match her intelligence. Dark-haired, bright-eyed, fun-loving but capable of deep feeling, she was a girl to arrest the attention of the least romantic schoolboy.

Her family had come from Wales, and her father had been drawn to Elwood by the tinplate industry. The Harrys were middle class—moderately well to do, Episcopalian, inclined to conservatism (one gathers) in their social thinking, and not unconcerned with their social standing. Except for a general interest in books and ideas, they had little in common with the rough-and-ready democracy practiced by the Willkies.

Wendell and Gwyneth had already become acquainted in school and sometimes he asked her to help him with his Latin—whether from a real need for help or from a desire for her companionship. It was Bing, however, who brought him to Gwyneth's home, and encouraged an intimacy that brought Gwyneth, for the next six or seven years, closer to him than was any other person. It also reinforced the new attitude toward school work that Bing had inspired; and it aroused him for the first time to a serious interest in religion.

The approach to religion of Wendell's parents had been primarily rational and moral. Now the boy found that it might also have an esthetic and emotional appeal and that this satisfied some hitherto unrecognized need. And, characteristically, he did not stop half way, by merely becoming a member of the Episcopal Church. To his brothers it seemed that his whole attitude had changed. His habit of swearing, which like many adolescents he had cultivated as a sign of maturity, was abandoned. In his spare time, instead of joining in the normal leisure activities of the other boys, he mowed the church lawn and acted as janitor—without pay, of course, since the church was small and far from rich. He also became the lay reader, and was so deadly serious that Robert, worldly and skeptical after a couple of years at the University, found him "insufferable."[24]

Those who say a boy of sixteen cannot be genuinely in love are mistaken. Instances may be rare, but they do occur, and this was one. Even loyalty to his family meant less to him than his love for Gwyneth. Moreover, this love colored all his boyish dreams of the future; when he talked to Gwyneth about them, they were always of a kind of success that would permit him to offer her, after they were married, every luxury that she might wish to buy. When he left for a summer job in the West (this was in 1909), he pleaded with her, while they walked to the railroad station, to say that she loved him, and the letters that he wrote her during the summer were filled with the same plea.

Yet even a devotion so intense as this did not completely submerge his individualism and love of fun. Gwyneth made a point of being British in ancestry rather than Welsh, and Wendell delighted to tease her with tales of Britain's political sins and with the assertion that if Britain and Germany ever went to war (already their rivalry was apparent), he would fight on the German side. He would also resist her efforts to make him dress more neatly or to be more conventional in his manners (she objected to his habit of eating apples core and all!), arguing vigorously that externals were unimportant. And even with her, he loved argument for its own sake, so that sometimes she was not quite sure which side he was on.

Gwyneth's response to Wendell's passionate attachment is a little hard to define. She was younger than he and had had a more conventional upbringing. She admired and took pleasure in his eager intellect, was touched but sometimes embarrassed by the depth of his devotion, and seems to have retained, unlike her lover, a degree of objectivity in viewing their relationship. Nevertheless, this relationship remained mutually satisfying during the years that led to maturity.[25]

4

Meanwhile there was another trait in Wendell that romance could not subdue—his love of work. Loafing was something that all his life he found impossible. Even during a short vacation from school or college, he would get restless and say to Fred, "We ought to be doing something."[26] And Herman Willkie's determination to put all his children through college made it necessary for them to do all they could (at least during the summer, for Wendell seems not to have worked during the college year, though Robert and Julia did) to earn their expenses.

In the summer of 1908 Wendell, though a youngster of sixteen, undertook to do a man's job in the local Tin Plate Works, the largest of the many factories that had sprung up during the boom days when the supply of natural gas seemed inexhaustible. The boom, however, was brief, although the gas supply did not fail as suddenly and dramatically as has sometimes been stated. As early as July 3, 1896, the Elwood *Free Press* published the results of a survey by two experts sent by the Pittsburgh Plate Glass Company; one predicted that the gas supply would last three to five years, the other that it would last seven to nine years. The first prediction proved correct; the winter of 1900 brought a partial failure that forced some factories to close and forced all of them to make a decision on whether to move or convert to some other fuel. The Tin Plate Works was one that stayed, and this was a cause of much rejoicing, for it was by far the largest plant in the city. "In a sense, the Tin Plate was Elwood."[27]

In 1908, when Wendell got his job, much of the work was still done by hand, and the workers were divided into groups, each of which operated a "hot mill." Bars of steel "perhaps an inch thick," several inches wide and about two feet long were heated white-hot in a furnace, then removed by the "heater," using heavy tongs, and passed to the "roller," who was boss of the crew. The roller pushed them slowly between revolving massive steel cylinders. On the other side the "catcher" received them and returned them to the roller, who shoved them through again; then they were doubled, reheated, and again rolled thin; and this process was repeated until, in the judgment of the roller, the separate layers were of the right thickness for the use to which they were to be put. Another worker then cut the edges with heavy shears, and another man separated the sheets. The bundles of sheets then left the "hot mill" to be cut to size, "pickled" in acid (to remove impurities), annealed, cold-rolled, "pickled" again, annealed again, and finally covered with two thin coatings of pure tin. At this point the product was ready to be made into "tin cans," the use of which was increasing at a spectacular rate.[28]

Workers in the "hot mills" found conditions barely endurable. Robert Willkie says, "I have literally seen eggs fried on the floor." Some workers wore wooden clogs, while others half-soled their shoes with thick belting (without such protection leather shoes would quickly have scorched and curled). Visitors to the plant when it was dedicated, who because of the rain and mud were wearing rubbers, found that if they stood long in one place the rubber melted.[29] Ten or fifteen minutes of continuous labor was all a man could stand; then he was spelled by an assistant. Wendell's job was "catcher's helper."[30] He stuck it out for one summer; but that was enough.

The next year he joined Paul Harmon, who had temporarily left school, in Aberdeen, South Dakota, where the government's opening up of free land for homesteading had just touched off a boom. For a week he worked as a dishwasher in the restaurant where Paul was cashier; then the proprietor, Charly Shortridge, offered him a job running a "hotel"—an old circus tent covering as many makeshift bunks as could be crowded under it, which he put up behind the restaurant, charging fifty cents a night.

It was a matter of pride with Wendell to fill the place each night. With typical enterprise and energy he scoured the streets, and became adept at persuading drunks that it would be worth while to spend a half dollar (if they had it) to sleep in the "hotel" rather than in the gutter. Many of them were so disreputable that Shortridge refused to let them pass through the restaurant; so the seventeen-year-old boy had to drag them up an outside stairway and down again. His employer was impressed: "That boy will amount to something some day," he told Paul Harmon.

Presently, however, Wendell "got itchy feet" and decided to move on.[31] Farther west, he promptly lost the $300 that he had made, when he bought an apparatus for making cement blocks; too late he discovered that it was impossible to get cement. So he started again from scratch, hopped a freight train headed west, and helped cut hay on a Montana ranch until the farmer's daughter became too friendly. Next, still moving westward, he tried his hand at driving loads of tourists through Yellowstone Park;

but this was not like driving a bakery wagon around Elwood, and only good luck saved him, on his first trip, from breaking his own and his passengers' necks. Finally he headed back to Elwood for his last half year of high school.

5

But in Elwood, too, he found excitement—a strike at the Tin Plate Works.[32] The main issue—surprisingly for that period—was the open shop. The Amalgamated Association of Iron, Steel, and Tin Plate Workers, perhaps grown too complacent with their closed shop, seem to have resisted the inevitable trend toward mechanization, along with company efforts to increase the efficiency of the workers.[33] The company reacted by resolving to break the union and accordingly announced an open shop policy. The union accepted the challenge, and on July 1 the men walked out in fifteen plants in various states.

In Elwood, at first, the strike was relatively effective and without disorder. Even when the company began importing workers from the East (on July 3 and again on July 9 special trains carrying strike-breakers were run inside the plant, where the men received free board and lodging), there was no violence. But as the days dragged by with no sign of the company's yielding, with the plant gradually returning to production, and with discouraged local workers trickling back to their jobs, tempers wore thin. Crowds began to gather at the gates to jeer the workers when they entered or left. On July 21 the company applied for an injunction against picketing. The *Daily Record* reported: "The bill states that the 'aforesaid pickets, including women, are strikers, or persons in sympathy with the defendants, make loud noises for the sake of frightening and terrorizing and intimidating the employees.' The crowds jeer and hoot, as the bill states, and call them 'scabs' and vile and offensive names."

Herman Willkie was the union's attorney. He had advised against the strike, pointing out that industrial progress could not be prevented. But now that the strike had come, he did his best to protect the union from legal coercion; and at a hearing on July 26 in the Federal District Court at Goshen, before Judge Francis E. Baker, he presented his case so effectively that the injuction was denied.

At this point the company's district manager announced that he and other district managers had been called east by the company president and ordered to keep their plants open or quit; and that in his opinion, if the Elwood plant could not operate as an open shop, it would be permanently closed. The *Daily Record* in a front page editorial denounced the strikers: "Sympathy can no longer stand in the way of our future. It is purely a matter of dollars and cents." The police force (charged with not having tried to preserve order) was increased to a total of twelve. A group of citizens prepared a petition urging the Governor to intervene.

The records do not show, however, that anybody got hurt; although four West Virginia strike-breakers were convicted of carrying concealed weapons and had their fines paid by the company, and a fiery Welshwoman named Ann Todd was arrested after dousing some workers with a pailful of cow manure and water. Herman Willkie defended her, and the *Daily Record* reported, "The case is being hard fought." In the end she was found guilty of disturbing the peace and was fined a dollar and costs.[34]

But the disturbance gave the company an excuse to renew its application for an injuction, and Judge Baker held another hearing on August 25. Company attorneys presented sheaves of affidavits that the strikers and their sympathizers had been guilty of violence and intimidation. But Herman Willkie was ready with as many more denying the allegations, as well as others to the effect that the strongest affidavits against the strikers had been sworn to by men who were "police characters," professional strike-breakers, and illiterates. Judge Baker found the evidence too conflicting to permit a decision and scheduled a rehearing for September 21.

It was somewhere near the end of August that Wendell got back from the West to begin his final semester of high school, and became his father's assistant. (He carried only three courses in school instead of the usual four.) In this capacity he was present at his father's talks with the union leaders and, when his father advised seeking the aid of Clarence Darrow, joined them in a memorable visit to the famous lawyer. Darrow staggered them by asking a fee of $20,000, and $1,000 a day in court; but he approved of the way the case was already being handled and, in fact, told them that they did not need him. So Herman Willkie continued as the union's counsel at $25 a day. Darrow seems to have taken particular notice of Wendell and to have addressed to him some friendly remarks.[35]

When the rehearing was held, however (after being put off for two days to September 23), the company reported its decision to postpone the application indefinitely, since the strikers were returning to work and violence had ceased. This was true. The strike had failed, though it nominally continued for many months. And here, as far as the records go, the case ended.[36]

6

On January 7, 1910, the *Daily Student* of Indiana University, under the headline ANOTHER WILKIE ARRIVES (the University publications always had trouble spelling Willkie's name), reported: "Another of the tribe of Willkie has enrolled in the University. The new arrival is Louis Wendell. Two have just left, one is now a sophomore—and others are expected to arrive in years to come." Evidently the Willkie name meant news to many of the 1135 students at the University.[37]

The item is, however, a little misleading. Julia was doing graduate work in classics while teaching in the Bloomington High School. Robert was also teaching, in a smaller high school, but would return to the University the following year to complete his course in the Law School. Fred was in the class of 1912.

To save money, Julia, Fred and Wendell (and the next year Robert) lived together in a rented house near the campus. This establishment resembled the Willkie home in Elwood in its haphazard living arrangements (for Julia's many gifts did not include one for home-making), in its acceptance by friends as a social center, and in the vociferous arguments that were continually in progress. It differed in that the older boys (emancipated from the Sunday School atmosphere of home) were joined there by campus comrades in poker games that were not less exciting because the stakes were necessarily small.[38]

The reputation implied in the news item above had probably been earned mainly by Julia and Bob, who were in the same class, and who in an unconventional family were the most ruggedly individualistic. Julia was also the most brilliant.

One of the first things that Julia did after Wendell arrived was to introduce him to Dr. Lillian Gay Berry of the Classics Department. He at first found little to say, and Miss Berry (thinking of his older brothers, as so many people seemed to) said bluntly, "Well, Wendell, I don't know whether I'm going to like you or not." Instantly he "flashed back," "You *will* like me!" And she did—although, surprisingly, he said little in her class and impressed her as being rather shy. Later, after becoming famous, he wrote to tell her how much inspiration he had gained from her classes: "I have said a hundred times so that I can say it directly to you now without any touch of flattery, that if I had to make a choice and select the best of all my courses, I would select the course in Latin under Lillian Gay Berry."[39] In a lighter mood, when she telephoned him on a trip to New York and told her name, he asked, "Is this Miss Berry from Indiana University?" and on being told that it was, declared, "The office will close for the day!"[40]

Willkie's life at the University, as elsewhere, has been over-dramatized. Most of his friends[41] do not remember his wearing red turtle-neck sweaters or chewing tobacco;[42] they do not remember him as a "rough-neck" or as being in dress and manners notably different from other students. As for campus activities, the *Daily Student* did not have occasion to mention his name for more than a year after his enrollment; then, on January 18, 1911, there appeared a cryptic announcement: "IMPORTANT. All Sophomores see or call up over the phone this afternoon Hickam, Payton, Richman or Willkie." The next mention of him is again more than a year later, on April 17, 1912.

There is no mention of one event that is vividly remembered by many of Willkie's contemporaries, and in which all agree that he was a leader—"the riot at the Harris-Grand." The Harris-Grand was a theater (pre-movie), where the students usually sat in the balcony, and, if the show was dull, enlivened it by varied vocal effects and typical undergraduate humor. Memories are vague as to the occasion of the riot, but for some reason the police were called in to keep order; and, with the infallible gift that police officers have for doing the wrong thing in dealing with college students, they apparently seized the first person they came to, a boy named Bill Sutherland, who had only one arm, and hustled him out of the theater. Bob and Wendell, sitting near, rushed down the stairs in pursuit, with shouts that brought others swarming after them. They quickly overtook the officers, and even the intervention of a crowd of non-collegians, always ready for a fracas with the boys from the University, could not prevent the release of the prisoner and considerable damage to the dignity of the law. The triumphant students returned to the theater to see the rest of the show. It was not until later that Bob and Wendell, becoming aware of pain in their backs, discovered that they both had stab wounds, apparently inflicted by one of the town toughs.[43]

Rumors that Wendell spent a night in jail following this episode are certainly untrue.[44] Likewise, no other testimony bears out that of a local judge that he sent one or "both" (there were three) of the Willkie boys to jail when a demonstration by several hundred University students following a "wet and dry" election threatened to develop into another battle between the students and the town boys.[45] But such stories have a certain value as showing the impression that Willkie left on people's minds—that when there was fight, he was likely to be in the front of it.

7

He also seems to have been in the thick of campus politics. His Elwood chum Paul Harmon had entered the University in the fall of 1910, and a year later Wendell proposed to make him president of the sophomore class. Paul laughed at the idea; he was not a fraternity man, nor was he particularly prominent. But he agreed to be a candidate; and so effective was Wendell's campaign that on October 5 the *Daily Student* announced his election.[46]

It may have been even earlier that Wendell joined in an attempt to democratize the election of officers of the Student Union, an organization which, along with other contributions to the social life of the campus, sponsored a series of entertainments and musical programs. Though there was a popular election of the officers, it was a cut-and-dried affair, and non-fraternity men were never among the nominees. Wendell's campaigning produced reforms, and later, according to some accounts, he took the lead in organizing the non-fraternity men in an alliance with Beta Theta Pi against most of the other fraternities to elect Paul McNutt president of the Union.[47]

Wendell's career in campus politics, however, was not uniformly successful. In the only contest in which he himself ran for office, he was defeated. This was in the spring of 1912, in the election of the board of the *Arbutus,* the University annual put out by the senior class. The heads of the business and editorial staffs received pay as well as honor, and these inducements led Wendell and his close friend and fellow-politico, George Henley, to announce that they were candidates for Secretary of the Board of Managers and Editor-in-Chief respectively, and to try to pool their support. Their opponents were Dwight Cragun and Chester Teeter, and the space given the contest by the *Student* suggests that it aroused widespread interest.

The election evidently took place at a meeting of the then junior class, and was the first popular election of the kind, since heretofore the members of the outgoing board had appointed their successors. In this situation Wendell hoped to gain an advantage by going to the University Medical School in Indianapolis and securing the proxies of thirty-six medical students, who were nominally members of the class but as a rule took little interest in campus activities. The opposition had had the same idea, but when they discovered that Wendell had beaten them to it, they quickly devised a counter-stroke. Their floor manager, Earl Stroup, mounted the platform and, waving a sheaf of papers, implied that he "held the power of revocation of most of the Willkie proxies." Accepting the claim at face value, and rejecting the advice of some of his friends, Wendell made a motion that the proxies be not accepted; and this was quickly passed. Too late he discovered that Stroup had been bluffing and had held only blank sheets of paper. In the final vote Wendell lost 129-91 and Henley 113-86. Still, the combination was not wholly a failure; three of its candidates were elected to the editorial board.[48]

The *Daily Student* of April 17, the day before it mentioned Wendell's candidacy for the *Arbutus* board, carried another story in which his name appeared—that of the mock Democratic National Convention staged by the Jackson Club, the student Democratic group. As a member of the Club, he took a significant though not a leading part in the convention, heading the Pennsylvania delegation; and he took a stand—which he maintained with increased conviction for the remaining thirty-two years of his life—in support of Woodrow Wilson, the liberal Governor of New Jersey, who was challenging, in a dramatic contest, the candidate of the Democratic organization, Senator Champ Clark of Missouri. At the end of the year Ben Scifres, newly elected president of the Jackson Club, appointed Wendell to its five-man Executive Board.[49]

8

Such partisan activities, however, did not claim Wendell's whole attention. Unsought honors and responsibilities came his way, especially during his senior year, and support the opinion of a contemporary that "he was universally admired, liked and respected."[50] One of these, especially, is hard to fit into the picture of him as the campus radical. On October 18, 1912, the *Daily Student* reported: "The tradition committee is now organized and a list of Freshmen that come under the green cap ruling is being made. The Committee intends to locate all Freshmen in school that are violating this ruling. . . . This committee this year is made up of Lewis Willkie, President . . ." (Ten days later the *Student* explained, answering a query about the "Board of Traditions," that it had been organized in 1911 and consisted of four men from each of the three upper classes, appointed by the respective presidents.)

Further evidence that Wendell had become a solid citizen of the University appears in his appointment as a "student marshal." These marshals, whose chief duties were to prevent disorderly conduct by students at athletic contests and to "act as ushers at University functions," were chosen by the faculty from lists submitted by student organizations. The requirements were that they should be "representative students, popular among the student body, possessing influential ability, and whose scholarship is above question."[51]

After this, it is not surprising to read in the *Student* for December 12 that Wendell had been elected president of the Boosters' Club for the winter term. The aims of the Club, one supposes, were what the name implies; its most publicized activity was the promotion of a state-wide interscholastic basketball tournament, in which ninety-five teams participated. A staggering amount of work must have gone into making arrangements for housing and feeding the teams, printing tickets and programs, securing the referees, and handling finances—not to mention working out a schedule! These responsibilities, assumed entirely by the students, would seem to have been good preparation for running a Presidential campaign.

And in this instance nobody questioned Wendell's organizing ability. The tournament was an unqualified success.[52]

Other items accompanying Wendell's picture in the 1913 *Arbutus* are: "Executive Committee Student Council. Interclass Athletic Committee." Altogether, his achievements in extra-curricular activities were distinguished although not spectacular.

The same can be said of his academic career as an undergraduate. His official transcript shows, for his entire course at Indiana University, including his final year in law school, 108½ credit hours of A, 112½ of B, 15½ of C, and 1 of D (Hygiene).[53] Picking up where he had left off in high school, "he loved to argue with his professors"; in general they seem to have respected him, recognizing that his main motive was not mere love of argument but genuine intellectual curiosity.[54] Such was the feeling of his history professor, James A. Woodburn, who wrote to him early in 1940: "You were a promising student and have well fulfilled those early days of promise. . . . In our classes in history and politics in those days at Indiana I used to think of you as a pretty good Progressive."[55]

Wendell in turn remembered a number of professors with gratitude and respect: Ernest H. Lindley in philosophy, Dr. Harding in history, Dr. Hepburn in law[56] (who later told Ernest K. Lindley, the son of Professor Lindley, that Willkie was "the most stimulating student I ever had").[57] There was some truth but more humorous exaggeration in his remark on receiving an honorary LL. D. from Yale in 1941: "I spent four years . . . as an undergraduate student with one determined and dogged purpose and that was to prove that all college professors and presidents were stuffy fellows."[58]

Perhaps his most celebrated academic exploit came in his junior year. An elementary economics course led him, in the summer of 1911, to Marx's *Das Kapital*[59] (then as now a work less often read than talked about), and then to works by Herbert Spencer and Edward Bellamy. Desiring a still better understanding of socialism, he besought the head of the Economics Department, Dr. Weatherly, to offer a formal course in the subject. The professor was willing if Wendell "could drum up ten students who were interested. I had to buttonhole almost everyone in the university before I could get the ten. No wonder they thought of me as a Socialist."[60]

What he was, in truth, was a free thinker, in the full sense of the phrase; a youngster passionately interested in ideas for their own sake. Evenings and weekends he spent browsing in the library, picking out books here and there that for one reason or another aroused his interest, scanning them rapidly to get their drift, fixing in his memory passages that seemed especially significant, and occasionally taking one home for thorough study. The University librarian, Dr. Jenkins, is reported to have remarked wonderingly: "I don't see how Wendell does it. He leads his classes, is in the midst of every campus activity, and causes the faculty endless trouble; yet he is more widely read than any other boy I have ever known."[61]

This picture strikingly resembles one given by Mrs. Willkie thirty years later: "You should see our apartment in New York early on a Monday morning after Wendell has been reading the night before. It is littered with books. He may be reading history, and it suggests something in literature, or just the other way. When he is through, he has delved into a dozen books and has them lying all around."[62] It is clear that his years at Indiana University were, above all, a time of intellectual growth.[63]

9

Through these stirring years Wendell's love for Gwyneth, now a student at Butler University in Indianapolis, had not diminished. True, the religious seriousness that had accompanied the first phase of his attachment had lost its intensity (there is no record of his having been connected with any religious organizations while at the University), but perhaps Gwyneth herself had found this seriousness a little tiresome. In the summer there were parties and dates between vacation jobs. (One summer when Robert and Wendell worked on a farm in northern Indiana, Wendell would walk four miles to and from town to mail his letters to Gwyneth.)[64] During the college year, as often as he could afford it, he would visit her at Indianapolis, deluging her with roses and chocolates. But what rather attracted her, still, was that she found in him "the personification of devotion and high principles."[65]

There were, however, two sources of dissension between them. One was Wendell's stubborn refusal, as in the past, to accept Gwyneth's argument as to the importance of conventional refinement of dress and manners; the other was his condemnation of fraternities and sororities. At Butler, in defiance of his wishes, she had joined Kappa Alpha Theta, and this action led to a certain awkwardness in their relations, since fraternities and sororities monopolized the social life at both Butler and the University. Many years later she wrote: "The fact that he did not belong to [a fraternity] caused some embarrassment when he visited me at Butler. This . . . seem[s] petty to me now but then it was important."[66] Moreover, she was confident that fraternity life "would give him the polish he lacked," and that this would be a gain for him as well as for her.

Accordingly, when George De Hority came to her during Wendell's senior year with the plea that she use her influence to get him to accept an invitation to join Beta Theta Pi, she agreed. And, having failed to move him by argument, she decided on direct action. She delivered an ultimatum: he must either join the fraternity or give her up.

One cannot help wondering how she could fail to realize the strength of Wendell's commitment. Although he had good friends in the fraternities as well as out of them, he had fought against them in campus politics and denounced them with complete and considered conviction as being in principle undemocratic. As late as the middle of his senior year (January 3, 1913) the *Student* reported that at a meeting to discuss organizing the non-fraternity men, "Lewis Willkie said amid much applause, 'I am an unorganized man, and I am proud of it. But I am not in favor of an organization because I do not see the need of it.'"

On the day the ultimatum arrived, his roommate, Maurice Bluhm, found him pacing up and down the room, disheveled and distraught. His explanation—"If I don't join a fraternity, I'll lose my girl, and if I do, I'll lose my soul"[67]—sounded melodramatic, but his suffering was not feigned. The dilemma might be an old one, but for him the conflict of loyalties was intense and the choice was tragic. In the end, toward the close of the year, he became a member of Beta Theta Pi.

After he had been initiated, he sent his pin to Gwyneth. With it went a brief note: "I have dedicated my life to you. 'In thee have I put my trust; let me never be confounded.'"[68]

III

Coming of Age

1

In June, 1913, when Willkie received his A.B. degree, he had still before him a year of work to earn his LL. B. But he was now twenty-one, and with a younger brother and sister to be put through college by his parents, he felt that further study ought to be self-financed.

The first job that presented itself came through the good offices of Professor Woodburn, who recommended him as a teacher of history at the Coffeyville, Kansas, High School. He was offered the position and accepted.[1] He held it for a little more than a year—from September, 1913 to early November, 1914—when he resigned to take a better-paying job as a chemist with a sugar company in Puerto Rico.

Biographers have done little with this brief chapter in Willkie's life. But it is the one period when, judging by later letters from his students, he achieved an absolute and unalloyed success. What "Pat" Bing had been to Willkie and other students at Elwood, his star pupil now was to the young people of Coffeyville.

And his influence was exerted in an even greater variety of ways. He not only taught history, but coached the basketball team (as well as a girls' team), which won six of its ten games, and a track team which won all its meets; organized a debating team; advised the literary society; and took charge of the Hi-Y Club,[2] which he "built up to include in its membership over one-half of the boys in the high school."[3] The school annual in 1914 contained a cartoon showing him giving a vigorous oration; it was captioned: "The 'Pep'perpot of C. H. S."[4]

The letters from Willkie's former students are so loaded with superlatives that one might be inclined to discount them as reflections of teen-age emotionalism, if they were not, on the whole, so lively and literate and filled with concrete details. It may also be noted that the students' enthusiasm was shared by their elders. Charles T. Carpenter, the member of the school board who had arranged Willkie's appointment, became one of his closest friends, and wrote to him in 1937 (after an article about him had appeared in *Fortune*): "I love to remember the radiant and eager young man who lived among us and won such enthusiastic devotion from his pupils, associate teachers and outside friends."[5] And one of these "associate teachers" had written him a few months earlier (after seeing him in a

"March of Time"): "I shall never forget the table for four at Mrs. Somebody's boarding house, nor the extravagant praise of your personality in which we three girls indulged ever so often."[6]

It is the statements of his students, however, that properly count for most in the total picture. One of them wrote with friendly irony that in 1940 she had voted "the Republican ticket for the only man who could ever have caused me to do it, the one who had educated me to be a Democrat . . . in that English History class, with the primary subject well supplemented with issues of the day."[7]

He also supplemented his subject with literature, as another student remembered (along with other details): "I dare say that this former Coffeyville student is not the only one who remembers with a great deal of pleasure the versatile young man with the engaging gold-toothed grin and apparently boundless energy. He was the sponsor of the Hi-Y, chief talker-up at every 'pep' rally, and I don't know what besides, outside of classes; and he actually taught us history and made us like it! We all went into deep mourning when he left . . . I have a particularly vivid picture in my mind, of our teacher on the one day in each month when he declared a holiday from English history and sat on one corner of his desk, swinging a long leg and reading O. Henry to us."[8]

Willkie seems to have had a marvelous gift for kindling in his students a pictorial imagination—for making them *see* the scenes and actors on the stage of history. "I have always wanted to tell you," wrote another of his students, "just how much you meant to me as a teacher . . . to this very day, every word, look and gesture of yours are remembered as plainly as if it took place only yesterday. . . . I just can't feel that the world war [I] will ever amount to much as history unless it were possible for you to delineate it to some history class. The battle of the Marne is puny to me, because I can never forget your description of England's defeat of the Spanish Armada. . . . In fact, back in my brain you came to very nearly being the History of England itself. You had such remarkable powers to make others see just what was taking place, that it was as hard to separate you from history, as it is hard to separate an excellent actor from the play he is interpreting."[9]

Yet making students *see* history was not mainly an end in itself but rather a means of making them *think* about what they saw, of bringing them in contact with ideas; and this fact comes out in still another letter: "you will never know how much we missed you after you left. I was enrolled in your civics class. . . . There were two things that you told us in that class that I have never forgotten. One was to cultivate a larger vision in world matters, and to keep in touch with world affairs and to do our duty as citizens when we reached the voting age. I remember your saying that there was as much romance in present day events as there were in ancient times. The second thing was that the most perfect form of government today was that of England. I have always tried to keep in touch with the political affairs of England since that time. . . . I cannot think of anything that I would rather do right now than to listen to you give a lecture on world affairs. There are so many things happening every day that we 'little folks' get confused about it all and miss a great many of the really important things of our day."[10]

It was the girls in his classes who penned the tributes so far quoted. But it is reasonable to assume that the boys were not less responsive but only more reticent. One of them declared: "The writer was one of the student body who was especially benefited by the influence and inspiration of this man whom we knew as Lewis Wendell Willkie."[11] Another one recalled: "I took every subject you taught, and have since remarked you were the best teacher I ever had. . . . you lifted that whole school more than you ever realized. . . . So all these years I have wondered what became of you. We all thought you were going to the top."[12]

Another letter refers to the only recorded fiasco in Willkie's activities at Coffeyville High School: "Do you remember the basketball team's experience in Bartlesville [Oklahoma] some 23 years ago when we made the trip from Coffeyville down here to play a game of basketball only to find upon our arrival that we were supposed to play football?"[13] Willkie *did* remember it: "I frequently laugh and tell friends the circumstances of our going to Bartlesville under the misapprehension that we were football players instead of basketball players. As a matter of fact, I was the presumptive coach of the team and I did not know a great deal about the difference between the two games. However, I do not have a single sour memory of the year I spent in Coffeyville."[14]

The note of affectionate reminiscence in this letter runs through all his acknowledgements. To the teacher and table companion who avowed her admiration for him he responded: "I have always lived with gusto and with pleasure but I really think the happiest time I ever had was while I was teaching at Coffeyville." And he added: "It was my first real adventure in standing on my own feet."[15] To one student he replied: "Your interesting letter brought back a flood of memories that are very dear to me. I have been in a good many parts of the country since I left Coffeyville but I never enjoyed anything so much."[16] And to another he commented that "the year I spent at Coffeyville was the most enjoyable since my boyhood. I . . . reveled completely in new contacts and experiences."[17]

The idyll ended in early November, 1914. He had entered teaching to earn money to complete his law course and, delightful though he had discovered teaching to be, his choice of a profession was still the law. So when his brother Fred, who was now a chemist with the Fajardo Sugar Company in Puerto Rico, urged him to accept a similar job at a salary considerably higher than the $85 a month that he was getting at Coffeyville,[18] he accepted.

His students were crushed. The school annual for 1915, in listing the noteworthy events of the year, recorded: "November 6th. Willkie Day. A special service was given in chapel for one of the best friends C. H. S. has ever known. . . . Mr. Willkie told of his regret in leaving C. H. S. in one of his characteristic speeches . . . A gloomy student body filed to classrooms."[19] Later the whole school went to the station to see him off, with cheers and tears. One girl rushed up and kissed him. Then, as he was in danger of being mobbed by his admirers, the train pulled out.[20]

2

His new job did not begin as soon as he had expected, and he accordingly enrolled as a special student at Oberlin, where his younger brother Edward was already enrolled, to take additional work in chemistry.

When he began his duties in Puerto Rico in January, 1915, however, he found that he needed little technical knowledge. His job was that of running repeated simple tests during the refining process and recording the results. It was not skill that was called for (the manager of the plant told Willkie later,[21] "You broke more test tubes than anybody else that ever worked there"), but conscientiousness in performing a monotonous but necessary job throughout a twelve-hour working day.[22]

Nevertheless, as with every other experience, Willkie made his Puerto Rican sojourn another step in his education. When his day's work was over, he turned to the study of the subject that always fascinated him more than any other—people, and how they lived. In the evening, in any town or village, the people would gather in the plaza, where there were always palm trees and benches, and always something going on—music or some sort of impromptu show. Willkie liked to join the crowd—or sometimes simply to stand and watch.[23]

But there were some aspects of Puerto Rican life that he found less to his taste, when he encountered them on the trips that he took to all the readily accessible parts of the island: the grinding poverty of the masses, the hitherto unimagined squalor of their existence, their almost total illitracy, and their merciless exploitation by the propertied class, especially the owners of sugar plantations. There was even, during his stay, a brief but violent rebellion by the workers against their masters,[24] and he never forgot what he saw on a casual ride with the manager of a sugar plantation. A half-starved participant in the rebellion "stumbled out of the sugar cane, where he had been hiding . . . The manager hacked at him with a cane knife, all but cutting off his shoulder, without stopping his horse or the conversation." Some quarter of a century later he told his friend Gardner Cowles, in answer to a question, that this was one of the things "that had kept him from thinking like a typical American millionaire."[25]

A more obvious and immediate effect of this and other new experiences was the weakening of his long and ardent and, on the whole, happy romance with Gwyneth. When he returned to Elwood in the summer of 1915, having saved enough money from his six months in Puerto Rico to see him through his final year in law school, the old tie was broken.

One naturally looks for a cause, for a story, for some dramatic climax; but according to the testimony of both parties, they simply drifted apart. Coffeyville was a long way from Indianapolis; and Puerto Rico still farther from Elwood, where Gwyneth, after graduating from Butler, had returned to teach. "We both felt," Gwyneth wrote later, "that it had gone on too long."[26]

There is some evidence, however, that it was Wendell who did most of the drifting.[27] It is natural to wonder whether the rift may not have had its beginning in Gwyneth's ultimatum about the fraternity,[28] although his note of submission contains no hint of bitterness. That there was *some* story, some aspect of the separation that one or both found painful to recall, is suggested by episodes in later years that he related to his brothers Robert and Edward. Once in Chicago he looked up Gwyneth's address and took a taxi to her home—but did not go in.[29] On another occasion he was late to a luncheon date with Edward, and explained that he had happened to meet Gwyneth on the street. The meeting had not, it seemed, been wholly happy; to his casual remark that life seemed to have treated her well, she retorted, "Yes, but you didn't."[30]

There is no neeed, however, to dramatize the relation. Meetings between them were certainly few. Gwyneth in her turn married, apparently happily; and when Wendell tactfully inquired of a common friend whether she and her husband could afford to send their children to college (an inquiry that implied a continuing interest but not much information), she was able to report that they could.[31] In 1940, although Gwyneth strongly resented the publicity that ensued when someone dug up the story of her youthful connection with Willkie ("I shall never forgive those Tribune reporters for barging into my home"),[32] she consented toward the end of the campaign to appear on a radio program in support of his candidacy;[33] and she was amused when during the campaign her five-year-old son Robert clinched an argument with a play-mate as to whether he knew who Wendell Willkie was by asserting: "He almost got to be my father."[34]

During the brief remainder of Willkie's life they kept in touch mainly by letter. On June 14, 1941, he wrote to her: "I called you when I was in Chicago but [was] unable to reach you.

"While in England I had several talks with people from Swansea [the Harrys' home before they left for America] and also flew over Swansea on my way to Ireland. I wanted to tell you about it.

"I hope you approve of what I am trying to do to assist Britain and ourselves in the present struggle for liberty. I remember with what ardor you always sang 'Britain [sic] Rules the Waves.' I hope it continues to be true."[35]

She answered in a chatty letter, telling of her mother's illness, an accident to her sister, and the prospective enrollment of her daughter at the University of Wisconsin; and he replied in kind.[36]

What seems to have been the last exchange of letters was occasioned by the request of Alden Hatch and Mrs. Hatch that Willkie help them secure an interview in connection with their biography of him. He told Gwyneth of the request and added: "Obviously, and for many reasons, I did not want them to, if in any way it would be contrary to your wishes."[37] Though reluctant to incur further publicity, she agreed to the interview, "feeling that it is your wish." She then thanked him for a photograph of himself that he had recently sent, and added: "You would be greatly amused if you could hear my children reading to me every bit of news in the paper concerning you. You are surely a hero to them."[38]

On this pleasant note the record ends.

3

When Willkie returned to Indiana University in the fall of 1915, after two years of absence, most of his old friends were gone; and he now accepted without reserve the chance to make new friends that was offered by his membership in Beta Theta Pi. He roomed near the fraternity house, spent much time there, and took an active part in fraternity affairs.

In these affairs he still stood by his equalitarian principles. He opposed a clique that he felt was too powerful in the fraternity and was using its power to further the personal interests of its members; and when this clique proposed as the chapter delegate to the national convention a man who Willkie felt was unsuitable, he put up a candidate of his own, Harry Shackleford, making the nomination at the end of an eloquent speech about fair play. Shackleford was elected.[39]

From partisan campus politics, however, Willkie during this year remained aloof—although he did take part in a vain attempt to persuade the city council to allow students of legal age to vote in Bloomington.[40] His only other involvement in political activity came in the spring of 1916, when the Jackson Club chose him to organize another mock Democratic National Convention. It was scheduled for Saturday, April 30, and Willkie did his best, in the face of Wilson's certain renomination, to stir up interest. That he had difficulty is suggested by a notice in the *Student* at the beginning of the week: "Chairman Lewis W. Willkie is very anxious that anyone who can make a speech, fill an office, control a delegation, or participate in the affair at all, should communicate with either the national committee or the chairmen of the state delegations."

What the student body *was* interested in, suddenly and unpredictably, was the baseball game with Purdue, also scheduled for Saturday. At a Boosters' Club meeting Monday night, someone proposed an all-university excursion to Lafayette. Enthusiasm was instantaneous. "Not even a thing like a national convention will be allowed to interfere with the trip to Purdue, and the Jackson Club sent word that their big mock Democratic convention, which was to have been held in the Gym on Saturday, would be postponed if the excursion was decided upon." The postponement of the convention turned out to be permanent. (Indiana lost the baseball game by a lopsided score.)[41]

There had also been another change of emphasis in Willkie's career. He was now concentrating more intensely on his studies. His only regular extra-curricular activity during this year was debating. The *Student* of June 3, 1916, lists him among twenty-eight men who had taken part in one or more of sixteen debates during the year, of which Indiana had won nine. (Another member of the team, Basil Walters, recalls that "Willkie, always a free wheeler and his own thinker, was not a particular favorite with the coach.")[42]

It must have been his earlier reputation as a public speaker, surviving his two-year absence, that led to his election as class orator, which the *Student* reported on October 11, 1915. But it was his solid work during his last year that brought him the other important honor conferred on a Law School senior: "forty-three volumes of a law encyclopedia . . . worth $280," given to the "best all around student."[43]

The last episode in Willkie's university career fulfilled the promise of drama implied in the *Student's* item on his arrival six and a half years before. As class orator he was to speak at the Law School graduation exercises, which this year, contrary to custom,[44] were separate from the general Commencement ceremony. He entitled his speech, after a recent book by Woodrow Wilson, *The New Freedom*. No text is known to exist, but the main theme, conceived with characteristic boldness and stated with characteristic fervor, was the need for a new state constitution which would permit Indiana to emulate Wilson's program—such measures as the Federal Reserve Act, the Clayton Anti-trust Act, and the establishment of a Federal Trade Commission—to regulate, for the common good, the activities of the banking and business interests. He may also have added, or interspersed, some caustic comments on the Law School and its faculty.[45]

It is clear that the speech caused a sensation. Twenty-four years later, after Willkie's spectacular triumph at the Philadelphia convention, the occasion was recalled by William Lowe Bryan (from the secure position of President Emeritus) with tolerant amusement. "I shall never forget Wendell Willkie's oration at his law class commencement. He made the most radical speech you ever heard. Willkie later said he was scared, fearing that they (the faculty) would interfere with his graduation, but of course they wouldn't do that."[46]

With his diploma safe, Willkie went back to Elwood to join his father and Robert in practicing law, although his brother declared later that Wendell "never did consider staying in Elwood unless he could have made some political contact at the state level."[47] A year or two of actual practice, however, would be of value in any position that he might later choose.

Some stories of his months in Elwood have survived. One is that in his first case he opposed his father, who punctured the balloon of Wendell's eloquence and won the case by remarking casually to the jury, "I believe my son will be a great lawyer, he can make so much out of so little."[48] Another is of a case in which Wendell and Robert worked together for a client who was suing for $50 damages in an automobile accident. Although they had told him that the case was hopeless, they found it going their way and amended the complaint to ask for larger damages. Then, as prospects became still brighter, they repeated the process. In the end they won a verdict for $150.[49] Most of the cases were small ones in Justice of the Peace courts around the county, but they probably provided Willkie with as good experience as he could have found anywhere.

When business was slack, the law office became, like any place where two or more Willkies got together, a forum for discussion and debate, among themselves or with whoever might drop in. And of course such sessions were not confined to the office. On his way to work one morning Calvin Sizelove saw Willkie standing on a street corner arguing energetically with the newly elected Socialist mayor, John Lewis; on his way home to lunch he saw them in the same place, still in earnest discussion. He could not swear that it had been uninterrupted, but saw no evidence to the contrary.[50] An even more prolonged session took place on the occasion of Paul Harmon's wedding. It started the evening before and was continued next morning and at the wedding reception. When train-time for the honeymooners threatened to end it, Wendell climbed aboard.[51]

Among more conventional activities were those connected with his membership in the Masons and the Elks. Although in later life he was emphatically not a "joiner," he always liked people, and during these light-hearted years it was natural for him to accept invitations to join fraternal orders. He became a Mason in 1913, was active in the local lodge when he was in Elwood, and transferred to an Akron lodge when he moved to that city. He also joined the Elks, and his friend Phil Hamm later recalled "when I was Exalted Ruler of our Elks and you were Esquire—how dramatic[ally] you performed your post in both the Opening and Closing of the Lodge and especially in the degree work."[52] Similar is the recollection of Abe Levi of a speech to the Elks that "stood them on their heads."[53]

To conclude this catch-all of recollections of Willkie's life in Elwood during early manhood, there is an episode that contributed to an idiosyncrasy much publicized in later years—his refusal to drive an automobile. These vehicles were just coming into general use, and Bob had a 1911 Overland at which all the brothers tried their hand. Wendell, however, "was never interested in anything mechanical."[54] Moreover, he was likely, in the midst of an argument, to forget altogether that he was supposed to be holding a steering wheel, and to start talking with his hands. This happened once when Edward was with him; the car turned over, pinning Ed face down underneath; and Robert remembers Wendell on his knees beside the car frantically digging with his hands to get the gravel away from his brother's face so he could breathe. "It was the one time I ever saw him really scared."[55] He did not immediately give up driving, and even had a car of his own (a Ford) during his first months in the Army. But before he was sent to France he sold it, and never got another.[56]

4

Among these minor happenings during Willkie's year in Elwood, one major sequence of events stands out. In September, 1915, George De Hority had married a girl from Rushville, Louise Mauzy, and had asked Wendell to be one of the ushers. In the activities preceding the wedding he was more or less paired off with one of the bridesmaids. She had chestnut hair and blue eyes, unlike Gwyneth, but she had the same vivacity and love of fun. She was slightly built and fragile beside the gangling six feet two of her escort; but as a newspaper reporter noted later, she had a jaw as square as his. Her name was Edith Wilk, and Wendell made some obvious joke about the similarity of their names.[57]

Edith Wilk's ancestors on her mother's side had been Scotch-Irish and had come to America before the Revolution. Her father's grandfather had come from Germany. She had been born in Nashville, Tennessee, where her father was a building contractor, but the family—there was one sister, Erema—moved to Rushville when Edith was seven years old and remained there. (The Rush County Court House was built by Mr. Wilk.)[58] Edith entered Indiana University in September, 1908, and left in December, 1909, at the end of the fall term—just before Wendell entered.[59]

A year after their first meeting, Edith arrived in Elwood to act as librarian. (The records of a meeting of the library board on September 5, 1916, include the item: "Chairman reported that a Miss Wilk of Rushville, Indiana would accept the position of librarian here at $65 a month.")[60] It seems likely that Wendell had a hand in her appointment (he became a board member the following January), along with George De Hority and his wife, who found herself a bit lonely in Elwood.[61] At any rate, once Edith had arrived, Wendell lost no time. Although at first she had dates with other men, he soon "swept her off her feet."[62] Still, she was not a girl to surrender easily—she had a mind and will of her own. And it was probably her desire to take her own time in making her decision, and to make it in a relatively calm atmosphere, that led her in mid-November to ask the library board to choose a successor as soon as possible so that she could return to Rushville.[63]

Wendell, however, was not to be put off. Travel between Elwood and Rushville necessitated a roundabout trip through Indianapolis, but during the next few weeks he "practically commuted."[64] In the end, Edith consented, though some of her friends thought it an odd match; she had always been an eager participant in the social whirl, and Wendell did not even dance. "I think Edith married him for his brains," was the judgment of Mary Sleeth,[65] a close friend of the Wilk family who later became the manager of the Rush County farms in which Willkie invested much of his modest fortune. But this overlooks the innate charm, undeniable though unstudied, that drew to him innumerable persons of both sexes. Especially, he seems to have aroused in women the desire to mother him. He remarked to Robert after the 1940 election that if all the women who had smiled at him and wanted to straighten his tie had *voted* for him, he would have won.[66]

Meanwhile, events were shaping in Europe that would take small account of lovers' longings and plans. For this was early 1917, and Germany's unrestricted submarine warfare was forcing Woodrow Wilson to abandon his policy of strict neutrality. The successful slogan of his supporters in the 1916 election had been "He kept us out of war"; and his famous "too proud to fight" statement had certainly represented, in its upshot if not in the adjective, the majority sentiment of the American people. But he was not willing to abandon a cardinal principle of international law and traditional American policy—"freedom of the seas"—even at the cost of war.

Willkie's admiration for Wilson had been shaken by the earlier policy, for his family had a long-standing hatred of German militarism; and the "radical" ideas which had attracted him during his university days did not include pacifism. But now his faith was restored. And when war came, on April 6, he was ready.

The War Department, however, was not ready. And the often repeated statement that Willkie enlisted as a private on the day war was declared is untrue.[67] He may have made some inquiries or taken some steps leading to military service, but nobody was quite sure about what was best to do. Finally, the Government announced that an Officers' Training Camp would be activated at Fort Benjamin Harrison, near Indianapolis; and on May 7 or 8 Robert and Wendell went to Indianapolis to sign up. Wendell was called on May 11 and Robert on May 13.[68] On August 15 they both received commissions—Wendell as a first lieutenant and Robert as a second lieutenant.

It was at the beginning of this period that the Army made the mistake that led to a permanent reversal of Willkie's first and middle names. As he explained later to a former Coffeyville student, the red tape involved in getting the error corrected would have been "endless";[69] and since he had never liked "Lewis," anyway, and had always been called "Wendell" or "Wen" by his family and close friends,[70] he was satisfied to let the change remain.

After getting his commission, Willkie was one of a group of fifty—along with his friend and fellow Indiana alumnus Donald Thornburgh—who were sent to Harvard for a month's special instruction in infantry tactics by a staff of French officers. On weekends, under the stimulus of Willkie's interest, the two would visit some historic spot—Plymouth Rock, Bunker Hill, or Lexington and Concord; and Willkie would imagine himself in the position of those who had helped make history and would try to relive the experience. Once they went as far as New Haven to see the statue of Nathan Hale.[71]

As it turned out, this was the only feature of their stay at Harvard that was of any value, for on September 15[72] the Army characteristically assigned them to the 325th Artillery (perhaps because their names were near the end of the alphabet). This was a light artillery regiment, as was the 326th; and together with the 327th, a heavy artillery regiment, formed a brigade that was kept together during the war. Willkie and Thornburgh joined it at Camp Taylor, near Louisville, Kentucky; and there, and later at West Point (now Fort Knox), Kentucky, the brigade marked time for almost a year.

The young officers protested against their new assignment vigorously and insistently, but a hard-boiled old major finally told them that they should be grateful, since in this war the artillery was going to be a much more pleasant assignment than the infantry. As for their fellow officers, "Hell, they don't know anything either. All they know is the nomenclature. *I* will do the teaching around here."[73]

The monotonous routine of life at Camp Taylor was broken for Willkie, in January, by his wedding. It was planned as a church wedding, in Rushville, the afternoon of Saturday, January 12. Donald Thornburgh was to be best man, and Willkie was to bring the wedding bouquet (white orchids and lilies of the valley) because a storm had been predicted, and the florist refused to send it.[74]

But on Friday night occurred the heaviest snowstorm ever recorded in Louisville, followed by bitter cold. The first problem that Willkie and Thornburgh faced the following morning was to get from the camp to Louisville. Cabs and street cars were immobilized; but someone suggested that by walking across the camp and a subdivision of the city they could reach an interurban line which was sure to be running. It was heavy going, however, and on the way Willkie froze his ears.

They would have suffered still more if a woman had not seen them floundering along the street in front of her home, and invited them to come in and get warm. But Willkie was almost too miserable to appreciate her kindness; he paced up and down, groaning with the pain in his ears and the generally dismal prospects.

At last they reached the city, picked up the flowers, and after a long delay got a train for their destination. But after struggling along painfully to a little town about twenty miles from Rushville, it got hopelessly stalled. Unwilling to give up, they visited the local livery stable and tried to hire horses to ride to Rushville, but the owner refused. Fortunately, telephone lines were still open, and Wendell was able to call his waiting bride and explain his predicament; and he found solace during the rest of the day and the evening at the town's one small hotel by telephoning every hour or so to say: "Edith, the trains aren't running yet, but you aren't going to change your mind, are you?"[75]

On Sunday morning they got to Indianapolis and went to Thornburgh's home, where his mother went over the bouquet and picked out the wilted or frozen flowers. But their leave had been only for the weekend, and they were both due back in camp Monday morning. So Willkie did more telephoning, this time to the regimental commander, who extended his leave, but not Thornburgh's.

The wedding finally took place on Monday, in Edith's home; and the bouquet that Wendell had been at such pains to bring, she carried perhaps even more fondly than if it had been fresh from the florist's.

On Tuesday morning Wendell had to be back at Camp Taylor; but Edith followed him and found a place to live in New Albany, just across the Ohio from Louisville.[76] Here she stayed for two months, until Wendell was ordered to the artillery school at Fort Sill, Oklahoma, on March 25. Thereafter, because of ill health, she gave up trying to follow him.[77]

5

One dramatic detail of his stay at Fort Sill survives—a voluntary parachute jump, which he liked to recall later, although at the time he apparently said nothing to his friends. According to the version that he gave to a later friend, A. C. Blinn, Willkie had made some casual remark about not being afraid to jump from a balloon, and "quite an argument developed resulting in a $50 wager that I didn't have the nerve to do it." So they went to the commanding officer and told him the story. "I expected him to say 'Get the hell off the place and mind your own business . . .' But instead of that, he said, 'Why sure, it's all right with me. I have some French parachutes I would like to try out. Do you want to use one of those or do you want one of ours?' 'Well,' I answered, 'I will take one of ours.' They put the parachute on me and told me how to pull the rip-cord. . . . The instructor was a very nice chap; as the balloon was slowly going up he talked to me most casually, asking me where I was from, what I was going to do after the war, whether or not I was married, etc., etc. Finally we got up to about 1,500 or 2,000 feet; he looked at the instruments and said, 'Well, if I were going to jump I would do it now,' so there wasn't anything for me to do but go over the side of the basket, which I did, pulled the rip cord as I had been instructed, landed safely and collected $50."

At this point Blinn could not help asking, "'Wendell, why in the world would you do such a crazy thing?' I will never forget his answer. He said, 'If you are going into war you can't be a coward.'"[78]

On June 7 Willkie rejoined his regiment at Camp Taylor, just before it was moved, on June 15, to West Point, Kentucky,[79] where it was kept for almost three months more.

The picture of the young officer that emerges from the recollections of many members of his unit is clear, consistent, and strikingly attractive. It is true that in certain respects he did not live up to the standards traditionally prescribed for an officer. The Army had no more success than Gwyneth in polishing its "diamond in the rough."[80] "Sloppy," and even "slovenly," are the words used invariably to describe his dress and bearing. He never tried to correct the slight stoop that was still, as in boyhood, habitual; he wore shoes that were too big; at meals he would unhook the collar of his blouse and pull up his sleeves; he would show up for regimental review in a uniform that was wrinkled or improperly buttoned, or both; and if reprimanded, he would say afterwards: "What do they want, Arrow Collar ads, or men to fight a war?"[81]

These shortcomings were offset, however, even in the eyes of most of Willkie's superiors, by his general competence and capacity for work—traits concerning which the testimony is equally uniform. In addition, he interested himself in the personal problems of the enlisted men in his battery. At Camp Taylor he found that many of them were boys from farms or small towns in Indiana or Kentucky, totally unsophisticated and often lost and lonesome amid the vast impersonal operations of the Army. Sundays, when there were few duties to take their minds off their troubles, were especially bad; and Willkie made it a practice to go through the barracks and try to cheer them up. He would begin bluntly, when he saw a soldier moping, "What's the matter with *you?*" But after he had got the men to talk, he would listen sympathetically to their stories and do his best to help them.[82]

In fact, he refused to accept the hard and fast line traditionally drawn by the Armed Services between officers and enlisted men. Sometimes a group of men sitting around and talking would hear someone coming and get ready to spring to attention; then they would hear a casual voice call out, "It's just me; sit still"—and Willkie would make his appearance. Often he would go into the kitchen early in the morning and read the newspaper, chatting pleasantly with the mess sergeant. He also—alone among the commissioned officers of his outfit—sometimes took exercise with the enlisted men; and in a favorite game called "Swat the Kaiser," he showed that he could "take it" with the best of them.[83]

This democratic attitude met with less approval from some of his superiors than from his subordinates; and one of the latter happened to overhear the colonel lecturing Willkie for associating too freely with the enlisted men. Willkie retorted: "I'm going to associate with these men as equals after the war—and I'm also going to do it now."[84]

And in later life, after he became famous, Willkie was still happy to "associate with them as equals." When his campaign train stopped in Bakersfield, California, one of the men of his battery fought his way through the crowd until near enough to get Willkie's attention, and called out "Battery F" and his name. Instantly the candidate recognized him, reached down and hauled him up on the platform, and stood with his arm around him while the crowd cheered.[85] This was good politics, obviously; but his greeting to his old comrades was equally hearty under other circumstances. When Henry Sherrard happened to be in Rushville shortly after Willkie's trip to England in early 1941 and called at the Willkie home, he explained to Mrs. Willkie, who came to the door, that he was Willkie's old battery clerk; and Willkie, overhearing the words,, shouted, "Show him in!" and greeted him warmly by name after twenty-two years.[86]

Early in September the regiment was moved to Camp Upton, Long

Island—where Willkie and his friend Shackleford Miller were surprised and delighted to meet their wives, who had managed to follow them there. But after five days—on September 9, 1918—they sailed for Europe, on the small and crowded British ship *Canada.*[87]

During the voyage, there was one break in routine, when the troopship got separated from its escorting destroyers and was thought to be in danger from German U-boats; and officers were stationed at strategic points with orders to shoot if necessary, in order to prevent a possible stampede if an attack came. One of them, Percy Ruch, captain of another battery, became violently seasick and finally sent for Willkie, who was scheduled to relieve him later. Willkie arrived cheerful and fresh, having been touring the ship on his own, with the sympathetic inquiry: "Why didn't you send for me sooner?"[88]

No submarine appeared, however, and the regiment arrived safely in Glasgow. It then went by train to Winchester for a brief rest period, and here Willkie once more assumed the role of history teacher. With another officer, he organized hikes to nearby points of historic interest, where he would give informal lectures about what had happened there and why it was important. The trips quickly became popular; at the end, nearly two hundred men went along.[89]

From Winchester the troops had been scheduled to go by train to Southampton, but a railway strike compelled them to march—twenty-five miles a day under full pack. Despite their months in service, some of the men were unready for such an effort; and occasionally, when one of them approached total exhaustion, Willkie or Miller would carry his pack. The frequent irony of Army life was brought home to them when, during a rest period in a small town, they were sitting dirty and dishevelled beside the road; and a couple of passing MP's, brisk and spic and span, made an English girl exclaim to her companion: "My, aren't these American officers handsome!"

At Southampton they were marched directly on board the boat, where most of the men simply collapsed; but Willkie and Miller stood on the bow and watched the coast fade away, and talked about "what it was all going to lead to." They landed at Le Havre, where they got their first sight of wounded soldiers.[90] Next, as one member of the unit later remembered, "we hiked to the crest of that almost topless hill, which the French termed a rest camp. . . . Then by train to Bordeaux and on to Camp De Souge, where we arrived late one afternoon detraining in a cold, drizzling rain in a soggy, sandy terrain, dotted with pine trees planted by one of the long line of Louis', kings of old France. What an uninviting place!"[91]

Here the unit was put through still another period of training, this time in French artillery tactics—which some officers thought was a waste of time.[92] But at long last the brigade was judged to be ready. Orders came to proceed to the front. The trains were waiting.

Then the Armistice was announced.

This was perhaps what put an end to one of Willkie's cherished ambitions, that of being promoted to captain. It is surprising, at first glance, that he had received no promotion during almost fifteen months of wartime service after first receiving a commission; but the explanation is simple. The officer personnel of the entire regiment had remained almost unchanged, and nobody else had been promoted, either. Some vacancies developed, however, around the time of the Armistice, and an order came through that these were to be filled. Willkie was recommended for promotion to captain, and the recommendation was approved, but the actual promotion never came.[93]

Willkie's disappointment was intense. And in fact, after leaving the Army, although in formal statements he was always careful to say that he had been "recommended for a captaincy," he wore a captain's insignia whenever he had occasion to put on a uniform.[94]

6

Yet Willkie's Army life was not a total loss, for he was able to turn it to professional advantage. Soldiers who were court-martialed for violations of the military code could ask any officer to defend them,[95] and the evidence suggests that Willkie was called on more frequently than any other officer in the brigade. He was especially active after the Armistice, when the men were eager to get home and discipline was difficult to maintain. Toward the end, he was trying a case almost every day,[96] and even then had more requests than he could accept.[97] In fact, the colonel of another regiment in the brigade, known as "Spike" Hennessey, who although a Regular Army man was generally sympathetic to the enlisted men in his unit, made Willkie a sort of unofficial "public defender."[98] This was of course congenial work, for Willkie was naturally on the side of the men, whom, since "he disliked the Regular Army and all its ways,"[99] he looked on as the underdogs. (In fact, most of the offenses were minor.)

All accounts agree that he won a large percentage of his cases. His success was partly due to his skill in the courtroom (he would often say to Percy Ruch, who worked with him on a number of cases, "You get the evidence, and I'll try the case"),[100] but even more to his thorough knowledge of military law, which he studied constantly. Once he thought he was going to get his client off because the offense was not covered by Army regulations; but a further search showed that it *was,* and he "remarked regretfully that he would have to try the case on its merits."[101]

Another reason for his success was his ingenuity in legal—and sometimes extra-legal—maneuvers. Typical is a case remembered by several persons which grew out of the accidental killing of a French farmer's cow during artillery practice by a battery of the 327th. It was due to a minor oversight, for which nobody could be seriously blamed; but Stephen Noland, the first lieutenant, offered to take the responsibilty. An ill-tempered major, however, brought charges against the second lieutenant. Willkie was engaged for the defense, and held a conference to plan the case—in a room next to the major's office, where the latter was sure to overhear. Willkie outlined his plan, which included calling witnesses to prove the major's incompetence, and also charging the major with favoritism, since Noland had offered to take the blame. Next morning the charges were withdrawn.[102]

Cases involving enlisted men, though more numerous, were probably as a rule routine, not likely to be remembered by anybody but the defendant. One such was that of Sergeant William Arnold, who was court-martialed for being out at a dance beyond his time. There was no way, this time, to get around the evidence, and Arnold "was broken for thirty days and given K. P. duty."[103]

His legal activity, however, did not prevent Willkie from planning a brief escape from Camp Gennicarte—a thoroughly uncomfortable "mud camp" where the brigade had been sent soon after the Armistice—and having a fling at sight-seeing. No one was supposed to get leave who had not been in France for six months, but Willkie argued that Miller, as regimental adjutant, ought to be able to wangle one—and he did. Since there were no leaves for Paris, they chose as their stated destination a small town just to the north of the capital. This would give them twenty-four hours in Paris on the way and another twenty-four hours on their return. (MP's stamped the passes of all soldiers as they arrived in Paris, and if they did not leave within twenty-four hours they were arrested.) Ignoring the Parisian cabarets and "high life" that attracted so many service men, Willkie and Miller saw as many historic places as they could in the allotted time, and then talked the chief of the Military Police into allowing them another day without an intervening visit to their alleged destination.

They then decided to return by way of Nice, where they were disappointed to learn that no men in uniform were allowed at Monte Carlo (evidently Willkie considered this to be of historic interest); and on their second day there, Miller happened to see on the YMCA bulletin board a notice of a telegram for him—telling him that the regiment was moving out the next day. They got back to Camp Gennicarte with some seven hours to spare, before leaving at six a. m.[104]

During the next few days they moved first to Camp Bassens and then to Camp Paulliac, "where we embarked" (as one officer afterward recalled) "to the sweet strains of 'Homeward Bound' on the old ship 'Antigone.'"[105] They sailed on February 15[106] for Newport News, where Mrs. Willkie and Mrs. Miller again surprised their husbands by their presence; and after a few days at Camp Chillicothe, Ohio, they were mustered out on February 28.[107]

Willkie's twenty-two months in the Army brought no significant change in his character or opinions. His equalitarianism had perhaps been strengthened, along with his distaste for regimentation and red tape—but these traits were strong already. He had seen new countries, and old cultures—but he had always been free from the insularity that limited the thinking of many fellow Midwesterners.

It was characteristic that, although he must have resented many aspects of Army life, he later remembered most clearly the better part. Twenty years later, in a letter to an officer of the regiment who, like many early acquaintances, wrote to express pleasure at his success, and recalled "the young, lean lieutenant," "free-speaking" and "candid," Willkie replied: "You brought back to my mind very many pleasant memories. . . . I do not . . . know what has become of most of the fellows. They were all very dear to me and I hope life has been very kind to them and to you."[108]

IV

Akron

1

Willkie could now return to his career as a lawyer. Two other careers, however, he briefly considered—teaching and politics. The suggestion that he enter teaching came from Ernest H. Lindley, a professor at Indiana University during Willkie's student days, but in 1919 president of the University of Idaho. Willkie had written to ask him if there were any opportunities for young lawyers in Idaho, and Lindley replied that there were, but that he would like to have him on the faculty of the University Law School. In telling the story later to Ernest K. Lindley, Willkie said that the offer appealed to him, and that he would have accepted it but for one fact. The salary would not begin until fall, and he had to begin earning money at once.[1]

The political opportunity would perhaps have been even more tempting. The story has often been told of how Dale J. Crittenberger, the Democratic leader of Madison County, tried to persuade Willkie to become a candidate for Representative from the Eighth Congressional District, assuring him that he would win the election. Before giving his answer, however, Willkie consulted Frank C. Dailey of Indianapolis, an old friend of his father and later an unsuccessful candidate for Governor. Dailey discouraged him; granting that he might win one election, he pointed out that the district was normally Republican, and that the prospect of a successful political careeer in Indiana was decidedly dim. Instead, Dailey offered to help him get a position in Akron, Ohio, with the Firestone Tire and Rubber Company, with which he had connections.[2]

Willkie acknowledged the force of the objection. Besides, as noted, he needed money at once, and the next election, in November, 1920, was a year and a half away.

His father would have liked to return to the pre-war set-up with Robert and Wendell as his partners. But his mother—whether through jealousy and dislike of her sons' wives, as some Elwood residents thought, or, as another son, Edward, more generously suggested, because she desired for them greater success than Elwood could offer—was violently opposed.[3] Wendell himself, in a letter applying for a job at Firestone, gave as his motive the "conviction that the future of a lawyer in a town of 10,000 is very much limited" and his consequent "great desire to become connected with the legal department of a corporation such as you represent." The letter, together with Dailey's recommendation, won him the job. He began work on May 16, 1919. His salary was $2,500 a year.[4]

In 1919 Akron was booming, on a larger scale but in the same spirit as Elwood had been twenty-seven years before. On the day before Willkie began work at Firestone, two front-page headlines in the *Beacon Journal* proclaimed "HALF BILLION WORTH OF GOODS TO BE MADE IN AKRON THIS YEAR" and "PERMITS [for building] MILLION AND HALF IN DAY"; and the back pages were filled with advertisements that promised a suburban paradise to the workers whose influx pushed the population from 69,000 in 1910 to 208,000 in 1920. (The city was so crowded, in fact, that when Willkie arrived, in the midst of some convention, the only available accommodation was a cot in a hotel lobby.)[5]

The national scene was almost equally stirring, and national sentiment was on the whole equally optimistic. In January the "noble experiment" of the Eighteenth Amendment had been ratified by the required number of states and would go into effect a year later. In May and June the House and Senate respectively passed the Nineteenth Amendment, permitting women to vote, and swift ratification by the states was assured. The millenium, if not quite achieved, seemed not impossibly remote.

Nor had the concern with national problems, along with the fever of money-getting, yet extinguished the war-born enthusiasm for an international organization to prevent future wars. Woodrow Wilson, though still in Europe, had sent the Covenant of the League of Nations to the Senate for approval; and on May 17 the violently isolationist owner and editor of the Akron *Beacon Journal,* C. L. Knight, in an editorial summarizing and praising a speech by Senator Borah attacking the League, concluded disconsolately: "But this fatal break with American traditions, this rushing into entanglements against which the forefathers warned the nation, this hysterical plan to put on America's shoulders the burden of centuries of misrule in Europe . . . has been nurtured with such misrepresentation, with the vast powers of governmental prestige and publicity behind it . . . that the belief in Washington today is that it will be sanctioned by the Senate." He had, of course, despaired too soon.

The views of Knight and Borah were not changed by an event that coincided in time with the editorial—the flight of a U. S. Navy plane from Newfoundland to the Azores on the first lap of the first air crossing of the Atlantic.

Willkie's work at Firestone was not particularly exciting or challenging. Harvey Firestone, Sr., was among the relatively enlightened industrialists of his generation who considered it good policy to provide various "fringe benefits" for employees, and one of these was free legal advice and aid.

This was what Willkie was hired to provide. If a worker wished to make a will, if he was involved in a lawsuit, if some creditor threatened to attach his wages, he could go to Willkie—who declared later that he wrote "several thousand wills," was consulted about "various problems" by "hundreds and hundreds" of employees, and "tried their simpler cases in the courts."[6]

Willkie's love of action and drama, however, inevitably made his duties seem routinely dull. So, despite several salary raises and an offer to give him $10,000 a year if he would stay,[7] he resigned on December 31, 1920, and the next day joined the law firm of Mather and Nesbitt. He took a cut in salary, to $3600; but, at Mrs. Willkie's insistence, he demanded a partnership in the firm, and this was promised, and given, at the end of a brief probationary period.[8] The firm then became Mather, Nesbitt, and Willkie.

Mrs. Willkie, because of ill health, had remained in Indiana until after the birth of their son Philip, on December 7, 1919.[9] In the meantime her husband had lived in a rooming house at 157 South Balch Street. For a time after Mrs. Willkie's arrival, they shared with another young couple, the Hubert Hannas, an apartment on Rhodes Avenue. Then they bought a modest home at 180 Beck Avenue, where they remained until they left Akron. [10]

For a short time, however, Willkie cherished some notions that were something less than modest. As he told it later (in a 1940 campaign speech in Akron), "I landed here at the height of the boom in Akron, and I saved a little money [he had confided earlier in the speech that his "total accumulation" at the time of his arrival was $100], and we got to speculating, a small group of us, in real estate here in South Akron.

"We would buy lots, and then a great rush would come and we would sell them shortly thereafter at a profit, and I . . . accumulated about $30,000 in a year." At this point an official high in the Firestone organization flattered him with some unsolicited advice. "I was just a boy and occupied a very junior and unimportant position . . . He said to me, 'Wendell, have you got any money?' I said, 'Yes, I have a little money,' and I had all this in cash. Firestone stock was then about $190 a share. He said, 'Wendell, Firestone stock is going to $500 a share, and if I were you I would buy some of it.' Well, I sat down and figured it out that night, that I have 30 thousand, and then if I borrowed 30 thousand more, if that stock went to $500 . . . I would make enough money to go back to Indiana and really amount to something."

But the economic recession of 1921 upset his calculations. "Firestone stock dropped to 50 instead of going to 500, and . . . I was . . . left with an indebtedness of 10 or 12 thousand dollars. . . . I did not survive at this bar through any love of work—I survived through the necessity of making money. I applied myself to the bar because I had to. Otherwise I would have starved."[11]

The 1921 recession also had another effect on Willkie's career; it brought him to prominence in the affairs of the local American Legion group. In the brief post-war boom many former service men had found jobs in Akron, especially in the rubber industry. Between the spring of 1920 and the spring of 1921, however, the number of workers in the rubber factories fell from 70,000 to 25,000 and the monthly payroll from $9,500,000 to $2,500,000.[12] Thousands of veterans were stranded in the city, jobless and penniless.

The first result, as far as the Legion was concerned, was that nine different posts in the city, finding the struggle for existence too stern, combined to form Summit Post No. 19. That Willkie, formerly a member of Firestone Post No. 301, was a leader in the reorganization may be inferred from the fact that in the first election, on May 2, 1921, he was elected First Vice Commander (690 votes were cast).[13] When, a few months later, the Commander resigned on leaving the city, Willkie succeeded him. The next year he was elected to the office, and so held it for a year and a half.

As commander, he fell heir to heavy responsibilities. "Through its prominence Summit Post had come to be looked on as the leading place for a veteran to go, outside of the Red Cross, when he needed financial help or aid in solving any of the problems that beset so many of the discharged veterans of the Great War. Bonus applications were filled [sic], help obtained for reinstating government War Risk insurance and scores of other perplexing details worked out to assist the veteran.

"Willkie insisted that all these activities be carried on full blast despite declining membership and revenues of the post."[14] No veteran was turned down, whether he was a member of the post or not. Often the help consisted of buying a railroad ticket back to his home town in Kentucky or Tennessee or West Virginia. At one point, debts were $75 and available funds totaled $56. The other officers resigned; but Willie stuck it out, and had the executive committee appoint replacements.

One problem was that the new post, despite the depression, had leased relatively luxurious clubrooms, at what soon became a ruinous rent. Willkie negotiated with the owners, secured several reductions in the rent, and finally persuaded them to let the post cancel the lease altogether, so as to move into cheaper quarters.

Still, however, the post's financial position was desperate, and in September, 1921 it sponsored a benefit concert by the famous contralto Madame Schumann-Heink, a favorite with service men because of her generosity in their behalf. "But advance sales were going very slowly. To speed them up the group urged the commander to plug the concert and explain the post's plight to civic groups. Someone suggested a talk at Kent State as a starter." Willkie went, made a speech, and left a few tickets. The next day the dean called and asked for more. There were apparently other speeches with similar results, for when the concert was given, the Akron Armory was packed, and the post cleared $3,000.

2

No doubt it was Willkie's activities in connection with the Legion that brought him into demand as a public speaker, especially on patriotic occasions. He delivered eulogies of Washington and/or Lincoln to the Rotary Club on February 1, 1922, and again on February 21, 1928; to the Kiwanis Club on February 10, 1926; and to the Akron Real Estate Board on February 19, 1928.[15] He always spoke extemporaneously, and little of what he said remains in print, but from the last of the speeches mentioned, a few sentences are preserved. After asserting that both Washington and Lincoln "became President through force of circumstance" and that "neither strove to make the Presidency the end of his desires," he added that "it was in their native simplicity when they were elevated to lead this nation that they showed their greatness. They did not become complex and difficult for their fellow citizens to understand. They remained themselves, and that fact should come home to every man who studies their lives and seeks to draw lessons from them."

Willkie also played a notable part in a pageant presented on July 4, 1923 before an estimated audience of 5,000 persons—"the greatest attempt locally to depict American history: the signing of the Declaration of Independence and the growth of the nation." Willkie played the role of Lincoln and at the appropriate point "recited the Emancipation Proclamation and struck the shackles from the arms of a slave." In the picture of him made up for the role, he bears a striking resemblance to the Emancipator. His face, though young, is less full than in later years; and there are the same rugged features, the same deep-set eyes, the same unruly mass of dark hair.

Another frequent theme of Willkie's public appearances was government. He discussed "The Meaning of the Constitution" before the Rotary Club on September 24, 1923 and before the Civitan Club on December 13 of the same year. On the second occasion (and perhaps the first), he traced many of the "government . . . and economic ills of the present day" to the fact that the direct representation provided for in the Constitution had been "changed to indirect democracy by the influence of blocs and organizations."

His Jeffersonian principles came to the fore again when he talked to the Exchange Club on March 31, 1925 on "A Great American Evil—Too Much Law." "There has grown up a belief that it is possible to control the country morally by the passage of sumptuary laws. One example is . . . the passage of a law to control liquor traffic. . . . I wonder whether [if] millions spent in the enforcement of the liquor amendment were expended in the education of young men and women, if we would not be nearer sobriety than we are now."

Another frequent theme of his eloquence was the folly and futility of war. On March 26, 1925 he addressed a meeting of the No More Wars Society; and on July 2 of the same year, before the Rotary Club, instead of waving the flag and hailing America's military victories, he pleaded for peace. "I do not care whether peace comes through leagues, courts, international agreements or otherwise. I only ask that the children of today be so educated to the futility of war that peace will come in the next generation." And four years later he was still preaching the same doctrine, at an Armistice Day banquet of the Knights of Columbus: "Why is it that we divorce ourselves from 2000 years of Christianity and go out on the field of battle to hunt our fellow men and hide in a dugout like rats? This is not manly—it is not human; but it's war." Nevertheless he concluded (by what stretch of logic the account leaves unclear): "If there were another war, I'd go again."

This pacifist strain, no doubt rooted in his native idealism, was strengthened by his admiration for Newton D. Baker, an Ohioan who had been Wilson's Secretary of War. Willkie admired Wilson for his ideals and moral steadfastness, but it was Baker who moved him to personal devotion. The occurrence at the 1924 Democratic convention that struck him with the greatest force was Baker's fight for a platform plank endorsing the League of Nations. Describing the convention to the Akron Kiwanis Club on July 16, he told how "Newton D. Baker, a pacifist who had by some peculiar fate been thrown in as Secretary of War during the greatest war in history, pleaded for the League of Nations issue. He begged that the committee [on resolutions] endorse the issue without qualification or referendum.

"But the committee would not listen. Then came a speech by Baker in which he gave a minority report on the action taken by the committee, which was not only the greatest speech in the country but the greatest speech in the world. . . . I saw hard, stern men, men of the Western plains, cry during the plea for the issue, a plea against war, and a plea for the thousands of mothers and fathers in the country."[16]

Twenty years later, the passion aroused by this experience had not faded. In a statement written for John Temple Graves' column in the Birmingham *Age-Herald* in the late summer of 1944, Willkie again recounted Baker's fight. "I shall never forget those early morning hours when Baker, physically a slight man, would return exhausted to his room to tell us—ardent, young, and uninitiated in the obduracy of mentally set politicians

—of his battles in the committees and to get fresh stimulation from our naive and infectious belief that so just a cause, so ably advocated, could not lose."

Nevertheless, he lost—first in the committee and then on the convention floor, despite "the greatest speech in the world," which Willkie still remembered. "I sat in that room across the street [Baker said, referring to the meetings of the Resolutions Committee] for five days and nights and heard talk about 'expediency' and 'votes' until I am sick. I am talking about life and death and love and duty. . . . We have no logic for luck. There is no calculus for expediency. But we do know how to do that which is right, and that is the only rule we need to follow if we want to win and deserve to win in politics."[17]

His speech eulogizing Baker reveals the quality of Willkie's early idealism, which was clearly one source of his popularity as a public speaker. But part of his success was due, on the other hand, to the fact that he never took *himself* too seriously: that he never talked down to people, never set himself apart, never seemed conscious of himself but only of his subject. And for all his earnestness, there was a kind of zest in his speaking, a kind of ingenuous enjoyment of what he was doing, that few hearers could resist.

His manner of accepting a speaking engagement was still more spontaneous and light-hearted. His friend Edson Oberlin recalls the pattern of a typical telephone conversation with Willkie in which such an engagement was made.

"Will you speak at a bankers' convention next Friday?"

"Sure. What time?"

"Ten thirty."

"O. K. Pick me up, will you?"

But his seeming casualness was always tempered by a shrewd estimate of what was appropriate to the occasion and the audience. On the way to the meeting he would ask a series of questions. "Where are we going?" "How many people will be there?" "Is it stag or mixed?" "What do you want me to talk about?" "How long do you want me to talk?" When the time came, he would be ready.

Sometimes, however, he got himself into a situation that would have embarrassed a person of more limited resources. One morning about 10:30 a man telephoned to say that his group was holding a convention and that at the last minute the main speaker, scheduled for 11:30, had been unable to appear. Would Willkie fill in? "Sure. Where is it?" The man told him. But in the hasty conversation the nature of the meeting was not made clear. So Willkie, arriving a few minutes early, entered the back of the auditorium and walked about, looking and listening in the hope of discovering what was going on. But time was getting short, and he remained as much in the dark as ever. Finally he approached a man who was standing alone and inquired confidentially, "Say, what the hell kind of a meeting is this, anyway?"

The answer would have staggered almost anyone else: "It's the Northern Baptist Convention." Even Willkie was momentarily taken aback. But not for long. When he got to the stage, he began with his usual aplomb. And when he ended, he received his usual ovation. (But he told Oberlin once, when the latter expressed envy of his readiness in speaking: "I never got up to make a speech in my life that my knees didn't bump together the first thirty seconds.")[18]

As the years passed, however, his constant speaking became a drain on his time and energy that could not be ignored; and, according to a *Beacon Journal* story on May 24, 1928 (when he was made a director of the Northern Ohio Power and Light Company), "he withdrew when the demands got too heavy, after making a reputation that still brings demands for his services." [19]

3

Willkie's gift for speaking also served him well in the political activities that filled his early years in Akron. As it happened, a number of like-minded young lawyers arrived in Akron at about the same time as Willkie. They included Joseph Thomas, Robert Guinther, Cletus Roetzel and Aldrich Underwood, and together they joined the local Democratic Club (presided over by an older and more conventional party man, Cornelius Mulcahey) and "began to make things hum."[20] Guinther said later, "Willkie and I would cover the area, backing Democrats in 1920. He was a natural as a speaker."[21] As "Young Democrats," all were supporters of the League of Nations, which was then the great political issue; but perhaps none was so ardent as Willkie. Thomas recalled: "The activities of the Young Men's Democratic Club catapulted him into the 1920 League of Nations campaign and he carried the League's banner high on every possible occasion. His speeches were made whenever and wherever he could get an audience. He spoke from trucks parked on Akron's street corners. A friend once took him to a Rotary Club luncheon as a guest. When it came his turn to be introduced in the course of the routine presentation of visitors, Willkie startled everyone present by making a League of Nations speech." He boasted later that he had made an "even thousand" speeches for the League.[22]

These activities brought Willkie into association with Ohio's most prominent Democratic statesmen, Governor James M. Cox, the Presidential nominee in 1920, and Newton D. Baker, Secretary of War in Wilson's cabinet. According to his own account,[23] it was his loyalty to the latter that led him to the high point of his political careeer in Akron—his attendance, as a delegate, at the 1924 Democratic National Convention in Madison Square Garden. Fearing that the Democrats would repudiate the League, Baker "ran as a delegate at large . . . and, at his suggestion, I ran and was elected as a delegate from my home district in order to serve him in his contemplated fight for a straight-out platform endorsement of the League of Nations."

Aside from the issue of the League, there was another source of controversy at the Convention, namely, the Ku Klux Klan. An attempt was made to write into the platform a resolution condemning the Klan by name, and this, during a "tumultuous session," was defeated by a single vote. Mulcahey and Willkie, of course, voted for the resolution.[24] Willkie declared, however, in a speech made to the Kiwanis Club after his return (described as "one of the most scholarly addresses before any luncheon club in months . . . a brilliant word picture of the convention"), that "there was no occasion to fear" the Klan, and told the familiar story of how, after he had voted for Smith, "he received a telegram from the Klan in Akron, asking him 'when he had joined the payroll of the Pope.' To this, he said, he sent a reply that was appropriate to the occasion, as he was getting short of funds."[25] (This suggests that his actual answer was, as has sometimes been reported, "When I ran out of money," but other sources give as his retort, "The Klan can go to hell.")[26]

The intensity of the conflict over condemning the Klan and endorsing the League presaged a similar division of sentiment concerning the candidates; and the balloting was, in fact, almost interminable, with McAdoo consistently getting about 550 votes, far short of the necessary two-thirds, and Smith from 330 to 350, while each of the "favorite sons" hung on stubbornly in the hope of becoming the compromise candidate. The Ohio delegation first supported Cox, then switched to Baker,[27] and finally, on the 74th ballot, decided to let each delegate vote as he wished. Some would have liked to swing the delegation solidly to Smith; but, as Willkie told the Kiwanis Club, "because . . . one delegate said that he would demand a poll from the floor if the delegation went for Smith, there were fifteen delegates that were afraid 'of the goblins will get you' [a reference to the Klan] and refused to side with the remainder for Smith." In the end, of the delegation's 48 votes, Smith got 20½—from delegates "that were not afraid of what the W.C.T.U., the Epworth League or Joe Seiber and his forces would say about them back home."[28]

On the 91st ballot Willkie shifted from Smith to John W. Davis, later cast two votes for former Ambassador to Germany James W. Gerard,[29] and then, after Smith and McAdoo had agreed to withdraw following the 99th ballot, joined in the final drive for Davis, which brought his nomination on the 103rd ballot. This, according to a statement made to the *Beacon-Journal* on his return, had been Willkie's aim all along.

In summing up the whole political situation, Willkie admitted that "Davis will never have the appeal to the common people that Smith has," but held "that with John W. Davis and Calvin Coolidge in leadership of the two great parties, we shall have an able and dignified presentation and analysis of the issues, which will be corruption in office, the League of Nations and tax reduction."[30]

There is one more comment to be made on the 1924 Democratic convention. Many reports make clear that the man who scored the greatest personal triumph at the convention was not one of the candidates for the nomination but, instead, the 1920 nominee for Vice President, now back in politics after a winning fight against infantile paralysis, and acting as spokesman for Al Smith. His name was Franklin D. Roosevelt. One reporter called his famous "happy warrior" speech nominating Smith "the most perfect nominating speech I ever listened to. . . . he has poise, charm, extraordinary sweetness. He spoke with great moderation, using well chosen words, smiling at his audience as if he were talking to them by his own fireside."[31] There is no contemporary record of Willkie's reaction. But one of the strongest reasons for his later distrust of Roosevelt was the latter's failure to support Baker's fight for endorsement of the League. The fight was lost, he charged, "largely because the New York delegation, under the leadership of Franklin D. Roosevelt and others, voted two to one against it."[32]

In the fall campaign Willkie seemingly played no great part; and thereafter he seems to have withdrawn from the political scene, except for one local political battle in 1925—to prevent the Akron public schools from being controlled by the Ku Klux Klan. (Back in Indiana Herman Willkie was also fighting the Klan. "He practically dropped his law practice for almost a year to make speeches against them whenever and wherever he could get an audience."[33]) In the early summer of that year, three of the seven members of the city's Board of Education resigned, charging that the policies of the majority were dictated by the Klan. As a result, "one hundred or more citizens" held a meeting on June 19 and organized the Non-Political Public School League. "Despite repeated requests from [the chairman] and others that personalities and vituperation be left out of the fight, numerous speeches were made in which the Ku Klux Klan was assailed as the source of the recent school board situation.

"'I think we are all of one mind,' said Wendell Willkie, the first to take the floor after the three resigned school board members had explained their stand in resigning. 'Sometimes in a crisis there is a doubt as to the course to be pursued. But I do not believe any honest citizen has any doubt what to do in this case.

"'This man Hanan (Exalted Cyclops of the Summit County Klan and leader of the four remaining members of the school board) has thrown down the challenge he controls this city. Let me take it up and fight it out. I do not think that he does. I think if we properly organize and fight that the people who believe in the American form of government are in sufficient number that we can elect four members to the Board of Education who will express the true selection of this city.'"[34]

Later Willkie was appointed to a five-member committee to make nominations for the November elections;[35] and when three of the committee's four candidates, including Willkie's friend Robert Guinther, were victorious, "political prophets" predicted the end of the Klan's power, noting that this was "the only political fight in which endorsements of the hooded order have been smashed since the organization of the order in this city."[36] Apparently their judgment was correct.

Concerning Willkie's withdrawal from politics, it may be surmised that, with the Klan no longer to be feared and American membership in the League of Nations no longer to be hoped for, he saw no local or national issue urgent enough to distract him from his legal career.

4

This career, after he joined the firm of Mather and Nesbitt, was on the whole a brilliant one. His success, as all his associates agree, was based on two things: his capacity for work and his skill in the courtroom. One friend declares without reservation: "He was the hardest working and fastest thinking lawyer at the local bar."[37]

The same friend remembers that he was often at his office at seven in the morning and still there at seven in the evening. He even "insisted on bringing his lunch to the office with him on the theory that he could get more work done if he did not have to go out to eat. With some difficulty . . . Nesbitt dissuaded him from this practice." Another friend recalls that sometimes he would drop in at Willkie's office in the evening, and find him lying on a rug on the floor, with a pile of books in front of him and another propped against them, reading.[38] Furthermore, unlike some lawyers, he was eager to get things done without delay. When a client came to consult him on a matter that involved a visit to some particular place or person, his regular response was: "Got your car here? . . . O. K. Let's go."[39]

Mather and Nesbitt had been an effective team; the former, genial and society-loving, made contacts and brought in the business, while the latter tried the cases.[40] For a brief period Willkie served as Nesbitt's understudy; but his energy and alertness, together with his eloquence, were gifts too great to be wasted in a supporting role, and soon he was trying cases on his own.

Some features of his courtroom technique have stuck in people's minds. First among these was his forcefulness. One observer even declares that his chief tactic was "main force."[41] And certainly to some extent and on some occasions he would simply overpower—by the vigor, the intensity, the conviction with which he spoke—the arguments of the opposition and the judgment of the jurors. "I never saw a lawyer," one witness testifies, "who could make a jury swallow so often."[42] Although not so massive physically as he later became, he was a formidable figure; and he had the thick, dark mane of hair that was later to become so familiar, with the forelock that would never stay in place and that he would throw back with a dramatic toss of his head that fascinated his audience.[43]

But his strength did not lie merely in words and gestures, nor in the elusive thing called "personality." No member of the Akron bar was his equal in quickness to see and take advantage of every opening provided by the opposition, every unforeseen turn of events.[44] And in pressing an advantage he could command a variety of moods. He was not always thundering at witnesses and jurors. He preferred rather to assume an air of friendliness—which was all the more effective because it reflected his natural liking for people. And he also had a sense of humor. It is these qualities that are notable in a story dug up by columnist Tony Weitzel at the time of his nomination:

"Attorney George Hargreaves recalls a case Willkie fought against those one-time giants of the Akron bar, Rockwell and Grant. Rockwell and Grant seemed to have an air-tight case. Witness after witness went to the stand, testified that a certain vehicle involved had not had 'adequate space' to get by the bus it smashed into. As Willkie got up to make his final argument, Rockwell and Grant looked triumphantly at the jury.

"But Willkie wasn't licked. He seized upon the phrase 'adequate space.' Wasn't it funny, he mused, that every witness for the Rockwell side had used that same phrase. Of course, he insisted, it couldn't be possible that somebody had got all the witnesses into a room and staged a dress rehearsal.

"The jury chuckled and they went out and stretched and talked politics a while and came back and handed the verdict to Willkie. 'Doesn't he remind you of Lincoln?' a juror confided to Hargreaves."[45]

Other characteristics of Willkie as a lawyer that impressed his associates were his complete honesty with clients or prospective clients—his habit of telling them exactly what he thought; his willingness to accept a client who had a good case but not much money; his absolute incorruptibility when offered what were in effect bribes; and his preference for fighting a case through rather than compromising it.[46]

It was a striking tribute to Willkie's ability and integrity that on March 6, 1925, at the age of thirty-three, he was unanimously elected president of the Akron Bar Association,[47] which at that time had about one hundred members.[48] And in a special centennial issue of the *Beacon Journal* on July 21 of the same year, Willkie was among seventy-two "Citizens Prominent in the Development of Akron" whose photographs were reproduced with appropriate notations.

It is evident, therefore, that he had already made his mark in Akron before taking his most famous case, that of Harvey Firestone, Sr., against William H. Kroeger. The latter had been the manager of a large real estate development owned by Firestone, and Firestone had held in his name fifty-seven shares of stock in the Akron *Times.* Kroeger contended that when he left Firestone's employ, the stock had been given him outright in payment for his services. In 1925, however, the Scripps-Howard newspapers bought the *Times,* and the stock rose in value. Firestone then sued Kroeger (in May, 1925) to recover the price of the stock, about $70,000, on the ground that Kroeger had remained merely the nominal holder.[49]

Willkie agreed to take the case for Kroeger and, after a year of legal maneuvering, got it settled out of court, shortly before it was to have come to trial, to Kroeger's satisfaction. Naturally the case was one that Akron had watched with interest, for Firestone's wealth and prestige were immense; and Willkie's victory enhanced the general estimate, already high, of his courage and legal skill.[50]

Not all his cases were won, however. His firm was counsel for the Northern Ohio Traction and Light Company (later the Northern Ohio Power and Light Company), and in this capacity it was often called on to defend suits for damages allegedly caused by the Company's streetcars. Thus, from a sentimental standpoint, Willkie was often on the wrong side; in the popular mind, the Company was the villain, trying to avoid just payment for injuries inflicted on innocent persons through the carelessness of its employees, and in many cases not all Willkie's legal knowledge and courtroom skill could do more than minimize the damages assigned by the jury.[51] On the other hand, of course, the damages sought were often outrageously disproportionate to the injuries sustained. In this difficult position, Willkie seems to have won general respect, if we may judge from a *Times-Press* editorial on his departure from Akron: "as the legal representative of great power organizations in their national litigation, he can put to good usage [sic] the acumen and fair dealing with which he has helped materially to maintain good public relations in Akron for the N. O. P."[52]

5

Despite the brilliance of Willkie's professional success, however, what is still more important to his biographer, in the Akron chapter of his life, is the light thrown on his personal character. Now for the first time we find him arrived at maturity and stability, permanently committed to a particular career, making a place for himself in a particular community.

In this connection a number of perhaps not very significant traits and habits have been dwelt on by various writers: that he was a chain smoker of cigarettes; that he never drove a car; that he rarely carried a watch (but was usually on time, and once remarked, with reference to his wife's habit of keeping the household timepieces ahead, that he had spent much of his life "in a state of chronological inaccuracy");[53] and that he was incorrigibly casual about clothes and food. (When his hat became shabby, his wife would buy a new one and substitute it;[54] when he was finally brought to the point of getting a new suit, she would make him order three;[55] and no matter how carefully his clothes were pressed, they looked, after an hour or two, as if they had been slept in.) Sometimes if engaged in an interesting task or conversation, he would forget all about mealtimes,[56] and at the table he would often become so absorbed in a discussion that he paid no attention to what he ate; as when, at dinner with Paul Harmon in Colorado Springs in 1940, the waiter kept putting trout on his plate and he kept eating them mechanically, while he talked, for an inordinate length of time; or when, invited to the home of his brother Edward, he consumed a whole pound of cheese, brought in as an appetizer before dinner, while he kept up an animated conversation.[57]

He was, in fact, almost wholly indifferent to his physical surroundings. If there was furniture on which he could loll or sprawl without discomfort —a chair solid enough so he could throw a leg over the arm or a desk on which he could put his feet while he argued—these were the essentials, and he asked for nothing more. Except, of course, books to read when there was no one to argue with. Like his father he had a passion for books and his home was always overflowing with them. (Years later Mrs. Willkie told with gleeful irony of the interior decorator whom she consulted about doing over their apartment in New York. She arrived, and cast a disapproving eye on the welter of volumes. "But don't you know, Mrs. Willkie," she said in a professionally patronizing tone, "that books aren't being used much now?")[58]

Thus, his passion for ideas, for work, for success—that is, for mastering his profession and winning his cases—left him little time for unrelated activities, even for playing the role of husband and father. His brothers Robert and Edward thought (at a later date) that, unlike their father, he devoted too little personal attention to the upbringing of his son.[59] Yet he was far from indifferent, and desired for Philip especially the interest in ideas and the independence of mind that he himself possessed. His friend Paul Harmon recalls an evening in the Willkie home when Philip was a youngster, during which Willkie kept prodding or mildly heckling the boy about various subjects; and when Harmon mentioned the matter afterwards, he replied cheerfully, "It will sharpen his wits."[60]

Later, in letters to members of his family, Willkie deprecated, tolerantly, his wife's protective attitude toward their son. Writing in August, 1936, to tell his sister Julia that Philip was soon to enter Princeton, he remarked, "His mother insists that he is too juvenile to go to college. [He was, in fact, only sixteen.] I tell her that she is of that frame of mind because her memory is not distinct as to how juvenile we seemed to others when we undertook a similar adventure."[61] The next year he wrote to his brother Edward in Belgium to ask if he knew of "some responsible and morally satisfactory man who understood both German and French and who had an automobile who could take him [Philip] on a motor trip through those two, and perhaps other countries. . . . I don't care for him to stop at the finest hotels or anything of that kind but I would like for him to see the countries with somebody who really understands them and at the same time could develop his knowledge of those languages." But this plan was given up in favor of a six weeks course at Heidelberg University. "I personally thought the trip idea was the best but his mother seemed to think there was a lot of protective advantage in being with a group."[62]

This difference of opinion between husband and wife was evidently not serious. But what *would* have troubled many women married to such a husband was his lack of interest in conventional diversions. In the early years of their marriage, however, Edith's ill health would have precluded much social life even if they had wanted it; taking care of her young son left her with little energy to spare. And if she was a bit lonely during her husband's long hours at his office, and once asked plaintively why he could not work a shorter day, like many other young men of their acquaintance, she was satisfied with his answer: "I won't be a clock-watcher. I'm going to make a place for myself."[63]

Later, it is true, she remarked a little wistfully (after fame had come, but before it had taught her caution), "I don't feel as if Wendell and I had ever had time to play in our lives."[64] Her husband, also, especially during the years in New York, sometimes voiced the same regret. To an old friend in Coffeyville he wrote in 1937: "I have thought many times that I would like to pay a visit to Coffeyville, but there is always at hand some immediate job to be done which prevents me from doing just what I want to do."[65]

These statements, of course, do not come from the Akron period of the Willkies' life, but it was in Akron that the pattern of their life was set. A study of the pattern suggests, however, that such remarks need not be taken too seriously—that, on the whole, what they really wanted to do was what they did. Certainly neither of them had much taste for "social life" and its trivialities. Once, Mrs. Willkie told a reporter, a friend had accused her of lacking wifely ambition. "You never do anything for your husband. You never give any big parties, or dinners, or plan any excitement for him at all." And she had to plead guilty. "'But then, you know,' she continued, 'Wendell Willkie feels that there is so much to learn, and he is so eager to gain a right understanding of fundamentals, that we just don't find much of a place for those things.'"[66]

They never found much place, either, for the celebration of anniversaries, which Willkie always forgot. But his wife took the sensible view of this, also. "I think it is nice when men remember birthday and wedding anniversaries, but it is not important. The really important thing is how they treat you every day." And she added, smiling, "I have no complaints."[67] Her husband, in turn, was appreciative of this attitude: "I had the good fortune," he wrote in 1937 to an old Indiana friend, "to marry a sane Indiana girl with a rare capacity to bear with a restless and altogether unsatisfactory husband."[68]

Certainly, however, his wife would never have admitted the justice of this self-characterization. "I can find more pleasure in just walking down the street with Wendell Willkie than in anything else I know of," she asserted in 1940;[69] and if she did not mean this, and other comments of the same kind, she was a consummate actress. For the rest, she made him comfortable at home, kept him presentable outside, and did not bother him about domestic details. In his campaigns for office and in his advocacy of unpopular causes she stood quietly but unfalteringly by his side.

It is evident that, as the years passed, the widening scope of his activities left her to some extent in need of building a life of her own. But she was able to do it. And, on the whole, it is hard to imagine that a different choice of partners in marriage could have led him to greater achievement or her to greater happiness.

6

Outside his home and his office, Willkie was gregarious but not a "joiner." (Nor was his wife.)[70] Hugh Johnson said, "His liking for people —all kinds of people" (in later years one could have found exceptions)— was "almost an obsession";[71] he sought companionship because he liked people and enjoyed friendly argument or exchange of ideas—not because he needed help in killing time. Thus he joined the Exchange Club, the University Club, the Akron City Club, and the Portage Country Club.[72] The last of these—a rather swank organization—he joined "at the suggestion of his partners and with reluctance," since "he didn't play golf and his relaxation was limited to an occasional social drink." But he liked occasionally to sit on a bench by the last hole of the golf course and make friendly and unsubtle jokes as other members returned perspiring from their rounds, elated or dejected.[73] It was impossible for him to take such an activity seriously.

The same was true of card playing. It has been said that in Akron he "earned a reputation as . . . a great poker player."[74] But two friends of his early years do not recall ever seeing him play cards, and one distinctly remembers hearing him inveigh against it as a waste of time.[75] Later he developed a fondness for rummy[76] and solitaire[77]: the former on long trips with one or two close friends, with whom he had already canvassed pretty much the whole realm of ideas; the latter as a means of clearing his mind when he arrived at an impasse in the writing of a speech or article.

He had a similar lack of enthusiasm for fishing, as may be inferred from his slightly acid remark in 1940 that a Presidential candidate must be a fisherman.[78] He did, indeed, belong to the Bras Coupe Fishing and Hunting Club of Quebec, and sometimes went there on fishing trips with friends from Akron; but he preferred to sit and read while the guide caught the fish, which Willkie on returning would display as his own, putting on an imitation of a boastful angler.[79]

This was the kind of humor—amiable and obvious—that Willkie enjoyed. But occasionally it backfired—as when he undertook to have a little fun with a clerk of the Northern Ohio Power and Light Company, to which his law firm was counsel. Mrs. Willkie had left town on a vacation, admonishing her husband not to forget to pay the electric bill, which would soon arrive. Characteristically, however, he forgot to pay it, and one night, arriving home, he found "on the doorknob a red tag, notifying him that his electric service would be turned off unless he paid his bill the next day." This made enough of an impression so that he remembered to stop at the Company office the next morning. Noting that the young man at the cashier's window did not recognize him or his name, Willkie pretended to be angry about the notice, and to become more so as the clerk "tried to smooth the matter over by being polite and sympathetic." He threatened to sue the Company if service was discontinued, disparaged the Company's lawyers, and declared that he would like nothing better than to get them into court and show them up, since he was a lawyer himself. Still anxious to placate the customer, "the clerk leaned over the counter" and "in a confidential tone" remarked, "I don't think they're so hot either." Willkie suppressed his mirth and paid the bill without more ado.[80]

The ability to enjoy a joke even when it was on himself was, like his choice of associates and leisure activities, a reflection of his inner security and self-reliance; and this in turn, along with his moral idealism, led him to reject vehemently the notion of seeking personal connections for the sake of social or professional advancement.

Two stories illustrate this attitude. In his earlier years at Akron, when he still had his career to make, his friend William F. O'Neil of the General Tire and Rubber Company once invited him and Mrs. Willkie to a dinner party, accompanying the invitation with the remark, "You'll meet some rich people who can give you some law business." Willkie declined the invitation. "We're not going to keep up with the Joneses," he said. "We're going to keep up with the Willkies. I'll come to your house any time you want, but I don't want to meet your rich friends."[81]

This episode did not affect the friendship between Willkie and O'Neil. But a somewhat similar experience involving an unnamed acquaintance aroused deep and lasting resentment. Willkie was still nominally an Episcopalian, and in Akron he and Mrs. Willkie were accustomed to attending the smaller of the city's two Episcopal churches because they liked the rector, a Dr. Atwater. This, the acquaintance told him, was a mistake. He ought to attend the larger and more fashionable church, St. Paul's, where he would make professionally profitable contacts with some of Akron's wealthier citizens. Willkie was furious.[82]

In later years his attitude remained the same. In New York he and Mrs. Willkie often attended the Fifth Avenue Presbyterian Church because they liked the minister, Dr. John Sutherland Bonnell. But after he entered public life, Willkie was so violently repelled by the idea that somebody might think of him as trying to win votes by a display of religion that he actually cut down on his church attendance.[83] The same motive brought him into conflict with his advisers over whether, in his speech accepting the nomination, there should be some expression of religious sentiment at the end. Willkie declined to use the word "God" but finally agreed to "almighty Providence."[84] In his last years he was wont to say to his friends, "You understand, of course, that I am not a deeply religious man";[85] and behind the smile one could discern an edge of irony, and of contempt for conventional displays of piety.

In general, it is clear that he had little taste for theological speculation or for the traditional forms of Christian worship. Creeds and rituals were things that he apparently felt no need of. Where religion was needed, it seemed to him, was in the relations between human beings. But his plea was not for mutual "tolerance" by members of differing religious groups

There is irony as well as comedy in the action of a Catholic group in Akron who, thinking that he must be a Catholic because of his attacks on the Klan, invited him to be a marshal in their parade![86] His plea was for the breaking down of all barriers between men, for the equalizing of opportunities, for the setting up of common and not competitive goals that men could work for. Perhaps the time was ripe, he once told his friend Charles Nutter, for a new religion, since the existing religious organizations seemed to be out of touch with the needs of the present day.[87] In the meantime, he was willing to work for the realization of his ideals with all men of good will.

This, then, is the picture of Willkie that emerges from the records of his ten years in Akron: an eloquent and earnest public speaker; a courageous and public-spirited citizen; a hard-working and resourceful lawyer; a man endowed with self-reliance, a sense of humor, a hatred of hypocrisy, and a moral idealism unconfined by formal creeds.

7

The decision to leave Akron was not made lightly.

Many persons have testified to the intensity of Willkie's ambition. And it is true that when he engaged in any kind of activity, he wanted to master it; when he entered any kind of contest, he wanted to win. He threw himself into every undertaking without reserve, and with the determination to push it through to the desired conclusion. If this is what is meant by "ambition," Willkie had it.

But when the chance came—at the age of thirty-seven—to go to New York as counsel for a billion-dollar corporation, at a salary of $36,000 a year,[88] he hesitated. He had no complaints about life in Akron. He told Hugh Johnson later, speaking of this period: "I thought I was fixed for life. I wanted to stay right there."[89] And ten years after leaving he said in a radio speech that he had spent "perhaps the happiest and most satisfying years of my life" in Akron.[90]

No doubt he was exaggerating a little, however, when he went to his friend Underwood one evening after getting the offer and said, "I've got a terrible decision to make, and I want to tell you about it." To Underwood it did not seem a terrible decision; it seemed the chance of a lifetime, which it would be unthinkable to refuse. But Willkie dwelt on the contrasting ways of life between which he was choosing. Here he could have "a nice house," close friends, a sense of belonging to a community. He thought his personal life would be much happier than amid what seemed to him the rootless, ruthless existence in a city like New York, with its ceaseless competition and strife. (He said nothing about his professional eminence in Akron, and the prominence in business and financial circles to which it had led—as evidenced by directorships of the Ohio State Bank, the South Akron Savings Association, the Acme Mortgage Company, and the Northern Ohio Power and Light Company.)[91]

His friend had the feeling, however, that Willkie was playing the role of Devil's Advocate, and that he really wished to be persuaded of the wisdom of the change. So Underwood suggested—quite sincerely—that in order to be happy he *needed* the excitement of constantly renewed or varied or more compelling challenges such as the new environment would bring. Willkie acknowledged the soundness of the argument.[92]

Another probable reason for his hesitation was that he would no longer be so completely on his own, but would have to carry out policies made at a higher level. To resolve this doubt he went to Chicago to see his old friend Maurice Bluhm, who was in the employ of the Milwaukee Railroad (where he eventually became General Counsel and Vice President), and to ask how he liked working for a great corporation. Bluhm's answer was that he found it pleasant and satisfying.[93] And probably, again, this was the answer that Willkie wanted.

Yet there were to be moments of nostalgia. Throughout his life he retained much of the simplicity of taste and outlook that he had acquired in Elwood. (He liked later to tell the story—when "some of his friends used to tell him that he ought to spruce up a bit"—of meeting an old friend from Indiana and informing him "that he was a member of Akron's leading law firm. 'Well,' said the friend, 'you still look like an Indiana farmer to me.'")[94] He took New York in stride, but the record does not show that he ever changed the opinion about big city life that he had expressed to Underwood. In later years he wrote to his university friend Robert Lang: "Maurice Bluhm told me . . . that you were always wondering why I left Indiana. I live perhaps, a more strenuous and varied life by so doing but I sometimes wonder whether I have lived on in as much ease and contentment as I would have lived if I had stayed in my own state."[95]

It is easy to be nostalgic, perhaps, about "the road not taken," after the chosen road has led to a spectacular success. Nevertheless, the break was not made without a severe emotional wrench. To the 125 persons who attended the farewell dinner given him by the Akron Bar Association a week before he left, he declared: "The most difficult thing I ever had to do is leave Akron. . . . I never would have considered leaving Akron if I had realized it would be so hard to sever my associations here."[96]

Nor did he feel, when he arrived in New York, the elation that might have been expected. For once his optimism was overbalanced by a presentiment of disaster. Though more experienced men were still predicting unlimited economic prosperity, some prophetic genius made him turn to his wife and say: "Billie, we've come too late."[97] But a still longer view of the future would have shown him that, with reference to the career that lay before him, the time was exactly right. The depression that brought ruin to so many others, gave rise to events that opened to him the road to greatness.

So ends the Akron chapter of Willkie's life. He arrived in 1919 as just another young lawyer, not knowing exactly the shape of the success he sought. He left in 1929 with his feet on the path that would lead him, not indeed to the White House, but to a position where he exercised an influence over his countrymen far greater, and far better, than that of many men who have held America's highest office.

V

Commonwealth & Southern vs. the New Deal

1

Willkie's new job was nominally that of junior partner in the law firm of Weadock & Willkie, counsel to the Commonwealth & Southern Corporation. The senior partner, John C. Weadock (pronounced "Wed-duck"), lent the firm prestige, but it was Willkie who did the work for C & S, to which he devoted himself exclusively.

He began work on October 1, 1929, twenty-nine days before the most memorable session in the history of the New York Stock Exchange signalled the onset of the Great Depression. Years of steadily rising stock prices had created the seductive illusion, even among financial leaders, that the rise would go on forever. In June the *American Magazine* published an interview with Bernard Baruch, later an adviser to three Presidents and one of America's most widely admired "elder statesmen," in which he prophesied: "In broad and general terms progress is on the march. The economic condition of the world seems on the verge of a vast forward movement." And in August another family magazine of vast circulation, the *Ladies' Home Journal,* printed an interview with John J. Raskob, conservative financier whom Al Smith had made National Democratic Chairman in 1928, of which the tenor was indicated by the title, "Everybody Ought to Be Rich." With such impressive authority, it is not surprising that everybody rushed to get into the market. And the certainty of a rise in price made it safe to buy stocks, not outright, but on the thinnest of margins. Eventually there would be enough profit to pay for them in full—or to buy more on margin.

But in early autumn the mood of the market changed; prices stopped rising; some even declined. There were sharp day-to-day fluctuations. Then on October 23 came a terrifying plunge; and on Tuesday, October 29, the bottom dropped out. In a hysterical attempt to get out of the market before they were utterly ruined, investors dumped 16,410,030 shares onto the floor of the Exchange. Tens of billions of dollars of what owners had assumed to be real wealth suddenly vanished, leaving countless persons, including many who had always thought of themselves as prudent and responsible, in a daze of bewilderment and despair.

And this was only the beginning. Even those who could afford to hold their stocks, and were encouraged by the slowness of the general economic decline to believe that renewed prosperity was indeed "just around the corner," had only a temporary reprieve. The common stock of United States Steel, for instance, which during 1929 reached a high of 261¾, and sank to 150 before the end of the year, went down in 1930 to 134⅜, in 1931 to 36, in 1932 to 21¼. General Motors stock fell during the same period from 91¾ to 7⅝.[1]

The common stock of the Commonwealth & Southern Corporation meanwhile dropped from a high of 23¾ to 1⅝. And though Willkie in October, 1929 was only the newly appointed junior partner of the law firm serving as counsel to C & S, a brief history of the corporation is essential to Willkie's biography.

The utilities holding company is a corporation which typically holds a controlling interest in the common stock of the operating companies, that is, the companies that actually produce and distribute electric power (or gas). In testimony before a Congressional committee in 1935 Willkie summarized the benefits of holding companies by quoting the man who at that time was his chief opponent in the controversy between C & S and the Tennesee Valley Authority, David E. Lilienthal: "The spread of rural electrification, the amazing advances in telephony, the rise of superpower systems—these and many other technological developments so intimately related to the public welfare are directly attributable to the holding company. Perhaps most important of all, to the holding company must go the credit for the unprecedented flow of capital into the public utility industry making possible extensions and improvements of service."[2]

At the date of this testimony, however, Lilienthal had joined the critics who viewed the holding company as a mere parasite on the operating companies (a "financial tapeworm"). He demanded "a clean-up of an intolerable situation."[3] What made the situation worse was that control of the operating companies was often achieved by a relatively small initial investment. Two practices made this possible. One was the issuing of securities of which only a small percentage carried voting rights. The second was "pyramiding," whereby "intermediate" holding companies were set up, which in turn were controlled and exploited by another holding company—a process which could be indefinitely repeated.[4] These practices made it possible for a small group of men, like that headed by the notorious Samuel Insull, to gain control of a vast network of operating companies which they could rule for their own profit.[5]

Regulation by state authorities was almost impossible, even when these authorities were not bribed or coerced into permitting illegal practices or exorbitant rates. And even the Federal government, President Roosevelt declared, was helpless. In a message to Congress in March, 1935, urging legislation that would entirely abolish public utility holding companies, he declared: "Regulation has small chance of success against the kind of concentrated wealth and power which holding companies have shown the power to acquire in the utility field."[6]

Despite the prevalence of unsavory practices, however, and despite later allegations, there seem to have been few sins to be charged to the account of C & S. It was chartered in Delaware on May 23, 1929, and was authorized to issue 60,000,000 shares of common stock (of which about 34,000,000 were actually issued) "without nominal or par value," along with option warrants for the purchase of half as many additional shares, at $30 a share (the expectation was that the price would rise far above $30); and 2,000,000 shares of preferred stock (of which 1,500,000 were actually issued) with a guaranteed dividend of $6 a year. The chief agents in forming the corporation were Bonbright & Company, and it was formed by exchanging stock with three other large holding companies, the Commonwealth Power Company, the Southeastern Power and Light Company, and the Penn-Ohio Edison Company, whose combined assets were given as $1,042 million and their combined annual gross earnings as more than $135 million.[7] The shares of common stock were valued at $19 for purposes of exchange[8] (somewhat lower than would have been justified by the current market value of the stocks for which they were exchanged), but on May 29, in "over the counter" trading, it was quoted at 23¼ bid, 23¾ asked.[9] By the beginning of July, C & S had acquired 90 per cent of the stock of the companies, and was about to add a fourth, the Columbus (Ga.) Electric and Power Company. It had already, on June 25, announced its first quarterly dividend of 1/80 of a share (equivalent to a 5 per cent stock dividend), payable September 1.[10]

The moving spirit in the new corporation was Bernard Capen Cobb.[11] He was at first chairman of the board, the president being Thomas W. Martin, who had been president of Southeastern Power and Light. But Martin was a Southerner who "hated New York,"[12] and in June, 1932, he retired from the presidency,[13] and Cobb took it over while remaining chairman of the board.

Cobb was primarily a production man, not a financier, and although Willkie was later given credit for many reforms, most of them were initiated by Cobb. In early January, 1930, less than eight months after the corporation was organized, the four intermediate holding companies were eliminated, and during the year all the operating companies in Ohio, Pennsylvania, Michigan, and Georgia were consolidated into one company for each state.[14] Thus he made substantial progress toward reducing the number of operating companies from the original 165 to the 11 of which it was finally composed.[15] These were Consumers Power (Michigan), Central Illinois Light, Southern Indiana Gas and Electric, Ohio Edison,

Pennsylvania Power, Tennessee Electric Power (TEPCO), Alabama Power, Georgia Power, Gulf Power (Florida), Mississippi Power, and South Carolina Power. The holding company owned all the common stock of these companies except 2 per cent of TEPCO's; together they produced 95 percent of the gross revenue of the system.[16] Obviously they fall into two groups, the Northern and the Southern, which, as it happened, were about equal in size.[17]

Cobb was also responsible for setting up, a year after the original organization of C & S, a new service and management company, with the same name but chartered in New York. Its aim was to give the operating companies "the advantage of combined power for buying apparatus, equipment and supplies; of technical services such as engineering, financial and legal advice; of advertising, publicity and other public relations services; and of intangible services that the large organization maintained in New York City is able to give quickly and easily. None of the operating companies could afford to maintain so complete a staff at its own expense." All the stock of the new corporation was to be owned by the operating companies and all services were to be supplied at cost. (In practice, the operating companies were billed at a fixed rate—in January, 1935, it was 1.15 per cent of their gross revenue—and any profit was returned to them.)[18]

This was apparently an innovation in utility holding company practice, which other companies were said to be watching with interest. It not only eliminated one of the most flagrant abuses charged against utility holding companies, whereby the holding company owned the service company, compelled the operating companies to employ it (in construction, for instance) at arbitrary prices, and kept the profits; it was also an at least partial answer to the allegation that a holding company had no legitimate function. In 1938 the C & S service company won the approval of the Securities and Exchange Commission, which found that "the services could be rendered at a reasonable saving to associate companies over the cost to such companies of comparable services performed by themselves or by independent persons."[19]

Not even the highest measure of enlightened management, however, could have enabled the Corporation to avoid the effects of the depression. During the first full year after its organization, the gross earnings of the C & S system were more than $147 million. But during the next three years, as the depression gradually paralyzed the nation's industry, and the demand for power was reduced, these earnings declined at an average rate of more than $1 million a month. For the year ending May 31, 1933, they were less than $109 million.[20]

To understand the effect of this decline, one must understand something of how public utilities differ from other industries in their financial operations. A large initial investment is necessary for the construction of power plants (either steam or hydroelectric), transmission lines, and distribution systems, but thereafter the cost of producing and distributing electricity is relatively low.[21] Large profits are in theory impossible, however, because maximum rates for the sale of power are normally fixed by state commissions. This arrangement is necessary because utilities constitute a "natural monopoly." As in the communication and transportation industries, competition is simply wasteful. To build two sets of facilities to serve the same area would nearly double the cost to consumers. But without competition and without government regulation, a company could force its customers to pay whatever it might choose to ask—the only check being that at a certain point small customers would stop using electricity and large industries would start producing their own. Hence, regulation, allowing a "fair return" on investment—and no more—becomes a necessity.

This "fair return" does not ordinarily permit profits large enough to provide capital for expansion, which must be obtained by issuing bonds or new stock; and the "provision for retirement reserve" (or "depreciation") required, and often fixed, by law does not really provide for amortization of the company's indebtedness; it represents simply the depreciation of the physical properties and the need for their eventual replacement. As Lilienthal told the Congressional committee investigating TVA: "private utilities, like railroads, do not amortize their capital structure. They never pay off their debts but refinance."[22]

The result is that a large part of a utility company's gross earnings goes to pay interest on its indebtedness; this, along with dividends on preferred stock, constitutes "fixed charges" that may be larger than operating expenses. Also fixed, to a great extent, are taxes and provision for retirement reserve.[23] Thus, during the early years of the depression, while the gross earnings of the C & S sytem were being drastically reduced, many of its liabilities remained substantially unchanged. Only operating costs could be cut; these were kept at about 40 per cent of gross earnings. But taxes remained about the same, between $14 and $15 million; the provision for retirement reserve remained between $9 and $10 million; interest on bonds and dividends on preferred stock of the operating companies remained approximately the same, something over $40 million. The balance, if any, went to the owners of the common stock of the holding company.

For the year ending May 31, 1930, this balance had been about $24 million, equivalent to 70 cents a share, a return of approximately 3 per cent on the $24 a share for which the stock was selling just before the crash.[24] But for the year ending May 31, 1933, the balance applicable to dividends on the common stock had shrunk to $340,000, or about one cent a share; and thereafter, although gross earnings began gradually to rise, taxes and expenses rose faster, so that for the year ending December 31, 1934, the balance had changed into a deficit of more than $1.5 million. This deficit had to come out of dividends on C & S preferred stock, which were accordingly cut from $6 to $3 in 1935. (The arrears that accumulated thereafter had to be paid up before any dividends could be paid on the common stock. By the beginning of 1940 they amounted to about $22.5 million.)

What these perhaps dull statistics show is that Commonwealth & Southern was on the whole honestly organized and operated; and that the heavy loss suffered by the early buyers of the common stock was simply a part of the national misfortune called the Great Depression.

This conclusion does not alter the fact that when Willkie in 1933 became president of C & S, he was taking on a tough job. On the other hand, it offered a challenge, and he accepted it confidently.

This confidence, as far as it rested on his ability, seemed justified. At the age of forty-one he headed one of America's great corporations, with assets of more than a billion dollars and annual gross earnings, at the lowest point in the depression, of more than a hundred million depression dollars. He had come far from his father's unpretentious law office in Elwood, which he had left in some uncertainty of mind only fourteen years before. How had this spectacular advancement come about?

In line with his general aim of unifying the system, Cobb had decided that the operating companies ought to have a uniform legal policy. When, for instance, officials appeared before a regulatory body in one state, they might take a position or advance an argument that would run counter to what officials of another company were saying in another state. Cobb's first choice for the job was George Roberts, a member of a prominent New York law firm which had numbered among its clients Cobb and his associates in organizing C & S. Roberts declined, but gave Cobb a piece of advice: "Go around to the operating companies and pick out the best young lawyer you can find. Bring him to New York and give him the job."[25]

Meanwhile, in Akron, one of the principal clients of Mather, Nesbitt, and Willkie was the Northern Ohio Traction and Light Company. (In 1926 it became the Northern Ohio Power and Light Company, and in 1930, after C & S began consolidating its operating companies, the Ohio Edison Company.) The general manager, A. C. Blinn, could not help noticing, from the first, Willkie's capacity for work and the promptness as well as the effectiveness with which he handled whatever matters were brought to him. (He also, according to a later account, "eliminated so much graft" in franchise renewals through his "persuasive and aboveboard handling of them" that the company "became known as a reformed utility.")[26] Blinn therefore urged Cobb, "not once but many times," to make a point on one of his visits to Akron of watching Willkie in action. He "never received the slightest response," however, until one day, in the wake of rumors that Willkie's law firm was about to be dissolved, Cobb said without preface, "If the Mather firm breaks up, don't let Willkie get away."[27]

In his new job Willkie more than justified Blinn's good opinion. Energetic and decisive, yet easy to work with, he soon began to be talked of as a successor to Cobb, whose health was increasingly precarious. In 1932, by way of testing him, Cobb relieved him of many of his purely legal duties and made him his assistant; and on January 24, 1933, the board of directors approved Cobb's request that Willkie be made president of C & S.[28] Cobb stayed on as chairman of the board, although progressively less active, until June 20, 1934, when ill health forced his retirement. Willkie then assumed complete authority as chief executive officer of C & S, at a salary of $75,000.[29] (He is said to have turned down a later offer by the board of directors to increase his salary with the comment that $75,000 was the salary of the President of the United States, and that was enough.[30] It is also said that he refused two other jobs, either of which would have paid him $250,000.[31]) He abolished the position of chairman of the board as "too damn stuffy. I would have to be dignified."[32]

2

Thirty-nine days after Willkie became president of Commonwealth & Southern, Franklin D. Roosevelt became President of the United States. And immediately thereafter he initiated a project which, as it developed, forced Willkie to become his antagonist in a prolonged struggle which eventually became a sort of focus for the opposition of American business to certain aspects of the New Deal.

This project was the Tennesseee Valley Authority (later abbreviated almost universally to TVA), and the controversy concerning it, especially its relations with the C & S subsidiaries operating in the area, is one that no conscientious biographer can approach without misgivings. The issues are in themselves so complex and difficult to define, they are so entangled with personalities and politics, they involve (if one wishes to decide where the rights and wrongs of the controversy lay) so vast an amount of technical information, that one would like to bypass the whole affair. But it occupied so large a place in Willkie's life for so many years, and had so decisive an effect upon his career, that it must be made a part of the record.

TVA was one of the "alphabetical" agencies through which the President and his advisers launched a many-fronted attack on the depression. As announced by Roosevelt a month before his inauguration, it seemed primarily an expression of his enthusiasm for conservation and his eagerness to put people to work. The main stress was on reforestation and (almost incidentally) flood control, and on the number of men who would be given employment. But the bill introduced into Congress immediately after his special message on the subject on April 10 was sponsored by Senator Norris of Nebraska, a relentless critic of the utility industry and an ardent advocate of public power; and among its provisions was one giving TVA the power to build and own transmission lines, without regard to whether or not they duplicated existing lines.

It was natural for Willkie to take the lead in opposing the part of the bill that authorized duplication. The Tennesseee River swings in a great arc from its headwaters in western Virginia southwest across eastern Tennessee, loops into northern Alabama, forms for a brief distance the northeast boundary of Mississippi, moves north to cross Tennessee once more, and continues north across Kentucky to empty into the Ohio. Four of the six Southern companies of C & S (excluding two small companies, Gulf Power and South Carolina Power) operated in the area.

In his testimony before the House Committee on Military Affairs on April 14, Willkie pointed out the implications of this clause. He argued that "to take our markets is to take our property. If this market is taken away, this property is valueless." He also noted another provision permitting TVA to cancel a contract with a private company on two years' notice, and pictured the plight of a company that had come to depend on TVA power and suddenly received notice of cancellation. "There is not a bond house and there is not an investor, with the provisions of this bill as they now are, that would buy securities of any of these companies." As an alternative, he promised: "If you will make that power, we will absorb it into our system as fast as we can; which means, in effect, that we will have to cease the building of generating plants and absorb that power." He was even willing to let the government set the price: "if we buy this power and you have the privilege to say to us at what price we shall sell it to the ultimate consumer, how can we get any advantage?"

Or if Congress considered it "imperative to pass the bill in its present form," permitting the government, if it wished, to take over the power industry in the area, then the bill should be passed. But then the government should be willing to offer "fair compensation" to the utility companies, just as it did to the farmers whose lands were flooded by the dams.[33]

In other circumstances, his testimony might have had an effect. But Roosevelt was the man of the hour; his words and actions had brought hope to millions; and an overwhelmingly Democratic Congress was willing to give him any legislation he asked for. The bill was passed substantially as written, and when Roosevelt signed it on May 28, Willkie himself issued a hopeful statement. Declaring that he and the heads of the companies in the Tennessee Valley area were "in favor of the administration's plan for the development of the valley," and that they had also "offered no objection to the government developing such hydrogenerating plants . . . as might be thought necessary in connection with the government's flood control and navigation program," he noted that advocates of the measure had stated on the Senate floor that transmission lines would not necessarily be built "if the electric distribution companies are willing to contract for the purchase of electric power generated by the government and distribute the same to their consumers at reasonable rates. This we have at all times been willing to do."[34]

This optimism, however, failed to take account of two things. One was the intensity of the public distrust of the power industry, bred by the Insull and similar scandals and a long history of predatory action by individual companies in charging what the traffic would bear—a history documented in a many-volumed report made by the Federal Trade Commission after exhaustive investigation. This distrust was bound to be reflected in Congress. Some Congressmen honestly shared it; others saw the political expediency of professing it; and a combination of both these motives made still other persons, in the Administration as well as in Congress, eager by any means to foment feeling against the power companies.

On the same day, for instance, that Roosevelt signed the original TVA bill, a statement was issued through the office of Secretary Ickes which charged that the Alabama and Tennessee Power Companies, which had been buying power at Muscle Shoals, had been using government facilities there to transfer power from one private company to the other, thus lessening purchases of government power, in violation of the contract; and some newspapers made it appear that the companies had been simply stealing the power. The heads of the two companies, Thomas W. Martin and Jo Conn Guild, wired Roosevelt that the story was "unqualifiedly false" and demanded a full and immediate hearing.[35] They did not get it; and when, months later, they were cleared by an investigation, the public heard nothing about it, although the original story had rated front-page headlines in all the papers. Willkie believed that the story had been invented in retaliation for his testimony against the bill.[36]

The second fact that Willkie failed to take into account (necessarily, since it was not yet known) was the attitude of David E. Lilienthal, one of the three-man board of directors of TVA, whose special responsibility was power. Lilienthal was a man with a vision, which he later expressed with force and eloquence in *TVA: Democracy on the March*. He saw the Tennessee Valley as it was; not only the slashed and eroded forest hillsides, the exhausted and gullied fields, the washed and stony roads, the dilapidated farm buildings, the somnolent and static towns, but the people who lived there—gaunt, ragged and unlettered, beset by malaria and malnutrition, without the ambition or the means to abandon the bankrupt pattern of the past. And he saw it as it might be; the forests and fields restored, the homes repaired and painted, the people decently fed and clothed and endowed with energy and hope, their bodies and minds set free to build a better life. There was an almost mystical quality in Lilienthal's philosophy as he later stated it: "that resource development must be governed by the unity of nature herself" and "that the people must participate actively in that development."[37]

The means to make this dream come true was mainly power—power from the great dams that he envisaged along the river and its tributaries; power to turn the wheels of new industries, power to light the homes and lighten the labors of the farmers and their wives and children. And to achieve this end, it must be cheap, so that people would use it freely; there was no reason why the price should include a profit for private companies that wished to distribute it. The dams belonged to "the people," and "the people" should benefit from the power they produced. The cost, he declared, appeared in the account books of TVA, "but the benefits appear on the balance sheet of the region and the nation."[38]

Besides his vision, he had a keen mind, a flair for rhetoric, an unyielding temper, and a confidence in his own rightness that was no less strong than Willkie's, and that bred a certain degree of ruthlessness in dealing with opponents.

It is to Lilienthal's credit that he did not try to hide his aims. His statement of TVA's power policy, issued on August 24, 1933, had all the earmarks of a manifesto, as the following assertions will show. "The business of generating and distributing electric power is a public business." "The interest of the public in the widest possible use of power is superior to any private interest." "The right of a community to own and operate its own electric plant is undeniable," either "by acquiring the existing plant or setting up a competing plant." The aim of TVA in regard to power will be "the accomplishment of the social objectives which low cost power makes possible. The Authority cannot decline to take action solely upon the ground that to do so would injure a private utility." Eventually, "to make the area a workable one and a fair measure of public ownership, it should include several cities of substantial size, such as Chattanooga and Knoxville, and ultimately one city of more than a quarter million, within transmission distance, such as Birmingham, Memphis, Atlanta, or Louisville." Detailed accounting will "permit of comparison with privately owned plants," and "supply a 'yardstick' and an incentive to both private and public managers."[39]

A few weeks later he added a comment on the yardstick principle which was to be so important in the ensuing controversy. "Public ownership of power is just another means of public control. . . . If State utility commissions are not giving this public control, then it may be necessary for the government itself to step in and by distributing power itself show what is a fair rate to charge. This is the yardstick method."[40] The insistence that TVA provide such a yardstick obviously precluded sale of TVA power to private companies "at the switchboard," and also the later proposal of "power pooling."

Guessing at what the "yardstick" would show, Lilienthal the next day announced the rates for TVA power to domestic consumers. There would be a flat rate of $1.50 a month to the ordinary "small user," on the assumption that he would use on the average 50 kilowatt hours a month; for those who used more there was scale starting at 3 cents per KWH and decreasing with the amount, so that 200 KWH a month would cost $4.50.[41] Comparable rates for C & S companies in Alabama and Georgia, established in early 1933 (before the creation of TVA) and uniform for both states, were $2.58 and $5.95, far lower than the national average.[42]

The private utilities asserted, then and later, that TVA rates were possible only because of subsidies from the Federal government. For the time being, however, with only the power from Wilson Dam at Muscle Shoals available to the TVA, and with TVA policies still to be worked out in practice, both sides were willing to adopt a live-and-let-live attitude. On January 4, 1934, after much negotiation, Willkie and Lilienthal signed a contract providing that C & S would sell TVA certain properties in Alabama, Mississippi, and Tennessee, in order to provide a yardstick area, and would buy TVA's surplus power; in return, TVA would not try to compete with C & S companies in areas which they already served. The contract was to run for five years or until Norris Dam began producing power.[43]

3

It is doubtful that, given Lilienthal's philosophy and Roosevelt's willingness to back him, such an agreement could have been more than temporary. At any rate, by the summer of 1936, when the completion of Norris Dam terminated the contract, events had occurred which clouded the issues that were in contention and hardened the attitudes of those who were contending; until Willkie could say truthfully, in a letter to Roosevelt that was itself conciliatory, "The present status is one of practically open warfare."[44]

The first of these events was the so-called Ashwander suit, brought by a small group of preferred stockholders of the Alabama Power Company to prevent the sale of property by that company to TVA under the January 4 agreement. It was charged by Willkie's enemies that he had not bargained in good faith, and that the suit was brought with his foreknowledge and approval.[45] The charge rests on the fact that the suit was backed by the Edison Electric Institute (a trade association of the utility industry), of whose board of trustees Willkie was a member. Willkie vehemently denied it, in a telegram to Presidential Secretary Steve Early on November 19, 1934: "Press dispatches quoted various officials on the President's recent trip that the power companies are behind the recent litigation preventing the transfer of property to TVA. The President or you or others may infer this to mean that the Commonwealth & Southern Corporation or some of its operating units are behind such litigation. I say to you that any such statement made to you by anybody is an absolute and unqualified falsehood and readily demonstrable as such."[46] Nevertheless, many New Deal partisans believed the charge, while Willkie in turn believed that it was a calculated slander. (The Supreme Court in its decision said: "there is no question that the suit was brought in good faith.")[47]

On the other side Roosevelt declared in a speech at Tupelo, Mississippi, on November 18, 1933, after praising the community for being the first to buy all its power from TVA: "What you are doing here is going to be copied in every State in the Union before we get through."[48] So far as this was more than mere rhetoric, Roosevelt was probably thinking of other "valley authorities." He certainly never advocated public operation of the entire power industry. But leaders in that industry might be excused for taking it, along with Lilienthal's earlier statement, as a declaration of war.

For nearly a year after this date, however, Willkie's public utterances remained generally temperate in content and tone. In a speech on "Government and Private Ownership," delivered on September 26, 1934, to the American Statistical Association, he praised the TVA directors as "men of intelligence, energy and devotion to the work they have undertaken." And in his argument for private ownership of the utilities there was no attempt to blur the issue with emotional attacks on "socialism." "I believe [the facts] demonstrate that private operation is the best . . . because it will best serve the public and at the lowest cost. That is the test by which privately owned operation as well as publicly owned utility operation must be measured. If I evade that test for the interest which I serve, I shall fail and I should fail." (Three years later, in an *Atlantic* article called "Political Power," he said the same thing: "But there is nothing sacred about private operation of business. The utilities have no God-given charter for existing. . . . The only question which the people are interested in . . . is: *What is the best way to generate and distribute electric power economically?*")[49]

He then listed—as he was to do so many times in the future—the factors that, he held, gave TVA an unfair advantage over the private utilities. First, the Public Works Administration was offering outright grants of 30 per cent of the cost (later the upper limit was set at 45 per cent) of distribution systems built by municipalities which bought TVA power; private companies must pay the entire cost. Second, Wilson Dam with its power plants had cost $60,000,000 but was down on the books of TVA at $20,000,000; private companies (he implied but did not say) would have had to pay interest on this difference of $40,000,000. Third, TVA paid 5 per cent of its gross earnings in taxes; Willkie's company in that area paid 20 per cent. "If the factors which I have mentioned are equalized, the Tennessee Electric Power Company could, on its present volume of business, double its net income and still reduce its industrial rates . . . to 10 per cent below the TVA rates . . . and reduce rates for domestic and commercial consumers 35 per cent below the rates charged by TVA in that nationally famous yardstick at Tupelo." In addition, he pointed out that TVA had free use of the mails, reduced rail fares for its personnel, a one-third reduction in railroad freight rates, and the ability to borrow money at lower rates because its bonds were guaranteed by the United States Government.[50]

If there is an aggressive note in Willkie's concluding remarks, it was more than matched by Lilienthal in a speech to the Rotary Club of Birmingham a month later, in which he declared that "Birmingham and Wall Street" were linked in the fight against TVA, and charged "Wall Street" with "the desire to retain control of the country and to continue the sending of a stream of money from other sections of the country to its vaults. . . . To these great concerns the Birmingham district is a kind of colonial possession to which proconsuls are sent to administer colonial affairs."[51]

Willkie answered him a week later before the same audience, and in the same tone, in "The Other Side of the TVA." "I have no doubt that you will soon hear that the headquarters of the Tennessee Valley Authority are to be removed to your state, where, as I recall, the law provides they should be located; and that no proconsul from Knoxville will issue edicts affecting your interests. . . . If my memory serves me right, proconsuls were not representatives of private business but of government, and, as I recall, they are classic in world history as the extravagant and wanton spenders of the taxpayers' money."[52]

The two men met in debate on January 21, 1935, at a joint meeting of the Economic Club of New York and the Harvard Business School Club. The main subject was utility holding companies in general—which, it had just become known, Roosevelt was planning to abolish. But Lilienthal dwelt at length on the sins of the utility companies as a justification for TVA's yardstick policy. Willkie in reply also made a calculated appeal to emotion. He had a large and sympathetic audience[53] and he made the most of it.

His beginning, it is true, was temperate: "if we can present the facts, as I honestly know and understand them, I do not believe we need be apprehensive about the future of the industry." And he gave the facts as he had given them before. But this time he added shrewd dramatic touches. Asserting that municipal power plants had a long record of inefficiency, he quoted a letter written by Roosevelt in 1926 to Thomas W. Martin, president of the Alabama Power Company, complaining that Warm Springs and neighboring communities were "suffering from the usual high cost and inefficient service of small local power plants," and inquiring indirectly whether power could be obtained from "a high tension power line" near by, reputedly owned by the Alabama Power Company. The result was that the latter purchased the local plant, made it a part of the system, and provided both a reduction in rates and an improvement in service which Roosevelt had often praised.

Willkie was shrewd, too, in presenting another of his arguments against TVA—that there was already an excess of generating capacity in the Tennessee Valley. Declaring that a frequent charge against the utilities was that "they imprudently overbuilt their generating capacity in 1929 and 1930 and now expect the consumer of electric energy to pay a legitimate return on such excess investment," he pointed out that this had been done partly at the request of President Hoover as a means of combating the depression, and that many utility executives had complied, but with misgivings. On the other side, "I remember how one forceful, dynamic, and attractive figure, Mr. Samuel Insull, said of such faint hearts that they were entirely mistaken; that it was impossible to overbuild the requirements of electric generating capacity for this country . . . that the industry should sell such securities as were necessary to provide the money with which to do such construction work. He was, of course, tragically mistaken."

Willkie was also willing to invoke now, although incidentally, the fear of "socialism." One group of those advocating government ownership of utilities was composed of persons "enamored with European economic and social concepts." Their beliefs were held with a kind of "religious phrenzy . . . against which no amount of argument or factual presentation will prevail." (He later viewed with alarm "abandoning the tradition of 150 years in this country, that government should remain entirely outside the field of private enterprise.")

Passing by these, and also the second group (political demagogues "whose conversion lies in the conversion of their constituents"), Willkie came to the third group, who had been "led by subversive propaganda to the belief that abuses have arisen in the utility industry which can be corrected only through government ownership." His line of argument here was that abuses in private industry had their counterpart in government: "human nature operates the same whether one is employed by government or whether one is employed by private capital. Honesty and integrity characterize in large preponderance both spheres of activity and influence. Restraint, regulation and control are required in each."

His peroration reveals the spirit and technique of his crusade to save his companies and the utility industry in general; it foreshadows his "crusade" in 1940. "Those who oppose the utility organization . . . assume an attitude of superior virtue and patriotism. They seek to paint us who represent private enterprise in the utility business as anti-social, unpatriotic and the despoilers of men. I yield to no government official, be he high or low, in my social obligations, love of country or fellow feeling for the struggling masses of humanity. I do not like to make personal references, but I want to say to you that no duty has ever come to me in my life, even that in the service of my country, that has so appealed to my sense of social obligation, patriotism and love of mankind as this, my obligation to say and do what I can for the preservation of public utilities privately owned. All that I have observed, all that I know and all that I read teaches me that I could do nothing nobler for the future financial stability and political good of my country or the social and economic well being of my fellow citizens, than to stand firm against this foolish fad and fancy of the moment."

In cold print the closing comments are extravagant to the point of absurdity, and the opposition in 1940 quoted them with relish. One feels that the speaker has been hypnotized by his own rhetoric. Yet it was this very capacity for unqualified surrender to conviction that gave him, in part at least, the extraordinary power over an audience to which many persons have borne witness. It was also characteristic that he found for his belief a moral basis. The issue, as Willkie saw it, was simple justice. His company had been honestly and efficiently managed; now the government was trying to destroy it.

The conflict was, in fact, basic. And while Willkie continued to plead his case in the court of public opinion, where he correctly considered that the final judgment would be rendered, the private power industry—this time with his approval—took action in the nation's courts of law. On November 25, 1934, the Edison Electric Institute announced its intention of attacking the whole TVA power policy as unconstitutional; and Lilienthal commented: "The mask is off. The few men in New York City who, through the holding companies, control the electric supply of 130,000,000 people, have stepped from behind the 'widows and orphans,' the preferred stockholders, the ice men and the coal men and are now speaking in their own behalf. We now have, in the open, a clear issue between the people who use electricity and those who have controlled it."[54] Roosevelt's reaction was apparently the same. While the Ashwander case moved slowly up to the Supreme Court (Judge W. I. Grubb of the Federal District Court in Alabama on February 22, 1935, issued an injunction against the sale of the Alabama Power Company properties to TVA and against PWA grants and loans to municipalities to build competing systems),[55] while TVA feverishly rushed to complete some projects and begin others so as to present its opponents with a *fait accompli,* while Willkie fought by increasingly frequent speeches and articles to a widening audience to sway public opinion, the Administration got a still sympathetic Congress to pass an amended TVA Act which specifically granted the Authority the right to make contracts such as those that were being challenged in the courts (this would remove the argument that the Authority had gone beyond the intent of Congress) and authorized it to borrow up to $100 million at an interest rate of not more than 3½ per cent, on the credit of the United States Government.[56]

Once again Willkie led the opposition. Now, as two years earlier, he was among the first to testify against it at the hearings by the House Military Affairs Committee. What he wanted was limitation and not expansion of the Authority's power. He urged five amendments, which would have compelled TVA: (1) to comply with the same system of accounting that private utilities had to comply with; (2) to charge a rate that would bring "a fair return on the property devoted to this business"; (3) to "stand on its own bottom" in borrowing money; (4) to file its rates with the Federal Power Commission; (5) before selling power to a community served by a private company, to buy the distribution system or, if this was impossible, to institute condemnation proceedings.[57] The Committee must have found his testimony persuasive, for it amended the bill to provide that TVA accounts should be audited by the Comptroller General, that it should not sell power under cost, and that it should not duplicate facilities; but Administration pressure removed the amendments,[58] and Roosevelt got the bill he wanted.

He also got what he wanted, for once, from the Supreme Court, which on February 17, 1936, settled the Ashwander suit in favor of TVA. (A *Times* headline read: TENNESSEE VALLEY SHOUTS WITH JOY.) Specifically refusing to consider the constitutionality of the Act as a whole, it affirmed the right of the Authority to sell surplus power from Wilson Dam and to buy the properties that it had contracted to buy.

How Willkie's mood had changed is shown by the fact that when the suit was brought, he heatedly denied any connection with it, whereas he now deplored, in words sharp with disappointment, the dismissal of the suit. The companies must continue, he declared, "to ask Congress and the Administration to stop the further invasion of their property rights and the profligate spending of the tax-payers' money."[59] And he pointed out how narrow was the issue that the Court had chosen to decide: "The threat of the TVA to take the government into the power business and to drive the companies out was not under consideration."[60]

4

This decision closed one chapter of negotiation and litigation between the power companies and TVA, and opened another. In the meantime, early in 1935, the Roosevelt Administration had brought forward a measure that carried a still more direct and immediate threat to the existence of Commonwealth & Southern. This was the Public Utility Holding Company Act, generally referred to as the Wheeler-Rayburn Bill. Its aim was to drive such companies out of existence. "Why have any?" asked Roosevelt at a press conference three years later.[61] As finally passed, after months of wrangling, in a characteristic Congressional rush to adjourn, the law set a limit of three years on the existence of all public utility holding companies except those controlling "a single integrated system" of power production and distribution, and gave to the Securities and Exchange Commission the authority to decide which companies came under the rule. (This was the provision which became known as the "death sentence"—a phrase which Willkie first applied to it.)[62] As a preliminary measure, all holding companies must register with the SEC.

Once again Willkie found himself the leader of the opposition to New Deal legislation. In 1933 he had been the logical spokesman of the utilities against that part of the TVA Act authorizing duplication of facilities, because his own companies were most immediately affected. Now, however, he was the leader in a fight that affected about three-quarters of the industry.[63] How, during his two years as president of C & S, had he achieved this eminence?

He had achieved it, first, because among utility executives he was one of the least vulnerable to the criticisms commonly made of utility practices. Cobb had eliminated most of the intermediate holding companies and had set up the non-profit service organization, and at the beginning of 1933 he and Willkie wrote off more than half a billion dollars in "watered stock" values. The 1934 annual report of C & S, signed by both men, contained the statement: "The comparative balance sheet reflects a $563,123,255 charge to surplus undertaken to reduce the book values of investments in subsidiaries to par or stated values therefor."[64]

"Watered stock" was a phrase often in the mouths of critics of the utilities—as of course it was often a fact in utility accounts. It meant, simply, stock that had been given a "book value" higher than the tangible assets that it represented. The profit to the utilities came in the inclusion of these paper values in the "rate base" on which a "fair return" was permitted. What deserves to be a classic instance was given by Senator Bone of Washington in House hearings on the original TVA bill: the Northwestern Electric Company built a hydro-electric plant on the White Salmon River in southern Washington at a cost of $1,300,000. Against this actual investment the company issued $10,424,000 in securities, and charged rates which enabled it to pay "12 or 13 per cent a year on this phantom issue."[65]

C & S had been guilty of no such sins. In the action referred to, it was simply writing down the stocks from their pre-depression market value to a realistic estimate of their worth.

Another fact that ought to have won the praise of the reformers was that when Cobb retired and Willkie became sole boss of C & S, most of the bankers on the board of directors resigned and were replaced by heads of operating companies.[66] This was, as Willkie said, "another step in the established policy of the Commonwealth & Southern Corporation to unify more completely its functions and operations. . . . the practical effect is to make the system one large operating unit."[67]

Finally, the frequent charge of exorbitant rates could not be made of C & S. Willkie asserted (and nobody challenged the figures) that in 1934 the average consumption of C & S domestic customers was 718 KWH a year against a national average of 630 (14 percent higher), while the average rate was 4.35 cents per KWH against a national average of 5.29 (18 per cent lower).[68] And on the whole these low rates were not, as TVA partisans declared, the result of that agency's competition or example. The idea that low rates would mean greater use and ultimately greater profits was no brain-child of Lilienthal. It was C & S engineers who, with this principle in mind, developed the so-called "objective rate," of which Willkie was properly proud. "For each customer under this plan, base bills are established. These base bills are the consumptions for each month of the year preceding the adoption of the plan, figured under the 'Immediate Rate.' Whenever the customer increases his use so that his bill, figured under the lower or 'Objective Rate,' is equal to or greater than his base bill, the 'Objective Rate' automatically applies. . . . after one year's operation of the plan, nearly 70 per cent of the residence customers of the Georgia, Tennessee and Alabama Companies . . . were being billed under the low 'Objective Rate.'"[69] The "objective rate" was first put into effect by the Alabama Power Company in October, 1933, and such an action must obviously be the result of months or years of planning and study.[70] Lilienthal did not announce the TVA rate until September 15.

And while rates were going down, holders of C & S common stocks were going without dividends. Some critics of the utilities, of course, insisted that this was as it should be. Lilienthal in his debate with Willkie doubted "the existence of any substantial equity for common stocks in a large part of the operating utilities of the country"[71]—that is, that the common stocks represented any genuine assets; and a question to this effect was implied when Senator Wheeler asked Willkie at a Senate hearing: "What reason have you to believe, or what reason had you to believe, that you could earn dividends upon that common stock of these operating companies?" But Willkie answered with conviction that, "Taking the allowable rate of return on the fair value of the property and eliminating any claim of any write-up that ever existed, Commonwealth & Southern could make close to a dollar a share on its common stock."[72] Instead, he was taking the long view: "If we take some punishment, we can build up."[73]

Willkie had also set the TVA an example (and not vice versa) in building up domestic use by "intensive selling of electric-current-consuming devices, such as ranges, refrigerators, washing machines and other appliances. During the year 1934 the units of the system sold $10,501,820.20 of such appliances, 80 per cent being on the deferred payment plan." (The operating companies by themselves could not have financed such a program.)[74] There is doubtless some exaggeration in the statement that one of his first acts "as president of C & S was to hire 500 new salesmen of appliances,"[75] but there is no doubt that he pushed the campaign as vigorously as he could, in view of the charges of the industry's critics "that we were subsidizing the sale of appliances" and thus preventing local dealers from making a profit—charges that in some states resulted in laws "prohibiting the sale of appliances by utilities."[76] TEPCO, for instance, enlisted in its drive two out of three of its entire force of employees—elevator boys, meter readers, and bus drivers as well as office workers. It also employed thirty-five Home Lighting Girls to bring "class, sex appeal and free lighting advice" to Tennessee homes—and to sell "more or stronger bulbs." And it hired seven agricultural experts to think up new gadgets for electrifying farms.[77]

The effectiveness of the C & S campaign is shown by the figures. For the year ending May 31, 1930 (the first full year after C & S was organized, and before the depression had had much effect), the system's industrial and commercial sales of electricity totaled approximately 4.5 billion kilowatt hours; residential (including farm) sales were 467 million. For the year ending December 31, 1934, industrial and commercial sales had fallen 13.5 per cent, to 3.9 billion KWH, but residential sales had risen 33 per cent to 621 million KWH. Most of this increase had come from a higher average use per customer—544 KWH in 1930, 718 KWH in 1934. In the same period, the gross earnings from residential electric customers rose from 18.3 per cent of total gross earnings (including those from gas and transportation) in 1930 to 23.5 per cent in 1934; and this was in spite of a 24.5 per cent cut in residential rates—from 5.769 cents per KWH to 4.353 cents.[78]

In fact, the whole record of C & S was so good that Senator Wheeler, a bitter critic of the industry, complimented Willkie at the end of his testimony against the Wheeler-Rayburn Bill before the Senate Committee on Interstate Commerce: "I am frank to say to you that probably if there had not been any more abuses in some companies than there have been in yours . . . you probably would not have been faced with some of the provisions that you are faced with at the present time."[79]

5

The other factors that pushed Willkie to the front of the stage were personal. In the first place, he was willing to talk, on any occasion and to any audience—as many of his colleagues were not. They may have had the public-be-damned attitude of the old-style tycoon like Samuel Insull, who in his one face-to-face meeting with Willkie rebuked him for challenging Insull's expressed desire to silence the critics of the utilities: "Mr. Willkie, when you are older, you will know more."[80] They may simply have been inarticulate in public, though decisive in private. Or they may have been, in these depression years for which they had been so long and loudly blamed, afraid to challenge a popular and aggressive Administration. But Willkie was by nature equalitarian, schooled from childhood to enjoy and excel in argument, and unafraid of anybody. There is an apt comment in a letter from an old friend written in 1939: "In following this controversy from the sidelines, via the press, *The Saturday Evening Post, Atlantic,* and *Time* the thought occurred to me that you were having the time of your life." (He added, "I say this with all respect to the Willkie family tradition as I have never seen or known a member of same who has not welcomed such a fracas.")[81]

At almost the same time Cal Tinney was making a similar comment in his column in the New York *Post:* "Comes TVA and the scrapping starts Willkie vs. the U. S. gov't. Willkie would take a page adv. in a paper. Willkie would make a speech at the *Herald Tribune* Forum. Willkie would be interviewed at the depot before going to Washington.

"'What are you going to Washington for, Mr. Willkie?' 'Oh, to see that my contempt for the New Deal remains founded on familiarity.'"[82]

Other writers also had fun with the picture of Willkie rampant among cowering Wall Street lambs, confronting the Roosevelt Administration. "Wall Street was in more of an uproar than Washington during Willkie's fight with the TVA. Leading financiers, brokers and corporation executives begged Willkie to 'pipe down for the sake of all of us.' He wouldn't. They offered various settlements 'under the rose'; Willkie said it would be settled in public.

"Willkie just couldn't see it their way. A group of top-flight men from Wall Street, including Willkie, were summoned to a White House conference. They didn't like what the President had to say, but none of them said so.

"Others there said that Willkie, while maintaining respect for the office and character of the President, told in no uncertain terms what he thought. Willkie scared the wits out of the other Wall Streeters, and all the way back to Manhattan on the train they were looking over their shoulders."[83]

In short, he became the utilities' spokesman because nobody could stop him. At the same time, nobody denied his skill. He was equally at home in every situation, although his technique varied. Confronting a Congressional committee, he presented a temperate and rational argument, but was unyielding on the main point. In the Senate committee hearings on the Holding Company Act, he made his case for his own company, as Wheeler's compliment showed. To the House committee he himself proposed a list of specific measures (thirteen in a memorandum that he submitted immediately afterward) that were stringent enough to justify his claim that they would correct every abuse legitimately charged against utility holding companies. In effect, he consented to everything except the "death sentence."[84]

Meanwhile, he also sought his end by an appeal to public opinion. Senator Bone insisted that "millions of people are demanding . . . something infinitely more drastic than the present bill";[85] and Senator Wheeler suggested that the alternative to "the strictest kind of regulation by the Federal government" would be an irresistible popular demand for government ownership of the whole industry.[86] So far as these statements are true, they show the need for such a campaign as Willkie waged.

The 200,000 stockholders of Commonwealth & Southern were always within reach, and his general policy of keeping them informed about their investment was now given a special bent. Even before his testimony to the Congressional committees, he had sent them a letter attacking the Wheeler-Rayburn bill and urging them to protest.[87] He acted openly, of course, and he avowed and defended his act before the House committee two weeks later,[88] as he did in a speech toward the end of the year: "As far as I am personally concerned, in my duty as trustee to 200,000 utility security holders, I have only one possible regret: if by spending more money legitimately the Commonwealth & Southern Corporation could have prevented this destructive act from being passed, then I am very sorry that I did not authorize such additional expenditure."[89]

He also turned to the press, with newspaper releases that were given increasing prominence, and with periodical articles to a steadily widening audience. He addressed his fellow utility executives in such trade magazines as *Electrical World, Electrical South, Public Utilities Fortnightly,* and *Forbes Magazine;* ventured into intellectual fields with articles in the *Wharton Review* and the *Journal of Land and Public Utility Economics,* and reached out to the general public in *Current History.*[90] Moreover, many of his speeches were reprinted and given wide distribution by the Edison Electric Institute and by C & S itself, as well as by other firms whose executives approved of Willkie's approach.

It was probably as a speaker that he was most effective and popular, and by May, 1935, his reputation was such that he was invited to address the annual meeting of the U. S. Chamber of Commerce. His address was entitled "The New Fear," and was another brilliant rhetorical effort. He began with a reference to Roosevelt's inaugural address: "In perhaps the darkest hour in our nation's economic history he thrilled and inspired us, and few will forget that challenging sentence—'The only thing we have to fear is fear itself.'" Two years later the statement was still true; it was fear that was causing the lag in America's economic recovery. But this was a different fear—one inspired in American business and industry by "the hostile attitude of Government itself."

Willkie illustrated this hostility from his own field. "Every week for the last two years . . . there have emanated from this city, drastic and defamatory statements regarding public utilities and public utility holding companies." He then proceeded skillfully to identify his cause with that of business in general; listing the alleged abuses of the utility industry, he told his hearers, "If all or any of these counts warrant the sentence of death and dissolution, I am looking at an audience filled with representatives of corporations ready for the hangman's noose."

He followed with a scathing attack on the Wheeler-Rayburn bill, and then developed what was to become a familar theme. If the utility industry were freed from the fear of this legislation, if the Government would cease making grants and loans to municipalities to duplicate existing distribution systems, and if it would cease selling subsidized power in competition with the private companies, then this industry would undertake a program of expansion that would "do more to lift this country out of the depression . . . than the Government itself can do with all of its expenditures."

Willkie closed with a characteristic emotional appeal. "The loaning of money to municipalities to build duplicate distribution systems does not distribute wealth; it destroys it. The building of duplicate government transmission and distribution lines does not communize or share property; it annihilates it. . . . The utility industry requests these reasonable protective safeguards to which I have referred, under the principles of simple justice. It prays for them in the name of millions of unemployed, to thousands of whom it could give employment if permitted to pursue its lawful purposes under Constitutional Government. Will you not help us to accomplish this program and thus take people off the dole and put them on the payroll?"[91]

Such passages from a speech made on such an occasion help to explain how Willkie aroused such enthusiasm among the enlightened members of the business community. As they saw it, he combined realism with idealism, opposition to the extremes of the New Deal with social responsibility. He spoke with eloquence but without fanaticism, with sincerity but without self-righteouness. And he had a program of his own instead of merely desiring to undo the work of the New Deal.

It is true that, as already suggested, not all businessmen agreed with him. Perhaps especially in the utility industry itself there were those who resented both his willingness to compromise, to admit the evils of the past, and his determination, if compromise proved impossible, to fight to the finish, and in the open. Their habit of mind was to resist all change that threatened to limit their profits or their power; their habit of action was to work behind the scenes to influence individual legislators or administrators. And, assuming that his ultimate motives must be the same as theirs, they viewed his professed idealism as mere hypocrisy, and labeled him among themselves "The Jesus Christ of the utility industry."[92]

But such criticism was always behind his back. In a showdown, he was the boss. Once during the fight against the Holding Company Act, a large group of utility executives met in Washington to discuss what line the industry should take in the Congressional committee hearings. Opinion was divided, but Willkie got his way, as usual, and went back to New York. The next day, however, the opposition set out to reverse the decision, and showed such strength that the supporters of the original agreement asked Justin Whiting, who was representing C & S in Willkie's absence, to put in a hurry call for help. Whiting records the sequel.

"He arrived on the evening train. We were all assembled at the hotel, about sixty to seventy strong. Wendell walked into the room, faced the group and said: 'What's the reason for not going through with what we agreed to last night?' The most vehement objectors of the day sat there and did not say a word. No one would pursue the argument. He turned to our group and said, 'What's the matter with you fellows?' The testimony later went in as agreed."[93]

6

In the end, it was his cynical opponents themselves who brought about the passage of the "death sentence." Preferring their own time-tested methods of influencing legislation, they proceeded to deluge Congress with "inspired" letters and telegrams opposing the Wheeler-Rayburn bill. The true nature of many of the messages was obvious at once; a Senatorial investigation of utility lobbying, chaired by the liberal Senator Black, was quickly under way; and soon newspaper headlines spread before the public gaze lurid accounts of power company employees forced to sign messages on pain of dismissal, of thousands of telegrams signed with fictitious names, of millions of dollars spent by the utilities to defeat the bill.

The public resentment thus aroused was doubtless the decisive factor, along with Administration pressure and a feverish rush for adjournment, in finally wringing from the House, which had repeatedly rejected it during months of wrangling with the Senate, reluctant passage, by a single vote, of the "death sentence." Roosevelt signed the bill on August 26.

But though Willkie had lost the fight in Congress, there were still the courts; and on November 23 he announced that C & S would refuse to register with the Securities and Exchange Commission, as the Act required, and would bring suit to test its constitutionality. At the same time he recognized, as he told the Bond Club of New York on December 19, that "courts settle questions but they do not dispose of problems."[94] He still hoped that Congress could be persuaded to reconsider the "death sentence," and he coupled every denunciation of the Act with a statement of the regulations that were desirable. Moreover, if this Congress refused to modify the Act, there were other Congresses to be elected in the future.

In January of the election year 1936, therefore, he was glad to get his first chance to reach a really national audience in a March of Time movie about TVA.[95] For the first time, also, he now took to the air on the national radio networks, repeating the familiar arguments but using language more scathing than he had yet employed. On March 5, 1936, on the NBC network, he excoriated TVA. On April 16, on CBS, he assailed the Holding Company Act and the motives of its supporters. "The price which the American public has paid in order that the politicians could thus enjoy their hatreds has been incalculable. One essential part of that price is the existing unemployment."[96]

As the months went by, new avenues of publicity, new doors of communication, were opened to him. *Fortune* featured him and his company in its May, 1937, issue; *Life* did the same on November 18; in August the *Atlantic Monthly* had printed his essay on "Political Power"; on January 6, 1938, he engaged in a debate with Attorney General Robert H. Jackson on "America's Town Meeting of the Air."

But as far as his immediate aim was concerned, he failed. The 1936 elections established the New Deal more firmly in power than ever, and on March 28, 1938, the Supreme Court upheld the Holding Company Act in a suit brought by Bonbright and Company. As usual, the Court avoided a specific pronouncement on the constitutionality of the Act; but the utilities gave in. The fourteen companies which had refused to register with the Securities and Exchange Commission now appointed a five-man committee, including Willkie, to cooperate with the SEC (which had shown itself unexpectedly moderate in exercising the wide powers accorded it) in carrying out the "death sentence."[97] In regard to his own company, Willkie was reported on December 4 to have proposed to the SEC a tentative plan for bringing C & S into conformity with the Act.[98] And he was already working on a program to integrate the Michigan and Ohio properties by buying the utility systems that lay between them.[99]

Commonwealth & Southern passed out of existence, after years of negotiation and litigation between its management and the SEC, on July 15, 1949. The Holding Company Act did not, however, bring the catastrophic effects upon the utilities that Willkie had prophesied. On the other hand, he was probably right in his argument that the "death sentence" was unnecessary. He was almost certainly right in his contention that it and the policies of TVA frightened utility investors, delayed the expansion of the industry, and to some extent prolonged the depression.

The one clear effect of Willkie's fight against the Utility Holding Company Act was the enhancement of his reputation.

VI

Defeat and Victory

1

Meanwhile the fight against TVA had been continuing; and a final statement of the issues may serve as preface to the closing chapter of the story. Willkie's case contained two main items: first, that the much publicized "yardstick" was dishonest—"rubber from the first inch to the last," as he once put it;[1] second, that government subsidizing of municipal distribution systems to duplicate the existing systems was still more flagrantly unfair.

The first comment concerning the yardstick is that it was unnecessary. Plenty of data already existed to enable electrical engineers to calculate accurately the cost of electric power under the conditions existing in any particular place. Lilienthal himself commented in 1944: "The particular rates embodied in the TVA schedule were not to be an absolute standard of precisely what should be charged for electricity everywhere in the country. . . . The example this valley has supplied is a yardstick in a much more important sense. It has demonstrated . . . that drastic reductions in electric rates result in hitherto undreamed of demands for electricity in homes and on farms."[2]

But this second definition of "yardstick" was not new, either, as has been shown already; although TVA was able to illustrate it more dramatically than the C & S companies. Why this was possible is suggested by Willkie's caustic comment in a radio broadcast: "If they gave the power to the domestic consumer, he would use still more."[3] Somewhere there was a minimum rate below which the producer could not go without losing money, no matter how great might be the volume sold. And this rate was not, and could not be, the same for TVA and for private companies.

To this differential, two main factors contributed. One was that whereas the total cost of private hydroelectric plants must be allocated to power, part of the cost of TVA dams was allocated to flood control and navigation. This is proper—flood control and navigation are worth something and ought to be paid for. But the comparison in cost with private power is thereby invalidated.

When, for example, TVA presented its statement on allocations (more than a year after it was due under the law), the cost of all the installations at Wilson, Wheeler, and Norris Dams was given as (in round figures)

$94 million—the identical figure that an accounting company later placed on TEPCO as a "going concern." Of this, $2.6 million (2.8 per cent) was spent exclusively for flood control; about $4 million (4.3 per cent) for navigation; and about $24 million (25.5 per cent) for power. The remainder, $63.5 million (67.5 per cent) was spent for facilities (mostly dams) essential to all three functions. In the allocations, 20 per cent of the total was charged to flood control, 28 per cent to navigation, and 52 per cent to power.[4] Yet if these three dams had been built for power alone, they would have cost 93 per cent of the total—all except what was spent exclusively for navigation and flood control. This meant that in figuring its rates TVA could write off 41 per cent ($38.6 million) of its total investment on which private companies would have had to pay dividends and interest. If these averaged 5 per cent, the advantage to TVA would be almost $2 million annually.

It was Willkie's contention, furthermore, that TVA's allocations were *deliberately* dishonest: "The facts are that the money is not being spent for navigation or for flood control or for soil reclamation. These are but the constitutional excuses. The money is actually being spent to put the United States government into the power business."[5] Moreover, flood control and power production are incompatible; the former demands that normally the reservoirs be empty, the latter that they be full.[6]

The answer of TVA's defenders was that flood control and navigation *were* important, and that certain types of dams in certain situations *could* serve both for flood control and power.[7] And once the dams were built, the power was there; not to use it would be indefensible. Finally, after all, it belonged to the people of the area and should be used for their benefit, without profit to the government.

It was an honest answer. TVA had to be considered as a whole. The fact was that the building of multi-purpose dams in areas already served by private power companies created a new situation, for which no policy had been established. To work out such a policy peaceably required a conciliatory attitude on both sides, a readiness for concession and compromise. And this did not exist.

A second fact that made incommensurable the cost of TVA power and that of private power was that TVA, with the credit of the United States behind it, could borrow much more cheaply than private companies. Lilienthal said in 1938 that TVA in computing its rates used a 3½ per cent interest rate (the maximum specified by the TVA Act of 1935), but that actually it should have been much lower.[8] Willkie said in 1935 that his companies had to pay 4½ to 5 per cent interest on their bonds.[9] It seems a conservative estimate that the Federal government can always borrow money for 1½ per cent less interest than can private corporations. On an investment of $88 million (the cost assigned to the Wilson, Norris, and Wheeler Dams minus what was spent exclusively for flood control and navigation), considering only the 50 per cent which C & S companies normally had in bonds, that is, $44 million, a private company would have to pay $660,000 more than would the government. (If the preferred stocks were included—roughly 25 per cent of the total capital, at 6 or 7 per cent, the difference would be doubled.) Willkie's charge that it was unfair to use low government interest rates in setting up the "yardstick" was therefore justified.

Lilienthal, however, did not think so. "The lower cost of money to the Government is an advantage inherent in Government operation itself. . . . If by increased efficiency in other respects, that differential can be overcome [by the private companies], that is one thing. If it cannot, I think it is just inevitable that the trend will be in that direction," i.e., in the direction of government operation of the electric power industry.[10]

Combining the items of allocation and interest (and omitting dividends on preferred stock) the total advantage to the government would be $2.66 million dollars, or slightly less than 3 per cent of the total investment of $88 million. But in terms of gross earnings, this sum would represent 20 to 30 per cent.[11] If the whole C & S system could have enjoyed these advantages, its annual net income would have been increased more than $30 million—close to a dollar a share on C & S stock.

Taking into account, therefore, only the advantage to TVA from the allocation of costs in multiple purpose dams and from lower interest rates, that advantage is seen to be overwhelming.[12]

The other main issue—duplication of transmission lines and subsidies for the purchase or construction of municipally owned distribution systems—is at bottom a question of morals rather than mathematics. Lilienthal before a House committee defended the direct sale of power to consumers by saying that it occurred in an area "where 98 per cent of the farmers had sat ten years without service with transmission lines running right through the valley."[13] The explanation was simply that it was not profitable to serve them. The head of the Tennessee Electric Power Company, Jo Conn Guild, testified in the "Nineteen Companies Suit": "We are always anxious and pushing out to serve our whole area more completely." "A great many times we go out and serve rural areas where it would not be profitable at first but where we hope it will be profitable." But in answer to a question he had to say: "We're not an eleemosynary institution. We have to make a profit sometime."[14] Lilienthal's position evidently was that people should not be deprived of the benefits of electric power because a private company could not make money in supplying it.

And he was right. Nobody could legitimately object if the government supplied this need. The odd thing is that Lilienthal did not make this unsatisfied need a major issue in the controversy with the private companies; that he left it to *Fortune* to point out, in 1937, that "there are more than 200,000 farms in T. E. P.'s service area but only 8,000 of them are T. E. P. customers"; that its experts in farm electrification "can't do much for the mountaineers and backwoods farmers, whose business T. E. P. won't take at less than $18 per month per mile of distributing line."[15] One would like to know what Willkie's comment on these facts would have been if Lilienthal had forced him to make a comment. But the latter chose to concentrate on the issue of municipal ownership in cities that were already getting adequate service.

Nor did Lilienthal greatly emphasize the issue of "spite lines," of which Willkie's journalistic critics made so much.[16] The picture as seen by TVA partisans was presented by a number of farmers from northwestern Georgia, in homely and sometimes ungrammatical English, to the Congressional committee investigating TVA. First, the companies tried to discourage them from organizing a rural cooperative to buy power from TVA, by letters or agents telling them that the whole project was a fake and that they would never get electric power; or that they would only get it after many years; or that in getting it they would incur a life-long burden of debt. When these efforts failed, the companies began building "spite lines" along the routes laid out for the lines of the cooperative, ignoring or overriding the objections of the land owners, trying to persuade members of the cooperative to abandon their commitments and buy private power instead; or drastically lowering rates (presumably not on the power—if rates were "uniform"—but on the lines) to keep the customers they already had. The farmers naturally fought this unneeded and now unwanted activity, and the "practically open warfare" of which Willkie wrote to the President threatened to become physical as well as verbal and legal.[17]

On the other hand, Willkie contended that it was TVA that was the aggressor;[18] and this view is supported by a company description of what is apparently the identical situation concerning which the Georgia farmers testified to the Congressional committee. It occurs in testimony offered to the Federal Power Commission in 1959 by J. J. McDonough, president of the Georgia Power Company; and in it the account given by the farmers is turned precisely upside down. "Early in 1936, the Company announced a construction program pursuant to which 1,000 miles of rural lines would be built, a portion of which were to be constructed in Northwest Georgia. Shortly after this announcement, the TVA instigated the formation of the North Georgia Electric Membership Corporation (NGEMC) organized to distribute TVA electricity in Northwest Georgia. The NGEMC immediately commenced to construct distribution lines in

Northwest Georgia, and to duplicate many of the Company's rural lines. Persons soliciting for NGEMC sought to obtain as customers persons who had already agreed to take service from the Georgia Power Company, informing those persons that the Company had never seriously intended to furnish service in the area and that failure to take service then from NGEMC would prevent their friends then without service from getting any service whatever."[19]

A fair conclusion seems to be that the leaders on both sides, convinced of the justice of their cause, permitted their subordinates to assume that any tactics were legitimate. In addition, it is clear that before the creation of TVA the companies had been slow in extending service to rural customers, and that the example and competition of TVA *did* (as its partisans claimed) stimulate the rapid expansion of this service.[20]

In regard to government grants to municipalities to duplicate existing distribution systems, the issues are equally complicated, as well as controversial. Lilienthal steadfastly rejected Willkie's basic demand that in any permanent settlement his companies should be free from TVA competition in any area where they continued to operate. The TVA director felt that this amounted to saying that "the private companies had monopoly rights to supply electricity even if the people who conferred those rights, the consumers, wished to supply themselves with this basic service."[21] He insisted that "electricity performs a public service and that unless it is exercised by private corporations with fairness, with efficiency, without financial jugglery and with a due sense of responsibility to the paramount public interests involved, the public at any time may itself assume the function of providing itself with this necessity of community life."[22]

But *do* communities have the right—and does the Federal government have the right to help them—to replace the service that *is* supplied "with fairness with efficiency, without financial jugglery"? On the whole it cannot be said that C & S operating companies had failed to meet this test When TVA finally took over the property of TEPCO, in August, 1939, there were friendly words for Willkie and his company. Mayor Thomas E. Cummings of Nashville declared, "Tennessee Electric Power has always given us the very best service. We regret that it is leaving the State of Tennessee . . ." U. S. Representative Joseph Byrnes, a strong supporter of TVA, said: "We have always regarded Mr. Willkie as a friendly enemy . . . he has always given us fair treatment and excellent service." And Mayor Edward D. Bass of Chattanooga, where there had been an especially bitter controversy over municipal ownership, averred that "no community was ever served by a finer utility company."[23]

Nevertheless, the company had no chance of competing with TVA. C & S rates might be—and *were*—among the lowest in the country,[24] but they were still higher than TVA's. As for industrial rates, Lilienthal told the Congressional investigating committee in 1938 that it was TVA policy to charge "what the traffic will bear";[25] but in the spring of 1937 "TVA indicated that no matter [at] how low a cost the Tennessee Electric Power Company might produce electric energy, it would deliver the same amount at a lower rate."[26]

And TVA's advantage was not merely economic but also psychological. People in the Tennessee Valley wanted public ownership not merely because rates were lower—though to some families in the area during the depression a dollar or two a month was not a negligible matter—but because they idolized Roosevelt, wanted what he wanted, and thought he wanted municipal ownership; and also because of the intense rivalry between communities, based on the prevalent view that "the city which first acquired TVA power would have an edge which competing cities would never be able to cut down."[27]

This psychological factor Willkie presented vividly in discussing Chattanooga's vote for municipal ownership, during the House committee hearings on the TVA bill of 1935. TVA had located there the headquarters of the Electric Home and Farm Administration, it had brought in many employees and engineers, and "three weeks before election day they announced that they were going to build Chickamauga Dam twelve miles from the city, at a cost of from $12,000,000 to $15,000,000. You just cannot stand that. Any city will go under those circumstances."[28]

And if a city did "go," what would happen to the private company? There was no incentive, even, for a city to accept Roosevelt's view that "they ought to offer a fair price" to a company for its distribution system.[29] For (in Willkie's words to a Congressional committee) "the PWA comes along and offers to give a city 45 per cent, absolutely free and loan them the balance, at very low rates of interest and on long-term money, and that city says to you, 'Now, we will buy your system rather than duplicate,' although saying to you all the time, 'You have got to sell it cheap because we can get 45 per cent free.'"[30]

Willkie's resentment against such tactics led him to an act of which his enemies made political capital—a contribution of $20,000, solicited by the Chattanooga Citizens and Taxpayers Association to help finance a campaign against municipal ownership in the city election held on March 12, 1935. He showed his feelings in a comment on the wide publicity given to the contribution during the TVA investigation in 1938: "The Commonwealth and Southern Corporation made its contribution on condition that the committee keep complete records of its receipts and expenditures and file the same with the proper public authority . . . The only regret the Commonwealth & Southern Corporation has is that if a larger contribution could have overcome the propaganda and contributions of the Federal Government and the Tennessee Valley Authority, that it did not make such additional contribution."[31]

As a matter of fact, the officials of TVA had maintained an exemplary neutrality in the election;[32] the TVA program itself was the "propaganda" that brought approval of municipal distribution, by a vote of 18,852 to 7,837.[33]

TEPCO officials, however, were far from neutral. They gave leaves of absence to a considerable number of TEPCO employees to campaign against municipal ownership; they also arranged to have two "ghost lots" within the city limits bought and registered in the names of more than a hundred TEPCO employees so that they would be eligible to vote (though in the end they did not do so because "there was so much talk in the papers");[34] after the election, they sought an injunction against a PWA loan to the city to buy the distribution system (or duplicate it);[35] and they supported a petition for a referendum on an ordinance forbidding the construction of duplicate facilities, which was circulated under false pretenses during registration for a primary election in 1938.[36]

TEPCO also, just before the election, withdrew its advertising from the pro-public power and generally liberal Chattanooga *News,* edited by George Fort Milton;[37] and it later paid excessive rates for advertising in the *Free Press,* originally a free advertising sheet owned by Roy MacDonald, the conservative operator of a grocery chain, when it became a regular daily in 1936.[38] It also gave the Chattanooga *Times,* which was editorially against municipal power, a much lower electrical rate than other customers in the same class. (The paper was cleared of any complicity.)[39]

These actions, which no testimony connected with Willkie, have no bearing on the main issue; they only reveal the lengths to which old-line power executives were willing to go in fighting, as they felt, for the very existence of their companies against competition which they regarded as uncalled for and unfair.

My conclusion is that the whole fight was unnecessary: that TVA could have achieved its goals by working with the private companies, selling or pooling its power, and having provisions for lowering rates and extending service written into the contracts. Or if Lilienthal and others believed that TVA must keep control of its power in order to carry out the intent of Congress and to realize fully the potential economic and social gains of the project, then the only fair procedure was to negotiate the outright purchase of the private power facilities throughout the area; and without (in Willkie's words) holding a gun to the head of a utility and saying, "Sell at our price or we will duplicate."[40] Competition was confiscation.

In the end, of course, the purchase was made. It remains only to trace the events which led to this settlement of the long controversy.

2

The truce arranged by Willkie and Lilienthal at the beginning of 1934 came to a formal end on August 1, 1936, when Norris Dam began producing power, and TVA, exercising its option under the contract, gave notice that it would end that contract in three months, and that thereafter there would be no restrictions on the area in which it would operate.[41] Unless a new agreement could be negotiated, the private companies would be faced with competition from TVA that in the nature of things they could not meet.

The one man who could effect such a settlement was Roosevelt. From the beginning Willkie sought a hearing from the President, but for many months he did not succeed. Apparently they did not meet until December 13, 1934,[42] shortly after the beginning of the Ashwander suit and Willkie's denial of any part in it, and Willkie's and Lilienthal's speeches to the Birmingham Rotary Club. The battle lines had already been drawn, but Willkie told reporters after the meeting that he and Arkwright (president of the Georgia Power Company) "were very favorably impressed with President Roosevelt's attitude on the power question. He did not believe, however, that the companies he represented could operate at the low rates charged by TVA."[43]

It was after this meeting that he sent his famous telegram to Mrs. Willkie: "Charm greatly exaggerated. I did not tell him what you think of him."[44] But to Roosevelt himself, having established a personal relationship, he wrote on January 6, 1935, a note that showed him to be, when he wished, the equal in tact and diplomacy of the President himself: "Various people mention to me from time to time statements credited to you in conversation, regarding the Commonwealth and Southern Corporation. It is reported to me that you say we have a very progressive management in Georgia in regard to rates while such is not the case in regard to the other Southern operating companies in which we are interested." After a firm denial, he concluded: "I have the feeling that men who have particular causes to advance report to you information about the operation of our companies which is either not correct or is so shaded as to advance their own respective causes."[45]

Roosevelt's answer on January 8, though brief, was a masterpiece: "Thank you for your letter. I am glad to have your statement. I hope you give as little credence to the statements you hear about me as I do to the many statements I hear about what you do and say."

This gave Willkie a further opening, and on January 10 he wrote, after referring to "the graciousness of your letter": "If at any time I can be of any service to you . . . in working out the vexed utility problem, I am at your command. I am extremely anxious to bring the whole utility problem to a workable solution and have the hope that if certain misunderstandings can be cleared away, that such an objective is not at all impossible."

Apparently, however, Roosevelt did not respond, for the next important meeting of the two did not take place until May 20, 1936. The next day Willkie wrote to the President: "I am writing to tell you how much I appreciate the opportunity you gave me yesterday to explain to you the position of the Commonwealth & Southern subsidiaries within the competitive area of the Tennessee Valley Authority and their complete inability to finance under present circumstances. I appreciated greatly your statement that you hoped early this summer to talk the whole matter over with me again,[46] with a view to a possible solution of the relationship between the private utilities and the government. . . . The present status is one of practically open warfare and . . . the utilities in that district naturally feel that they are fighting for their lives . . . This is the explanation of the numerous lawsuits that have been started recently—the necessity for which no one regrets more than I do. . . . I want you to know that I feel the problems should be settled by agreement and I am of the opinion that you, and you alone, are the one person who has the power to bring such a settlement about."[47]

This letter must be taken at face value. Willkie was always willing to negotiate. His vehement public attacks (like his radio address on March 5, 1936, entitled "Who Pays the Bills for TVA?" in which he called TVA "the most useless and unnecessary of all the alphabetical joy-rides"; repeated one of his favorite quips about the cost of the project, that "the Tennessee River waters five states and drains the nation"; and declared that "whenever a householder in Tupelo, Mississippi, switches on a light, everybody in the United States helps to pay for it"),[48] along with the "litigation" of which TVA partisans naturally complained, were not intended to annihilate his opponents but to strengthen his bargaining position. He was fond of saying: "Courts settle questions, but they do not dispose of problems";[49] and he remarked toward the end of 1937, during the hearing of the "Nineteen Companies" suit by the Court of Appeals: "Anyone who has had anything to do with composing differences knows that one of the very best times to bring a solution is during pendency or trial of litigation."[50]

But at this stage, there seemed no basis for a settlement. Willkie could not consent to TVA competition because, he held, no private company could match TVA's subsidized rates; Lilienthal was equally firm in refusing to grant the companies a monopoly.[51]

In the early fall of 1936 it seemed that the President might break the deadlock. He saw Willkie and Arkwright on August 25[52] and apparently discussed the situation created by the expiration of the contract between TVA and the C & S companies, with special reference to power pooling.[53] On September 20 he announced that a conference on this topic would be held on September 30. The tone of the announcement was temperate and optimistic. "The public interest demands," he said, that such government projects as TVA and Bonneville (on the Columbia River) "be made to serve the greatest number of our people at the lowest cost and, as far as possible, without injury to existing actual investment." He reported that he had been conferring for several months with experts and with representatives of various interests and added: "These conferences indicate agreement to a remarkable degree that this objective can best be obtained by" power pooling. He noted that the contract between TVA and C & S—"a rudimentary form of power pooling"—had established a precedent and provided experience. He described the plan as "cooperative pooling of power facilities within each region, including those of the federal projects, the privately owned facilities and the municipal plants, through joint use of the existing transmission line networks under control of the members of the pool. . . . I am advised that by this means investment in transmission lines and generating facilities can be kept to a minimum, service strengthened, and large economies in operation effected."[54]

Such an arrangement would have been a victory for Willkie. It would have meant abandonment of the "yardstick" idea, the end of competition, and the establishment of uniform rates throughout the area. It would also have meant, as Arthur Krock pointed out, a reversal of Roosevelt's previous policy.[55]

The conference was held as scheduled, but apparently the discussions were largely technical. Afterwards a brief and noncommittal statement was issued jointly by Willkie and Frank McNinch, chairman of the Federal Power Commission: "It appeared from the discussion of the experience here and abroad that there might be savings made in the pooling of transmission which would be beneficial to the public and investors. Consequently it was agreed that during the next few weeks there would be explored further and in detail these possibilities.

"In the meantime, the TVA and the Commonwealth and Southern Corporation are to see whether they could not agree on an extension of the present agreement between them."[56]

Work on the second item began the next day, and on October 10, the White House announced a three-month extension of the old agreement, with a few modifications. It was obviously a temporary truce to give the President time to decide what he wanted to do.

Despite the meager results of the power pooling conference, Willkie called it, optimistically, "an act of political statesmanship calling for an equal degree of business statesmanship on his part." "The only possibility of failure" that he could see lay in the attitude of "the 'die-hards' on either side of the question." His own view was that "a tremendous investment of public funds has been made in the Tennessee Valley; that a great volume of 'dump' power and a smaller but important percentage of 'firm' power will be available there for all time; and that the statesmanlike thing to do is to negotiate a permanent settlement."

This eagerness for a settlement, however, as the story pointed out, was "not shared by the entire power industry . . . Among the more frequent comments is that TVA is facing imminent failure . . .; that it will be defeated eventually in the courts; and that no action is required by the utilities at this time to bring TVA to terms." "Many utility men" were convinced, moreover, that Roosevelt's conciliatory attitude was inspired by the coming election and that the attitude was temporary.[57]

With unconscious irony Willkie sent a clipping of the story to Roosevelt.[58] The irony lay in the fact that the die-hards in the industry were right; the die-hards in the Administration were still in control—because Roosevelt was one of them. There were no more power pooling conferences; and after Roosevelt's crushing victory over Landon in the November election, rumors began to spread that Lilienthal and his supporters were successfully attacking the plan.[59]

The rumors continued; and on January 6, 1937, Willkie finally sent to the President a long letter which he had prepared for presentation at the conference on September 30. He had not presented it, he said in the covering letter, because "at the opening of that conference you requested that the discussion be limited to the subject of the pooling of transmission. . . . I thereafter refrained from sending it to you because of the political campaign . . ."

The original letter is perhaps the best single statement of his position that Willkie ever wrote. He began by saying that "the creation of a power pool is not, in and of itself, a solution of the problem." "The real problem" was competition; and the TVA policy of duplicating distribution systems (he enclosed a map showing "the exact nature and extent" of this) made it impossible for the C & S companies in the area "to operate efficiently or with decreasing rates."

And he showed why. "Out of every dollar of revenue received by our companies in the southeast from all of their customers, we expend approximately 24¢ for labor, 13½¢ for taxes, 38½ for cost of borrowed capital (bonds and preferred stocks) and 19½ for materials and supplies." (He left it to Roosevelt to figure that this left 4½¢ for dividends on common stocks.) The only possible cut in costs was in the third item; fortunately, "there is prevailing today the most favorable money market that has existed for over fifty years." But it did the Southern companies no good; nobody would buy their bonds, and their preferred stocks (though regularly paying full dividends) were selling for as much as forty points below par. On the other hand, the Northern companies, "free from the uncertainties caused by the operations of the TVA as presently conducted," were "able to refund their senior securities on such a basis that a similar refunding of our southern companies would save them over six million dollars per year in interest and preferred dividend charges. And this is equal to one-half the amount they receive annually from their more than 400,000 domestic customers in the south." (A little arithmetic would show the President that, except for TVA, the companies could cut their domestic rates in half.)

Still more serious than the companies' inability to refund their securities before maturity was "their inability to meet their maturing bond issues or to raise capital for new constructions." The holding company had met the need by advancing them $20 million; but now (Willkie no doubt got a bitter pleasure out of this jab) the Holding Company Act, if upheld by the courts, would make such advances impossible.

"We are therefore justified, it seems to me, in asking the Government either to buy as systems all of our electric utility business in the southeast," or else to free it from competition. If the first alternative was chosen, the price should be set by "fair negotiations" free from coercion, or "by a disinterested tribunal in condemnation proceedings." If the second alternative was accepted, he would undertake to organize all the private companies in the area into a pool to buy and distribute all of TVA's power; or else arrange "a complete interconnection" of both private and government generating and transmission facilities, with neither controlling the property of the other and with distribution left to the private companies or existing municipal systems. Any savings (including those from a refunding made possible by a permanent agreement) would go toward lowering rates, improving service, or extending service into rural areas where it had heretofore been uneconomical.

Finally, if the government was really interested in a yardstick, it should buy (again, at a fair price) one unit of the C & S system and operate it "for a substantial number of years" under an accounting system and other regulations the same as those imposed on the private companies.

As a parting shot Willkie wrote: "I should be unfair to my own convictions if I did not say to you on this occasion that I personally believe that private operation is far better for the public than public operation and that there is absolutely no occasion for a Government yardstick. . . .

"I do not, however, feel that I have the right to sacrifice the property of others in the advocacy of my own convictions and I have no illusions about the power of the Federal government to destroy our operations. . . . I feel that my first duty is to do all that I can to protect the property of the over three hundred thousand security holders for whom I am one of the Trustees and to seek the continued employment of our ten thousand employees in the TVA area."[60]

Twelve days went by without an answer. In the meantime, Senator Norris had delivered a violent attack on C & S, strongly implying that no negotiation was possible; and Roosevelt (nearly four years after taking office) had appointed a committee, headed by Secretary Ickes, to draw up a national power policy and report in two weeks! Then Willkie issued a statement to the press: "In the absence of a statement from the President, I cannot believe that the President has turned 'thumbs down' on further power pooling conferences, which he initiated last September. For me to believe this would be for me to believe the charges made when the President called the original conference, viz., that his object in calling the conference was political strategy."[61]

Eight days later (and eight days before the expiration of the extended contract between C & S and TVA) the statement came. At a press conference the President made public a letter to the heads of the Federal agencies that had been represented at the first conference, stating that there would be no more such conferences. The reason he gave was that the "Nineteen Companies" had secured a "sweeping preliminary injunction" against TVA.[62]

It was a lame excuse. Willkie in his letter of May 21 had warned that "a further and more comprehensive lawsuit" would "probably . . . be necessary"; and on May 29 the suit was brought, challenging the constitutionality of the whole TVA power program. But TVA lawyers by a series of legal maneuvers delayed a hearing on the suit, while TVA engineers rushed their projects. Accordingly, on August 19 the companies sought an injunction to "restrain the TVA from further activities, pending the determination of the suit brought on May 29." On December 14 the injunction was granted by Judge John J. Gore in Federal District Court, although he specified that projects already begun might be completed.[63]

All this Roosevelt had of course known. And when a reporter at the press conference mentioned Willkie's comment that "the suit was pending at the time of your September conference" and "you did not require that they withdraw the suit," the President answered defensively, "He would not have withdrawn it if I had required it. Obviously the situation was changed by the sweeping character of the injunction."[64]

But what had happened to Willkie's letter? The answer is given in a memorandum for the President (who had sent the letter to Chairman

Frank McNinch of the FPC) dated "1/22" and initialed "HMK." (Who HMK was does not matter.)

"Mr. McNinch left this for the President saying:

'This is our recommendation on how the letter (from Willkie) should be handled at the present time. The letter (Willkie's) was very carefully prepared and we do not think the President should reply right now.' Mr. McNinch then said that the President has before him, awaiting his signature, the draft of a letter to the Govt conferees (copy of which was to go to Willkie) giving, as a reason for not continuing with the conferences, the fact of the injunction. Mr. McNinch thinks that in addition to that reason (which was all they could find), the President can also refer to the issue raised in the last paragraph of the third page of Willkie's letter." (This was the fourth proposal, concerning the setting up of a yardstick. What exactly McNinch had in mind is uncertain.)

Accompanying the memorandum was the following letter to Willkie to be signed by Presidential Secretary Marvin McIntyre. It was sent on January 25.

"The President has held your letter of January sixth, transmitting your unmailed letter of September 30, 1936, hoping that he would be able to find time to reply to it personally. So many other matters have pressed for immediate attention that this has proved impossible.

"He has therefore asked me to acknowledge its receipt and that he hopes to have time within the near future to consider the numerous suggestions that you have submitted."[65]

Seven and a half years later, after reading another letter from Roosevelt, Willkie said: "I've been lied to for the last time."[66] The episode just related helps to explain the statement.

Willkie did not know, however, the full extent of the President's double-dealing in regard to the power pooling conference, as revealed in a letter that Roosevelt wrote to Senator La Follette before the conference. The latter protested on September 26: "Your power policy is a great source of strength to you. . . . It would be a major disaster to have even the impression created that you have given an inch of ground to the enemy in the power fight." The President's answer must have reassured him: "At the power conference there will be no concessions and no statement of plans. My policy, of course, remains exactly the same."[67] The only difference between them was that Roosevelt thought a conciliatory pose would win more votes. After the election it could be dropped.

3

Willkie must still have had some hope, however, that he could win the President over, for he sent to the White House copies of the letters that he wrote to Lilienthal in a final effort to reach an agreement. The conclusion of his last try is worth quoting: "If any of the various suggestions that we have made do not appear feasible to the government, I wish to say that we will consider any other solution. We name only three measures that the solution should include: (1) That our employees be taken care of; (2) That there be no destruction of property; (3) That if any property is left to us it will be left unmolested to such an extent as to permit us to finance it.

"I appreciate that in discussions involving such consequential and controversial subjects, personal feelings may momentarily be aroused; to me the solution of this problem is so vastly more important than any of us that if ever under momentary intensity I manifest any personal feeling I want to be the first to express my regret.

"You have vast quantities of power to dispose of. We can make available a market for much of it. Surely there is some solution by which these naturally coalescing forces can be reconciled for the good of both and for the welfare of the public."[68]

Here the matter rested—except for Willkie's continuing campaign for public support—for another nine months. Then he thought he saw another opening. The President at his press conference on November 9 intimated that if the utilities would revise their rate-making procedures by accepting the "prudent investment theory" (that is, that the investment on which a "fair return" was to be made should be "the historical cost of properties" instead of the "cost of reproduction now," which would ordinarily be larger and which had been the generally accepted standard), they could expect to enjoy a virtual monopoly, subject to the right of municipalities to operate their own systems. But, he said, not many would wish to, if the private companies lowered their rates.[69]

This certainly seemed like an olive branch; and though Willkie from previous experience knew that it might turn out to be poison ivy, he was willing to take a chance. He wrote to the President the same day repeating his plea for a negotiated peace. "I read with great interest your statement in the morning newspapers in regard to the public utility situation. . . . I have throughout felt and feel now, that through common counsel and cooperation a right and just solution can be reached within the broad framework of the social and economic objectives laid down by you. . . ."[70]

For some reason it suited Roosevelt to have another meeting, though the opening of the trial of the "Eighteen Companies" suit (Alabama Power had been excluded) would have given him an excuse for refusing. (On May 14, 1937, the Circuit Court of Appeals had voided Judge Gore's injunction as against the public interest, but had ordered the original suit to be tried on its merits. The trial opened on November 15, before a special three-judge court.)[71] They met on November 23, talked for two hours, and got nowhere—except to agree that $1.5 billion should be spent on utility expansion. In a press conference the same day with ten selected reporters, Roosevelt said he had tried to convince Willkie that the government did not wish to compete with private companies, and that therefore the utilities need not hesitate to undertake the needed expansion. Willkie answered that "they couldn't sell the securities." But when the President asked him why, he could only repeat that "the general feeling" was responsible. Roosevelt took obvious pleasure in picturing his easy triumph over an opponent who appeared not much more than simple-minded.[72] As for the memorandum that Willkie had left, the President had not had time to read it.

The memorandum suggested that if the government would repeal the "death sentence" clause in the Holding Company Act and if TVA would keep its books honestly and refrain from competition with private companies, the utilities would reform their rate-making procedures by eliminating all the write-ups of stock values that the Federal Trade Commission claimed to have found, and accepting, after this date, the valuation of property according to the "prudent investment" method.[73] But nothing had really changed, and in a press conference on January 14, 1938, the President announced a flat rejection of Willkie's proposals.

Meanwhile, the "Eighteen Companies" suit had clearly been going against the companies. Their bill of complaint contained four heads: that TVA's power program would destroy much of their business; that the "yardstick" was unfair; that TVA had solicited large industrial customers, offering them "arbitrary, non-compensatory, confiscatory and discriminatory rates"; and that TVA had conspired with PWA (the Public Works Administration, headed by Ickes) to force sale of municipal distribution systems at unfair prices.[74] Willkie himself testified, and gave a dramatic illustration of TVA's effect upon the companies. TEPCO had reached an agreement with Monsanto Chemical Company to supply 50,000 kilowatts of power for a new plant at Columbia, Tennessee. But in the end, Edgar Queeny, head of the company (as well as a pillar of Old Guard Republicanism who was later a violent critic of Willkie's liberal views), called it off. "Our directors are unwilling to hazard a several million dollar investment whose success is entirely dependent upon the continuity of its power supply, at contract rates which we believe are insecure without a guarantee from Commonwealth and Southern." Willkie offered to post $1.5 million of first mortgage bonds, but Queeny declared that "in view of . . . competitive operations" by TVA, this was "not a satisfactory guarantee." Instead, he signed a contract with TVA.[75]

When Willkie ended, TVA counsel James L. Fly, after a conference with his staff, said, "No cross examination," and Willkie remarked, "I am sorry."[76] But it did not matter. The court "conceded that damages had been done the companies by TVA," but declared that this was irrelevant because "the companies seek injunctive relief and not money damages."[77] Earlier it had ruled out discussion of rates and of alleged TVA propaganda.[78] These rulings pointed the way to its final decision handed down on January 21. It refused to agree that TVA was "a sham and a pretense" to conceal the real aim of putting the government into the power business; it denied that there had been anything but legitimate cooperation between TVA and PWA; it ignored most of the other issues that the companies had tried to raise. It declared: "These complainants have no immunity from lawful competition even if their business be curtailed or destroyed."[79] Government competition was obviously "lawful."

Willkie had evidently foreseen this decision; evidently, too, he expected it to be upheld by the Supreme Court. On January 15, the day after Roosevelt's press conference, he issued a dramatic public statement urging that TVA buy out TEPCO in its entirety. He defended the record of his companies, again pointed out that the municipalities wished to buy only the distribution systems and not the generating and transmission facilities, which would "be reduced to the value of junk." He suggested that the price be "fixed by negotiation or . . . determined by three arbitrators—one to be named by the President, one by the Supreme Court of the United States, and one by the utilities." He concluded: "I make this suggestion as a last resort in a desperate situation."[80]

Lilienthal's response was as self-righteous as usual: there was "no such crisis as he describes" and no loss need occur "if the problem is approached, not in the spirit of trying to win a debate in the newspapers, but by a calm and rational analysis of the problem and by sincere negotiations. By this method the whole problem can be worked out without any such radical scheme as he has suggested."[81]

Either he had second thoughts, however, or some higher authority (which could only be Roosevelt) thought Willkie's proposal not impossibly "radical." At any rate, on March 6 Lilienthal suggested that the municipalities combine to take over all the facilities in a large area. Willkie welcomed the proposal as "what I have long advocated" and advanced the idea that a price be recommended by a board composed of persons "not hitherto involved." He nominated Clarence Dykstra, Karl T. Compton, and Felix Frankfurter.[82] Lilienthal replied that the Board could not delegate its responsibilty to private citizens but that he himself would negotiate.[83]

For a time the negotiations went well. TVA engineers defined the area that they thought TVA should take over (including parts of Georgia, Mississippi, and Alabama as well as Tennessee) and Willkie agreed.

(There were of course other utility companies in the area, but there seems to have been an informal agreement among them that Willkie should act as spokesman for all.) On the other hand, Lilienthal finally agreed not to compete with private companies outside this area.[84]

The negotiations stalled, however, on the question of price. Lilienthal insisted that it be the original cost of the facilities less accrued depreciation; Willkie maintained that it should represent the value of the company as "a going concern." The independent accounting firm engaged by TVA, with Willkie's approval, to appraise the properties, accordingly produced two estimates. It gave $81 million as the original cost of the electrical properties. From this Lilienthal deducted $24 million for depreciation, leaving $57 million. When Willkie refused to consider this, he raised the offer to $67 million; but Willkie, whose figure from the accounting firm was $94 million (the value as "a going concern") held out for $90 million.[85] Here matters rested—partly because Lilienthal suffered a prolonged illness, and partly because of a Congressional investigation of the whole TVA project that lasted from May to December.

This grew out of a longstanding feud between Lilienthal and Arthur E. Morgan, chairman of the board of directors, with the third member, Harcourt A. Morgan, on Lilienthal's side. Among the many causes of dissension was the relation between TVA and Willkie's companies.

Almost from the beginning, apparently, there had been friction between Lilienthal and A. E. Morgan, but Roosevelt, who hated having to take sides in such family quarrels within his administration, tried to smooth things over, and for a time succeeded. But eventually, on March 2, 1938, Morgan publicly demanded a Congressional investigation. Roosevelt then released a memorandum from Lilienthal and H. A. Morgan, dated January 18, listing a number of charges against A. E. Morgan and demanding his resignation. The latter issued a long statement defending himself and again demanding a Congressional inquiry; and when Roosevelt said he would make his own investigation, and called the directors together, Morgan refused to answer his questions, and was dismissed from his post.[86] But at least he got his investigation; the record of it fills fourteen volumes.

Apparently Morgan had always been uneasy about Lilienthal's power policy. He approved of power pooling, which Lilienthal opposed. He once consulted Willkie as to whether a letter written by Lilienthal purporting to state Willkie's position actually did so, and joined Willkie in preparing a memorandum that *did*.[87] In the end, he also joined Willkie in condemning the accounting method that justified the "yardstick" rates, in charging that Lilienthal had tried to give the public a distorted idea about Willkie's position and policies, and in attacking Lilienthal's "policy of gaining a market for TVA power by gradual and partial penetration of private utility territory, with the inevitable conflict, duplication and waste which that policy involves . . ."[88]

From the welter of charges and counter-charges, often couched in explosive language, the picture emerges of two essentially honest but stubborn men, involved in a clash of philosophies and personalities. On the whole, making allowance for the fact that a majority of the committee were Democrats who would naturally approve of persons and policies that Roosevelt supported, and that the committee counsel, Francis Biddle, shared their attitude, TVA still made a reasonably good showing. Nevertheless, the general result seems to have been the strengthening of TVA's critics.

Willkie saw the affair as another chance to get his case before the public and was eager to testify. But the Democratic majority paid him the tribute of postponing his appearance, originally scheduled for August, until after the November elections. It can hardly have been an accident, either, that he was finally called to testify on the day before Thanksgiving, when it might be supposed that the story would attract a minimum of attention. But Willkie's name was now news; and the stratagem failed.

Once again, possibly before a larger ultimate audience than ever before, Willkie listed his grievances against TVA, and the benefits to the national economy of a fair settlement. He told his story as he wanted to tell it, in spite of Biddle's skillful and hostile cross-examination; sometimes with eloquence, always with assurance. His aim now was to get a fair price for the properties that he felt he had no alternative except to sell. He told of Lilienthal's offer of $67 million, and of his answer that by accepting it "I would violate my obligation as a trustee, that the Government might destroy the property but that I was not going to give it away . . ." What TVA wanted, he charged, was to buy the property "at a price that will make their yardstick rates work." And he proposed dramatically that, since his suggestion of a board of private citizens had been rejected, the Securities and Exchange Commission should be authorized to set a price, which he promised to accept.[89]

It seemed, however, that he had got nowhere; for two weeks later Julius Krug, appearing in place of Lilienthal, told the committee that Willkie's proposal was "visionary," "impracticable," "over-simplified," and "studded with jokers"; and he came back to the charge of monopoly, accusing C & S of trying to build a "Chinese Wall" to protect itself from competition.[90]

4

And then, suddenly, at the beginning of February, 1939—after the Supreme Court had ruled for TVA in what had finally become the "Fourteen Companies" suit;[91] after Roosevelt had made public a statement from the SEC that it had no authority to arbitrate in the controversy over the price of TEPCO;[92] and after Willkie conceded defeat by saying that there would be no more litigation against TVA[93]—something happened. On February 1 Krug and another TVA representative, Joseph Swidler, conferred "all day" with Willkie;[94] and on February 2 they announced an agreement for the sale of TEPCO's electrical properties for $78.6 million. The municipalities would buy the distributing systems; TVA would buy the generating plants and transmission lines; most of TEPCO's employees would be kept. Negotiations would continue for the purchase by TVA of other C & S properties in Mississippi and Alabama.[95]

This meant that the holders of $49 million of TEPCO bonds and of $24 million of preferred stock would be paid at par value; the remainder would go to C & S for the common stock—the first recognition by the government, according to a *New York Times* article, "of 'equity' or common stock value in utility systems."[96]

Only one man could have been responsible for so sudden and sweeping a change in the government's position, and that was the President. But why did *he* change?

In some quarters Harry Hopkins, now Secretary of Commerce, was given credit for the Administration's conciliatory attitude toward business.[97] And it is true that in a speech on February 24, he praised the C & S-TVA settlement: "the government demonstrated its good will by settling on generous terms. It struck a peace that will be a lasting peace and a good peace because it is a generous peace."[98]

But, close to Roosevelt though Hopkins was, it seems likely that it was mainly the logic of events that persuaded the President to adopt a new policy. For one thing, he was a politician, and the political events of 1938 may have given him second thoughts on a number of subjects. Not only was he uniformly unsuccessful in his efforts to "purge" conservative Democrats by supporting their opponents in the primaries, but in the general election the Republicans had made a vigorous comeback, and were now a formidable minority in Congress, especially in the House.

This Republican resurgence was largely due to the economic recession that increased in severity from August, 1937, to July, 1938, and that brought the nation's "Business Index" to its lowest point since 1933. The previous year had been relatively prosperous and, although unemployment remained high, complete recovery seemed at last to be really "just around the corner." Roosevelt was even led to the incautious boast, "We planned it that way." But the 1937-38 recession showed that the country's economic illness was far from cured, and perhaps the President was beginning to wonder whether the cause of its continuance might not lie nearer than the Hoover administration—whether there might not be something in Willkie's contention that the "general feeling" of insecurity among American businessmen was an important factor in prolonging the depression.

Finally, Roosevelt was outgrowing the insularity of his early years as President; and in Europe forces were now loose whose whirlwind energy was stirring waves that reached even the Western edge of the Atlantic. In March, 1938, Hitler annexed Austria; in September he dictated the Munich agreement which, as Willkie later said, "sold Czechoslovakia down the river"; and while Willkie and Krug were settling the price of TEPCO, the Fascist Franco, with the aid of Hitler and Mussolini, was destroying the last remnants of Republican resistance in the Spanish Civil War. At such a time America needed to be economically strong and politically united.[99]

One step more was necessary, an act of Congress. With Willkie and TVA's supporters now united, this looked like a routine matter, and the Senate quickly passed a bill which authorized TVA to issue $100 million in bonds to finance the TEPCO purchase and to carry on other activities, with no restrictions. But in the House, ironically, the majority now shared Willkie's former views, and passed a bill which limited the bond issue to $61.5 million, restricted operations of TVA to specified areas, forbade it to compete with private companies, required it to submit its accounts and fiscal policies to the General Accounting Office, prohibited the Federal government from backing the bond issue, requiring a sinking fund to be established to amortize the bonds, required payment to the Federal government for all properties allocable to power, and forbade payments to the states in lieu of taxes.[100]

These restrictions, a writer in the *Times* observed, were "in no small measure . . . attributable to the cumulative efforts of Wendell Willkie."[101] But the result of the action, which had no chance of being accepted by the Senate, was to block the purchase. Weeks of bickering followed, with neither the House nor the Senate willing to yield, while Willkie urged them to "keep their shirts on."[102]

But finally he himself got together with Representative May of Kentucky, the most powerful opponent of TVA, along with L. J. Wilhoite and S. R. Finley of the Chattanooga Power Board, who for four years had been waiting impatiently for the city's vote for municipal power to be put in effect, and worked out a compromise. The bond issue was to be for $61.5 million, of which about $45 million was earmarked for the purchase of TEPCO and $6.5 million for the purchase of C & S properties in Alabama and Mississippi. All other restrictions were dropped, but in effect TVA was prohibited from expanding the area of its operations without specific authorization from Congress.[103] On July 15 the bill was passed by both Houses; on July 26 it was signed by the President; and on August

16 one of the main headlines of the *Times* read: "TVA TAKES TITLE TO POWER FOR STATE OF TENNESSEE: $78,000,000 PAID WILLKIE."

The ceremony took place in the National City Bank of New York, where a whole floor was vacated to provide space for the several hundred persons in attendance. It lasted three and a half hours, as first Lilienthal and then the representatives of all municipalities involved handed Willkie checks for their share of the properties—often accompanied by friendly words. Even Lilienthal praised him as one "who has done a real job of selling electricity at low rates," to which Willkie replied with humorous inaccuracy as he took the check for $44,728,300, "This is sure a lot of money for a couple of Indiana farmers to be kicking around." "It was a banner occasion for Mr. Willkie," wrote the *Times* reporter, "and he appeared to enjoy every moment of it as it represented what his legion of friends both in and out of the utility industry have described as a 'one-man victory over the competitive inroads of the Federal government' into the power business."[104]

It was Willkie, however, who struck the only sour note in connection with the proceedings. In a press statement he declared: "We sell these properties with regret. We do so because we could not stay in business against this subsidized government competition. . . . this sale does not represent the true value of this investment . . . But the loss will not be in vain if it serves to arouse the American people against government invasion of their business. In looking to the future I plead with the government for two principles": "that the government should discontinue its competition with private business outside the Tennessee Valley" and "that these government agencies should keep their books on a completely honest basis."[105]

This statement seems out of character; Willkie was never one to hold a grudge. And Lilienthal cannot be blamed for the tartness of his answer: "The statement does violence to the fact recognized in all quarters that the terms of the settlement with Commonwealth and Southern were eminently fair . . .

"I regret Mr. Willkie's reopening of the controversy, since the effect will be to frighten potential investors in badly needed utility expansion everywhere without any reason for alarm except the impassioned statements of the recognized spokesman of the utilty industry."[106]

From this exchange one thing is clear. The contest between Willkie and the New Deal was not yet over.[107]

VII

The Private Life of a Public Figure

1

It is odd that during Willkie's rise to national fame, the personal image is temporarily blurred. The intimate friendships of his university days, of his Army life, of his Akron career, seem to have had few counterparts during the first years of his life in New York. As far as anecdotes or personal reminiscenses are concerned, the early thirties are almost a blank.

One reason, it may be assumed, is that he spent most of his time working. He enjoyed working, he was ambitious, and in his first years there was much to learn, despite his Akron experience, about the utility business in general and Commonwealth & Southern in particular. Nor did he relax after becoming president. He spent perhaps a hundred days a year in visiting the operating companies—not merely on routine "inspection tours," but to become familiar with and to share in decisions about operations, financing, and any special problem that a particular company might have.[1]

And he had his own unique way of coming to know the territory in which his companies operated and of gaining background knowledge that would be helpful in solving problems and deciding policies. He traveled by automobile, accompanied by C & S experts from New York (he himself always disclaimed a knowledge of technical matters, though with his lively curiosity and retentive memory he must have acquired a vast amount of information) and presumably by officials of the local company. This necessitated a motorcade of several cars; and sometimes when Willkie had a particularly troublesome problem that he wanted to think through, he would insist on being alone in the last car.[2] When the party stopped at a town that he was not familiar with (he made it a point to visit, at some time or other, every town of more than 2000 population that his companies served),[3] he would leave his companions entirely and "go first to the local newspaper editor, then in turn to the town library, to the Chamber of Commerce, and to the Superintendent of Schools."[4] And, when the occasion offered, he would simply stop and talk with people on the street.

This comprehensive knowledge, along with his natural force of character, made him the real boss of C & S. On the other hand, according to the head of one of his operating companies, "he expected operating heads to assume responsibility and . . . where a mistake was made he would express himself about it but he would never let the operating man down, never. . . . I have settled wage contracts for the entire [Ohio-Edison] company and told him afterwards of the results and invariably he would say, 'Well, if you think that is a fair settlement, it is all right with me.'"[5] But this also makes clear that it was Willkie who exercised final authority. He himself declared later that the "suggestion that as President of Commonwealth and Southern I did not manage the system would strike as exceedingly humorous those then connected with the company."[6]

Besides being the executive officer of C & S, he was also (though the title and even the profession had as yet hardly come into existence) its director of public relations. A friend of his university days has suggested that he was the first big business executive who realized the importance of public opinion and who set out to "sell" himself and his company to people in general;[7] and a later associate who had seen much of the business world declared, "He was the greatest public relations man I've ever met."[8] But it took time to compose the speeches, articles, press releases, and statements to Congressional committees that he produced at a steadily increasing pace. In New York he regularly arrived at his office at 8:30[9]—a fantastic hour in that city. And, just as he originally carried his lunch to his office in Akron so that he would have more time to work, so now he often had his lunch sent in—thus violating another item in the ritual of big city business. He even worked in his office on many weekends and holidays.[10]

He *did* take time during the early years to go sight-seeing with his family, repeating the pattern established during his Army days by visiting famous historic places in the vicinity of New York. And he also took conventional, though brief, vacations: a trip to Bermuda in the summer of 1930; a week in the Adirondacks in 1931, where Mrs. Willkie and Philip were spending a longer period; and a month with them in Europe in 1932 when they spent the summer abroad. On this occasion he went with his brother Edward, whose firm (Libby, McNeil, and Libby) stationed him in Belgium from 1926 to 1938, on an automobile tour of Belgium and Luxembourg, and evidently the brothers had fun; though Wendell was at a disadvantage through not being able to speak French, and once when they were flirting with a couple of pretty barmaids, he accused Edward (not unjustly) of mistranslating.[11]

In June, 1933, he took time out to go with Mrs. Willkie and Philip to see the Chicago World Fair. The next summer he took a vacation trip to Puerto Rico; and in 1936 he took his "last real vacation" at Bay View, near Petoskey, Michigan, with Mrs. Willkie and Philip.[12] From this date on, whenever he could escape from his duties as president of C & S, and later from his self-imposed and still more pressing duties as an unpaid public servant, he went to Rushville, Indiana, where he found relaxation in visiting his farms. It also became his habit to spend Christmas there.

The story of these farms illuminates his character in several ways. He bought the first one, 350 acres, on January 6, 1935; a second, of 390 acres, in September of the same year; and others at intervals through 1944, the year of his death. In the end he owned about 1,600 acres.

His main reason for buying the first one was his characteristic generosity. Mrs. Willkie's father, who had had his financial ups and downs, had suffered, like millions of other Americans, from the depression; and he had reached an age where it was difficult to start again. It was Willkie's idea to give him the job of managing the farm, and thus to help him, while letting him think that it was *he* who was conferring the favor.[13]

After Mr. Wilk's death, Wendell turned over the management of his farms to Mary Sleeth, an old friend of the Wilk family, who was by profession a librarian. Her first response to the offer was, "Why, Wendell, people will think you're crazy having a woman manage your farms." But he answered, "I've got where I am by doing things other people thought were crazy"; and eventually he persuaded her to take the job.[14]

He had, of course, another motive for buying land, namely, as an investment—the safest and most satisfying. He had had enough of buying industrial stocks in 1921 in Akron. Bank stocks, however, still seemed a sound investment, and after he had paid his debts, he began putting his savings into stock of the Ohio State Bank. But this proved to be an even more costly investment than that in Firestone. The depression forced the bank to close, and Willkie, under Ohio law, became liable for twice the listed value of the stock he owned. He was still paying assessments on it when he was nominated for President in 1940.[15] When again he was in a position to invest, he chose land. He would say to Mary Sleeth, "Here is something that is *yours*. You don't have a board of directors sitting around a table spending your money."[16]

Since the farms were an investment, he wanted them run in a businesslike manner, and he was always definite and detailed in discussing his plans with Miss Sleeth. But (as in his dealings with the heads of the operating companies of C & S) he gave her complete responsibility for carrying them out. His agreements with his tenants, likewise, were always exact, so that they knew what was expected; and he wanted them to make money both for themselves and for him. At the same time, he was interested in them as human beings. He urged Philip to get acquainted with one of them for whom he had a particular regard. And if a tenant had bad luck, he would say to Miss Sleeth, "Don't press him; don't take away his self-respect."[17]

Since in 1940 Willkie was thought of both by his supporters and his opponents as a representative of American business, especially big business, it is worth while to pause to consider his attitude toward wealth. A writer in *Life* opined in 1940, "He retains much of the small-town youth's bedazzlement with success"[18]—meaning of course financial success. Other writers took note of such thrifty habits as having his shoes re-soled (which reminds one of the famous picture of a hole in the shoe of a later Presidential campaigner) and taking the subway or a taxi when most men in his position and drawing his salary would have had a private chauffeur.

It is true that he did not spend money carelessly—perhaps because it had sometimes been so hard to come by in his youth—and that when he did spend it he wanted to get his money's worth. He often said to his son, "Don't reach. If you can't get a thing for what it's worth, don't buy it."[19] On the whole, his attitude toward money was that of a rational, civilized citizen of a democracy. He wrote to a university student who was the son of a friend: "If I had my life to live over . . . I would do the thing that I most wanted to do in the location that I most desired to live in . . . I have pursued the 'Will o' the Wisp' of larger earning capacity, and I do not believe the receipt of such has the slightest to do, providing of course one is above the mere subsistence level, with either happiness or satisfaction in life."[20] And he practiced this philosophy. He could have had a larger salary from his own or from other corporations, but declined. After 1940 he could have named his own fees for as many lectures as he cared to give. Instead, his innumerable speeches were made only for causes that he considered worthy, and he would accept no compensation. When *One World* became a fabulous best seller, he put the royalties into a trust fund for benevolent purposes.[21] And he gave up a "research and magazine" idea that he had talked about with Henry Luce because "there would be too much danger of it getting to be a commercial magazine enterprise."[22]

For to him money was a means and not an end. It was something to be used, first, to maintain one's independence of thought and action. In a letter to Edgar M. Queeny, multimillionaire Missourian leader of the Republican Old Guard, who had accused him of taking his ideas from Thomas Lamont, Willkie replied: "Neither he nor you nor any other man influences my opinions beyond the logic of what he has to say. I never have been awed by such great wealth as yours, nor afraid of defending a Communist such as Schneiderman if I thought his cause was just. I wear my sovereignty under my hat."[23]

And money was to be used, in the second place, to aid those who did not have it but would spend it to good purpose. He once named over to a friend forty boys whom he had helped through college.[24] On the other hand, he declined a loan to an old Elwood friend to set up a business that he was sure would fail (he gave his reasons); but he was ready to lend

$15 to an Akron acquaintance to buy tools so that he could get a job in the Brooklyn Navy Yard.[25]

At his death Willkie left an estate appraised at about $850,000[26]—a fortune small in comparison with those of most of his associates, and with what he could have made had he considered wealth an end in itself.

Besides financial security, however, his farms brought him a kind of wealth that *was* an end in itself. Whenever the pace of his existence became too gruelling, or whenever he had a great decision to make, he left the sunless canyons of New York's financial district, and went back to the quiet streets of Rushville and to the spacious surrounding fields. He loved the land, he loved growing things, he found in the unhurried movements of nature an escape from the demon of restlessness by which he was so often driven. "I dream of the day," he wrote in 1937 to an old friend, "when I can return to the simple environment of some Indiana farms which I have purchased and in connection with which I am attempting to create an environment of the type I like best. I suppose it will never happen and until the end I shall live in the restless activity of so called big business. I dream, however, the other way."[27]

The unashamed sentiment of his attachment to rural Indiana had its counterpart in an equally unsophisticated humor—broad, earthy, elemental. Though capable on occasion of incisive if unsubtle wit, his favorite brand of humor was one for which there is no exact word in formal American English, and which is variously known in the vernacular as "kidding," or "ribbing," or "joshing." The *New Yorker* tolerantly presented as an example his telling a visitor to one of his farms that a hog's name was "Waterman"; and answering the inevitable question, "Is that his real name?" with "No, just his pen name." "He adores jokes like that."[28]

His characteristic humor is shown more clearly, however, by an episode involving another visitor. Willkie liked to show off his farms, especially to friends from the city, and to explain the progressive agricultural techniques used by his tenants. This time the display of a prize bull led to a lecture on artificial insemination as a means of breeding better cattle, and on how remarkable it was that the semen from a bull could be put into a test tube, shipped to a distant point, and used to inseminate a number of cows. When at this point a feminine member of the party was led to exclaim, "Oh, no!" Willkie kidded her unmercifully. Why was she so upset? he inquired. Was it the cow she was sorry for? Or was it the bull? The party was swept away by a tide of hilarity.[29]

2

Nevertheless, far removed as he was from the stereotype of the corporation executive, he took New York in stride. It is true that one friend remembered him as being, on his arrival, "in some ways a pretty crude country boy,"[30] on whom his boss, B. C. Cobb, and his partner, John C. Weadock, worked to impart some polish. Whether they had more success than Gwyneth and the Army before them remains a question. They *did* persuade him to have a gold filling in a front tooth replaced with a porcelain one.[31] But they never taught him how to wear his clothes so that they would stay pressed, nor to remember to get haircuts when he needed them. They never broke him of the habit of putting his feet on his desk, of throwing his leg over the arm of a chair, or of chain smoking. They never erased his Indiana accent, or his habit of saying, or doing, what was natural.

He was aware, of course, that to be natural is, in the eyes of many persons, to be queer. But this did not worry him. When Robert's daughter, then a student in college, remarked to him, "You know, I think all the Willkies are a little queer," he answered, when he could stop laughing, "Yes, of course we are. But the thing is, we talk about it ourselves."[32] (Other people talked about it, too, however; Senator Van Nuys of Indiana once answered a question about them by saying, "Yes, he knew the Willkies well—smarter than Christ, but a little queer.")[33]

One trait that some companions considered queer was his capacity for complete absorption in the discussion of some idea, to the point where he would completely lose track of his surroundings. Once when Paul Harmon was on a visit to New York, the friends had dinner at the University Club and then decided to walk over to Broadway. Willkie, talking steadily, started to turn off Fifth Avenue in the wrong direction, and when Harmon tried to correct him, demanded with humorous aggressiveness, "Are you trying to tell me which way Broadway is? I *live* here." "Yes, I'm *trying* to tell you," Harmon answered—whereupon Willkie shouted to the nearest pedestrian, half a block away, "Hey! Which way is Broadway?" He was amazed to find that Harmon was right.[34]

The same habit of mental concentration, whether in discussion or reflection, is revealed in a story of a political trip through Idaho, when his car was caught in a blinding snowstorm. The driver could not see the road; the rest of the party sat on the edge of their seats in dread of imminent catastrophe. Miraculously, they arrived safely in Boise, where Willkie was to attend a banquet and give a speech; but when someone asked how they had managed to get through the storm, Willkie, looking puzzled, turned to a friend. "What storm?" he asked.[35]

Another trait that sometimes surprised people was his obedience to impulse—not in regard to matters of policy or principle, but in response to unexpected situations, often humorously and always without regard to consequences. During the hectic period of speech-making and public appearances that preceded the 1940 convention, he was scheduled to visit Hartford, Connecticut, and Providence, Rhode Island; and to save time, his friend Sam Pryor, National Committeeman from Connecticut, was piloting him in a private plane. The Hartford speech was a success; but afterward, at an informal gathering of prominent local Republicans, Pryor got word that the fog was closing in at the Providence airport. As it happened, drinks were just being passed around, and Pryor told Willkie, "You can either drink that mint julep or you can go to Providence and make the speech." Willkie retorted, "I'll do both!" and dashed out to the taxi with the glass in his hand. He was still holding it when he reached the airport.[36]

This was the sort of thing that gave nightmares to his political advisers. But sometimes such an impulse would result in sheer triumph—as at a Lincoln's Birthday gathering at Indianapolis in 1943, where Willkie was to give the main speech. It was to be broadcast, and so one of the earlier speakers, Mrs. Dudley Hay, National Committeewoman from Michigan, got a whispered request from the chairman to kill a little time. She did so by telling of her experiences at Elwood when Willkie had given his acceptance speech. She did not meet the candidate; but after the ceremonies, when she and her husband were standing on a street corner "knee-deep in beer cans," she got an unexpected thrill when a car drove by carrying "a very weary Wendell Willkie"—so near that she could have touched him. At this point the main speaker jumped up, strode across the stage, gave her a resounding kiss on the cheek, and said for the delighted audience to hear, "When you go back to Michigan this time, Regina, you can tell them that Wendell Willkie kissed you."[37]

If this impulsiveness posed problems, both in business and politics, it was also one source of Willkie's immense popular appeal. Many ordinary folk, endlessly frustrated in their desire for independence, were eager to identify themselves with this man who seemed the embodiment of their secret wish.

And if some of his associates in business and industry were inclined to look askance at his unconventional ways, he had a more damaging criticism to make of them. Though he liked many of them personally, respected their knowledge of their own field, and did not think them to be, on the whole, less honest and high-minded than members of Congress or of the Roosevelt Administration, he found that few of them were interested in *ideas*. "You can't imagine what limited intellectual interests business men have," he told Irita Van Doren, the person to whom, more than any other, he turned to supply the deficiency; and she noted by way of confirmation that he mispronounced words not uncommon in literary circles, which he had encountered in his reading but had never heard used by his associates.[38]

The reason was that they spent their leisure time in entertaining each other, in activities at their clubs and country clubs and yacht clubs, either in New York or, on week-ends, at their suburban estates. Willkie spent his in reading or in talking with like-minded companions. His clubs were mostly those in which intellectual or professional interests took precedence over purely social functions: Lawyers, University, Century, along with the Economic Club and the Town Hall Association, of both of which he served as president toward the end of the thirties.[39] And although he and Mrs. Willkie were listed in the Social Register from 1936 on,[40] there is no evidence that this much sought-after distinction brought any change in their lives.

It is true that they lived in a fashionable area—at 1010 Fifth Avenue, on the edge of Central Park. But this was more or less an accident. They had taken an apartment there on arriving in 1929, had found it comfortable, and had simply stayed. Restless though he was in many ways, still, in regard to the ordinary business of living, Willkie was conservative. He disliked changes of residence, just as he disliked giving up old clothes and getting new ones, just as he disliked changes in the kind of clothing worn. (He clung to B.V.D.'s long after most men had abandoned that type of underwear.)[41] He and his wife also kept the Indiana small town habit of not locking the door when they went out.[42] He liked an accustomed pattern of everyday existence, because it did not distract him from more important matters.

How far Willkie departed from the stereotype of the business executive is humorously suggested by Russell Davenport, his most intimate and influential adviser in the 1940 campaign, in his account of how he and Willkie became friends. As managing editor of *Fortune,* Davenport first met Willkie at a round table conference on unemployment sponsored by that magazine, and "casually invited him for a week-end at his Norwalk, Conn., home, never thinking Willkie would accept.

"But Willkie did, and at the last minute, too, throwing Davenport into a panic.

"'I didn't belong to a golf club, but I wangled a special golf pass for the weekend. I had the tennis court rolled and my sailboat spruced up. Everything was shipshape.'" But when Willkie came, all he wanted to do was talk.[43]

When there was nobody to talk to, Willkie read. Still, as in youth, strenuous days did not exhaust his energy, sleep seemed a waste of time, and often in the morning his chair in the library of his apartment would be surrounded by piles of books. Sometimes, however, instead of pursuing one topic through a variety of sources, he would read a work straight through from cover to cover—even a multi-volume work like the

Dictionary of American Biography.[44] And when a book of normal size engaged his interest, he hated to stop until he had finished it. His habit in such cases is revealed in a note to Thomas W. Lamont (chairman of the board of J. P. Morgan and Company, and an exception among Willkie's non-literary business associates, who was drawn to the young Midwesterner in part by their common zest for books and ideas, and who became an intimate friend). "Many thanks," he wrote on January 4, 1943, "for sending me 'English Social History' by Trevelyan. I read it Saturday night and Sunday morning. I do not know when I have been so absorbed."[45]

At the same time he sent a note of appreciation to the author, and the reply of the distinguished British historian must have warmed his heart:

"Dear Mr. Wendell Willkie,

"Your letter of January 4th, just arrived, has given me the greatest pleasure. I am pleased to think that my book should have been readable enough to keep an extremely busy man up all night.

"And as that busy man is engaged in business which is so valuable to the world, and which I follow with such hearty approval, my pleasure has been particularly great. [This was when many of Willkie's own countrymen, including some ex-isolationists, were berating him as an enemy of Britain because of his strictures on colonialism following his world tour.]

"When next you come to England will you please write to this address and let me know, so that I can get you down here for a couple of nights. The Master's Lodge of this College [Trinity] is a good place from which to see Cambridge and Cambridge folk."[46]

Willkie was also on friendly terms with some American professors, one of whom was Felix Frankfurter of the Harvard Law School, soon to be appointed Associate Justice of the United States Supreme Court. Their first meeting occurred in March, 1938, when Frankfurter gave an address at the Harvard Club in New York, to an audience composed largely of lawyers and leaders in business and finance. The speaker was known to be a friend and adviser to the President and was widely considered to be one of the main architects of the New Deal. Evidently his speech was in keeping with his reputation, and when at the end of it he invited comment or rebuttal, some of Willkie's friends nominated him to reply. The result was a knock-down-drag-out argument that lasted for three hours, and in which the partisan audience rejoiced at Willkie's ability to hold his own against so redoubtable an opponent. (It has been said that within a few days five different publishers had invited him to write a book.)[47]

Many of those who applauded Willkie's performance, however, would have been baffled by the sequel; a letter which he wrote to Frankfurter next day saying that he wished to apologize if he had used too extreme language, and expressing his admiration of Frankfurter's character and achievement. The answer was equally magnanimous: "We met in the simple, direct way in which Americans should meet who have a common concern about great public issues, even though they may view them on the basis of different experiences and are preoccupied with different interests."[48]

This ability to combine intellectual disagreement with personal respect, springing in part from a love of ideas for their own sake, was something that he encountered too infrequently among businessmen. Few of those who heard him debate with Frankfurter would have cared to read the Harvard Law professor's study of *Law and Politics,* which an interviewer noticed lying on his desk a year and a half later.[49] He even toyed with the idea of writing a book himself on the philosophy of law, at the suggestion of Tom Bevans, an editor of the publishing firm of Simon and Schuster, but never found the time to carry out such a long range project.[50]

As this item suggests, his intellectual interests were not confined to the contemporary scene. In history he continued and broadened the reading that had fascinated him since his university days. England in the eighteenth and nineteenth centuries and the American South before the Civil War were special but not limiting interests. He bowled over a reporter in Rushville in 1940 by reciting the names and dates of all the British prime ministers since the reign of George I.[51] And he astonished Irving Stone, in talking of the chapter about himself in *They Also Ran,* by his comments on the subject of the book Stone was then writing, Jessie Benton Fremont, and "on her father, Senator Benton, and her husband, John Fremont, which showed me pretty clearly that Mr. Willkie knew as much about these characters of the period as I did after years of close study."[52]

Naturally, Willkie was delighted to review for the New York *Herald Tribune* Lord David Cecil's biography *The Young Melbourne,*[53] and he discussed the early career of Queen Victoria's first prime minister with the authority of a scholar and a deftness of style that few scholars could command. It was entitled "Evening Star of the Great Day of the Whigs," and a quotation characterizing the Whigs of that great day will show, in contrast to his usual rough-and-ready eloquence, how carefully he had worked on the style. (Writing it was, he told a friend, "the hardest job he'd had in years.")[54] "Rowdy, reckless and robust, they could eat their twelve-course dinners, dance until dawn and gamble, drink and make love until breakfast—and still put in a hard day's work on their estates or in Parliament. The quality for which we envy them is not their morals, which were questionable, nor their principles, which were largely expedient, but their amazing vitality."

Willkie was, as he wrote to Robert Kintner in sending him a copy of the book and the review, "inordinately proud of this—almost childishly so."[55] One reason was that he felt it would give him standing in the literary world. He perhaps did not feel really inferior to literary people, as is sometimes said,[56] but he certainly enjoyed feeling that he was one of them, and he invested the world in which they moved with a glamor that he did not find in business. He must have been delighted with the acknowledgement of the book and review that he received from Julia Peterkin, author of the widely read novel *Scarlet Sister Mary,* who told him that it was "not fair for the review of a book to be better written than the book."[57]

Earlier he had taken time out from his activities as a utility executive and public defender of private enterprise to give a dinner for the writers of Charleston, South Carolina,[58] of whom Josephine Pinckney was perhaps his most ardent admirer. Another Southern literary friend was Ellen Glasgow, to whom he sent "My affectionate congratulations on the Pulitzer Prize" in 1942[59] for *In This Our Life.*

Although Willkie found relatively little time for reading fiction, he read the work of Faulkner and Hemingway long before either had been awarded the Nobel Prize. The *New Yorker* profile recorded that "at a recent Gridiron dinner in Washington he stopped at William Faulkner's table to tell the author how much he had enjoyed 'Sanctuary'"[60]—although a literary friend later commented that "enjoy" did not exactly describe his response in spite of his admiration for the power of certain passages.[61] There is no qualification to be made, however, of the praise he gave to *For Whom the Bell Tolls.* In thanking Hemingway for an autographed copy, he wrote: "I am glad to have this. I have read the book. It is one of the really great books I have read in the last several years."[62]

These opinions may be thought conventional, no matter how sincere. Nevertheless, his taste was not determined by what was fashionable. His first meeting with Edna St. Vincent Millay, long after the tide of her popularity (and, it must be said regretfully, her inspiration) had passed, led him to write this touching note: "I cannot tell you what a joy it was to meet you last night. I have admired you for years. I am indebted to you for coming up and introducing yourself."[63]

If this note implies, as it is natural to assume, admiration of the poetry as well as of the person, it shows that, as one would expect, Willkie's literary taste was not "highbrow." Though he read Faulkner and Hemingway, he continued unashamedly to admire O. Henry, whose entire works he read through aloud to his son several times,[64] as he did Tennyson's *Enoch Arden,* where Victorian sentiment appears in full flower. And his library contained sets of such nineteenth century standbys as Dumas, Scott, and Thackeray, along with Kipling and Mark Twain.[65]

Willkie's interest in literature, it almost goes without saying, was in content rather than in technique, and this was true even of poetry. Though he could quote verse at length, he had little sense of rhythm; and when his memory was at fault and he substituted for the original word another of similar meaning, he might ruin the meter of a line without being aware of it.[66]

Perhaps an even greater source of pleasure than fiction and poetry was drama. The theater was one of the few attractions that could lure him away from work or books or conversation. In the early summer of 1932, for instance, when Mrs. Willkie and Philip were in Europe, and when his brother Robert was stationed in Brooklyn, he welcomed the chance to take Robert's older daughter, a student at Smith College, to various Broadway productions. After going a few times she announced to her parents, "Uncle Wen has seen these plays before!"[67]

And, like any theater enthusiast, he enjoyed meeting and knowing the stars of the stage. He sent a copy of *The Young Melbourne* and his review to Katherine Cornell; he wrote to Tallulah Bankhead after their first meeting: "I want to tell you what a joy it was to meet you last night. . . . You have no more ardent admirer of your theatrical accomplishments than I"; and his correspondence also contains an appreciative note to Gertrude Lawrence.

To a degree, his entree to the world of letters and of the theater (for the other arts he seems to have had little enthusiasm, although he occasionally attended concerts or recitals) was provided by Irita Van Doren, who as editor of the Sunday book review section of the *Herald Tribune* possessed a wide circle of literary acquaintances. The *New Yorker* used the word "salon," with its connotations of personal charm and intellectual sophistication, to describe the circle over which she presided, and certainly she fascinated many people, especially men.

Among these was Willkie, and it is clear that the fascination was mutual. The initial tie may have been a common interest in the history of the South, for Mrs. Van Doren was a granddaughter of the Confederate General Brooks, in whom Willkie had become interested before he knew of the relationship. But later she became not merely his adviser in literary matters but his confidante in regard to political matters as well, and even in regard to his personal affairs. She helped him, for instance, in the delicate task of composing the letter to Roosevelt immediately after Pearl Harbor—an answer that would express his complete support of the Administration and at the same time his desire not to take a position in it.[68] She also aided him with another piece of writing—the one that he was most proud of, *One World;* and though the book is emphatically his own both in substance and style, the absolute rightness of expression no doubt owes much to her critical taste. She worked with him too on the proofs of Alden Hatch's *Young Willkie* in early 1944—though it was evidently

Willkie himself who was responsible for many of the factual errors in that work. In many ways she was his closest friend.

3

This account of Willkie's friendships in the world of intellect and letters leads to the final item in this analysis of his personal character. What was the *quality* of his relations with other human beings?

One element that went into this quality was Willkie's extraordinary power over people—a power to attract them, to excite them, to make them lay aside the opinions of their cooler moments—that can only be described in a metaphor by calling it "personal magnetism." Over and over one encounters the judgment that in this respect he had only one rival among contemporary public figures (many persons would not even have excepted Roosevelt); and, by those whose memories go further back, only one rival among twentieth century Republican leaders. "With the exception of T. R and F. D. R.," wrote Nicholas Roosevelt, a journalist and diplomat of long experience, "I know no one in public life in our time who had greater magnetism than Wendell Willkie."[69] His brother Robert, who became a colonel in the Army and was deeply devoted to the three thousand men in his outfit, as they were to him ("he never court-martialed a boy . . . if any outsider stepped on his boys they had a protector; if they had problems they had a sympathetic ear even after fourteen hours of labor; they knew the old man 'knew his stuff'"), nevertheless averred: "Wen could have taken that loyalty in a few days if he had come into that outfit and he had tried."[70] Even Old Guard Republicans sometimes, after hearing him speak, experienced a temporary conversion.

It is true that (to continue the metaphor) under certain conditions of polarity, magnets repel as strongly as under other conditions they attract. Some of Willkie's enemies genuinely believed him to be an egotist and opportunist, who used his magnetism to gain his selfish ends, who accepted men's help and offered no return, who was arrogant in his assurance and resentful of criticism.

The record contradicts these charges. He had nothing to gain in the Army by being on the side of the men. He had nothing to gain in Akron, politically or professionally, by crusading for the League of Nations or fighting the Klan. And in his last years, his devotion to impersonal goals is almost unexampled in American political history.

At the same time, he was not a fanatic. He had an innate liking for people as people, regardlesss of their accidental status in society. He could be as friendly to a barber as to a banker. On the same day that he wrote to Thomas Lamont to thank him for Trevelyan's *English Social History,* and to Trevelyan himself, he wrote a note to his barber, Vincent Gengarelly: "My dear Vincent:

"I am terribly sorry not to have written you before this but I just learned that you had been ill. . . . I am afraid I have been a little remiss about haircuts and I know Mrs. Willkie will be glad when you are back on the job. I do hope that you are recuperating in good order and will soon be completely rid of the ailment."[71]

This letter also illustrates what strikes one most strongly in reading his correspondence—in direct contradiction to the most serious charge against him—namely, his *considerateness*. The president of Commonwealth & Southern was never too busy to answer promptly and warmly letters from former students in Coffeyville or friends of his years in Elwood. Among the many such letters is one to Millie Garrison-Burton, who had once been the stenographer in the Willkie law office. On March 30, 1937 she wrote from Seattle recalling "many fond memories of my associations with the firm of Willkie and Willkie. . . . I would like a line from you, Wendell, just for old time's sake. Would like to know about Julia, Robert, Charlotte and Edward too.

"I remember you once willed me your third interest in the old Oldsmobile and a life estate in your love and affection. Does that still hold?"

Almost by return mail, on April 5, he answered that her letter had "brought back very, very many pleasant recollections both of school days and of the old law firm. I am perfectly willing to write a codicil to the will affirming your interest in the old Oldsmobile and a life estate in my love and affection.

"Julia is in Canada, Bob is in the Philippines where he is now a major in the Army, Charlotte is in Hawaii where her husband is temporarily stationed in connection with his work in the Navy, Ed is in Antwerp, Belgium, where he represents Libby, McNeil Company and Fred is in Scotland. I alone remain in this country and in view of some of the happenings here of late, I feel as though I am a foreigner.

"I am happy to learn that the years have dealt with you kindly and that you show no touch of age except the graying of the hair. As far as I am concern[ed], the reverse is true. My eyes have become dimmer and I therefore have to wear glasses, my teeth are decaying and I have to consult the dentist regularly, my waistline has grown until I am now referred to as heavy-set and with it all I have become somewhat lazy. Otherwise, I am fine, enjoying life and like all the rest of my acquaintances, cursing the New Deal."[72]

Even with his mother he seems to have remained on almost uniformly good terms, for she once told his wife that Wendell was the only one of the boys who had always been polite and respectful towards her.[73] (This was unjust to the others, for they were always dutiful and often more than that.) It is pleasant, at any rate, to record one moment of tenderness towards him. She wrote on January 9, 1938 (perhaps after hearing his radio debate with Robert Jackson), "I am writing this note to tell you how proud I am of you, and of your standing in this great nation.

"And to remind you that you lost a little pin which you prized highly about twenty years ago, remember? . . . help me to think to give it to you when we meet again."[74]

In the casual contacts of everyday existence Willkie was equally sensitive to other people's feelings. So small an incident as the inadvertent failure to greet an acquaintance when leaving an elevator led to a note of apology and an invitation to lunch.[75] Still more revealing is the following letter to a *Time* staff writer (written three days after the preceding): "Thanks for your letter of the nineteenth. Of course I understand; don't ever be bothered by such a thing. I appreciate you have your editorial problems and it won't make me feel badly when you don't print a statement you ask me to prepare for you."[76]

As for alleged ingratitude to those who had helped him politically, he was, in fact, deeply disturbed by such suggestions. In the summer of 1943 he wrote to Eugene Stetson, who had worked for him in 1940: "I was much distressed to learn the other day that you are upset towards me. I am not speaking politically, I am speaking personally. Undoubtedly, I have failed to thank you adequately for all that you did for me in the last campaign. . . .

"In the last three years I have received literally hundreds of thousands of letters. It has taken every cent I have been able to make to adequately take care of the mail and pay my own traveling expenses which I insist on doing wherever I go to make a talk or on other trips. In addition, during that time I have written a book, numerous articles, many speeches and practiced law, the latter pursuit being necessary with my limited accumulation to support my program. The result is, frankly, that I have not been able to see my friends the way I would like to have had [sic]. I think, however, if you saw my problem you would understand. I shall feel very badly if you do feel ill towards me."[77]

It is apparently true that he sometimes became angry at criticism of his policies, even when offered with the friendliest intentions. Nicholas Roosevelt, for instance, thought it foolish for Willkie to oppose Dewey for governor of New York in 1942 before he was nominated, and said so. "For saying this to him I was for a while in his bad graces."[78] But the breach was temporary, and Roosevelt's final impression was of his "rugged, bear-like, warm-hearted personality."[79]

Over against this flare-up of resentment may be set the experience of

Irving Stone, who in *They Also Ran* gave a picture of Willkie that was not unsympathetic on the whole but critical in some particulars. He tells the story in a letter written just after Willkie's death. "When I arrived in New York this May [1944], Mr. Willkie called me and asked me if I could come down to his office for a chat about the book. . . . We talked for about three hours . . . We spent the major part of our visit . . . discussing the manner in which impressions are created in history, and how difficult it is, first to get them on the record straight, and second to keep them straight. To this end, Mr. Willkie discussed many phases of my chapter about him, discussed them in the warmest and most kindly manner, despite the fact that some of my judgments about him were critical. He did not challenge my facts, but he told me some very interesting stories to show how some of the implications arising from my facts were not strictly accurate. He did this in all humility; there was no attempt to force an opinion on me, nor yet to improve his position in history except as he felt a broader understanding would be helpful."[80] More informally, Stone wrote to Willkie himself soon after the interview: "I read my chapter about you this morning, and I must say that you are a damn good sport. There are several things in there for which you might legitimately have wanted to take a poke at me."[81]

This objectivity on Willkie's part also appears in his later attitude toward men who had been in some sense his opponents. In writing to Morris Ernst, noted liberal lawyer, his regret at being unable to lunch with him and Lilienthal, he remarked: "Dave is very able; also, I have a good deal of affection for him."[82] He was willing to recommend James L. Fly, the extremely aggressive counsel for TVA, for admission to practice in the Federal District Court of the District of Columbia. And in doing so, he came to the point: "Mr. Fly is a very positive individual but he is also a very honest one and a very able one."[83] He wrote to Roosevelt an unsolicited letter warmly recommending Ben Cohen, one of the authors of the Holding Company Act, for appointment as Solicitor General.[84] After the 1944 Republican convention he wrote to Senator Joseph H. Ball, who as leader of Stassen's campaign in the Wisconsin primary was in some degree responsible for Willkie's devastating defeat, "Now that the intensities which arose before the convention have had time to subside, I think it would be very wise if some of these days you and I had a good talk.

"The next time you are in New York, why don't you give me a ring?"[85]

On the other hand, he felt that some issues were so fundamental that certain positions in regard to them were demonstrative of a profound flaw in the moral character of the persons who took such positions; and toward these persons it was impossible for him to be friendly, or to affect a friendliness that he did not feel. The isolationism of Hamilton Fish and the xenophobia of Colonel McCormick deserved, he felt, to be publicly condemned; and he had not the politician's gift for combining public condemnation with private cordiality.

No better summary estimate of Willkie's character can be given than that by his friend Roscoe Drummond: "He was an engaging, disarming, compelling, fascinating, stirring personality. I choose these adjectives carefully. He had few of the little graces, though in his personal relations he could show an extraordinary and imaginative sensitivity. He was a warm-hearted, unwavering, loyal friend and expected the same loyalty in return."[86]

The total picture of Willkie's character is an appealing one. It shows breadth of interest, firmness of conviction, magnanimity in personal relations.

It is true that some of the illustrations of these qualities are drawn from a later period than that at which the story has yet arrived; and this fact calls for a final comment. In part it is due to the lack, in earlier years, of the indisputable documentary evidence that only personal letters can supply. Were such evidence available, we may be certain that in many respects it would simply clarify, without changing, the portrait that has been drawn. But it is also certain that the last four years of Willkie's life brought to his character greater breadth, greater depth, and greater elevation.[87] The greatness of the issues brought to full realization the potential greatness of the man.

In the Willkie of the thirties, though the figure is brilliant and attractive, one meets at times a brashness of assumption, a partiality of vision, an extremity of expression that show a lack of complete maturity. The Willkie of the forties has acquired humility, takes the long view, and speaks with a fervor that fits the life-and-death decisions with which the nation is confronted.

VIII

From Business to Politics

1

The first person to connect Willkie's name with the Presidency, in a place where it would be widely noticed, was Arthur Krock in his column in the *New York Times* on February 23, 1939, although Edward E. Whiting of the Worcester *Telegram* had preceded him by almost a year.[1] He naturally did not commit himself very far; in a survey of possible candidates he introduced Willkie by means of a brief, humorous imaginary conversation, which ended: "If he's a Republican—is he?—you can't wholly count out Willkie. . . . 1940 will be a little early to bring out a utilities man. But if anything like that can be put over, I'd watch Willkie. He still has his haircuts country style."[2]

Krock's caution was understandable, for the reasons hinted at, which thousands of persons were to repeat in the years ahead. First, he had recently been (and, in fact, still was at the time Krock wrote) a registered Democrat. Second, he was a big business executive, with an office a block from Wall Street, and in the branch of big business, the utility industry, which had become almost a symbol of corruption.

A further objection, which Krock did not make explicit, was that he had never held a public office, either elective or appointive, and was assumed to have little knowledge of politics. This assumption, of course, was not wholly correct. He had been all his life an avid student of American history; and during his first years in Akron he had seen, from the inside, a good deal of the working of American politics, both local and national. And in 1932 he had gone to Chicago, though not as a delegate, to work for the nomination of his old idol, Newton D. Baker. It may seem that he was still a little naive politically in thinking that Baker had a chance; but certainly he was no longer so when the convention was over, after observing the efficiency and ruthlessness of the Roosevelt machine. "I've seen history in the making," he told his father-in-law on his return to Rushville, "and it isn't the way they tell it in the books."[3]

He had even had a little experience in local politics in New York as a member of the Democratic organization of New York County—better known as Tammany Hall. In 1935 both he and Mrs. Willkie were elected to the County Democratic Committee (along with James A. Farley, Frank C. Walker, and Bernard Baruch).[4]

Oddly, perhaps, one finds him during the early years in New York on the side of Tammany and against Roosevelt's reform administration in Albany. But he evidently regarded Roosevelt—no doubt remembering the 1924 convention—as an opportunist, and he was not without sympathy for Jimmy Walker, New York's personally charming playboy Mayor, whom Roosevelt removed from office after an investigation that brought national fame to Judge Samuel Seabury. Willkie felt that such investigations were more often inspired and guided by political expediency than by a desire for better government; and he was temperamentally, even more than most Americans, on the side of the underdog.[5]

Willkie voted for Roosevelt, however, in the 1932 election, despite his doubts. His lack of enthusiasm is evidenced by the fact that although he was asked to give $5,000 to the Democratic campaign fund, he actually gave $150. And by the end of 1935 he was saying publicly, "I wish I had my money back."[6] Nor was he disconcerted by a resultant telegram sent (and made public) by three Akron friends, who apparently enjoyed his own brand of humor:

"Dear Wendell:

. . . Before you became a plutocrat you were a good Democrat and we are astounded to know that you contributed only $150. . . . If you are quoted correctly, attach evidence of such contribution to a draft on us through the First Central Trust Co. and we will reimburse you."

Willkie retorted in the same vein (also with a copy to the press): "Thanks for the publicity which you undoubtedly anticipated you would share. I am still a Democrat but not a socialist, therefore I feel I am justly entitled to my refund. I am accepting your offer and . . . will donate my refund when, as and if received to the Akron unit of the Red Cross."[7]

He voted for Landon in the 1936 Presidential election, without fanfare and probably without enthusiasm. His feelings are indicated in a letter to Robert on August 17 of that year: "Your commander-in-chief, Franklin D. still causes me great worries and concern. All my life, as you know, I have been an ardent Democrat and here I find myself after one is elected with almost a phobia on the subject."[8]

In 1937 he voted for the Fusion candidate for Mayor of New York, Fiorello La Guardia; and in the 1938 state election his vote helped re-elect Governor Herbert H. Lehman—by a slim margin—over the young racket-busting District Attorney, Thomas E. Dewey. He still considered himself a Democrat, for in a speech at the New York *Herald Tribune* Forum in October, 1938, he referred to the Democratic Party and added, "of which, incidentally, I am a member."[9] He did not register as a Republican until 1939—and then partly because of the urgings of his son and his wife.[10]

That he took no part after 1932 in other than municipal politics was due to his position as a utility executive. In a letter written early in 1940 to an Indiana newspaper man, he gave as one reason for not supporting the Presidential aspirations of his university classmate and fraternity brother, Paul McNutt, the fact that "since I became an executive officer in the utility industry, I have completely eschewed any relationship with organized politics."[11] And he wrote to his friend Joseph Daniels on the same topic: "I have one ambition as a utility operator and that is to get involved in no presidential or other political campaigns."[12] Whichever party he might support, he would be accused of acting solely in the interest of his company.

A final comment on Willkie's political experience is that during his years of battling the New Deal he had learned much about the workings of Washington politics. Few persons outside the highest government circles can have had a clearer understanding of how political power is exerted.

2

All these facts, however, were unfamiliar to the public, to whom Willkie was known (as far as he *was* known outside of financial and industrial circles) as a spokesman for business against the government. Until 1938 the main theme of his speeches, articles, and press statements had been the injury to the stockholders of C & S and its subsidiaries that would be, or had been, done by New Deal legislation, and the related but subordinate idea that what was bad for them was bad for the country.

But in 1938 he began, in public addresses, to deal with themes wider than the economic effects of quarrels between business and the government; to attempt a clarification of the basic principles of democracy, not as incidental but as antecedent to the settlement of those quarrels; and to look beyond the boundaries not merely of one aspect of the national life but of the nation itself. In his "Foundation Day" address at Indiana University on May 4 he undertook to give a definition of "liberalism," and he did so without even one specific reference to the utility industry. Instead, he related his definition to American life as a whole. Liberalism, he said, is "an attitude of mind," and its goal is "individual freedom." Liberalism had therefore fought, under the leadership of Theodore Roosevelt, Woodrow Wilson, and Robert La Follette, Sr., against the concentration of power in the hands of private individuals controlling vast economic organizations; now, he said, it must oppose the concentration of equally great power in government commissions, leading to "a government of men, instead of a government of laws—in which the favor of a commission chairman determines the conduct of an industry that may be employing several hundred thousand people and owned by several million stockholders."[13]

And the fight was now more important, because then—when he had been an undergraduate—the trend was toward freedom, not only in America but throughout the world. But now the trend had been reversed: Mussolini, Hitler, and Stalin were denying the value of individual freedom and asserting the absolute supremacy of the state.

It is significant that this reference did not lead to a further attack on the New Deal as the enemy of "free enterprise" but to the charge that political expediency made new style "liberalism," as exemplified in the national Democratic leadership, willing to overlook the repression of far more basic liberties. "The true liberal," he asserted, "must be . . . outraged when the government permits the Mayor of Jersey City to throw union organizers in jail—or eject socialists from the town—merely because the Mayor of Jersey City is Vice Chairman of the Democratic National Committee."[14]

One may also note that, in comparison with Willkie's earlier speeches, there is a difference in the quality of the eloquence with which he ends—that it is quieter, deeper, stronger. "I should warn you, however," he told his audience of university undergraduates, "that liberalism is neither easy nor sensational. Very rarely is it called upon to storm the barriers with flags waving, and very rarely can it rely simply on a good heart to determine the merit of its cause. Frequently you will find yourself in the minority, and sometimes you will find yourself alone.

"The fact is that the liberal attempts to do the most difficult thing in the world—namely, to strike a true balance between the rights of the individual and the needs of society. He is like a man rowing a boat who, when the boat swings to the right, pulls on the left, and when it swings to the left, pulls on the right. Liberalism sticks to the middle of the road, speaks quietly and insists on the color of no man's shirt. If its voice seems small in the present tumult of shouting—if its ranks seem thinned among the regiments in uniform—let that be a sign to you, who have been educated in its spirit, to recognize the urgency of its cause."[15]

Both "the rights of the individual" and "the needs of society" were involved in what Willkie was coming more and more to emphasize as the basic failure of the New Deal—its failure to eliminate unemployment. Typical are two essays, "Brace Up, America!" in the *Atlantic Monthly* for June, 1937, and "Idle Money, Idle Men" in the *Saturday Evening Post* for June 17. In both he began with "the grim and inescapable fact" that after six years of the New Deal "we have as many people unemployed as at the beginning"[16]—that is, more than ten million. In both he found the cause in the attitude of the Federal government, and in both he identified three policies as being chiefly to blame. The first was the repressive regulation of business by government commissions: "while a straight-jacket will keep a man out of trouble, it is not a suitable garment in which to work."[17]

The second was excessive government spending. "As in Gresham's law—'bad money drives out good money'—these huge indiscriminate government expenditures, many of them in direct competition with business, have scared private investment into hiding."[18] The third was excessive and ill-conceived taxation—on large personal incomes, on capital gains, on undistributed profits—which destroyed the incentive to invest in productive enterprise, and encouraged investment in untaxed, and unproductive, government securities.

One might wonder, in passing, why Willkie wished to publish two articles saying the same thing at the same time. The answer is that he was writing for different audiences, and in consciously divergent styles. The *Atlantic* article is written for an intellectual audience; its tone is generally serious; the language, though clear, is relatively sophisticated; there is an appeal, at the end, to thoughtful idealism: "This program does not call upon us to sacrifice any of the moral gains of recent years. We do not have to get rid of the idea of 'truth in securities.' We do not have to abandon any plan for 'social security' for the aged and the unemployed. We do not need to annul our provisions for collective bargaining, or reject the principle of federal supervision over industrial activities."[19]

In the *Post* article, the tone is more folksy, the humor is more homely, the final appeal is to common sense. In speaking of spending, he does not refer to Gresham's law, but makes vivid the metaphor of "pump-priming": "every boy who has ever been on a farm should understand it. When you went to get the horses out of the barn in the morning, you led them over to the pump and filled the waterbuckets. But first you poured a glass of water down the pump to get it started. That little glass of water and a few quick strokes of the handle were all that you needed before the pump started to flow."

"Government pump-priming doesn't seem to work that way. The amounts poured down the pump are not small; they are enormous. And still the water doesn't flow."[20] And the conclusion is totally unadorned and down to earth: "if we balance up the books, where are we?

1. We still have those 11,000,000 unemployed. Nobody can get away from that fact.

2. We have lying idle in the banks several billion dollars of money for investment.

3. We have need for all that money, and more, to be spent for the capital expenditures of industry.

"And if we can add Item No. 2 to Item No. 3, then we can largely get rid of Item No. 1. When the people of America feel strongly enough about it, they will force the Government to abandon those hostile policies that make this achievement impossible."[21]

No reader can miss the new note in the speeches and articles here referred to: the substitution of a national point of view for that of a single industry, and the addition of human values to economic values. The second concern is most clearly shown in his increasingly frequent and vigorous defense of civil liberties. At a Columbia University Alumni Luncheon on November 1, 1939, he discussed the violation of individual rights by Congressional committees. What is significant now is that the hostility to business men that had been shown by some of these committees is mentioned mainly as a preface to a denunciation of the House Committee on Un-American Activities (known as the Dies Committee because it was headed by Congressman Martin Dies of Texas).

Willkie began with a joke: "my private papers, telegrams, bank accounts, brokerage accounts, and so forth, have been examined so many times that I no longer even attach to the wires to my wife the stereotyped word, 'Love,' because I am afraid that when it becomes public it may be subject to erroneous inferences." But he quickly became serious. "Let me say to you that the democratic process cannot go on, and will be gradually undermined, if men can be put upon the witness stand without the protection of counsel and without any adequate opportunity to answer. There is no more cruel way of destroying the reputation of a man than by publicity through inference and innuendo. It has been done to hundreds of businessmen and public figures heretofore, and I can speak of it now because it is not my kind that is being investigated . . .

"This must be stopped, both with commissions and Congressional committees."[22] (Willkie did not mention the Dies Committee by name, but later, in answer to a question, he confirmed that he had been referring specifically to it.)[23]

The broadening strain of idealism in Willkie's thought finds its most eloquent expression in a creed which he twice publicly stated toward the end of 1939—once in an article in the December issue of *Readers Digest* entitled "The Faith That Is America,"[24] and again in a speech to the Congress of American Industry on December 8, entitled "Free Men."

"I believe in America because in it we are free—free to choose our government, to speak our minds, to observe our different religions;

—Because we are generous with our freedom—we share our rights with those who disagree with us;

—Because we hate no people and covet no people's lands;

—Because we are blessed with a natural and varied abundance;

—Because we set no limit to man's achievement: in mine, factory, field, or service in business or the arts, an able man regardless of class or creed, can realize his ambition;

—Because we have great dreams—and because we have the opportunity to make those dreams come true."[25]

To be sure, this might be taken, by American businessmen as well as by conservative magazine editors, as a kind of pulpit oratory calling for conventional applause by all respectable persons. And this impression would naturally be strengthened by his warning against the "temptation to surrender the responsibilities of a free citizen, to say to the government: 'During the emergency, you take charge. You tell us what to do, what to think. You fix the prices and production, control the press and the radio.'"[26]

It is even possible to understand the sense of betrayal that some of these persons later felt. Willkie himself did not yet see how far the change in his thinking was to lead him. Yet anyone who cared to, could see that a change was taking place.

3

After reciting his creed to the Congress of American Industry, Willkie closed his speech with a pun on the title of the sensationally best-selling book *Life Begins at Forty*. "If in the next few months we can restore the functioning of free enterprise, we shall find, perhaps, that life begins in '40."[27] It seems obvious that he was thinking of the 1940 election. Was he also thinking of his own possible candidacy?

If so, he had some excuse. On November 21, General Hugh S. Johnson, redoubtable one-time boss of the ill-fated National Recovery Administration, later a columnist who delighted in bludgeoning the New Deal, said in a talk at a Bond Club luncheon in New York that Willkie would make "a very strong candidate" for President (his own later version of what he said was that "if Mr. Willkie were nominated, he would make a powerful candidate and, if elected, a great President.")[28] "I have seen that guy in pretty tough circumstances," the General added, "and he always came out with his head above water."[29] An enterprising reporter telephoned Willkie at Atlanta, Georgia, sure of a comment that would be news, and got it: "In view of the speed with which the Government is taking over my business, shortly I'll have to be looking around for a new job. General Johnson's is the best offer I've had thus far."[30]

Willkie's previous popularity as a speaker sank into insignificance in comparison with the flood of invitations ("2,000 of them in a few days," said Johnson,[31] no doubt with pardonable exaggeration) that now poured in upon him. But the explosive response to Johnson's casual judgment and Willkie's casual joke was of course not causeless. Behind it lay the years of battling for his company against a hostile government—in Congressional committee hearings and investigations, in court cases, in well publicized conferences with the President, and most of all in the sale of TEPCO to TVA at something like his own price, which got page one headlines across the country as well as extended and dramatic treatment in the weekly news magazines. Behind it lay his many articles in trade papers; his many speeches to national organizations of bankers and business men, whose members went home to spread the gospel; his radio speeches and his appearance in a "March of Time" newsreel; his write-up in *Fortune,* the bible of the business man; a brilliant journalistic portrait in the *Saturday Evening Post* (Alva Johnston's "The Man Who Talked Back"); his own article in the *Post,* along with two in the *Atlantic;* his speech at the dedication of the Indiana State Building at the New York World Fair, where he received top newspaper billing over Will H. Hays (former Republican National Chairman and Postmaster General, at this time the "czar" of the movie industry, who for many years had kept Hollywood productions pure), Governor Clifford Townsend and Senator Sherman Minton;[32] and most of all, in the view of many observers, his radio debate with Attorney General Robert H. Jackson on January 6, 1938, in the "Town Meeting of the Air."

This was the best and probably the most popular public affairs program that radio ever produced, and this particular debate was one of the liveliest, with applause (and occasional boos and cries of "No") from the studio audience punctuating every answer in the question period that followed the formal speeches. Thoughtful people throughout the country had a chance to hear Willkie in the kind of situation where he was at his best. In print, it does not appear that he had much of an edge on his opponent, who spoke ably and to the point.[33] But Willkie's personality evidently had an overwhelming impact on the radio audience. It was even intimated that the meeting put a decisive end to an Administration attempt to build Jackson up as Roosevelt's successor.[34]

As a result, many business men had doubtless been saying long before the appearance of Krock's column that Willkie would make a good President. Sometime in 1938 he showed to one columnist, Jennings Perry, "a large sheaf of letters, carefully preserved, suggesting that he run."[35] And in 1939 such suggestions began appearing more and more frequently in print. On March 3 one appeared in the *Herald Tribune* over the name of G. Vernor Rodgers; and on March 27, in *Newsweek,* Raymond Moley followed Krock's lead by referring to "a few timid 'feelers' about Wendell Willkie as a possible candidate."[36] On May 22, David Lawrence (who was then far from the acid reactionary of later years) was more positive: "His name is one that fits the demand the Republicans are making for confidence and fair dealing in the government's relations with business."[37]

By midsummer there was so much support that *Time* took notice of it in its July 31 issue, with a cover photograph of Willkie and an extended article in which the writer observed that "Wendell Willkie (a life-long Indiana Democrat) is today the only business man in the U. S. who is ever mentioned as a Presidential possibility for 1940. . . . Into Willkie's office come 500 letters weekly, all urging him to keep up the fight, many predicting that it will wind up with him in the White House. . . . When friends ask him whether he intends to be a candidate, he answers, 'Wouldn't I be a sucker to say "Yes"?' "[38]

After this, the fact that many people wanted Willkie for President was no longer news. What *was* news, from now on, was anything that had a bearing on whether that wish would be fulfilled. In this situation, Johnson's opinion and Willkie's response were the answer to a newsman's prayer.

That Willkie was still uncommitted is shown by the fact that despite the 2,000 invitations, he gave only one major speech in December (to the Congress of American Industry on December 2, which must have been scheduled long before), one in January (at Wooster College on January 29), and none in February. There was also only one important article, a rather brief piece in the *Saturday Evening Post* of December 30 entitled "With Malice Toward None"—an attitude that he urged the Administration to adopt.

But if he was not campaigning for the nomination, neither was he allowed to forget it. Arthur Krock found in the Johnson episode an excuse for a full column plugging Willkie's candidacy.[39] On January 16, when he spoke as a member of a panel at the Sales Executives Club, he "received an ovation" when another panelist remarked that "the business outlook would be good 'if we had a Presidential candidate like our honored guest, Mr. Willkie.'"[40] And the letters kept coming in. At Wooster College he told the press that he had received "thousands" of letters urging him to run for President, and attributed them to the comments of Johnson and Krock.[41] Krock promptly came through with another.[42]

One of the letters, which must have been both pleasant and unexpected, was from the chairman of the Chattanooga Power Board, L. J. Wilhoite, who had been in some sense his opponent through years of controversy and negotiation. If there was anybody who knew of anything personally discreditable to Willkie in the struggle between C & S and TVA, it should have been Wilhoite, yet he wrote: "It is becoming more and more apparent every day that Mr. Roosevelt will not be a candidate, and that gives me an opportunity to vote for you. So please don't put cotton in both your ears."[43]

The plea was unnecessary. Willkie was now definitely weighing the possibility of a try for the Republican nomination. To Russell Davenport, who happened to be with him when he read in the paper of the death of Senator Borah on January 19, he commented: "This gives me a chance."[44] Nothing further was said on either side, but the connection was obvious. Borah had been one of the most influential Republican Senators—and one of the most violently isolationist.

A little later Willkie made a public statement on the nomination which showed him to be as honest and irrepresible as ever: "if the nomination were given me without any strings, I would have to accept it. No man in middle life and in good health could do otherwise.

"But I couldn't go out and seek delegates and make two-sided statements. I value my independence. That's what I've been fighting for all these years."[45] This was no way to make friends and gain influence among the politicians; but it was the way he felt, and he said it. In the same spirit, when a friend advised him that it was politically inexpedient to accept election as a director of the First National Bank of New York, he retorted: "If I have to predicate everything I do on what may happen to me politically in the future, life is not worth living."[46]

But Willkie's most startling display of independence was an article called "Fair Trial" that appeared in the *New Republic* on March 18. It began like merely another warning against the increasing power of the Federal government, now aided and abetted by the Supreme Court. (A week before, in his third article in the *Saturday Evening Post,* entitled "The Court Is Now His," he had blasted the Court for having effected a "silent revolution" by abandoning precedents concerning the government's power to regulate business, impose taxes, and shape the social life of the population.) And his appeal for "equal treatment for all under the law" and denunciation of devious methods devised by "district attorneys" whereby a man "can be punished for a political opinion," did not prepare his readers for the examples that he gave.

The first was Eugene V. Debs, founder of the American Socialist Party, sentenced to ten years in prison in 1918 for making an anti-war speech. "Debs, a pacifist with a strong labor following, had been a nuisance for some time, and the authorities wanted to get him out of the way."[47] The second surprise example was Huey Long, who at one time had become "a real threat" to the continuance of the Roosevelt Administration. "The Bureau of Internal Revenue accordingly tried to get at Huey via the income tax route." A number of his subordinates were indicted, though Huey himself escaped—to be assassinated. Thereupon the Long machine made peace with the Administration—and "the government dropped the prosecution."[48]

Perhaps most Republicans would not have minded this—if indeed they read the *New Republic.* But they would have been staggered by a sentence that soon followed: "Anyone who wants to go through the records can have a fascinating and disturbing time checking up on Mooney, Billings, Sacco, Vanzetti, and others."[49] For these, during the twenties and thirties, were legendary names: symbolic, among left-wing groups, of capitalist society's determination to destroy its critics; demonstrative to right-wing groups that such a determination was justified; vaguely annoying to the vast majority of Americans, who did not wish to face unpleasant doubts about the justice of their country's courts. That all four men—Mooney and Billings convicted of murder in the bombing of a "Preparedness Day" parade in San Francisco in 1916, sentenced to death but finally released after years in prison; Sacco and Vanzetti convicted of murder in a payroll robbery in Massachusetts in 1921, sentenced to death and finally executed in 1927 under circumstances that aroused protest throughout the world—were innocent of any crime but that of being theoretical anarchists is now widely, though not universally, agreed. But in 1940 their names were poison to any well-bred politician.

But Willkie made this reference merely in passing, and then went on to defend, as victims of political persecution, the two most unpopular men in the United States—Fritz Kuhn, head of the Nazi German-American Bund, and Earl Browder, head of the American Communist Party. The former had been sentenced to from two and a half to five years in prison for misappropriating $500—"although the Bund gave him unrestricted power over expenditures and apparently did not care about the $500."[50] The latter was sentenced to four years in prison and fined $2,000 for having once traveled on a fake passport—though, since that act had occurred so long ago as to come under the Statute of Limitations, he was nominally tried for perjury in having later sworn in applying for a passport that he had never had one before. (This set a precedent, followed in the Hiss case and others, for circumventing the Statute of Limitations.) Was he convicted, Willkie asked, "because he made a false statement on a passport application, or because he was a member of the Communist party?"[51]

He concluded: "It is well to remember that any man who denies justice to someone he hates prepares the way for a denial of justice to someone he loves."[52]

4

Civil liberties have never been a popular issue in America, despite our general devotion to fair play. Nobody but Willkie would have signed his name to such a manifesto if he had the remotest notion of seeking the Presidential nomination. Yet in the next article that he published he took a long step toward avowing his candidacy. In "We the People," in the April issue of *Fortune,* he presented the fullest statement that he had yet made of his political and social philosophy. It was in effect a political platform.

Yet he began (after a brief "Petition" to the Federal government) with another jibe at the politicians: "the American people tend to suspect political candidates. They know that each is told by his advisers to put on a smile as automatically as a hat, to be photographed going to church [Willkie did not go to church], and to play with his grandchildren if he has any [Mr. Roosevelt during the early years of his Administration had often been photographed with "Sistie" and "Buzzie" Dall, the children of his daughter Anna]—or with somebody else's grandchildren if he hasn't. The candidate should be a fisherman. [This was rather hard on Mr. Hoover, who no doubt really enjoyed fishing.] But above all he must be careful about what he says. If he is talking in the country districts, he should say one thing; in the city, another. In order to avoid offending this or that pressure group, he may be advised to straddle colossal issues. If he believes in an issue advocated also by his opponent, he is instructed to remain silent lest he give support to the enemy. And should he object to these machinations and try to assert a little independence, he is assured that, once elected, he can ignore all that has gone before."

And then, as he was to do so many times in the future, he appealed to the people over the heads of the politicians. "The American people are not dumb. They know all about this. . . . the American people do not give their vote to policies; they give their vote to *men*. They vote for the man who, in their opinion, will not let them down."[53]

But of course one thing essential to the judgment of a *man* is an *honest* statement of what policies he believes in; and this Willkie went on to give. His criticisms of the New Deal were familiar; but his comment on government spending developed a new idea—that such spending should be an *investment;* though "sometimes, in the very nature of its trust, the returns on its investment must be intangible returns, as in the case of hospitals, for example. Yet good economic investments can be found. Slum clearance, for example, should be carried much further than it has been."[54]

Such suggestions are far from radical—except possibly to the Old Guard. But other passages echo Roosevelt in the first flush days of the New Deal. "Government, either state or federal, must be responsible not only for the destitute and unemployed, but for elementary guarantees of public health, the rehabilitation of farmers, rebuilding of the soil, preservation of the national forests, clearance and elimination of city slums, and so forth. The need for these public works . . . has been felt and answered by every civilized government in the world today."[55]

A still more striking departure from recent themes was his stress on the importance of international ties: "today the world is so closely knit, the oceans are so small, and the peoples of the world are so dependent upon each other, that it is not realistic to make domestic policies without considering their relationship to foreign affairs. . . . It makes a great deal of difference to us—politically, economically, emotionally—what kind of world exists beyond our shores."[56]

His first application of this principle was a condemnation of the Congressional isolationists who had blocked loans to Finland with which to buy arms for defense against the Russian invasion. After all, "there can be no question which is right and which is wrong. . . . We are opposed to war. But we do not intend to relinquish our right to sell whatever we want to those defending themselves from aggression."[57]

His second application was a defense of the reciprocal trade treaties negotiated by Secretary of State Hull: "What could be simpler or more in accord with common sense? What could be better qualifed to benefit us, the people, *as a whole?* Of course we have to make sacrifices. But the point is that, owing to the way the agreements are negotiated, the sacrifices are always, and should always be, less than the benefits gained." And he followed to the end the logic of his position: "the best foreign policy for the United States is one that will, in the long run, help to raise the standard of living of the rest of the world."[58]

So here he stood—a low-tariff, anti-isolationist, Bill-of-Rights Democrat, in rebellion against the New Deal not because of its aims but because of its arbitrary exercise of power. He would accept the nomination from the Republicans if it were offered "without any strings." But he wanted people to know what he thought.

He had already begun to step up, a little, his campaign to tell them in person. And here too there were surprises. At Toledo on March 4, along with the familiar attack on "big government," he presented a powerful indictment of the sins of big business during the years before the depression. "In the inflation and false prosperity following the World War, business men, drunk with power, and a public, drunk with money, broke down the safeguards protecting individual liberties. . . . In the money-mad period of the twenties the heads of some of our corporations forgot their primary function—that of running a business enterprise in a way that would be sound for the worker, the consumer and the investor. Instead . . . they began playing with corporate structures as with a child's building-blocks, becoming promoters rather than businessmen. And some financiers in Wall Street and elsewhere, instead of serving as a link between the savings of the people and the enormous capital needs of industry, became jugglers of finance, concerned primarily neither with the investor nor the investment, but with making money and securing power . . . putting pressure on this man or that newspaper, or this or that group, so that opposition would be eliminated."[59]

And such criticisms of business were not made only in public to conciliate the critics of business who might be critics of *him;* he had also told off business men to their faces, in private. General Johnson reported a meeting of industrial leaders where, after "a succession of die-hards and clock-reversers had excoriated the New Deal and the President in total condemnation," Willkie was called on for his opinion. He gave it: "that this nation was disgracefully laggard in social and other reforms, that gross abuses of our capitalistic system were long overdue for regulation, that any attempt to frustrate or prevent those corrections would be both futile and disastrous," and would convict American industry of "not deserving that independence of action without which no profit system can hope to function."[60]

Willkie followed the Toledo speech with one to the Commonwealth Club of San Francisco on March 15, another to a Town Hall audience on April 4, and another to the Boston Chamber of Commerce on April 5. In these speeches, and in "We the People," Willkie still was only testing public responsiveness to his views. In an interview with McAlister Coleman published in the *Nation* of April 15, he denied that he expected or desired to be nominated. "I have, however, been very anxious to put over certain ideas." As a result, he had been asked if he would accept the nomination. "In order to preserve my intellectual integrity I have said yes, if it were on a platform in which I believed. I have, however, consistently refused many offers of financial help, all offers to seek delegates, and any kind of political assistance."[61] This was true.

5

During this period of watchful waiting, the three events that were most decisive for Willkie's future all occurred on April 9.

One was his appearance on the radio program "Information, Please," deservedly the most popular quiz show at the time. The central interest in the program lay, not in a tension contrived out of little facts and big money, but in the character of the permanent members of the cast: Clifton Fadiman as master of ceremonies, and John Kieran, Franklin P. Adams and Oscar Levant as members of the panel. (On this occasion Christopher Morley, a more or less regular stand-in for the other members, replaced Levant.) All were informed, articulate, and witty; each possessed a distinct and forceful personality. A big name was no guarantee that the guest member of the panel would not sit mute and embarrassed through most of the program, or get flustered and hurry to give the wrong answers. Willkie was the first big business man to appear.

When the time came, he was as uninhibited and as much at ease as before a Congressional committee. He quoted, with only a minor slip, the Preamble to the Constitution, defined "carpet-bagger," explained what a "pocket veto" is, discoursed on the "farm bloc," and showed a considerable knowledge of literature. No one could resist the warmth, the enthusiasm, the humor, the intelligence, that radiated from him. *Life* in a special write-up added to the effect by picturing his zestful, boyish grin as he answered a question or offered a wisecrack.[62]

The second significant event on April 9 was that Oren Root, Jr., a grandnephew of Elihu Root, one-time Republican Secretary of State, decided that Willkie was his candidate for President; and, to learn whether many other people shared this sentiment, and if so, to channel it, he sent out to a selected list of persons copies of a simple "declaration," with space for fifteen signatures, affirming that the signers were in favor of Willkie's candidacy. He sent a copy to Willkie, whom he had never met (although he had heard him speak), explaining: "Today I have mailed copies of the enclosed to a couple of thousand people. This is only a feeler and a very small beginning of what must follow to dramatize your unquestionable availability. I did not inform you in advance because I wished to be able to say not only that you had not sponsored it but also that you had not even known of it."[63]

As a matter of fact, Willkie and Russell Davenport, who at this time was his principal political adviser, felt that it was too early for such a move, but when they talked to Root, his enthusiasm partly won them over.[64] Even if Root had been asked to stop the movement, however, he could not have done so. Five days later he had had to print 20,000 "declarations." "My telephone has not stopped ringing since they were sent out."[65] On April 13 a friend inserted a small classified advertisement in the "public notices" columns of the *Herald Tribune:* "Wendell Willkie for President! Help Oren Root, Jr., organize the people's demand for Willkie. Send Root a contribution at 15 Broad Street, New York."[66] The response to this was also startling. Root had to move out of his law office (taking a leave of absence from his firm) and establish a special headquarters.

And now, almost spontaneously, Willkie Clubs began to spring up all across the country, the members of each animated by the same missionary zeal that had moved Root himself. A month later there were 200 Willkie Clubs; by mid-June there were 750, and "new ones were forming at the rate of 20, 30, 40 a day. . . . at least 50,000 volunteer Willkie workers were in the field, handing out Willkie buttons, getting signatures on petitions . . . over 750,000 pieces of Willkie campaign literature had been mailed from the

Manhattan Volunteer Mailing Committee."[67] Not all this activity stemmed from Root's "declarations"; but certainly they were a major cause.

But it was the third event that occurred on April 9 that, with the sequel it portended, was decisive in Willkie's winning the nomination. This was the invasion of Denmark and Norway by Nazi Germany. It brought a frightening end to the "phoney war" into which the European conflict had subsided after the destruction of Poland and which had lulled many Americans into a state of cynical or hopeful security. It foreshadowed the successful attack on Belgium and the Netherlands a month later, and, after the briefest of breathing spells, the annihilation of the French defenses. It jolted many Americans into a new look at the outside world and their relation to it. And among these was Willkie.

The record of his attitude toward events in Europe during the thirties is almost non-existent. The rise of Hitler, Mussolini's invasion of Ethiopia (which in effect killed the League of Nations, to which Willkie had once been so passionately attached), the passage of the Neutrality Act of 1935 (an example of folly and cowardice hardly matched in American history), the bloody triumph of despotism over democracy in the Spanish Civil War;[68] and, on the other side of the world, the Japanese invasion first of Manchukuo and then of China itself—all these passed without public comment from Willkie.

This silence is hard to understand. One can only assume, difficult as the assumption is, that he was so exclusively occupied with his struggle to save, first, his company and, second, the country, from being ruined (as he saw it) by Roosevelt's domestic policies, that foreign affairs simply got shoved out of his mind. We even find him in 1935, before a Congressional committee, jeering at the idea that TVA power might be needed in a war, and dismissing it as propaganda.[69]

Even after the outbreak of war in Europe in 1939, when he wrote "The Faith That Is America" (which he closed with such a lofty and stirring creed), the greatest evil that Willkie could find in the war was that it threatened America's "freedom," "because in a modern war people destroy the very things they say they are fighting for. It is because we wish to preserve our free democratic system that we must remain at peace"—and must be on guard lest the Administration, "under the guise of 'emergency,'" demand still greater power over the lives of private citizens.[70] This was spoken like a true Republican.

He possessed, however, the power to learn, and change. The Russian invasion of Finland and the Nazi invasion of Denmark and Norway roused him to the belief that America must do all in its power, short of open war, to aid the democracies. Presiding at a dinner of the Economic Club on April 10, he said, "There is one thing we are all agreed upon, and that is that the British and French way of life shall continue in this world."[71] The implications of this statement, as he spelled them out during the next ten weeks, were the decisive factor at the Philadelphia convention.

6

From this point on, Willkie's popular fame seemed to increase in geometrical progression. Now his name was on many tongues as a Presidential possibility. On April 16, Kenneth Simpson, New York National Committeeman who was violently anti-Dewey, proposed him as keynote speaker at the National Convention, but withdrew the suggestion when it was pointed out that Willkie was a potential candidate.[72] (Governor Harold Stassen of Minnesota was named instead.)

It also became clear that some persons in the Roosevelt Adminstration were beginning to take note of the Willkie boom. In his Town Hall speech of April 4, in discussing civil liberties, Willkie said he had been told that "a certain board official in Washington" had been keeping a file on him, and had declared: "We are going to get him if it is the last thing we ever do."[73] Roosevelt, asked about it at his press conference next day, laughed it off: "Of course nobody takes things like that seriously."[74] But Willkie had the last laugh, though a wry one. On April 15, a news story revealed the intention of the SEC to investigate the alleged political activities of the Georgia Power Company, which was reported to have collected political contributions from its employees during the primary election of 1938; in which, the story noted, Roosevelt had been badly beaten in his attempt to "purge" the conservative Senator George.[75]

Arkwright and Willkie were quick to deny the charge. And the SEC hastened to avoid political entanglements. Chairman Jerome Frank announced: "Several months ago a complaint was made to the Commission regarding the Georgia Power Co. . . . The Commission has come to no conclusion as to whether there were any irregularities. The complaint made no charges against Mr. Wendell Willkie."[76]

Who was responsible for the news story remains unknown. But in view of the unfounded charges made in 1933 against the Alabama and Tennessee Power Companies after Willkie had testified against some features of the TVA bill; the fact that the primary had taken place two years earlier, that no complaints had previously been made, and that the charges were never substantiated; and the methods used by Roosevelt's subordinates to discredit Willkie during the campaign—in view of all this, one would be simple-minded not to take the charges against the Georgia Power Company as a left-handed compliment to Willkie's growing political strength.

An indeterminate amount of his strength lay in the support of a number of wealthy New Yorkers who were now active in pushing his candidacy. One was Colonel Henry Breckenridge, Assistant Secretary of War in Wilson's administration, who on April 7 publicly urged the Republicans to nominate Willkie, declaring that Taft, Vandenberg and Dewey had "demonstrated their unfitness" by their isolationist statements.[77] Among others who at that point worked less openly were Harold E. Talbott, later Secretary of the Air Force under Eisenhower; Rauol Desvernines, a prominent lawyer who was an anti-New Deal Democrat; Frank Altschul of the banking firm of Lazard Frères; Harry Shackleford of Johns-Manville, a fraternity brother of Indiana University days; John W. Hanes, Under Secretary of the Treasury during the early years of Roosevelt's administration, who had resigned in protest against Roosevelt's fiscal policies; and Harold Gallagher, a member of the law firm that Willkie later joined. In addition there were Sinclair Weeks of Massachusetts, afterward United States Senator and later Secretary of Commerce under Eisenhower, and, most important of all, Samuel F. Pryor, vice president of Pan American Airways and National Committeeman from Connecticut, who was a member of the Committee on Arrangements for the National Convention and became chairman on May 17 following the sudden death of the previous incumbent. More active than any of these, at the beginning, was Charlton MacVeagh, a friend of Davenport's with similar literary and philosophical leanings, who took the lead in establishing the Willkie Mailing Committee and sending out copies of "We the People."[78] (Davenport himself decided on May 2 that he must give his full time to the Willkie cause and resigned as managing editor of *Fortune*. He did so against Willkie's advice,[79] and he was careful to state for public consumption that he was working on his own, "without any authorization from Mr. Willkie. I do not contemplate forming any organization, raising any funds, or making any of the routine moves of a campaign.")[80]

Popular support was also growing. In the Gallup Poll published on May 8, he was suddenly fourth on the list of candidates preferred by Republican voters. It is true that he was preferred by only 3 per cent, as against 67 per cent for Dewey, 14 for Vandenberg and 12 for Taft; but a month earlier he had not had enough support to be listed at all.

Willkie himself had maintained a very modest speaking schedule, addressing only non-political audiences, and insisting: "I am not electioneering. I have not spent a nickel." He was only trying, he said, "to win popular support for certain principles in which I believe."[81] (He was still busy with C & S affairs, arguing against the SEC that to break up the holding company, in view of the low residential rates and high average use throughout the system, would be "detrimental to the public interest.")[82]

His only major speech was at a meeting of the American Newspaper Publishers Association at New York on April 25, which he followed with a press statement clarifying some of the things he had said. Most striking was his comment on the war. "It may well be that the most effective way of keeping out of this war will be by helping the democracies in every way possible, within the limits of international law. . . . if the totalitarian states prevail the odds are very substantial that we shall have to meet them in armed conflict when they have been victorious over the democracies and are truculent and strong."[83]

The platform for his candidacy was now complete. It remained to be seen whether the Republican party, to which he was now to speak directly, would approve it.

He spoke to them first at St. Paul on May 11. This speech was arranged by John and Gardner Cowles, Jr., publishers of influential newspapers in Minneapolis (the *Star* and *Tribune*) and Des Moines (the *Register*) and of the magazine *Look*, which in its class was second in popularity only to *Life*. As liberal and non-professional Republicans, they were the kind of people that Davenport (who shared Willkie's distrust of professional politicians) wanted his candidate to meet, and he introduced them one evening in New York about April 20. They talked until 2 A. M., and the Cowles brothers, like so many others, succumbed to Willkie's magnetism and decided at once that here was the man for the Republicans to nominate. But they could not approve his strategy—if it could be called that—which was simply to wait, while his popular support continued to snowball. They argued that it was the delegates who made the decison in the end, and that Willkie must be known to *them*. They invited him to come either to Des Moines or Minneapolis, promising to get together all the convention delegates from the state and all the county chairmen to hear him. Willkie was reluctant, but they finally talked him into it. "What have you got to lose?" they asked. As it happened, Minnesota Republicans were planning a meeting on May 11, and Willkie was invited to speak.

The next step was to get Harold Stassen, who in those lean years for the Republicans had got himself elected Governor of Minnesota at the age of thirty-one, to make the introduction. It was John Cowles who made the request, and though Stassen had no wish to be associated with Willkie's candidacy, which he thought had no chance, he was willing to introduce Willkie as one candidate among others, with the statement that he was glad to have as many of the candidates as possible present themselves to local Republicans.[84]

It was on this date, Willkie said later, that "he had first taken seriously his campaign for the Republican nomination."[85] But of course there are degrees of commitment. He had always said he would accept the nomination *if* it were offered him. And as this possibility became less remote, the idea of exerting some effort himself began to seem less absurd. On his way to Minnesota, therefore, he stopped in Chicago to see his brother Edward, whom he told what he had told everybody else—that he had not yet made up his mind and that he did not know whether to take seriously all the talk about his running for President. But he also said that if the St. Paul speech was a success, he would then go all out for the nomination. And he went so far as to say that if he *did* get the nomination, he wanted Ed to take a leave of absence from his job and go with him on the campaign train.[86]

If the speech had been a failure, Willkie would probably have gone back to sit on the sidelines—with less of a chance than before of being called into the game. He had, after all, something to lose. And it almost *was* a failure. The Cowleses had bought radio time, and Willkie had prepared a careful script. But he had never learned—never really *did* learn, in fact—to read a speech effectively before a microphone. It would not have seemed possible for him to give a dull speech. But this time he did.

And of course he knew it. So, when the microphone was turned off, he threw the speech away, literally. Then while the sheets floated down on the persons sitting in the front rows, he launched into an extemporaneous denunciation of the New Deal that totally erased the previous impression. He talked for twenty minutes and was cheered for ten. He gained half a dozen of the Minnesota delegates then and there; and he convinced Stassen that he had a real chance of winning the nomination.[87]

He also, apparently, convinced Stassen of something else. Though he said that he had more respect for Stassen than for any other man in American political life,[88] he also warned: " I say to him, in all seriousness that if he, as key-noter of the Republican Party, attempts to put the Republican Party on record as saying what is going on in Europe is none of our business, we might as well fold up."[89] When the time came, Stassen heeded the warning.

7

And now Willkie plunged. Before, nobody could push him into an active, direct effort to win the nomination; now, nobody could hold him back. In the next five weeks, he gave speeches in at least fourteen cities: Indianapolis; Des Moines; Somerville, New Jersey; New York City; Kansas City; Akron; Denver; St. Louis; Lincoln, Nebraska; Omaha; Washington; Boston; Hartford; Providence; and Brooklyn. And these were frankly political speeches, usually to Republican audiences. (He also worked in a Commencement address at Colgate University, where he received an honorary degree and told the graduates, "All the fun in life comes from being unafraid. . . . Be yourself . . .")[90]

And now, with Denmark and Norway, Belgium and the Netherlands, engulfed by the murky tide of Nazism, with France tottering and Britain standing alone, Willkie dwelt with new and urgent persuasiveness upon two themes: first, the need for all possible aid to the Allies—that is, finally, to Britain—short of war; second, the need for a tremendous speed-up in the building of America's military strength, and the unfitness of the Roosevelt Administration to carry out the job. But it was on the first that he was most insistent—in St. Paul, in Kansas City, most of all, in Akron: "I should like to ask Secretary Hull to ask the democracies, publicly and openly in the name of the American people, what help—short of troops—the American people can give."[91]

It is curious that after such aggressive statements in the supposedly isolationist Midwest, Willkie should have taken a less clear line in the supposedly internationalist East, saying in Boston on June 14: "personally, in spite of my belief that we would [sic] help the Allies in every possible way, I have been against getting into this war, or any other war, and I still am";[92] and in Brooklyn, four days later (although he spoke feelingly of the fall of France and of "the brutal power and force of the totalitarian armies"): "It is the duty of the President of the United States to recognize the determination of the people to stay out of war and to do nothing by word or deed to undermine that determination."[93] There is clearly a change of emphasis here. And the natural though unwelcome assumption is that Willkie, forgetting his brave words in "We the People," had shifted his ground because some of his supporters had urged him to; and that he partially yielded, as he was to do in the campaign itself, to the pressure of persons who thought mainly in terms of votes.

Even the isolationists, however, were eager for America to build its own defenses; and so his attacks on the Administration for having failed in this duty were eagerly approved by all Republicans—even though the party members in Congress had solidly and consistently opposed, up to this time, any increase in military expenditures. Willkie's criticism, however, was basic: that New Deal policies had left the nation economically weak and emotionally divided in the face of a now desperate need for strength and unity.

The development of this theme in the Akron speech is typical: "the government has sought power, and won it, by sowing discord among the people and the people's enterprises. . . . we say to the New Dealers and the trouble-makers: 'Let us work together. We have had enough of discord.

"'Let us bring together the industrial brains of this country, and the labor of this country, and the young men and women of this country, and everyone who belongs to this country and lives in it.

"'And let us take our vast resources out of the earth and transport them to our factories; and let us assign each factory a job for the defense of this nation; and let us gear these jobs one to the other, so that each will fit, so that there will be a minimum of waste, and so that our army, our navy, and our air force may be adequately equipped as quickly as possible.' "[94]

The quality of this quotation will perhaps help to explain Willkie's sensational success in winning the approval of his audiences. This success was reflected in the Gallup Poll of May 31, which showed him the choice of 10 per cent of Republican voters, though he was still in fourth place; but two weeks later he had 17 per cent of the vote, and was second. In the final poll before the convention, made public on June 21, he had 29 per cent. Dewey was down to 47, Taft and Vandenberg to 8.[95]

The next day Willkie went to Philadelphia.

IX
The Philadelphia Convention

1

The miracle was not yet complete, but it was authentic. Willkie had not yet won the nomination; but even to have got this far was, under the circumstances, an unprecedented triumph. A year before—six months, three months, two months—it would have been incredible. To a certain extent it still was. What were the forces behind it?

One myth can be dismissed at once. Willkie was not sold to the public by any group of public relations experts working either collectively or separately. The claim of one of them that "the 'Willkie boom' was one of the best engineered jobs in history,"[1] and of another that he contributed $10,000 worth of his *time*,[2] are ludicrous. At best the public relations men were belatedly following the lead of Oren Root, helping to crystallize a sentiment that was already there. They were no different from numberless other individuals—some of them personal friends of Willkie who held high positions in the business world, others obscure persons in the smaller cities and towns throughout the country—who were all working with unflagging ardor, doing whatever came to mind, to advance his candidacy.

The kind of things that Willkie's friends could do was vividly illustrated by the "Hoosier Box Lunch" gathering that his fraternity brother Harry Shackleford and another Indiana University alumnus, Guy Lemmon, took the lead in arranging on May 21, in order to "take the curse of Wall Street off him" by suggesting the rural Indiana environment in which he had grown up. They hired the Manhattan Center; they designed a "little Red Schoolhouse" as the theme of the decorations; they sold box lunches for a dollar; they had Willkie introduced by one of his former English professors, Dr. William Howe, a kindly and unpretentious person whose genuine pride and affection were reflected in his words and manner; and they drew an overflow crowd. Moreover, Shackleford was able (with the aid of Donald Thornburgh, who was on the staff of CBS) to talk the Columbia Broadcasting System into giving Willkie's speech a free broadcast over a 99-station hook-up, on the ground that the speaker was a *public* figure and not a *political* figure. Undoubtedly the meeting added momentum to the Willkie drive.[3]

But the most powerful agency in Willkie's rocket-like ascent to a dominant position at the convention was the press. The Luce publications (*Fortune, Time,* and *Life*), the *Saturday Evening Post,* and *Readers Digest* made him known to a mass audience. The *Times* and the *Herald Tribune* gave him full news coverage and sympathetic editorial treatment in New York and a large surrounding area; the Cowles brothers, in the last two months before the convention, helped introduce him to the Middle West. A number of columnists, as noted, worked to stir interest in his candidacy. And as the convention neared, newspapers throughout the country gave him more and more space.

But in the end, every factor in the Willkie build-up goes back to the man himself. The magazines wrote him up because they knew their readers were or would be interested. They published his articles because they knew people would read them. And he forged into the headlines not because newspaper reporters or editors were initially prejudiced in his favor, but simply because what he did and said was news.

This personal gift for gaining a hearing was no less evident in his political campaigning than it had been in other activities. He disdained, as "We the People" had suggested, the time-tried shifts of the professional office-seeker. "The curse of democacy today," he told a St. Louis crowd, after praising Winston Churchill for facing up to the grim truth, "in America as in Europe, is that everybody has been trying to please the public. Almost nobody ever gets up and says what he thinks."[4] And whether they liked what he thought or not, he was gambling that they would like him for saying it. "I'm the cockiest fellow you ever met," he said to another audience, this one in Kansas City. "If you want to vote for me, fine. If you don't, go jump in the lake." But he grinned when he said it, and added, "and I'm still for you."[5] No political candidate had ever talked to them like this before—and they loved it.

He was equally frank with reporters. "I don't know Joe Pew," he remarked casually of the multi-millionaire oil man and ultra-conservative boss of the Pennsylvania Republican organization (and presumably of its 72 votes at the convention), "but I am 100 per cent against his policy of turning the Republican party back to the days of Harding and Coolidge."[6]

With the same frankness, he did not hide his hope that Roosevelt would be the Democratic candidate: "I want to see us beat the champ: I don't want to see us beat Tony Galento."[7] (Galento, known as "Two-ton Tony" or "Beer-barrel Tony," was an earnest but not a serious contender for the heavyweight boxing championship held by Joe Louis.) Later he explained, "He's the author and ablest advocate of the New Deal, and the people have a right to hear from him." And besides, it would be a good fight: "I'd like nothing better than to stand up and trade swats with him."[8]

Apparently he did stand up and trade swats with Harold Ickes, in an off-the-record debate at the banquet of the American Society of Newspaper Editors in Washington on April 19, "on the third term and 1940 issues."[9] Ickes was widely and justly noted as a master of the art of verbal combat (a "well known gladiator," as Willkie called him a little later with friendly humor),[10] but Willkie caught him off guard. "With occasional swipes at the New Deal [these are Ickes' own words], he said in effect that there were many men in the New Deal who were as capable of being President as Roosevelt. . . . I was his candidate, he declared, and he rang the changes on this to the amusement of the audience and his own satisfaction."[11] Even though the debate was not publicly reported, it was worth a good deal to Willkie to have won the favor of that particular group; it gave him, according to one who was present, a "big political push."[12]

In a less genial mood, he met head-on the charge that being a business man disqualified him for the nomination. "Since when have American business men been barred from running for or holding public office?" And again he voiced his desire to "meet the champ." "I would like to go out on the stump and debate with the President the question of whether the job I did in utilities was not far better than the job he has done the last seven years."[13]

Such apt and unstudied comments Willkie could and did toss off without effort or inhibition. He was, in fact, equal to any occasion. In another off-the-record performance, at the National Press Club in Washington on June 12, when a reporter asked him without warning, "Mr. Willkie, why did you leave your party?" he "shot back: 'I did not leave my party. My party left me. I am a Jeffersonian Democrat and I have never deviated from the principles of Thomas Jefferson. . .' " The answer brought a storm of applause.[14]

2

But there was one force working for Willkie that was more powerful than all the others, which owed him nothing, which he could not influence, but which made him for the moment its favorite. This was history. "I would like to think," he remarked in discussing his popularity, "that it means I'm a hell of a fellow . . . but I think it means . . . I represent a trend, or am ahead of a trend."[15] The trend he had in mind was a reaction against the New Deal's hostility to business coupled with the desire to retain certain government controls. People "want business to have a chance again, but they want to keep the social controls over it. That's the idea I symbolize."[16]

No doubt this estimate was in part correct. But there was another trend that was pushing him still more strongly toward his goal—the trend of sentiment toward aid for the Allies, and still more toward aid for Britain, after Britain stood alone. Just as Roosevelt's crusade against the utility industry created the role of opposition leader, and Willkie stepped into it, and rose to fame; so now Germany's attack upon her neighbors created a life-or-death need for fearless and forceful leadership in the United States—and, since this was an election year, in both political parties. But the Republican party did not have it. The Old Guard was in control.

And since Willkie's main opponent through most of his four years in politics was not the New Deal but the Old Guard, it is necessary to understand what that entity is. Essentially, it consists of those Republicans whose central belief is that *rights* are derived from *property*. It follows that the principal function of government is to protect the property of those who have it and to help them get more. It is not the function of the Federal government—or even of local governments, beyond a meager minimum—to assume responsibility for the welfare of the entire population: to aid in housing them, to aid in educating them, to aid in keeping them healthy; not even to aid them when unemployed or beyond working age. The Old Guard has its own interpretation of the phrase in the Preamble to the Constitution "to provide for the general welfare."

In this philosophy, taxes are always an evil, though to some extent a necessary evil; labor unions are always an evil and are not necessary; civil liberties are a nuisance, since there are no rights except property rights that the government is bound to protect, and these may even be jeopardized by freedom of speech and association. Efforts to prevent discrimination against minority groups are met with the ancient argument for inaction, "You can't change human nature."

And if the government is not to assume responsibility for the welfare of even its own citizens, it will naturally not acknowledge any responsibility (unless dictated by self-interest in the narrowest sense) for the welfare of the people of other nations. "Economic Toryism," racial and religious intolerance, "narrow nationalism"—all these go together, as Willkie later said.

It is the isolationist convictions of the Old Guard that concern us here—convictions that during the twenties and thirties had been shared by the country as a whole. Republicans and Democrats alike professed to believe that war never involves a moral issue, that there is no "right" or "wrong" side, that any apparent distinction between aggressor and victim must be ignored. They also believed that from the economic and political, as well as from the moral standpoint, wars in Europe and Asia could not seriously affect American interests.

Isolationist sentiment had been strengthened rather than weakened by the Italian conquest of Ethiopia (which, in fact, triggered the Neutrality

Act), the Spanish Civil War, and the Japanese invasion of China. Even the rise of Nazism caused only vague uneasiness: the occupation of Austria in March, 1938 was accepted without serious protest; the Munich agreement in September, 1938, though it aroused many Americans to anger for the first time, was generally looked on as concerning only France and England; the total occupation of Czechoslovakia in March, 1939, though decisive for French and British policy, caused no upheaval in America; and when the war actually began in September, 1939, with the German attack on Poland and a consequent declaration of war on Germany by France and Britain, the dominant response of America was a strident clamor to keep out.

But the treacherous, murderous, and spectacularly successful invasion of Denmark and Norway, Belgium and the Netherlands, was a different story. They were geographically nearer; the ties of sentiment were stronger; and the attacks upon them were totally without excuse. Here was naked aggression; here was treachery and butchery; here was a nation run amok. And here was a war machine of unimagined power, that in a matter of days rolled over, or swept around, defenses that had been years in building; that achieved in a single month what the German armies of World War I could not achieve in four years, so that by the middle of June France was prostrate and paralyzed at the feet of Hitler, and Britain stood alone—and, after Dunkirk, all but empty-handed—with only twenty miles of water between her and the end of nine hundred years of national existence.

More than twenty years have now dimmed the memory of what numberless Americans felt during those fearful weeks in the spring of 1940: the sick, black, horrible sag of spirit under the almost physical impact of the German victories, incredibly rapid, irretrievably complete. It was not merely individual men (and women, and children) that were being bombed and machine-gunned into physical extinction; it was not merely nations that were being broken and enslaved; it was the whole of Western civilization, the whole tradition of Greek and Christian culture, that was being hurled into a bottomless abyss. No imagination could picture the means by which Europe could ever be freed from the fatal grip of a nation that had renounced humanity. Only under the spell of Churchillian oratory—the greatest, one may think, that men have ever heard—could one cherish, briefly and blindly, the hope of what reason declared to be an obviously impossible reversal of events.

To the Old Guard, of course, nothing had changed; there was no need to go into the war and no difficulty about staying out. And for a time it seemed to have a majority of Americans on its side. On May 5 a group of Protestant clergymen, including some of the most prominent in the nation, such as Harry Emerson Fosdick and John Haynes Holmes, issued an anti-war manifesto, pledging themselves "to have no part in any war."

"War itself is the enemy," they declared; and insisted that non-violence was the only effective policy.[17] Two weeks later a *Times* headline read "500 Scientists Ask U. S. to Avoid War." Their statement was: "The continuance of progress now largely depends on the scientists of neutral nations. American scientists can best fulfill their share of this responsibility if the United States remains at peace."[18] Such views were also held by many prominent individuals, from Norman Thomas, perennial Socialist candidate for President, and the idol of many non-Roosevelt liberals, to the one-time hero of the first solo flight across the Atlantic, Charles A. Lindbergh, who expounded with energy and clarity the doctrine that America's only duty was to herself. "Above all," he told an audience on May 19, "let us stop this hysterical chatter of calamity and invasion that has been running rife the last few days."[19]

There was, however, an opposing group whose members grew more numerous as the Allied defeat became more catastrophic. To these persons the only adequate response was an immediate declaration of war on Germany. In late May the *Herald Tribune* declared editorially: "The least costly solution both in life and welfare would be to declare war on Germany at once."[20] And on June 9 "an immediate declaration of war against Germany" was advocated by "30 Notables" (as the headline put it) including such persons as Herbert Agar, Stringfellow Barr, Bishop Henry W. Hobson, Frank Kent, Walter Millis, Lewis Mumford, and retired Admiral William H. Standley.[21]

The whole country, in fact, was a turmoil of conflicting opinions passionately held, in which many persons sought a moderate course between the two extremes—all possible aid to Britain without war. It was this middle course that William Allen White, veteran liberal Republican editor of the Emporia, Kansas, *Gazette,* undertook to implement by founding the Committee to Defend America by Aiding the Allies.[22] The response was overwhelming.[23]

Among those who aspired to lead the Republican party, Taft and Vandenberg stood, as a matter of principle, for isolation. Both were men of integrity, as politicians go; but both were at this point intensely provincial in their outlook. No doubt they sympathized with the Allies, despite the anti-British bent of Middle Western Republicanism, but some sort of habitual mental myopia made them see the war as remote and irrelevant to America's proper concerns. So, while the front page headlines recorded the obliteration of European civilization, some inside headline would read "Vandenberg Urges 'Insulated' America"[24] or "Strict Neutrality Urged by Taft."[25] The Senator from Ohio even appeared to resent the intrusion of the war into his solemn campaign to persuade the people of America that he was the man to rid them of the evils of the New Deal.

"This is no time for the people to be wholly absorbed in foreign battles simply because the newspapers with screaming headlines devote the first three pages exclusively to Europe."[26] And although Vandenberg on June 9 modified his stand, and acknowledged that the United States had a stake in a victory for the Allies and should therefore offer aid; he still insisted that if they were defeated, America's interests were "not inseverable" from theirs.[27]

As for Dewey, the *Times* commented editorially on May 29: "Discovering Mr. Dewey's view on questions of foreign policy has not been an easy matter."[28] It did so while praising him for saying, at last: "Our convictions and sympathies are wholly and unhesitatingly with the Allied nations." Whether America should offer something more than sympathy, however, he still seemed disinclined to say. He preferred rather to attack the Administration for not building up American defenses and, at the same time, for leading the country into war.[29] This, he guessed, was what the Republican rank and file wanted.

He guessed wrong. Rank and file Republicans could see as well as Walter Lippmann that the record of Taft and Dewey on the issue of America's attitude toward events in Europe was "a record of having been deaf, dumb and blind in the presence of every warning and every epoch-making development."[30] In fact, the accusation that the President was leading the country into war was an attack on Roosevelt for his reaction to Italy's declaration of war on France at the moment when France was beaten. Speaking at the University of Virginia, the President said: "On this 10th day of June, 1940, the hand that held the dagger has plunged it into the back of its neighbor." He then promised: "we will pursue two obvious and simultaneous courses: we will extend to the opponents of force the material resources of this nation; and, at the same time, we will harness and speed up the use of those resources in order that we ourselves in the Americas may have equipment and training equal to the task of any emergency and every defense."[31]

There is no doubt that this speech expressed the feelings of the great majority of Americans, Republicans and Democrats alike—all possible aid to Britain short of troops. And this was what Willkie alone of the Republican candidates had been advocating—clearly, earnestly, repeatedly.[32]

3

The convention was to open on Monday, June 24. Willkie arrived on Saturday—thanks to reporters who paid his fare when he discovered, at the Pennsylvania Station, that he had left all his money at home.[33] This was a fitting prelude to the wildest show that the methodical managers of the

Grand Old Party had ever been forced to watch at a national convention. And the man who made it so was Willkie. From the moment when he appeared on a Philadelphia street, he was surrounded and followed by "a cheering crowd," while he amiably tossed off answers to "reporters, or anyone else, who asked him questions."[34]

And it was not only the general public that was fascinated: "delegates from State after State hastened on arrival" to see what manner of man it was that had crashed the gates of the GOP and was threatening to take it over—this Wall Street liberal, this ex-Democrat who had led so brilliantly the battle of business against the New Deal, who was afraid of nothing, who had an answer for everything, who could win over an audience with a grin and a wave of the hand. The "500 young salesmen" that the Willkie Clubs had recruited "to 'sell' Mr. Willkie to the arriving delegates"[35] had nothing to do but get out of the way as the latter swarmed to the two-room suite in the Hotel Benjamin Franklin that was Willkie's personal headquarters. (The modest accommodations were apparently Davenport's idea,[36] and he got the headline that made his point: "Taft Forces Engage 102 Rooms, Dewey 78, Willkie 2, Gannet 48 and a Club."[37] In reality, there were three other headquarters, including a special one "to align the women delegates and alternates behind Willkie."[38])

From the time Willkie moved in, there was a solid line of delegates from the elevator to his door. One group after another would go in and fire questions at him, which he would answer, sitting on the floor or sprawled over a chair, with "astounding frankness."[39] On Monday, according to one story, he "shook hands and talked with more than 600 delegates and alternates."[40] By midnight Tuesday "he had personally talked to all or a part of the delegations from 34 states."[41]

Moreover, he seemed to know, as if he had been a politician all his life, when to abandon his free-wheeling, wise-cracking attitude and become a model of tact and diplomacy. At a breakfast Wednesday morning with the Ohio delegation,[42] he praised Taft and said he "wanted Ohio's support only if and when they became convinced the Ohio Senator could not win."[43] Later the same day he met "about half" the New York delegation; again he was generous with praise for Dewey, Taft and other candidates "and made no attempt to sway delegates from their first ballot pledges."[44] Perhaps it was on the same day that he met the Indiana delegation and told them, with reference to his career as a utility executive, "If you can find any successful accusation against me, I want you to be against me."[45] Earlier in the week (at one A. M. Monday!) he had welcomed about twenty-five members of the Missouri delegation and answered their questions for about three quarters of an hour. "I guess," the leader commented later, "he won most of the delegates over to himself right then."[46] (The evening before he had attended a "get-acquainted party" of 3,000 supporters at the Academy of Music, sponsored by the Pennsylvania Willkie Clubs.)[47] And later in the morning (presumably after daybreak) he visited the Texas delegation.[48]

Somehow or other, he even got time to talk to individuals. He paid a courtesy call on Hoover early Wednesday evening, and described his reception as "pleasant and satisfactory";[49] though the fact is that Hoover always resented Willkie's intrusion into the Grand Old Party. A more profitable conversation had been held Sunday morning with Rolland Marvin, Mayor of Syracuse, who happened to see Willkie in the hotel lobby, introduced himself, and was lucky enough to get a few moments of uninterrupted conversation with the candidate. It was good luck for Willkie, too; Marvin was looking for someone more to his taste than Dewey, and decided he had found him. A few moments later, he sought out Willkie again, and told him so. Willkie's response was, "If you'll come out in favor of my nomination, it might tip the scales"; and Marvin, impressed by this directness, did so.[50]

No previous Republican convention had experienced anything like Willkie's personal impact. As the columnist Raymond Clapper put it, "All other candidates are trembling in mortal terror of this whirlwind that is wrecking delegations all around the convention. Rumors fly through the throngs of delegates about desertions to Willkie. Delegates won't stay hitched."[51] In part this reflected the temper of the whole community, which was seething with Willkie supporters and Willkie sentiment. "Unlooked for crowds"—all wanting Willkie—descended on the city; hotels set up beds and cots in conference rooms; fraternity and sorority houses at the University of Pennsylvania were requisitioned.[52] Obviously Akron was not the only city to "send a large group of plain American citizens down to Philadelphia to support [Willkie's] candidacy."[53]

And despite the earnestness of these uninvited guests, they and the natives alike seemed automatically to create a carnival atmosphere. Countless Willkie jokes were told and retold: of the Midwestern delegate whose daughter was undergoing an operation and who got a telegram from the surgeon: "Operation successful; daughter doing fine; drop Taft and vote for Willkie"; of the cab driver who turned down a fare because the man was wearing a Taft button on his coat; of the pedestrian hit by a street car and carried, a mass of bruises and broken bones, to a hospital, where his first words to the nurse, as he struggled back to consciousness, were, "Where's your Willkie button?"[54]

Some true stories were as hilarious as the fictional ones—if they *were* fictional. "Suits back from the hotel valet [at the Bellevue-Stratford] . . . had Willkie literature in the pockets. One man found a Willkie brochure in his pajama pocket when the pajamas came back from the laundry."[55] Perhaps among this literature was a copy of the pamphlet described in another story. The Willkie headquarters that passed it out must also have been infected by the gay madness that was sweeping the city. " 'Win,' sad to relate [the pamphlet read], was anything but a model boy. He was always in trouble; fighting, tipping over the neighbors' privies, using his Sunday School text cards from the Methodist Church to play a gambling game with his brothers and sisters. . . . Then [wrote the reporter who had discovered this treasure or had it thrust upon him] in flagrant contrast to the story of law enforcement told in Mr. Dewey's biography, the Willkie brochure goes on to describe 'Win' as a kid who loved to fight the cops."[56]

No wonder the managers of the other candidates were at a loss as to how to cope with such delirious conceptions—especially since they seemed to work. (A Missouri delegate remarked that Willkie's campaign was "unfair to organized politics.")[57]

They did not know, either, how to cope with the flood of messages that inundated the delegates—all urging Willkie's nomination. On Thursday, June 20, four days before the convention was to open, "thousands of letters, telegrams and petitions" descended on the chairman of the New York delegation, William F. Bleakley.[58] The next day it was "tens of thousands," and Kenneth Simpson asserted that he had received more than 100,000 in the last twelve days: "I have never seen anything like it." At the same time the Associated Willkie Clubs of New Jersey announced that the "declarations had been signed by 300,000 persons in that state, and that they expected 100,000 more signatures before the convention opened."[59] And now the "Willkie amateurs" found a use for the declarations. Some went directly to the delegates themselves; others, returned to a Willkie headquarters, were swiftly delivered to the appropriate delegates by the Volunteer Mailing Committee.[60]

Yet even the Willkie Clubs, for all the size and zeal of their membership, can hardly have been responsible for the vast urge of the populace to tell their delegates what they wanted. And what they wanted was Willkie. On Tuesday "it was estimated that nearly a million messages from all parts of the country had been received here since the delegates began to assemble last Saturday, almost unanimous in their demand for Mr. Willkie."[61] Dewey supporters tried to discount them, but on Wednesday "it was admitted that all New York delegates were under tremendous pressure from their home districts to vote for Mr. Willkie."[62] On the same day the chairman of the Missouri delegation said "that he had not had time to read all of the telegrams that arrived yesterday, but that of more than 100 he had opened, all except one expressed a preference for Willkie."[63] At the headquarters of the Texas delegation, when somebody posted on the bulletin board a telegram "from a Texas clergyman who wished the delegates good luck," some wag wrote underneath it with a blue pencil: "At last a telegram that don't mention Willkie."[64]

Besides the telegrams, there were countless letters—probably, as a rule, from persons less sophisticated and well to do; although a reporter who examined those received by Kenneth Simpson found that they "were from all sorts of persons . . . on stationery ranging from the cheapest type to business letterheads and engraved and embossed personal stationery."[65]

Such a description suggests that the messages were completely genuine —and this is true. The story circulated then and later by Democratic opponents, Republican enemies, and ignorant or biased commentators, that the messages were somehow faked, is false. It was perhaps not unnatural for persons who remembered the phoney telegrams against the Holding Company Act five years before (even though Willkie was not responsible) to speculate that the same tactics were being repeated, especially as no such flood of communications had ever occurred at a previous convention. But even a writer for the *New Republic,* a periodical which was grossly unfair to Willkie during the campaign, agreed that "most of the names" on the "declarations" were "those of real people, who wanted our long-lipped, tousle-haired Indiana friend for President."[66] As for the telegrams, these could have been checked, if desired, by the Senate Campaign Expenditures Committee, headed by Democratic Senator Gillette of Iowa, which listened to allegations of impropriety and "agreed unanimously that information laid before it in several suggestions for an inquiry into the Willkie prenomination campaign lacked facts to warrant committee action 'at this time.'"[67] (Possibly the Democratic members hoped that something would turn up later. But it never did.) No honest person can doubt that the statement by a leader of the Willkie Club of Buffalo was true of the situation everywhere: "every signature to the petitions was genuine [there were 11,000 of them], every telegram was genuine, and our operations were forthright and open."[68]

There is, to be sure, a superficial persuasiveness about the argument that occurred to Harold Ickes, who at a press conference "remarked sarcastically upon the circumstance that apparently thousands of citizens in all parts of the country knew instinctively who their delegates to the Republican national convention were . . ."[69] Ordinarily, of course, people do not know. But here, precisely, is what made the 1940 convention different; Willkie's supporters cared enough to find out. The editor of the Elwood *Call-Leader,* for instance, casually suggested on June 4: "Citizens of Madison County can do their part . . . by dropping postal card[s] to their convention delegates, urging them to support the former Elwoodian."

The next day he announced: "This column has been swamped by requests for the names and addresses of delegates." More often, perhaps, it was a local Willkie Club that took the initiative. A writer for the Washington *Post* remarked ironically: "Willkie's innocent amateurs stole a march on rivals by sending out to radio stations some records urging his admirers to write and wire their delegates."[70] What is remarkable is that a million or so people accepted such suggestions.

The press, of course, was continuing to do its share. On June 20, the Scripps-Howard newspapers came out editorially for Willkie: "With all due respect to other Republicans who seem to have a chance, Willkie stands out among them like an oak in a thicket."[71] The *Herald Tribune* saved its endorsement (in a front page editorial) for June 27, the day of the balloting. And the *Saturday Evening Post,* on June 22, practically got out a special Willkie issue, with a brilliant article by Hugh Johnson carrying the tongue-in-cheek title "I Am Not Nominating Him," and another article by Willkie himself, "Five Minutes to Midnight." These added to the Willkie groundswell.

4

There was still the question, however, for Willkie and his advisers: Could this vast popularity be converted into convention votes? What did he have, as the convention opened, in the way of solid political support? And, observers were asking, what did he have in the way of an effective political organization?

To begin with, there were the half dozen Minnesota votes that he had won by his St. Paul speech. Second, he expected at least 6 of New Jersey's 32 votes as a result of his polling 24,240 write-in votes in the primary on May 21.[72] He was also sure of 6 of Rhode Island's 8 votes after Governor William H. Vanderbilt endorsed him on June 15, and he had been promised all of Connecticut's 16 after the first ballot, when they were to go to Governor Raymond E. Baldwin as a favorite son.[73] On June 23, however, Baldwin withdrew and announced that Connecticut would go for Willkie on the first ballot; and at the same time Mayor Marvin of Syracuse took a group of New York delegates into the Willkie camp.[74] In addition, he could count on strong support from his native Indiana, and was hopeful about the results of his speeches in California, Colorado, Iowa, Kansas, Massachusetts (after it stopped voting for its favorite son, Joseph W. Martin), Missouri and Nebraska. Willkie himself had predicted on June 12 that he would have 70 votes on the first ballot (a majority of 501 would be needed to win), and added: "The nomination will be made on the sixth or seventh ballot and the nominee will be the free choice of the convention. My supporters say I will be the nominee, and I think I should be."[75]

As the opening day of the convention approached, however, some of his supporters began to be worried by the lack of an organization. Taft and Dewey had been working for months, not only covering the country on speaking tours to make themselves known to the public, but building alliances with state and county chairmen, planning every detail of convention strategy. And each, to start with, controlled a powerful Republican organization in his own state. (Dewey showed his strength two weeks before the convention opened by engineering the ouster of Kenneth Simpson as national committeeman from New York. Taft's machine was so solidly put together that it was still functioning, with the same leaders, twelve years later at Chicago.)

But apparently all Willkie had done, the day before the convention opened, was to get Congressman Charles Halleck of Indiana to make the main nominating speech and Congressman Bruce Barton of New York to second it. Arthur Krock and Turner Catledge, in a long talk which Willkie initiated about midnight Saturday, were astonished to find that he had no floor manager and professed not to know what the duties of one would be.

Telling the story later, Krock wondered if Willkie was quite as naive as he seemed; and of course the answer is that he was not.[76] He had attended a couple of conventions himself, and, in the six weeks since May 11, he had not lacked for advisers. The delay in setting up a team to operate on the floor of the convention was evidently deliberate, in line with the strategy of making the whole campaign appear spontaneous and nonprofessional.

It was now time, however, for the professionals to come forward, and on Sunday evening a meeting was held in the suite of John Hamilton, the National Chairman, at the Hotel Bellevue-Stratford. Hamilton himself, of course, had to be strictly neutral, and was not present, but seems to have been sympathetic to Willkie's candidacy.[77] The group included such early adherents as Pryor, Weeks, Simpson and Baldwin, along with Halleck and Barton, and Davenport and MacVeagh. Recent recruits were Marvin and Walter Hallanan of West Virginia.[78]

On Monday Willkie announced another significant addition to his forces, Governor Ralph Carr of Colorado. One key figure, however, was still missing from the Willkie line-up. This was Stassen, who refused to commit himself, even in private, until after he had given the keynote address on Monday night. As soon as it was over, however, he got in touch with John Cowles and suggested a meeting with Willkie at two A.M. It took place as scheduled, with only Willkie, Stassen, and the Cowles brothers present. Stassen's price for supporting Willkie was the job of floor manager during the balloting. Apparently it was still open, and Willkie quickly agreed.[79] Then they sat until four A. M. going over lists of delegates and discussing key men. Stassen made public the announcement just before noon on Wednesday, after informing Dewey and Taft, and telling the Minnesota delegates that they were free to support their individual choices.[80] His appointment to the post clearly gave another boost to Willkie's candidacy.

5

In the meantime, the convention had got under way. Hamilton, as National Chairman, called it to order shortly before noon on Monday, June 24, but no important activity was scheduled until 9:30, when Stassen would take over as Temporary Chairman and deliver the keynote address.

The sensation of the first day was an action intended to "stop Willkie." A group of Republican Congressmen, including "about forty members of the House and five Senators," issued a statement signed by eight Representatives, demanding the nomination of "a leader with a past record consistently supporting Republican policies and principles and whose recognized position and recent pronouncements are a guarantee to the American people that he will not lead the nation into a foreign war."[81] The target of this document could only be Willkie. He responded with a characteristic statement: that he felt "particular gratitude" to those who had issued it.[82] And he was not being sarcastic. More sharply than anything that he himself could have done, it dramatized the difference between his stand on foreign policy and that of his rivals.

The isolationists got little comfort that evening from Stassen's keynote speech. He belabored the Democrats satisfactorily and asserted that only in the hands of the Republicans would the nation be safe. But he did *not* say, as Hamilton, Taft, and Dewey had said, and as many of his audience would have liked him also to say, that Roosevelt was leading the country into war.

The next day, however, the isolationists went to work again, with a full-page newspaper advertisement sponsored by "The National Committee to Keep America Out of Foreign Wars," and addressed "To the Delegates to the Republican National Convention, and to American Mothers, Wage-earners, Farmers, and Veterans." To this fairly inclusive audience its message was, in screaming capitals: "STOP THE MARCH TO WAR! STOP THE INTERNATIONALISTS AND WAR-MONGERS! STOP THE DEMOCRATIC PARTY!"[83] The last admonition, however, was obviously disingenuous. What it meant was, "Stop Willkie!" The chairman of the committee was Republican Representative Hamilton Fish of New York.

Nothing else of great significance happened during the day. The convention was mainly killing time while waiting for the report of the Resolutions Committee, in which isolationists and non-isolationists were reportedly waging a see-saw battle over the foreign policy plank in the platform. Echoes of the battle could be heard when Hoover addressed the convention on Tuesday evening. Although he approved sending "supplies of materials and munitions to those nations who are fighting for their freedom," he admonished his hearers "not to exaggerate our immediate dangers," and asserted: "It is nonsense that we cannot defend freedom here even if the Old World fails." By entering the war, we should "not assure liberty in the Old World"; we should instead "be sacrificing the last sanctuary of liberty" at home.[84]

What he was really saying was that America should send Britain its sympathy, but not much else. And this was also the substance of the platform plank on "National Defense." The platform was to have been adopted on Tuesday evening, but the foreign policy plank, as indicated, was knotty, and required much smoothing. But by Wednesday it was ready, and nobody needed to worry about splinters. It took a firm stand for "Americanism, preparedness and peace." It pledged defense of "the United States, its possessions and essential outposts from foreign attack," affirmed the Monroe Doctrine, deplored "explosive utterances by the President directed at other governments which serve to imperil our peace."

In the end it came out with two cheers for Britain, which it did not name; advocating "the extension to all peoples fighting for liberty, or whose liberty is threatened, of such aid as shall not be in violation of international law or inconsistent with the requirements of our own national defense."[85] Skeptics could point out that the two key phrases—"violation of international law" and "requirements of our own national defense"—could be variously interpreted. Hamilton Fish described it complacently as "an unqualified anti-war plank."[86]

6

And now at last the convention could get down to its real business, the nomination of a candidate. It was the opinion of many observers that Hoover, who had been discreetly running down the other candidates,[87] had tried to jump the gun and stampede the convention by his speech the night before. But though they cheered him wildly at the beginning, and throughout applauded the verbal hand grenades that he hurled at the New Deal, the familiar monotony of the delivery dampened their ardor; at the end, the applause was as much from relief as from approval, and an attempted parade failed to get started. Before the Wednesday night session, he let it be known that his name would not be formally placed in nomination.

Ordinarily nominating speeches are as vacuous and deadly dull as platforms. The flattery and platitudes fall with a hollow thud that is clearly audible above the automatic applause. The "demonstrations" that follow are—except perhaps to those taking part—equally synthetic and wearisome. But 1940 was different. Even the demonstrations for Taft and Dewey acquired a sort of defensive intensity from the Willkie threat.

The permanent chairman of the convention, who would guide it through the nominations and balloting, was Joseph W. Martin of Massachusetts, Republican leader in the House. He was widely respected as a practical politician of the best sort; moderate in his views, loyal to his party and his friends, personally honest and not personally ambitious, anxious to give every side in an argument a fair hearing, and always preferring a genuine compromise to a bitter-end fight. His handling of the convention was superb.

The procedure was that at the beginning the whole roll of states was called, so that each could make known its intention, before the nominating speeches were given. Immediately the Dewey strategy went awry, for Alabama unexpectedly yielded to New York to put Dewey's name in nomination. This meant that he would be the first to be nominated, as soon as the roll call was completed, and his supporters were not ready for the demonstration; some had not even arrived. Next Arizona yielded to New York for the nomination of Frank Gannett of Rochester, conservative publisher of a chain of newspapers. Arkansas then yielded to Ohio for the nomination of Taft. The succeeding delegations passed, while the crowd waited eagerly for Indiana to be called. But Indiana passed. The Willkie partisans were bewildered. Martin asked, "Is Indiana sure that it wishes to pass?" But the response was, "Indiana passes, yes."[88] At the end of the roll call, however, Indiana announced that it was changing its pass and would nominate Willkie. The relief and pleasure of the audience found voice in a great burst of applause. (The order of nomination was not affected by the delay, and Willkie was to be fourth.)[89]

After the roll call came the actual nominations. Those of Dewey and Taft were on traditional lines, except that there was noticeable stress on their life-long membership in the Republican party. And the demonstrations likewise were of the usual sort. Dewey's supporters, though not fully prepared, managed to *ad lib* successfully for 24 minutes, until the chairman reminded them, "We have a busy program before us tonight." Then came an intermission of interest while Gannett was nominated and the Taft people got ready for their turn. It came, and they marched and cheered and waved their standards and banners for 19 minutes before yielding to the chairman's gavel.

Then it was Willkie's turn, and "the galleries went wild from the beginning."[90] Again the "Willkie amateurs" outgeneralled their opponents.

Knowing that Taft and Dewey delegates would boo the speech, they reversed the traditional procedure of not mentioning the candidate's name until the end. Instead, Halleck mentioned it at the end of the second paragraph, and "a tremendous roar went up" from the galleries.[91] It did not silence the oppositon, but it disrupted their plans and put them on the defensive.[92] Moreover, it was a fighting speech, deliberately defiant of Willkie's critics and calculated by means of that defiance to enlist the passion of his supporters. Even in listening to the radio broadcast, one could not fail to sense the power of the Willkie movement or the fury of the opposition that it generated.[93]

The chairman himself, caught in the middle, has described how Halleck, "with a manner too brash," provoked "a blast of hostile reaction which almost blew him off the platform," and how he himself "quieted the crowd" and told him, "Get in there and finish it!"[94] But he does not do justice to the even more potent blast of favorable reaction from the galleries. When Halleck declared that Willkie "can keep us out of war," "a resounding chorus of boos came from the floor. The galleries responded with 'We want Willkie.'" When Halleck asserted that the Willkie boom had grown "without a political organization, and with no campaign fund," another storm of derisive boos arose, to be answered and drowned by "We want Willkie!" And when he asked, "Is the Republican party a closed corporation? Do you have to be born in it?" the boos were lost in a thunderous chorus of "No." When he had finished, "the galleries turned themselves loose with a mighty Niagara-like roar," while some of the delegates, "glaring angrily at the cheering spectators, were booing back."[95] Presently the audience settled into the chant "We want Willkie!"—"the volume of which," commented another observer, "startled many a seasoned convention-goer."[96]

"The crowds are shouting louder now," wrote another reporter after Halleck finished. "Chairman Martin hits the desk with his huge gavel, the size of a hunk of drain pipe. The audience takes it as an incentive to cheer harder. He appeals—'Will the convention come to order?' 'No,' shouts the gallery crowd. Bang, bang, bang, goes the gavel. 'We-want-Willkie!' chants back the crowd. . . . Either Wendell Willkie gets the nomination or the nomination won't be worth much."[97] When Martin again tried to get order by saying, "The Chair must remind the occupants of the galleries that they are the guests of the Convention," he got a shouted answer from one ebullient Willkieite: "Guests, hell! We *are* the convention."[98]

The Willkie forces apparently *did* slip up in not planning a demonstration after Halleck's speech. But Willkie's friends among the delegates showed the true Willkie spirit and went ahead. The burly Mayor Marvin wrested the New York standard from the hands of angry Deweyites to spark the parade, and other states joined in. Fights broke out, also, in the Virginia and Washington delegations, and there were minor scuffles elsewhere, but the parade got started and kept going. It was twenty minutes before the Willkie supporters consented to let Martin call for the seconding speeches. Then the convention recessed.[99]

Meanwhile, hundreds of Willkie enthusiasts who had not been able to get into the hall were parading through the streets of downtown Philadelphia.[100] But too many of them had got in to suit the managers of the other candidates, and there were immediate charges that the galleries had been "packed." An investigation revealed, in fact, that "the Committee on Arrangements had issued thousands of tickets bearing the legend: 'Republican National Convention—June, 1940—Special Admission—June 26th—Entrance 23.'"[101] Thereupon Colonel R. B. Creager of Texas, Taft's floor manager, angrily declared: "[Pryor] admitted having them printed. He said he did so because he thought there would be especially large crowds tonight. I say he had them printed in the interest of Willkie. None of them were turned over to anybody but Willkie supporters."[102] Martin persuaded him not to take the issue to the convention floor,[103] but he declared that the following night "extra precautions would be taken so that only legitimate holders of official tickets might gain admission."[104]

Pryor later explained, after stating that he *had* issued standing room tickets: "Those tickets went to the average people in the street who, I knew, were ardent supporters of Wendell Willkie. Every regular ticket was numbered and alloted. Taft had as many standing room tickets as anyone; the only restriction on these tickets was that of the fire marshal who closed the doors when the hall was legally full. A political party belongs to the people; it is not a country club—not a private organization."[105]

This statement still leaves vague the answer to the crucial question of how the tickets were distributed. But essentially the statement is correct. The galleries were "packed" with Willkie supporters because the city was packed with them, because the country was packed with them—because they were *there,* struggling to get in, and Taft and Dewey supporters were not. And despite Colonel Creager's "precautions," the crowd the following night was still more partisan. A reporter jotting down notes during the balloting asked the logical question: "What about tonight? . . . how is it that they got in again, and that now there are 14,000 instead of a mere 2,000?"[106] The obvious answer is that even among the guests of delegates and others who were supporting rival candidates, a great majority were cheering for Willkie.[107]

So the story about the "packing" of the galleries, like the story about the faking of the messages, turns out to be itself a fake.

7

There were more nominations on Thursday morning—Hanford MacNider of Iowa, Senator Vandenberg of Michigan, Senator Bridges of New Hampshire, Senator McNary of Oregon, Governor James of Pennsylvania, and Governor Bushfield of South Dakota—all favorite sons, and none except Vandenberg considered by many persons to have a chance. This was the calm before the storm that everybody knew would break at the afternoon session, when the balloting would begin. (Betting odds on Willkie against the field were "even on Tuesday, dropped slightly on Wednesday, fell as low as 1-to-4 just before the balloting began on Thursday, when rumors of a Taft-Dewey deal began to be accepted as fact.")[108] In the meantime, "the Republican leaders," as William Allen White reported, were in a mood for "an anything-to-beat-Willkie program." But they could neither agree among themselves nor control the delegates in a convention that was "unbossed and unbuttoned."[109] (Part of the unbuttoning was being done by the messages that were still demanding Willkie's nomination—making some delegates "jittery" and others "irate."[110] Western Union delivered 40,000 telegrams on Thursday and Thursday night alone.)[111]

At 4:30 p.m. on Thursday, Martin called the convention to order. He had previously consulted with representatives of each of the leading candidates,[112] and it was agreed that there would be a recess after the second ballot. Willkie had wished to push on without a break, and Martin therefore promised Stassen that after the recess he would try to have the convention reach a decision that night if it were at all possible.[113]

The clerk began calling the roll. The first votes for Willkie—2 from Arkansas—drew a cheer, which was repeated ever more loudly with each addition; and at every pause the irrepressible chant—"We want Willkie!" —exuberant, expectant—beat like surf upon the harassed delegates. On the floor, too, confusion reigned, and there were repeated protests that delegates could not hear what was going on and "that many people are in the aisles buttonholing delegates who have no right to be on the floor of the convention."[114] But finally Martin got a semblance of order.

The experts were surprisingly unanimous in predicting the course of the balloting. Dewey's chances would come early (he was claiming 450 votes on the first ballot, out of the necessary 501; Taft was conceding him 279; neutral observers gave him about 350); if he did not win by the third ballot, his support would disintegrate. Some would go to Taft (who claimed 328 first ballot votes, was conceded 200 by the Dewey forces, and was generally expected to get 275), who with this addition to his solid core of "organization" support and the expectation of inheriting strength from fading favorite sons, would then make his bid. If he failed, Willkie was the likely winner. The strategy of his leaders was to keep his vote low (about 70) on the first ballot and gradually increase it on succeeding ballots for the psychological effect; but the reporter of this plan felt that it might be difficult to keep his first ballot vote below 100.[115]

He was right. Willkie got 105 votes, drawn from 24 states and the Philippines. Many of the votes came in 2's and 3's, as the personal enthusiasm of individuals made them break with the majority. Connecticut's 16 votes made up his only solid delegation; the next largest were 12 of New Jersey's 32, 9 of Indiana's 28, 8 of New York's 92, 7 of California's 44, and 6 each from Minnesota and Missouri.

Dewey confirmed the experts by getting 360 votes, headed by 61 from New York. The big surprise was that Taft got only 189. Vandenberg had 76, James 74. (Pew had promised that Pennsylvania would stick with James "to the bitter end";[116] and when after the second ballot Stassen proposed to talk with the Pennsylvania boss, Willkie said "No."[117] He did permit Baldwin to talk to Pew after the third ballot, but Pew was still sticking with James, and Willkie said, "Pew be damned!")[118] Besides the favorite sons who had been formally nominated, Senator Capper of Kansas was given his state's 18 votes, and Martin got 33 from Massachusetts. There was also Hoover with 17.

On the second ballot, Dewey still led with 338, a loss of 22. The Taft forces were again disappointed by a vote that was up a meager 14, to 203. The big gainer was Willkie, who added a net of 66 votes from 21 delegations, losing only one vote from Utah, and ended with 171. His most significant gains were 9 from Maine, 7 from Massachusetts, 7 from Missouri, 5 from New Jersey, 5 from New York, 4 from Pennsylvania.

The clamor from the galleries increased; the note of exultation was stronger. While the vote was being tabulated at the end, the familiar chant went on, incessant, unwearied: "We want Willkie!" The vote was announced, and Martin, imperturbable amid the tumult, recessed the convention at 6:55.

The balloting began again at 8:47. The delegates had not dawdled over their dinners. The hopeful and the fearful alike had surrendered to the feverish urge to have the issue settled. And the galleries were determined to miss nothing.

The third ballot proved the experts right about Dewey, who lost 28 more votes, although he still led with 315. But they were confounded for the third time by Taft's weakness. This time he added only 9, for a total of 212. Willkie swept past him with another sensational gain to 259. His 88 new votes came from 25 states, as favorite sons released or were deserted by their delegates. The crowd roared as he gained 19 from Massachusetts (by the end of the roll call another delegate had come over). It was disappointed when the New York announcement gave him a gain of only 4; but when a roll call forced by Delegate Walter Mack brought him 10 unreported votes, it was thunderous with joy.[119] A third prolonged outbreak acclaimed the announcement showing that he had pried another 10 Pennsylvanians out of the grasp of Mr. Pew. And at every pause in the proceedings, the reiterated refrain "We want Willkie!" burst forth with hypnotic fervor. (Willkie himself, in his hotel room, was naturally enjoying the proceedings. "When Tennessee showed a gain for him on the second, he chuckled, 'That's where I had that T.V.A. fight; I'm supposed to be unpopular down there.'" And "after one particularly loud outburst of cheering . . . he said: 'There goes that paid-for gallery again; there ought to be an investigation.'")[120]

And outside the convention hall, as if that hall were the nation's brain, as if the radio networks were its nerves, "the people of the United States," whose name had been taken in vain so often by convention orators, found their own pulses quickening in response to the turbulent passions of the floor and galleries. All across the country, in weather-beaten farmhouses, trim suburban homes, palatial apartments, crowded tenements (whose dwellers forgot for the moment that they would automatically vote for Roosevelt on election day), men and women sat by their radios and shared the drama, while the long June day drew slowly and serenely to a close. Magazines were laid aside, bridge games ceased, drinks stood untouched, bedtime hours were forgotten. Between ballots the more enterprising added their items to the tide of telegrams that still flowed unceasingly before the eyes of delegates who were at last beginning to believe what they read: "We want Willkie!"

At the end of the third ballot the Dewey forces would have liked an adjournment,[121] but after a short conference Martin, his outward calm unruffled, called in a matter-of-fact voice for the fourth ballot. It began at 10:07.

On this ballot there were fewer dramatic moments. Dewey was clearly beaten, but was still able to hold 250 votes—a quarter of the whole—and it was not clear where these would go. Willkie was now ahead, with 306, but his advance had been slowed; he had added but 47 votes from 20 delegations, the largest gain being 8 from New York. Taft, on the other hand, was at last beginning to show his predicted strength. He added 42 votes and went into second place with a total of 254. Now was the time for him to make his drive; the rumors circulated that "the so-called bosses of Pennsylvania and Illinois had joined forces in a 'stop-Willkie' cabal . . . 'It's in the bag now for Taft,' said the agents who scurried about the aisles spreading the tidings of impending doom for Mr. Willkie."[122] But, the writer added, "somehow, somewhere, it got out of the bag, if it was ever there." It was clear, at any rate, that the fifth ballot would be crucial if not decisive. (Only four times previously had a Republican convention gone beyond the fifth ballot.) Neither of the two main contenders could afford to lose ground, even relatively. And, astonishingly, neither did.

The Dewey delegates were now scrambling to get on the band-wagon —if they could discover which it was. From the first state on the roll, Alabama, 4 Dewey votes went over to Willkie; from Florida 7, from Georgia 4, from Illinois 7, from Indiana 4. Iowa gave him 7 as its delegation finally quit on MacNider, Kansas 13 as Landon capitulated. The galleries were in a frenzy as New York gave him 40 new votes for a total of 75 out of 92. His final total was 429—a gain of 123.

But Taft also had been gaining. His assiduous cultivation of the obscure men in the city halls, the county courthouses, the state capitols, the men who keep the party machinery running, to whom party regularity is the supreme personal and political virtue, was paying off. (On the fifth ballot, the spokesman for the Washington delegation announced to "great applause," "Washington casts 16 votes for a real Republican, Senator Robert Taft," and was promptly rebuked by Martin: "This is a Republican convention, and all of the candidates before this body are Republicans."[123]) He also ended with a gain of exactly 123 votes, for a total of 377. A long struggle seemed possible.

At the end of the fifth ballot the Taft forces asked the Chairman for a recess.[124] But Martin kept his promise to Stassen, though the hour was growing late and the delegates were growing tired. The pressure was increasing, and the pressure was on Taft. The telegrams kept flooding in, the galleries kept up their chant, unfaltering, ever more confident: "We want Willkie!" The wall of conservative resistance, based on the mental habits of a lifetime, reinforced by resentment and incredulity, still held. But at any moment it might crack.

At 12:20 a.m., Martin called for the sixth ballot. It was clear at once that the Willkie drive had not lost momentum, though Taft was hanging on doggedly. Alabama gave Willkie 1 new vote, California 8 (but Taft gained 10), Colorado 1 (but Taft gained 2), Florida 3 (including 1 from Taft), Idaho 2 (including 1 from Taft), Illinois 7 (but Taft gained 3), Indiana 3 (including 2 from Taft), Maryland 1, Massachusetts 2—and then the crack appeared. Vandenberg released the Michigan delegates, and 35 went over to Willkie.[125] The galleries were delirious. But Martin finally restored order and the roll call continued. It showed the wall still holding. Willkie's gains, though consistent, were small: 1 from Minnesota, 2 from Mississippi, 5 from Missouri ("great applause"),[126] 6 from New Jersey ("great applause"—the delegation was now solid), 1 from New Mexico, 3 from New York ("great applause"), 3 from North Carolina. Then the crack widened. In the Oklahoma delegation, 13 Taft votes went over to Willkie.

This was the end, and everybody knew it. Oregon asked to be polled and then, after giving 3 votes to Taft, announced that all 10 would go to Willkie. Pennsylvania passed, but the other states swung into line, and when Virginia gave Willkie 16 of her 18 votes, the fight was over.

At this point, though it no longer mattered, Pennsylvania announced her 72 votes for Willkie ("great applause");[127] and Governor Bricker of Ohio, forcing his way to the platform, moved that the nomination be made unanimous ("great applause"). But Martin, still in command, ruled the motion out of order, and continued the roll call, though a score of chairmen were now on their feet shouting for recognition to change their vote. Eventually they got it, and at 1:15 the clerk announced 998 votes for Willkie, with 2 delegates absent.[128] Then Bricker was allowed to make his motion, which was seconded by J. Russel Sprague of New York, who thanked the delegates and pledged Dewey's support. David Ingalls of Ohio made a similar statement for Taft. The motion was seconded again by Senator Thomas of Idaho (one of the group responsible for the anti-Willkie statement on Monday, who had said that he would not run for re-election if Willkie was the nominee);[129] and again by Governor James. It was passed without dissent. And even Hoover sent a message of congratulation to be read to the convention. (But later, he refused comment to reporters: "I wouldn't like to make any statement about Mr. Willkie without having time to think it over.")[130] Then Stassen expressed *his* thanks, and moved a recess. At 1:57 the Chairman laid down his gavel, while the gallery crowds departed, exhausted and jubilant.

Reporters had already made a rush to Willkie's hotel. How would he take his victory—this man who had been so brash, so self-assured, so ready with wise-cracks; who had told an audience with a considerable show of truth, "I'm the cockiest fellow you ever met"?

He took it well. "I am very happy, very humble, and very proud."[131]

The remaining business of the convention was the selection of a candidate for Vice President, always a prerogative of the Presidential nominee. Willkie, impressed by the way Martin had handled the convention to this point, asked the latter for suggestions, and Martin strongly recommended McNary. It was characteristic of the candidate that he held no grudge against the Oregon Senator for his part in the "Stop-Willkie" attempt on Monday. It was also characteristic that he wasted no time. "Call him up," he told Martin.

McNary's first response was to his credit. "Hell, no, I wouldn't run with Willkie."[132] But, like Martin, he was a good party man, and after

Landon, too, urged him to accept, he did so; though he remarked somewhat plaintively: "I wish they had imposed this chore on someone else."[133]

As soon as the nomination was made, the Democrats hastened to point out that Willkie and McNary held widely different views; that the Vice Presidential nominee had been a consistent supporter of public power, high tariffs, and an isolationist foreign policy.[134] But if such a combination of candidates seems strange, it is to be remembered that in the United States, unlike many European countries, there has rarely been any sharp doctrinal division between the major parties, and that within each party there has been room for widely divergent views. Party affiliation is largely a matter of habit, or of immediate self-interest, as far as that can be discerned, or of allegiance to some compelling personality; not, as a rule, the result of adherence to established policies and principles. A party's main reason for existence is to win elections, and it is therefore almost inevitable that the candidates for the two chief offices should represent not only different sections of the country but also different interests and ideas. The *New York Times* might editorialize that McNary was "a poor choice,"[135] but at a meeting of Roosevelt's cabinet that afternoon, "it was the general opinion that the Republicans had nominated their strongest possible ticket. The President spoke particularly of McNary."[136]

With the Vice Presidency taken care of, the Presidential nominee made a brief appearance before the convention adjourned. "I stand before you," he told the delegates, "without a single pledge, promise or understanding of any kind except for the advancement of your cause and the preservation of American democracy. . . . And as your nominee I expect to conduct a crusading, vigorous, fighting campaign; to bring unity to America . . . that this way of life shall not pass from the earth."[137]

So far, so good. But at the end he said, "And so, you Republicans, I call upon you to join me." This seemed to many a painful confirmation of what they had thought—and said: that he was not a "real Republican." And of course they were right. This, in fact, was why the American people had insisted on his nomination.

8

For it *was* they who nominated him. The persisting stories that there was something improper or underhanded about the way he won, or at least that his victory resulted from some elaborate secret plan and organization, are only ficton, inspired either by disbelief in democracy or by hatred of Willkie. The true story is what has just been told, and there is nothing more.

Such stories, in fact, are refuted merely by the sequence of events that led to his nomination. In the first place, nobody *would* have planned such a campaign, and in the second place, nobody *could* have. To have ignored the primaries, to have ignored entirely (until the last six weeks) the party organization, to have taken positions, publicly and repeatedly, that were directly at odds with party policies that had been dominant for two decades—these, taken together, comprise a course of action that only a lunatic would have followed if his exclusive aim had been the nomination.

And, second, his success was due in part to events in other countries, and their repercussions in America, that nobody could plausibly have prophesied. Who in America foresaw Hitler's attack on the neutral countries and his swift destruction of them and of France? And who would have believed that Willkie's rivals for the nomination would all have been so blind as to believe either that these events in Europe *really* did not affect America in any crucial way, or else that this was what the American people wanted to be told?

Moreover, there is simply no evidence that anything of importance went on that anybody could not see. Nobody ever disproved Willkie's statement about what his campaign had cost: "I have expended less than $4,000 in traveling expenses and telephone bills and paid it all myself." He estimated that "the total expenditures of all groups engaged in his campaign would approximate $25,000"[138]—not so much, Arthur Krock noted, "as was used by the Republican candidates in the Wisconsin primary alone." "If a great fund had been expended," he insisted reasonably, ". . . the signs would be clear and obvious to the seasoned observers" at the convention.[139] And Walter Lippmann denounced the Old Guard for attacking Willkie "because there are rich people who support him—a most despicable attack in view of the fact that there are many more rich men and many more private interests behind Taft and Dewey."[140]

As a rule, the accusations and insinuations have been confined to generalities. When they have been specific, and capable of being checked, they have been found to be false. One example is a book called *One Man: Wendell Willkie,* published in late 1943. Among the book's innumerable lies, so assured and circumstantial (though the sources are always anonymous) that it is hard to imagine anyone's inventing them, two will serve. A Georgia delegate to the convention confesses that he changed his vote to Willkie on the second ballot because ordered to do so by a banker who had a mortgage on his farm (and implies that the banker in his turn had orders from the Georgia Power Company). But the record shows that on the second ballot Willkie got no Georgia votes. Still more extraordinary is the assertion, in an attempt to show that Willkie ran behind local Republican candidates, that while Willkie lost Pennsylvania the Republican candidate for Governor carried it by 279,000. The fact is that in 1940 there was no gubernatorial election in Pennsylvania.[141]

More damaging to the truth, however, are occasional articles by reputable journalists, who assert that he secured the nomination by means of a widespread organization of bankers and businessmen. One is surprised to find such stories sanctioned by reporters like Thomas L. Stokes and Arthur Krock, in articles in the *New York Times Magazine* in 1952 and 1956, respectively, in discussing the national conventions. The former tells of meeting on the train, when leaving Philadelphia after the convention, a woman who, like her husband, had been a delegate from a Western state. They had come as supporters of Hoover, "but my husband's banker called him long distance and told him we should switch to Willkie, which we did." The narrator comments: "Her husband certainly knew, whether she did or not, that his own banker's call was, in turn, the result of a long distance call to him by a representative of international finance and foreign trade interests in New York who had an organization at work on this sort of chore, as was revealed later."[142] Seeming confirmation is given by Mr. Krock when he says: "The concealed Republican organization that had been formed for Willkie in an industrial-financial network suddenly rose to the surface at Philadelphia and routed the majority combination that was divided between Robert A. Taft and Dewey."[143]

Ordinary readers can hardly be blamed for accepting such statements. They are, nevertheless, simply and totally untrue.[144] Many persons who worked closely with Willkie to win the nomination, and whose honesty there is no reason to question, have emphatically denied that such allegations contain even a grain of truth.[145] And finally conclusive is the testimony offered by the great majority of the reporters who were present at the convention—including Mr. Krock, who in 1940 denied flatly the rumors spread by workers for the other candidates, that "some remarkable secret organization, skilled in politics and heavily financed, has been doing spadework which is responsible for the Willkie boom."[146] A writer for *Newsweek* likewise asserted that "the newspaper men who have covered Willkie know that there was nothing about his campaign that did not meet the eye."[147] Robert Bendiner in the *Nation* called Willkie's victory the result of "a genuine popular revolt."[148] He was echoed by Edward T. Folliard in the Washington *Post,* who described it as "a tremendous and historical revolt of the people against the politicians."[149] Walter Lippmann maintained that Willkie's support was "as nearly spontaneous as anything that we have ever seen. . . . it is a popular uprising of men and women who have responded, as free people ought to respond, to good leadership when good leadership is available."[150] Roscoe Drummond averred that the convention simply "responded to the battering waves of popular demand. Willkie was no more 'put over' on the Philadelphia convention than Babe Ruth was 'put over' on the New York Yankees. It was obvious to the party leaders that Willkie could hit and it was assumed that he could be managed without too much difficulty."[151] Raymond Clapper's comment was: "The people have saved the Republican politicians from themselves and have forced them to nominate Willkie. That's all there is to it."[152]

Anyone who challenges this collective affirmation does not wish to know the truth.

And this unique popular uprising which is attested by so many writers calls for one more comment. It illustrates the genius of American democracy for acting with wisdom in a time of crisis—if the crisis is great enough. One shudders at the thought of what would have happened if the nomination had gone to Dewey, unsure of himself and susceptible to pressure, or to Taft, too sure of himself and terrifyingly provincial. Inevitably the campaign would have been fought on the isolation-intervention issue, and although Roosevelt would certainly have won by a far larger majority than he gained in defeating Willkie, the country would have been torn apart. The President would have feared to make the destroyers-for-bases deal in the middle of the campaign; Selective Service might well have been filibustered to death in the Senate; the passage of Lend-Lease would have been more than doubtful; the extension of Selective Service in the summer of 1941, which passed the House by a single vote, would certainly have been defeated. It is not too much to say that Willkie's nomination, and his fidelity to the principles by which he won it, made America far better prepared, materially and morally, for Pearl Harbor and its sequel than it would otherwise have been; and so shortened the war by months or years, and lowered the cost by tens of billions of dollars and hundreds of thousands of lives.

And more than this, it gave Willkie a position from which to tell the American people, during the next four years, many things (besides those directly related to the war) that they needed to hear; and at the same time it brought him experiences which prepared him for this high station and its duties. It gave him the wisdom, the will, and the opportunity to be, for four years, the conscience of his country.

X

The Election Campaign: Organization and Policies

1

At the end of the convention, Willkie announced, "Now I'm going to sleep for a week,"[1] and boarded the private yacht of publisher Roy Howard for a leisurely cruise back to New York. But first he "surprised Philadelphia newspaper editors by calling at their offices to express his appreciation of the 'fair treatment you have given me.' "[2]

By the time he reached New York he was ready, with a resilience that amazed his friends, to plunge into his new job of running for President. "Bring on Roosevelt!" he remarked cheerfully.[3]

As a preliminary, on July 1, he resigned his old job as President of Commonwealth & Southern. In the office where, for seven and a half years, he had directed the affairs of the vast corporation, he was received by the staff with a warmth that revealed affection as well as pride. Reporters found everyone eager to talk about the man who was now the talk of the entire country, and to affirm the unstudied friendliness, the innate equalitarianism, that millions of their countrymen had somehow sensed from afar.[4] In New York as in Philadelphia, he was a hero. When he went that night to Radio City Music Hall to see himself as an actor in a film of "Information Please," the crowd recognized him and cheered until he had to rise and acknowledge the applause. Again three days later, when he indulged his love of the theater by going to see *Life with Father,* the applause that he received was only surpassed by that which greeted the line in the play where "Father" exclaimed, "God! Why does God make so many fools and Democrats?"[5] (Had his campaign manager packed the galleries?)

The fact was, however, that he now had no campaign manager. The organization so hastily assembled to carry out the final phase of the fight for the nomination was not the kind that could carry to a successful conclusion the four months' political war that lay ahead. Willkie's first task, indeed, was to choose his staff.

The terms in which this problem presented itself to him were unique. Normally the candidate is an office-holder who already has some sort of personal political machine, often the party machine in his state, which has been tested and strenghtened in the fight for the nomination. Or if it should happen that a non-professional like Hoover or Eisenhower is chosen, then he lets the national party organization—that is to say, the National Committee—run his campaign.

But Willkie had no machine of his own and he was not prepared to accept the party machine. Not only had that machine suffered two successive catastrophic defeats, but those who ran it had been for the most part opposed to his own nomination. He felt, rightly, that his success reflected a popular revolt against the Old Guard leadership. To submit meekly to that leadership now would be to betray the forces to which he owed his place. On the other hand, it was equally unthinkable that the party organization should be ignored. And there was a third group of citizens from whom he expected much. Believing that Roosevelt would be the Democratic candidate, he counted on the third term issue to alienate a large segment of the opposing party.

If anybody could unify these three forces, it must be the candidate himself. But how to do it was the problem, and the solution was not easy. The first step was to appoint an "advisory campaign committee," headed by Stassen and composed mainly of party professionals, including some of those who had aided Willkie at Philadelphia, along with a few who had worked for his chief opponents.[6] In addition, the selection of a national chairman was delegated to another committee, chosen from the ranks of the National Committee and headed by Walter Hallanan of West Virginia. Its function was mainly advisory, however, for it is the traditional prerogative of the Presidential candidate to choose his own man.

The main issue was whether or not Hamilton should be retained. It has been asserted that each of the leading candidates had made "a personal pledge, if nominated," to continue Hamilton as National Chairman, and that Willkie broke his promise.[7] But it is not clear that the pledge on Willkie's behalf was authorized, although the candidate at this point had nothing personal against Hamilton.[8] He did, however, have a certain amount of distrust of professional political organizers,[9] which had not been lessened by his experience at Philadelphia. Moreover, however little Hamilton might have been responsible for the 1936 debacle, many persons would naturally think it wise to name someone in no way associated with that catastrophe. But what really lost him the appointment was a circumstance in his private life that contained, as many of Willkie's advisers felt, the seeds of a national scandal.[10]

The final solution was reported in the press on July 9. The National Chairman and nominal campaign manager was to be Joseph W. Martin, who was to serve without salary. Hamilton was to be retained as Executive Director and his salary of $25,000 was to continue.

This was another move toward achievement of party harmony. If anyone could mediate between conflicting personalities and points of view,

Martin was the man. And now it was his turn, as it had been McNary's a few days earlier, to take on an unwanted "chore." Willkie simply refused to take "No" for an answer, and again he had party loyalty working on his side as well as personal charm. ("As he talked on," Martin wrote later, "I became conscious of the fact that I *liked* Willkie.") Martin had one motive for refusing, as he candidly confessed in his memoirs, that he could hardly mention at the time: "I had no desire to jeopardize my standing with Republicans in the House by running a campaign for a candidate toward whom many of them were hostile." But to his surprise, he found that they also wanted him to take the job.[11]

Many details still remained to be settled. But obviously no complete campaign plan could be worked out until it was known that Roosevelt would actually be the Democratic candidate. On July 9 Willkie took off by plane for a three weeks' vacation at Colorado Springs, whither he had been invited by Governor Carr.

2

But despite the glamor still attendant on Willkie's every act and word, the eyes of the nation were now turning toward Chicago, where, on July 15, the Democrats were opening their national convention. If there was less promise of drama, it was because most persons had little doubt as to the outcome. It seemed obvious that, having refrained so long from saying that he would not accept renomination, thereby effectively thwarting the aspirations of other possible candidates, Roosevelt wanted the nomination and would therefore get it. The main point of interest was how he would proceed.

By way of preparation for his coup, the President set out to calm the fears of the isolationists, almost as strong in one wing of his own party as among the Republicans. In the message on national defense that he sent to Congress on July 10 he declared: "[On September 21, 1939] I said that this government must lose no time or effort to keep this nation from being drawn into the war, and I asserted my belief that we would succeed in those efforts. We have succeeded. I believe we shall continue to succeed."[12] The same line was taken in the keynote speech of Speaker Bankhead of the House of Representatives, who asserted (with typical Congressional redundancy) that the Democrats had "done everything possible . . . to so conduct our foreign relations that every precaution would be taken to keep us out of involvement in a foreign war," and rehearsed with apparent pride the sorry tale of the surrender of sovereignty and the retreat from responsibility embodied in the neutrality legislation from 1935 to 1939. The following evening Senator Barkley, in his speech as permanent chairman of the convention, repeated the ignoble boast. The isolationists were also allowed to write into the platform, adopted on Wednesday afternoon, the assertion: "We will not participate in foreign wars, and we will not send our Army, navy or air forces to fight in foreign lands outside the Americas, except in case of attack."[13]

At this point, however, the issue had ceased to be important; for Barkley, at the end of his speech on Tuesday evening, had delivered a message from the President which, while it pretended to leave the convention free, actually left it no choice. "Tonight," Barkley concluded, "at the specific request and authorization of the President I am making this simple fact clear to the convention.

"The President has never had and has not today any desire or purpose to continue in the office of the President, to be a candidate for that office or to be nominated by the convention for the office.

"He wishes in all earnestness and sincerity to make it clear that all the delegates to this convention are free to vote for any candidate."[14]

But this "simple fact" was neither simple nor a fact—except to the simple-minded. Had the words meant what they purported to mean, there was no reason why they could not have been said a week before, a month before, a year before the convention began. But now it was the second night of the convention, only a few hours before the balloting was to begin. For two days the majority of the delegates had been wandering helplessly in a fog of uncertainty. The two avowed candidates, Vice President Garner and Postmaster General Farley, could gain little support as long as there was any likelihood that Roosevelt would run again.

The reception of Barkley's announcement was curious. A few minutes earlier, his mention of the President's name had set off a tremendous and apparently genuine demonstration. But now the excitement seemed largely synthetic, and after it had run its course, Barkley recessed the convention.

On reconvening, the delegates adopted the platform without discussion, as the Republicans had adopted theirs. In neither case did any delegate question the obvious effort of the isolationist faction to tie the hands, in regard to foreign policy, of the man they feared would be the candidate. For the rest, the platform praised the New Deal record of reform and reviewed once more the horrors of the "Hoover depression." The Democrats had won two Presidential races by successfully attaching to their opponents the ball and chain of responsibility for economic disaster, and there seemed no reason to abandon the strategy.

What happened that evening lent support to their belief. It was clear that to most of the 25,000 persons who jammed the hall Franklin D. Roosevelt was the symbol of salvation from bitter experiences not yet forgotten.

More partisan even than the Willkie supporters at Philadelphia, they booed vigorously when the aged and long revered Senator Carter Glass of Virginia attacked the third term while nominating Mr. Farley. Sure of victory but impatient of any delay, they did not hesitate to make vocal their impatience as the balloting dragged out to what was indeed an unconscionable length. Each state, though assigned a definite number of votes, could send an unlimited number of delegates, each of whom might have only half a vote, or even less, and the polling of a delegation, which was often demanded, was a tedious process. But at last the balloting was finished. The count (before the formality of making the nomination unanimous) was 946 for Roosevelt, 72 for Farley, and 61 for Garner, with only a handful scattered. The galleries (here also there was the rumor of "wholesale distribution of fraudulent tickets . . . in an attempt to pack the galleries with Roosevelt sympathizers")[15] were exultant, but many delegates were far from happy.

They were still less happy twenty-four hours later, after the President had forced them to nominate Henry Wallace for Vice President. Wallace, like Willkie, was looked on by the professionals as strictly an amateur, despite his years in Roosevelt's cabinet; and unlike Willkie, he possessed no discernible popular appeal. But Roosevelt's resolve was so unyielding that he had written, and would have delivered, a statement refusing the nomination if Wallace had not been accepted.[16] The pressure that he was able to exert, however, was successful. Another long-drawn-out ballot ended, after midnight, with Wallace the winner—and with more than a few sullen faces among the delegates.

But Roosevelt was Roosevelt, and he won them back. His acceptance speech, radioed to the convention immediately after Wallace's nomination, was a masterpiece of persuasion, which almost made the convention believe that it had really drafted him, and that he had simply responded, like any other patriotic citizen, to the call of duty: that in "a conflict between a deep personal desire for retirement on the one hand, and that quiet invisible thing called conscience on the other," the latter had won.

And now that the nomination was actually his, he could afford to play down his claim to have kept the country at peace. His words were in strange contrast to those of Bankhead and Barkley a day or two earlier, to his own a week earlier. Now he threw down the gauntlet to the dictators. "I do not recant the sentiments of sympathy with all free peoples resisting such aggression or begrudge the material aid that we have given them. I do not regret my consistent endeavor to awaken this country of ours to the menace to us and to all we hold dear.

"I have pursued these efforts in the face of appeaser fifth-columnists who charged me with hysteria and war-mongering, but I felt it to be my duty, my simple plain inescapable duty, to arouse my countrymen to the danger of new forces let loose in the world."[17]

To access justly the issues of the campaign, one must come to a conclusion about Roosevelt's real motives for seeking a third term. Taken by itself, the manipulation of the convention was a morally shabby affair. Had the President trusted without reserve the democratic process, he could simply have said, at any time, "I will not seek the nomination, but I will accept it"—and he would have got it. But apparently he and his advisers felt not only that the outcome must be absolutely certain but that it must appear unsought.

But was this policy motivated mainly by the desire for continued personal power, or was it really dictated by "duty" and "conscience"? Here the President must be given the benefit of the doubt. It is fair to assume that before the outbreak of the war in Europe, and perhaps even after it, as he said, he had intended to retire, and had intended to say so "clearly and simply at an early date." But any forceful leader naturally hesitates to make a statement that will drastically weaken his influence, as such a statement by a President must do. And in this instance the war in Europe made Roosevelt still more reluctant to loosen the reins. It is easy to see how, after the Nazi conquests between April and June, he honestly felt that no one else could meet the crisis so well.

Moreover, the Democrats had no other candidate who seemed likely to win, or to be able to handle the problems that he would face if he did win. Garner and Hull were too old; and the former was a conservative Texas rancher in no way qualified to deal with either domestic or foreign problems, while the matter was colorless, cautious, unimaginative, in many ways provincial. Farley was an able and faithful manager of party machines and campaigns, engagingly honest and modest, but with no obvious preparation or capacity to guide his country through a war-torn world; and he was also a Catholic. Of other cabinet officers, Harold Ickes, incorruptible but irrascible, had many political enemies and few political friends; Henry Wallace was distrusted as a visionary (not without reason, as the sequel showed); Harry Hopkins, uniquely valuable as Roosevelt's personal aide, not only lacked his chief's magnetic personality but probably had even more, and more bitter enemies in both parties; Paul McNutt was somehow never able to convince the public that he was a statesman in much more than appearance; and neither Congress nor the state governors' mansions contained any particularly distinguished leaders. (Lehman of New York might be excepted, but he was a Jew.) Whether by plan or accident, Roosevelt simply overshadowed all other potential candidates.

What undoubtedly clinched the President's decision was the nomination of Willkie. It was obvious that no one else would stand a chance of beating the amazing Republican nominee. And this fact at once put the President under tremendous pressure, not only from the vast number of persons whose jobs depended on a continuance of Democratic power but from many sincere idealists who looked at the Republican record in Congress and shuddered at what might happen if the Republicans controlled the government.

3

In accepting the nomination, the President also launched his campaign, combining, as only he could do, a lofty discussion of principles with a shrewd partisan appeal. Thus in one sentence he strove to give the impression of being dedicated only to the nation's welfare, of standing above the dust and heat of party strife: "I shall not have the time nor inclination to indulge in purely political debate." To this Willkie retorted: "I predict that Mr. Roosevelt will be out on the stump before this election is over."[18] But Roosevelt was already on the stump; and in another sentence, after a ringing defiance of the dictators, he deftly planted in the public mind the seed of a doubt that may well have done more than anything else to defeat his opponent: "If our government should pass to other hands next January, untried hands, inexperienced hands, we can only hope and pray that they will not substitute appeasement and compromise with those who would destroy democracy everywhere, including here."

Willkie, listening in Colorado Springs to the convention broadcast, must have realized something of the shrewdness of the thrust. But his immediate feeling was one of exultation. Reporters noticed with surprise that he was visibly nervous as he listened to the convention proceedings, until the tremendous demonstration that greeted Barkley's first mention of the President's name. Then he relaxed, and remarked with a cheerful grin: "Boy, I think my worries are over. That is the anwer, I think."[19]

Now that his opponent had been named, Willkie and his aides could concentrate on the strategy of the campaign. Part of this strategy was being made clear already by the way he was spending his "vacation." This, one reporter declared, had "the appearance of the closing days of a campaign . . . full of all-day conferences with Republicans, anti-New Deal Democrats and independents, handshakes and autographing for a horde of admirers, hurried automobile drives and airplane flights over the Rocky Mountain region, numerous interviews with the press and the inevitable barrage of newsreel and newspaper photographers."[20] In Salt Lake City, where (the day after attending a rodeo in Cheyenne, Wyoming) he had gone to participate in the celebration of the anniversary of the city's founding, he told newsmen that he was there because "I wanted to see the people and I wanted to have the people see me." An inquiry whether he did not think he was answering some questions "too frankly" brought first a hearty laugh and then the serious answer, "I don't know about that. But I do know that I am just going to be myself during this campaign."[21] It was simply not in him to accept the friendly advice of Senator McNary at their first meeting: "Don't forget, young fellow, in politics you'll never be in trouble by not saying too much."[22]

The same self-confidence appeared again in his initial determination to compose his own campaign speeches. Asked early in July whether he would have a "brain trust" to help him compose his acceptance speech, he replied tersely, "No, I roll my own."[23] And three weeks later he asserted his intention to "write all my speeches myself."[24] These statements must have worried the GOP leaders: first, as an indication of the candidate's political inexperience, and second, as evidence of his independence. His confidence was presumably based on his campaign for the nomination, when he *had* composed a number of speeches in rapid succession, and delivered them with obviously great effect. Most of these, however, had dealt with relatively simple and familiar themes, and had been delivered to relatively select audiences of business and political leaders. They did not call for omniscience concerning the innumerable issues that must be argued during a Presidential campaign; nor was there need to calculate their appeal to people of all social groups and political persuasions.

Organization Republicans had also reason to be disturbed by the implication that the candidate would allow no one to tell him what he was going to say. What they wanted to find in his speeches was a powerful partisan approach, combined with an appeal to the self-interest of many different groups of voters; and presented so as to camouflage, by oratorical sleight-of-hand, the inescapable contradictions. That a candidate should simply stand up and say what he thought, filled them with consternation.

The trouble was not that Willkie was unwilling to listen to his Republican advisers. He was as willing to talk with them as with anybody else, and he listened to Hoover and Colonel McCormick of the Chicago *Tribune,* with whom he had little in common either in temperament or opinion, as he did to William Allen White, who became one of his warmest friends. There was, in fact, no subject on which he did not wish to get the best informed opinion that was available, as he showed by his enthusiasm for a conference on agricultural problems arranged at his request by Governor Wilson of Iowa. It was held in Des Moines on August 5, and attended by four Republican governors and four Republican candidates for governor, as well as by sixty-five other farm state representatives of agriculture, ranging from college professors to dirt farmers. Although the meeting was not open to the public or the press (presumably so that everybody could speak frankly), Willkie told reporters that "no holds were barred."[25] The trouble was, from the standpoint of party orthodoxy, that in the end he came to his own conclusions and stated them in his own words.

4

The traditional acceptance ceremony, dating from a more leisurely and less sophisticated age, was already an anachronism. Franklin Roosevelt's precedent-shattering flight to Chicago in 1932 to make his acceptance speech directly to the convention was inspired, like so many of his actions, by a prophetic recognition of changing times. But Willkie, however forward-looking on great issues, desired in this instance to follow the old forms. The main reason for the delay was not that he was not ready to deliver it in June, for "We the People," with a few changes, would have served admirably; and only partly, perhaps, because he wished to repeat the pattern of his whirlwind finish in the campaign for the nomination. His chief motive seems to have been personal: the desire of a man who had never been quite at home in Wall Street, who had kept the essential simplicity of small-town life, to share his triumph with the people among whom he had grown up, whom he still thought of as his friends. (On the day of the balloting for the nomination, "business in the stores nearly reached a standstill . . . Practically every house in town had the radio turned on"; and when Willkie's nomination was certain, a police sergeant remarked: "It looks as if they might tear Elwood down."[26]

It is true that Willkie was not unmindful of the political advantage of stressing his small-town ties. But what Ickes, in his famous taunt about "a simple barefoot Wall Street lawyer,"[27] chose not to see was that Willkie had never outgrown his early background and that this political gesture was natural and sincere. On the other hand, he ignored Willkie's forthright declaration in the acceptance speech itself: "I am a businessman . . . formerly connected with a large company"—a connection "of which I am very proud." The candidate's utter lack of affectation was revealed again a day or two later at Rushville, when he told reporters with candid humor: "There is one error I want to correct at once, this talk of being a Rush County farmer. I am purely a conversational farmer. I have never done a stroke of work on a Rush County farm in my life, and I hope I never have to."[28] And he stubbornly refused to pose for photographers while wearing overalls or sitting on a tractor.[29] "I can't fake things," he explained. "I can't play any part but Willkie."[30] At the same time he refused to publicize the genuine love of the land that was noted by an old acquaintance: "He enjoys driving through the country. He likes to see things grow. That's the reason he bought farm lands. He likes the earth and he likes to see it producing."[31]

Nevertheless, the decision to hold the notification ceremonies in Elwood posed practical problems whose magnitude he and his managers did not at first foresee. They underestimated the enthusiasm, the curiosity, the proprietary interest which countless Americans felt toward the man whom they considered that they had nominated. It was Philadelphia over again on a vaster scale. Instead of the few thousand, at most, that Willkie originally expected to address (in a sentimental gesture) from the steps of the small old high school building, it soon became evident that the audience would number tens if not hundreds of thousands. The local committee that had been making plans passed on the responsibility to the Republican State Committee, which in turn called on the National Committee. Homer E. Capehart, an enterprising Indianapolis businessman who was later to be United States Senator, was given charge of the arrangements.

His task became increasingly formidable. Into a community of 11,000, twenty times that number were expected to come. Special trains were bringing 40,000. Hundreds of buses were coming from nearby states. No one knew how many thousand private automobiles would be moving along the four roads leading into town. A sensation was created by a boy who had ridden a bicycle from Texas, distributing Willkie buttons along the way.[32]

Capehart, however, went at the job with energy. The high school was now out of the question as a site for the ceremonies, although Willkie still insisted on a brief appearance there. The main event was to take place in 40-acre Calloway Park on the edge of town. Here a speaker's platform was erected with room for a thousand persons. In front of it were placed seats for 30,000 (exhausting the supply of folding chairs throughout the area). Loudspeakers were set up to make the address audible over a square mile of territory. An area of 160 acres was rented and cleared of crops to provide parking space, with more available if needed. First aid stations, rest rooms, and drinking fountains (150 of the push-button type, plus other sources of supply) were set up. An army of concessionaires were licensed to sell hot dogs and hamburgers, soft drinks, and souvenirs (besides the countless local entrepreneurs whose stands lined the streets). Thirty-odd tents were made ready to serve as headquarters for various political organizations, special groups of visitors, and representatives of the press and radio. Doctors and nurses were to be on duty. Indiana supplied 140 state police (200 according to another account); and 400 uniformed officers and 225 plain-clothes men were assembled from other cities. The railroads built special platforms at the stations. New telegraph outlets were opened; new telephone cables were laid. In one way or another American "know-how" met the unprecedented problems involved in handling the greatest crowd ever assembled in America outside a large city.[33]

The vast throng, estimated by one expert at a quarter of a million (though of course nobody really knew), assembled on the appointed day in a festive, harmonious and hopeful spirit. (By midnight of the preceding day there were already 1,200 cars in the parking lot.)[34]

Willkie arrived shortly after noon from Rushville, which he had reached at midnight Thursday after a plane trip from Colorado. (He had spent Friday, despite an intense heat wave, in visits to his farms.) It had been prudently arranged to have his train stop outside of town, at a spot revealed only to newsmen, lest he be mobbed by the crowd of admirers waiting at the station. He had, however, to drive through the streets; and the surgings of the crowd, unsubdued by the furnace-like heat, were sometimes beyond the power of his police escort to control. Several times the procession was brought to a halt as people fought their way toward Willkie's car and reached up to shake his hand. The grounds around the high school building were solid with humanity, and when, after a hard struggle, he gained the rear entrance, he was almost overcome, and had to sit down in one of the classrooms to recuperate.

But he was soon himself again, leaning out the window while he lighted a cigarette and remarking with a grin to the delighted crowd, "they didn't use to let me do this in this building." Proceeding to the front steps, he again joked with his audience—"It looks like it's going to be a hot time in the old town tonight!"[35]—before saying the few dignified, if unavoidably trite sentences that he had come to say. "The simple precepts I learned in this school, truth, honesty, integrity, are still the precepts that will conquer the world today."

Then came the struggle back to the car, and continuance of the long ordeal of inch-by-inch movement through the broiling streets. When he arrived at the park, "it took police fifteen minutes to open a narrow lane twenty yards long between his car and the steps to the platform." In the meantime, it had been discovered that the speech itself had been left in Rushville, whence it was rushed in a car with a special police escort.[36] But at the appointed hour, 3 P. M. Central Standard Time, he was ready to be notified by Chairman Martin that he had been nominated for President, and to deliver his acceptance speech.

5

It fell flat. Not absolutely, but in comparison with what his admirers had expected. It disappointed thousands of those who had come long distances to hear it from the speaker's own lips and millions of those who listened to the radio broadcast.

In retrospect, this anticlimax is not surprising. It could almost be explained, in fact, by physical causes alone, beginning with the mere size of the crowd. To draw a unified response from the huge straggling assembly would have challenged the most skilled speaker under the most favorable conditions. And Willkie was *not* skilled in the art of reading a prepared address before a microphone. When he sought to be emphatic, the stress was likely to fall on the wrong phrase; when he was calm, his voice tended to become monotonous.

To these difficulties was added a temperature of 102 in the shade. The breathless heat wilted the spirits and dampened the ardor of even the most eager listeners, many of whom had already been on the spot for hours. The candidate himself, on whom the hectic parade through the town could not have been without effect, stood (wearing the coat and tie that the occasion seemed to demand) facing the full, scorching glare of the afternoon sun. The sweat ran into his eyes and onto his glasses, blurring the type and making effective reading still more difficult.[37]

But perhaps a still greater obstacle to his success was psychological—the fact that no possible performance could have matched the expectations of his audience. No other person in history had appealed so suddenly and powerfully to the imagination of the American people. Roosevelt still kept, of course, the idolatrous loyalty of millions. But millions of others had turned to Willkie, in the belief that he could offer them a simple way—not easy, perhaps, but at least clear and direct—to avoid or surmount the difficulties and dangers that lay so menacingly across America's future. They were in the mood for a crusade, as Willkie was in the mood to lead one.

But what should it be a crusade *for,* or *against?* The cold fact was that divergent aims made unity impossible. Some of his hearers were Old Guard Republicans who hated Roosevelt and all his policies, both foreign and domestic; who wished to cut all ties with Europe and cancel all the social changes inaugurated by the New Deal. Others were willing to approve the reforms in principle, while urging that the time had come to call a halt. The majority of these were probably internationalists; but in the West and Middle West there had been a long tradition of liberalism in domestic policies accompanied by insularity in regard to world affairs. On the other hand, there were many bankers and businessmen who felt that Roosevelt's domestic policies were ruinous, but were heartily in accord with his outlook on world affairs. How was it possible to compose a speech that would please all these, and still other, factions?

The proposed Selective Service Act was a case in point. Under the impact of events in Europe a bill to conscript young men for military service had been introduced in Congress, and had become a burning issue. Many persons besides the incorrigible isolationists were opposed to a peacetime draft, and most Republican leaders, whatever their personal convictions, felt (although the polls gave them little support)[38] that here was an issue on which the President could be defeated—first by the vote of Congress and then by the vote of the country.

On this issue Willkie refused to commit himself before his acceptance speech. The President, although known to favor the bill in principle, did likewise. Like Congress and the rest of the country, he was waiting (although convinced at this point that Willkie was "merely playing politics")[39] to hear what his rival would say. Senator Edwin Johnson of Colorado, an outspoken opponent of the measure, was right in saying that its fate depended on Willkie. "If he approves it vigorously, a dozen timid Democratic Senators and fifty election-conscious Congressmen will be free to support it, since it will then be no longer a campaign issue. If Willkie straddles the issue, Congress will follow suit."[40]

On such clear-cut questions the candidate's dilemma was plain. Whichever side he took, many hearers would be disappointed, some bitterly offended; if he refused to take sides, all groups would accuse him of cowardice. But in regard to other issues, especially those involving social and economic reforms, he faced a difficulty of a different sort. He not only saw clearly that, for better or worse, these changes had come to stay, and that to repudiate them would be political suicide, but he himself approved of them. They were the outgrowth of practical needs that, in the name of mere justice and humanity, had to be met, and that could in many instances be met only by using the resources of the Federal government.

But while approving the ends, he condemned the means that had often been used, and the spirit that had often been shown, in the effort to achieve them. He considered that the spokesmen for the New Deal had often been unfair and arrogant, self-righteous and self-seeking, professing a concern for people but acting from a concern for votes. But he had to face the fact that this distinction between aims and methods was hard to define and dramatize in terms that ordinary people would understand.

6

These were among the difficulties that Willkie faced. How did he meet them?

Re-read calmly, at a distance of two decades, the acceptance speech strikes one as being far from ineffectual.[41] It is true that his opening statement seemed almost calculated to inflame the wounds inflicted at Philadelphia on those who wanted "a real Republican." "Party lines are down. Nothing could make that clearer than the nomination by the Republicans of a liberal Democrat who changed his party affiliation because he found democracy in the Republican party rather than in the New Deal party."

When, however, he presented a nostalgic picture of his own boyhood and of the opportunities that "the American way of life" had placed before him, followed by the assertion that he wanted to make those opportunities available to the new generation, he was following a fool-proof tradition in American electioneering; and in recalling that his own ancestors had fled from Old World oppression to New World freedom, he was shrewdly forestalling an attack on his German ancestry.

But in proceeding to dwell on the horrors of Hitler's Europe, whence millions of sufferers were again turning their eyes toward America, he was saying what many in his audience would rather have forgotten. He acknowledged the naturalness of his hearers' feelings: "instinctively we turn aside." But the future crusader for "One World" would *not* turn aside: "Yet—instinctively also—we know that we are not isolated from those suffering people. We live in the same world as they, and we are created in the same image. In all the democracies that have fallen, the people were living the same peaceful life that we live. They had similar ideals of human freedom. . . . Try as we will, we cannot brush the pitiless picture of their destruction from our eyes, or escape the profound effects of it on the world in which we live."

If eloquence on this subject was not what his audience had come to hear, still less did they welcome the grim conclusion to which he pursued the theme. "No man is so wise as to foresee what the future holds or to lay out a plan for it. No man can guarantee to maintain peace. Peace is not something that a nation can achieve by itself. It also depends on what some other country does. It is neither practical, nor desirable, to adopt a foreign program committing the United States to future action under unknown circumstances." This was the best thing said on foreign policy by anyone in either party during the campaign, but it was a view that could hardly be popular.

And now he had come to the one issue on which the nation was most anxious to know his stand, the word for which Congress and the President had been waiting. What would he say about Selective Service? "I cannot ask the American people to put their faith in me without recording the conviction that some form of selective service is the only democratic way in which to assure the trained and competent man-power we need in our national defense." (Some die-hard isolationists afterward professed to find the statement noncommittal, but Willkie quickly set them straight.)

How strongly he felt on this topic, and how strong the pressure on him had been, is suggested by what he had told reporters in Rushville the day before, after distributing copies of the speech. Characteristically, he asked them, "Boys, what do you think of it?" and one correspondent, saying what many thought, answered, "It is a fine speech, but if you want to win the election you will come out against the proposed draft." Willkie's reply came "quick as a shot": "I would rather not win the election than do that." And when a discussion ensued of the advantages that he would gain from such a stand, he closed it with: "Some of those who want to advise me on political strategy have said the same thing. They have urged me at least to ignore the issue if I am not willing to oppose the draft. I will not do it."[42]

Nor did the speaker hedge on aid to Britain, being battered for the sixth successive day by the first great Nazi air attacks; pointing out that from the standpoint of sheer self-interest Americans must see that the defeat of that country and the loss of its fleet would be a "calamity" that would leave America "exposed to attack." "The President of the United States recently said 'we will extend to the opponents of force the material resources of this nation and at the same time we will harness the use of those resources in order that we ourselves in America may have equipment and training equal to the task of any emergency and every defense.'

"I should like to say that I am in agreement with those principles, as I understand them . . ."

After all, however, he was campaigning for himself and not for Roosevelt. Here, as on domestic issues, compelled by conviction to approve the President's general aims, he was compelled by expediency (if nothing more) to assail his methods. And once launched on an attack, he was not inclined to stop half way. "There have been occasions when many of us have wondered if he [Roosevelt] is not deliberately inciting us to war. . . . The President's attacks on foreign powers have been useless and dangerous. He has courted a war for which this country is totally unprepared—and which it emphatically does not want."

These charges are manifestly unfair—though behind most of them are half-truths, or at least quarter-truths, and as campaign statements go, they are not immoderate. But the speaker was hardly consistent when he went on to boast: "I promise, by returning to those same principles that overcame German autocracy once before, both in business and in war, to outdistance Hitler in any contest he chooses in 1940 or after."

There was no doubt, however, as to where he stood on the main issue.

That it *was* the main issue shows again how far a man's political career may be shaped by external events, quite beyond his control. Willkie had originally sought the nomination in order to oppose certain aspects of the New Deal's domestic policy, and had hoped to fight the campaign on those issues and, later, the third term issue. Yet now he found himself devoting to these topics only the less important half of his acceptance speech.

He made the transition well: "The promises of the present administration cannot lead you to victory against Hitler or against anybody else. . . . It does not preach the doctrine of growth. It preaches the doctrine of division. We are not asked to make more for ourselves. We are asked to divide among ourselves that which we already have."

At this point he delivered what was obviously intended to be the punch line of his attack, a spark to set off an explosion of applause, a slogan to be used throughout the campaign. "The New Deal doctrine does not seek risk. It seeks safety. Let us call it the 'I pass' doctrine. The New Deal dealt it and refused to make any more bets on the American future." But speech-writers can never tell what will succeed and what will not. This particular verbal firecracker fizzled; it scarcely rippled the surface of the apathy that had settled over the sweat-soaked, heat-drugged audience.

If such anti-New Deal sallies failed to strike fire, the speaker was not likely to arouse enthusiasm by declaring himself a "liberal" and subscribing to a long list of Roosevelt reforms. "The doctrinaires of the opposition have attacked me as an opponent of liberalism. But I was a liberal before many of these men had heard the word, and I fought for many of the reforms of the elder La Follette, Theodore Roosevelt and Woodrow Wilson before another Roosevelt adopted—and distorted—liberalism.

"I learned my liberalism right here at home in Elwood. From the factories that came into this town many years ago, large fortunes were made by a few individuals, who thereby acquired too much power over our community.

"These same forces were at work throughout the rest of the nation. By 1929 the concentration of private power had gone further than it should ever go in a democracy. . . . I believe that the forces of free enterprise must be regulated. I am opposed to business monopolies.

"I believe in collective bargaining, by the representatives of labor's own free choice . . . I believe in the maintenance of minimum standards for wages and of maximum standards for hours. . . .

"I believe in the Federal regulation of interstate utilities, of securities markets and of banking. I believe in Federal pensions, in adequate old-age benefits and in unemployment allowances. I believe that the Federal government has a responsibility to equalize the lot of the farmer, with that of the manufacturer . . .

"I believe in the encouragement of co-operative buying and selling, and in the full extension of rural electrification."

Thus Willkie went down the line in support of the essential measures of the New Deal's domestic policy. And, again, he faced the task of making clear his reasons for opposing the regime by which these measures had been initiated. This time he attacked not only the way in which they were administered—the partisan spirit and the inefficient procedures—but the defeatist philosophy, as he saw it, by which good intentions and initial gains must eventually be nullified. "American liberalism does not consist merely in reforming things. It also consists in making things. . . . To be free, man must be creative. . . . I believe that in our industrial age there is no limit to the horizon of the United States . . . Only the strong can be free. And only the productive can be strong."

A quarter-century of change has blunted the point of this charge. We accept America's fantastic productivity as a matter of course, and no one remembers Roosevelt's declaration, "Our industrial plant is built. . . . Our last frontier has been reached"; or his acceptance of the doctrine of a "closed economy" that was implicit in several New Deal programs. It seemed to Willkie that the Administration was not only willing to accept as inevitable, but determined to promote as desirable, a planned economy in which there was no room for the free growth of industry. Such a purpose was reflected not only in the NRA and the AAA but in a tax system which penalized productive investment by placing high taxes on income derived therefrom while refusing to tax unproductive government securities in which capital naturally took refuge. It was largely because of these policies, Willkie argued (and believed), that "the New Deal has failed in its program of economic rehabilitation"; and he added: "I charge that the course this administration is following will lead us, like France, to the end of the road."

And now, having finished his argument, Willkie made his most dramatic gesture. Picking up the President's remark about being too busy to engage in "purely political debate," he retorted: "I do not want to engage in purely political debate, either. But . . . I do not think that the issues at stake are 'purely political.' In my opinion they concern the life and death of democracy.

"I propose that during the next two and a half months the President and I appear on public platforms together in various parts of the country and on those platforms debate the fundamental issues of this campaign."

Here, at last, after the failure of so many well planned appeals to the emotions of the audience, one actually succeeded. The somnolent crowd awoke with a roar of applause to so bold and unorthodox a challenge to "the champ."

When the applause ceased, he listed the now familiar issues which he wished to debate. He added: "I make this proposal respectfully to a man upon whose shoulders rests the burden of the State. But I make it in dead earnest."

He was in dead earnest, also, as he neared his conclusion: "I am saying to you that we cannot rebuild our American democracy without hardship, without sacrifice, and without suffering. . . . In these months ahead of us every man will have to work a little harder.

"Every man and every woman will feel the burden of taxes."

He ended with a plea for unity and a promise to achieve it. "The Democratic party today stands for division among our people, for the struggle of class against class and faction against faction, for the power of political machines and the exploitation of pressure groups. Liberty does not thrive on such a soil.

"The only soil in which liberty can grow is that of a united people. We must have faith that the welfare of one is the welfare of all."

The speaker laid down his manuscript. The crowd applauded, partly in relief, loosened its sweaty clothes, and began to move toward the parking lot and the railroad station. The great day was over.

The national response, so far as it got into print, was partisan and superficial. The Democrats were dutifully disdainful, although not all of them followed the party line with the push-button servility of Senator Minton: "It was the worst major political speech I ever listened to." Roosevelt himself airily maintained his pose of being too busy not only to engage in debate but even to note what his opponent was saying.

Among Republicans, Senator Vandenberg was among the few who appeared genuinely enthusiastic, calling the speech "one of the greatest of our generation," and adding sensibly: "In this day of desperately complicated issues it is impossible for frank men to agree with each other on everything." (But the next evening in Rushville he was sharply critical.)[44] Hoover was still hopeful: "It was the call of a strong man to strong men and women." Taft professed himself "satisfied"[45]—which was probably as much praise as Willkie cared for from that quarter.

Newspaper editorials were generally laudatory (the speech read better than it sounded), although the Chicago *Tribune* confined its praise to the speaker's candor and courage. The minority pro-Roosevelt press was naturally cool. The Louisville *Courier-Journal,* perhaps the most ably edited of this group, concluded: "He made a fine pep-talk and that was about all." The *New Republic,* however, in a generally fair account, called it "a shrewd and skillful job."[46]

The quotations from the address that are given above speak for themselves. In a situation where complete success was almost ludicrously out of reach, Willkie did the best he could. Years later Russell Davenport made what may well stand as a final comment: "Everybody worked on it and nobody liked it. I still don't know what we could have done to make it better."[47]

XI

The Election Campaign: "The Willkie Slump"

1

The tremendous crowd which inundated Elwood for the acceptance ceremonies showed that during the seven weeks since Willkie's triumph at Philadelphia, the flood tide of popular enthusiasm had not receded. The Gallup Poll's second report, published on August 25 but based on polling conducted before the Elwood speech, showed him still holding the 49 per cent of the popular vote that had been given him three weeks before, and clinging to a slight majority of electoral votes, although twenty had gone over to the Roosevelt column.[1]

New elements in his strength were perhaps the sour taste left in many people's mouths by the proceedings at the Chicago convention, and the continued military lull in Europe (not broken until early August), which, as always, made some people feel that Roosevelt's leadership could be dispensed with.

It was true that the third term issue had not caused the general defection from Democratic ranks that Willkie had expected. Most of those who announced their support of him had, like Al Smith, broken with Roosevelt already, on other issues, and held neither public office nor standing in the party organization. Still, it might be hoped that their revolt was symptomatic of a widespread feeling, and four members of the group—John W. Hanes and Lewis W. Douglas, who had been Under Secretary of the Treasury and Director of the Budget earlier in the Roosevelt administration; Alan Valentine, president of the University of Rochester; and Mrs. Roberta Campbell Lawson, president of the General Federation of Women's Clubs—agreed to head a Democrats for Willkie organization aimed at translating this feeling into votes.[2]

But in the next few weeks, and before Willkie's active campaign had even begun, a catastrophic change took place. The third Gallup report, published on September 20 but reflecting the country's sentiment two weeks earlier, showed Roosevelt getting 55 per cent of the popular vote and leading in all but ten of the forty-eight states. He would have received 453 electoral votes; and 35 of Willkie's 78 were from four states hovering on the verge. These results confirmed a *Fortune* poll reported a week earlier in which 53.2 per cent of all persons questioned declared themselves for Roosevelt, as against 35.6 for Willkie.

Nor were the polls the only omens of disaster. Private guesses almost unanimously concurred. On September 3 Erwin Canham reported in the *Christian Science Monitor* that "a certain degree of pessimism prevails in New York, Washington, and many other 'political circles' in the East" about Willkie's chances.[3] Five days later the *New York Times* reported, as "an opinion pretty generally held in Washington," that "the Republican Presidential campaign is currently undergoing a definite slump."[4] At about the same time, Ernest K. Lindley, traveling from Washington to the West Coast and back, found everybody asking one question: "What has happened to Willkie?"[5]

For one thing, there had been the general letdown that followed the acceptance speech. Until then, Willkie had been a miracle man, and many people, as the Richmond *Times-Dispatch* observed editorially, had "expected the impossible."[6] On August 17 these persons were forced to face the facts of life in the United States in the year 1940.

The fact that many people liked least, and that Willkie made them face but could not make them accept, was that isolation was no longer possible. For twenty years the Old Guard had been unreservedly isolationist; and it still was. When the Selective Service Act was finally passed by the Senate on August 28, twelve Republicans (including Taft and Vandenberg) were recorded against it and only eleven for it, including McNary, whose vote was an obvious concession to the need for party unity. Of the other ten, seven were from New England.[7]

In the House, on September 7, the repudiation of Willkie's leadership was even more decisive, with 112 Republicans against the bill and only 52 (including the reluctant National Chairman) for it. The House measure, moreover, included a crippling amendment, proposed by Hamilton Fish of New York, limiting the increase in the armed forces to 400,000 and calling for a 60-day delay while efforts were made to recruit this number. The Republican vote on this provision was 140 for, 22 against.[8]

Thus Congressional Republicans lent support to the biting comments of Harold Ickes in answering Willkie's acceptance speech: "No fine words about the candidate's foreign policy will quiet fears as to what will happen if, in the event of a Republican victory, Hiram Johnson becomes chairman of the Senate Committee on Foreign Affairs and Hamilton Fish, chairman of the House Committee on Foreign Relations."[9]

It is easy to believe that, as Willkie on the day of the House action told an audience at Rushville, he had received "a great deal of advice," mostly in the form of "suggestions that I should compromise my principles or modify my views." He responded, characteristically, with a declaration of independence: "Let me say to you people of Rush County . . . that I will not compromise my principles or modify my basic philosophy to gain the office of President.

"Whether you or others like it or not, I never, during the course of the campaign, will state anything in which I do not believe. I will not talk in quibbling language."[10]

There was certainly no quibbling in the statement in which, three days later, he took issue with more than 85 per cent of his fellow Republicans in the House: "I hope that, as a result of the conference between House and Senate conferees, the Fish amendment is eliminated."[11]

The issue here was not merely that of isolation or intervention, but also that of party solidarity and party leadership. The traditional American two-party system of politics cannot operate without some measure of coherence within each party. It is true that the right of individual members to dissent on any given question has also been traditional; but that the party nominee for President should be on one side of an important issue and 85 per cent of the party's members in the House on the other side sounds more like a Broadway musical than an actual situation. What a majority of Congressional Republicans were doing was presenting the candidate with an ultimatum: declaring that they and not he would speak for the Republican party.

And they cannot have been blind to the consequences. They did not need Walter Lippmann to point out that "Mr. Willkie cannot make speeches advocating conscription and the policy of extending to Great Britain 'the material resources of the nation,' and expect the people to follow him if his own party does not follow him. . . . The party cannot offer the country a national leader for the next four years if in the weeks after he accepts the nomination they reject and repudiate his leadership."[12] Either they thought that Willkie could be coerced into at least a semi-isolationist position; or else they were willing, if he stood firm, to see him defeated.

This was the battle that Willkie was to fight for the rest of his life. The quarrel with the New Deal, which had drawn him into public life, became a minor issue. The crying need was for national unity on an internationalist philosophy; and if this involved a second front against the Republican Old Guard while continuing his earlier campaign against the New Deal, Willkie was willing. That this brave decision, like his resolve never to say what he did not believe, was sometimes disregarded during the hectic weeks of the campaign was a fact that, afterward, he admitted, regretted, and atoned for.

2

There were, however, other and less basic causes of friction between Willkie and the party regulars, and for these the latter were not always to blame. One matter in regard to which it is hard to acquit Willkie of impetuousness and bad judgment was his attack on the Russell-Overton "industrial conscription" amendment to the Selective Service Act. Opponents of a peace-time draft had been quick to raise the cry that while men were to be conscripted, business was to remain free, and that while individuals would be making sacrifices, corporations would be making profits. An obvious counter-move by proponents of the measure was to add a clause providing that any industrial plant whose owner refused to cooperate in the national defense program could be seized and operated by the government.[13] This was calculated to appease many voters, and it seemed relatively harmless. Not many firms were likely to turn down government contracts.

For some reason, however, it made Willkie see red. "It may be that the American people want to come to the point where they want to Sovietize or socialize (you can take your choice of terms) American business. If they do, it's O. K., but I want to present the issue."[14] It is true that the amendment contained sweeping phrases and undefined terms, such as "facility," as well as vagueness in regard to procedures, which obviously made it subject to abuse. Willkie might, however, have pointed out such weaknesses in temperate language while stating (as he did two days later): "I am wholly in favor of providing the government with enough power to force a recalcitrant minority of the industrial community to cooperate with our defense program."[15]

Perhaps Willkie thought he had an issue on which he could make an effective appeal for votes. But he must have noted that a majority of Senate Republicans had approved the amendment, and it would have been prudent, if winning votes was mainly in his mind, to ask experienced politicians whether they thought this a good way to do it; or, if he felt that a real principle was involved, to ask himself whether it was important enough to warrant a public statement condemning so many prominent persons in his own party, and inviting retaliation. A dozen or more Democrats (not all of them New Dealers) arose in the Senate to defend the amendment and to assail its critic as the mouthpiece of "big business," while their Republican colleagues sat in bitter silence.[16]

Not all the Republican leaders that Willkie offended were in Congress. He had hardly been nominated when he tossed a hand-grenade into the midst of the party fund-raisers by asking that they accept no campaign contributions of more than $5,000, no cash contributions of more than $10, and no contributions whatever from corporations; and he added that nobody need expect a political reward in return for a contribution.[17]

This policy was in line with the second Hatch "clean-politics" bill (then lying in a House committee pigeonhole, but immediately brought out and passed),[18] which was intended to prevent elections from being unduly influenced by the expenditure of either government or private funds. The policy was not, however, in accord with the traditional practice of either party; and Willkie's statement is said to have so infuriated the chairman of the Finance Committee of the Republican National Committee, steel magnate Ernest Weir, that he immediately telephoned Willkie and threatened to resign.[19] One can understand his anger when one reads later the statement of Senator Gillette of the Senate Committee on Campaign Expenditures that in 1936 the Republicans had received $1,060,000 from the Du Pont, Rockefeller, and Pew families.[20] But Willkie would not retreat.

The same feud flared again a few weeks later. The Hatch Act had set a limit of $3,000,000 on the amount that a party could spend in one year, but local organizations were specifically exempted, and the exact meaning of the law was not clear. Henry P. Fletcher, one-time National Chairman and now counsel to the Republican National Committee, prepared an elaborate and no doubt legally valid argument that each of the three Republican campaign groups—the National Committee, the Willkie Clubs, and the Democrats for Willkie—could spend up to $3,000,000. But again the candidate rebuffed his advisers. He was determined that the combined total expenditures of the organizations working for him on a national basis should not exceed the stated figure.[21] He declared: "I think this is a fine time to clear up the abuses which have for so long existed in our politics—and I'm not saying that one party has been more responsible in the past for these abuses than the other."[22]

There were good reasons for Willkie's stand. Corruption was to be one of his main charges against the Democrats: corruption in the political machines—Hague, Pendergast, Kelly-Nash—that controlled many big-city governments; corruption in the use of WPA funds; corruption in the soliciting of money from corporations (the Hatch Act forbade campaign contributions by any firm holding government contracts) under the guise of "advertising" in the Democratic campaign booklet. Obviously Willkie could not press his charges unless his own hands, and those of his party, were clean. Moreover, aside from this particular issue, it would seem that Willkie's aims—to try, not to outspend the other party, but to limit the expenditures of both; and to raise money by giving many people a chance to contribute and so feel thal they were sharing in a common effort, rather than seeking massive gifts from a few persons whose very names aroused popular distrust (and who might or might not be moved by altruism)—were the aims that made sense.[23]

There was also another motive for Willkie's stand—a private aversion, amounting almost to a horror, of any obligation that might result in pressure for action that he would regard as unethical.[24] Whether or not this made sense politically, it was a fact.

These two specific disagreements between Willkie and a majority of regular Republicans need not in themselves have been serious. They reflected, however, a split that divided Willkie's supporters from top to bottom: a split, first, between opposing views of what a political party should be and how it should be run, and, second, between two irreconcilable social philosophies.

The meeting at Colorado Springs early in August, at which Fletcher's interpretation of the Hatch Act had been turned down, included also Martin, Hamilton, Pryor, Stassen, Weeks, Charles B. Goodspeed (Treasurer of the National Committee), Oren Root, and Russell Davenport. The *New York Times* story of the meeting included the comment: "Some of the Republican leaders appeared to be a little annoyed at the inclusion of Mr. Root in the conference and the attention focused on him by Mr. Willkie. It is known that there has been some resentment among 'organization' Republicans at the emphasis placed by Mr. Willkie on the clubs and on the independent Democratic movement."[25] The "organization" was willing, since the thing was done, to forgive the young, independent enthusiasts whose Willkie Clubs had won the day at Philadelphia—*if* these personal devotees of the candidate would now pass quietly out of the picture and leave the campaign to be run by those who knew how.

But this the Willkie Clubs declined to do. Willkie was *their* candidate. Throughout the country they had organized and channeled the spontaneous support for Willkie into an irresistible force. Why should they cease their activity now? And why should they not have a voice in the party councils? After all, the professionals had run the campaigns of Hoover and Landon.

It would have been strange indeed if Willkie had not lent a sympathetic ear. He was humanly grateful for their support in winning the nomination, and he knew that it was essential in winning the election.[26] Roosevelt had beaten Landon in 1936 by almost 11,000,000 votes. If, as one might naturally assume, the voters who had remained loyal to the Republican party in that unparalleled disaster constituted a "hard core" of support that could always be counted on, then the problem was to win over to Willkie's side the millions of independents and of disillusioned Democrats without whose votes his cause would be hopeless.

This obvious fact, however, many of the party professionals declined to face. The Old Guard insisted that the country was still "normally Republican," and that Landon had been defeated because his views were "too much like Roosevelt's," so that many "real Republicans" had not bothered to vote.

Such persons were probably less angered by Willkie's cultivation of the Democrats than by his support of the Willkie Clubs. True, Mr. Hoover and his admirers must have ground their teeth when Willkie remarked toward the end of July: "I do not know of any reason why any Democrat who subscribed to and believed in the 1932 Democratic platform or believes in the historic principles of the Democratic party or who was a Woodrow Wilson Democrat, should not vote for me instead of the President"; and the question of one reporter as to how Republicans "would react to this statement" was very much to the point. Willkie replied, however, plausibly enough, that both groups would be united "in opposition to the policies and practices of the Roosevelt administration, particularly with reference to domestic questions."[27]

At any rate, this situation could be regarded as temporary. It did not threaten the permanent control of the party by the Old Guard. But the Willkie Clubs *did*. And the friction between the latter groups therefore continued and increased. The rumor of "organization" resentment found its way into the *Times* again on August 23[28] and again on September 1, when a writer commented on the "evident dissatisfaction on the part of the Old Guard over a disposition on the part of new elements in the party to crowd them out of the picture."[29] The question was, however, as to who was crowding whom. By this time, as an apologist for the Old Guard admits, "Nothing could placate the Republicans except the elimination of the amateurs from key positions on Willkie's staff."[30] ("Amateurs," obviously, could not be "Republicans.")

In the meantime, it was evident that the "organization," from whatever causes, was continuing to drag its feet. Toward the end of August two writers in the *Christian Science Monitor,* editorially friendly to Willkie, discussed this fact. One noted a total lack of organized effort to "win whatever may be available of the labor vote."[31] The other commented more generally: "There are many signs this year that the behind-the-scenes organizational work on the Republican side is not proceeding as normally. Nobody seems to know exactly how the National Committee stands. Various important sub-officials have not yet been appointed. The work seems far behind and in some ways half-hearted." On the other hand, "the Willkie Clubs seem to have done fairly well."[32]

One is tempted to wonder, reading this account, what Hamilton was doing to earn his $25,000 salary. (Martin obviously had his hands full in Congress and, moreover, had never claimed to possess any organizing genius.) But perhaps the split was really too wide to be bridged. Perhaps there were too many "organization" Republicans who were sure that Willkie would lose, and were not sorry. They had assumed at the time of the nomination, as Roscoe Drummond later wrote, that Willkie "could be managed without too much difficulty. . . . How wrong they were! How deeply they regretted their decision. What a relief when Willkie wasn't elected."[33]

Willkie himself was trying his best "to live in both worlds."[34] In a final effort to achieve harmony before setting out to stump the country he called a conference of Republican leaders from twenty-one states to meet in Rushville on September 5.[35] At the conclusion of the conference Pryor announced smoothly to newsmen: "Mr. Willkie settled every question that any State chairman or national committeeman had in mind, not only as to the timing of his campaign, but on several issues and organizational problems. Most important of all, he left us no doubt that he was the candidate of the regular Republican organization and that he was going to cooperate in the campaign with every regular Republican candidate. . . . Henceforth . . . the Republican National Committee will have sole jurisdiction over the campaign."[36] Willkie confirmed Pryor's statement by telling the gathering: "This is also a campaign for the election of Republican Senators and Congressmen. I hope you will support them all to the limit so that the pernicious doctrines of the last few years will be completely eliminated from America."[37] On the surface, it looked as though the "organization" had won.

To a certain extent this is correct. Willkie went as far as he decently could (and sometimes a little farther) to conciliate the "organization" Republicans. When he stood out against them, as in regard to campaign financing and the Selective Service Act, he did so not merely from personal moral convictions but also from a conviction as to what was best for the party. The legend that he systematically ignored or snubbed them in the weeks following his nomination is without foundation. No Presidential candidate has ever been more thoroughly "covered" by reporters, and if any person—of any party—who wanted to see him was ever turned away, that person's name is not recorded.[38]

It *is* recorded that he sometimes conferred "briefly" with visiting Republicans, and it is true that throughout his political career he was apt to exasperate Very Important Persons (often inadvertently) by keeping them waiting while he talked to people like cab-drivers and clerks—who were of no importance except that they were human beings and fellow citizens. What really annoyed the VIP's, however, was not that they did not get a chance to give advice, but that their advice was often not followed. Nor did Willkie shrink, as did Roosevelt, from telling people that he did not agree with them.

Still, he did not, as a rule, go out of his way to irritate his fellow Republicans. He had a natural liking for people; although he had no illusions about politics he did not consider it a dirty business; and he had no desire to split the party, nor, in 1940, any notion of reforming it farther than was necessary to win the election.

So he was willing to meet the established leaders of the party more than half way. He followed the traditional pattern in choosing his running mate (who also had publicly opposed his nomination); in the interest of party harmony he gave up his novel idea of having the campaign run by a three-man board; and instead of exercising his prerogative and following the usual practice of a Presidential nominee in picking a personal friend to be National Chairman, he picked a man whom all factions respected. He asked Taft and Dewey to help in his campaign, and accepted their supporters as his aides and advisers. He walked softly in his dealings with Congress, except when his concern for the national welfare compelled him to speak out on crucial issues; so that Walter Lippman, confusing the desirable with the possible, blamed him for not taking action "to make the party leaders in Congress . . . bring the party organization into line."[39] He tried at first—until the Democrats taunted him with being the candidate of isolationists and appeasers—to keep foreign policy out of the campaign and to put the emphasis on domestic issues, where he felt that a much closer approach to unity was possible.

And he swallowed his personal aversions to individuals. He did not want to see Hoover, but he saw him. He can hardly have cared much for Colonel McCormick of the Chicago *Tribune,* but he saw him, three times,[40] and listened while the Colonel urged, as Willkie later recalled, "that I should adopt his peculiar foreign policy which seemed to consist mostly in worrying about the danger of being invaded through Canada."[41] He even took back, at the urging of his advisers, his cutting remarks about Pennsylvania's boss Joseph Pew (when asked by a reporter a few days after the convention whether he had heard from Mr. Pew, he had retorted, "No, I haven't, and as far as I'm concerned, that's only half of it"), and let it be known that he had "asked for and obtained the full support" of the man whom he looked on as almost the embodiment of everything in the Republican party to which in his heart he was opposed.[42]

He went further. The old saw about strange bedfellows never received a more dramatic illustration than when Willkie, practically in the same breath, denied Henry Wallace's charge that the Republican party was the party of appeasement and welcomed the support of the bitter-end isolationist, Senator Hendrick Shipstead of Minnesota;[43] or when he praised Senator Hiram Johnson of California—a man who twenty years before had helped break the heart of his hero Woodrow Wilson and who was now fighting every move to aid England or prepare America for war—as "a true liberal."[44] It is true that Johnson and Shipstead were men of integrity, however misguided. But it must have been a bitter decision that brought Willkie, an internationalist all his life, to accept them as allies.

The truth is that if Willkie made a mistake in his dealings with the Republican "organization" and its established leaders, it was, as he later realized, in being too conciliatory, in sacrificing his independence and even, to some extent, his integrity, to the unattainable aim of party unity.

The full significance of the dissension within the party was, however, not yet clear. Rumors of such strife are a regular feature of campaigns, and it is hard to say how far the situation just described contributed to the "Willkie slump" and to his subsequent defeat. Probably it cost him support not so much among rank and file Republicans as among independent voters who drew the conclusion that reaction still reigned in Republican councils and that even with a new and personally attractive leader (and *was* he the leader?) the party could not be trusted.

3

In the meantime, the Democrats—at least the overwhelming majority who had remained faithful to what Willkie during the campaign called the "New Deal Party"—were on the whole united among themselves as well as in opposition to Willkie. The threat of war, crowding domestic issues off the stage, which set Republicans against each other, drew the Democrats together. It is true that eighteen Democratic Senators were recorded against the Selective Service Act when it was first passed by the Senate. They were, however, merely dissident individuals who wielded little power in the party councils and commanded—on this issue, at least—no popular following. Nor was Willkie more to their taste than Roosevelt.

On the other hand, the traditional components of the party—the Southern conservatives, the Northern liberals, the big city workers—were solidly united behind the President's foreign policy and solidly against the isolationism which Congressional Republicans had been working for twenty years to establish as their party trademark.[45]

Hence, no influential Democrat raised any protest against the attacks on Willkie which Roosevelt and his henchmen had lost no time in planning. The nomination took place in the early morning hours of Friday, June 28. Saturday morning papers carried a statement by Mr. Farley (and a similar one by Speaker Bankhead) that the question posed by Willkie's nomination was: "What set of forces, economic or social, are to conduct our government—the historic American processes, or some new and somewhat foreign methods of concentrated control?"[46]

This was the first of many low blows struck at the Republican candidate during the campaign. If the point of the question now seems obscure, we need only recall that a term then in everybody's mouth was "blitzkrieg" —the "lightning war" by which Hitler had conquered first Poland, then Norway and Denmark, then the Low Countries and France. Reporters had seized on it as an apt epithet to describe the outward course of events at

Philadelphia. Now an attempt was being made to associate Willkie's campaign with Hitler's, not only in its overwhelming effect but in its methods and motives—secret machinations on the one hand, autocratic power on the other. It laid the foundation, furthermore, for an attack on Willkie through his German ancestry—an attack of which there were many early rumors.

The idea that there could be anything un-American about Wendell Willkie was, however, so patently absurd that it was immediately abandoned as a campaign weapon. What is significant here is not the episode but its revelation of the spirit in which the Roosevelt administration responded to the challenge of Willkie's candidacy.

Before entering on this topic, however, it is only fair to make clear that an American Presidential election is traditionally a dirty business. Morals suffer as well as manners; honesty is cast aside along with courtesy. Men who are normally truthful and good-humored indulge deliberately in half-truths and whole lies, spread malicious insinuations and downright slanders, annihilate straw men and conjure up bogey-men; in short, do anything whatever that they think will discredit the opposing candidate in the eyes of the voters.

Yet there are some grounds for the hopeful belief that the voters, after all, are not taken in; that Willkie was right in saying, "The American people are not dumb. They know about all this"; and that they accepted as a matter of course Willkie's famous remark about "campaign oratory." They make their choice on the basis of a few elementary issues and personal qualities. This is not to say that the electorate is never tricked, or that if a lie is repeated often enough and loudly enough it will not sometimes be believed—like the lie that Willkie's joking comment was a cynical admission of total insincerity. Nor is there an implication that in a political campaign *no* moral standards apply. There are some things, one would like to believe, that decent people will not do—or tolerate.

Even this limited optimism, however, is shaken by the viciousness of the attack that Administration strategists launched against Willkie as soon as he was nominated, and continued throughout the campaign.

Mr. Farley himself has revealed the origin of the comment quoted above. "On the day of the nomination Steve Early called me and read a statement the White House had prepared for me to release. . . . I objected to the word 'foreign,' but there was no arguing with the White House." Equally revealing is his account of the next day's cabinet meeting, where the outcome of the Republican convention was naturally a main topic of discussion. "'We will have to break down the aura they are trying to build up around Willkie,' Roosevelt said. 'I want the Senators and Congressmen to start in on him Monday.'

"Ickes said that a vigorous campaign should be directed at once against Willkie. . . . The President told him to 'go to it.'"[47]

The initial attacks, however, were more or less run-of-the-mill. Senator Norris, whose long battle against abuses in the utility industry had made him incapable of fair or factual judgment on anything associated with that industry, immediately labeled the candidate "Insull the second," adding: "The power trust was behind him and gave him the nomination."[48] Senator Pepper followed up, on the Senate floor, with some typical left-wing oratory about the utilities and Wall Street.[49] Senator Lucas remarked, more reasonably, that if Willkie was interested in unifying the country, he could start with his running-mate.[50]

All attacks, according to the Democratic strategy, were to be delivered by Roosevelt's lieutenants: the Commander-in-Chief was to pose as being too busy with affairs of state to be even aware that a political campaign was in progress. He regularly professed to newsmen, in fact, that he had not had time to read or listen to Willkie's speeches. (Of course he was too intelligent not to want to know what his opponent was saying, and one of his secretaries, Grace Tully, has testified: "He listened to several of Mr. Willkie's speeches on the radio, and read all of them.")[51]

One may doubt that such purely tactical maneuvers result directly in much gain or loss of votes. What may have made this one important was that it infuriated Willkie, led him sometimes (as at the beginning of his active campaign) to adopt an angry tone that alienated potential supporters, and strengthened the hand of the Old Guard in trying to push him into more sweeping attacks on the President than he would have wished to make in a calmer mood.

More directly, the pose served Roosevelt well, in that it gave him an excuse for refusing Willkie's challenge to a series of platform debates on major campaign issues. In such give-and-take contests—unless they had been formalized into a pair of set addresses—there is little doubt that Roosevelt, accustomed to preparing his speeches with the aid of a group of master rhetoricians and to calculating the effect of every phrase, would have been at a disadvantage in the presence of the ebullient Willkie—although it is true that in his press conferences he showed himself a master of verbal fencing.

But while the President was obviously taking the sensible course in refusing the challenge, Ickes did less well in his answer to the acceptance speech; he called the challenge "cheap bravado," "reflecting upon the dignity and striking at the prestige of an office which, as a candidate himself for the Presidency, it ought to be his zealous duty to uphold and defend."[52] To this, Willkie promptly and effectively retorted that Mr. Roosevelt was not only President but also a candidate for reelection and ought to be willing to discuss with the voters his reasons for requesting an unprecedented third term.[53]

For the time being, however, Roosevelt saw no reason to change his tactics, and let the verbal barrage against Willkie be continued by his underlings. Of these, one of the most assiduous was Edward J. Flynn, boss of the Bronx Democratic organization and successor to Farley as Democratic National Chairman. He conceived his function in the campaign, as he remarks complacently in his autobiography, to be that of drawing upon himself, through a continuous series of attacks, the fire which Willkie would otherwise have directed against Roosevelt.[54] Most of his assaults, however, were picayune and personal—like the charge, first made by Ickes but promptly megaphoned by Flynn, that although Willkie had been denouncing Democratic political machines, he himself had belonged to one of the most notorious, Tammany Hall. This was really pointless, since the Republican candidate readily admitted that in 1935 he had been elected a member of the New York County (Manhattan) Democratic Committee, to which the name "Tammany Hall" is often applied. At the same time, the term is inseparably associated in the public mind with the secret, sinister and corrupt machinations of a small group of New York City political bosses, and it was this that Willkie obviously had in mind when he replied that the charge was "bunk"—a response which, according to Flynn, showed that Willkie was "emotionally unstable—he likes to give it but he can't take it."[55]

Contrary to the impression given by Flynn in his book, there were plenty of other Democrats who were willing to "take on Willkie"—and to use the same techniques. Solicitor General Francis Biddle in a speech delivered in Seattle a week after the Elwood acceptance characterized him as "a businessman who doesn't like regulation and therefore hates the New Deal. . . . The Weirs, the Pews, the Grundys, the Girdlers, will not fear him because they know his record." (Biddle knew his record too, and therefore knew how far from the truth this statement was.) On the same date Senator Joseph Guffey of Pennsylvania was dispensing the same doctrine at Wilkes-Barre, calling Willkie "a false front for Wall Street," whose "real supporters" are "the potential war profiteers, the politicans for profit, the same type of fascist reactionaries who led the great democracy of France to its destruction."[56] (The fall of France was invoked with nauseating frequency to support the arguments of both parties.) Taking "Wall Street" as a symbol of everything reprehensible in the world of business, industry, and finance, these attacks can be translated into the slogan, "A vote for Willkie is a vote for Wall Street."

A few days later Henry Wallace, accepting the Vice Presidential nomination so grudgingly offered him, chimed in with statements more restrained in phrasing but more deadly in their insinuation. "I do not wish to imply that the Republican leaders are wishfully or consciously giving aid and comfort to Hitler. But I do want to emphasize that the replacement of Roosevelt . . . would cause Hitler to rejoice."[57] ("A vote for Willkie is a vote for Hitler.")

When Willkie tried to defend his party, Flynn rushed forward to repeat the charge, and added: "Neither can Mr. Willkie answer for the beliefs and conduct of his other supporters and the many who exist solely on promoting religious and racial prejudices.

"Mr. Willkie can repudiate their support—as he has in one case, at least —from now until doomsday. The fact still remains that these fellow travelers still support him, by disseminating the vilest sort of anti-Roosevelt propaganda."[58]

Such statements were themselves the vilest sort of propaganda. At the beginning of the campaign Willkie had declared truly that he had taken a stand "against race hatred, bigotry and Hitlerism" "long before I even thought of being a Presidential candidate." "I consider anti-Semitism in America as a possible criminal movement and every anti-Semite as a possible traitor to America."[59] A week after his Elwood speech he said: "I repudiate any committee or individual who is supporting me on the basis of racial or religious prejudice."[60] Four days later he responded to praise from the rabble-rousing "radio priest," Father Coughlin, by saying: "If I understand what his beliefs are, I am not only not interested in his support—I don't want it. . . . I don't have to be President of the United States, but I do have to . . . live with myself."[61]

Even in an election, one would think, such a stand deserved something better than what was, in effect, the Democrats' repeated assertion: "A vote for Willkie is a vote for anti-Catholicism, anti-Semitism, and white supremacy."

These libels by leading Democrats, continuing without intermission from the date of his nomination until the election, must have been particularly hard to take because Willkie himself, though he enjoyed vigorous verbal combat, had no taste for this kind of calculated venom directed against particular persons. At a conference in early August when mention of Henry Wallace's name had drawn boos from his audience, Willkie praised Wallace (without irony) as "a fine gentleman and a scholar," and added: "I want to conduct this campaign upon the basis of the very fundamental issues that are involved and not upon the question of personalities."[62]

Nor were the professional politicians the only offenders against honesty and decency. They were frequently joined by the left-wing intellectuals whose influence in the New Deal had once been strong, and who were still, on the whole, its partisans. An extreme example was a special supplement put out on September 2 by the *New Republic,*[63] under the editorship of Bruce Bliven,[64] entitled "This Man Willkie." In it Willkie was branded "a front man or fixer" ("These are admittedly smear words," said the writer, with a venomous affectation of ingenuousness, "but it is hard to think of more respectable synonyms") for that section of the business world "which has one of the worst records for shady practices in American history." The indictment then proceeded on the assumption that "since he was the front man for the entire Commonwealth and Southern system, it is fair to hold him responsible for the misdeeds of his subordinates throughout that system." (This was equivalent to holding Harry Hopkins responsible for every act of everyone associated with the WPA.) Included in what he was responsible for were the allegedly nefarious stock market manipulations involved in the formation of Commonwealth & Southern "in the spring and summer of 1929"; and the case against him was carried to the point where he was said to have been "one of those responsible for the speculative orgy" which ended with the great stock market crash of October, 1929. (Until October 1, 1929, Willkie had been a hard-working young Akron attorney. And he did not become president of Commonwealth & Southern until 1933.)

Still more flagrantly dishonest was the detailed account of how one or two minor officials of Consumers Power Company of Michigan, another Commonwealth & Southern subsidiary, had tried to bully workers into staying out of a CIO union. The "unfair labor practice" had undoubtedly existed, as the U. S. Court of Appeals found, in a decision handed down on June 27, 1940, sustaining a "cease and desist" order against the company by the National Labor Relations Board. But Willkie's defamer failed to state that the decree was based largely on technicalities, and that the Court sharply censured the National Labor Relations Board for its handling of the case. "Many specific findings of fact . . . are unsupported otherwise than by suspicion, surmise, or guess." The NLRB "went far afield and much that is irrelevant and unimportant is incorporated. . . . It may well be, as contended by the petitioner, that its officers . . . endeavored, in the utmost good faith, to be impartial with respect to union organization and to redress grievances as soon as they were apprehended. . . . much that is sinister has been read into acts that might well have been perfectly innocent."[65]

This judgment accurately describes the method of the author of the *New Republic* article, for which the editors must share responsibilty. If the Georgia Power Company employed the Pinkerton detective agency, then the truth could not be, as President Preston Arkwright declared, that the Pinkerton agents merely "checked the receipts on street-cars and buses of this company. . . . These services are perfectly legitimate, universally employed, not only by street railway companies, but by every other concern with respect to employees who handle money." The truth had to be that the company was hiring "labor spies." And the editors never printed the report that they had requested of the AFL's Southern Publicity Director, James Barrett, "on the background of the labor relationship existing on the properties of the Georgia Power Company"; possibly because it would have illustrated, in Barrett's words, "the appreciation that Labor has for the splendid labor relationships with the Georgia Power Company."[66]

And if the Central Illinois Light Company bought a few tear gas guns and shells, it could have done so with no other purpose than using them on its own employees, even though the company had never had a strike, and the business manager of Local 702 of the International Brotherhood of Electrical Workers declared: "This company has never used tear guns or other weapons. As a statement by me previously said, their labor policy has been and is '1,000 per cent satisfactory.'"[67]

Once more it must be said that the effect of this attack in terms of votes cannot be measured and may easily be overestimated—although Mr. Flynn and his cohorts saw to it that the *New Republic's* lurid light was visible far beyond the limits of its usual circulation. Now the Democrats could add to their list of slogans: "A vote for Willkie is a vote against labor unions."

Against these concerted attacks by many foes on many fronts, the Republican candidate had to fight almost single-handed. Few Congressional Republicans rose to defend him. No platoon of high Federal officials could be ordered into action on his side. Senator McNary had made it understood at the beginning that he would not wage a very active campaign, and his acceptance speech, although in some ways effective, embarrassed Willkie by a vigorous demand for higher tariffs.[68] The National Committee was apparently satisfied to let him "go it alone." And the young and relatively liberal Republican governors who had rallied around him were little known to the nation at large. Only toward the end did many Republican leaders with national reputation enter the fight.

This situation was perhaps not wholly uncongenial to Willkie, who, contrary to Flynn's assertion, could both "take it" and "dish it out," never was at a loss for rebuttal remarks, and had a gift for getting headlines. But it was impossible for the public not to perceive the lack of party support; and this perception may have been more decisive with the independent voters who would decide the election than was the flood of Democratic propaganda.

One may therefore conjecture that the effect of such slanders as those of Flynn and the *New Republic* was not so much on the immediate as on the ultimate fortunes of their object: that after Willkie's defeat, as popular enthusiasm waned, and as his enemies in the party became more numerous and implacable, the poison slowly spread, infecting the minds even of honest men, and contributing to his political downfall in 1944.

4

What was hurting Willkie more at the moment than the attacks of his adversaries was the march of world events. Every surge of German aggression, bringing always nearer the danger of American involvement in the war, caused an upswing of Roosevelt sentiment; and early in August Hitler opened the "Battle of Britain." On the day of Willkie's Elwood speech the column of the *New York Times* military analyst, Hanson Baldwin, was headed "Battle of Britain Nears Peak," and while Americans in Elwood were sweltering in the sun, dwellers in British cities were being seared by the heat of their burning homes. Even the factual and unsensational headlines of the *Times* told a story that none could ignore: "400 Nazi Planes Bomb British Coast"; "Nazis Intensify Air Raids on Britain as 500 Planes Pound at Strongholds"; "1,000 Nazi Planes Raid Britain; 144 Shot Down"; "London Area Bombed in Rush Hour; Many Dead"; "600 Nazi Planes Raid London Area Again"; "London Bombed in Four Areas; Fire Near St. Paul's"; "1,000 Incendiary Bombs Rained on London"; "700 Planes Give London Worst Pounding of War."

While the headlines shouted their story day after day and week after week, the picture pages with equal persistence thrust it before people's eyes: pictures of formless heaps of rubble where houses, shops, and churches had once stood; pictures of the victims, living and dead, being dug out of the debris by weary workers; pictures at night of ruined walls outlined against the infernal glare beyond; pictures of bombed-out crowds cheering a grim-faced Churchill in his greatest hour.

No American could stand unmoved at such a drama. And of the emotions that a vast majority of Americans felt—pity, admiration, anger, a rising resolve that Britain must not go down—Franklin Roosevelt was the symbol. Other men, perhaps including Willkie, had seen the menace of Nazism sooner and more clearly. But against the unbroken record of wrong judgments by a majority of Republicans, Roosevelt loomed as a prophet almost of Old Testament proportions. No words of Willkie or anyone else could destroy that image.

And Willkie could appeal *only* with words, while Roosevelt could point to facts—things that, whoever deserved the credit, had been done or had come to pass during his administration. This was true even in regard to domestic affairs. Willkie could declaim against continuing unemployment, but working people had at least not been allowed to starve; and besides, under the impact of Roosevelt's defense program (opposed until June, 1940 by the Republicans) jobs were opening up. Willkie might also denounce the New Deal for persecuting business; but, with Roosevelt still in the White House, business was beginning to boom.

The situation was even worse, from a Republican point of view, in regard to national defense and foreign affairs. Willkie might view with loud alarm the lagging program of arms production and call Roosevelt a bungling administrator, who also, in talking about "weapons in hand and on order," was juggling with facts—and America's helplessness after Pearl Harbor would prove him right; and he might call for a single head of defense production, remarking with justice, "It is time for the bunk and conversation to end and time to get the machinery going,"[69] and Roosevelt after a year and a half of such prodding would finally do what Willkie suggested; but at present Roosevelt could make well publicized though "non-political" inspection trips to shipyards and arsenals—so long disused, now coming resoundingly to life—and point with pride to ships and guns and tanks and planes that were actually being brought into existence. (On July 29, at Norfolk, Virginia, he was "greeted by cheering crowds that lined literally miles of streets.")[70] Willkie might demand more effective aid to Britain, but Roosevelt was the man who could give it. And Willkie might support Selective Service and put courage into timid Congressmen of both parties; but when the bill was passed, the credit went to Roosevelt. Willkie's act of statesmanship alienated many Republicans and gained no votes from Democrats.

Roosevelt exploited his advantage with his usual skill. At his press conference the day before Willkie's acceptance speech he made the exciting announcement that he was "negotiating directly with the British government for acquisition of naval and air bases on British possessions in the Western Hemisphere" and "with Canada on problems related to hemisphere defense."[71] On the following day, while Willkie was speaking, Roosevelt was reviewing Army war games near Ogdensburg, New York, involving, according to the President, "the greatest peace-time assemblage of American troops in eighty years";[72] and in the evening he held a conference with Canada's Prime Minister MacKenzie King. Both events claimed headlines the next day beside those devoted to Willkie's speech. (The *Times* reporter said the conference was "hastily arranged."[73] Did it merely happen to coincide in time with the Elwood speech?) The next day the actual terms of the defense pact with Canada were announced, providing for the establishment of a "Permanent Joint Board on Defense" to "commence immediate studies relating to sea, land and air problems, including personnel and materiel."[74] And the next day brought the announcement that study was being given to a proposal that the United States should patrol Canadian waters, thus freeing Canadian destroyers for service in protecting the approaches to British ports.[75] By such actions and announcements Roosevelt gave convincing substance to his claim of being too busy for "political debate."

His great triumph of this kind was the engineering of the agreement to give Britain fifty "over-age" destroyers in return for American bases on British territory in the Atlantic and the Caribbean. Britain's existence was threatened not only by German planes but by German U-Boats. The steady rise in British shipping losses did not make as exciting reading as the bombing of British cities, but the record of it was scanned no less anxiously by those who looked behind the headlines.

Talk about ways of helping meet Britain's desperate need for destroyers began to be heard almost as soon as Roosevelt had the nomination safe. By August 2 this talk had become common enough to draw a question from a reporter at a Willkie press conference. In response Willkie declared that "no representative of the Administration has approached me on any phase of the problem or as to any agreement," although "individuals have discussed the matter with me . . ."[76]

This did not stop the talk, and a week later a similar query drew the admission that some of the persons with whom he had discussed the question had "left their status in doubt." He added that his "general views on the foreign policy and the vital interests of the United States in the present international situation" were well known; but he declared, "As to specific legislative or executive proposals, I do not think it appropriate for me to enter into advance commitments or understandings."[77]

As a matter of fact, the question of getting Willkie's approval of an offer by Churchill to trade West Indian naval bases for the fifty destroyers had been discussed at a cabinet meeting on August 2, and Roosevelt had immediately telephoned William Allen White and asked him to be the intermediary. What he wanted at the time was not merely Willkie's personal approval but also an agreement to bring pressure on Republicans in Congress to give *their* approval.[78] But Willkie, as White tried to explain, was hesitant, lest he make Congressional Republicans more restive and resentful than they were already inclined to be.[79]

In taking this position Willkie was undoubtedly prudent; how little influence he had on Congress was shown by the vote on Selective Service. Still, he might have been wise to accept a later invitation from the President, after the decision had been made to act through an executive order rather than Congressional legislation, "to join with the President to the extent of issuing a statement simultaneously with the announcement of the destroyer deal, declaring that he had knowledge of it and approved it."[80] But again Willkie shied off, laying himself open to the charge that Ickes confided to his diary: "He wants the Administration to make all of the moves and run the risk of making all of the mistakes."[81]

On the other hand, such an act would have laid him open to assault, from within his own party, as a tool or secret confederate of the man whom according to orthodox Old Guard doctrine he ought to be trying by any and all means to defeat. Ever since the Philadelphia convention the Republican isolationists and other Roosevelt-haters had been whetting their knives in anticipation of the moment when Willkie might make a misstep or lower his guard. If he had admitted that he had come to a secret agreement with Roosevelt on an action that came closer than anything yet to active intervention in the war, they would have leaped into action. Roosevelt, perfectly aware of this, aimed at getting Willkie to share the risk, while he himself got most of the credit. As on many later occasions, especially before Pearl Harbor, the President sought and got Willkie's support; and had the double satisfaction of seeing his policies approved and of knowing that the split in Republican ranks had been made wider. Of course it was not Roosevelt's fault, but only his good fortune, that the Old Guard leaders were what they were.

On August 16 the first report of the destroyers for bases deal was allowed to appear in the press; and after a sufficient interval for the public to get used to the idea, Roosevelt announced on September 3 that such an agreement had been put into effect by executive order. In return for the destroyers the United States was to receive 99-year leases of sites for naval and air bases in Newfoundland, Bermuda, the Bahamas, Jamaica, Antigua, St. Lucia, Trinidad, and British Guiana. In addition, there was a superfluous promise from Churchill that the British fleet, whatever happened to Britain itself, would never be surrendered.

The President plainly showed his elation in making the announcement to the press. "It was inevitable," as one reporter noted, "that under the circumstances he must have been thinking of the tremendous point he had scored over Wendell L. Willkie, his political antagonist."[82]

It was indeed a master stroke, approved not only by the majority of Americans who wanted "all aid to Britain short of war," but also by an unexpectedly large proportion of isolationists, since it made more plausible the argument that America itself could repel any attack by a European power and was also a long step toward the "hemisphere defense" which was a favorite catch-word in some isolationist circles. Even the Chicago *Tribune* gave editorial approval to the agreement itself, while charging that Roosevelt's primary motive was to aid Britain rather than to defend America.

In the Republican party, however, there was a powerful faction who called the agreement an "act of war" and insisted that it should have been submitted to Congress; and while Willkie *did* emphatically approve the end, he felt constrained to deplore the means. "The country will undoubtedly approve of the program to add to our naval and air bases and assistance given to Britain. It is regrettable, however, that the President did not deem it necessary in connection with this proposal to secure the approval of Congress or permit public discussion prior to adoption."[83] But the Republican record in Congress again supplied ammunition for the Democrats; and for once Flynn's comment was fair enough: that if the President "had waited for the present Congress to come to agreement either for or against such aid to England, the war might be over while they were still arguing about it."[84] Nevertheless, Willkie felt called upon, after a conference with Vandenberg[85] and probably other Republican leaders, to issue a still stronger statement, calling the bases for destroyers deal "the most arbitrary and dictatorial action ever taken by any President in the history of the United States."[86]

Thus the bitter division between Willkie and many members of his party increased tremendously what was perhaps his greatest disadvantage in the campaign; a disadvantage that was neatly summed up by Turner Catledge: "Mr. Roosevelt can act, while Mr. Willkie can only talk, and talk for the most part about the President's acts."[87] There was simply no way for Willkie to eliminate this disadvantage.

XII

The Election Campaign: The Western Swing

1

If everybody else thought the election was lost before the campaigning started, Willkie did not. All he needed was a chance to talk to people, face to face, with unstudied directness, contemptuous of oratorical artifice or mechanical aids.

But when he got the chance, with the opening of his formal campaign, his actions (even a friendly reporter said) "astonished his friends and alarmed his followers."[1] His customary good humor seemed at times to have gone sour, his good sense was constantly being swamped by waves of angry emotion. He was like an over-eager fighter trying for a first-round knockout, throwing wild punches which often missed his opponent and left the attacker floundering off-balance.

His first major speech was scheduled for September 16 in Coffeyville, Kansas, scene of his brief but triumphant career as a teacher of high school history. But this was to be preceded by a barnstorming tour through Illinois and Missouri, beginning in Chicago on September 13. His day in that vast, variegated, raucous, and anarchic Midwest metropolis was in some ways an apt beginning for the epic campaign that was to come.

From the moment when he arrived at the Union Station at 8:30 a.m. (exactly on schedule), his managers and advisers were faced with what was to prove in many ways their hardest problem—how to stretch a program in which every moment was already planned for, to include the impromptu speeches, and the extensions of scheduled speeches, that the candidate could not be restrained from making. More than a thousand people met him at the station, and he made an unplanned speech to them. He spoke again to "three or four thousand" persons at the Union Stockyards; to "friendly throngs" at the Western Electric plant in Cicero; to 5,000 listeners at the Carnegie-Illinois Steel Company plant in South Chicago; and again at the American Giants Baseball Park on the South Side (the color line in organized baseball had not yet been broken), where "nearly 15,000 Negroes listened with interest and attention." These were the four talks that had been planned; but in between he had given "half a dozen" others and "was so hoarse that he could hardly speak."[2]

The generally cordial reception that he was given spurred him on.

"They said I couldn't come into a section of Chicago like this," he told the Stockyards workers with his customary bluntness, "but you see me here. I have worked as hard as any guy in the crowd. I can do as much work as any damn one of you. I call on you to join me in this great crusade to build a great, strong, free America."[3]

If this group of hearers, and others like them, were not ready to join a crusade against the New Deal, they still responded to Willkie with at least as much warmth as a Republican candidate could reasonably expect—if not a good deal more. And when he toured the financial and shopping districts in the Loop, the wildly cheering crowds that jammed the streets and leaned perilously from skyscraper windows must momentarily have lifted the spirits of his least optimistic adherents.

No doubt this friendly and festive atmosphere stimulated the off-guard attitude that led him into one of the most celebrated of his campaign statements. Beginning his speech at the Western Electric plant he revealed by some casual reference to Chicago his unawareness that he was now in the suburb of Cicero. This is the sort of error that every campaigner makes and is expected to make, and when nudged by the local chairman and reminded of where he is, he simply apologizes, makes a joke if he can think of one, and hastens to begin his speech. But Willkie's response (to a shouted correction from the crowd) has deservedly become a classic. "O. K.," he remarked with amiable good fellowship, "to hell with Chicago."[4]

It is not likely that this slip, despite its noisy echoes, lost him many votes. Another appeal, on impulse, to the prejudice of his Cicero audience, if it had been as widely reported, might have hurt him more: "I doubt if there's a Harvard or Groton boy in the bunch!"[5] This implied not only a kind of inverted snobbishness but a simple-minded ignorance of the fact that it was he and not Roosevelt who had the support of the vast majority of Harvard and Groton graduates. And he spoke again in the same spirit on the following day, with reference to Democratic nonchalance about the national debt: "I never made any pretense of being any remarkable fellow, but I do now the rules of addition. I learned them in an Indiana public school. My talk over the radio is unpolished, but I can tell spinach any time I see it."[6]

Such out-of-character comments can only be explained by the intensity of his resentment against the unscrupulous attacks of his opponents. To the same resentment, together with pressure from the Old Guard, must be ascribed his comments on American foreign policy. It is commonly said that only in the final furious days of the campaign did he lower himself to lay hold of the propaganda line that Roosevelt was leading the country into war. The painful fact has to be recorded that from the beginning of his active campaign, abandoning the honesty of his acceptance speech, he aped the extravagance of the isolationists: "if you elect me President . . . no American boys will be sent to the shambles of the European trenches. I will make this country so strong economically, I will build a defense program so great, I will teach the doctrine of national unity so much, that no dictator will dare to strike or touch this great free land of ours."[7]

For this blatant appeal to fear and vanity no defense is possible. Willkie knew, and had said in his acceptance speech, that "no man can promise to maintain peace. Peace is not something that a nation can achieve by itself." In another candidate, it is true, such an abandonment of principle might be excused as a reflection of the accepted ethics of Presidential campaigns. But the speaker here was Wendell Willkie—who had won the nomination precisely because he had convinced the American people that he could be trusted when he said, "I will not compromise my principles."

For the rest, during his Chicago visit he hammered at such safe and sound themes as the corruption of the Kelly-Nash machine which then controlled Chicago and of Democratic bosses in general; the ability of the Republicans to bring about industrial recovery; and (to his Negro audiences) a promise of equal rights for all: "I say to you that during my administration there will be no discrimination between people because of race, creed or color in appointments to federal positions."[8]

At the end of the day Senator Brooks (whom Willkie had warmly endorsed for reelection despite his isolationist record) estimated that the candidate had been seen by nearly a million people.[9]

But the second day was a disaster. In his first speech, at Joliet (which was followed by others at Morris, Ottawa, La Salle, Peoria, Galesburg, and Rock Island), he made the sensational charge, in attacking Administration foreign policy, that Roosevelt "telephoned Mussolini and Hitler and urged them to sell Czechoslovakia down the river at Munich."[10] It was evident to everybody that the charge, as worded, could not be sustained, and his press secretary, Lem Jones, immediately issued a statement admitting that Willkie had "misspoken" and restating the charge as he had intended to make it. The candidate restated it himself at Peoria, and if the wording was changed, the substance and spirit were not softened. "At Munich—you remember when they sold Czechoslovakia down the river, the first nation that was taken over by this heinous Hitler [Austria had of course been the first]—what was Franklin Roosevelt doing? Was he standing up, fighting for democracy? Oh, no, he was telephoning Hitler and Mussolini and Chamberlain, urging them to Munich, where they sacrificed Czechoslovakia. Why, the most presumptuous statement ever made by man is that this fellow has helped to preserve democracy throughout the world. . . . I say to you, and I say it to you deliberately, and not as if in the heat of a political campaign: 'Of all the men I know who have any acquaintanceship with international affairs, Franklin Roosevelt is the least qualified to lead the country through this crisis period.'"[11]

And while indicting Roosevelt as an appeaser in the past, he did not drop the charge that he was a warmonger in the present. In another speech, protesting his own sincerity in promising to keep the country at peace, he added, "If you elect my opponent, you will have no such guarantee. Please, please, without regard to me, do not vote to send American boys to the shambles of a European war."[12]

These words—and several thousand others—were delivered in a rasping voice that did nothing to temper their harshness and that from time to time threatened to give out altogether. Some of his friends might have been forgiven if they had hoped, at this point, that it would.

Yet the charge concerning Czechoslovakia was not made casually, nor did it involve a surrender of principle. It expressed—in extreme terms, to be sure—one of Willkie's basic criticisms of the Roosevelt administration, namely, the isolationist trend of its early years. Yet at first glance there seems no reason to have made it an issue, since Roosevelt's present foreign policy was in general one that Willkie approved of; and it certainly would not make more plausible Willkie's pretended fear of a desire by the President to lead America into the war.

The reason lay in the Democrats' resolve to make a major campaign issue out of the isolationist record of the Republicans. Willkie himself could hardly be labeled an isolationist or appeaser, but the charge *could* be made against the party of which he was the candidate. To this he had to make some answer; and since he could not deny (although he consistently minimized) the fact that his party *had* been isolationist, and since he considered that the best defense was a good offense, he retorted that the record showed, if one looked back only a little way, that it was not he nor any other Republican who had led the trend toward isolation, but Franklin Roosevelt himself.

Probably Willkie in his own thinking went back to the Democratic National Convention of 1924. But his public indictment, outlined in his San Francisco speech on September 21, began with the London Economic Conference of 1933, which met in May of that year, as a result of Roosevelt's urging, to work out a plan for stabilizing the currencies of the important nations of the world as a prerequisite for the revival of international trade. But after two months, and after various specific proposals had been watered down, because of Washington opposition, to what was not much more than a pious hope, Roosevelt publicly condemned even this as showing "a singular lack of proportion and a failure to remember the larger purposes for which the Economic Conference was originally called together."[13]

What had happened was that in a characteristic reversal of policy (which he characteristically never admitted) Roosevelt had abandoned the idea of international economic cooperation in favor of a managed economy at home. Willkie went on to argue that this action had delayed economic recovery in Europe and throughout the world, and that the continuance of the depression had aided the Nazi revolution, while keeping the democracies weak and divided. Furthermore, regardless of formal agreements, the economic condition of the world was partially dependent on that of the United States; and Roosevelt's domestic policies, by postponing recovery at home, had contributed to the chaos abroad. Finally, Roosevelt's 1937 attack on the Supreme Court, unhinted at during the 1936 campaign, had disunited the American people and distracted their attention from the ominous events in Europe; and "the very next year was the year of Munich."[14]

Nobody will ever know how far this line of argument is valid—although it found strong support in a speech by Winston Churchill only three years before.[15] On the other hand, there was another item in the Roosevelt record on foreign policy of which Willkie might have made more than he did—the President's approval of the Neutrality Act of 1935. The "Nye Committee," which was supposedly investigating the munitions industry, had convinced the American people that the primary cause of modern war is the greed of munitions-makers; and events since 1918 seemed to prove that the results of war, whatever its causes, were wholly evil. The conclusion was that it was both possible and right for the United States to avoid involvement in "Europe's wars." To achieve this end, Congress passed a law which renounced America's traditional claim to freedom of the seas and drastically curtailed both commercial and individual contacts with belligerent nations. It resolutely refused to make any distinction between aggressor and victim.

This triumph of cynicism, stupidity, and cowardice over common sense and common decency was heartily approved by Roosevelt and the American people. It encouraged Mussolini in the invasion of Ethiopia which he had undertaken; it helped make possible the triumph of Franco and Fascism over democracy in Spain; it convinced Hitler that America would never oppose his purposed conquests until her own soil was attacked.

By the time of Munich, Roosevelt and some other Americans were coming to their senses. But the country as a whole was still immovably mired in isolationism; and its military unpreparedness was appalling. All the President could do was indulge in exhortations; and in one of the latter, addressed to Hitler, he had to admit: "The government of the United States has no involvement in Europe and will assume no obligations in the conduct of the present negotiations."[16] One may feel that if the American government was able to do nothing but talk, it would have done better to keep silent. But Roosevelt must have thought that even Hitler would be to some degree sensitive to American opinion, and that any act which might tilt the balance toward peace ought not to be foregone.

Nevertheless, the Munich agreement *was* a sellout—and Roosevelt approved. That he temporarily shared Chamberlain's delusive hope of peace is shown by the testimony of Lord Halifax, to whom Roosevelt confided that immediately after the Munich agreement he had sent the Prime Minister "the shortest telegram I ever sent, two words: 'Good man.'"[17]

So Willkie was right. And what gave his charges a solid moral basis, even then, was the fact that at the time of Munich, Roosevelt neither repudiated his admirers' claims that he should share the credit for preserving peace nor accepted any responsibility for the terms on which peace had been bought. Secretary Hull stated on September 30, 1938: "As to immediate peace results, it is unnecessary to say that they afford a universal sense of relief. I am not undertaking to pass upon the merits of the differences to which the Four-Power Pact signed at Munich yesterday related."[18] And a month later, when the bargain did not look so good, Anne O'Hare McCormick wrote: "In Washington those who deplore the 'surrender' continue to acclaim proudly the role played by the President."[19]

But all this, two years later, was past and forgotten. The President had since become, more than anyone else but Churchill, a symbol of resistance to aggression. That charges, however just, of past isolationist tendencies could now alienate his internationalist supporters was a notion not less than fantastic. Nevertheless Willkie held to it and continued to press the issue despite his initial ill success.[20] Votes or no votes, he would not have it said without rebuttal that Roosevelt was a better internationalist than he.

2

With the campaign two days old, one thing was clear to friends and enemies: it *was* a crusade, and Willkie was leading it. No Republican since Theodore Roosevelt—no Republican *but* Theodore Roosevelt, in fact, and he only under the Progressive banner—had hurled himself with such ebullience into a Presidential campaign. He was acting on the principle that he had stated in "We the People": "the American people give their vote to *men*." Add to this the breach between him and the party leaders, and the campaign was bound to be a one-man show.

At any rate, it was a good show. The stage was the whole country (except the South, where he had originally intended to campaign,[21] but did not) and the audience was the whole people. At the center, producing the illusion that it was fixed, while the whole theater revolved about it, was the campaign train. Long before the election, it had become a legend.

The legend is one of disorder verging on anarchy. Raymond Clapper, no unfriendly critic, wrote on September 20: "Seldom has there been more chaos in a Presidential campaign. Congressional cloakrooms echo with stories of confusion, hurt feelings, unanswered telegrams and letters, crossed wires and general disorganization. . . . the Willkie train . . . seems to operate with all the confusion of an amateur road show."[22] To a certain extent, it *was* an amateur road show. And Clapper was summarizing the opinion of Congressmen and correspondents, whereas amateur shows play to unsophisticated audiences, and plain folk may applaud what would be mercilessly panned by Broadway critics. Willkie was thinking solely of his audience; theirs was the only verdict that counted.

Though overshadowed by the star, the cast, as well as the helpers behind the scenes, deserve more than passing comment. First, there was the candidate's wife, tiny and trim beside his rumpled bulk, always cheerful, always gracious (after the one rebellion at Colorado Springs against the loss of privacy, when she frustrated a corps of waiting photographers by washing her hair),[23] always wearing a smile that never grew fixed or artificial, thinking her own thoughts but letting her husband do the talking, summoning a sense of humor to give immunity against rare affronts—as when a woman in an endless line of handshakers at some reception paused, looked her up and down with critical deliberation, and observed, "Well, it don't take much looks to beat Eleanor, does it?"[24]

Equally indispensable, though somewhat less in the public eye, was Willkie's younger brother, Edward, who had agreed to the tentative request made by his brother in May. Even bigger, physically, than Wendell, equally genial but more even tempered, an admirer of his brother but a typical Willkie in his independence and outspokenness, he stood guard outside Wendell's quarters and amiably fended off the visitors who could not be permitted to trespass on the candidate's desperately overcrowded hours. "I wasn't so easy to brush off," he remembered with a grin, "because I stood in the aisle."[25] In addition, he was one of the few people who could exercise a real restraining influence on his brother.

The older brothers, Bob and Fred, were also on the train for brief periods. It was difficult for a Willkie to keep out of any contest when there was an excuse to become involved; but in recent years they had been less close to Wendell than had Edward, and there were also fears that the Democrats might try to capitalize on their connection with the liquor industry. (Both had positions with Seagram's.) Bob, however, was able to make one contribution: when the laundry got lost, he was able to lend Wendell a set of underwear. Fred had made a similar offer, but Wendell replied, "I'll be damned if I'll put on silk underwear."[26] Also on the train for extended periods was the candidate's son, Philip, an alert and engaging young man (from Princeton, not Harvard), enjoying the excitement but shunning the limelight.

Willkie's press secretary was a young ex-newspaperman named Lamoyne A. Jones, universally called Lem, who had until two months earlier held a similar position with Dewey. Willkie at first dealt directly and informally with the press, answering any question put to him at any time by any reporter. Since the latter was under no obligation to share the answer until it was in his paper's headlines, bitterness intensified until the whole corps of newsmen rebelled and demanded that he hire an experienced man to handle all releases to the press. Agreeing, Willkie told them to pick their own man. They picked Jones, and Dewey generously advised him to accept what looked like a definite step upward.

But when he arrived at Colorado Springs, got a brusque welcome from Willkie, and saw the appalling conditions that he was expected to correct, he almost quit. Typical was the treatment of correspondence. Cartons were stacked about full of unopened letters, which nobody could think of anything better to do with than distribute to the Willkie Clubs for answers; with the result that some notable public figure, making an offer of personal support, would get back a form letter advising him to contact his local Willkie Club. The next day, however, Jones flew to Cheyenne with Willkie and had a chance to talk with him. Willkie's intense convictions and forthright speech won him completely: "I had never met anybody like him." From then on, until he stood beside his friend's hospital bed and watched him die, he was Willkie's man.[27]

Another friend whose loyalty never wavered was Harold Gallagher, a member of the New York law firm which Willkie later joined. His was the difficult task of routing the train and keeping it on schedule, and despite innumerable pressures, he was generally successful; except for a few occasions when the railroad was responsible, the train stayed approximately on time.[28] It was he, also, who knew how many extra passengers the train could accommodate at a given time and, together with Hamilton, sent that number of tickets to the party chairmen of he states along the route, who had the responsibility for distributing these tickets to local Republicans. Candidates for minor offices rode between stops; candidates for state-wide office rode all the way across the state. As far as Willkie and his staff were concerned, no favoritism was shown.[29] Some of the guests were probably hurt because they did not get to see and talk with Willkie personally; but the pace and pressure of the campaign simply made such situations inevitable.[30]

The person on whom Willkie leaned most heavily in discussing policy and preparing speeches was Russell Davenport. At their first meeting they had found themselves speaking the same language. It was Davenport who had opened to him the pages of *Fortune* on which to spread the challenge of "We the People"; Davenport who had then resigned his job to help win the nomination, when the Willkie boom had been only a cloud the size of a man's hand on the political horizon. If his favored position was resented by the "regulars," that was their hard luck. With Davenport was his wife Marcia, the novelist and biographer of Mozart.

To help prepare the formal speeches, Willkie (who by now had recognized the impossibilty of composing them all himself) had engaged Elliott V. Bell, former financial writer for the *New York Times* and later Bank Commissioner under Governor Dewey. Working with him was Pierce Butler, Jr., son of the Supreme Court Justice and a leader of Democrats for Willkie. And on the West Cost Davenport invited a young lawyer with liberal views, Bartley Crum, to join the team. The usual procedure was for Davenport to discuss a speech with Willkie and take notes, then talk it over with Bell, Butler, Crum, and sometimes John Hollister, and then produce a speech and submit it to Willkie for approval. On the whole, the team worked in harmony, and ended the campaign on friendly terms.[31]

The research staff numbered twenty persons, who had one car to themselves, and whose filing cases "overflowed from their compartments onto the platform between cars."[32] Willkie's steady campaigning, during which the intended number of "major" speeches was constantly raised, kept them digging up material at a furious rate; and their task was complicated by the fact that, despite the filing cases, much research had to be done in New York. How lavish Willkie was in the use of material is shown in James A. Hagerty's recollection of a day when he gave three speeches (in Dubuque, Iowa, Freeport, Illinois, and Madison, Wisconsin) any one of which "would have furnished a satisfactory lead for the newspaper story of his campaign on that day. No other Presidential candidate that I have known—and I have covered three others—would have made three good speeches of entirely different character in one day."[33]

Representing the "regular" Republican organization among Willkie's advisers were John B. Hollister, a former Congressman who was now the law partner of Senator Taft, and Representative Charles Halleck of Indiana, who had made the nominating speech at Philadelphia. This representation was felt by some party leaders to be inadequate, and there were rumors of resentment.[34] Possibly some Republicans also resented the presence of Butler; and they certainly resented the presence of Root, who was on and off the train throughout its travels.

A less controversial figure was Walter O'Keefe, popular radio entertainer, who was chairman of the "entertainment division" of the Republican campaign and also worked diligently to improve Willkie's speaking technique, especially when addressing a radio audience. He had the good sense not to aim at any essential change but in small ways he made Willkie's delivery smoother and more effective.[35] One reporter commented that "he stopped shouting at folks on the far edge of the crowd and began to pitch his voice in conversational tone into the microphone."[36] And another declared: "To have heard him at Elwood and then at San Francisco was to have wondered if he could have been the same man."[37]

It was also O'Keefe who, when Willkie's voice deserted him, first called two specialists from Chicago and then engaged the permanent services of a Hollywood throat specialist, Dr. Harold Barnard,[38] who was flown to Kansas City by Robert Montgomery, and who kept the candidate's voice more or less in working order during the seven weeks of campaigning that remained.

Not the least spectacular group in this tumultuous cavalcade was the reporters. No previous candidate had been so assiduously covered. The radio, newsreel, and newspapermen who were permanently assigned to the train totalled seventy-five[39] and some of Willkie's friends thought that they created much of the impression of disorder that they so zestfully described.[40] Busy as the candidate kept them, there was still time for talking and drinking—in which Willkie himself, ever restless and seemingly never wearied even at the end of a day of incessant speechmaking, would often join them, speaking as freely as ever. And though some were politically hostile, most of them seem to have liked him and respected him personally. One of them, James L. Wright of the Buffalo *Evening News,* wrote to him four years later, after his defeat in the Wisconsin primary: "The fellows who travelled with you throughout the campaign four years ago are very fond of you. . . .

"Fred Pasley was just in the office and we were talking about the friendships that developed on your trip and the unusual steps newspapermen took in guarding you against unfortunate publicity. Some of those you knew nothing about. For instance, I remember that night in Salt Lake City after we had returned from the rodeo in Ogden when you told us of your plan to spring on President Roosevelt your challenge to a series of debates. . . . You did not ask the newspapermen not to print it but they knew that they shouldn't, and no one leaked. As a matter of fact, after we left your suite that night we stood at the elevator and pledged ourselves against any disclosure. The secret was kept inviolate."[41]

The Presidential campaign train is now a thing of the past, exiled by the jet plane from the world of fact to the realm of legend. With it has vanished the most vivid symbol of the democratic process as it is manifest in a national election in the United States; the noise, the confusion, the enthusiasm, the frequent frustration, the infrequent exaltation, the unremitting pressure, the sense of involvement in a common cause. And this symbol has never been presented to the nation in such perfection as it was in the campaign train that carried Wendell Willkie in 1940.

3

At Rock Island on Saturday afternoon Willkie's vocal cords gave out, and he could only whisper to the crowd, "The spirit is willing, but the voice is weak."[42] Two other scheduled rear-platform talks were called off entirely.

Fortunately, the next day was Sunday, and his practice of not campaigning on that day, together with pressure from Dr. Barnard, his brother Edward, and others, made it possible for his throat to get a rest. The next morning, in fact, his voice was so near normal that at the first stop on the way to Coffeyville, at a place called Pleasant Hill, he again held forth at greater length than had been planned, and "was given another talking-to on the way to his next stop," where, obeying orders, he spoke "less than a minute."[43]

His speech at Pleasant Hill showed him as confident as ever: "I took a little rest over the weekend, and I have never felt better in my life. If any of you people have a couple of wildcats that you would like to have finished off, please send them up immediately." But the tone of such utterances was now more relaxed and less aggressive than on the first two days. "I want you to look me over and see what kind of a fellow I am . . . whether you can entrust [sic] me to run the affairs of the government."[44] Even the joke about recognizing spinach sounded more amiable, and his disclaimers of personal distinction now made the proper point: that nobody—neither he *nor* Roosevelt—was the "indispensable man."

Monday afternoon he was in Coffeyville, where the Elwood drama was reenacted on a smaller scale, moving old inhabitants to comparisons with the day, ten years before Willkie was born, "when the Dalton gang raided a Coffeyville bank and four robbers and four residents were killed."[45] This time, however, there was no anticlimax; Willkie was not trying, as in the acceptance speech, to do the impossible, under impossible conditions. Here, moreover, in contrast to Chicago, he felt himself to be among friends; and he won his audience by a felicitous tribute to Coffeyville's most famous son, the great baseball pitcher Walter Johnson, who introduced him.

The speech itself was a comprehensive indictment of the Roosevelt administration, not marred by any suggestion of personal rancor. Willkie charged the President with paternalism on the one hand and incompetence on the other; with being simultaneously desirous of power and incapable of using it effectively; with not being frank with the people in regard to either foreign or domestic policy and with muddling both. "The charge

I make against Franklin Roosevelt is that he . . . has lost faith in the American people," "offering us the gold brick of safety without sacrifice." Apostrophizing "that vast, mistaken, deluded government of ours in Washington," Willkie pleaded: "Give our country back to us. It belongs to us. We want it. We love it and are not cynical about it. . . . We should like if necessary to suffer for it, so that we may pass it on intact to other generations."[46]

Only once did the speaker try to stir irrational fears: "I warn you . . . if . . . you return this Administration to office, you will be serving under an American totalitarian government before the long third term is finished."[47] This was nonsense and Willkie knew it.

Almost before the applause had ended, the train was on its way to Tulsa, Oklahoma, where another great crowd heard him invoke the great Democratic names in American history, claim to be their legitimate heir, and assert his inability to understand why any real Democrat should hesitate to support him. He was still hoping to split the opposing party.

The high hopes raised by the size and enthusiasm of the Tulsa audience received a blow the next day at Amarillo, Texas, where only 3,000 took the trouble to hear him attack the third term and Democratic bossism. But at Albuquerque, New Mexico, there were 15,000, to whom he expressed not merely a desire for a partisan victory but also a passion for national unity: "I hope I win. If I lose, you will find me upholding the hands of the government in this critical time."[48] But at Phoenix, Arizona, on Wednesday he descended to the most blatant sort of appeal to the narrow self-interest of a cattle-raising region, reviving a picayune controversy over the purchase by the Navy of a small amount of Argentine beef. He proclaimed, referring to the rehabilitation of the American economy, "I can tell you one way. Have the American Navy eat American beef instead of Argentine beef."[49]

In San Diego, before a crowd of 30,000, Willkie was again guilty of inconsistency when he praised California's Senator Hiram Johnson as a "true liberal" (glancing at the "liberalism" of Roosevelt). For Johnson, undoubtedly the most admired public figure in the state, was in his views on domestic problems a liberal in much the same sense as Roosevelt, while in regard to foreign policy he was among the most irreconcilable of isolationists. But this was only another instance of the fantastic pattern of Republican disunity by which the candidate was constantly plagued. His choice in California was between Johnson and Hoover, who was conservative as well as isolationist. In the end, he got the grudging support of the aging Senator—who in his turn had a hard decison to make.[50]

Nobody knows how many votes Willkie won or lost by these gyrations and maneuverings. Nor can one estimate with any accuracy the effect on the voters of the sheer physical drama of such a campaign as his. Marquis Childs considered it "evident" that "crowds and crowd reaction . . . meant little."[51] But for Childs himself, and for some others on the campaign train, it was a memorable if sometimes harrowing experience—a mingling of melodrama and comedy, of epic scope and sometimes lyric intensity, which he strove to capture in his descriptions: of the packed stadium at Tulsa, under a full moon; of the departure by air from Albuquerque at dawn, when "everyone, even, amazingly, Willkie, was in a subdued mood";[52] of Willkie talking to a gay crowd in Fresno, while migrant workers in ragged clothes lay about on the grass, apparently oblivious; of the girl in Missoula who came up to Childs and looked him in the eye with "something of candor, something of contempt: 'You can go on wearing that if you want to,' her eyes on the official Willkie badge on my lapel, 'but it isn't going to do you any good.'"[53]

It is possible that the greatest effect was on Willkie himself. He "said at the end of his Western tour that he saw the light of a spiritual hunger in the thousands of faces turned up to him."[54] He can hardly have supposed that this hunger would be satisfied merely by the election of a Republican President. "The American people . . . put their trust in *men*." That so many of them, lost and bewildered, seemed ready to put their trust in *him* was not in his eyes an invitation to use them for his own purposes but the drawing up of a contract obligating him to serve their interests—and the interest of the rest of the people as well. As president of Commonwealth & Southern, he told his hearers, "I never forgot to fight for and protect the interests of those who were paying me. When I am President of the United States, I'll fight for and protect your interests."[55]

Perhaps it is in this sense of nearness to so many of his fellow citizens and the resulting sense of responsibility to all of them, born during the crescendo of popular enthusiasm at Philadelphia and brought to maturity (though not always kept in sight) during the prolonged intensity of the campaign, that we may find one answer to what for many persons is the central mystery of Willkie's life: why, after so many years as a leader, however popular and enlightened, of one segment only of the national life, he should be transformed so swiftly into a citizen of the world, a crusader for human rights, a seeker for intangible goals, a fighter for just but lost causes. And this sense of kinship with common men and women, this kind of intuitive and exalted democracy, struggling into view through all the grime and glamour of the fight for votes, was one of the things that gave effect to Willkie's campaigning.

He had left Chicago on Saturday morning; on Wednesday evening he was in San Diego, his energy undiminished, his spirits as high as ever. A man in the crowd shouted "Roosevelt!" and Willkie shot back, "There you are, one man in a hundred thousand!"[56] Thursday morning he headed for Los Angeles by automobile, stopping on the way to tour the great North American and Douglas airplane factories, where an unbudgeted hour of asking questions about production put him behind schedule, despite cancellation of one part of the announced program. This was a ceremony to mark the start of production by North American of an advanced type of training plane—a ceremony planned by the Company, at whose request Willkie had included it as part of his campaign. His own words in a letter a year and a half later tell the story. "When I arrived at the plant, the President of the Company, who had invited me, had been called to Washington for conference with Mr. Knudsen and, although there were airplanes scattered all over the yard, there was not a single plane that could be christened. . . . Within two weeks the North American Company received a large contract for the manufacture of several million dollars of planes for the Federal Government."[57] (The letter continued: "As you know, it is the religion of my life to save the enterprise system. One of my fears has always been that cowardice and self-seeking of some of the representatives of the enterprise system may make it impossible for anybody to do so.")

But he gave his speech anyway, and if the presence of company officials was forbidden by the White House, it was, after all, the presence of the workers that counted. The main thing was for the candidate to be seen, and everywhere crowds were waiting for him, growing larger as he neared Los Angeles. In the downtown section the streets were packed solid and the crowd out of control. He had been scheduled to pose with the Mayor on the steps of City Hall and say a few words, but "he never got within fifty feet" of the Mayor or the microphone.[58]

His major address in the evening was made part of a super-colossal spectacle in true Hollywood style, and drew a crowd estimated at 75,000, who were given a generally sober analysis of New Deal economics—the same analysis that Willkie had given many times before. One new feature, however, was a proposal for a study of the whole problem of taxation by a committee composed of "government officials, members of both Houses of Congress, businessmen, representatives of labor, and tax experts."[59] But again he cheapened his speech with "campaign oratory" calculated to inflame the fear of war. Recalling the Democrats' 1932 campaign promise "to reduce the cost of government 25 per cent," and the President's recent promise (in his speech to the Teamsters' Union) to carry out the 1940 Democratic platform pledge "that America would fight in no European war," he added, "I hope and I pray that he remembers the pledge of the 1940 platform better than he did the one of 1932. If he does not, you better get ready to get on the transports."[60]

On Friday the campaign train moved up the Central Valley to Sacramento, and Willkie spoke at Bakersfield, Tulare, Fresno, Madera, Merced, Modesto, and Stockton, to crowds ranging in size from six to ten thousand. He again praised Johnson as a "fighting liberal," tried to take the curse off his utilities connections by promising to complete the great Central Valley power and irrigation project, turned heckling to laughter by a cheerful retort to "you Democrats," jibed at Roosevelt's "non-political" speeches (he was making one that day at the University of Pennsylvania), and when a man at Tulare called out, "I want a job," again showed himself to be swift on the uptake: "You're just like 9,600,000 others in the United States. They are crying for jobs, and there is no reason why we can't stimulate the domestic economy of the country to such an extent that it will provide jobs for all."[61]

The San Francisco speech, to another huge and partisan audience, was an attack on Roosevelt's foreign policies during the thirties, repeating and elaborating in more measured terms the charges made at Peoria a week before. And, with London reeling under the second successive week of Nazi bombings, he urged continued "aid to Britain, our first line of defense and our only remaining friend," "to the limits of prudence and effectiveness, as determined by impartial experts in the field." (Where the impartial experts could be found, he did not say.) He also called for "economic aid" to China, "the acquisition and development of Pacific air bases," and American leadership in reconstructing the postwar world. "We must work for a higher standard of living not only here in America but in other countries as well."[62]

On Sunday he crossed Oregon, greeting the people who assembled to see him (when he got to Portland there were ten thousand at the station and five thousand at his hotel), but making only brief and nonpolitical speeches. (He was again troubled by hoarseness.) To newsmen he declared himself "pleased at the size of the crowds" during the past ten days "and their willingness to listen to him."[63]

On Monday he was back on the firing line. In Portland he derided the Democrats' charge that he was opposed to government development of hydroelectric power: their "line of argument is that Wendell Willkie will presumably go out with a spade and dig up Bonneville and Grand Coulee." But on the crucial question of distribution, he hedged, proposing that the people of any particular region should decide whether the facilities should be publicly or privately owned.[64]

In Seattle, in a major speech, he made his first serious attempt to break the Democratic hold on the votes of labor. Some Republicans may have thought that he was hedging again when he endorsed, as he had done at Elwood, the social goals of the New Deal, including "minimum guarantees" to labor. But the issue for him was not the ends but the means. Social benefits have to be paid for somehow, he argued, and the only permanent solution is the creation of more jobs in productive, profit-seeking business ventures. But this solution had not been sought. "The New Deal candidate does not believe there are any more jobs, whereas I know there are."[65]

Here was in fact the root of Willkie's quarrel with the New Deal, of which the central principle (if one can make *any* general statement about that vague, varied, ever-shifting blend of theory, expediency, and sentiment) was that some sort of managed economy is the only alternative to the endlessly recurrent cycle of boom and bust that results from making the profit motive paramount, and that such economic expansion as might be possible must be planned, initiated, and guided by the government. But the argument against this theory was hard to state in simple terms, and still harder to make attractive to men whose last memory of a Republican administration was three years of apparent paralysis while the depression deepened; and to whom Roosevelt was a symbol not only of relief from physical destitution but of the recognition of workers as human beings. On the other hand, by accepting New Deal aims and admitting past abuses on the part of business, Willkie was bound to alienate the many Republican reactionaries to whom any government regulation of wages and profits was "creeping socialism."

Again, as in regard to foreign affairs, Willkie was faced with a set of circumstances which no Republican candidate could have overcome.

But the campaign went on. Tuesday, September 24, found him crossing Montana, responding to boos and catcalls at Missoula (there was also a tomato thrown, reportedly by a ten-year-old boy) with his usual unperturbed retort that these were the only arguments that his opponents could offer; conferring at Butte with eleven labor leaders "selected by the workers to question [him] on his views on labor," and denouncing centralized government and Secretary Ickes to a crowd of fifteen or twenty thousand;[66] bidding—but without affectation—for the friendliness of ordinary folk by recalling, at Miles City, that thirty years earlier "I blew into town in a box car and almost got pinched" (word of this remark apparently preceded him to Glendive, where someone shouted, "Is this better than riding the rods?" and Willkie responded jovially, "It's a lot better!")[67] and in South Dakota "that he had once washed dishes in Aberdeen."[68]

From the Dakotas he swung south to Omaha, where he delivered his first major speech on the perennially unsolved problem of agriculture. "The problem arises out of the fact that the farm population, comprising 24 per cent of the total, gets only 12 per cent of the income." He approved the aims of Administration policy—"to remove burdensome surpluses . . . and bring agricultural products and income to parity"—and promised no change in the present program until a better could be worked out. Soil conservation, commodity loans, rural electrification, "an adequate system of farm credit," crop insurance—all these New Deal measures he heartily approved. In addition, he urged an attack on the problem of distribution, by seeking lower transportation costs and encouraging cooperative marketing. But the real solution, once more, lay in an expanding national economy: the removal of unemployment, the discovery of new uses for agricultural products, the development of export markets through international trade. And instead of appealing to the selfish interests of each class—as he charged the Administration with doing—he would "convene a White House conference of all our great groups—farm, factory, labor and consumer"—to devise a united attack on evils that affected all.[69]

The next evening in Madison, Wisconsin, still the center of Midwestern political insurgency, he faced a strongly anti-Republican audience, including a large number of irreverent university students, who, as he walked across the stage, chanted "hip—hip—hip." But he won a hearing with a grin and a wave of the hand, and then shrewdly denounced the dictatorial tendencies of the New Deal: the "court-packing" plan, the attempted "purge" of conservative Democrats in the 1938 primaries, the unprecedented third term candidacy.[70]

From Madison he made a swing through Iowa, and returned to Chicago fifteen days after he had left it. Into this brief space of time he had crowded some 8,000 miles of travel and a hundred-odd speeches. At the end of it the pattern of the campaign was established: the technique, the tempo, and the issues.

The over-aggressiveness had vanished, but the evangelical fervor remained; and his voice, less recklessly though still relentlessly used, did not again desert him, although it displayed varying degrees of hoarseness. He was still most persuasive when his words were least studied, and often an impromptu peroration would arouse an audience that had found little excitement in his earnest reading of a set speech. He had been right in his answer to a group of friends who at the beginning of the tour had adjured him to proceed with system and circumspection: "to put up a fence around himself, to lay down a simple and clear campaign line and stick to it, and to give up speaking without a manuscript."[71] He thanked them and agreed that the advice was good. But, he insisted, he was simply not that kind of person, and he could not change. He must say what came to him, trusting himself always to be sincere. Moreover, Willkie's plan was to be seen and heard in person by as many people as possible; and this simply precluded the meticulous preparation, with the weighing of every phrase and intonation for their possible effect on a nation-wide radio audience, that marked the campaign utterances of President Roosevelt.[72]

The main lines of attack on the Administration had also been laid down: in Coffeyville, that it had lost touch with, and trust in, the people, and had become paternalistic in principle and cynical in practice; in Los Angeles, that it had adopted a defeatist economic philosophy, seeking to share what wealth existed in a static economy instead of allowing free enterprise to create an expanding economy that would bring greater wealth to all; in San Francisco, that its foreign policy, isolationist during the mid-thirties, opportunist then and later, had contributed to the coming of war; in Seattle, that it had promised the workers social gains that could be paid for, once more, only by an expanding economy based on recognition of the profit motive; in Omaha, that the aims of its agricultural policy were commendable but the administration often partisan and inefficient. And over and over he charged the New Deal with being allied with old and corrupt political machines; he attacked the third term attempt as evidence of a lust for power that might well lead to dictatorship; and he challenged the good faith of the President's promise to keep the country out of war.

No doubt many Democrats were angry and many Republicans disgruntled at Willkie's campaign; its success could not be judged until November; but it provided a superlative center ring for the Greatest Show on Earth—an American Presidential election.[73]

XIII

Election Campaign: Crescendo and Conclusion

1

Strenuous as the two weeks Western trip had been, it was as nothing compared to the five weeks that followed, during which Willkie fought for the populous states from the Midwest to the East Coast, where almost half the electoral votes were in the balance.

From Chicago, without a pause, the campaign train headed East, where Willkie was scheduled to address the New York State Republican Convention at the Empire Race Track in Yonkers on Saturday evening, September 28. When he had finished his wide-ranging attack on the New Deal (coupled with the positive note that he was to sound so often during the next four years: "The time has come when the government must cease giving to the people. The time has come for the people to give to the government"), his 45,000 hearers refused to let him go until he had twice returned to the microphone to acknowledge and intensify their riotous enthusiasm.[1] (They might have been less enthusiastic had they seen Willkie several hours later, in Sam Pryor's apartment, strenuously arguing John L. Lewis into promising support.[2])

Monday morning found him back in the Midwest, speaking in South Bend, before crossing the Michigan line and proceeding by way of Niles, Kalamazoo, Jackson, Ann Arbor and Wyandotte to Detroit, where he addressed 12,000 members of the National Federation of Women's Republican Clubs; characteristically mingling satire ("What I want to know," he jibed at the threadbare argument about changing horses in midstream, "is how we got in the middle of the stream") with exhortation ("Democracy has given you the fullest, freest lives of any women in history. . . . Now the time comes for you to give to democracy").[3] Earlier in the day he had asked whether his audience thought Britain made a mistake in exchanging Chamberlain for Churchill; and told them, in demanding a single head of defense production, "Why, you couldn't even run a church social with a committee without a chairman!"[4]

In Michigan's industrial centers the vigor of his campaigning brought fully into the open, for the first time, the intense partisanship of labor. Memories of the famous "sit-down strikes" by the automobile workers, and of Republican opposition to the National Labor Relations Act, flared into violence unmatched in any Presidential campaign in recent generations. The candidate's impromptu speeches in Detroit were interrupted by boos, and fruit was thrown at him in the streets; in Pontiac the next day he and his wife were bombarded with eggs, and for the only time in the campaign he publicly lost his temper. Readers across the country were treated to a picture of his face, dripping egg and contorted with fury, as he lunged in the direction of his assailant. But later, when the Pontiac City Commission sent him a formal apology, he replied that he had "nothing but the friendliest feelings for Pontiac and the people of Pontiac"; and on hearing a rumor (false, as it turned out) that a boy had been expelled from high school for the egg-throwing, he wired the superintendent: "I hope you can in your judgment lighten the punishment. He was probably more misled than offending."[5]

Despite such episodes, he still felt that if he could get his opponents to listen, he could win them over. In Flint and Lansing he sought out worker audiences, paid them the compliment of an attack on people with "minds closed to reason," and then reasoned from the premise of continuing unemployment to the conclusion that only a revival of private enterprise could give jobs to all. And again in Toledo, after speeches at Grand Rapids (where a stone was hurled through the window of the dining car as the train was leaving) and Adrian, he toured the factory section, undaunted by the sullen or angry faces and voices that he everywhere encountered.

In Cleveland, however (after talks at Sandusky, Oak Harbor and Elyria), he could take heart, for his ovation "exceeded any previously received,"[6] and 20,000 partisans packed the auditorium. They heard a scathing indictment of the Administration record on defense: "The defense job that lies ahead of us is appalling . . . We are terribly late . . . The Administration has played politics with preparedness." Yet, despite this military weakness, "I would continue my efforts to aid the heroic British people—the only people in the world today who are fighting with their lives for liberty."[7]

From Cleveland he went back to his offensive on the labor front, traveling through the great industrial area of the Mahoning valley, pleading with workers to keep an open mind and listen to his evening speech in Pittsburgh. It was delivered—after twelve short afternoon talks in the area—to 35,000 people at Forbes Field, and consisted, like the Seattle speech, of whole-hearted endorsement of the aims, together with a sharp attack on the administration, of the Roosevelt labor policy; and a promise "to tie labor into the councils of our government"—partly by appointing as Secretary of Labor an actual labor leader. "And it won't be a woman, either," he added, drawing laughter and applause that seemed to justify his assumption of Miss Perkins' unpopularity. (Roosevelt, listening, judged this to be another Willkie blunder, where he had his joke but offended women voters.[8])

Then eastward again, with talks at Harrisburg, Coatesville, Lancaster and half a dozen places in Philadelphia before his closing speech to 25,000 persons in Shibe Park—another rousing attack on the defense record of the New Deal, which has simply "lacked the ability to get things done." From this relatively solid foundation, however, he once more took off on a flight of campaign oratory: "Not only does the hope of America and this way of life depend upon us winning, but the hope of the continuation of this way of life anywhere in the world depends upon us winning this fall."[9] Next came five speeches in Brooklyn, in which he attacked the "whispering campaign" against his German ancestry and pleaded for the preservation of civil liberties. The latter topic was again his theme, after the Sunday respite, as he crossed and recrossed the grimy metropolitan area of New Jersey: Union City, Jersey City, Hoboken, Hackensack, Kearney, Paterson, and a host of smaller municipalities, ending with a night speech in Newark. Throughout the day he belabored the notoriously ruthless and corrupt rule of Mayor Hague of Jersey City, "a welcome guest at the White House." "I say that [Roosevelt] cannot represent the democracy that I stand for while he seeks to perpetuate his power through petty Hitlers right here at home"—"the greatest bunch of corruptionists and racketeers," he had said in an earlier speech that day, "that ever existed in America."[10]

And whatever he said, it was heard. People might come to cheer or to jeer, but they came. Three times he spoke to audiences of more than ten thousand people. The pattern was the same the next day when he toured Manhattan and the Bronx, seeking out the places, like the Garment District and Harlem, where the opposition was strongest, and claiming and getting a hearing.

But the dominant theme this time (though even in short speeches he tended to make forays in several directions) was the threat of war: a theme on which, despite the extravagance of earlier statements, he had never before so recklessly rung the changes. "Is there anybody here who really thinks that the President is sincerely trying to keep us out of war?" "Are there any international understandings to put us into the war that we citizens do not know about?"[11]

These ominous insinuations were projected against an ominous world background. The great night bombings of Britain were beginning, but it was clear now that she would hold out indefinitely, and the longer the war went on, the more likely it was that America would be drawn in. Nor was the recent formal adherence of Japan to the Axis a hopeful sign that the war would be confined to Europe.

Again that evening he raised the cry of "War!" in a radio program where he answered a list of questions carefully selected from the mail. "We are being edged toward war by an administration that is alike careless in speech and action."[12] And he used another question as an excuse for the charge (which was likewise neither new nor honest) that although the principle of Social Security was sound, benefits would never be paid if the present Administration stayed in office because the country would go bankrupt.

He had begun his tour of Manhattan long before noon; he left it at ten minutes past midnight to stump New England. One day was devoted to Connecticut, with appearances (in company with Governor Baldwin) at Bridgeport, Stamford, Norwalk, Waterbury, New Britain, Hartford, Westport, Fairview, Shelton, Derby, Ansonia, Naugatuck, Bristol, Middletown, Meriden, and Wallingford before his main speech at New Haven to a crowd of 40,000. The relatively unexciting subject, chosen because of the economic interests of the area, was a program for government aid to small business, which, he charged, had suffered far more from New Deal restrictions than had "big business."[13]

Next morning he began at New London and went on to Rhode Island; where with Governor Vanderbilt he received a hearty welcome at Westerly, Riverpoint, Woonsocket, Pawtucket, and Providence, as well as in Joe Martin's home district at Attleboro, Massachusetts. His main speech at Narragansett Race Track—again to a crowd estimated at 40,000—was once more shrewdly aimed at his audience. In this textile manufacturing area, he approved the provisions of the National Labor Relations Act and the Wages and Hours Law, and promised to enforce them not only in the North but in the South as well; admitted the need for tariff protection against "the unfair competition of the enslaved labor of totalitarian countries," but still placed the hope of permanent prosperity, as well as security from foreign aggression, in greater industrial productivity.[14]

He hammered away at similar themes next day in New Bedford, Fall River, Brockton, and Lynn. But in his evening speech in Boston, to an audience that filled the National League ball park, he went back to the threat of war, with a blatant appeal to Irish Anglophobia: "we shall not undertake to fight anybody else's war. Our boys shall stay out of European wars." Yet after this appeal to prejudice, he made a passionate plea for unity, for freedom from the "social and racial tensions" that Goebbels was trying to foment and that Hitler was counting on so strongly.[15]

2

This plea, though sincere, had a special motive. The Colored Division of the Democratic National Committee had just issued a pamphlet stressing

Willkie's German ancestry, comparing his winning of the nomination with Hitler's methods of gaining power, and accusing his father of being a leader of anti-Negro sentiment in Elwood, which was described as "an un-American anti-Negro community where members of our race are forbidden to live."[16] That there were no Negroes in Elwood was apparently true,[17] but the general tone and content of the pamphlet were so patently slanderous that a number of Democratic leaders, including Negroes, were quick to condemn it. Even Flynn, after two days of silence, felt obliged to state that it "was not submitted to the publicity division of the Democratic National Committee prior to its issuance," and that "to issue this stupid pamphlet" was "a disservice to our great President and his party."[18] The following day he asserted that only one copy got out and that this was reprinted only in Republican newspapers; but reporters told of copies being passed out freely from a four-foot-high stack, along with a printed circular showing "a man painting a sign saying 'No Negroes allowed,' with the railroad station labeled 'Elwood, Ind. Home of Wendell Willkie.'" This circular Flynn *did* take responsibility for, asserting that neither Willkie nor his father had ever protested the exclusion of Negroes from Elwood.[19] (Willkie had not lived there for twenty years, and his father had been dead for ten.) And four days later the first pamphlet was reissued, with only a few of the most venomous lies and insinuations omitted.[20]

This increasing virulence in the anti-Willkie campaign (though the spirit had been the same from the beginning) was due to fear—fear all the more intense because of the smug confidence that it replaced. For Willkie at last had turned the tide. Americans admire a fighter against odds—and few Presidential candidates had ever fought more furiously in the face of greater odds. Eggs and tomatoes earned him votes, as he deplored the national decline of baseball "because the number of hits compared with the number of pitches has been so small."[21] His spontaneous wisecracks were often irresistible. ("What about the man up a tree?" called a young man from a lofty branch to which he had climbed for a better view. "Washington is full of them!" the campaigner shouted back.)[22] And his energy was unflagging. Listening, after the passage of so many years, to recordings of his speeches late in the campaign, one is startled at their oratorical effectiveness. The voice is hoarse, but it has power. Occasionally, at the beginning of a speech, it fails; "but it is in a good cause," and it returns as he warms to his work. And hour after hour it goes on, reasoning, ridiculing, exhorting, pleading. If the goals of the crusade are not always sharply defined, the driving passion is genuine.

And now, at last, he was getting greater support from the party. The Willkie Clubs, indeed, had never lost heart; and now, as the testimony of many political reporters makes clear, something of the same fervor that had swept the nation in June was being re-aroused. In New Jersey, for example, it was noted on October 28: "The work of the Willkie Clubs is easily the outstanding feature of the campaign . . . There are 386 such organizations now working in different parts of the State . . . using sound trucks, newsreels, newspaper advertising, radio programs, circulars, house-to-house canvassing and every other conceivable approach, and are carrying the fight right into enemy territory with meetings at factory gates, in Negro neighborhoods, and other places where the President has been strong."[23] This pattern of activity was repeated in many states.[24]

The changed atmosphere even brought a changed attitude in many "organization" Republicans who had been cold to Willkie's candidacy. Until now, there had doubtless been many states like New Jersey where "neutral observers" found "the Republican organization . . . more interested in electing its State and local candidates than in working 100 per cent for Mr. Willkie."[25] In Chicago, also, the "Illinois Coordinating Committee," headed by Werner Schroeder, was accused of "double-crossing" Willkie and devoting all its money and activity to the campaigns of local candidates.[26] And in San Francisco, again, Republicans who had worked "outside of the Republican party" for Willkie's nomination were "rebuffed" when they wished to work with the Republican organization for his election and were compelled to join the Willkie Volunteers.[27] But as the campaign began to gather momentum, and Willkie once more appeared to have a chance, it is reasonable to assume that most Republicans—even the members of Congress who had publicly flouted his leadership—wanted to be in on a possible victory.

Moreover, such party leaders as Dewey, Taft, and Landon were now stumping vigorously for the candidate; even Hoover broke his silence with some acrimonious blasts at the New Deal; and in Washington, Chairman Martin called a meeting of House Republicans, from which they emerged with endorsements of Willkie.[28] Meanwhile, such dramatic personalities as Hugh Johnson and Clare Boothe lent their varied satirical talents to the cause.

Non-political notables also joined the Willkie parade. Joe Louis appealed earnestly for his election; and if some of the champion's impromptu comments sounded more like praise of the New Deal, they were no more confused or confusing than what was being said by many people with greater intellectual pretensions. Other stars of sport who had earlier pledged their adherence were some of the greatest: Helen Wills Ruark, Robert T. Jones, Jr., and Gene Sarazen. At the same time it had been announced that Hollywood support for Willkie was being organized by Gloria Swanson and Robert Montgomery; and in his election eve broadcast he was joined by Mary Pickford and Bing Crosby. Popular novelists and playwrights likewise came forward: Bess Streeter Aldrich, Nina Wilcox Putnam, Kathleen Norris, Lloyd Douglas, Rex Beach, Irvin S. Cobb, and the candidate's fellow Indianan, Booth Tarkington. Toward the end of the campaign a group of "Writers for Wendell L. Willkie" sponsored a full-page advertisement in the *New York Times;* the list of names including among others Maxwell Anderson, James Branch Cabell, John Erskine, Ellen Glasgow, John Kieran, and Grantland Rice.[29]

Less was now heard about hurt feelings and disorganization. As Willkie headed west from Boston, Roscoe Drummond commented: "In New England, Willkie has done everything political precisely right."[30] Leaving Boston, he spoke in Haverhill, Lawrence, Lowell, Worcester, Springfield, Pittsfield, and Albany; the next day in Schenectady, Amsterdam, Utica, Rome, and Syracuse (two street-corner speeches besides the major evening effort); then Rochester (six speeches), Batavia, Niagara Falls, and Buffalo; next Ohio—Mansfield, Marion, Bellefontaine, Hamilton, Springfield, Dayton, and Cincinnati; then across Indiana and Illinois to St. Louis, where an estimated 28,000 jammed into the arena before the police locked the doors on thousands more, and gave him "easily the most enthusiastic" reception of the campaign;[31] then four more speeches in Missouri and back to Springfield, Illinois; northwest to Minneapolis, via La Crosse, Winona, Red Wing, Hastings, and St. Paul; east through Wausau, Green Bay, Appleton, Oshkosh, Fond du Lac, and Milwaukee; on to Chicago, where (notwithstanding his earlier profane remark) the "demonstration was easily the most tumultuous of the entire campaign";[32] back to New York, where he arrived at 7:30 p.m., toured the Bronx and Manhattan, including the Lower East Side (whose dwellers might boo him but at least knew him), and after three formal speeches gave another at the *Herald Tribune* Forum —which he repeated in part for newsreel photographers before his train pulled out at 1:27 a.m. and headed west; west to Harbor Creek, Erie, Sharon, and Greeneville, Pennsylvania, Warren and Akron, Ohio; east through Jamestown, Salamanca, Hornell, Elmira, and Binghamton, New York, to Scranton and Wilkes-Barre, Pennsylvania; back to New York at noon next day, through crowded streets where boos were drowned by cheers to the World Fair—then through Harlem, where the boos were louder, to half of the Fordham-St. Mary's football game as the guest of Father Gannon—then to Queens and Brooklyn and a major speech before leaving at midnight for Illinois; after the Sunday breathing spell, across Illinois and Indiana (with a speech to 75,000 at Indianapolis) to Louisville, Kentucky; east again through southern Ohio and West Virginia; on to Maryland and Delaware and finally, after two days of intense campaigning in New Jersey, to the Saturday night wind-up in Madison Square Garden, where a crowd that jammed the building and solidly filled the streets for blocks around emitted a triumphant roar at every phrase he uttered, no matter what it was.

3

Small wonder that Democratic leaders became first uneasy and then frantic as the President maintained his pose of being too busy with affairs of state to spend time making speeches. "Into the White House poured telegrams and telephone calls from all parts of the country . . . warning that Willkie was making great headway and that the President had better begin to do some campaigning. . . . The political leaders were learning in their local districts that, as far as votes for a President are concerned, the American people refuse to be taken for granted. They want to hear the campaign issues debated by the candidates."[33]

To be sure, as Rosenman remarks, "The President was very adept at using non-political speeches—especially during his campaigns—to derive political benefits."[34] Moreover, he was reluctant "to put himself in a position of making it possible for Willkie to say that he (Willkie) had smoked him out"[35] and for some time clung to his original plan. This included a speech on September 20 at the University of Pennsylvania, where he received an honorary degree, after which he toured the Philadelphia Navy Yard and held a press conference on the progress of the national defense program; a speech on September 28 dedicating the Washington airport (where 240 Army planes and 168 Navy planes put on a spectacular show); a tour on September 30 of Maryland defense plants and installations; a speech on October 5 at the dedication of three schools in Dutchess County, New York, built with the aid of Federal funds; a trip on October 7 to the Watervliet Arsenal, Albany, and Saratoga; a highly publicized tour of defense installations in Pennsylvania and Ohio on October 10-12, with a formal speech at a Federally financed housing project in Pittsburgh, another at Akron, Ohio, and a Columbus Day address from his special train at Dayton, Ohio; and a radio address opening the annual "Mobilization for Human Needs" on October 13.

By this time, however, the pretense that such activities were non-political was becoming absurd, even without Willkie's frequent sarcastic comments, and on October 15 the President gave it up and announced two formal campaign speeches. Two days later the number was raised to five.

It is this writer's judgment that if Roosevelt had not taken this decision, he would have lost the election. But once it was taken the picture changed. Millions of voters needed only to hear once more the familiar voice, confidently assuring them that all was well, forcefully recalling to memory the benefits brought by the New Deal, ridiculing—sometimes savagely, sometimes almost gleefully—Republican indictments, claims and promises. Nor was this campaigning less effective because of the evident zest with which, dropping his pose of being above the battle, he returned to the political wars. "I am an old campaigner," he confided in his first speech at Philadelphia, "and I love a good fight."[36]

He could enter it, furthermore, with a good conscience. He had, in his acceptance speech, stipulated that he would feel free to correct misrepresentations by the opposition, and "misrepresentations" was a mild term for some of the things Willkie had been saying: among others (to use Roosevelt's words in his Philadelphia speech, which do not go much beyond the truth), "that the President of the United States telephoned Mussolini and Hitler to sell Czechoslovakia down the river; or that the unfortunate unemployed of the nation are going to be driven into concentration camps; or that the Social Security Funds of the government of the United States will not be in existence when the workers of today become old enough to apply for them; or that the election of the present government means the end of democracy within four years"; or "that this Administration wishes to lead the country into war."

With so little time left, Roosevelt shrewdly confined himself, on the whole, to two main lines of argument: that in domestic affairs the New Deal had brought economic recovery, and that in foreign affairs the Administration had worked consistently for peace while preparing efficiently for defense against military attack. And even for a less able orator, with a less skilled and experienced team of speech-writers, it would perhaps not have been difficult to make the arguments stick. Willkie's charge that New Deal measures had actually delayed economic recovery could not be proved, whereas the contrast between 1932 and 1940 was visible on every hand. And although Willkie could—and did—prove that the Administration had been laggard and incompetent in building a national defense,[37] its lack of vision and its ineptitude showed like inspired foresight and miraculous achievement compared to the incorrigible myopia and the unwavering obstructionism of the isolationists who dominated the Republican party. In his Madison Square Garden speech (the day after Mussolini had invaded Greece), Roosevelt quoted statements by Fish, Hoover, and Vandenberg in 1936 and by Taft early in 1940 opposing increased military appropriations. He cited measure after measure aimed at strengthening the Armed Forces and acquiring strategic materials, which a majority—often a large majority—of Republicans in the House and Senate had voted against. As for aid to Britain, he recalled Republican votes against the repeal of the arms embargo in the fall of 1939, and declared that the opposition in the House had been led by "Martin, Barton and Fish."[38]

Thus was coined the most famous slogan of the campaign. The crowd gleefully picked it up, and when in subsequent speeches Roosevelt (or other

Democratic campaigners) returned to the theme, his hearers seized every opportunity to chant hilariously "Martin, Barton and Fish." Willkie said later, "When I heard the President hang the isolationist votes of Martin, Barton and Fish on me, and get away with it, I knew I was licked."[39]

But Roosevelt's most strenuous efforts were devoted to the least laudable end—to persuade the voters that he too had the will *and* the power to keep America out of war. In Philadelphia he asserted: "Throughout [the last eight] years my every act and thought has been directed to preserving the peace of the world and more particularly the peace of the United States —the peace of the Western Hemisphere. . . . It is for peace that I have labored; and it is for peace that I shall labor all the days of my life."[40] This was reasonable enough; but in his Madison Square Garden speech his desire to appease the anti-war extremists led him to a profoundly disingenuous defense of the 1935 Neutrality Act: "In 1935 . . . your government undertook to eliminate the hazards which in the past had led to war. . . . We made it possible to prohibit American citizens from traveling on ships belonging to countries at war. Was it right? We made it clear that American investors, who put their money into enterprises in foreign countries, could not call on American warships or soldiers to bail out their investments. Was that right? We made it clear that we would not use American armed forces to intervene in the affairs of the sovereign republics to the south of us. Was that right? We made it clear that ships flying the American flag could not carry munitions to a belligerent, and that they must stay out of war zones. Was that right?"[41]

This statement was disingenuous because it presupposed a theory about the causes of war which, as his acceptance speech showed, he no longer believed in. It was disingenuous because now he did *not* believe that the provisions he defended were right, to say nothing of those that he did not mention, such as forbidding the sale of munitions even on a "cash and carry basis" (this was, in fact, the "arms embargo" the repeal of which in the fall of 1939 he had blamed the Republicans for opposing!) It was disingenuous, finally, because it confused the real issue by dragging in the totally irrelevant and justly discredited policy of money-motivated intervention in Latin America.

In other words, Roosevelt went far towards admitting the justice of Willkie's attacks on him for having been an appeaser and isolationist. He did so, obviously, in order to answer Willkie's other charge that he was now deliberately leading the country into war.[42] "The effects of this," writes Robert E. Sherwood, "were felt powerfully in the White House during the last week in October. I had to read the letters and telegrams and reports that flooded in and . . . I was amazed and horrified at the evidence of hysteria."[43]

The situation led Roosevelt in his speech at Boston to answer Willkie's unprincipled appeal to isolationists (Irish and other) with an equally unprincipled and strident assurance. "I have said this before, but I shall say it again and again and again. Your boys are not going to be sent into any foreign wars." Upon this, the *Christian Science Monitor* pointed out editorially that any war except a civil war is a "foreign" war, and told the candidates: "It is misleading to let Americans believe that you can single-handedly keep America out of war. . . . You should both cease to make this impossible claim. You should both be more frank, more fair, with the citizens of the United States."[44]

But frankness and fairness were now out of the question on either side. The prolonged and intense emotional strain to which Willkie had been subjected and the extent to which it undermined his normal good humor and fairmindedness, were revealed in his reaction to the climax of Roosevelt's Boston speech: "That hypocritical son of a bitch! This is going to beat me!"[45] That Roosevelt was being hypocritical is true; but Willkie was at this point the last man who had a right to say so. In fact, the treatment of the war issue during the last two weeks of the campaign was, as Sherwood said, "a national disgrace." Both candidates simply let go all hold of fact, reason, and moral principle. Not only did they know that promises to keep America out of war were meaninglesss; they must both by this time have known that Germany could not be beaten without full-scale participation by the United States; that a negotiated peace was impossible; and therefore that American involvement was inevitable. Yet instead of preparing their countrymen morally for the inevitable war, each sought to build a false sense of security—contingent on *his* being elected.

One would like, nevertheless, to say something in their defense. Although the majority of Americans had made up their minds that they would go to war rather than let Hitler win,[46] the psychological residue of twenty years of isolation prevented them as yet from facing the fact that these were the only alternatives.

Moreover, it was not clear that an immediate declaration of war on Germany would hasten Hitler's defeat. There was no land front on which to fight, no likelihood that one could soon be opened. What seemed most important was to get arms to Britain as fast as possible—for immediate defense and perhaps ultimate attack. Under these circumstances it was perhaps the part of wisdom to turn away deliberately from the long range view, concentrate on building military strength, and leave to the logic of unforeseeable future events the decision as to how that strength was to be used.[47]

But none of this excuses Willkie's assertion (in effect) that Roosevelt's election would mean war, nor Roosevelt's answering assertion that it would mean unbroken peace. For these statements no excuse exists—except that they were made during a Presidential campaign.

4

This irresponsibility of the principals was exceeded by their partisans. And if as between Roosevelt and Willkie the latter was more at fault, the reverse was true of their respective supporters. Violently as many Republicans hated Roosevelt, no high ranking member of the party was guilty of such total contempt for honesty and decency as was consistently displayed by Democrats of the highest standing.

On the theme that "a vote for Willkie is a vote for Hitler," Governor Lehman declared: "Let there be no mistake about it: nothing that could happen in the United States could give Hitler, Mussolini, Stalin and Japan more satisfaction than the defeat of . . . Franklin D. Roosevelt."[48] (In fact nobody knew or could know whether this was true; and true or not, it was still dirty politics.) Vice President Wallace chimed in with the statement that Nazi agents were under orders to help Willkie win. "The friends of the totalitarian powers have decided that the stupidity and lack of leadership of the Republican candidate qualify him as their candidate."[49] This was the man whom Willkie had earlier defended as "a fine gentleman" and "a scholar."[50]

By some sort of self-deception, however, Wallace professed not to be casting any personal slur on Willkie, and this must also have been true of his friend Dorothy Thompson, who took the same line (achieving the difficult feat of being pontifical and hysterical at the same time) in a column that the *Herald Tribune* refused to print, and who declared flatly in a radio broadcast that "a vote for Wendell Willkie is a vote for Fascism."[51]

Most violent of all was Mayor La Guardia, who charged that Willkie had shown himself "willing to sacrifice the best interests of our country and our relations with foreign countries in order to win favor from hyphenated citizens, from foreign propagandists, and to get on the good side of minorities which are controlled by dictator enemies of the country."[52]

In the same spirit of vilification, La Guardia and others harped on the old theme that the nomination was gained through the machinations of big business,[53] and revived the *New Republic's* lies about the anti-labor activities of some of Commonwealth & Southern's operating companies. Typical of this line of attack was Senator Mead's lurid picture of Willkie's labor record as president of Commonwealth & Southern as "a grim story of hired labor spies, tear gas, company unions, as well as intimidation and coercion of company workers."[54]

These are only a few instances of the malignant and fantastic—and deliberate—falsehoods that were repeated with shameless pertinacity by Democratic leaders. And these men—Lehman, Wallace, La Guardia and Mead, along with Ickes and Jackson, who also joined in the abuse—were men of far greater integrity than the general run of politicians. Once more it is evident that in a Presidential election normal standards of conduct simply do not hold.

What effect these tactics had is anybody's guess. But, on the other side, there is remarkable unanimity of opinion as to the effect of a similarly venomous diatribe against the President by his erstwhile supporter, John L. Lewis. The leader of the United Mine Workers and the CIO offered Willkie his endorsement with no strings attached other than acceptance of the principle of collective bargaining and a general promise of fair treatment for labor, which Willkie could give in good conscience. And he felt that Lewis's support could provide a dramatic and effective rebuttal to the sort of libel mentioned in the last paragraph, and might even modify the antagonism of the workers by whom he had been jeered, cursed, stoned, and spat upon in the cities of Michigan and Ohio.

Hence he disregarded the warnings of his advisers. But for once they were right. In a rhetorical eruption extravagant even for him, Lewis poured forth his hatred of Roosevelt: assailed him as a traitor to labor ("Where now are the tears for the 'ill--housed, ill-clothed, and ill-fed?'"); accused him of "over-weening, abnormal and selfish craving for increased power"; charged that, in an effort to conceal the failure of his economic policies and to satisfy his lust for power, "his motivation and his objective . . . is war"; and adjured the mothers of America to vote against "the candidate who plays at a game that may make cannon fodder of your sons." Overshadowed by these dire and vengeful prophesyings was his listing of Willkie's promises and his assertion of the belief that Willkie would keep them. He closed with the promise—or threat—to resign as president of the CIO if Roosevelt was elected and thus "save our great movement . . . from the embarrassment and handicap of my leadership during the ensuing reign of President Roosevelt. . . . Sustain me now, or repudiate me."[55]

The speech was delivered on October 23. The chorus of condemnation that straightway rose from the ranks of labor was all but universal. Even most of the heads of CIO unions bitterly denounced Lewis as being himself a traitor—"the Benedict Arnold of the labor movement," as one of them phrased it.[56] Only a few left-wing leaders approved—presumably on the war issue—his stand. The district leaders in his own United Mine Workers were divided, while the rank and file remained unshaken in their devotion to Roosevelt.

Lewis's speech, therefore, won few votes; whereas some of the fury that it engendered was bound to overflow onto Willkie. How clearly this was seen by responsible Republicans was revealed in a meeting at Chicago where Albert Lasker was trying to raise substantial funds for the campaign from a group of well-to-do Republicans. They listened to the broadcast of Lewis's speech. When it was finished, Lasker broke the silence: "Now, gentlemen—having heard that speech in our support, you will understand why the need of the Republican Party is truly desperate."[57]

The hate-mongering on both sides, exemplified by the speeches of Lewis and other national figures, rose to a crescendo of fury in the last days of the campaign. Republicans circulated stories (some of them apparently true)[58] of union members being ordered to attend Roosevelt rallies. The President, in turn, in his Brooklyn speech, picked up a statement by a Philadelphia citizen—"The President's only supporters are paupers, those who earn less than $1,000 a year and aren't worth that, and the Roosevelt family"—and declared, "There speaks the true sentiment of the Republican leaders." In the same speech he called attention to the presence in the Communist *Daily Worker* of full-page anti-Roosevelt and pro-Willkie advertisements, and spoke of the "unholy alliance" between "the extreme reactionary and the extreme radical elements in this country."[59]

As election day approached, each side put out stories of discreditable statements or actions by the other. Democrats told of an airplane flying over New York dropping handbills which "purported to ask votes for Roosevelt, naming a long list of names of one religion"[60]—the implication being that the Republicans were appealing for anti-Semitic votes by representing Roosevelt as favored by the Jews. (Republicans had indeed—in Philadelphia again!—raised the religious issue by plastering billboards with the slogan: "Save your church! Dictators hate religion. Vote straight Republican ticket.")[61] On the other hand, Republicans told of the circulation of rumors that if Willkie won, there would be an end of relief, all Negroes would be sent to concentration camps, and children would have to go to school on Saturday.[62]

There were also (as throughout the campaign) the nasty stories about the candidates' private lives that are a regular part of an American Presidential election. One day toward the end of the campaign a delegation of local Republicans approached the campaign train and insisted on seeing the candidate, while refusing to state the nature of their mission. Finally Edward yielded and led them to his brother's quarters, where with much hesitation and embarrassment they finally asked if the story was true that Willkie had fathered an illegitimate child. Willkie leaned back and looked them over; and then, with the broad and reckless humor that his associates knew so well, retorted: "Well, gentlemen, that cancels out the story that I don't have any balls."[63]

5

To the candidates, however, the arrival of the hour of decision brought a more sober mood. The election eve broadcasts of both were generally impersonal and dignified, though overtones of the Willkie "crusade" still lingered. And it was still *his* crusade: "I have made no commitments of any kind, directly or indirectly, to any man or any group of men."[64] He declared, with manifest sincerity, that he felt no bitterness. Roosevelt expressed confidence in, and Willkie pleaded earnestly for, national unity when the election was over, whatever the outcome.

As he waited for the votes to be cast, Willkie knew that the odds were against him. His mood, just before the final Madison Square Garden speech, is brilliantly recorded by one of the reporters on the now legendary campaign train. "It was a rough, raw, rainy November day. Willkie, after resting throughout the morning in his compartment, stepped outside for a brief walk along the siding and of course, most of the press and radio representatives followed him and as always, it ended up in an informal, off-the-record press conference. . . . And in typical Willkie style, he went around the ring of men who were with him asking each in turn how he figured the election. I shall always remember how he took the 'no's' for in one or two cases they were pretty forthrightly expressed. I think his attitude then, as I look back on it, was indicative of the man who said, 'To hell with everything. If I can't beat the isolationists in Wisconsin, I would rather not be President.'"[65]

On the morning of Election Day Willkie told Lem Jones that only a miracle could bring him victory. He repeated that he had made no commitments and was now making his first one. "If the miracle does happen, there will be a place in the White House for you."[66]

But if Willkie was intellectually prepared for defeat, it was not in the nature of so intense a competitor to accept it emotionally. And at best there can be few more dismal places than the election night headquarters of the losing candidate. It is credible that, as one reporter wrote, "Mr. Willkie looked more and more grim as the trend of the returns" became clear, and no one need have been surprised at his reluctance to admit defeat, though the hour grew late and his wife sensibly remarked, "I wish Wendell would get ready to go home."[67]

Yet many radio listeners will remember the heartiness of Willkie's answer to a query as to how he felt, "I feel fine." And at his death a veteran reporter recalled that "on the night of his defeat he was magnificent when he came into the ballroom of the Commodore Hotel and told the hundreds of admirers there, not a few of whom were visibly crying, that he had just begun to fight and that the crusade he was leading would be carried on."[68]

And the next day at lunch, a friend found him "frank, cheerful, fair, and appreciative. He showed no bitterness against F. D. R., nor did he seek to blame anyone in his entourage for his defeat. He admitted mistakes of political judgment. He had warm praise for all who worked for him. His was the reaction of a big man in adversity."[69]

There was one Republican, however, who did not share the general gloom. This was Dewey, who at a small private party was obviously feeling no pain as the radio returns showed a growing margin for Roosevelt.[70] And his mood is understandable. He had (playing the game of politics "by the book," as always) worked hard and well for the election of the party candidate. Now that the election was lost, it was not unnatural that his thoughts should turn to the consequent heightening of his chances in 1944. But the episode sheds light upon the always uneasy relationship between the two men.

There is also on record a picture of how the news of victory affected Willkie's opponent in his Hyde Park home. "One of those present said it was received in a silence weighted with something like gloom and foreboding. Another heard the President sigh heavily as he sat alone by the fire. For the first few minutes the shadow and the burden of the years to come seemed to fall on the President-elect."[71]

Later Willkie would know and like better (though never without reservations) his election opponent. But now his feelings were still strong, and his telegram to Roosevelt was carefully worded: "Congratulations on your re-election as President of the United States. I know that we are both gratified that so many American citizens participated in the election. I wish you all personal health and happiness." To those who regard politics as a kind of game, this will sound grudging, but to have gone farther would have seemed to Willkie to be hypocritical. Roosevelt's reply showed that he got the point: "Please accept my sincere thanks for your message of congratulation. I greatly appreciate the assurance of good wishes for my health and happiness, which I heartily reciprocate." At 10:30 A.M. Willkie made a short radio broadcast to the nation, in which he thanked those who had voted for him, and added: "I accept the results of the election with complete good will. The popular vote shows the vitality of our democratic principles and the adherence of our people to the two-party system."[72]

Obviously he was not worried by any prospect of the destruction of the American democratic system during the next four years.

6

Hardly less fascinating than the spectacle and drama of a Presidential election is the post-mortem: the attempt of experts and amateurs to answer the question, "What happened? Who voted how, and why?"

The facts, as distinguished from the guesses, are as follows. Willkie carried ten states—Colorado, Indiana, Iowa, Kansas, Maine, Michigan, Nebraska, North Dakota, South Dakota, and Vermont—with a total of 82 electoral votes. (Hoover in 1932 had 59, Landon in 1936 had 8; Dewey in 1944 had 99.) Roosevelt carried the remaining thirty-eight, and received 449 electoral votes.

The popular vote was much closer. Willkie polled 22,304,755, Roosevelt 27,243,466. Willkie received, roughly, 1,000,000 more votes than Hoover in his landslide victory in 1928; 6,600,000 more than Hoover in 1932; 5,500,000 more than Landon in 1936; 300,000 more than Dewey in 1944 or 1948. He lost New York State by 224,000 votes; Dewey four years later, after a brilliant two-year record as Governor, lost it by 317,000.

It was later alleged by the Republican Old Guard that Willkie ran far behind the Republican candidates for other offices. This is untrue. In the thirty-one states (leaving out the Solid South) where there were elections to the United States Senate, Willkie's percentage of the vote for President was greater in nine states, including Massachusetts and New York, than the percentage of the vote for Senator received by the Republican candidate; the same in one state, Indiana; and lower by not more than 1.6 per cent in eleven others, including Illinois and Pennsylvania. With reference to the vote for the United States House of Representatives, Willkie's percentage was greater in nine states (all Western or Border states) than the combined vote of the Republican candidates; in one, Missouri, it was the same; in twelve, including Michigan, Ohio, New York, and Pennsylvania, it was lower by not more than 1.5 per cent. Among thirty contests for governor, Willkie's percentage was greater than that of the Republican candidate in seven states (he carried three that elected Democratic governors), and was lower by not more than 1.7 per cent in six others.[73]

The only "facts" in an election are the votes. Attempts to explain *why* people voted as they did are only a guessing game in which even professionals, after assembling what are assumed to be relevant data, still have to make a leap in the dark. Nevertheless, the lure of the game is irresistible, and guesses have degrees of plausibility. By interviewing a certain number of selected voters one can draw inferences that have a certain measure of validity, depending on the choice of people interviewed, the way the questions are worded, and the truthfulness of the answers. Or one can study the vote cast in relatively small areas where the population is in some important respect relatively homogeneous: the slum section or the colored section of a large city, for instance, or a community made up largely of persons whose origin can be traced to a particular nation.

Mr. and Mrs. Herman F. Willkie

ding: Wendell, aged 11,
d Fred
ed: Bob, Ed, and
Mr. Willkie

os:
d Press International

Willkie at seventeen

Left: At Culver Military Acade
Left below: At Indiana Univers
Below: In 1917.

Edith Wilk

Gwyneth Harry

otos: United Press International

Mr. and Mrs. Wendell Willkie at the Philadelphia Convention

Photo: Wide World

The use of such methods has made clear beyond reasonable question that economic status was the most important factor in determining people's votes in the 1940 election. In general, the rich and well-to-do voted for Willkie, the poor for Roosevelt. The Gallup Poll estimated that in the "upper income group" (which, one finds, is made up of those with an income of $50 a week or more) only 28 per cent voted for Roosevelt; in the "middle income group" ($20 to $50 a week) 53 per cent voted for him; in the "lower income group" (less than $20 a week, including all receiving relief) 69 per cent voted for him. Related to these data are those concerning occupational groups. The estimated percentage in each group that voted for Roosevelt was: business, 34; professional, 36; white collar, 48; farmers, 54; labor, 66.[74] It is noteworthy that Willkie carried no states containing much industry, except Michigan (by 7,000 out of more than 2,000,000) and his home state, Indiana (by 25,000 out of about 1,700,000).

Another analyst, Samuel Lubell, made a similar finding. He also found that Willkie received a heavy vote in counties that "were predominantly German-speaking in background," whereas Roosevelt had overwhelming support among Poles, Norwegians, and Jews.[75] Probably here again, the balance favored Roosevelt.

Other factors, not susceptible to statistical analysis, have been much talked about as having influenced the election one way or the other. Democrats complained (as always) that the Republican candidate got better treatment by the press and also far greater financial support. That these charges were true was, however, unimportant. They were also true in 1932 and 1936, and in 1944 and 1948. For good or ill, the power of the press in a national election is small. And so, apparently, is the power of money. Undoubtedly the Republicans outspent their opponents in all the five Presidential elections from 1932 to 1948; yet in each they were beaten by a decisive margin.

In their turn, Republicans, including Willkie, pointed an accusing finger at two reprehensible ways in which Democrats allegedly obtained votes: the misuse of funds by government agencies, especially the WPA, and the machinations of big city bosses. But WPA officials did not need to bring pressure on workers to vote for Roosevelt. And, leaving aside the relatively rare instances of outright fraud on a large scale, such as seems to have regularly taken place in Jersey City during Mayor Hague's administration, the so-called "machine vote" is no different from the "Chamber of Commerce" vote. In each instance, people vote for the candidate whose election they think will best serve their own interests.

One other matter looms large in the minds of many persons: the organization and management of the campaign. Over and over, people have earnestly declared that if the Republican "organization" had cooperated with Willkie or if Willkie (and his "amateurs") had cooperated with the "organization" (depending on the speaker's bias); or if the planning had been more efficient and the campaign train less disorderly; or if Willkie had been more willing to take advice about both the technique and the content of his speeches, and had repressed his impulsive wisecracks; *then* he would have won.

These arguments are plausible, but they do not fit the facts. Willkie's huge popular vote, unmatched by any other Republican before Eisenhower, is proof of the effectiveness of his campaign, and the "if's" of his adverse critics are unimportant. As William Allen White commented a few days after the election: "Mr. Willkie was speaking to the masses. He could not consider precincts, districts, States, regions. He was plunking for the middle class, where a few crafty advisers might have got him more electoral votes and cut down his popular vote and impaired his power as a leader."[76]

It has been said that "the so-called vote of the masses is a myth,"[77] and that what really counts is efficient party organization. But the fact is that, in a Presidential election, a good "organization" is the result and not the cause of popular enthusiasm; it is effective not because the county chairmen are happy, but because ordinary people are willing to get out and work. Where the Republican "organization" dragged its heels, the Willkie Clubs did the job that it was supposed to do—and did it better. Twenty years later Joseph Martin declared: "The Willkie clubs were a tonic that the Republican organization needed. They brought enthusiasm, aggressiveness and color into the campaign—and they raised a great deal of money."[78]

It should also be remembered that, as Martin remarks, "No Presidential campaign rolls along smoothly."[79] Eisenhower in 1952 ignored the "regulars" fully as much as Willkie did in 1940; and had he lost, there would have been the usual recriminations, as there were in regard to the campaign waged by Stevenson. On the other hand, Dewey, who was no amateur and whose record as Governor of New York demonstrates his ability as an organizer, made every effort in 1944 and 1948 to placate all factions of the party, to offend no one, to make no mistakes, to leave nothing unplanned; while his 1948 opponent, Mr. Truman, despite the regional, doctrinal and personal dissension that demoralized the party "organization" completely, took his case to "the people" in a strictly one-man fight—and won.

Finally, the critics of the "disorganization" of Willkie's campaign should take note of the comment of Harold Ickes, written on Election Day, concerning the Democratic effort: "But if we do win today, and as I sit here I believe that we will—we can thank God for it and not ourselves. We haven't deserved to win. . . . I have never seen such incompetent and inept management—if it deserves the name of management at all."[80]

So it is personalities and issues that are decisive—that somehow, finally, *do* get themselves impressed on the minds of the voters, with whatever degree of accuracy or inaccuracy. As between the two—issues and personalities—Willkie had already asserted his belief in "We the People" that "the American people do not give their vote to policies; they give their vote to *men*"; and despite occasional—and sincere—disavowals,[81] this belief governed the general conduct of the campaign. And the main reason why Willkie lost—why in some instances he ran behind other Republican candidates—was that he was running against Franklin D. Roosevelt.[82]

One corollary of this conclusion is that many particular issues and strategems that seem important to those who are campaigning have actually little effect; they appeal only to voters who already like or dislike a candidate for reasons of their own. There is no evidence that the Democrats took many votes away from Willkie by picturing him as a front man for "Wall Street," or "Big Business," or "the power trust." In fact, it was in the farm states just west of the Mississippi, where suspicions of the forces so labeled are traditionally the strongest, that Willkie made his best showing. On the other hand, Willkie's attempt to dramatize the third term issue, by persistently referring to the "third term candidate" and prophesying the end of democracy in America if Roosevelt was elected, was similarly ineffective.[83]

What pulled Roosevelt through, what no Republican attacks could alter, what won him the adherence of the majority of voters, was that he stood in their minds as the man who had *done* something to mitigate the evils of the Great Depression—who had given food to millions who were facing starvation, who had renewed hope in millions who had begun to despair, who had treated the unemployed and underprivileged as human beings instead of statistics.

Moreover, for whatever reason, the depression was ending. Even a casual traveler (like the present writer) through the East and Midwest during the late summer of 1940 could not escape the impression of America as an awakening giant, in the act of throwing off some evil spell. Factories were smoking, farmers were harvesting abundant crops. And unemployment was declining at a spectacular rate. Even businessmen were disposed to find a bright side to the New Deal.[84] There was nothing wrong with Willkie in the minds of the voters except that he represented the party that was popularly believed to have caused the depression and that he was attacking the man who was popularly supposed to have cured it. In the minds of "the masses" and many "independent" voters, he had no issue; whereas, the Democrats *did* have an issue, namely, the reactionary record of the Republican party.

In foreign affairs the situation was similar. Willkie would get the votes of the isolationists, no matter what he did or said. But he also had to have the votes of some at least of the internationalists, the aid-to-Britain-even-if-it-leads-to-war group. And these persons saw no reason not to support Roosevelt, while they found a powerful reason for not supporting Willkie in the isolationist record of his party. They would be alienated further by his reckless charges that the President was deliberately leading the country into war. This desperate expedient no doubt won Willkie votes in the Midwest, but just as certainly it lost him votes in the East (conceivably, the 224,000 by which he lost New York State). It is a good guess that the anti-war hysteria which so alarmed the Democrats existed mainly among those who already distrusted the President, so that both Willkie's attempt to exploit this hysteria and Roosevelt's attempt to allay it by unconditional promises of peace were as pointless as they were unprincipled.

In brief, Roosevelt won because a majority of the American people liked him personally, approved of his social and economic policies at home, and trusted to his energy, experience, and right-mindedness in meeting the Nazi menace from abroad. No Republican candidate could have won. No other candidate could have done as well—or come near doing as well—as Willkie.

XIV

England and Lend-Lease

1

For a hundred years before 1940 it had been the rule, broken only by two Democrats, Cleveland and Bryan, that a defeated Presidential candidate retired to private life and never again sought an elective office. But in this respect, as in so many others, 1940 was different. For there were many Americans into whose lives Willkie had brought something new, which they did not wish to give up. In the five days following his defeat, he received 30,000 letters and telegrams "from every part of the country . . . from people in practically every walk of life,"[1] but mainly "from middle class men and women." They were not letters of condolence: the note most often struck was "What now?" and the attitude was "something akin to personal worship" of Willkie, combined with assurances that he would "be in the White House in 1944." Willkie himself commented that "the writing indicates something in the nature of a spiritual revival."[2]

Throughout the brief remainder of his life the messages kept coming. They strengthened his feeling of nearness to "the people," of confidence in them and of responsibility to them; and reinforced his inclination to view politics and political parties not as ends but as means—not as a way of life or as entities commanding loyalty but as instruments to be used.

There was other evidence besides the letters that his following had not forgotten him. When, on November 17, he left New York for a vacation in Florida, word of his presence quickly spread through the Pennsylvania Station "and he was soon the center of an enthusiastic crowd . . . The campaign cry of 'We want Willkie!' spread through the waiting rooms of the terminal . . ." (Mrs. Willkie was heard to remark laughingly, "I thought all this would be over.")[3] Again on November 29, when he returned briefly to New York to address the annual dinner of the National Interfraternity Conference, he was given "a tremendous ovation . . . The chant 'We want Willkie!' rose spontaneously from the crowd as he entered and when he left, and broke in on the proceedings from time to time. Even after he led them in the toast to the President, holding his glass high in a sweeping gesture, there were cries 'We still want Willkie!'"[4]

This continuing popularity was perhaps partly the cause and partly the effect of the way he took his defeat, which was wittily described a few months later by the writer of "Topics of the Times." "It would be news of the most sensational kind if the reporters ever found Wendell Willkie in a despondent or surly mood. . . . The loss of [the Presidency] does not seem to have cost Mr. Willkie a moment's lost sleep or a single sigh in his waking hours.

"It's fine in a public man to be a good loser and harbor no grudges. . . . Just the same, it would be a tribute to the office of the President of the United States if Mr. Willkie managed now and then to look a bit wan and thoughtful . . . How would a lady feel if she had told a man that she can only be a sister to him and he picks up his hat and goes whistling out of the room?"[5]

Another sign of his popularity was the continuing "enormous pressure to make talks," which as he indicated to David Sarnoff in refusing an invitation to address the Economic Club, actually worried him: "one thing I do not want to do is keep talking every few days. The people of the United States rapidly get weary of a man expressing his opinion on all kinds of subjects, particularly when he holds no official position."[6]

His first response to the pressure was an Armistice Day broadcast to the nation, and more particularly to his supporters.[7] The sober tone was set by the opening admission: "Many things were said during the campaign which, in calmer moments, might have been left unsaid or might have been worded more carefully." But, he added, "I can truthfully say that there is no bitterness in my heart. I hope there is none in yours." This did not mean, however, that the elected government ought to be free from criticism. "We must constitute a vigorous, loyal and public spirited opposition."

And the emphasis was on the adjectives. "Let us not . . . fall into the partisan error of opposing things just for the sake of opposition." And once more he endorsed the aims of the New Deal: "we must fight for the rights of labor, for assistance to the farmer and for the protection of the unemployed, the aged and the physically handicapped." At the same time he declared that government "must not dominate our lives" and restated his program for encouraging business. He also restated his foreign policy—aid to Britain "to the limit of our ability" but short of war—"unless attacked."

He saved for the end what his audience, both friends and enemies, were most curious to hear about—the future of the Willkie Clubs. Nothing like them had ever existed in American political life, and having no precedent to follow, he must have done some hard thinking. To cut himself off from them would be to destroy them, and with them a powerful force for the realization of the goals he sought. On the other hand, such a personal organization would inevitably savor of dictatorship and provide a prominent target for his enemies in both parties. There was really only one possible decision, which he announced to his supporters as tactfully as he could: "In your enthusiasm for our cause you founded thousands of organizations. It is appropriate for you to continue them if you feel so inclined. . . . It is not, however, appropriate to continue these organizations in my name. . . . 1944 will take care of itself."

One problem that Willkie always faced and never solved was the translation of his personal popularity into political power. It was, in fact, insoluble as long as he was basically at odds with the dominant faction in the party which he had chosen as the instrument for achieving his aims for the nation. And since that faction refused to change—though individuals occasionally *did*—Willkie had to fight it.

This was not the fight that he thought he was getting into when he entered politics; nevertheless, it was destined to dominate his life during the years that remained. Between him and the realization of every one of the ideals that he came to believe in with more and more impelling earnestness—economic justice, racial equality, international order—stood the Republican Old Guard. As he had tried to reform the utility industry—to restore public confidence by making such confidence deserved, and to prevent government competition by showing that it was unnecessary—so now he was to undertake the far more difficult task of restoring the Republican party to power by making it worthy of such a restoration.

And in the end this was a better fight than the one he had planned: better for him because it engaged more fully his intellectual powers and his moral passion; better for the country because the imperfections of the New Deal, though real, were unimportant and temporary, while the need to destroy isolationism was desperate and the need to defend basic human rights is never-ceasing; and better as a human drama because of the courage and tenacity that were called for by what was essentially a one-man fight. For although he had many friends and followers, they were never organized—and under the circumstances could not be organized—for the effective exercise of power.

In the meantime, the Willkie Clubs were dissolved. This action, taken at a meeting in New York on December 14, attended by about 150 delegates, was accompanied by a resolution which urged the members to form new organizations at local and state levels to encourage intelligent interest and responsible participation in public affairs. To this aim Willkie lent encouragement in addressing the delegates next day. "One of the difficulties of American life has been its failure to call its ablest and best men into public service. . . . I hope in five or ten years or even in two years I will see many among you running for Congress, the Senate, Governorships, and office in your own community."[8] No lofty statement of principles, however, could alter the fact that the driving force behind the Clubs had been the desire of the members to make Willkie President. Without this purpose the Independent Clubs of America (as it was decided to call them) were bound to lose their vitality. They kept alive for a year, but after the attack on Pearl Harbor, the national office was closed, with Willkie's approval.[9]

The dissolution of the Willkie Clubs was calculated to conciliate "regular" Republicans, and this seems to have been Willkie's consistent aim during the two months following the election. There was, it is true, a report that he desired a "gradual absorption of party power into the hands of the more progressive elements of the party and an ousting of the more reactionary leaders."[10] Nevertheless, he wrote to Robert P. Allen in early December emphatically denying "the statement in your column that I have had difficulty with some Republican committeemen or Congressmen."[11] It is clear from Allen's answer, however, that the desire for harmony was not reciprocated, for the columnist declared that he had his information from "responsible party figures" in Congress.[12]

There is further evidence of Willkie's desire for party unity in the position that he took when Martin's announcement that he would soon resign as National Chairman threatened to touch off a struggle for power. He refused to put forward any candidate of his own,[13] although consulted by "more than half the members" of the National Committee; only stipulating, in a joint press conference with Martin, who approved the statement, that the new chairman be a "liberal, forward-looking fellow, with energy and drive and capacity."[14]

As always, however, he was more interested in national unity than in party unity. In the Interfraternity Conference speech, referring to the campaign, he deplored the "pure vilification and personal argument" engaged in by some on both sides, which "did not change any votes." "I hope," he went on, "to contribute something to the constant . . . elevation of public discussion in America." Even after a vehement plea "to help the fighting men of Britain to preserve the rim of freedom which is constantly shrinking," he asserted that this was "an honest issue that must be determined by the American people after full, free discussion. It does no good to say of the man who believes that we must send help to that rim of freedom that he's a war-monger, or of the man who believes that America should protect herself wholly within these shores that he's a fifth columnist, or a Nazi or something else. [Ickes in a Town Hall address had called Lindbergh a Fascist.][15] . . . My faith in democracy is such that I believe the collective judgment of the people, after listening to both sides, may be wiser and better than [the judgment of] those, whoever they may be on either side, who think the wisest course of discussion is to destroy your opponent rather than answer his argument."[16]

This faith would have served Willkie well in a new career of which at one time there seemed to be a possibility. His friend Donald Thornburgh wrote him on December 5 that he was being "seriously discussed" as the new president of Stanford University; but the question had been raised whether he might leave in 1944 to go back into politics. Willkie replied on December 18: "You may say to anyone, with full authority, that I do not intend to devote my time to any form of organizational politics."[17] He would certainly have been tempted by such an offer. But in the end it did not come.

The activities just chronicled were interruptions in a six-weeks vacation that Willkie permitted himself at Hobe Sound in Florida, where, he said on leaving New York, "I am just going to read, fish and rest. I am not even going to talk politics."[18] He did, however, have to face a social issue. When he learned (as Cleveland Amory tells the story in *The Last Resorts*)[19] that Jews were excluded from Hobe Sound, he delivered an ultimatum: the restrictions must go, or *he* would go. The policy was changed.

2

Willkie ended his vacation on January 5. The surprising thing is that he was able to stand aside so long. For, with the election out of the way, it was possible for the American people and their leaders to face up to reality; and the great night bombings of Britain (on December 29, in London, "the havoc was comparable only to that wrought by the Great Fire of 1666")[20] had brought a perceptible hardening of the general attitude toward Germany. William Allen White's Committee to Defend America by Aiding the Allies, with half a million members in 760 chapters, had become so aggressive that when its aged and amiable leader, defending himself against the charge of "war-mongering," incautiously remarked, "The only reason in God's world I am in this organization is to keep the country out of war," there was an immediate upheaval, and the New York chapter retorted publicly, "We will not be intimidated by the word 'war-monger.'"[21] White had not intended, obviously, to be so sweeping, and when he resigned a few days later, saying that the job was too demanding and that a younger man was needed, he added a denunciation of "appeasement" and a plea for complete support of the President's program.[22]

The Roosevelt policy that White recommended had also hardened. Some commentator has observed that Roosevelt's pre-Pearl Harbor procedure in dealing with the growth of Nazi and Fascist power consisted of sudden spurts of aggressiveness and steps toward intervention, alternating with long periods of seeming indecisiveness during which public opinion overtook and moved far beyond the Administration's position.[23] After the election, at any rate, the President pushed ahead. On Armistice Day he delivered a speech decrying "the unpatriotic efforts of some of our countrymen to make us believe that the sacrifices made by our nation [in World War I] were wholly in vain."[24] (Yet a campaign speech two weeks before had contained a sweeping defense of the Neutrality Act of 1935, which was the result of precisely such "unpatriotic" efforts.)

In the same spirit, on December 29, in a radio address to the nation, the President declared that "never before since Jamestown and Plymouth Rock has our American civilization been in such danger as now." He poured scorn on those who sought to escape danger "by crawling into bed and pulling the covers over our heads" and derided the judgment of "the American appeasers" who were saying that "the Axis powers are going to win anyway." As for the role of America: "We must be the great arsenal of democracy."[25] And this general policy was made specific eight days later in the President's message to Congress, which contained the proposal for aid to Britain that was later to be known as Lend-Lease.

The intensity of the isolationist reaction to this trend of sentiment and policy can be indicated by a few random quotations. California's Senator Hiram Johnson was bitter but fatalistic: "Those in command of us are perfectly mad to be a part of the game. When it is propitious, from their point of view, they'll take us in."[26] Boston's Cardinal O'Connell thought the "war propagandists" should be silenced: "They cannot be real Americans, because real Americans think of their own country first."[27] Senator Bennett Clark of Missouri suggested an appropriation by Congress to be called "The King's royal tax for the support of the British Empire."[28]

To these attacks the President replied in his message to Congress: "principles of morality and considerations for our own security will never permit us to acquiesce in a peace dictated by aggressors and sponsored by appeasers." To Hitler's "new order" he opposed the concept of "a world founded upon four essential human freedoms"; freedom of speech, freedom of religion, freedom from want, and freedom from fear (of war).[29]

The Lend-Lease proposal was spelled out in a bill introduced into Congress on January 10 (designated—the clerk insisted by coincidence—"H. R. 1776"). The crucial Section III read as follows: "(A) Notwithstanding the provisions of any other law, the President may, when he deems it in the interest of national defense, authorize the Secretary of War, the Secretary of the Navy, or the head of any other department or agency of the government: 1. To manufacture in arsenals, factories and shipyards under their jurisdiction, or otherwise procure, any defense article for the government of any country whose defense the President deems vital to the defense of the United States. 2. To sell, transfer, exchange, lease, lend, or otherwise dispose of, to any such government any defense article. 3. To test, inspect, prove, repair, outfit, recondition or otherwise to place in good working order any defense article for any such government under Paragraph 2 of this Subsection. 4. To communicate to any such government information pertaining to any defense article furnished to such government under the proposed bill. 5. To release for export any defense article to any such government. (B) The terms and conditions upon which any such foreign government receives any aid authorized under Subsection (A) shall be those which the President deems satisfactory, and the benefit to the United States shall be payment or repayment in kind or property or any other direct or indirect benefit which the President deems satisfactory."[30]

The sweeping powers given to the President surprised even his supporters, and invited Republican attack. Taft commented: "it authorizes the President to make war on any nation in the world and to enter the present war if he wishes to do so, as he apparently does."[31] Dewey chimed in: "I strongly favor every possible aid to Britain short of war [but the bill] would bring an end to free government in the United States."[32] Hoover warned Congress, in a somewhat more restrained statement, against "the enormous surrender of its responsibilities."[33] Landon called it "a slick scheme to fool the taxpayers," adding, "We have a great and very real interest in English success. But to say that our national security rests on her victory is a misstatement."[34]

Willkie thus found the two preceding Republican candidates for President and his two closest rivals for the 1940 nomination, as well as other leading Republicans, leagued against the bill, and he therefore reconsidered his initial refusal to comment on it.[35] As he wrote to Robert P. Allen on January 17, "when Hoover, Landon, Dewey, Taft, and Vandenberg all came out in a frontal assault on the Lend-Lease Bill, I thought I owed a duty to speak for it."[36] And this duty was not merely to the country: it was also to the Republican party, as he made clear in addressing a meeting of the Women's National Republican Club on January 18. "But let me say to you that if the Republican party in the year of 1941 makes a blind opposition to this bill and allows itself to be presented to the American people as the isolationist party, it will never again gain control of the American government."[37]

His press statement five days earlier had of course been more restrained. "It is the history of democracy that under such dire circumstances, extraordinary powers must be granted to the elected Executive. Democracy cannot hope to defend itself in any other way." He did indeed urge "thorough debate" of the bill in Congress, and suggested amendments to insure that Congress would "retain in its own hands the fundamental power to declare war" and that there would be an automatic review of the law at some specified date "not too far in the future." Nevertheless, he expressed the hope that there would not be "opposition to granting power to the

Administration just because it is this Administration. . . . The people chose this Administration and we must abide by that choice." He hoped also, he said, that debate would "be confined to the merits of this bill. Appeasers, isolationists or lip-service friends of Britain will seek to sabotage the program of aid to Britain and her allies behind the screen of opposition to this bill. . . . I refute the statement that American security is not involved in a British defeat."[38]

The Republican reaction was swift. Colonel McCormick in the Chicago *Tribune* for the first of many times read Willkie out of the party: "The party will take leave of its late standard-bearer with the hope that it will never again see him or he it."[39] Landon commented tartly: "There is no essential difference between Mr. Willkie's position and Mr. Roosevelt's position, which is to go to war if necessary to help England win. If Mr. Willkie had revealed it before the Republican convention he would not have been nominated, and if Mr. Roosevelt had revealed it before the election he would not have been re-elected."[40] Among prominent Republicans only Senator Austin of Vermont approved Willkie's position.[41] Even some who were friendly feared "that his stand would weaken his control over party organization and strengthen the isolationist bloc"; while others complained "that it tended to stir up controversy within the party at a time when harmony was being sought to present a solid front to the New Deal."[42]

It was, of course, precisely this lack of any principle higher than party unity that Willkie believed would bring destruction to the party. Hence, all attempts to prevent his speaking out were useless. He himself declared just after issuing the statement that he had "been subjected to considerable pressure, with threats" from persons whom he did not name.[43] One such episode, in fact, made him so angry that he went home and spent most of the night composing his statement for the press.

He made another public appeal for Lend-Lease a few days later. Appearing at Town Hall to listen to a Town Meeting of the Air debate on the topic between Frank Kingdon and Norman Thomas, he was asked by the moderator, George Denny, if he would like to comment. His characteristic answer was: "I, who opposed Franklin Roosevelt, call upon all Americans to give him such power in this most severe crisis, I believe, in the history of America, so that we can debate with him in another election." Also characteristic was his crushing retort, delivered with a good-humored smile, to Thomas's repetition of the threadbare theme that the election had offered the voters no choice on the war issue. "I would like to remind you that when Mr. Thomas says that the American people had no choice except to vote for Mr. Roosevelt or myself, they also had the privilege of voting for Mr. Thomas. Mr. Thomas went all over this broad country of ours preaching the same doctrine of narrow isolationism that he preaches tonight. If I recall the results of the mandate of the American people, Mr. Roosevelt got some 27,000,000 votes, I got some 23,000,000 votes, and I have never seen a public record of how many Mr. Thomas got."[44]

But Willkie himself felt impelled during his remarks to pay lip-service to the conventional kind of patriotism, of which isolationism was a natural result. "If I believed," he said, "that Britain could collapse and America could survive economically, then I would not take a single risk in [sic] involving this country in any foreign entanglements." This was not true.

3

Having done what he could, at this point, for the Lend-Lease bill, Willkie took off on a visit to Britain. Before leaving, he explained to the press how he had come to take the trip. "I was writing an article, and I put down a statement about Great Britain. Then I thought, how do I know that? The idea popped into my head, why not go to the source? Why not go to England and find out? I called Secretary Hull and made arrangements to go."[45] And he quickly expanded his aim: "I want to talk to as many people as possible and get their view of the probable social and economic consequences of the war and their ideas of what form life in England will take after the war is over."[46]

The President was more than agreeable to the plan. Steve Early issued a statement saying that Willkie had not asked to see the President, but that the latter would "of course" be glad to talk to him if he wished. "Meanwhile," the statement continued, "the President has asked the Secretary of State, who has an appointment with Mr. Willkie, to give him all the information the government has received on conditions abroad and to fully outline to him the policies of this government and the reasons therefor." Willkie, immediately told of the statement by reporters, was quick to take the hint: "I'm deeply appreciative. I'll be glad to talk with the President."[47]

And again Willkie had stirred the imagination of the public. During his hour and forty minute conference with Mr. Hull at the Carlton Hotel, "several hundred people had jammed into the hotel to see them. As Mr. Willkie came out of the elevator and came up beside the Secretary, the people closed in so quickly that hotel attendants had to clear a path. A highly agitated woman shoved through the group and grabbed at Mr. Willkie's coat. 'Bless his heart! Bless his heart!' she cried."[48]

"The first meeting Willkie remembered having had" with the President "during the latter's second term"[49] (the third would begin the following day) was cordial, and they exchanged bantering remarks for the benefit of their hearers. "Mr. Roosevelt laughingly said that he wished 'Wendell' were going to be put out on the cold inaugural stand tomorrow taking the oath instead of himself. Mr. Willkie replied that when he got to London in the midst of all the excitement, Mr. Roosevelt would want to change places with him once more."[50] Afterward Willkie told reporters that the meeting had been "delightful." On his side, Roosevelt (as Frances Perkins records) "took an immediate liking to Willkie and he hadn't expected to. . . . The next day he talked to me about it. 'You know, he is a very good fellow. He has lots of talent.'"[51]

What they said in private was not revealed except for Willkie's general comment that they "talked of many things involved in the growing crisis and particularly of American production schedules."[52] One detail, however, has been recorded by Robert E. Sherwood, and it shows how swiftly they arrived at complete frankness. Roosevelt asked Willkie, while in England, to see Harry Hopkins, and Willkie "did not greet the suggestion with much enthusiasm. . . . Indeed, he asked Roosevelt a pointed question: 'Why do you keep Hopkins so close to you? You surely must know that people dislike him and resent his influence.' Willkie quoted Roosevelt as replying: 'I can understand that you wonder why I need that half-man around me.' (The 'half-man' was an allusion to Hopkins' extreme physical frailty.) 'But—some day you may well be sitting here where I am now as President of the United States. And when you are, you'll be looking at that door over there and knowing that practically everybody who walks through it wants something out of you. You'll realize what a lonely job this is, and you'll discover the need for somebody like Harry Hopkins who asks for nothing except to serve you.'"[53]

When Willkie left, he took with him a hand-written note from Roosevelt to Churchill: "Wendell Willkie will give you this. He is truly helping to keep politics out over here." The President added: "I think this verse applies to you as it does to us:

> Sail on, O Ship of State!
> Sail on, O Union strong and great!
> Humanity with all its fears,
> With all the hopes of future years,
> Is hanging breathless on thy fate!"[54]

A crowd of some 300 persons gathered to see Willkie's plane take off at 8:30 a.m. on January 22. After stops at the Azores and Portugal, he arrived at a "Western port" on the afternoon of Sunday, January 26.

Immediately, his visit took on proportions that he had not foreseen. On the day he arrived, the London *Daily Express* printed an open letter telling him what he should see and do.[55] At a press conference the following morning, 200 newsmen were present.[56] Within three days of his arrival he was getting 500 letters a day, most of them inviting him to visit some particular place. He had to hire three secretaries to send his regrets.[57]

All this was not because he had sought the limelight. When first asked about press conferences, he replied, "I came here to listen, not to make speeches,"[58] and he made it clear that he had no official status: "I am here as Wendell Willkie. I am representing no one."[59] His tact was exemplary and his diplomatic reticence as complete as it was disarming: "I don't want to get in wrong, so I'm saying nothing about my conversations with ministers."[60] "His broad non-committal smile [was] often his only answer to very leading questions."[61] "He declined to discuss any phase of the relationships between the United States and Britain, declaring that the proper place for such utterances was at home. Likewise he deemed it improper to discuss this country's domestic affairs."[62] He amiably evaded a question about the possible transfer of more destroyers, by saying: "The people of the United States decided that I shouldn't have anything to say about that. There is only one head of the U. S. government."[63]

And he did not forget his original purpose, namely, to gather facts: facts about what Britain had and what she needed in the way of war materials, how fast she was producing them and how much the bombings had hurt; and facts about what hopes and plans were in men's minds for shaping the national life and international relations when the war had been won.

In this purpose he found everyone eager to cooperate, though perhaps there were some who were a little unclear as to what the point of it all was. It was natural that a newsman should ask him what "practical use" he intended to make of what he learned. Willkie's reply, though indirect, pointed to the real answer: "I don't know what you mean by practical use, but I do make speeches and write sometimes."[64] What everyone sensed was that here was a man eager and able to tell Britain's story to the people of the United States.

He therefore had a chance to meet and talk with practically everybody of importance. On Monday he saw Foreign Minister Anthony Eden in the forenoon; had lunch (an hour and three quarters) with Churchill and Mrs. Churchill (to whose charm he did not forget to pay a compliment; adding "Don't ask me what we ate—fish, I think—I was too interested talking to notice");[65] met Harry Hopkins; talked with Labor Minister Ernest Bevin; and had dinner with Lord Stamp, head of the London, Midland and Scottish Railway. In between he held two press conferences and toured the bombed-out center of London.

On Tuesday he visited St. Paul's Cathedral; attended a session of the House of Commons (where he heard a fiery attack on the Government for suppressing the Communist *Daily Worker*); saw Westminster Cathedral and talked with Cardinal Hinsley, Primate of the Roman Catholic Church in Great Britain; lunched with Labor Party leaders Clement Attlee and

Arthur Greenwood; held separate conversations with Montagu Norman, Governor of the Bank of England, and Sir Kingsley Wood, Chancellor of the Exchequer; and had dinner with Lord Beaverbrook, minister in charge of airplane production.

Two more days were spent in London, and the list of important people with whom he had conferred was lengthened by the addition of Sir Robert Kindersley, President of the National Savings Committee; Sir Andrew Duncan, Minister of Supply; Harold Laski, unofficial philosopher of the Labor Party;[66] various members of the Trades Union Congress; General Sikorski, head of the Polish government in exile; Quo Tai-chi, the Chinese Ambassador; Herbert Morrison, Minister of Home Security; Viscount Simon, the Lord Chancellor; A. V. Alexander, First Lord of the Admiralty (who discussed with him for an hour and a half "British needs and naval affairs" and showed him the famous Map Room); and Alfred Duff Cooper, Minister of Information.[67] One meeting, which he probably enjoyed as much as any, did not get into the press. Somehow or other he managed to save an evening for a meeting with Rebecca West and other leading literary figures, which had been arranged for him by Irita Van Doren (to whom they sent gay cablegrams).[68]

On Friday he visited Dover and inspected the invasion defenses along the Southeast Coast. On Sunday he toured the north of England, stopping in Birmingham and Coventry (victim of the first German attempt to destroy an entire city by indiscriminate night bombing); and on Monday visited Liverpool and Manchester. He left Manchester Tuesday morning to fly to Dublin, where he had a long talk with Prime Minister De Valera; flew back to London in the afternoon for tea with the King and Queen; left London just after midnight by train for Bristol, where in the morning he made one last tour of inspection and recorded a message to be broadcast to Germany, in which he stressed his "purely German" ancestry and asserted that both he and "the great majority of my fellow countrymen of German descent . . . reject and hate the aggression and lust for power of the present German government";[69] and left for the airport at 9:15 a. m.

The aim of the Irish trip was to try to persuade De Valera to change his policy of strict neutrality, although Churchill told him that the attempt was hopeless.[70] And the Prime Minister was right (although Willkie in public called the visit "definitely worth while" and spoke of his "delightful meeting" with De Valera),[71] despite his "brutally frank" attempt to make the Irish leader face reality. "He told De Valera that Ireland ought to grant harbor facilities and airplane fields to Britain"; he pointed out the part played by American friendship in the winning of Irish independence and predicted that if England fell while Ireland remained neutral, the Irish "would stand condemned in the eyes of Americans"; he added "that it was foolish to think that Ireland could escape involvement in this conflict simply by remaining neutral and that Hitler would strike Ireland just whenever he got ready."[72] He made De Valera admit that if Germany landed parachute troops in Ireland he would call on Britain for aid, and asked him why, therefore, he was unwilling to seek her help beforehand and put her in a position to give it effectively. But this question De Valera simply refused to discuss.[73] In truth, Willkie had been too optimistic. Britain was now paying the penalty for the prolonged injustice and stupidity of her treatment of Ireland.

The meeting with the King and Queen was more pleasant. Willkie had received the invitation as soon as he landed, but had put off acceptance of it as long as he could, thinking other things more important than a chat with royalty. But their genuine friendliness won him over. He drank a Scotch and soda with the King and joked with the Queen, whom he liked because of her simple manner and sense of humor.[74] "You are doing a better job on me than you did on another person," he told her with an oblique reference, which she understood, to the isolationist views of Ambassador Joseph P. Kennedy. But this time, though the words of her reply might have been humorous, her tone was not: looking at him "steadily and simply and without any pretense of play or attempt at stage-acting, she said: 'Well, Mr. Willkie, it wasn't because I didn't try on him!' "[75]

As the Queen responded to him, simply and naturally, so did almost everybody in England. He took the country by storm. His visit became nothing less than a love affair between him and the English people.

Willkie was of course prepared to fall in love with England. In another man, in fact, the praise that he poured out at every opportunity might have seemed fulsome. Asked for his impression of the British people, he replied, "During the few hours I have been here I have found their spirit magnificent. I like their nerve."[76] He called the Commons debate about the *Daily Worker* "the most dramatic example of democracy at work anybody could wish to see."[77] Viewing the burned-out bookstores in Paternoster Row, where three million volumes had been lost, he commented: "They have destroyed the place where the truth was told."[78] After touring five typical air-raid shelters in the company of Ellen Wilkinson, Labor Member of Parliament, he observed: "I have never seen such spirit. . . . this was an emotional experience that I will never forget."[79] Talking with leaders of the Trades Union Congress led him to affirm his "complete agreement with their aspirations and purposes."[80] As for Churchill, the visitor (in almost Churchillian style) "doubted whether ever in history any man had been more ideally suited to the particular task he was called on to perform than was the Prime Minister of Britain, with his qualities of inspirational leadership, his large comprehension, his dauntless courage and his long experience."[81]

Of the country as a whole, he proclaimed, "No nation in the world was ever more united in a cause than England is united now."[82] And of his personal reception he declared: "To say that I am staggered . . . would be putting it mildly. It has been the experience, the thrill of a lifetime. But the calm, precise, magnificently efficient turning of your wheels of industry is, perhaps, an even greater thrill."[83] His final statement before leaving was: "What I said when I arrived over here still goes. Anything I can do in America to help Britain in her fight for freedom, I certainly shall do."[84] In autographing his photograph for the newspapers he wrote, "With affection for the British people."[85]

On the other side, Willkie's absolute genuineness, his total lack of front, his "boundless energy and radiant high spirit" (even the editorial writer for the *Times* of London tended toward superlatives),[86] were irresistible. In the air-raid shelters he was recognized at once, and there were cheers for the United States and cries of "Send us all you've got!" and "We aren't down!"[87] "Cried one elderly woman: 'We can take it. You go home and tell them that.' 'I certainly will,' replied Mr. Willkie.

"In another shelter people got up from their beds to cheer and clap him. A mouth-organ player struck up 'The Star-Spangled Banner', and the crowd joined in." "The thing that got me," Willkie told a reporter (who told the nation), "was the spirit down here. One guy gave me part of a cup of coffee. . . . A woman dashed up to me at a sort of side turning, caught my arm, 'Come and see my baby,' she said. The kid couldn't have been a week old."[88]

"The very unconventionality of his approach," the *Times* further editorialized, was a "tonic," to which everyone responded. As he was leaving the Foreign Office with Eden, who had urged him to get the opinions of ordinary people, he caught sight of a workman repairing some bomb damage to the roof and shouted: "Hey! What do *you* think about the war? Do you want to keep on fighting?" Only momentarily confounded, the man replied: "Well, 'Itler eyn't dead yet, is 'e?"[89]

Entering a public house, Willkie explained pleasantly, "I just wanted to look around one of your pubs." The proprietor responded by producing a half-bottle of champagne: "I was going to keep this for armistice day, but you are as good as an armistice day to us and we will have this together."[90] Seeing a group of soldiers, he said, "I'd like to buy those guys a drink," and did so. Challenged to a game of darts, he cheerfully accepted and as cheerfully lost. He complimented the barmaid, who laughed and told him that her hushand was in the Armed Forces, to which the guest laughing in turn responded: "Fancy pulling that husband stuff on me!" A wag in the bar shouted: "'If the missus only knew!' and Wendell, quick as you like on the comeback, says, 'What! does your missus know when you go out?' "[91]

As he was driving to Lambeth Walk on Saturday afternoon, "several hundred people, recognizing him quickly, surrounded the visitor, cheering and shouting. Somebody shoved a bicycle in front of him and, amid more cheers, he cycled along Lambeth Walk. Dismounting, he encountered a woman who invited him into her house for a cup of tea, pointing to a heap of rubble which a bomb had made of her home."[92]

Outside of London, the enthusiasm was, if possible, still more intense. In devastated Coventry he was "engulfed in a wave of cheering people . . . who had waited hours for his arrival . . . As the procession of cars moved slowly through the bombed streets, people ran to their doors to cheer. At almost every corner there was a lookout man who passed the word around as soon as the cars appeared. Children waved the Stars and Stripes from doorways of half-ruined houses. Workmen paused in their work of rendering blitzed homes habitable to give a cheer." In Birmingham, "thousands of people held up his entry to the Council Chamber while they sang and cheered him."[93]

In his hotel at Manchester next morning, he was told that the German radio, broadcasting in English, had urged the people of Lancashire to organize demonstrations against him. By way of answer, he stepped out onto a balcony, and "several hundred people . . . waiting for a glimpse of him . . . yelled, cheered, and sang 'Marching Through Georgia.' . . . Back in the room, Mr. Willkie said, 'That seems to settle that. I guess these German guys haven't been reading the papers.'" Throughout the day, he "was feted, mobbed, swept off his feet, and cheered. He talked to A. R. P. workers, soldiers, women and children who had lost their homes. Wherever he went squads of police had to clear his way through crowds. A woman wanted him to hold her baby. Mr. Willkie grinned. 'I'd love to, ma'am, he said, 'but I'm scared. I'm so darned awkward I might drop him.'"[94]

At Liverpool the story was the same. "As he descended the Town Hall steps to enter his car, he was mobbed by hundreds of people who . . . tried to shake hands and pat him on the back." At the docks he walked up to a group of workers "with a cheery 'Hello, boys' and the dockers jostled to shake him by the hand amid cheers and cries of 'Good old Willkie., '"[95]

Occasionally a sterner note was sounded, and he was greeted with cries of "Let us have the stuff."[96] On the other hand, there were touches of comedy; both unintentional, as when "an elderly lady presented him with a bottle of beer and kissed him on both cheeks," and deliberate, as when a group of students "rigged themselves out in ridiculous costumes and . . . fitted up an imitation coach and four drawn by a bony nag," with "a placard proclaiming: 'This Is Not Wendell Willkie.'"[97]

This in a way was the ultimate tribute, even more than the *Times'* editorial, which found his attitude "immensely heartening" and spoke of "the spontaneous response of the man and woman in the streets to a spontaneous gesture of American friendship and sympathy." But perhaps the highest tribute of all was that of Winston Churchill, who confessed to Willkie the doubt and discouragement that the outside world never had grounds even to imagine, and asked his guest whether he thought that Britain really would pull through. Willkie's answer was no doubt, this time also, "immensely heartening."[98]

The passages quoted above speak for themselves in telling what Willkie's visit meant to the British in their time of greatest suffering. And they felt that their trust had been justified when they read of his testimony on Lend-Lease before the Senate committee. Eddy Gilmore of the Associated Press wrote to Willkie on February 21: "The people here all say, 'Willkie didn't let us down—he told them what he told us.'"[99] And the same reporter, in a letter written more than three years later, declared: "I often to this day hear British people say, when your name is brought up, that you certainly did give them a badly needed shot in the arm just at the time they needed it most."[100]

If the effect on England of so brief a visit by one man on a personal mission was all but incredible, the effect on Willkie was also profound. His conviction that America should support Britain at any cost, hitherto held primarily as an intellectual conviction, was now invested with personal passion. Now he *knew,* as he told the people of Coventry, "that in the face of totalitarian attack free men feel a common brotherhood."[101]

4

On his return trip, Willkie's friendliness almost got him into trouble. The *Dixie Clipper,* mapping a new trans-Atlantic route for Pan-American Airways, stopped at the island of Bolama off the coast of Africa; and Willkie, still eager to see everything and talk with everybody, made a call on a local tribal chieftain, who mistook his guest's questions about family organization for an offer of marriage to his daughter. The ingenuity of the crew members, however, prevented an international incident, and Willkie took away with him as a memento only a native sword, which he waved jovially at reporters when he arrived in New York.[102]

This might have been taken as a gesture of defiance to the isolationists. At Trinidad he had, as he later revealed, "received a cable message from a man who became one of the heads of America First that my reputation would be the subject of debasement in every town in America if I carried out my intention of testifying."[103]

Perhaps the man was also a member of Congress; for when, on February 8, the House of Representatives passed the bill by a vote of 260-165, only 24 Republicans (of whom 20 came from New England and the Middle Atlantic states) voted for it, while 135 were against it, in spite of Willkie's attempt to get agreement among Republicans on certain amendments in the hope that a majority of them would then vote for the bill.[104]

The majority of those who testified before the House and Senate committees opposed the bill. (Senator Wheeler had already publicly attacked it as another "New Deal triple-A farm policy—plow under every fourth American boy.")[105] Norman Thomas said it would "imperil the democratic structure of the United States."[106] Charles A. Lindbergh told the House committee that "the faults and causes of the war are evenly divided in Europe . . . it would be better for us and for every nation that the war in Europe end without conclusive victory."[107] Robert M. Hutchins said "'the American people are about to commit suicide' by drifting into a war for which they were 'morally and intellectually unprepared.'"[108] (At the same time a statement signed by 125 members of his faculty at the University of Chicago urged immediate passage.) Charles A. Beard, the eminent historian, called it "a bill for waging undeclared war."[109] Alan Valentine, erstwhile leader of Democrats-for-Willkie, declared: "No matter what . . . supporters of this bill may say, we know that they would have us go to war."[110] Landon also testified against the bill, and Dewey had been expected to do so, but at the last minute declined the Committee's invitation. (Perhaps he had been studying the Gallup Poll—this at least was Willkie's view—which on February 9 reported that 54 percent of the voters favored the bill without reservations, and that only 22 per cent were uncompromisingly opposed.)

Among those who spoke for the bill, besides Secretaries Hull, Stimson, Knox, and Morgenthau, were Reinhold Niebuhr, noted theologian; James B. Conant, then president of Harvard; and Mayor La Guardia. The final witness was Willkie. That famous tourist had arrived in New York, apparently as full of energy as ever, on February 9; the same day Winston Churchill, in one of his great war speeches, made a dramatic plea for aid—"Give us the tools and we will finish the job"—and stirred the ire of many Republicans by remarking: "In Mr. Willkie we have welcomed the great champion of the Republican party."

Willkie testified before the Senate Foreign Relations Committee on February 11. Although the hearings were not scheduled to begin until 10:00 a.m., and Willkie was not to testify until 2:00 p.m., a line began to form at the door of the Senate caucus room at 6.45 a.m., long before sunrise. Eventually an estimated 1,800 persons forced their way into a room with seats for only 500, while other hundreds remained standing outside. Nothing like it had ever been seen on Capitol Hill.

Inside, "nearly all members of the Senate, with their wives; about half the membership of the House; and representatives of the Cabinet and sub-Cabinet were on hand."[111] Many persons sat or knelt on the floor. Mrs. Henry Wallace, wife of the Vice President, stood throughout the hearing. Senator Murray, a member of the Committee, gave his seat at the table to his wife and perched precariously on a photographer's camera case.[112] Yet it was noted that the crowd in general was not made up of "mink-coated . . . women and sleek men" but "simple, ordinary looking people, plain people, but anxious to have their glimpse of the significant instant."[113] Three photographers somehow got up on a ledge near the ceiling, and someone exclaimed, "They're coming out of the woodwork!"[114]

Willkie arrived from New York at 12:30, and was met at the airport by "a cheering crowd." Arriving at the Senate Office Building, he was smuggled into the caucus room by "a circuitous route, through five different suites." It was then 2:28, and there was another half-hour delay "while the mimeographing machine was turning out copies of his prepared statement."[115] But finally the drama began.

Willkie's prepared statement was in general temperate and conciliatory—an appeal to reason, a plea for national unity. He summarized the isolationist point of view and rejected it as "too simple. It has no regard for the way the world is built." He noted that there were few people who did not sympathize with Britain and added: "If we are going to adopt a policy of aid to Britain, it is necessary above all else to make that aid effective." What was needed now was not money but "the disposition of certain equipment." The greatest threat lay not in the bomb damage to Britain's industries, which had been "relatively small," but in the fact that since May, 1940, she had lost "60,000 tons of shipping per week, almost three times her present rate of construction." "If we are to aid Britain effectively, we should provide her with five to ten destroyers per month"; and he added, with a glance at the bases-for-destroyers deal of the previous summer: "We should be able to do this directly and swiftly rather than through the rigmarole of dubious legalistic interpretation." He urged those who favored the bill to agree with the opposition on "the elimination of unnecessary authority." "It would be truly inspiring for us and liberty-loving people everywhere if this bill could be adopted with a non-partisan and almost unanimous vote."

He closed with a look toward the future. "No man can guarantee to you that the policy of aid to Britain will not involve the United States in war," but "it offers the best clear chance for us to keep out. . . . if Britain can stand through this summer, then at last the effects of our long-term assistance will begin to be felt. The tide will turn." And what was the alternative? "A future surrounded by totalitarian powers; threatened by dictators whose real desire is for conquest; betrayed by nations whose word is not to be trusted; loaded with armaments and domestic debt, and faced with a declining standard of living—such a future is not a future for Americans as we have known them.

"If we are to avoid such a calamity, we must now have courage. We must bravely do the things which we know ought to be done. And we must lay the moral, intellectual and spiritual foundations for the kind of world we want our children to inherit. That world . . . must be a world in which America will share with other nations the responsibilities—and the great prospects— of peace."

The most dramatic part of the hearing was still to come, as the opponents of the bill set about cross-examining the witness. First came Vandenberg, unspectacular and persistent, trying to pin Willkie down on "whether this policy of all-out aid to England does finally include our entry into the war," while Willkie skillfully hedged, insisting that the point was that *not* to aid Britain would *certainly* bring war.

The first mention of the campaign came from the mild-mannered Senator Gillette of Iowa, who inquired whether the witness had changed his views since the campaign ended. Obviously Willkie was prepared for this, and the answer came quickly: "Not in the slightest. As a matter of fact, in April, prior to my nomination, I made a speech in Akron, Ohio, in which I called upon the Secretary of State of the United States to ask Britain what we could do to help her."

"Perhaps in April," the Senator returned, "your speeches did not have the effect, Mr. Willkie. "

But Willkie flashed back: "They brought about my nomination. I was not elected, but I got the nomination."

Senator Bennett Clark of Missouri also brought up the campaign, and passages from Willkie's speeches charging or suggesting that Roosevelt was leading the country into war. The witness replied, unruffled: "I made a great many statements about him. He was my opponent, you know"; and when his questioner caught him up with "You would not have said anything about your opponent you did not think was true, would you?" his answer was still good-humored: "Oh no, but occasionally in moments of oratory in campaigns we all expand a bit." As Clark continued quoting, however, Willkie objected: "I do not see any reason in raking up old acrimonies." As the Senator kept on, the witness began to couple a protest with each answer: "I was much opposed to some of the statements the President made and I thought they were reckless and inflammatory. I would hesitate to say that now. What good does it do?" Finally, confronted with his campaign charge that Roosevelt "has unscrupulously encouraged other countries to hope for more help than we are able to give," he lost patience: "There was a current report at the time that we had made promises to France about what we were going to do. Again I protest. I struggled as hard as I could to beat Franklin Roosevelt and I tried to keep from pulling any punches. He was elected President. He is my President now. I expect to disagree with him whenever I please."

This reply brought such a storm of applause from the audience that Chairman George threatened to clear the room—an obvious impossibility.

To the aged Senator Johnson of California, who clung, not without dignity and pathos, to a position that the march of history had long since passed by, Willkie's manner was different. When Johnson said, "I think I can assure you that there is no immediate aid that we could give to Britain," he answered: "I respectfully, and with deference to the fact that you may have information that I do not have, cannot agree with you on that." He did agree that the bill should be fully debated: "I think that is what we have a United States Senate for."

The highlight of the hearing came near the end. Senator Nye of North Dakota had his turn at quoting Willkie's attacks on the President. He chose a statement made on October 20: "On the basis of his past performance with pledges to the people, you may expect that we will be at war by April, 1941, if he is elected." Willkie was apparently not quite sure as to the exact point of the question: "You ask me whether or not I said that?" Nye answered, "Do you still agree that that might be the case?" What he seems to have been asking was whether Willkie thought that America would be at war by April. But the ambiguous reference of the pronoun evidently left the witness still under the impression that what he was being asked was whether he had made the statement; and accordingly he replied with a grin, "It might be. It was a bit of campaign oratory." Enjoying the burst of laughter that followed, he seized the opportunity for a second wisecrack: "I am glad you read my speeches, because the President said that he did not."[116]

From the caucus room Willkie went to the White House and talked for an hour and a half with the President—who at his press conference earlier in the afternoon had played up Willkie's appearance at the Senate hearings by telling reporters that "they were at the wrong end of Pennsylvania Avenue."[117] What they said was not disclosed.

5

The day after Willkie's testimony on Lend-Lease was Lincoln's Birthday—an occasion in recent years for extensive Republican self-congratulation. But Willkie's speech to the National Republican Club in New York was mainly a warning and a challenge to the Republican party. Taking as his heroes not only Lincoln but also Washington and Lee, he declared that the memorials to them recalled and strengthened in him "a real faith that the

American people worship most, not partisanship, nor bitterness, nor vindictiveness in their party leaders, but love of mankind and magnanimity and tolerance and understanding."

On this note he turned to the history of political parties in America. "Parties in the United States are born and die in times of great crisis and struggle." The Federalist party was destroyed because it "became a party of negation. . . . And then in the time of Andrew Jackson there arose the Whig party, a party of opposition, a party of negation, a party that offered no other program to Jackson's except that Jackson was wrong, and it existed for some twenty-five years and then a great moral issue arose in America. And because the Whig party found nothing in that issue except compromise, except cliches, except the playing to local prejudices, it passed away.

"And in its place in the struggle for freedom came the Republican party. We were founded to preserve freedom. . . . But if we become like the Whig party, merely the party of negation, merely the party of opposition, merely those who find fault and who in one of the great critical moments of history find nothing nobler than compromise, this great party will pass from the scene. . . .

"Here we are at this moment, in this peaceful ballroom, untouched, happy, gay, buoyant and little troubled, and yet, within a distance that I traveled by a roundabout route within three days, bombs are dropping, destroying cities, lived in by free men, free men like us, and some men rise and say, 'That's no problem of ours. Let's preserve America alone.'"

"Free men like us"—there lay his real conviction, there was the source of his passionate crusade for help to Britain; not in the concept of national self-interest, however enlightened, to which he sometimes appealed, but in the faith, deeper than reason, that in the community of free men, national boundaries have no meaning.

When he finished, there was "prolonged applause," followed by the familiar chant, "We want Willkie!"[118]

At other Republican gatherings, however, the story was different. Dewey now discovered grounds for cautious approval of the bill in the amendments adopted by the House. But Taft was still opposed, and he asserted that Willkie's support of the bill was purely personal, insisting that there was "no justification in precedent or principle for the view that a defeated candidate for President is the titular head of the party." Representative Fish and Senator Nye, in other speeches, not only attacked the bill but, even more vehemently, attacked Willkie; with Nye declaring that the "campaign oratory" remark was "an insult to the American electorate" and an all but mortal blow to the two-party system.[119] This rant was echoed in the Chicago *Tribune,* which foamed at its editorial mouth and spluttered about "The Barefoot Boy as a Barefaced Fraud."[120]

More disconcerting to Willkie, and illustrative of the difficulties that he sometimes encountered in trying to aid the Administration, was Secretary Knox's hasty statement that "my position, as Secretary of the Navy, is against any further depletion of the United States fleet." Willkie answered: "Information given me by high authorities in the government after my testimony yesterday confirmed my views that we are in a position, without any injury to our Navy or national defense, to give Great Britain . . . additional destroyers." Reporters were quick to point out that the only "high government authority" whom Willkie had conferred with was the President himself.[121] Next day there was a conference between Knox and Roosevelt. But afterwards the Secretary said, "I have not changed my opinion"; Presidential Press Secretary Steve Early denied that there was any controversy; and Willkie was left without support.[122]

The Senate debate was long and the attacks on Willkie were bitter, but on March 8 the bill was finally passed by a vote of 60-31, with Republicans voting 17-10 against it. Two days later the House accepted the Senate amendments, Roosevelt immediately signed the measure, and five minutes later he approved a list of materials to be transferred to Britain and Greece. This particular battle was won.

Obviously Willkie's support for Lend-Lease did not change many Republican votes. Probably the bill would have passed in some form even without his support, though certainly not so soon and possibly not without crippling amendments. But if his influence was intangible, it was still powerful. For one thing, however much other Republican leaders discounted his views, they could no longer make the bill a party issue in Congress. Likewise, it was only as individuals that they could take their case to the country; and in this attempt they were frustrated by Willkie's vast personal popularity, which both reflected and strengthened the general approval of the measure.

The pattern was repeated time after time in the months that followed, as the nation readied itself, often confusedly and reluctantly, for the inevitable outbreak of war. Willkie became a sort of advance guard for the Administration, leading the demand for the steps that had to be taken, bearing the brunt of the attacks by the isolationists of both parties, and thereby to a certain extent giving the President freedom to devise specific programs for implementing the policy of saving Britain at any cost, and strengthening his hand when these programs were presented to Congress—or, if they were executive acts, to the public—for final approval.

It is a measure of Roosevelt's greatness that he fully recognized the magnitude both of Willkie's contribution and of the courage that he showed in making it. On the day Willkie testified, the President told reporters that "as far as he was concerned," Willkie's recent actions "had erased any rancor that might have developed during the heated Presidential campaign."[123] That this feeling was permanent is borne out by the testimony of every writer of reminiscences concerning him—most dramatically perhaps, by Robert E. Sherwood, in *Roosevelt and Hopkins:* "There is no doubt in my mind that Roosevelt had far more admiration for Willkie than for any opponent he ever faced . . . and was profoundly and eternally grateful for Willkie's persistent battle against the isolationism of the Old Guard in the Republican party. Once I heard Hopkins make some slurring remark about Willkie and Roosevelt slapped him down with as sharp a reproof as I ever heard him utter. He said, 'Don't ever say anything like that around here again. Don't even *think* it. You of all people ought to know that we might not have had Lend-Lease or Selective Service or a lot of other things if it hadn't been for Wendell Willkie. He was a godsend to the country when we needed him most.' "[124]

Willkie did not fully reciprocate this liking and admiration. He held no grudge for what was past, any more than the President did, but he was often impatient with the latter's indecisiveness, and he also felt that in their personal dealings Roosevelt was sometimes less than frank and fair. Nevertheless, he was not immune to Roosevelt's charm nor blind to his abilities nor unaware of how much they had in common. American history shows few, if any, instances of so close a relationship between a President and his defeated rival, nor one so rich in benefits to the nation.

6

In serving his country Willkie was also serving—perhaps even saving—his party. He provided a rallying point for the many rank and file party members, and for a considerable number of governors and other local leaders, who did not share the blindness and obduracy that with some notable exceptions prevailed among Republicans in Congress; and thus he made it possible for them to retain both their party membership and their self-respect. Walter Lippmann's comment at the time of Willkie's death was no less just than eloquent: "Although Willkie never succeeded in converting the 'old guard' and in restoring the party to its great federalist position, he was able to hold in check its tendency to sink into know-nothingism and reactionary obstruction. Thus, because of him, and of him alone, the Republican party has survived during these four historic years, has preserved its title and eligibility to govern in the world as it now is. If the ideas of his rivals in 1940 had prevailed, we should be today not on the slopes of victory, but isolated, divided, and desperately hard pressed."[125]

It was also because of Willkie that, after the war, such influential one-time isolationists as Senators Vandenberg, Wiley of Wisconsin, and Tobey of New Hampshire were able to reverse their stand and work so effectively for a bipartisan policy of international cooperation. In the words of Joseph Martin (who also at the time, though personally friendly to Willkie, was often on the other side), "This is Wendell Willkie's monument."[126]

Willkie saved the Republican party, however, against the will of its leaders, and his reward was repudiation. But this was a risk that he had taken with open eyes. "I can tell you one thing, though," he said in the spring of 1941 to an interviewer who had asked about the 1944 nomination, "if I could write my own obituary and I had a choice between saying I had been an unimportant president or a person who had contributed to saving democracy at a critical moment, I'd prefer the latter."[127]

Already, before Lend-Lease was finally approved, there were omens of what was to come. As his national popularity increased, his popularity in his own party diminished. A Gallup Poll report on March 2, surveying the change in Willkie sentiment since the election, showed that of all persons questioned, 22 per cent liked him better and 14 per cent liked him less. But among those who had voted for him, the trend was almost exactly reversed. Only 14 per cent liked him better, while 24 per cent liked him less.

Many Republicans, indeed, would have liked to read Willkie out of the party at once. At a meeting of the Young Republican National Federation held at Des Moines on January 30, while he was still in England, two angry anti-Willkie resolutions were proposed. One contained the statement: "The defeated Republican candidate for President has seen fit to travel to England, purporting to be there as a private citizen, when, in reality, he is there as the alleged leader of 22,000,000 Republicans who no longer consider him qualified to speak or gather information for them." The other declared: "In the last election the Young Republican League and the Republican party were deliberately sabotaged by a candidate of the Democratic faith on the Republican ticket whose campaign was epitomized by two words, 'me, too.'" These resolutions, however, were blocked by Martin, who issued a statement saying that he would "regret it" if the resolutions were "seriously considered."[128] But, in fact, a majority of those present showed their approval of Willkie's main position by passing a resolution urging all possible aid to Britain "consistent with building our own national defense and our determination to stay out of war."[129]

But at a meeting of sixteen Republican state chairmen held at Omaha at the same time, although anti-Willkie feeling was held in check once more by a message from Martin—"there is no place in the Omaha meeting for discussion of the lease-lend bill, which is the responsibility of Congress. This thing is not being handled on a party basis"[130]—the gathering showed its resentment by passing a resolution "expressing entire confidence in the Republican delegation in Congress," while pointedly ignoring Willkie.[131]

In the East, however, Willkie still had influence. When his friend

Kenneth Simpson died suddenly during Willkie's absence in England, the latter, while refusing to run himself for Simpson's seat in Congress,[132] backed the candidacy of another liberal Republican, Joseph Clark Baldwin, who won a special election on March 11. Willkie hailed his victory as a sign that "the doctrine of isolation is losing favor."[133]

Willkie won another victory at the meeting of the Republican National Committee on March 24, where a fight over policy was avoided, Martin was persuaded once more to sacrifice his personal inclination and stay on as National Chairman, and "there was general agreement" that Willkie "should be regarded as titular head of the party."[134]

This semblance of harmony, however, concealed a deep and bitter hatred of Willkie by many highly placed Republicans. Raymond Clapper was right when he wrote on February 12: "Wendell Willkie is the hated target of most of the influential politicians in the Republican party today. They are conspiring to get rid of him. They hate him more than they hate Mr. Roosevelt."[135] The resentment kindled by his triumph at Philadelphia, inflamed during the campaign by his endorsement of Selective Service and of the social aims of the New Deal, was made implacable by his aggressive fight for Lend-Lease. The Old Guard saw that a struggle for control of the party was inevitable, and that either they must destroy him or he would destroy them.

One effective weapon against him was fashioned out of his innocent little joke about "campaign oratory." Applauded so heartily at the Senate hearing because it was expressive of innate honesty and of the realities of American political life, it deserved the praise given it by William Allen White: "Only three times in public life have I seen such honesty. The pretension that a candidate's utterances are omniscient when everyone knows that he is talking damned nonsense is one of the large reasons why Americans lose faith in democracy."[136]

Willkie's enemies were able, however, taking his words out of context, to make it appear that he had confessed, not to having indulged in extravagant rhetoric in one particular sentence in one particular speech (it is true that he repeated the sentence, in substance, in other speeches, but this is beside the point), but to having been insincere in everything that he had said—every charge and every promise—during the whole campaign. And this lie, repeated day after day and year after year—and not merely by politicians indulging in campaign oratory on their own account, but by persons from whom one might reasonably expect some regard for simple truth, including (for example) a Roman Catholic Bishop,[137] a Yale Law School professor,[138] and the author of a syndicated column on psychology[139] —finally had its effect.

This result is supremely ironic, for Willkie's main failing as a politician was his inflexible adherence to principle. Yet to a certain extent he *was* responsible for it—not by his remark at the Senate hearing, but by the statements that in that remark he repudiated. For he *did* say things during the campaign that he did not believe to be true. "In the last campaign," he wrote in 1943, "I made some statements under political pressure. After the campaign, I made a resolution never to say or do any thing except strictly in accordance with my belief."[140]

Of course such yielding to pressure is common if not universal among Presidential candidates; while the grace to regret it and the will to atone for it are uncommon if not unique. Perhaps Willkie's subsequent unrelenting campaign against the isolationists in the Republican party stemmed in part from his recollection of having allowed them to persuade him, if only briefly and on one issue, to be false to his better self. If as a public leader he had slipped once from the path of absolute integrity, he would not do so again.

XV
From Lend-Lease to Pearl Harbor

1

The passage of Lend-Lease ended only one act of the historic drama in which the forces of isolation and those of intervention struggled for mastery of American policy, until the Japanese attack on Pearl Harbor ended the outward conflict.[1] This issue cut across all boundaries—of party, occupation, economic status, geographical location, national origin, and religion. Nevertheless, the interventionist group—defined by its determination not merely to aid Britain but to defeat Hitler at any cost—was to a certain degree uniform and comprehensible in its makeup. In general, its members were most numerous in the East and South, and included many business and professional men, as well as artists and intellectuals, and some political leaders; it was also strong in industrial areas and drew support from many workers—perhaps because of family ties with Europe, or because to unsophisticated minds the issue seemed simple and they sensed that the greatest threat to their security was Hitler and what he stood for.

Among those who led the movement were Harvard President James B. Conant; the editor of the Louisville *Courier-Journal,* Herbert Agar; the distinguished playwright and Roosevelt aide, Robert E. Sherwood; Episcopal Bishop Henry W. Hobson; Admiral William H. Standley; Colonel William J. Donovan; Mayor LaGuardia; Senator Claude Pepper of Florida; and former New York Governor Al Smith. The most powerful spokesman for the group was Wendell Willkie. (In early November Senator Bennett Clark of Missouri called him "the undisputed leader of the war party in the United States.")[2]

On the isolationist side was perhaps the most heterogeneous array of groups and individuals that, within the boundaries of the United States, had ever been drawn together in a common cause. It included, of course, the openly pro-Nazi membership of the German-American Bund; the more numerous and widely dispersed Communist claque—to whom, between September, 1939, and June, 1941, the struggle was merely an "imperialist war" initiated by Britain and France; native fascists like Gerald L. K. Smith, with a long record of hate-mongering against minorities; simple-minded heirs of the "Know-nothing" tradition like Verne Marshall, whose "No Foreign War Committee" achieved a brief notoriety at the end of 1940; high-ranking members of the Catholic hierarchy like Cardinal O'Connell of Boston, whose Christian principles, one is tempted to think, were not uncolored by an honest Irish hatred of Britain; men of unquestioned ability in industrial and commercial enterprise, like General Robert Wood of Sears, Roebuck; professional protesters like Norman Thomas, the perennial Socialist candidate for President; professional left-wing-turned-reactionary propagandists like John T. Flynn; soft-headed college presidents like Henry Noble MacCracken of Vassar and hard-headed ones like Robert Maynard Hutchins of Chicago; assorted political figures, ranging from the unaltered "irreconcilable" foe of the League of Nations, Hiram Johnson, and that impervious patriot, Representative Hamilton Fish, to such extravagant demagogues as Senators Burton K. Wheeler and Gerald P. Nye; unclassifiable eccentrics like Colonel Robert R. McCormick of the Chicago *Tribune;* and finally, also unclassifiable, and by all odds the most able spokesman for the cause, the nation's one-time idol, Colonel Charles A. Lindbergh.

The isolationist argument was powerfully presented by Lindbergh in "A Letter to Americans," published in *Collier's Magazine* (which was editorially interventionist) on March 29. He charged that America was "being led toward war with ever-increasing rapidity and by every conceivable subterfuge"—"by a group of interventionists, and foreign interests, against the will of a majority of our people." He drew the inevitable parallel with 1917, and a further parallel between interventionists in an unprepared America ("We have not as many thoroughly modern fighting planes in our Army and Navy combined as Germany produces in a single week") and the leaders in unprepared France and Britain in 1939.

And now, in contrast with 1917, with Hitler and his puppets in control of Western Europe and in alliance with a friendly or cowed Soviet Union and an increasingly aggressive Japan—what possible plan of victory could be devised? If Hitler had so far not been able to invade England, how could England and America ever hope to invade the Continent?

And he argued with almost equal force the difficulties of any foreign invasion of America—the breadth of the Atlantic, working for America and not against her; defenses planned and implemented without haste, a united people if an attack should come. "I believe that we can build a military and commercial position on this continent that is impregnable to attack . . ."

And what, after all, had America to do with Europe's ancient quarrels? "We should all be marching together toward one clear and accepted goal—the independent destiny of America. If we desire unity and strength among our people, we must turn our eyes back from these everlasting wars of Europe—back to our own country, to the clear horizons of a great American future."

For an answer the editors turned to Willkie. His reply appeared on May 10. He began by rejecting the allegation that the interventionists wanted war. Everybody, he declared, *wants* peace; but "no man can guarantee peace." Nevertheless, he refused to question the isolationists' good faith. "Their motives are high, their intentions are good, and some of their arguments are persuasive." The essential difference lay in his belief—which they rejected—in "the interdependence of the democratic world." "We . . . cannot agree that the United States is able, at will, to shut herself off from the rest of the world. . . . We do in fact have responsibilities toward other peoples; not merely moral responsibilities but political and economic responsibilities. . . . *The world cannot get along without the United States of America.*" This means "that we must be willing to stand firmly upon the principles that *we* believe in . . . that we must be willing to help keep those principles alive wherever man wants to keep them alive. If we don't, the principles will die, not only elsewhere but right here among us."

And, second, *"what happens in the rest of the world must inevitably have profound effects on us in America."* If Germany were to win, and with Japan control the rest of the world, then (assuming that they did not attempt a military attack) America would have two choices: to trade with the totalitarian countries *on their terms,* or not to trade with them at all. Either choice would be ruinous to a free economy and would eventually result in a totalitarian government at home. But, he is convinced, in such a world, war would be inevitable. "And by that time we should be fighting alone."

He did not dodge Lindbergh's challenge to produce a definite program. "I give to America a practical, specific plan. Furnish to Britain today and tomorrow and the next day, for her desperate need, ships—the ships in our docks, the ships in our coastal trade—until it hurts, the impounded ships of other nations, the ships we are building. Give to her destroyers, and if necessary [Willkie told reporters that events had led him to try to remove the phrase "if necessary," but that it was too late][3] see that those ships, with the ever-increasing production of American factories and farms, deliver their cargoes safely to the ports of western and northern England. Thus Britain will survive . . ." Eventually victory will come through "overwhelming superiority in the air."

In assessing this exchange, it is evident that in one respect Lindbergh had a moral advantage. He saw and could say that aid to Britain meant war for America—total war, of indeterminate duration. And Willkie, one must believe, saw it too but could not say it. The gospel of "victory through air power" was tempting; it did not lack fanatical and articulate preachers; and it *did* give Lindbergh an answer. But Willkie did not press it, and the conclusion must be that he was too level-headed not to see that war must come for America and that, even without a huge expeditionary force, it would be prolonged and bloody.

Should be, then, have spoken as did Bishop Hobson, in issuing a manifesto on behalf of the Fight for Freedom Committee (formed, on April 19, by the more aggressive members of the Committee to Defend America)? "Hitler cannot allow our goods to get to England; if he does, he will be beaten. We cannot allow our goods to be sunk in the Atlantic; if we do, we shall be beaten. The problem is simple, and the answer is a willingness to do whatever is necessary to insure a Hitler defeat. This means accepting the fact that we are at war, declared or undeclared."[4]

But while an avowed partisan could make such a statement, a national leader could not. The American people had indeed made their decision, but they were still not willing to admit it. On January 31 the Gallup Poll reported that 79 per cent of Americans were opposed to Lindbergh's suggestion for a "negotiated peace"; but on February 2 it stated that 85 per cent were opposed to entering the war. And in mid-April, after Hitler's first Balkan successes, 79 per cent were still opposed to sending any troops abroad.[5] Under these circumstances, if either Willkie or Roosevelt had endorsed the last sentence of Bishop Hobson's statement, it would have meant an incalculable lessening of their influence when that influence was most needed, and would have deeply divided public opinion when unity was most essential.

It is doubtful if the economic arguments—the theoretical lowering of living standards and destruction of the "free enterprise system" which each side asserted would result from the other's program—had any great effect on people's minds or emotions. Such threats were too tenuous in form and too remote in time to move men deeply. What *did* move them was the fear of war on the one hand and the hatred of Nazism on the other. And the latter was bound to prevail. Though the interventionists sometimes played down the moral issue and appealed to "enlightened self-interest," it was in fact the moral idealism of the American people—confused, self-contradictory, and inarticulate as it might seem—that guaranteed eventual American entry into the war. They hated the theory of Nazism—its exaltation of the state and annihilation of the individuatl, its belief in a master race and in slave races; and they hated still more violently the practice of it—the lengthening list of unprovoked aggressions against neighboring countries, the frightful persecution of the Jews, the calculated use of terror as a weapon through the wholesale slaughter of civilians. They could not help pitying those who were its victims or admiring those who fought against it regardless of the odds. They could not help responding to Willkie's ringing repetition of the phrase "free men like us."

2

There is no need to retell here the whole story of the nine months' "undeclared war" that existed from the passage of Lend-Lease to the attack on Pearl Harbor. During this time of tumult, Willkie hewed steadily to the line of trying to unite the country behind a policy of aid to Britain at whatever cost (though still avoiding the word "war"). His earlier reluctance to make speeches vanished, now that he had a cause to fight for. Whenever he had a chance to speak, he spoke, from one end of the country to the other.

Since, however, he never accepted payment for his speeches and always gave to charity the money received from magazine articles, he had still, somehow, to earn a living. No doubt there were many corporations that would have been glad to pay him a high salary for the use of his talents and his name. But he had dedicated himself, in the phrase that J. N. Darling used as the title of a profoundly moving cartoon at the time of his death, to "Courageous Public Service Without Reward,"[6] and he could therefore accept no position that would make too heavy demands on his time or that would place any limits on his freedom of speech.

The kind of job he wanted presented itself when he was invited to join the eminent law firm of Miller, Owen, Otis & Bailey (later Willkie, Owen, Farr, Gallagher and Walton). The initial invitation from his friend Harold Gallagher had come in January, 1940, when the forced break-up of Commonwealth & Southern was imminent. Willkie asked for time to think it over, however, and it was not until May that they talked again. By then Willkie had decided definitely to try for the Republican Presidential nomination, and he did not care to give his enemies a chance to charge that he was ashamed of his utility connections.[7] He joined the firm in April, 1941.

One wonders how he found time for *any* private activity. Only those who worked with him or one who has studied his correspondence can imagine the terrible pressure under which Willkie lived the last years of his life— greater, surely, than was endured by any American except the President himself; and the Presidency has a sort of built-in apparatus to protect the incumbent from just this kind of wear and tear, whereas Willkie operated with only two or three secretaries.

Every day brought its hundreds or thousands of letters from ordinary citizens; its dozens of invitations to make speeches; its innumerable requests to get people jobs, to endorse books, to secure a hearing for this or that proposal for saving the country or the world, to sign manifestoes, to serve as a director or chairman of organizations devoted to "worthy causes," to support or oppose this or that piece of legislation. And if he failed to comply with the last type of request, he was likely to be blamed for not exercising greater leadership. On one such occasion, he tried to explain his position in a letter to Arthur Krock: "I think the criticism you made of me was appropriate.

"I, however, do want to say that my failure to speak on some of the domestic questions, such as taxation, has not been due to any lack of appreciation of the point which you raise or from any lack of desire. I have had innumerable talks with Republican members of Congress. . . .

"You appreciate, I am but an individual. I have only so much time. In addition, I have to earn a living. It is difficult for one who is not in Congress, to follow the day to day fights on such matters as taxation, etc."[8]

But if he could not always follow what was going on in Congress, he was compelled by his role of public servant to know as much as he could about what was going on in the Republican party—to lead the fight to reform the party and get it to support an intelligent program. He had scores of advisers throughout the country—newspapermen, businessmen, local political leaders—with whom he had to keep in touch. Moreover, contrary to a wide-spread impression, he made a genuine effort to gain the good will of influential party leaders; sending notes of congratulation on appropriate occasions, according to suggestions by his advisers; writing political "bread-and-butter" letters after visits here and there; and warmly commending those who spoke out for the causes that he believed in.[9]

Despite all this, he conscientiously did his share of the firm's work, as is proved by his diaries and by the testimony of the partner who was closer to him than any other. "He participated in the firm conferences . . . was available for discussion on firm policies and other matters in relation to the business of the office . . . and was a most valued partner." In return, he received an income that "was very substantial, and had he been willing to take some of the things that he was offered, it could have been greater."[10] But he was interested in money only as a means to independence.

While preparing to join the firm, he was not idle. On March 24 and 25 he undertook to advance the cause of Canadian-American unity by visits to Toronto and Montreal, where hundreds of thousands of persons turned out to give him a more tumultuous welcome than had been accorded any previous visitor except King George and Queen Elizabeth in 1939.[11] And on the day of his return to New York, he spoke for United China Relief, presenting an eloquent exposition of the "One World" idea.[12]

Nor did his active partnership in the law firm bring a let-up in his public activities. In April, he wrote the answer to Lindbergh. On April 25 he spoke at Pittsburgh under the auspices of the YMCA fund drive; on May 4 at the dedication of a new Vultee Aircraft factory at Nashville, Tennessee; on May 7 at a "Freedom Rally" in Madison Square Garden; on May 25 at New York's Columbus Circle at a parade for United China Relief; on June 6 at the Chicago Stadium under the auspices of the All-Chicago Citizens' Rally Committee; on June 11 in New York at a United China Relief luncheon; on June 13 at a luncheon of the Society for the New York Hospital; on June 18 for United China Relief once more; on June 28 at a luncheon where he received "the 1941 Jewish War Veterans' award for American leadership"; on July 4 on an NBC Independence Day broadcast (his speech was translated into Spanish, Portuguese, German, Italian, and French for broadcasting to foreign countries); on July 15 on NBC's Blue Network in observance of Aid British Labor Week; on July 17 at a Labor Rally staged by the Fight for Freedom Committee; on July 23 in the Hollywood Bowl, for the Southern California Committee for National Unity; on July 24 in San Francisco for Americans United; on September 3 (after a vacation in Rushville) to a nation-wide radio audience, opening a drive to sell defense bonds; on September 6 at a Yugoslav Liberty Day luncheon; on September 17 at another United China Relief luncheon, and again on October 2 at a major rally for the same organization; on October 5 at the "It's Fun to Be Free" rally staged by the Fight for Freedom Committee in Madison Square Garden; on October 6 at a dinner of the National Republican Club in honor of Lord Halifax; on October 7 for the New York and Brooklyn Federations for Jewish Charities; on October 18 on a Blue Network symposium on "The United States and Japan Today" (he had a cold and his speech was read by Dorothy Thompson); on October 28 at an American Labor Party rally for Mayor La Guardia (who was running for re-election); on November 18 at a dinner where he received an award from *The Churchman* (independent publication of the Episcopal Church) "for the promotion of good will and better understanding among peoples." In addition, he had written articles for the *American Legion Magazine* (August), *Readers Digest* (October), *The American Magazine* (November), *Life* (November 3), and *Look* (November 4); and he had issued dozens of press statements.

The major theme in most of these speeches and articles (and a subsidiary theme in the rest) was the need for national unity to bring about the defeat of Germany and Japan.

This was one crusade in which Willkie did not fight alone. But the strength of the interventionist movement only intensified the fury with which the isolationists opposed it. The venom of some extremists is vividly revealed in an episode told by Mrs. Raymond Clapper, whose husband vigorously opposed isolation. "One day I received a package wrapped as a gift. When I opened it I found a miniature black coffin with a paper skeleton inside marked 'Your husband.'"[13] When Lindbergh told a huge America First rally in New York, "It is obvious that England is losing the war," "he was interrupted by wild cheers."[14] At a similar rally in Chicago, Wheeler spoke to "a stamping, shrieking crowd of 9,000 persons."[15] At another in Brooklyn, addressed by Senator Bennett Clark of Missouri, the crowd booed every mention of Hull, Stimson, Knox, Hopkins, and Willkie.[16] When Adlai Stevenson organized an aid-to-Britain rally in Chicago in early

June, he found that many local businessmen, though sympathetic, declined to be publicly associated with the undertaking for fear of economic reprisals.[17]

The interventionists, on the other hand, with a few notable exceptions, stuck to the issues and avoided personal abuse; and Willkie consistently defended the right of opponents to say what they thought. "I am so firmly convinced that our foreign policy as enunciated by the Administration and approved by the overwhelming vote of Congress is so right that we can finally convince all Americans of its wisdom if we keep the channels of public communication free and open, unclogged with bitter personal recrimination."[18]

In this statement he was rebuking the President, who in a press conference had compared Lindbergh to a notorious Civil War "Copperhead."[19] As a matter of fact, Lindbergh had been more temperate than many other isolationists. But after this episode (which led him to resign his commission in the Air Force Reserve) a note of increasing bitterness appeared in his speeches. He made no acknowledgement when Willkie again came to his defense. "I hope that the Administration will discontinue these constant and bitter attacks on individuals . . . Those of us who are doing our utmost to promote national unity, I believe, are entitled to the help, not the hindrance, of the Administration in our efforts."[20]

Yet, after all, there *was* in the very nature of the isolationist doctrine a kind of poison that more and more infected those who preached it. Lindbergh certainly was sincere when he told an audience on October 3: "I could not stand by and see [my country] going to destruction without pitting everything I had against that trend. . . . I have tried and I shall continue to try as long as it is possible to give you the truth without prejudice and without passion."[21] Yet this was the man who had declared: "Our government asks us to preserve democracy abroad by creating a dictatorship in our own country."[22] "We in America were given just about as much chance to express our beliefs at the election last fall as the Germans would have been given if Hitler had run against Goering."[23] "The three most important groups which have been pressing the country toward war are the British, the Jewish and the Roosevelt administration."[24]

This was too much even for Willkie, who called it "the most un-American talk made in my time by any person of national reputation. If the American people permit race prejudice to arise at this crucial moment, they little deserve to preserve democracy."[25]

More cautious language was used in a statement issued by a group of eminent Republicans headed by Hoover and Landon. The signers declared that they wanted Britain and her allies to win (Lindbergh had declared that it would be "a tragedy to the world . . . if the British Empire collapses"[26] and "I never wanted Germany to win this war"[27]) but that "in giving generous aid to these democracies at our seaboard we have gone as far as is consistent either with law, with sentiment, or with security. . . . Freedom for America does not depend on the outcome of struggles for material power among other nations."[28] But this statement is really as strongly tainted by nationalism as any of Lindbergh's: by the notion that American "civilization" is somehow superior to any other; by the implication that the people actually fighting against Hitler were inspired only by "material" motives; by the assumption that human ties and moral obligations exist in space and not in spirit and do not extend beyond a nation's geographical boundaries.

Such narrow nationalism did not and could not win the support of a majority of Americans, who were, moreover, repelled by the kind of support that it *did* receive. Religious bigotry, racial intolerance, fear of social change, personal resentments against individuals or society or "the government"—all these sought to gain respectability under the cloak of nationalism.

And this was natural. For once an arbitrary line is drawn that permits one group of human beings to look upon another group as inferior, then *any* group can claim the right to draw a line of its own. This fact Willkie saw, and stated, clearly. In 1944, opposing the reelection of Representative Hamilton Fish, he declared that it would be "a great service to all Americans to help terminate [his] political career," and added: "And this is true not alone because of his raising of the racial issue, but fundamentally because his narrow, nationalistic views and associations are the inevitable producers of anti-Semitism and a dozen other perils of democracy. Race antagonism is but one of the symptoms—narrow nationalism is the fundamental cause. This is the time for all men to be straightforward and unambiguous on this basic issue."[29]

3

Willkie's fight to unify the country, however, involved much more than answering the isolationists. A majority of Americans had already rejected the isolationist argument, but they still had to be brought to face the implications and accept the consequences of this rejection. They had, in short, to be prepared for war.

In this effort Roosevelt was once more willing to see his erstwhile rival take the lead, while he himself waited, apparently, for public opinion to continue its interventionist swing to the point where he could safely make another specific move to aid Britain. This is at least a possible interpretation of what appeared to be mere drift.

The immediate issue was convoying—the use of American warships to make sure that Lend-Lease materials were not sunk by Nazi submarines. Willkie had dodged the question at the Senate hearings on Lend-Lease—

and Roosevelt continued to dodge it. When on March 31 Senator Tobey of New Hampshire and Representative Sauthoff of Wisconsin introduced a resolution forbidding convoys, the President did not take up the challenge. On April 11 it was reported from an "authoritative source" that before facing this question he intended to "exhaust every possible alternative."[30] And he even tried to prevent Willkie from aggressive advocacy of such a measure; for on April 25 Lauchlin Currie, a Presidential assistant, wrote to Roosevelt: "In accordance with your instructions I telephoned Willkie and told him that some of our experts were not at all sure that convoys were the answer . . . He said he appreciated this information and asked me to keep him informed as he is now committed to this policy."[31] On the same day Roosevelt told a press conference that the government was "not considering naval convoys at this time."[32]

Perhaps the President's position was influenced not only by the "experts" but by the Gallup Poll, which on April 23 reported that 50 per cent of those questioned were opposed to convoys and only 41 per cent in favor, with the remainder undecided. So, at least, Willkie suggested a few days later: "The time to do something about these sinkings is past due. . . . I think that the Administration should not follow public opinion but should lead it. . . . I am waiting, as I know all the American people are, to be told the degree of destruction of supplies and a plan for protection."[33]

In the meantime, events were working against the isolationists. On April 6 the Germans invaded Yugoslavia, and three weeks later controlled the entire Balkan peninsula, despite Britain's gallant gesture in defense of Greece. During the same month the British, weakened by this effort after their first sensational victory in North Africa, had been driven back to the Egyptian border with heavy losses. And, as always happened after a great Hitler victory, American sentiment for intervention grew. On April 30 the Senate Foreign Relations Committee rejected Senator Tobey's resolution forbidding convoys, and another one by Senator Nye. And the New Hampshire Senator's constituents showed their feelings by sending him a yellow umbrella—Chamberlain had carried an umbrella to Munich—and other appropriate gifts, including "a quarter keg of tripe, a bag of fertilizer, a porcupine nose . . . and a package of petunia seeds."[34] (But in later years, it should be said, he changed his views, and became one of the staunchest Republican supporters of internationalism.) On May 15 the Senate approved a bill, previously passed by the House, permitting the President to seize and use as he saw fit all foreign ships lying idle in U. S. ports. (Republicans voted against it—100-51 in the House, 15-10 in the Senate.) And all the while an increasing number of famous persons, leaders of various national organizations, and committees created for the purpose, urged that war materials be delivered by convoys or by "whatever means is necessary."

At the center of this surge of feeling was Willkie. On May 7 he spoke at a "Freedom Rally" in Madison Square Garden, to which, police estimated, 110,000 persons sought to gain entrance. He was introduced by Mayor La Guardia as "the finest example of American unity—an American who puts his country before all party advantage."[35] (Nobody reminded the Mayor of *his* "campaign oratory" of six months before.) And he said what his audience had come to hear.

"Fellow Americans, there is no compromise—the world will be dominated by free men or it will be dominated by enslaved men. We cannot appease the forces of evil. We cannot make peace with those who seek to destroy our very way of life. . . . But some among us say we are weak and we are unprepared; that the British are bound to fail and that our own hope lies in locking ourselves behind our own defenses while freedom collapses about us. . . . This is a doctrine of confusion, fear and despair. . . . It is a cowardly doctrine, unworthy of our past and destructive of our future."

A month later, in Chicago, he made a still more eloquent appeal. It was, in fact, one of his greatest speeches,[36] and its reception by a crowd of 22,000 that packed the Chicago Stadium suggested that even in that stronghold of America First, isolationism was a minority movement.

Willkie began with a plea, already quoted in part, for a reasonable discussion of the issues, unclouded by personal rancor. He then dealt in forthright fashion with the common charge that in the 1940 election the voters had had no chance to express their views on foreign affairs: "As a matter of fact, in the very nomination of the candidates they expressed their views. . . . Frankly, I think one of the principal reasons why I was chosen by my party to be its nominee was because I had been more emphatic and consistent than any of the other candidates in urging all-out aid to Britain."

With equal frankness he admitted: "my conception of what constitutes effective aid to Britain has changed. I said . . . that England must win the war . . . but . . . I hoped, and said that top-speed production in the United States would be all the help necessary from us. . . . Now it is painfully obvious that production is not enough. It is now our job not only to produce the goods necessary for her survival but to deliver them by whatever means will be most efficient." "Our naval patrol does not stop the deadly toll; [but unless it is] stopped, or greatly reduced, England cannot survive." "I cannot tell you," he added, "the point at which we may become involved in war. Neither can any other American. [But] we of America must decide at once whether we will let Britain go down."

As always, he made a plea for unity, including, this time, a scathing attack on political opportunists of both parties: "there must be an end of petty politics. I have nothing but contempt for any Republican who hopefully keeps on the fence praying that at a later date he may inherit what he supposes will be the inevitable reaction toward isolationism and appeasement. . . . And I have equal disdain for those New Dealers and Democrats who cogitate and plan how America's present stupendous efforts can be translated into offices and power."

All personal feelings, in fact, and all special interests, must be subordinated (as the Administration was not yet willing to subordinate them) to the one aim of creating armaments: "We must gear ourselves for a united and complete effort in government, in industry, in labor and in agriculture. We must wipe out political blacklists. The fittest men to administer the defense effort, irrespective of their political affiliations or economic beliefs, must be brought to Washington.

"A master priority must be at once formulated. Our industrial capacity must be allocated, among our military, our naval, aeronautical, lease-lend and civilian needs . . . through a coordinated centralized authority under one man responsible to the President . . . Labor and industrial peace must come, and come quickly, whatever may be the sacrifice of ordinary aims." The national emergency "requires the organization of our whole economy into one vast, closely coordinated machine with every part adjusted to every other part and the whole thing ticking like a first-class watch. It can be done and it must be done."

Thus much for the means of insuring a victory over Hitler. But already Willkie had begun to look beyond the cessation of fighting and to consider how to avoid the pattern of catastrophe that had shaped itself after World War I. "Civilization cannot afford such another mistake," he had told an audience at Toronto on March 23. "We must begin now to shape in our minds the kind of world we want. We must not await the war's end to make these purposes clear. . . . we can, if we have the will, convert what seems to be the death rattle of our time into the birth pains of a better order."[37]

This was his answer to the isolationist argument that nothing would be gained and everything would be lost if America were involved in the fighting. The conflict, he kept insisting, was not merely a struggle for survival, it was an opportunity for advancement. The end to be sought was not merely the destruction of Nazi tyranny, it was the extension of freedom and democracy. Here, and not in a supposed national self-interest, was the motive that must unite and inspire the country in an effort more strenuous and all-embracing than any in its history. "We are beginning to . . . see in [a British] victory a chance to correct the errors of the past and to make democracy a reality for all men.

"In all those silent places of the earth where men are enslaved and dictators now seem permanently in power there will be lifting of heads as there was more than a century ago when men first heard of the Declaration of Independence. The myth of the invincibility of dictatorships will be ended. The creative genius of the people that collectivism and dictatorship now suppress will again be released—as the inventive genius of the American people was released in our own early days."

In this context, Willkie's concluding picture of America's greatness is untarnished by even a hint of nationalistic arrogance. For this greatness lies not in any unique quality that other peoples do not have, but in the achievement, imperfect though it may be, of that which all peoples desire and of which all are righful heirs. "The warlords of Nazi Germany boast that this country is powerless to thwart their long-laid plans of world conquest. America, they tell us . . . is torn with labor strife, with political dissension, with class and race antagonisms. And she is a democracy, they say, that fatal weakness. . . . Rent by conflicting counsels which democracy permits, America, they claim, will fall a prey to indecision until too late, when like an over-ripe fruit it will drop into the hands of the conqueror.

"That is the picture that the Nazis paint. But we in America see a picture they can never see. It is a picture that must be forever invisible to the eye of tyranny because it shows itself only to the inward gaze of free spirits.

"We see a nation slow to anger and unused to fear. We see a broad, rich and varied land. Here men, whose ancestors were hereditary enemies, work perfectly together, unmindful of those ancient feuds. Here stretches mile on mile of unfortified frontier. Men speak their minds, read what they please and worship in accordance with their consciences. A chance to earn a living, raise and educate a family, and be self-respecting, free individuals is all they ask. It is a peaceful nation, unused to military pomp and circumstance. Strangers may think it soft, divided, ineffectual. What they do not see is that, underneath, the love of country burns. Deeper than all the surface differences there runs the unifying devotion to our common heritage of freedom.

"And when that freedom is threatened, as it is today, this country will be found, as it has always been found in a great crisis, not divided but the *United* States of America."

4

Ten days earlier, the President had finally ventured to speak with something like Willkie's boldness. In a "fireside chat" on May 27 he proclaimed an "unlimited national emergency," and justified it in a powerful speech built upon the theme of "freedom of the seas." If this could be maintained, Hitler was beaten. "All freedom . . . depends on freedom of the seas. All of American history—North, Central and South American history—has been inevitably tied up with those words 'freedom of the seas.'" But this freedom was threatened by the "rate of Nazi sinking of merchant ships"—"more than three times the capacity of British shipyards to replace them . . . more than twice the combined British and American output of merchant ships today." "I say that the delivery of needed supplies to Britain is imperative. I say this can be done; it must be done; it will be done."

The extent to which this issue had now forced itself upon the country's attention can be measured by the reception of the President's speech. While he was speaking, the life of New York City practically came to a standstill. Telephone calls were down fifty per cent. Traffic in the streets almost ceased. At the Polo Grounds the baseball game between the Braves and the Giants, tied 1-1 at the end of the seventh inning, was halted for 45 minutes while players and spectators listened to the broadcast in complete silence.[38]

Nor was this intense concentration on the President's words limited to one section of the country. "No utterance by the President since he entered the White House," reported the United Press, "has had a response equalling in volume and approval that which was accorded to his speech on Tuesday night."[39] The isolationists attacked the speech with a fury that must have been heightened by a sense of futility. Willkie praised it, demonstrating a technique that he regularly employed during this period—giving Roosevelt a friendly pat on the back, accompanied by an adroit forward shove: "The President has stirred the whole world with his great message. It now lies within his power to unite the country in the singleness of effort and resolve which alone can make his vision come true."[40] Even Dewey broke his silence on the issue ten days later, with a ringing call for all-out aid to Britain, repeal of the Neutrality Act, and "safe delivery by our naval forces of merchant ships" carrying goods to anti-Axis nations.[41]

And then, after all this—nothing happened. On May 29 the main headline of the *Times* read: "Roosevelt Does Not Plan Convoys or Change in Neutrality Laws." With his popularity at a peak unequalled during the palmiest days of the New Deal (the Gallup Poll found that in May 73 per cent of the people approved of the President's policies and in June 76 per cent),[42] he did nothing. As early as May 10 Secretary Ickes commented bitterly in his diary: "I told McCloy yesterday that if I could have looked this far ahead and seen an inactive and uninspiring President, I would not have supported Roosevelt for a third term."[43] The country drifted, leaderless except for words, as it had done since the passage of Lend-Lease.

In the face of such Administration inertia, Willkie himself had moments of depression, although he tried to fight them off. "I know isolationism gains at times," he wrote to Bartley Crum on June 13, "but really,

Bart, I know if we keep at it we are bound to win. We cannot be as right as we are on that question and not prevail."[44] In a still less buoyant mood, writing to Joseph Alsop on July 3 to acknowledge some data on the shipping situation (he had just received from Lord Halifax the estimate that Allied and U. S. ship construction could not be expected to equal the present rate of loss before January, 1943), he confessed: "I sometimes become a little discouraged in the face of such situations as this one, but I guess the only thing to do is plug ahead. . . . Somehow I suppose we are coming out of all this some day and you and I and like-minded fellows have got to plug to see that there is something better after this."[45]

But the next day, in an Independence Day broadcast to the world, his voice had the old confident ring, though he did not deny the grimness of the present outlook. "Since the last celebration of this holiday in America, millions of people, just like us, who lived peaceful, contented lives, lived free lives, with the right to go about their life as they pleased, have been deprived of their liberty. And we also know that unless their liberty is restored, liberty cannot remain a permanent possession of America. . . . the overwhelming percentage of the American people are resolved that at whatever hazard or cost we will sustain the fighting men of Britain."[46]

And now, at long last Roosevelt once more replaced words with action. On July 7 American troops, with the approval of the local government, occupied Iceland, and the Navy was given the duty of keeping the sea-lanes open as far as that point—well over half way from the United States to Britain.

Two days later the President showed his appreciation of Willkie's support by inviting him to lunch at the White House. Willkie in turn assured him that the occupation of Iceland was approved by an "'overwhelming' number of the Republican rank and file"; and also took the opportunity (it was rumored and can well be believed) to repeat in private what he had been saying in public about the need for continued "aggressive leadership" in delivering war goods, for a unified program under a single head to produce these goods, and for an end to statements by members of the Administration that would arouse needless animosity and distrust.[47]

It was the second of these policies that was, at the moment, most urgent. There was an actual drop in plane production in May, and again in July—and the planes produced were still mostly trainers. On June 29 Hanson Baldwin declared that the Army had "not a single division yet ready for war"; that not one medium tank had been delivered, nor one heavy tank produced; that mechanized equipment was only "just beginning to be delivered." On June 14 the War Department asked for a fifty per cent cut in the production of automobiles for civilian use; but on July 24 William

S. Knudsen (who had a larger share of the scattered responsibility for production than anyone else) rejected the request because it would cause "dislocation" in the industry.[48] "Business as usual" seemed still to be the prevailing attitude. Lend-Lease exports through August 31, five and a half months after passage of the act, totaled only $190,000,000. Friction between labor and management was increasing.

Against this administrative fumbling, Willkie kept hammering away, as he had been doing for a year. In a speech at the Hollywood Bowl on July 23 (he had received a "tremendous ovation" on his arrival the day before at the Los Angeles airport)[49] he accused the President of having failed "in the most elementary task of management, the task of delegation, the task of calling in the ablest men in the country and giving them power to act." But his aim, as always, was unity, and he added that the remedy was "not more opposition but more support"; "we must get the kind of management we want, not through petty criticism, but through the enormous pressure of American public opinion insisting that a good job must be done."[50]

He went on again to defend the occupation of Iceland, and the President's power to order it. "It was the clear intention of the founders of this country that in emergencies the President should lead." The real danger was not from action by the President but from inaction, or even obstructive action, by Congress. "We may be in danger if Senators, instead of debating the real issues of this time, turn to personal invective, or take advantage of the Senate rules insuring fair debate to make debate impossible. We may be in danger if Congressmen become politically timid . . ."

And again he pictured the war as an opportunity for achievement. If the issue was seen "only as a sterile dispute between a war party and a peace party, we are led only to a paralyzing inaction and distrust—and the debate degenerates to personalities, to the imputation of motives, to smears and appeals to prejudice that make calm decision impossible." But if this danger was avoided, then: "As we move steadily forward it will be in the knowledge that each step is leading us closer to a vision of that new world . . . which if we are courageous, will little by little expose itself, until we see it whole.

"It is an exciting thing to be living in these times. For it is only in such times as these, when men are in doubt, and when they must struggle for the truth, that the great achievements of history are brought forth."[51]

In San Francisco the next evening Willkie re-asserted the constitutionality and the necessity of freedom of action by the President; and he also introduced a new theme, undertaking to reassure those who were uneasy at finding themselves on the same side as Communist Russia. "Russia has never been a military or trade menace to us," he declared, and added that even the ideological threat was now negligible.[52]

These statements were as timely as they were true, for the German invasion of Russia begun on June 22 had supplied the isolationists with new arguments. "Why not leave them alone to fight it out?" asked Hiram Johnson bluntly.[53] This had always been Lindbergh's desire. "If Germany had been permitted to throw her armies eastward in 1939 instead of 1941, the picture in Europe would be far different today."[54] Even less biased persons were disturbed because the war was now "not purely a world conflict between tyranny and freedom."[55] They could not see that this fact was irrelevant.

This was another source of the general apathy, the moral paralysis, the mood of drift, which gripped America during the summer months, and which brought the country to the verge of catastrophe. The original Selective Service Act had provided for only one year of military service. Without new Congressional action, those who had been first inducted would in October begin returning to civilian life, and the limit on the number in service at any one time would remain at 900,000.

Early in July, accordingly, a bill was introduced giving the government authority to keep selectees, National Guard units, reservists, and Regular Army men in service until six months after the end of the emergency and to send them wherever the national defense might require. Congress, however, seemed unaware that any emergency existed. The weakening, as time passed, of the fear and anger aroused by Hitler's Balkan conquests; the feeling that the Nazis were for the time being fully engaged in Russia (though it was all but universally agreed that Russian resistance could not last); the President's lack of leadership; the resentful belief of a large part of the public that the Administration had been less than frank in picturing the needs and accomplishments of the defense program at home; the audible protests of the draftees themselves, withdrawn from a comfortable civilian life to train (in many instances) with dummy weapons for a war of whose likelihood few were convinced;—all these operated against decisive Congressional action.

Belatedly awakening to the mood of Congress, Roosevelt first withdrew the request for authority to send draftees abroad, and then sent a special message. The issue seemed settled when the Senate passed, by a 45-30 vote (with Republicans voting, or paired, 16-8 against) a bill extending the period of service eighteen months and removing the 900,000 limit. But in the House, on August 12, victory came by the smallest possible margin: 203-202. With Pearl Harbor less than five months away, the change of a single vote would have reduced the military training program to something approaching chaos.

Willkie had made relatively few direct comments on the bill. But he had, not merely by giving unflagging support to the President's foreign policy but by pushing beyond and assuming the leadership which the President declined, focused public support and strengthened wavering Democrats, and so supplied the crucial impetus that carried the bill through.

He failed, however, to alter any Republican votes. The 133-21 vote of House Republicans against the extension of the draft was another 6-1 "no confidence" vote against the party's 1940 leader. And while the rank and file were far less antagonistic, the Gallup Poll on July 27 found that only 9 per cent of Republicans liked him better, and 38 per cent liked him less, than at the time of the election.[56]

5

The movement toward intervention was so widespread and was inspired by such strong convictions—it had the support of so many prominent and dedicated persons—that even Willkie did not dominate it, though he was its most influential spokesman. But in one minor skirmish, he was the star performer.

This was a Senate subcommittee investigation of alleged war propaganda in the motion picture industry. The first sortie was by Senator Wheeler in opposing the draft extension bill. He charged that the movie companies had ordered their employees to attend Willkie's Hollywood speech, and added: "Democrats follow Wendell Willkie, whom they were denouncing a few months ago. He is making their policies. He is telling them what to do. He is pushing the President. He and his little claque of Wall Street bankers, together with the motion picture industry, are trying to stir up sentiment to take us into war."[57]

A month later, as chairman of the Senate Interstate Commerce Committee, Wheeler appointed a subcommittee, headed by another isolationist, Senator D. Worth Clark of Idaho, to investigate his charge. The Motion Picture Producers and Distributors of America promptly retained Willkie as their counsel; and a reporter gleefully predicted that this "assures a battle."[58]

He was right. During August Willkie had broken his exhausting schedule and taken a vacation on his Indiana farms, and was returning to the battle with renewed vigor. Even before the hearings began, he made public a letter to the chairman which at once put the committee on the defensive. In it he raised first the issue of free speech. "From the motion picture and radio industries it is just a small step to newspapers, magazines and other periodicals. And from the freedom of the press it is just a small step to the freedom of the individual to say what he believes." He then questioned both the legal authority and impartiality of the committee, accused it (taking advantage of a speech in which Senator Nye had charged that the movie industry was engaging in war propaganda because most of its leaders were Jews) of being anti-Jewish, and finally cut the ground from under it by asserting that if the question was whether the movie industry was opposed to Hitler, "there need be no investigation. . . . We abhor everything which Hitler represents."[59]

At the beginning of the hearings, Senator Clark brought a sigh of disappointment from the audience by announcing that "under the Senate rules" Willkie would not be allowed to cross-examine witnesses. Senator Nye then took the stand and read a 41-page prepared statement. Before he had finished, Willkie had prepared a rebuttal, leading up to the conclusion that Nye had demonstrated, "without a bit of doubt, why this foolish show should be ended once and for all."

Willkie was, in fact, irrepressible. Toward the end of the session, after Nye had mentioned a few pictures to which he objected *(The March of Time* series, *Sergeant York, The Great Dictator, Escape, Convoy, Flight Command, I Married a Nazi)* but had been rather vague, under questioning by Senator McFarland (the one anti-isolationist member of the committee) as to what was in them, he suggested a private showing before the committee; whereupon Willkie seized a microphone to express enthusiastic and irreverent approval: "We'll be glad to supply them all and you can put them on right here in the committee room. That will make a real movie show out of this."[60]

The next day the witness was Senator Bennett Clark of Missouri, who in another long prepared statement charged that "dozens of pictures . . . are used to infect their audiences with hatred . . . and make them clamor for war." Willkie once more counter-attacked with "a barrage of letters and statements."[61] On the third day John T. Flynn read a statement so similar to Clark's that Willkie suggested that "John Flynn wrote them both." Characteristic of the tone of the testimony was the charge that the movie industry was "controlled by four or five men who cannot possibly have an American point of view." To this Willkie retorted: "The old monopoly humbug is dragged out to divert . . . attention from the real object of the investigation —the sabotage of the country's foreign policy."[62]

At the next session the witnesses were a couple of Hollywood gossip columnists, Jimmy Fidler and George Fisher. Willkie was not present, remarking with casual contempt, "I haven't any time to waste listening to one who makes his living purveying gossip even if the committee has." To this he later added: "the committee, in Fidler, had a witness to its liking—a gossip writer—one who makes a living by unsupported and unproven statements about other people."[63]

Here the case against the industry limped to an ignominious halt. When hearings were resumed a week later, and representatives of the industry got a chance to testify, their spirited denials were hardly necessary to make plain the hollowness of the whole investigation. On September 26, Senator McFarland challenged the chairman to submit to the Senate the question of whether the investigation should continue; and although Clark refused to commit himself, it was obvious that he had had enough. What Senator Downey said in defending his state's most famous industry was obviously true: "The potent propaganda is not movies about Hitler. It is Hitler himself."[64] So, even without Willkie, the hearings were bound to fail in their purpose of strengthening isolationist sentiment. But his presence made the failure resounding and farcical.

The main effect, perhaps, was on his own career. His part in the hearings won him the friendship of the movie industry and led eventually to his becoming chairman of the board of 20th Century-Fox, and hence a power in Hollywood. No doubt it still further increased his general popularity; though it may be conjectured that there were many Republicans, in view of their party's traditional preference for colorless conservatism, who wondered whether such a joyful indulgence of a gift for boisterous ridicule would be quite becoming to an occupant of the White House. Moreover, the hearings brought renewed national publicity to the "campaign oratory" issue. The most dramatic episode occurred when the subcommittee chairman commented that "during the campaign Willkie had made pledges that he would keep the country out of war but had later admitted that this was just 'campaign oratory.'

"Seizing the microphone, Mr. Willkie . . . shouted: 'You have been broadcasting that statement all over the country and in the Senate and it's an unqualified falsehood.' " Both of them appealed to the record, which of course supported Willkie.[65] But perhaps the exhumation of the charge would leave a stronger impression, especially among Republicans, than Willkie's denial.

6

Even before the hearings ceased, however, larger issues were beginning to grip the nation's attention. The occupation of Iceland in early July, and still more the issuance of the "Atlantic Charter" in mid-August (following the dramatic meeting at sea of Roosevelt and Churchill), with its reference to "the final destruction of Nazi tyranny," presented a challenge that Hitler finally felt compelled to meet. On September 5 it was announced that the U. S. destroyer *Greer* had been attacked by a German submarine on the way to Iceland and had retaliated by dropping depth charges, although apparently no damage was done on either side; on September 9, that the U. S. freighter *Steel Seafarer* had been sunk in the Red Sea by an unidentified plane; on September 10, that the U. S. freighter *Sessa* had been sunk on route to Iceland with a loss of twenty-four crewmen; on September 13, that the freighter *Montana,* and on September 23 that the freighter *Pink Star,* both American owned but flying the Panama flag and carrying foreign crews, had been sunk between Greenland and Iceland; and on October 4, that the U. S. tanker *I. C. White,* flying the Panama flag but carrying an American crew, had been sunk in the South Atlantic.

The President responded as he was bound to do. On September 11 he delivered a radio address whose obvious purpose was to carry the nation with him in a long step towards war. With painstaking simplicity and almost tedious repetition he pointed out that the German attacks proclaimed a determination to control the seas, and that this was an aim that America could not tolerate. "We have sought no shooting war with Hitler. . . . But when you see a rattlesnake poised to strike, you do not wait until he has struck before you crush him. . . . In the waters which we deem necessary for our defense American naval vessels and American planes will no longer wait until Axis submarines under the water, or Axis raiders on the surface of the sea, strike their deadly blow—first."

As always when Roosevelt made a fighting speech, Willkie was beside him. "The President has spoken as he should have spoken. He could not yield on such a fundamental right. This is the time for all Americans to rally to his support."[66]

And at last, Roosevelt admitted that he had been mistaken in approving the Neutrality Act. In an article in *Collier's Magazine* he wrote: "Although I approved this legislation when it was passed originally (August, 1935), and when it was extended from time to time, I have regretted my actions." He had come to see that "it could be made to encourage the very intentions and objectives of the aggressor nations"; and he had therefore, he said, on July 14, 1939, urged Congress to repeal it, but had been persuaded by Congressional leaders that this was impossible.[67]

The President followed this, on October 9, with a request that Congress repeal one part of the Neutrality Act and give him the authority to arm merchant ships. The President's reluctance to seek complete repeal of the Neutrality Act was no doubt largely due, as Turner Catledge said in an incisive analysis, to the certainty of Republican opposition in Congress. And he concluded: "There are many, and the number is increasing, who hold that Mr. Willkie is making a mistake—not measuring fully up to his responsibility—by not taking a strong hold on Republican machinery and bringing order out of chaos."[68] This was the same complaint that had been made by Walter Lippman with reference to the original Selective Service

Act. But the fact was that, now as then (and as Catledge partially admitted), Congressional Republicans were immovably committed by "conviction, opportunism and jealousy" (of Willkie) to an isolationist policy.

In view of this attitude on the part of Republican Congressmen, it was perhaps unfair of Willkie to call the Administration "faltering" and "vacillating" (as he did on October 6 at a dinner given by the National Republican Club in honor of Lord Halifax) for not pushing the repeal of the whole Neutrality Act—"a piece of hypocrisy and self-deception by which we tried to lull ourselves into a sense of safety." But he justified his right to such criticism by the position that he himself proceeded to take. "I recommend that the Republican party, through its membership in Congress, forthwith and forthrightly, candidly and courageously, take the lead in the repeal of the Neutrality Law.

"This must be done. It must be done for the sake of freedom. It must be done for the sake of America. And to put it on the narrowest grounds, it must be done for the sake of the Republican party. . . . there is no longer any possible excuse for the continuance of tactics which, however applicable in times of peace, are indulged in at the expense of the people's safety in times of emergency."[69]

He was equally outspoken in an article called "Patriotism or Politics" in the November issue of *The American Magazine*. He did indeed hold out the hope of a Republican return to power; but "only IF the Republicans, under that or some other name, will clean house of mere political obstruction and obstructionists and remnants of an outdated Toryism on domestic issues. Thus common cause can be made in a new political alignment with millions of Independents and Democrats in both the South and the North."[70] "I, for one, do not want to see the party languish and die through a policy of bigotry, shortsightedness and senseless negation."[71]

Willkie did not, however, limit his activity to personal argument and exhortation. In the Senate he was able to launch a surprise attack on the opposition by persuading Senators Austin of Vermont, Bridges of New Hampshire, and Gurney of South Dakota to introduce an amendment to the armed-ship resolution, calling for outright repeal of the Neutrality Act. This was on October 20, and he followed it up the next day by making public a letter to Republican members of Congress, evidently written by him and signed by 124 more or less prominent Republicans who had all been active in practical politics. This document asserted "that, whatever purpose the Neutrality Act may have served originally, it serves no useful purpose now; that its existence rather exposes the United States to the greatest threat in our history; that it in effect constitutes aid to Hitler; that in the sense that it proclaims our neutrality in a struggle in which neither the people nor the Congress have shown themselves neutral, it is both hypocritical and degrading; and that it is preventing a policy of aid to Britain and her allies which the American people overwhelmingly endorse."[72]

The signers, representing forty states, included six Governors, ten former Governors, twenty-six members of the National Committee, and eight chairmen of state committees. It was notable that the Midwest was sparsely represented; and certainly, as far as the "organization" was concerned, it was a minority report. It was, nevertheless, a dramatic gesture and, along with the Senate resolution, spurred Democratic Congressional leaders into action. They immediately introduced a resolution permitting American ships to enter combat zones and the ports of belligerent nations. Only one major article of the Neutrality Act remained—that giving to the National Munitions Board the authority to control the production, import, and export of munitions; and to this there was no objection.

A majority of Republicans in Congress were, however, incorrigible. Representative Lambertson of Kansas called Willkie the "Dr. Jekyll and Mr. Hyde of American politics," a "Johnny Come Lately to our political party," and the "No. 1 war-monger of America"; and his invective "brought applause from the Republican side of the aisle."[73] Two weeks later his colleague Dewey Short of Missouri launched into even more flamboyant vituperation against "Mr. Win-de War Willkie," a "belligerent, bombastic, bellicose, bombinating blowhard. . . . May God forgive me for having supported such an impostor, this fifth columnist, this preposterous man, this Trojan horse who is trying to split the Republican party wide open." He "was applauded for a minute by the Republican side."[74] It is doubtful that American history records another display of such blind and furious hatred by a party's Congressional delegation of the man who had been the party's nominee for President exactly one year before.

Willkie took the attack calmly, however, remarking that Short sounded like "many men when they represent a dying cause such as isolation. . . . His personal references remind me of the bad boy who, when he runs out of arguments, begins to make faces."[75]

Isolationism was indeed a dying cause. While Congress debated, the submarine attacks continued. On October 18 came news of a torpedo attack on the destroyer *Kearney,* which cost eleven lives; on October 22, of the sinking of the freighter *Lehigh,* flying the American flag, off the west coast of Africa, and the freighter *Bold Venture,* flying the Panama flag, south of Iceland; on October 23 of the loss of the American-owned tanker *W. C. Teagle,* in a British convoy; and on November 1, of the sinking of the destroyer *Reuben James,* on convoy duty near Iceland, with the loss of one hundred men.

This was the news that struck home most sharply. But American ears could not be deaf to the cry of agony arising from conquered Europe, as

Russian resistance spread hope and revolt among the enslaved peoples, and these were answered with inhuman reprisals. Day after day the headlines carried the heart-chilling story: "Nazis Slay Prague Mayor and City Council Members"; "Norway Warned to Comply with Nazi Rules or Starve"; "17 Czechs Killed, 55 More on Trial"; "Italy Shoots 18 in Dalmatia"; "Twelve Executed in Prague"; "Paris Announces 80th Execution"; "50 Frenchmen Slain in Nantes Reprisal"; "Germans Kill 200 Serbs in Reprisal."[76] Isolationists might warn against letting judgment be swayed by sentiment. But Americans have never looked with indifference on the torture and murder of people whose only crime was the desire to be free.

And while most people's gaze was fixed on the enemy across the Atlantic, those who read their newspapers a little more closely had long been aware that war with Japan was equally inevitable and was approaching even more swiftly, though without violence. Ever since the Japanese occupation of Manchuria in 1932, public antipathy toward Japan, and government misgivings about her ultimate aims, had been increasing. In the later thirties, the invasion of China, the increasingly arrogant utterances of her leaders, her soaring imports of oil and scrap iron from the United States, all gave evidence of her aggressive intentions. On September 25, 1940, Roosevelt ordered an embargo on exports of scrap iron to any country outside the Western Hemisphere except Great Britain. This order was aimed at Japan, and was evidently timed to precede the impending announcement (which came next day) of Japan's adherence to the Axis. Next came the seizure of French Indo-China from the powerless hands of the Vichy government, and in retaliation, on July 26, 1941, the United States and Britain jointly announced the freezing of all Japanese assets, and the shutting off of oil exports to, and silk imports from, Japan. Simultaneously, the Philippine armed forces were made a part of the United States Army under the command of General MacArthur. On August 1 the United States prohibited the export of aviation gasoline to Japan. And on August 11 Secretary Hull announced that there would be no further negotiations with Japan except on the basis of his "fourteen points" of 1937—of which the basic one was Japanese withdrawal from China.

At this point, obviously, a stalemate had been reached, which could only be broken (and was certain to be broken) by a Japanese resort to force. When, on October 16, the relatively moderate Prince Konoye resigned as premier and was replaced by the militarist Tojo, the writing on the wall was plain. And on November 4 a newspaper which was the mouthpiece of the Japanese Foreign Office published what was in effect an ultimatum: the United States must remove all trade restrictions and give Japan a free hand in China and Southeast Asia—or else! The sending of a special envoy to Washington immediately afterwards changed nothing; it was a fact—

as might have been guessed—only a trick. Any civilian, knowing merely what he read in the newspapers, could see that war was at hand. That the military commanders at Pearl Harbor should have been caught off guard, whatever instructions they did or did not receive from Washington, remains incredible.

Willkie, at least, was not blind to the trend of events in the Far East. On October 18 he warned: "Let us not delude ourselves. Berlin, Tokyo and Rome are linked by the dangerous dream of world conquest. . . . We must abandon the hope of peace."[77]

Meanwhile the debate in Congress ran its course, and on November 7 the Democratic resolution was approved by the Senate by a vote of 50-37. Only three Republicans—Ball of Minnesota, Barbour of New Jersey, and White of Maine—joined the three original sponsors. Twenty-one voted against it. In the House, on November 13, a last-minute Presidential plea, accompanied by a promise to end John L. Lewis's current coal strike, gained enough Democratic votes to secure passage by a vote of 212-194. Republicans voted against it 137-22. Of the affirmative Republican votes, California and Iowa contributed two each; the others came from New England, New York, and New Jersey.

Willkie did the best he could with this result. His press statement read: "The adoption of the amendment is gratifying. The close vote today in the House of Representatives, however, is unfortunate because it gives a false impression of the true sentiments of America toward the policy of aggressive aid to the democracies and of America's intent to maintain her right to freedom of the seas.

"Undoubtedly," he added, "the vote was in part retaliation by Congress for the Administration's negligence and muddling in the solution of our industrial labor relations program . . ."[78] But this was true only with reference to the Democrats. Throughout the year (as in previous years) House Republicans had followed the isolationist line with appalling consistency. Against Lend-Lease their vote had been 135-21; against the extension of Selective Service, 133-21; against Neutrality repeal, 137-22. No power of either words or events, no appeal to either reason or emotion, could shake such a monolithic refusal to change with a changing world. If anyone wonders why Willkie was repudiated by his party in 1944, these figures give some inkling of the answer.

Even after Pearl Harbor some isolationists, not all Republicans, refused to admit that they had been wrong. Senator Nye described the Japanese assault as "just what Britain had planned for us."[79] Norman Thomas complained in a speech to the Keep America Out of War Congress that "if the line of action followed by" that organization had been accepted by the government, "the war would have been averted"; and he indulged in "jibes at Secretary of the Navy Knox, Josef Stalin and President Roosevelt."[80]

But isolationism was in most cases a form of nationalism, and now the nation's existence was at stake. Senator Wheeler declared: "Everyone, regardless of party affiliation, must back up the President."[81] John T. Flynn spoke for America First: "This committee was formed to oppose America's involvement in European and Asiatic wars. Its counsel and advice were rejected at each step by the government. But the time for discussing that is past. We are now at war. . . . It is the duty of every citizen to stand behind the government . . ."[82] Lindbergh, as usual, was clear and to the point: "We have been stepping closer to war for many months. Now it has come and we must meet it as united Americans regardless of our attitude in the past toward the policy our government has followed."[83]

Some of these statements imply that the war could have been averted; and in recent years there has arisen a school of "revisionist" historians who have argued that Roosevelt deliberately maneuvered America into a needless war.[84] Such a view is the last refuge of fanaticism. Temporary peace could have been bought, undoubtedly, by American acceptance of the Japanese ultimatum mentioned above, and by refusal of all aid to Britain—that is, in effect, by becoming a partner of the Axis. But this was a price that the American people, like Roosevelt and Willkie, were too proud, too generous, and too wise to pay. And no other terms were possible.

But there is a grain of truth in the revisionist fantasy. If war had to come—*since* war had to come—it would be an immense moral advantage to the United States if the enemy made a large scale, dramatic attack. Given the continuing reluctance of a majority of Americans to accept an all-out war, only a clear-cut act of aggression could unite the country. It was therefore the Administration's policy in the Atlantic, where a war was already going on, to act at first with caution, and with increasing decisiveness only in response to Hilter's increasing belligerence; and in the Pacific, where the fighting was more remote, to draw a definite line, with all possible publicity, and dare the Japanese to cross it. This was not Machiavellian plotting; it was merely the exercise of good sense in meeting a specific situation which other nations had created.

The Japanese attack on Pearl Harbor was therefore—to an impersonal, overall viewpoint in which the death of three thousand men is merely a statistic—a tremendous stroke of luck, and must have brought to many Americans, after the initial shock, a feeling of profound relief. The fatalistic apathy that had gripped so large a part of the population vanished. At that moment the American people were united, in thought and will, as they had never been before.

XVI

The Home Front

1

The repeal of the Neutrality Act marked the end of another Willkie crusade. There was no longer any obstacle to unlimited material aid to the Allies. A declaration of war would eventually come, but it must wait upon events.

Meanwhile a new outlet for Willkie's restless energy presented itself: a trip to Australia and New Zealand. Rumors of another trip abroad began to circulate soon after his return from England, for in March he had been asked about "his reported consideration of a trip to the Far East to study conditions as he did in Britain."[1] At that time he declined to comment, but he must later have discussed the project with Roosevelt, for in a letter dated December 5 the President wrote: "It would give me very great pleasure if you would care to make a short trip to Australia. I could arrange the official procedure any way you like."

It is clear from the tone of this letter that Roosevelt was still appreciative of the results of Willkie's English visit, as well as of his continuing battle against the isolationists. The letter continued half humorously: "I think both of us should be extremely careful, if you go, lest it be said that I am sending you out of the country!

"It would, of course, be of great value to cement our relations with New Zealand and Australia not only now but in the future. There is always the Japanese matter to consider. The situation is definitely serious. . . . Perhaps the next four or five days will decide the matter.

"In any event I do wish you would let me know the next time you come to Washington as there are many things for us to talk over."[2]

The next four or five days did indeed decide the matter, for the letter has a postscript in longhand: "This was dictated Friday morning—long before this vile attack started."

The attack also decided many other matters. And at the same time it brought the necessity for many new decisions. What, for instance, was now the proper role for the leader of "the loyal opposition"? A partial glimpse of Willkie's state of mind is given by the comment made in mid-January by "a man who knew Willkie well": "The goddam fool wants to go into the trenches—can you imagine that!"[3] What is a little harder to imagine is that anyone "who knew him well" should have been surprised. But of course Willkie understood that his problem was not so simple. When, a few days after Pearl Harbor, an interviewer asked him about his own part in the war, he suggested following the example of the British and "keeping on with the everyday business of life and labor." "I see no reason to get excited or emotional. What we need is to keep our heads. . . . Why should a man wire the President an offer of services, or rush down to already overcrowded Washington?"[4]

Nevertheless, he recognized that his own position was exceptional, and on December 10 he sent the President the following letter.

"My dear Mr. President:—

"I congratulate you very much on your Tuesday night talk.

"I have your letter of December 5th, which I appreciate. I am unable presently to appraise the potentialities or the wisdom of going to Australia since the Japanese attack. Perhaps it would now constitute a nuisance. I will think about it further.

"I am coming to Washington Monday, and, if your schedule permits a free moment, would you have one of your secretaries let me know before that date if it would be convenient for me to call on you in accordance with the suggestion in your letter. Please disregard this if you are at all pressed for time.

"In case I do not see you Monday there is something I would like to say to you. Of late a few people, friends of yours, have suggested to me various ways in which they thought you might make use of me in our national emergency. Since they have talked to me about this, I am afraid they may have troubled you. You have incredibly burdensome and anxious days ahead and it should be plain to anyone that you can function with least strain and most effectiveness if you are free to choose your helpers and advisers for whom you must bear the responsibility, without any consideration other than your conception of the public welfare.

"What I am trying to say—honestly, but awkwardly I am afraid, because it is not easy—is this: if any such well meant suggestions are brought to you, I beg you to disregard them. There is on your shoulders the heaviest responsibility any man can carry and I would not add to it in the slightest degree. Even to volunteer a willingness to serve seems to me now only an imposition on your attention. Every American is willing to serve.

"In all sincerity, I am

Respectfully yours,"[5]

What Willkie is saying on the surface is that he wants the President to feel under no obligation to give him a job. What he is trying to suggest underneath is that he does not want a place in the government.[6]

On the Monday mentioned (December 15) Willkie lunched with Roosevelt at the White House and the two, as he told reporters, had a "completely frank" talk. Queried as to whether he planned to join the government in any capacity, he replied with a grin, "Of course you know that I am not running the government, although I sought to"; but then answered seriously that he had not been offered any job. Pressed as to whether he would accept one, he replied that at such a time *any* American would do what he was asked.[7]

As a matter of fact, ever since Willkie's championing of Lend-Lease, Roosevelt had been thinking about how to make the most of the position and ability of his recent rival. He told Miss Perkins, "I want to use him somehow. I want to offer him an important post in the government. Can you think of one? I want it to be an independent job . . . where the effect is non-political but important. . . . I think it would be a good thing for the country, it would help us to a feeling of unity."[8] Miss Perkins suggested the chairmanship of the Defense Labor Board, which was about to be formed, and, when Roosevelt agreed, she made the offer. But Willkie declined.

Both men, of course, recognized the delicacy of the problem. If Willkie became too closely connected with the Administration, he would lose his influence in the Republican party, and this would not only destroy any chance of a future political career but would leave the liberal elements in the party without a leader, and it would also destroy Willkie's independence and prevent him from criticizing the government. It may seem that the second result was one that Roosevelt would have welcomed. But in fact many of the things that Willkie criticized the President for not doing (especially during 1941 and the early months of 1942) were things that the President, also, knew ought to be done, but which he hesitated to do for either personal or political reasons; and Willkie's criticism helped to supply the justification or excuse that he wanted.

Nevertheless, Willkie was again approached by a "White House representative" in the fall of 1941. This time his reply was "that he was very much flattered but thought he would be more useful in the field of foreign policy if he were not part of the administration."[9]

There was one job that Willkie would probably have felt unable to refuse, namely, the one he had so often urged Roosevelt to create—that of director of the whole program of arms production. Such a suggestion was made from time to time in the press, as well as in hundreds of personal letters to the President during 1941,[10] but apparently the closest the President came to it was when, on the weekend of January 10, 1942, he talked to Harry Hopkins "of getting a three-man committee made up of Willkie, [Supreme Court Justice] Douglas and [Donald] Nelson to explore the matter for him and advise him about it." Hopkins, however, after warming to Willkie at the time of their meeting in England a year earlier, had recovered his normal dislike and "urged very strongly that this not be done, primarily because neither Douglas nor Willkie knew anything about production and because Willkie was apt to use it as a political football."[11]

Yet it seems likely that Willkie would have proved exactly the man to boss the arms production program. What was needed was not so much experience in "production" (William S. Knudsen had that, and failed) as the strength of character to demand authority and use it, to make decisions (one is almost tempted to say *any* decisions) and carry them out, and to be completely ruthless in subordinating to the general welfare the special interests of individuals and groups. This strength of character Willkie had. The appointment, however, went to Donald Nelson (and the program continued to lag for many months because of conflicts among his subordinates which he could not, or would not, end). The announcement was made about 6 p. m. on Tuesday, January 13.

The story of this announcement is worth telling in detail to illustrate the kind of devious dealings in which Roosevelt sometimes engaged and which were so infuriating to Willkie. On the day in question Winston Churchill was in the White House, near the end of his long visit to the United States to coordinate British and American plans for the conduct of the war. Earlier he had telephoned Willkie from Palm Beach, where he was getting a few days' rest and made an appointment, on this day, to renew the acquaintance begun in London. The meeting took place as scheduled, although what was said was not revealed.

During this visit Willkie also saw and talked at some length with Roosevelt, who that morning, according to Harry Hopkins, had finally been persuaded to do what Willkie had been urging for a year and half—appoint a single head of war production—and had also decided to make the announcement that afternoon.[12] But of this fact he said nothing to his guest.[13] Indeed, he seems to have changed his mind, for "in his regular press conference at 4 p. m. President Roosevelt told reporters that there would be nothing on defense organization."[14] But within the next hour and a half he changed it again; for at 5:30 p. m., Nelson (who did not yet know of the appointment), along with Vice President Wallace, was called out of an important meeting to see the President,[15] and the news was released immediately to the press.

Why Roosevelt said nothing of the appointment to Willkie, and why, after telling Hopkins that he would announce the appointment, he changed his mind for a time and decided not to, must remain matters of conjecture. But why he changed his mind again and *did* announce it is clear. He had seen or been told of the text of Willkie's address that evening to the Annual Conference of Mayors, which had already been released to the press, and which "literally blistered the Roosevelt Administration" for not appointing a single head of defense production.[16] As a result, he decided to forestall Willkie's criticism; and Willkie was forced, at an hour's notice, to make drastic revisions in his speech.

Still another event of the same exasperating kind occurred on the same day. Secretary Perkins, with Roosevelt's approval, had asked Willkie to be one of a number of "arbitrators" or "umpires" under the newly formed War Labor Board, and although he had given no answer, Early released the news of the invitation.[17] The embarrassment became mutual when Willkie declined. It was reported that "his associates" viewed the offer "as an act of 'trickery' intended to still the clamor for new faces in the defense picture without taking any of the basic control out of the hands of the New Dealers."[18] If Willkie felt the same way, who can blame him?

He was not one to hold a grudge, however, and he and the President remained on cordial terms. On February 21 Roosevelt wrote to invite Willkie to lunch "the next time you come to Washington, as there are a number of things I want to talk to you about."[19] One of these, as he went on to say, was the question of getting Hamilton Fish out of Congress. He represented the President's district, and to both Roosevelt and Willkie he was a sort of symbol of isolationism.

Willkie acknowledged the President's note on March 6, when he returned from a trip to the Pacific Coast, and they seem to have met early in April, for on April 15 Roosevelt wrote: "I did enjoy that little party the other night a lot. We did not get far on the Ham Fish matter."[20] To this Willkie replied on April 21: "I am confident Fish is going to be eliminated."[21] This prediction, however, was too optimistic. One of those organizing the opposition died, leaving "the whole matter . . . in some confusion";[22] the Old Guard rallied around; and Fish won the primary by a wide margin and the election by a narrow margin. Willkie gained only the increased hatred of a large section of the party, which found a partial expression in the many abusive letters that he received during the summer and fall, especially after Fish's reelection. One of the earlier ones, from Tulsa, Oklahoma, read: "I heard over the radio, that, you was favoring the defeat of Congressman Fish of Hyde Park district New York. I think that, in as much as you have been a damd democrat all your life, that it is impossible for you to understand the Constitution, the Supreme Court, and their creators, the Republican party."[23]

Republican animosity toward Willkie would have been still greater had it been known how close, at this time, were his relations with the President. One more episode involving the two men, although minor, is too pleasant not to tell. It occurred on the same momentous January day when Willkie went to the White House to see Churchill.[24] The President, after talking with Willkie himself, accompanied his guest to Churchill's room; then, following some general conversation, he remarked, "Well, I suppose you want to be by yourselves," and started down the corridor toward his office. Churchill waved away the servant who would have pushed the President's wheel chair and pushed it himself, to Roosevelt's obvious delight. This was a dark hour in the fortunes of America and Britain. Yet the two great leaders could enjoy their moment of fun; and Willkie likewise, entering into the spirit of the occasion, inquired of the returning Prime Minister, "Well, what do you want from us *now?*"[25]

2

There was one goal, however, toward which Willkie worked with Roosevelt's approval but necessarily without either his aid or his interference. This was the commitment of the Republican party to post-war cooperation with other countries in establishing some sort of world organization. This was probably a greater service than he could have rendered in any official capacity, even as direction of war production. Other men could do that job—at least, after a fashion. Willkie alone could do this job.

In arguing for intervention, he had held out the hope that a Hitler defeat would lead to a voluntary union of nations to prevent new aggression. Now, by a shift of emphasis, the means became the end, and for the rest of his life Willkie crusaded unceasingly to make America commit itself irrevocably to such a goal. America's rejection of the League of Nations had been, in his eyes, one of the great tragedies of history. "The League of Nations was the religion of my young life," he wrote on May 27, 1942;[26] and in order to prevent the recurrence of this tragedy Willkie sought to build a body of public sentiment so massive that no isolationist triumph would ever again be possible; and along with this, to force the leadership of the Republican party to go on record so precisely and so often in favor of international cooperation that no subsequent retreat from this position would be tolerated.

He attempted first to drive home the consequences (as he saw them) of America's rejection of the League: the fact that the attempt to avoid *any* kind of international obligations had only led to obligations incalculably costly. "Especially during the last two years it has become apparent to more and more Americans that if we *had* chosen an international move last time, the world would be very different today. Some, including the writer, go much further. We contend that if the democracies had acted in unison when Japan invaded Manchuria [Hoover and Stimson *had* wished to take a stand on this issue but had been rebuffed by their former European allies], or when Italy invaded Ethiopia, or when Hitler entered the Rhineland, the second *world* war might have been forestalled." And "the fact remains that we have had to take an international course anyway."[27] Now we are "paying the bitter price for our worship of expediency, our endless seeking of the easy way out. . . . today, when we can no longer put it off, today when the easy way is at last closed to us, the task is . . . almost infinitely hard."[28]

Furthermore, as the most powerful of the democracies after World War I, America bore the greatest measure of responsibility for the subsequent course of events: "for the failure of the democracies to get together during the last twenty years, the United States was largely . . . responsible. We . . . rejected [the League] outright. We rejected the World Court, we weakened the international economic structure, and we raised impassable tariffs." Americans were misled by "geographical" thinking. "The problems that led to World War II were geographical only in a very broad sense. The real forces at work were economic, industrial, scientific, social and political. These . . . are natural forces of modern civilization and they cannot be solved in terms of artificial boundaries."[29]

Yet, trusting as he did in the judgment of "the people," he partially absolved them from responsibility. "I am satisfied that the American people never deliberately turned their backs on a program of international cooperation in an organization for maintaining world peace. . . . They were betrayed by leaders without convictions who were thinking in terms of group vote-catching."[30]

Even internationalism, however, could take an evil form, namely, imperialism. Declaring it to be "the universal lesson of history that he who wins wars must maintain the peace," he added: "I do not mean to imply that the world is going to be subject henceforth to American imperialism, or even that we, in our sole discretion, are going to police other nations. That is not the American way."[31] "America must choose one of three courses after this war: narrow nationalism, which inevitably means the loss of our own liberty; international imperialism, which means the sacrifice of some other nation's liberty; or the creation of a world in which there shall be equality of opportunity for every race and every nation."[32]

And the sensible choice, the choice dictated by "enlightened self-interest," was in this case the morally right course as well. The end is freedom, and freedom is indivisible. In the "idea of equality lies the only sure hope of the future. . . . Let us keep that aim shining before us like a light—a light for the people of Europe, for the people of Africa, for the people of Asia, for the people of South America, and for the people of our own beloved land." "We cannot keep freedom to ourselves. If we are to have freedom we must share freedom."[33]

Such were the ideas that Willkie tirelessly attempted to impress on the consciousness of the public. One can only guess at the extent of his influence. Perhaps at this time—as he himself had conjectured in regard to his fight for the nomination two years before, and as was certainly true in the fight for Lend-Lease one year before—he was riding, or leading, a trend. This assumption will explain his surprising success in getting his views endorsed by the Republican National Committee.

The Committee met on April 20 to discuss ways and means of winning the fall elections; and although Martin, still chairman, was doing his best to avoid controversy, Willkie was determined to have a hearing for his views.

The resolution that he offered was in effect a party platform, in which post-war cooperation with other countries was only one item—although certainly in his mind the most important one. The main articles were not, on the whole, revolutionary: (1) prosecution of the war "relentlessly and without reservation" against the enemy powers; (2) "no peace with those powers except peace with victory" (an anticipation of Roosevelt's demand for "unconditional surrender"); (3) acceptance of "whatever just and reasonable international responsibilities may be demanded in the modern world"; and (4) determination to be "a constructive and energetic force in the conduct of the war effort," "through aroused and informed public opinion and through our elected representatives in Congress." The last of these was accompanied by a specific program, in which most of the items were already familiar.[34]

In this generally moderate statement, however, Willkie inserted several passages that clearly challenged the reactionary elements in the party. In one he asserted: "It has long been the proclaimed policy of the Republican party that a community of people cannot exist half slave, half free. The progress of human events, of science and technology, of communication and of political and economic institutions, has been such . . . that it is no longer realistic to limit this enduring principle to the shores of any single nation, however large." This was straight "One World" doctrine, and nobody but Willkie would have been bold enough to place it before the members of the Republican National Committee and dare them to turn it down.

Not less significant was another passage, in which Willkie qualified his warning against war-time "social reform": "We realize that the correction of social injustices can be made under the pressure of war which years of peaceful effort would have failed to bring about, such as, for example, the discrimination against the Negro citizen in industry, in labor and in the armed services of the nation. Such things we do not consider in the realm of social experiment. They are wrongs under the Constitution and we shall work to correct them." This statement failed to shock people because it sounded much like the verbal gesture customarily made in Republican platforms in an attempt to lure the Negro vote. The difference was that Willkie meant it.

It was therefore the internationalist plank in the platform that the Old Guard was eager to remove. Taft, always concerned to curb Willkie's influence, offered an alternative resolution—cold, negative, and non-committal, pointedly omitting any reference to post-war problems and policies. Questioned about this omission, he said: "I don't think we can say now what our definite policy of the peace should be. We ought to devote all our efforts to winning the war."[35]

But in this contest Willkie won. The resolution adopted by the Committee was essentially his, even to most of the wording, and included the statement about discrimination against Negroes. Although two or three of Taft's sentences were written in, and the statement about international cooperation after the war was slightly watered down, the subsequent comment of the Senator from Ohio was an obvious attempt at face-saving: "I think it was a great mistake for the national committee to express any policy at all at this time on post-war action, but the committee has drawn the teeth of the Willkie proposal so that no one can take exception to the language employed."[36]

Obviously the votes of many Committee members were dictated by unwillingness to go on record as favoring a currently unpopular position. It was undoubtedly true that "a majority of the members of the committee . . . would have preferred no declaration on foreign policy."[37] Undoubtedly, also, except for Willkie, they would have had their way; and their forced capitulation did not increase their liking for him. Neither did his comment, after the resolution was passed, that the "next job" was to nominate candidates "who believe sincerely these principles and their implications."[38]

This comment was aimed partly at Dewey, whose nomination for the Governorship of New York Willkie opposed without success. But he *did* succeed, in the New York State campaign as in the meeting of the National Committee, in getting from Republican leaders a clear verbal commitment to a post-war policy of internationalism. The state convention was not held until late in August, just as Willkie began his round-the-world tour. But before leaving, he put in print once more the ideas on foreign policy that he hoped the party would accept;[39] and once more the "organization" leaders hastened to agree with him, saying that his ideas were "elemental" and had often been advocated by Dewey. The platform plank headed "World Affairs" contained the substance of Willkie's statement.

3

Willkie's relations with Dewey are another story, which deserves telling in some detail. After Roosevelt, Dewey was the public figure who played the greatest part in Willkie's political career. As his standing with "regular" Republicans was damaged by his friendliness toward Roosevelt, it was damaged equally by his antipathy toward Dewey.

This antipathy was first widely publicized during the early months of 1942, in connection with Dewey's successful attempt to win the Republican nomination for the Governorship of New York. Those who think Willkie's great ambition was to gain the Presidency will find his conduct at this time incomprehensible. The true explanation, of course, is given in the statement by his friend Nathan L. Miller, a former Governor of New York: "Parties were to him mere instruments, not for political advancement or power, but to serve human needs."[40]

What this principle meant in human terms is seen in a moving passage by Walter White, long-time head of the National Association for the Advancement of Colored People: "One day as we were discussing in his office a suggestion that he be a candidate for the Governorship of New York, he expressed the conviction that ruled his thinking during the last months of his life. He was leaning back in his chair, with his feet on his desk. It was a little startling in that luxurious office to note that his shoes were half-soled. He watched an outbound troop ship, dreary in the dull gray paint of war, its deck crowded with young Americans pathetically absorbing their last view of New York Harbor. 'Look at those kids out there on that ship,' he said. 'I believe I can do more in fighting for what they believe and what they deserve by staying out of office, even including the presidency. I would gladly say to hell with the presidency and all political offices if I felt I could do more as an individual than as governor or president or anything else.' "[41]

These words were confirmed by Willkie's actions. If he had simply wanted to be President, he would have sought the Governorship of New York. As Joe Martin told him, it would be "a stepping-stone to the Presidency."[42] As Governor, Willkie would have controlled the State delegation to the National Convention in 1944, and he would also have been able to repel the accusation that he was an amateur. But Willkie refused to make the campaign. "I don't like the job," he told Martin.[43] He simply was not interested (except as any intelligent citizen is interested) in local problems. Hence, he not only refused to be an active candidate for the nomination, but rejected all efforts to draft him. When four Republican friends (Frank Altschul, Arthur Ballantine, William Chadbourne, and Robert Moses) called to discuss the question, they failed to see him because of a confusion as to the date of the appointment; and although Willkie later apologized, he did not ask them to come again.[44] When another admirer, Sydney Baron, publicly proposed that he run as an "all-party" candidate,[45] Willkie promptly declined. Despite this reluctance, another attempt was made later in the month by a bipartisan group including Russell Davenport, William and Herbert Agar, Roderick Stevens, Mrs. Raymond B. Ingersoll, Richard B.

Scandrett, Jr., Mrs. Helen Simpson, Mrs. J. Borden Harriman, and Herbert Bayard Swope. (Many Democrats were as unhappy about the prospective nomination of Attorney General John J. Bennett as their Republican counterparts were about that of Dewey.) Their "Draft-Willkie" movement was publicly announced on June 25, and David Dubinsky, head of the International Ladies' Garment Workers Union, promptly declared that he would support Willkie on any ticket.[46]

For several days Willkie did not repudiate this movement, and on July 1 Stanley Rinehart, the publisher, announced a state-wide "Draft-Willkie Committee" to organize public support for his nomination.[47] On July 2, however, Willkie firmly and finally refused to enter the contest: "I long ago declared that I did not intend to become a candidate, and I have no intention of becoming one. . . . I am attempting to bring about the adoption of certain principles by the Republican party and the development of a type of leadership that will win the confidence of the American people.

"If I can accomplish these suggestions, other people can have every office in the United States, as far as I am concerned."[48]

This statement settled the matter and left the field to Dewey.

There is no doubt whatever that if Willkie had been nominated, he would have been elected; and if he had been elected Governor of New York, it would have been very hard indeed to prevent him from winning the Republican nomination in 1944. And if he had wanted the gubernatorial nomination, he could probably have got it.

It is true that Dewey was also popular, as a result of his racket-busting career as district attorney, and in 1938 he had lost to the able and respected Governor Lehman by only 60,000 votes. Moreover, he had proved his party loyalty by campaigning vigorously for Willkie in 1940; and if he had not been a leader in the drive for aid to Britain, neither had he opposed it. Moreover, most of the leaders of the state Republican organization, including State Chairman Edwin F. Jaeckle and National Committeeman J. Russel Sprague, were on his side.

On the other hand, there were many people who disliked Dewey personally and distrusted him politically; Willkie's vote-getting record in the election of 1940 was at least as good as Dewey's in that of 1938, considering that his opponent was Franklin Roosevelt; his consistent internationalism, which had alienated Republicans in other parts of the country, had strengthened his support in New York, especially New York City; labor, too, was increasingly friendly, as was shown by Dubinsky's support; and he had powerful friends in up-state areas, including, besides Rolland Marvin, U. S. Representative (and former Senator) James J. Wadsworth and the majority leader in the State Assembly, Irving Ives.[49] And even if he had doubts about beating Dewey, nobody ever accused him of dodging a fight or being afraid to take a chance.

But he simply did not want the job. And he explained why to Lem Jones when the latter tried to appeal to his public spirit by pointing out that being Governor was a big job, and was worth while for its own sake: "In normal times, I might run for Governor of New York because of New York's economic importance to the country. But with things as they are, I believe my voice is more needed on the national and international scene than in a state office. And," he added, "don't tell me that I could get somebody else to do the real work of the Governorship while I concern myself with other things. When I take on a job, I do it myself."[50]

There was, however, another possible path to the Presidency—an agreement to support Dewey for the Governorship in 1942 provided Dewey would support him for the nomination for the Presidency in 1944. This was, indeed, so obvious a course of action that rumors of such an agreement began to circulate early in 1941 and appeared in the newspapers on April 9. Both men responded with quick denials. Willkie said: "This is no time, with the world in flames, to indulge in the nonsense of talking about candidacies. In no event would I enter such an alliance. I don't believe in political trading." Dewey was only a little less emphatic: "I have no political plans of any nature. With the nation confronting what may be the greatest crisis in history, it is ridiculous for anyone to make plans for six weeks ahead, let alone years ahead."[51]

Probably it is true that at the time there had been no discussion of such an agreement. What happened later, according to Willkie, is told in a letter that he wrote to Drew Pearson on June 26, 1942.

"The Dewey forces have been circulating a letter to this effect:

"Three or four months ago, presumably on the day of the Legislative Correspondents' Dinner at Albany, Mr. Willkie and Mr. Dewey met in a hotel room where also were gathered State Senator Fred Young of Lowville, New York, Speaker Heck and several other Republican leaders. During an animated conversation, Mr. Willkie is supposed to have said to Mr. Dewey, 'Tom, if you will assure me that you will not be a candidate for the presidential nomination in '44, I will support you for Governor.' Dewey is then supposed to have replied 'I am sorry, old man, but I am so far out in front now that I just can't make a promise of that kind.'

"No such conversation or any other, on that occasion, ever occurred.

"The facts are these—several months ago the representatives and associates of Tom Dewey proposed to me that if I would agree to support Tom Dewey for governor, they would assure to me the New York delegation at the Republican National Convention in 1944. I rejected their suggestion, saying to them that the proposal offended both my moral and my common sense."[52]

This letter shows why Willkie was the despair of many who would have liked to be his political supporters. What was wrong, from their point of view, in making such an agreement? And indeed, what is wrong with it from *any* point of view? Why should not two men agree to work together, in politics as in any other field of activity, to gain their respective ends, as long as these ends are not dishonorable?

Right or wrong, however, Willkie had an intense hatred of even the thought of a political deal. How could he tell, for instance, what positions Dewey might take before November, 1942—positions to which he himself, by making the deal, would be tacitly committed? Or what Dewey might do, or fail to do, by 1944—so that his support might be unwelcome? Even with a man whom he trusted and respected, Willkie would probably have refused to form such an alliance. And Dewey was emphatically not such a man.

Willkie's distrust is clearly shown in many statements that he made concerning the nomination for the Governorship—statements which naturally infuriated the Dewey partisans and disturbed many other Republicans who were anxious chiefly for a party victory.

"Pick a candidate about whose international views there is no question, and I'll campaign for him in every hamlet, town or city in the state if you want me to, or I'll keep still if you think that's best." These were Willkie's words to "influential friends who have questioned him about the nomination for governor." And he explained to one of them: "All I want to be sure of is that the candidate we nominate is not one who is for winning the war and against appeasement just because it is popular. . . . Frankly, I'd be more willing to accept as sincere the statement of an out and out isolationist who admitted he had been mistaken and now recognized the responsibility we have in this world today, than to accept the assurances of a wobbler who never had the courage to take a stand one way or another during critical pre-Pearl Harbor days but who was suddenly converted after war was upon us. If that means I'm dealing in personalities, well, I'm afraid I am."[53]

Willkie's doubts of Dewey were not removed by the latter's support of the Willkie resolution at the meeting of the National Committee, for in a telegram to New York Committeeman J. Russel Sprague, released after the meeting, Dewey declared: "I sincerely hope that issues buried in the bloodstained earth of Pearl Harbor and Bataan will not be allowed to injure our national or party unity in a battle over words of resolutions. . . . But we should . . . demand and procure a firm declaration that, as Republicans, we shall secure a lasting peace after we have won the war."[54]

In this statement nobody could fail to see, underneath the statesman's exhortation to unity, the politician's bid for eventual votes from the pre-Pearl Harbor isolationists who formed the great majority of the Republican leaders. And this accounts for the acidity in Willkie's comment: "I am puzzled. I am not sure from a reading of the wire whether he urged the committee to adopt isolation or for the United States to take a position of world outlook and cooperation. I am glad, however, that Mr. Dewey now commends the position taken by the committee on the subject. Mr. Sprague personally was very helpful in supporting the resolution that I drafted."[55]

Willkie's dubiousness seemed to be justified when C. Wayland Brooks, the Chicago *Tribune's* candidate for Senator from Illinois, who had won renomination in the primary by a huge majority, accounced receipt of a telegram of congratulation from Dewey, and went on to charge that anyone who stressed the pre-Pearl Harbor voting records of members of Congress was "promoting national disunity."[56]

Many Republicans, however, even among those who had not been isolationists, felt that Dewey's stand was now satisfactory. On May 9, opening his campaign for the nomination, he declared: "Enlightened national interest requires that out of this war we help to create a stabilized world. . . . We know that we can work together with other nations for war. We must learn to work with other nations for peace." [57] He even joined Willkie (and Roosevelt) in the attempt to unseat Hamilton Fish, saying in a letter to the Republican county chairman in Fish's district that he was "unalterably opposed" to Fish's renomination.[58]

On hearing this, Willkie (just back from a vacation in Rushville) applied the praise-and-prod technique that he had used on Roosevelt the year before. "Although Mr. Dewey does not say on what grounds his opposition was based, I am quite sure it must have been because of Mr. Fish's diehard isolationist position. . . . It will be good to have Mr. Dewey fighting with those who feel that persons with beliefs similar to those of Hamilton Fish, in both parties, should be removed from positions of public leadership throughout the State and the nation."[59]

Dewey's response, however, was not an advance but a retreat. Speaking in Fish's home district on June 6, he was quoted as saying: "I am opposed to the Congressman not for his views but for the misuse of his office by friends he has had."[60] Willkie accordingly delivered another and sharper prod without the praise. Declaring that Republican success in the election depended on a return to "the historically true position of the Republican party—namely, economic and social liberalism and a world outlook," he added that New York Republicans were "extremely fortunate" in having a chance to show their disapproval of Fish, "a sincere and outspoken advocate" of isolationism, who "opposed prior to Pearl Harbor practically all the measures" that would have prepared the country for war. "His views and his record are the important questions, not his friends. I hope the Republican candidates for various state offices, whoever they may be, stand forthrightly and directly on these issues and [do] not evade or confuse them."[61]

After this blast, Dewey insisted that he had been misquoted, and that what he had really said was: "This is even more than a matter of views. I am opposed to the Representative from this district not for his views only but because of the misuse of his office and the associates he has had."[62]

These statements would obviously only strengthen Willkie's distrust. While denying "emphatically," in a press statement, that he was engaged in a "stop-Dewey" movement, he made it clear that he would prefer almost any other candidate. He warned against "prenominating somebody in a rush," and stressed the importance, for the effect on national politics, of selecting a candidate whose "statements and past record must be such that we can absolutely trust his word."[63]

Since Willkie himself refused to seek the nomination, however, these warnings could not prevent it from going to Dewey, while they aroused the intense anger of Dewey partisans. W. Kingsland Macy, the Old Guard leader of Suffolk County, spoke for many in the Dewey camp when he quoted with approval an editorial which read: "We would not go so far as to say that the Willkie faction of the Republican party in the State would willingly throw away the State election this year to insure Willkie New York's delegates to the national convention in 1944, but it amounts to that when they attempt to nominate some other man than Dewey . . ."[64]

The truth was that Willkie was convinced ("leaving out of account all questions of principle, and I have serious differences of views with regard to certain principles from those advocated by Mr. Dewey") that if nominated Dewey would be "overwhelmingly defeated . . . I am anxious for the Republican Party to win. I want them to nominate someone who can win."[65] Most of the party leaders, however, were sure that Dewey could win and, like Macy, attributed Willkie's attitude to personal ambition and spite.[66]

The question remains of why Willkie's distrust of Dewey was so profound. In part, perhaps it was a matter of temperament. Outspoken and impulsive, disdainful of politics as a game of skill to be played for personal victory, he would hardly be drawn to so cool and calculating a player as Dewey. Perhaps, too, he felt that Dewey's activities as district attorney had been politically motivated—although racket-busting is a traditional and respectable means to political advancement. Probably, however, his distrust can be traced mainly to Dewey's indecisive stand on aid to Britain prior to the 1940 convention.

At any rate, Willkie did not like Dewey and he did not try to hide the fact. One evening shortly after the convention, when John Cowles was present in Willkie's apartment, Dewey telephoned to ask if he might come and discuss the campaign. Gaining Willkie's reluctant consent, he duly appeared and made a friendly and unqualified offer of support. This, of course, was good policy, whatever his personal feelings. Still, Willkie was not normally inclined to be unfriendly or to impute low motives, and his grudging acceptance of the offer reveals a deep-rooted antipathy.[67]

Willkie may have been partially won over by Dewey's hard work in the latter part of the campaign, for on November 14 he wrote with apparent cordiality: "I want to take this opportunity of letting you know how much I appreciate all that you did on my behalf during the recent campaign.

"Your unselfish efforts in many parts of the country did much, I am certain, to unify the party and awaken interest in the issues at stake. . . . I hope after I return from a week's rest, I will have an opportunity of really sitting down and talking to you. Again, many, many thanks for the grand job you did."[68]

But Dewey's initial condemnation of Lend-Lease once more aroused Willkie's suspicions, which were not allayed by a last-minute switch to support of the bill. And during the ensuing months of struggle against isolationism, Dewey gave relatively little help. (In the "Dewey" folder of his correspondence is a list of statements by Dewey, up to 1942, that could be interpreted as isolationist, and there are also his first and later statements on Lend-Lease.)

The question about Dewey, as Willkie saw it, was stated and answered in the letter to Drew Pearson already quoted in part. "I think you know me well enough to know that I am opposing Tom Dewey for the nomination, simply because I think he represents, perhaps unconsciously, those forces in the Republican party and in the country, which may, when this war ends, cause a repetition of the destructive attitude that kept America out of the League of Nations in 1919 and 1920."[69]

The question arose to haunt him again in 1944, and he died without having arrived at a certain answer. But it is evident that he feared the worst. "I am fully aware," he wrote to Bartley Crum early in 1942, "of what you say about the isolationist forces. They haven't given up the battle by a long shot, and it is up to us to see that they have no opportunity of riding to power again on a wave of reaction as they did years ago. Stopping them is not going to be an easy job . . ."[70] As for Dewey: "in measuring men I don't measure them so much by what they say—I measure them by when they say it. . . . It is easy to be against sin [i.e., isolationism] after it is apparent that it is sin."[71] It would be equally easy to cease being against sin if sin gave promise of becoming fashionable.

4

American membership in a world organization was, however, the goal of only one of the two great crusades to which, in the years after Pearl

Harbor, Willkie literally gave his life. The goal of the other was the protection and extension of civil liberties—that is, of basic human rights as these have come to be thought of in the Western world; and especially of equal rights, and equal recognition as human beings, for members of non-white races.

Although equalitarianism and a hatred of bigotry had always been part of Willkie's character, and although the campaign had sharpened his perception of human needs, it seems to have been the war that awakened him fully to the evils of racial discrimination. He saw that racial hatred was one cause of the war, that racial persecution was one of the evils that the war was being fought to destroy, and that racial discrimination in the United States was both an obstacle to victory and an absolute wrong.

Willkie's natural inclinations were further strengthened by his association with intelligent and educated Negroes like Walter White, through whom he met other gifted and dedicated Negro leaders. Thus the achievement of racial equality came to occupy, more and more, a central place in his vision of a better America and a better world.

In time of war, especially, while the need for national unity is greater, civil rights face a greater threat. "Under the stress and strain of combat," he told an audience at a luncheon sponsored by the National Conference of Christians and Jews, "intolerance always rises. Suspicion begins to grow and fingers are pointed. . . . We must preserve civil liberties for all or else our sacrifices in winning this war will be in vain."[72] To this end, in January, 1940, he joined with Mrs. Roosevelt, Mayor La Guardia, Dorothy Thompson, Herbert Agar, and others in establishing "Freedom House" as "a rallying point for all forces fighting for freedom and as a symbol of the fellowship of all who cherish it."[73]

And he was always ready as an individual to aid minority groups who were threatened with discrimination. When, for instance, such a group was formed in New York by Americans of German descent, together with aliens from enemy countries who were nevertheless loyal to the United States, in order "to stem the rising tide of thoughtless prejudice and to eliminate intolerance," Willkie lent his presence to a meeting where members displayed their loyalty by buying defense bonds; and he also wrote a statement to be issued in their behalf by Miss von Steuben (a direct descendant of the Revolutionary patriot), in which he declared: "This country's strength is the composite of persons of all descents—Irish, English, German, Italian and a myriad of other races, colors and creeds. No American has the right to impugn the patriotism of any other American because of the accident of his birth or race or religion."[74]

He returned to the theme at the inaugural dinner of Freedom House on March 19 when, as toastmaster, he "recounted at length the heroism of a Negro messman during the Pearl Harbor attack, and the subsequent efforts to identify him by name. He said that because of his black skin this man could not enlist in the Navy in any capacity except that of messboy and called for the correction of this 'injustice which makes a mockery of all our fine words.' "[75] Four months later in Los Angeles he expressed the same sentiment even more bluntly: "Democracy is what we're fighting for—so let's have it here."[76]

He was still more blunt, during the same trip, in pointing out to the leaders of the motion picture industry their own discrimination in refusing to give Negroes any but menial or comic roles. (Since his defense of the industry before the Senate subcommittee he had become a power in Hollywood. On April 10 he had been made chairman of the board of Twentieth Century-Fox.) At a luncheon attended by most executives and producers, after calling attention to discrimination in the industry, he added "that many of the persons responsible for Hollywood films belonged to a racial and religious group which had been the target of Hitler and that they should be the last to be guilty of doing to another minority what had been done to them." He was answered with applause.[77]

Willkie missed no opportunity to preach this gospel. One was a dinner in New York on June 17, "dedicated to the establishment of a memorial colony in Palestine in honor of the late Louis D. Brandeis," at which Democratic Senator Robert F. Wagner, author of the National Labor Relations Act and arch-New Dealer, was the guest of honor. As if acknowledging that his presence violated political propriety, Willkie remarked: "I doubt if I shall ever again aspire to public office, because there are certain causes in which I am so deeply interested, and I do not want my advocacy to be tainted with self-interest." Emphasizing once again the danger to minorities from war hysteria, he continued: "Bob Wagner has always fought for the weak, and while I am too old and fat to get into the firing line in this war, and while the people didn't see fit to grace me with a title two years ago, I will go out into the hustings, and fight at the bar of justice, for the rights of minority groups. I have no trust and faith in any extra-judicial proceedings under which any group will be deprived of their rights, under guise of war emergency."[78]

The last sentence may contain a reference to one of the most shameful episodes in American history: the unjust and unjustifiable removal (though it was later upheld by the Supreme Court) of all persons of Japanese blood from the Pacific Coast and their confinement—without any evidence of subversive activity, without trial, and without regard to the Constitutional rights which many could claim as native born citizens—in what were called "Relocation Centers," but for which "concentration camps" was the right name. It is perhaps a little surprising not to find Willkie taking a more definite stand on so clear an issue. But there is another indirect comment in an article in the *Saturday Evening Post* of June 12, entitled "The Case for the Minorities." This was written at the invitation of the editors, who explained in a note that, as an aftermath of an earlier article by Milton Mayer, strongly critical of American Jews, "many readers . . . suggested that the Post should ask Wendell Willkie to write an article expressive of the American attitude on minority groups."

Willkie began by once again calling attention to war as the source of intolerance. "The threat to racial and religious, even to political, minority groups springs in war-time from two things: an over-zealous mass insistence upon general conformity to majority standards, and the revival under emotional strains of age-old racial and religious distrusts." In the ability to resist these forces lies the real measure of a nation's greatness. "The height of our civilization, it seems to me, has been reached not by our assembly lines, our inventions or any of our great factitious development, but by the ability of people of varying beliefs and of different racial extractions to live side by side here in the United States with mutual understanding, respect and helpfulness." And this condition is to be valued not only as an end in itself but as a means to continued intellectual growth and spiritual vitality. "For minorities are rich assets of a democracy . . . the constant spring of new ideas, stimulating new thought and action, the constant source of new vigor. . . . The human mind requires contrary expressions against which to test itself."

Next he attempted, citing a long history of the persecutions of minorities in America—of Quakers by Puritans, of Indians by whites, of the Mormons, of the Abolitionists, of Jews and Catholics—to arouse in each reader the sense of his own responsibility. "For each of us has within himself the inheritances of age-long hatreds, of racial and religious differences, and everyone has the tendency to find the cause for his own failures in some conspiracy of evil. It is, therefore, essential that we guard our own thinking and not be among those who cry out against prejudices applicable to themselves, while busy spawning intolerance for others."

And not only in ourselves must we repress the evil, but in the government. "For government, which should be the very guardian of these liberties, is frequently, through excess zeal or desire for quick accomplishment of a purpose, the oppressor. . . . I have noticed, with much distress, the excessive wartime activity of the investigating bureaus of Congress and the Administration, with their impertinent and indecent searching out of the private lives and past political beliefs of individuals. Such methods, of course, are employed with the excuse of protecting the nation from subversive activities. So are those of the Gestapo."

"I have been appalled," he went on, spelling out his charges against those in positions of power, "at the callous indifference of high officers in the Navy to the obvious and undemocratic discrimination against Negroes, and disturbed to find similar discrimination too often in the ranks of industry and labor. I have been shocked to read that the Department of Justice seeks to revoke the citizenship of naturalized citizens suspected of foreign allegiance, rather than forthrightly to prosecute such persons for whatever crime they may be guilty of. . . . I have been sickened to see political parties flirting with the remnants of anti-Catholic Ku Klux Klanism and hesitating to denounce the anti-Semitism of Coughlinites and others.

"For now more than ever we must keep in the forefront of our minds the fact that whenever we take away the liberties of those we hate, we are opening the way to loss of liberty for those we love."[79]

There was one more step to be taken in Willkie's thinking about racial prejudice—a step that would reveal the inseparable connection between his two crusades. He took this step publicly in an address to the annual meeting of the National Association for the Advancement of Colored People in Los Angeles. "We have become," he said, "an adult nation of international interests and world outlook"; "we are learning in this war that it is not racial classifications nor ethnological considerations which bind men together. It is shared concepts and kindred objectives." Yet, while setting this new insight against the old imperialism embodied in the Axis powers, "we have practiced within our own boundaries something that amounts to race imperialism. The attitude of the white citizens of this country toward the Negroes has undoubtedly had some of the unlovely characteristics of an alien imperialism—a smug racial superiority, a willingness to exploit an unprotected people."

But now there is hope that the evil may be ending. "Today it is becoming apparent to thoughtful Americans that we cannot fight the forces of imperialism abroad and maintain a form of imperialism at home. . . . When we talk of freedom and opportunity for all nations the mocking paradoxes of our own society become so clear they can no longer be ignored."

He closed on a familiar note—a time of crisis brings both opportunities and obligations. "Our old world is breaking to pieces. And with its breaking arises the opportunity to fashion a new and better life. As always in periods of profound change and struggle, those who contribute most will have the most to do with fashioning the future. . . . You here today are leaders. You have been sore tried with many of the practices of our democracy. And it is right that you should be alert to every opportunity to remove the discriminations against your people. But you will find your largest opportunity to help your people in leading them to give their utmost to the preservation and advancement of our democracy. Thus by serving greatly they will share greatly in building among us a society in which all men will have justice and a real freedom."[80]

When had a national leader spoken to Negro Americans with such candor, such hopefulness, such an unpretentious taking for granted of a common dignity and common aims? "It is no exaggeration whatever," wrote Walter White, "for me to say that your going out there and making the speech you did has done more to lift the morale of Negroes than any other thing within the past year. They now see hope where before there was only despair."[81]

5

During Willkie's last years, when he moved so constantly and conspicuously upon the stage of national or world history, there are only rare episodes to remind one that he had a private life: that he had a wife and son; that he liked to talk *with* friends as well as *to* a public audience; that when human companions were lacking, his restless mind turned eagerly to the stimulation of books; that the place he thought of as "home" was a small town in Indiana; that he loved the feel of the soil on his farms near by, and the sight of the growing crops and livestock.

Nevertheless, these things were true; and one may suppose that when, on January 9, he and Mrs. Willkie saw Philip off for Annapolis, where he was to take a four-month course leading to an ensign's commission in the Naval Reserve, they felt the same mingling of pride and pain as millions of other American parents. Neither of them, however, cared to make a show of their personal feelings.

We catch another glimpse of Willkie's non-public life a little later in a talk which he gave at the New York Public Library on behalf of a campaign for books for service men: saying he had learned from experience "how important books are when the going is hard"; declaring that "no permanent disaster can come to a person who has the capacity to read"; and contributing two of his own "favorites," Lord Charnwood's biography of Lincoln and Ellen Glasgow's novel *In This Our Life*[82] (the moving story of a man in most ways ordinary who finds within himself the strength to defy his family and society in simply doing what decency demands).

Yet to all except Willkie's intimate friends, it is the public image that is real. And even to those friends, it seems, he rarely talked about himself. Philosophical ideas (in the broad sense of the adjective) and their social consequences; the human condition and human needs; plans of action to satisfy these needs—such were the things he talked about and thought about, which gave meaning and direction to his life. The personal desires that appear to govern the lives of most Americans—for physical ease or luxury, for material possessions, for power, for status—had little part in his make-up. Nor did he find satisfaction, as many Americans seem to, in activity for its own sake; nor, as fewer Americans seem to, in knowledge or art or religion as an end in itself, through speculation or contemplation or meditation. He was essentially a man of affairs, except that in this phrase the "affairs" are usually thought of as pertaining to a particular group or class, in a particular geographical and social setting; whereas the "affairs" with which, in Willkie's final years, some private demon drove him to concern himself were those of the human community as a whole.

Yet his idealism, despite its scope, was not abstract; it was rooted in his sense of the reality, the solidity, the uniqueness, of individual men and women, and his liking for them as they were. And so he threw himself without reserve into the common life, accepting every occasion to share with his "fellow Americans" (his favorite form of public address) his vision of a better world. On the evening after Philip's departure he appeared in the ring where Joe Louis and Buddy Baer were to fight for the heavyweight championship (with the proceeds to go to the Naval Relief Society), and brought down the house by remarking with a grin, "I took on a champion myself last year"; after which, never forgetful of the need for unity, he added, "And both my opponent and myself came out of the struggle firm and strong and united in the conviction that American democracy shall rule the world."[83] Later, in the fighters' dressing rooms, he congratulated Louis and was complimented in return. "That was a fine speech, Mr. Willkie. Yes, sir, that was the first speech I ever heard that I liked." Baer, to whom he offered condolences, took a good-humored revenge for Willkie's slip, in the ring, in referring to him as "Max" by remarking: "Yes, as you said earlier tonight, now we both know what it is to have taken on a champion."[84]

Two weeks later, as a guest at a dinner given by the Brooklyn Young Men's Chamber of Commerce in honor of retired Dodger pitcher Fred Fitzsimmons, he entertained the gathering with an account of "dodging 'pitchers' who hurled vegetables during the recent Presidential campaign" and with praise of "the ball-playing ability and delights of Brooklyn."[85]

In this speech, the reporter remarked, Willkie "eschewed topics such as politics and the war." But if so, this must have been a unique occasion. For he was profoundly troubled by the general attitude on the home front. Many persons in government and industry seemed inclined to proceed with "business as usual." On January 16 and again on June 18 the Truman Committee made public (over the protests of Donald Nelson) reports of confusion and inefficiency in war production that were little less than scandalous. Not until late March did the Army take steps to dim the lights of Atlantic seaboard cities which had brought destruction to dozens of merchant ships by making them perfect targets for night attacks by U-boats. On the other hand, there was widespread clamor for dispersing the Armed

Forces to protect the coasts, and even inland installations, from enemy attack. And in the meantime, the economic life of the nation was allowed to drift; not until the end of April did the President act decisively to regulate the civilian economy. Eight months after Pearl Harbor the Office of War Information asserted in a broadcast that "as a nation we are not yet more than ankle-deep in the war."[86]

From the beginning, Willkie was in the forefront of those seeking to arouse the country to the needed pitch of resolution. Two weeks after Pearl Harbor he spoke on a nation-wide broadcast, as he had thirteen months before, for the "loyal opposition," presenting the immediate prospect ("if we are honest") of "danger, hard work and iron resolution." But—"We must look beyond the bloody horizons of the present—must look out toward the shadows of the future which rise up like majestic phantoms of what may be our reward.

"Never—and I say it to you in measured words—never has there existed such hope for mankind as there exists today."[87]

And once again he applied to the Administration his technique of praise-and-prod. "It is a magnificent program," he said of Roosevelt's message to Congress outlining his goals in the production of weapons. "It is to be hoped that he immediately reorganizes his government and policies to the end that these accomplishments may be made possible."[88] To the Conference of Mayors in mid-January he spoke in the same stern tone: "we must become our own severest critics. We must impose on ourselves a discipline to match the fanatical fatalism of the Nazis and Japanese."[89] And again in a Lincoln's Birthday speech in Boston: "If the Japs go on as they are going in the Orient and the Indies, I should say, as a guess, that [the war] will continue from three to five years. It is going to be a long struggle and there will have to be tremendous sacrifice. There will be great loss of life. This death struggle of democracy against totalitarianism is the most tremendous thing in history."[90]

For Republicans he had a special message. He warned first, even more powerfully than in his earlier attacks on isolationism, against a negative attitude; and he condemned not only the "few who are imbued with the partisanship that blinds them to all other considerations," but also the "many more who would simply follow a passive course. . . . they counsel that the Republican party should not develop an affirmative policy at this time. . . . They insist that the United States, in the grief and distress and inconvenience that must be a consequence of the present conflict, will turn from the party in power. And they believe, therefore, that the Republican party will then come back into office on an inheritance of discontent.

"I have no faith in such a theory. . . . But even if I thought it would work I would still be against such a course. For I would not see the United States of the future made up of the backwash of the past. . . .

"To the Republican party I would say . . . Let us do more proposing than opposing. Let us exercise our freedom by developing our own policies. Let us work to put every resource of this great nation into the struggle for victory. Let us sacrifice every partisan advantage, if that is necessary, to win the war. Let us venture all, for all is at stake."[91]

This did not mean, of course, abstaining from valid criticism. He told a luncheon meeting of the National Women's Republican Club shortly after Nelson's appointment as head of the War Production Board that he had urged such action eighty-seven times during the campaign and thirty-seven times since. But he added: "It is our duty as a party and each in his individual capacity to do all we can to assist the man who has been appointed"; a "constructive approach," he argued, would be equally patriotic and—in the long run—expedient. "This is a time when people will separate the gold from the dross."[92]

His own proposal for speeding victory was: "Bring Douglas MacArthur home. Place him at the very top. Keep bureaucratic and political hands off him. Give him the responsibility and power of coordinating all the armed forces of the nation to their most effective use."[93] This particular suggestion, although undoubtedly popular, was perhaps a rather hasty one. But at least it dramatized the need for unity in military as well as in industrial planning.

It was also intended to dramatize the need for an aggressive leadership. "It sickens me," he said on February 26 at the annual awards dinner of the American Academy of Motion Picture Arts and Sciences, "to think of America in terms of defense. I am tired of hearing of defense efforts and defense rallies and even of defense bonds. We should be talking of conquering efforts, and victory rallies and bombardment bonds. But more than that, we should begin to think in terms of attack, not of retreat; we should begin to act in terms of striking, not blocking."[94] (But when, in July, he was asked about a second front in Europe, he replied that he could "speak only as an amateur," and that "amateurs can suggest methods of organization, but not actual military strategy.")[95]

This eagerness to get on with the war might have led him, as it led others, to impatient criticism of the British, who in Southeast Asia and North Africa had been suffering one military disaster after another—often, it seemed, from simple lack of energy, foresight, and competence. But Willkie saw the need for unity among America and her allies as well as among her citizens at home, and he defended the British on every occasion. In early June he acted as master of ceremonies at a tumultuous welcome given in New York to fifteen British and American war heroes; and after introducing them individually to the crowd that packed Madison Square Garden, he observed: "I like this picture of British and Americans standing side by side. You know, I've got no truck with those who seek to divide us either in war or in peace."[96] And again at the end of June, speaking at a luncheon of the British War Relief Society, he deplored current criticism of the British. "The British are a brave, heroic and self-sustaining people. . . . We must remember that we have not done wonders ourselves, yet. . . . every loyal American must scotch all criticism of the British war effort . . ."[97]

This, then, was Willkie's role as leader of the loyal opposition. Prize fights, hospital campaigns, war relief drives, party rallies, Hollywood dinners, welcomes to war heroes, symbolic events like the dedication of Lidice, Illinois (where 35,000 people assembled in the tiny village that was to be renamed for the Czech town wiped out by the Germans in one of the most sickening atrocities of the war), gatherings to honor foreign statesmen and monarchs (he was the main speaker at a farewell dinner to General Sikorsky, leader of the Polish government in exile; and at a White House luncheon for Queen Wilhelmina of the Netherlands he was seated at her right and the President at her left "as a demonstration of national unity")[98]—all these he viewed as opportunities to spur the government, to guide his party, to bring Americans closer to each other and to their Allies; stressing the harsh realities of the present war, but holding out the alluring possibilities of the future peace.

Willkie has often been disparaged as a "man of words"; and doubtless he envied those who could fight with other weapons, or command more tangible instruments of power. "They didn't do their job with words," he cried, in honoring the group of war heroes, while his audience cheered. "They did it with deeds. God bless them!" But in his time only Winston Churchill used words with greater power, and none used them for greater ends.

And what he did—though he always laughed at the idea when it was presented to him—was not without physical risk. The unceasing demands upon his energy which he was never willing to reject if the end seemed worthy were bound to take their toll. Already the doctor who had attended him during the campaign was telling him of what was to happen two years later. Dr. Harold Barnard, alarmed at his appearance when he visited Los Angeles in July, apparently gave him a warning which he followed up by mail on August 10. "At the risk of pestering you I would say again that you are too damn good a man to lose and unless you let up you are riding for a physical fall."[99] To Lem Jones he wrote even more urgently on the same date. "I hope Mrs. Willkie will prevail on the boss to take a vacation. I am distinctly worried about him, not so much for the present but for the future. At no time during the trip did I see him in such poor physical condition as when he was here. In all sincerity I feel that he is killing himself, and his trip abroad will only increase the strain he is under."[100]

But to such warnings Willkie would never listen. He had taken his good health for granted, with a kind of careless and innocent egotism—mixed, perhaps, with a dash of fatalism. His father and grandfather, he told Lem Jones a year later, when the latter tried to admonish him, had both died of cancer; and this, he said, was the way *he* expected to go when his time came.[101]

So, two weeks later, he set out blithely on a trip that was to be more grueling even than a Presidential campaign.

XVII

Around the World in Fifty Days

1

How little Willkie cared about New York State politics was evident when, two days after Dewey had been nominated for Governor, he took off on his flight around the world.

His reasons for going are most precisely expressed in a statement issued on his return, immediately after his confidential report to the President. "I went for three chief purposes:

(1) The first was to demonstrate to our Allies and a good many neutral countries that there is unity in the United States on . . . winning this war. . . . That was my own idea.

(2) The second purpose of my trip was to accomplish certain things for the President. . . .

(3) The third job I set out to do was to find out as much as I could, both for myself and for the American people, about this war and how it can be won—won quickly so that we can get back to our jobs again, and won securely so that the peace which follows it will hold."[1]

Ever since his return from England in early 1941 he had been thinking about a trip to other Allied countries; and when, in July, 1942, three friendly newspapermen in Russia cabled him to suggest a visit to that country,[2] Willkie jumped at the idea. On July 29 he wrote to the President proposing a trip "to the Middle East, into Russia and perhaps China."[3]

Roosevelt also jumped at the idea, particularly in regard to the Middle East. He immediately sent a memorandum to General Marshall: "I think that for many reasons Mr. Willkie should take this trip—especially to put some pep into the officials of Egypt, Palestine, Syria, Iraq, Iran, and China."[4] To Willkie he replied by telegram on August 3: "Am arranging for you to leave on any day after August 15 agreeable to you and to return between first and fifteenth of October. It is my thought that you could do the Middle East and that Russia and China could be subject to developments which you and I could talk over. . . . I hope you can come to see me at your earliest convenience so that we can have a good talk in regard to it and in regard to a lot of other things."[5]

The talk took place on August 7, following the luncheon for Queen Wilhelmina, and lasted until 4:30 p.m. Two days later Roosevelt sent a message to Stalin: "As you know, Mr. Willkie was my opponent in the 1940 election and he is today the head of the minority party. He is heart and soul with my administration in our foreign policy of opposition to Nazism and real friendship with your government, and he is greatly helping in the war work. For the sake of the present and the future I personally think that a visit to the Soviet Union by Mr. Willkie would be a good thing."[6] Stalin naturally agreed; and "Moscow newspapers gave prominent display . . . to dispatches reporting the forthcoming visit."[7]

One visit that Willkie would have liked to make was ruled out by the President.[8] India was in no condition to receive guests. Gandhi and Nehru were in prison, and a campaign of non-cooperation with the British was in full swing because of Britain's refusal to grant independence.

On August 20 Willkie had lunch at the White House and again discussed at length the coming trip. It was perhaps on this occasion that Roosevelt told him: "I've got a very great regard for you, even though we have differed politically in the past. I think you are Private Citizen Number One. And I just want to warn you. I know you've got guts, but remember, you may get to Cairo just as Cairo is falling, and you may get to Russia just at the time of a Russian collapse."[9] But while going this far in suggesting the seriousness of the military situation, the President failed to tell his "special representative" of the Western Allies' own military plans: that the "Second Front" was to be opened in November, not in Western Europe but in Africa—and that Stalin knew it.[10] This was, as Robert E. Sherwood later commented, "a circumstance incomprehensible to the Russians and the Chinese, and even to the British . . . "[11] And it was certainly less than fair to Willkie. Furthermore, Roosevelt never stated clearly and publicly that he and Willkie had agreed that the latter was to be essentially on his own, free to express his personal opinions as he saw fit.[12] On the other hand, leaving aside an occasional press conference remark indicative of some irritation, he took with good grace the blunt and controversial statements that Willkie was twice impelled to make.

In a news conference before Willkie's departure, the President gave him a handsome build-up, saying that his "mission in general would be to tell the truth about America's war effort" and, in talking to the leaders of neutral nations, to "compare what an Axis victory would mean as contrasted with a United Nations triumph." Willkie's words, the President felt, would carry "great weight." In addition, Willkie would deliver personal messages from Roosevelt to other leaders, including Stalin, and would perform other unspecified "special tasks."[13]

Before leaving, Willkie spent two hours with Secretary Hull, and talked to the Russian Ambassador, Maxim Litvinov. He also "sought the advice of State Department experts" as to the appropriate behavior in various places and situations. Their "first and strongest advice was to be himself—a course which they suspected he would follow anyway."[14]

Willkie told newsmen that he would be back by October 15. This was taken as an answer to those members of the Old Guard who were already charging him with not wanting to help the Republicans in the coming campaign.[15] In the meantime, he took occasion to help the Republican party in his own way, by delivering another blast at Hamilton Fish just before the primary and endorsing Fish's opponent, Augustus W. Bennet.[16] And when Fish won an overwhelming victory, Willkie still insisted that he must be defeated in the fall election.[17]

2

Willkie left New York on Wednesday, August 26 in a four-motored Army Liberator bomber converted to a transport, which had been named the *Gulliver* in honor of an earlier and still more famous traveler to remote places. It was piloted by Major Richard Kight (to whom, with the other six members of the crew, Willkie characteristically dedicated *One World*). Willkie's chosen traveling companions were Gardner Cowles, publisher of *Look*, and Joseph Barnes, former foreign correspondent for the New York *Herald Tribune,* both of whom now worked for the Office of War Information. The Armed Services were represented by Major Grant Mason of the Army and Captain Paul Pihl of the Navy (who, as it happened, was Willkie's brother-in-law, having married his younger sister Charlotte).

Egypt was the first destination. There were stops en route at West Palm Beach; Puerto Rico (where Willkie briefly saw his son); Belem, near the mouth of the Amazon; Natal, take-off point for the Atlantic crossing; Ascension Island, where the existence of an air base was still a military secret; Accra, on the African Gold Coast; Kano, in northern Nigeria; Khartoum, in the Sudan; and finally Cairo, on August 31. Already, in Nigeria and the Sudan, he had heard ominous rumors that recalled Roosevelt's warning—rumors that Rommel was about to capture Alexandria and that the British were planning to evacuate Egypt entirely. Cairo itself was "full of rumors and alarms," with pessimism the prevailing mood. A tight censorship made reporters anticipate the worst.[18]

Since one aim of his mission was to inspire confidence, Willkie immediately declared that although "he did not consider himself a military expert, he believed . . . Rommel was out on the end of a limb." With an eye to local morale, he stressed the importance of the Middle Eastern front and said he hoped one result of his visit would be "to focus United States attention on this area." Asked by an Egyptian newspaperman "whether the Republican party would advocate isolationism if it returns to power after the war," he retorted, "Not if I have anything to say." And to drive home the fact of American unity, he added: "If I am here as President Roosevelt's representative, it is because 130,000,000 Americans are all behind the President to beat the Germans."

For the benefit of American reporters he discussed the major league pennant races, professing worry over how the Dodgers had been doing since his departure. To American troops, after inspecting Army workshops and repair facilities, he remarked, "I just want to say I'm damned glad to see you, God bless you and give 'em hell." He also talked for forty minutes with Egypt's Premier Nahas Pasha, and took a sight-seeing tour to the Sphynx and the Pyramids.[19] The next day he had an audience with King Farouk (who at that time still seemed a more or less respectable monarch).

On September 5 he accepted General Montgomery's invitation to visit the front, where the British commander convinced him—by a detailed account of the battle (El Alamein) that had just been fought, a discussion of the overall strategy of the campaign, and exact figures on German losses and on the arrival of arms for his own forces—that Rommel had been definitely and finally stopped, and that shortly he would be driven back.

In the evening Willkie saw a different side of his host, as they sat on the steps of the trailer where Willkie was to sleep, "from which we could see whitecaps breaking on the sea under the moon and hear at our backs in the distance the pounding of his artillery against Rommel's withdrawing forces. He was in a reminiscent and reflective mood and talked of his boyhood days in County Donegal, of his long years in the British army, with service in many parts of the world, of his continuous struggle since the war began to infuse both public officials and army officers with the necessity for an affirmative instead of a defensive attitude."[20] With a touch of pathos he revealed that all his personal possessions had been stored in a Dover warehouse that had been destroyed by German bombs. He seemed to regret most the loss of his books.

All this, however, was aside from Montgomery's main point in sending the invitation. He told Willkie of the current low level of British prestige throughout the Middle East because of repeated defeats and of how this "interfered with his secret service and helped the enemy's." He did not wish, however, to make public officially the extent of the victory he was sure he had gained, lest the Germans should slip away before he received the three hundred American General Sherman tanks that he needed for an attack that he hoped would utterly destroy Rommel's army. A confident statement by Willkie, however, would strengthen the morale of pro-Allied elements in the Middle East without alarming the Germans.[21]

This was of course a congenial assignment. The two men agreed on the wording of a statement, Montgomery called a press conference, and Willkie said: "Egypt is saved. Rommel is stopped and a beginning has been made on the task of throwing the Nazis out of Africa."[22] He praised Montgomery as a "fighting field general," and paid tribute to the cooperation of different nationalities in the United Nations force, which he said symbolized the "future world spirit." [23]

Montgomery's strategy, however, ran afoul of the censor, who refused to pass Willkie's comments. Newsmen, not knowing the background, were surprised at the outburst which their announcement of the censorship provoked. "God damn it, boys," Willkie exploded, "nobody's got the right to censor anything I say. I'm a responsible person."[24] It must have been very pleasant to be told later by Winston Churchill: "Your visit to Cairo did no end of good and all your most sanguine forecasts were borne out by the ensuing battle."[25]

No real harm was done, however, since the message was intended chiefly for the other nations in the Middle East, and to these Willkie could carry it in person. Before leaving Egypt, however, he went to Alexandria, where two experiences strengthened his conviction that military and political problems could not be separated. One was a talk with the French Admiral Godfroy, whose ships lay idly at anchor, gathering barnacles, while he nursed his bitterness against the British and his loyalty to Petain; helpless, because he was "almost uneducated in any meaning of the war outside his simple officer's discipline."[26] The other was a talk with the British Admiral Harwood ("hero of the epic fight of the *Exeter* against the *Graf Spee*") and a group of his friends. What he got from them was "Rudyard Kipling untainted even by the liberalism of Cecil Rhodes."[27] (This was unfair to Kipling. But Willkie was only repeating a view that had been fashionable for forty years among literary "liberals" who had never read beyond the first line of "The Ballad of East and West.")

Willkie's next stop was Ankara, and there he continued to preach his good news; the official communiqués from Egypt, he insisted, had "failed to convey the extent to which the Allied desert army had triumphed."[28] "The truth is that Rommel is in a hell of a hole."[29] In Beirut, Lebanon, he revealed that current American plane production was 5,000 a month (60 per cent of them combat planes), and that while Allied shipping losses were 500,000 tons per month, America alone was producing 600,000 tons per month.[30] In Baghdad he informed his hearers that America "was distributing billions of dollars worth of lease-lend materials to the United Nations."[31]

And people believed him. How could they help believing a visitor who tossed diplomatic double-talk on the scrapheap and said exactly what he meant? In Jerusalem he said in so many words "that the purpose of his tour was to stimulate the people of the Middle East and other countries to make greater contributions to the war effort," and "that those riding the fence at present, who expect to come forward later to make demands that their actions had not justified, were mistaken."[32] From Axis propagandists this would have sounded like a threat. But there could be no mistaking Willkie's good will. "My country seeks no advantage," he said in Iran. "It wants no territory, no additional power and no control over others. But it does want to know who are those who fight with it—who are those who are willing to sacrifice for the common cause."[33]

The language that he used confirmed the impression of his sincerity. Such light-hearted use of American vernacular as "If you want to see the United Nations win don't just sit in the bleachers and throw pop bottles"[34] often put a strain on the interpreter, but when the meaning was made clear the audience was always delighted. People felt, and rightly, that he was talking to them just as he would talk to his own countrymen, without affectation or condescension.

And though his speech was sometimes blunt, it was never bullying. He had come not merely to talk and inform but to listen and learn. He listened through endless banquets in his honor—at ease in his plain blue business suit among immaculately dinner-jacketed and uniformed guests—to American and British diplomats, to prime ministers and monarchs. He listened to lawyers and engineers. He listened to people whom he stopped to talk to in the streets. He listened with special attention to what was said by students and teachers; and he was troubled that "nowhere . . . in the whole Middle East . . . except in Turkey did anyone suggest showing me a native school as a matter of national pride."[35]

In Turkey he listened to Prime Minister Saracoglu and other officials, appreciative of both their friendliness to the Allies and the country's geographical position that made it vulnerable to a German attack, and hence made neutrality necessary. In Beirut he listened to General de Gaulle and tried to understand him (as Roosevelt and Hull were unwilling to do for another two years);[36] and to General Spears, the British minister; and to an Arab official who said, "A plague on both your houses"; and to the President of American University, Bayard Dodge, who gave him "more hope and confidence in the future of those regions than all the others combined."[37]

In Jerusalem he spent an uninterrupted day listening to the stories of men representing every group in faction-ridden Palestine: the "very British" High Commissioner, Sir Harold MacMichael, who explained (as Willkie reported with quiet irony) "the distinctions an American finds it hard to see between a colony and a mandated area";[38] Arab leaders who wanted independence and an end to Jewish immigration; and Jewish leaders who wanted a Jewish state but were bitterly divided as to the kind of state they wanted and the best means of creating it. (The American Consul General, Lowell

Pinkerton, lent Willkie his house, which had two staircases, from which Arab and Jewish leaders alternately were ushered into the room where Willkie, Cowles and Barnes listened while they poured out their opinions and emotions.)[39]

Willkie in turn, after this exhausting experience, went to tell his story and present his questions to Henrietta Szold, the American Zionist, whom age had not hardened nor the agony of her people deprived of compassion for all suffering human beings. Afterwards he wondered a little wistfully whether it is "unrealistic to believe that such a complex problem as the Arab-Jewish one, founded in ancient history and religion, and involved as it is with high international policy and politics, can be solved by good will and simple honesty."[40]

Good will and honesty were, at any rate, the qualities that radiated from him on all occasions and gave rise to a spontaneous build-up of interest. He seemed, as he moved, to generate a kind of intellectual and emotional momentum that few could resist. "His instantaneous success in Turkey," wrote one correspondent, "brought him much more respect when he reached Beirut." In Baghdad the Royal Band was at the airport to welcome him, and "crowds lined the streets as he was driven to the palace"[41] for dinner with the Regent, Abdul Ilah, and conferences with Premier Nuri. At one place, at least, the people got their money's worth, when, "on an impulse, he stopped his car outside an Arab coffee shop and went inside to drink a cup of coffee," refusing a special seat and talking eagerly with those about him.[42] Such actions "apparently astonished and delighted the Arabs, who [wrote Ernest Lindley dryly] have not been accustomed to such behavior by high-ranking British and American visitors. According to one account, even veiled women on the streets of Baghdad cheered and waved to him."[43]

Here and there a resident representative of the State Department might be shocked at the visitor's unconcerned trampling down of the established proprieties, but there was, fortunately, nothing to be done about it. In the meantime, Axis propaganda withered beneath his ready wise-cracks. "If the Germans don't like it," he told a Turkish news conference where mention was made of Axis complaints and threats concerning his visit, "it's easy enough for the Turks to invite them to send along a leader of *their* administration opposition."[44]

Doubts of American unity vanished when President Roosevelt's recent opponent appeared as his personal representative, politely declining to discuss, without pretending to conceal, differences of opinion on matters not vital to the main purpose. "I don't want to discuss that," he said smilingly to a question about American policy towards Vichy. "My views don't correspond with those of the Administration."[45]

Fears of future American policy were dispelled when he declared his conviction "that after the war the United States intended to use its utmost efforts for the establishment of a world in which all men—irrespective of whether they are citizens of powerful or small nations—might live free and decent lives of their own choosing."[46]

It was obvious that Willkie was more than fulfilling Roosevelt's hope that he would "put some pep" into the Middle Eastern countries. From Ankara it was reported: "The Turkish press this morning reflected profound interest in and admiration for the Republican party leader."[47] The word from Jerusalem was that "Mr. Willkie's visit is having an extremely tonic effect upon the inhabitants of Syria, Lebanon, Palestine, Trans-Jordan and Iraq."[48] From Baghdad the London *Times's* "Own Representative" assured his readers that Willkie's visit "gives the greatest pleasure to all sections of the people."[49] Everywhere he was a symbol of the people's hope for true independence. As Edmund Stevens wrote later: "To the semi-colonial nations of the Middle East, who desire emancipation above all things, Willkie was the Four Freedoms taken out of the realm of the abstract and clothed in a rumpled blue suit."[50]

This was what Willkie meant to the Middle East. What did the Middle East mean to him?

It meant, in the first place, a social and economic system against which every atom of his American equalitarianism rebelled: "a small percentage of wealthy landowners" who were indifferent to "any political movement, except as it affected the perpetuation of their own status"; and "the great mass of the people" who "own no property, are hideously ruled by the practices of ancient priestcraft, and are living in conditions of squalor."[51] His comment was: "The urge and the strength to create do not come, as a rule, from those who have too much or from those who have nothing."[52]

He found, nevertheless, even among "the long-inert masses," a sort of blind groping for change; and among "a small group of restless, energetic, intellectual young people," "a growing spirit of fervid nationalism, a disturbing thing to one who believes that the only hope of the world lies in the opposite trend."[53] And it would no longer do "to say, as some people did say to me in Cairo and Jerusalem, that 'the natives don't want anything better than what they have.' "[54] "We have sent our ideas and ideals, and our motion pictures and our radio programs, our engineers and our business men, and our pilots and our soldiers, into the Middle East; and we cannot now escape the results."[55] No longer would the people of that region be content with "the veil, the fez, the sickness, the filth, the lack of education and modern industrial development, the arbitrariness of government."[56] And without a "new approach" by the Western nations, "a new leader will arise with a fierce fanaticism who will coalesce these discontents," offering the former ruling powers only the alternatives of complete withdrawal or total repression by force of arms.[57] In short, colonialism must go.

3

It was impossible that in the vast expanse of Russia—with German armies at the edge of the Caucasus oil fields, fighting in Stalingrad on the Volga, and besieging Leningrad; with every person engaged to the limit of his capacity in the war effort; and with all media of information rigidly controlled by the government—Willkie's visit would have as great an impact on the people as in the Middle East. But in the world at large, the echoes were even more resounding.

The first stop in Russia was at Kuibyshev on Thursday, September 17.[58] This city on the Volga, 500 miles southeast of Moscow, had been designated the temporary capital in 1941. Moscow, however, remained the real center of government, and Willkie wished to fly there directly from Teheran, but Ambassador Standley insisted that he follow the previously arranged itinerary.[59]

The fact is that Standley resented Willkie's visit. Having held the office of Chief of Naval Operations, he was accustomed to authority, and also to handling matters "through channels"; but Roosevelt's policy of sending a series of "personal representatives" (Hopkins, Harriman, Willkie) to do business directly with Stalin left him little more than a figurehead. As for Willkie, Standley was convinced from the start that his object was "more to enhance his political stature than to help the Allies get on with the war."[60] Nevertheless, he did his duty as he saw it, and was on hand to greet Willkie when the *Gulliver* landed at the Kuibyshev airport. The Russians sent only a minor Foreign Office official, S. A. Lozofsky, although the Deputy Foreign Minister, Andrei Vishinsky, was in Kuibyshev, and Standley "felt that our President's Special Representative had been slighted, and that the next move was up to the Russians";[61] but Willkie brushed this suggestion aside and promptly called on Vishinsky. He also asked Standley and the "Soviet authorities to reduce his social functions to a minimum."[62]

On Friday Willkie "was up at 7 A.M. to begin a fifteen-hour series of visits to agricultural units and factories . . . trying to meet and talk informally with workers and peasants."[63] In an aircraft factory the first worker he spoke to ignored his question and asked one of his own: "What about a second front?"[64] At a ballet that evening he was asked again: "When are Britain and the United States going to open up a second front in Western Europe?"[65] At a lunch next day at a collective farm "the Commandant of the Local Army Garrison . . . proposed a toast to 'The Second Front in Western Europe.' "[66] In a Moscow munitions factory the question was the same: "When are we going to have a Second Front?"[67] At the front near

Rzhev, he "heard from embattled Red Army men the now familiar query: 'How about a second front?'"[68] During this trip, also, "he stopped off whenever possible to talk to peasants" who were returning to their homes in recaptured territory; and always, when they found out who he was, "they plied him with questions as to what the United States was doing to help Russia win the war."[69]

Standley was sure that all the questions were "inspired." "I had recognized the phoney nature of the mass appeal of the Russian people to our visiting Special Representative."[70] But this comment only reveals the Ambassador's pathetic unawareness of what was going on around him. The writer of an Associated Press story during Willkie's visit observed: "To those Americans who have been working here since the announcement of the Washington and London agreements on the 'urgent task' of creating a second front in Europe in 1942, it is no secret that they have been getting a cooler treatment from the Russians, both officials and private citizens. . . . One learned Russian, who for years has been lecturing on the United States and Britain, remarked: 'Recently I have stopped talking on these two countries. My audiences ask me too many questions that I cannot answer. One of the foremost is why the United States and Britain cannot start a second front.' . . . Casual friends and bare acquaintances bring up the question of the second front and ask in no uncertain language why there isn't one."[71]

At any rate, no one can challenge the truth of what Willkie said on arriving in Moscow (on Sunday, September 20): "The second front has become almost a symbol for the Russian people of the kind of aid they feel they are entitled to receive from Britain and America. They appreciate the aid and materials, but they think it is inadequate. . . . I was asked about the second-front fifty times a day." But he refused to commit himself beyond saying: "All fronts belong to all the allies, and no nation can afford to be individually self-protective."[72] "He declined to give his own opinion on the second front question, on the grounds that it was not wise for a civilian, without knowledge of the military situation, to comment on it."[73]

This prudent position he abandoned before he left. In the meantime, he continued his high-pressure sight-seeing, gathering facts and forming opinions, and imparting to this normally humdrum process, as only Willkie could, a quality of high adventure. The day after his arrival in Kuibyshev he spent at an airplane factory (which had been picked up and moved from its location near Moscow in October, 1941, and was producing planes again in December). There he argued the case for capitalism against Communism with the young engineer in charge of production, until Major Kight told Barnes to explain that Willkie was not trying to convert him but only to get him to talk.[74] The next day he took a trip up the Volga (during which he found that steering the boat was a trickier business than he had anticipated);[75] heard of prodigious plans for power development on the river; and visited a collective farm, where he patted the cows admiringly but worried Admiral Standley by making advances to a bull who did not reciprocate his friendliness,[76] and where he again argued, with the manager, the issue of private ownership versus collectivism—and again got nowhere.[77]

There was, of course, as Willkie was at pains to point out to Americans, no mystery about this attitude. "Practically the whole upper and middle classes" had been wiped out by the revolution. The persons he talked to came from peasant families; their parents had had "no property, no education," no security, no hope of bettering their lot. The position of the present generation might not seem enviable to Americans, but it was a vast improvement over what had gone before.[78]

On his second night in Kuibyshev, Willkie went from dinner at the Chinese Embassy to the Bolshoi Theater to see a performance of Tschaikowsky's ballet *Swan Lake.* The theater established a precedent by delaying the performance fifteen minutes until Willkie arrived, when it announced that "The Honorable Wendell Willkie, Commissar and Special Representative of the United States, honors you this evening by his presence at our humble performance."[79] At the end of the ballet Willkie returned the compliment and established a precedent himself by leaping from his box to the stage, presenting a bouquet to the prima ballerina, Irina Tikomirova, and then kissing her, while "the audience cheered wildly,"[80] and shouted "WEEL-ki"[81] with a fervor that must have recalled the "We Want Willkie" chant of the past. This was an episode that, Larry Lesueur wrote a year later, "all Kuibyshev fondly remembers."[82]

The last night at Kuibyshev was devoted to a dinner given in Willkie's honor by Vishinsky,[83] before he moved on to Moscow. Here he received a warmer welcome. "There was a drizzling rain, but the flags were flying, and a good Soviet turn-out was on hand. . . . The visit, plainly, was already a success."[84] On Monday he was up early for breakfast with two reporters, and then, since no program had yet been arranged, he went for a walk through the streets, where he found himself apparently unnoticed, though the papers carried a short story on his arrival.[85] Then he saw Molotov, and the wheels started turning. Factory inspections, an interview with Stalin, and a visit to the front were put on the agenda. In the evening he heard a performance of Shostakovich's *Seventh Symphony* by the Moscow Symphony Orchestra. Tuesday he was taken in tow by a Mr. Molochkov, Chief of Protocol at the Foreign Office, for more sight-seeing and a jazz concert in the evening. The same evening he received word that Stalin would see him at 7:30 p.m. on Wednesday.

In the meantime, Standley, worried by having heard nothing about the appointment with Stalin, arrived early Wednesday morning at the guest house where Willkie was staying, and was infuriated at learning (first from the doorman!) that the appointment had been made directly, instead of through the Embassy. He demanded first whether Willkie was responsible; then expressed the determination to find out who *was;* became even more irritated when Willkie tried to calm him; and got still angrier when Willkie confirmed his inference that he was not to be present at the interview. He went with Willkie that morning, however, to inspect a munitions factory and then an antiaircraft battery outside the city, where they had lunch and where Willkie notably failed to amuse him by proposing a "drinking bout" between him and one of the young Russian officers.[86]

That afternoon the Ambassador gave a reception for Willkie, who again annoyed him by repeatedly leaving the receiving line to talk to various important people; and later the Ambassador was seen talking to his guest and "pounding a corner table until it bounced."[87] When Standley saw on the front pages of the next day's newspapers not only a picture of Willkie and Stalin, but another in which Cowles and Barnes were present (Willkie had invited them, with Stalin's permission, after the interview), it was the last straw.

Willkie left the Kremlin at 9:45. At midnight he climbed into a jeep and started for the front. At 9:30 a. m., in a "cold, driving rain," they arrived at the headquarters of General Lelushenko, commanding the Rzhev sector. The general explained in detail the operations on his front, and was visibly annoyed when Willkie asked him how long a front he was defending. " 'Listen,' he said to the interpreter, 'you tell Mr. Willkie I'm not defending anything—I'm attacking.' " At noon, without stopping for lunch, they drove to within about five miles of the front lines, where the party could see the flashes of shell bursts and view the debris of battle. During the day they met peasants already moving back to the ruins of their homes in territory recaptured only a few days earlier. That evening they had dinner with the General, and then left on the all-night trip to Moscow. Arriving Friday morning, Willkie "ate a big meal of ham and eggs, and went straight to bed."[88] The trip had been "the routine one which the Soviets had long since organized . . . for correspondents and distinguished visitors,"[89] but it was strenuous enough.[90]

But he was up again in the afternoon, visited a hospital, and talked with Standley. Once more he angered the Ambassador, by saying that some matters he had discussed with Stalin could only be reported personally to the President—"matters so secret that I can't trust them to the coded messages or even to the Ambassador."[91] (Standley was not happier when he learned later, from Stalin himself, that this had been by the wish of the Russian leader. "I gave [the information] to Mr. Willkie to take to the

President," Stalin told him bluntly. "Such matters can best be handled separately and directly between President Roosevelt and myself.")[92]

Friday evening Willkie went to the opera. Afterwards he spent most of the night at a gathering arranged by the American correspondents in Moscow and attended by some of the most influential Russian writers—Ehrenberg, Simonov, Voitekhov, and others. It was an off-the-record, no-holds-barred affair, and although in *One World* Willkie described the Russians as "critical but not antagonistic," he did comment on their "intransigence";[93] and to Alexander Werth (whom he invited to breakfast next morning at eight and who found him "a picture of health and vigor") he spoke of their "wild talk" and "abuse of the Allies."[94] No diplomatic official could have gained so clear a picture of what Russian intellectuals were thinking.

Later Saturday morning he inspected an elementary school, and commented: "Children are alike the world over. I heard one child reciting on the use of the comma. I told her that I was fifty-one years old and that I had been struggling with that problem for years and didn't know the answer yet."[95]

The climax of the visit was a banquet given to Willkie by Stalin Saturday evening, "with most of the Politburo present to do him honor."[96] Stalin even asked Willkie to choose the other guests—and there was another small tempest when Standley added some names to the list and a Soviet official suggested that he ought to get Willkie's permission.[97]

That the banquet was a generally festive occasion is borne out by Willkie's later boast to some young friends, "I drank fifty-three vodka toasts—bottoms up, glass over the head—and walked out of the Kremlin to my car."[98] One of these toasts was a characteristic gesture by Willkie himself. "Stalin chided the interpreters for translating in dull, flat voices, without emotion. Willkie promptly toasted the interpreters, 'the only ones who are working here tonight,'" and Stalin drank the toast.[99] But later the Russian leader showed himself less amiable. After a toast to the pilots of the Red Air Force, Stalin vehemently denounced the British for having "stolen" 152 Lightning fighter planes bound for Russia. (Stalin had told Willkie of the episode at their first meeting, and Willkie had discussed it with the British Ambassador Sir Archibald Clark-Kerr. The planes had been lying crated at a Scottish port, after the convoy carrying them had been turned back by German attacks, and Churchill, learning of the fact, "went to Averill Harriman and got them released for the defense of London.")[100] Willkie tried to ease the tension by remarking to Stalin, "You certainly keep your eye on the ball." Apparently he succeeded, for after a long explanation had been made in terms of golf and baseball, Stalin "chuckled" and agreed.[101] Clark-Kerr, however, naturally felt called on to answer, "saying that he admired Stalin's bluntness and would be blunt in reply. The Soviet Union, Great Britain and the United States were united in a common cause, he pointed out, and if any planes were diverted from Russia, it would only be to further the cause of all three." Stalin answered, "Nothing the British Ambassador has said will be taken amiss."[102]

Willkie, however, was not willing to let the matter rest. "In any great coalition, he said, there were always strains and misunderstandings, but we could not afford to lose sight of our common objectives. The British had held out alone for a long time before the Russians and the Americans were fighting by their side. If we stuck together now, he went on, we would beat the Germans surely. And if we could learn to stick together after the war, we would have a period of peace and prosperity such as the world had never known. He put his arm down and turned Stalin around towards him, almost violently, and then proposed a toast to the Great Alliance. Stalin drank it. . . . 'You are a plain-speaking man, I see,' Stalin said . . . 'I like plain-spokenness, but you wouldn't have stolen 152 planes from me.' "[103]

4

Earlier in the day there had been another instance of Willkie's plain-speaking which had been more to Stalin's liking. This was the famous statement on the second front, delivered to American and British correspondents. It read in part:

"There are certain facts that are important for Americans to know. . . . Five million Russians have been killed, wounded, or are missing. At least 60,000,000 Russians or nearly one third of the population are now slaves in Russian territory controlled by Hitler. Food in Russia this winter will be scarce—perhaps worse than scarce. . . . Fuel will be little known this winter in millions of Russian homes.

"Clothing except for the army and essential war workers is nearly gone. Many vital medical supplies just don't exist.

"Russian women by the millions, side by side with their children—some of them as young as eight or ten—are manning the machines in the war factories and running the farms. . . . Yet no Russian talks of quitting. . . . The Russian people have chosen victory or death. They only talk of victory.

"Personally I am now convinced that we can best help by establishing a real second front in Western Europe at the earliest possible moment our military leaders will approve. And perhaps some of them will need some public prodding. Next summer might be too late."[104]

At first glance this statement does not seem sensational. Nobody denied that a "real second front in Western Europe" was indispensable to final victory. The only question was, "When?" And many eminent persons were saying, "Now." Roosevelt himself had not given up the idea until the end of June. [105] On June 21 Lord Beaverbrook had called for a second front "at once."[106] At a New York "Rally to Support the President for the Opening of a Second Front Now," held on July 22, Senators Mead and Pepper and Mayor La Guardia were among the speakers. (Willkie sent a message of approval.)[107] On July 26, a British crowd of 50,000 assembled in Trafalgar Square to urge the same action.[108] Even at the time of Willkie's statement, the controversy was still going on.

But it was one thing for lesser men in America and Britain to urge a second front. It was another thing for Willkie to do so, speaking from Moscow, where he was understood to be in some sense a representative of the President. His words echoed in every capital in the world.

The echoes from America were mostly harsh. Many military leaders were naturally incensed by the comment about "prodding." So were many Republicans, who constantly sought to play up the role of the military in order to play down that of the President. So were many Democrats, who took the statement as an attack on the Commander-in-Chief. As for Roosevelt, he too seemed at first to be annoyed; for in his next press conference, when asked about the controversy caused by Willkie's statement, he replied that "he had read the headlines but had not thought it worth while to read the news stories themselves because they were speculative."[109] (To Willkie in Chungking Roosevelt was quoted as having condemned the statement itself, and he retorted with heat that although he was carrying out certain tasks assigned him by the President, "When I speak for myself, I'm Wendell Willkie, and I say what I damn please.")[110] At his next press conference, however, the President dismissed as "entirely political" stories of dissension between him and Willkie, and declared that "everything was all right as far as he was concerned in the Willkie mission"; pressed further, he added that "he was assuming that Mr. Willkie was carrying out extremely well just what he had asked him to do."[111]

The British on the whole took the matter calmly. In fact, two prominent members of the Labor Party, Lord Strabolgi and Emmanuel Shinwell, approved Willkie's stand.[112] The government leaders, however, were obviously irked. Deputy Prime Minister Atlee, in Canada, insisted that "there is no need for public prodding";[113] and Churchill, although he refused to comment directly, dwelt on the "undesirability of public statements or speculations as to the time or place of future Allied offensive operations."[114]

To the Russians, naturally, nothing could have been more gratifying. Now they could all say, as Willkie's admirers at the ballet in Kuibyshev had said, "dadou sumpathichny Americanets"—"what a charming American."[115] Stalin's response came when, a week later, he chose to publish his answers to three questions which Henry Cassidy of the Associated Press had submitted to him as a more or less routine matter, without any real expectation of a reply. Stalin observed, first, that "the possibility of a second front" occupied "a place of first rate importance" in the Soviet estimate of the military situation; second, that Allied aid to the Soviet Union, compared to the Soviet Union's own efforts, had been "so far little effective," and that he was only asking that "the Allies fulfill their obligations fully and on time"; and third, that "the Soviet capacity for resistance" was greater than the German capacity for conquest.[116]

This did not make Willkie's critics any more friendly; but it showed that his statement had faithfully reflected the mood of Russia's leaders. His own comment in Chungking was: "I hope Mr. Stalin's statements will bring the Russians' imperative needs forcefully to the attention of the United Nations. That was the objective of the statement of my personal views in Moscow last week."[117]

But why had he thought it necessary to be so blunt—especially since he had initially declined comment on the second front issue? For one thing, obviously, he had seen the desperate strain upon the physical and moral resources of the Russian people. "A hungry man, though he has the heart of a lion, cannot go on fighting."[118] And when he compared the Russian war effort with the fumbling and blundering that still went on at home, the refusal of many individuals and groups to make genuine sacrifices, it is little wonder if he thought his countrymen needed as hard a jolt as words could give.

It is clear in retrospect that a full scale invasion of the Continent in 1942 was not feasible. The Allies did not have enough trained men, enough weapons and equipment, enough ships to carry them, or enough planes to support them—especially since the United States, despite the priority given to beating the Germans, was fighting a full scale war in the Pacific. But in 1942 the situation was less clear; and in preparing Willkie for his trip, it is obvious that Roosevelt stressed only America's strength and not her weakness.

No doubt the decisive event in determining Willkie to make his statement was his talk with Stalin. It is clear that the Russian leader made a tremendous impression on Willkie, and that this impression was in many ways favorable. He could not help being moved when Stalin made an "appeal for the United Nations to put every ounce of energy into the war effort with the greatest possible speed. If the will was present, he said that seemingly impossible obstacles could be overcome. In the simple eloquence and sincerity with which he spoke these words he showed a tremendous power of persuasiveness."[119]

To a generation of Americans accustomed to think of Stalin as a mere monster (believing—on this topic alone—the words of those who were his accomplices and successors), Willkie's willingness to be impressed may appear naive. It may be pointed out, however, on the one hand, that almost every person who met Stalin was equally impressed; and on the other, that Willkie's admiration for Stalin was not without reservations. Despite his desire to increase American sympathy for Russia, the adjective he uses most often in describing the Soviet dictator is "hard"—"a hard face," "a hard, tenacious mind," "a hard man, perhaps a cruel man."[120] He was being only partly complimentary when he told Stalin: "I am rather glad your lot was not cast in America. You would have been a tough competitor." (Stalin was "obviously pleased.")[121]

What Willkie liked most—and the feeling was clearly reciprocated—was Stalin's almost brutal directness. He asked "searching questions, each of them loaded like a revolver"; he demanded "detailed reports" on Willkie's "trips through various factories";[122] he sought information about America's industrial development and advice on how Russia might emulate it.[123] The visitor also enjoyed his host's "robust sense of humor," his ready response to "unsubtle jokes and repartee" such as Willkie himself liked to indulge in. Stalin roared with laughter when Willkie told him, after praising Soviet schools and libraries: "But if you continue to educate the Russian people, Mr. Stalin, the first thing you know you'll educate yourself out of a job."[124] Finally, Willkie respected in Stalin, as in Churchill, a profound dignity arising from a sense of identification with the struggle for survival of a great people. When Willkie spoke of his eagerness to tell the American people what he had seen, Stalin asked if he might make a suggestion. Then he said: "Yes, tell America all that you've seen here. Tell Americans if you like that we need all the products they can send from their great workshop. But I would suggest that you understate the case rather than give anyone the impression that you are encouraging Americans to assume a patronizing attitude toward us."[125]

Willkie's final word from Moscow to his countrymen concerned his judgment of Stalin. "You may agree with him or disagree with him, condemn or praise the Russian social system, but don't discount his abilities or his purposes, for no man can leave Stalin's presence these days without admiration for his devotion to the cause of saving his people from Hitler's merciless hordes."[126]

Whether Willkie's appraisal of Joseph Stalin was too generous is a question that must await the verdict of history, rendered, after the passions of the present century have faded, in the light of the forces and events amid which the Soviet dictator moved. But a rash anticipation of the verdict might be that Stalin was a man of keen intelligence, the application of which was limited by his revolutionary background (and, in his last years, a growing paranoia); of great executive ability; of tremendous resolution and force of character; and of a fierce devotion to Russia, combined with but not submerged in, a lust for personal power. These qualities made him the one man that could have kept Russia from going down under the fury of Hitler's attack. He was also, obviously, in line with the long tradition of Russian autocracy, capable of total disregard of the sufferings of individual human beings and of total contempt for the "human rights" that are basic to Western democracy. He could nevertheless, when he chose, display great personal charm, which visitors from the West found it impossible to dismiss as a mere facade.

In the meantime, it needs to be made clear that Willkie's speeches and writings concerning Russia were not merely an essay in understanding but also a prophetic warning. Whatever Americans might think of Stalin, of the Communist system to which he was dedicated, and of the people whom he ruled, these together made up a massive fact: "that the Soviet Union, whether we like it or not, exists";[127] "such a force, such a power, such a people cannot be disposed of with a high hat or a lifting of the skirt. . . . Russia will be reckoned with."[128] For Russia and America there could be no course but cooperation or conflict. And the consequences of the latter were so appalling that all men of good will must work, as long as the choice was open, for the former. And they must do so *now*—"tomorrow might be too late." This was perhaps the strongest consideration behind Willkie's "second front" statement—not what effect American military policy might have on the course of the war itself, but (as he told the President on his return) what effect it might have on Soviet-American relations after the war.[129]

Yet Willkie's overall view of the future was hopeful and not fearful. "Russia is neither going to eat us nor seduce us. . . . that is, unless our democratic institutions and our free economy become so frail through abuse and failure in practice as to make us soft and vulnerable. . . . All we need to do is to stand up and perform according to our professed ideals."[130]

There can be no doubt that Willkie's visit to Russia contributed immeasurably to the temporary improvement of Soviet-American relations. The "Special Correspondent" of the London *Times* summed up the general judgment when he wrote: "Apart from his special mission as the President's personal envoy, Mr. Willkie told Russia in forceful and authoritative language of America's war effort, and his physical vigor, his abounding energy, and, in spite of the strain of work, his continual good humor made him an ideal envoy from the West. He never failed to pay high tribute to Britain's part in the war, and particularly to Mr. Churchill. . . . Nothing but good can come out of this visit for all the Allies of Russia as well as for Russia herself."[131]

5

On September 27 the *Gulliver* took off from Moscow and headed east. That night Willkie and his companions were in Tashkent, on the ancient caravan routes between Persia and China, where the party were "the first Americans who had been seen in that Central Asian city in many years."[132] The next night they spent in Tihwa, the capital of China's vast western province of Sinkiang. Here they were met by Hollington Tong, Chiang Kai-Shek's Vice Minister of Information, who accompanied Willkie throughout his travels in China. Here also was given the first of many ceremonial banquets, which led Willkie to remark in Chungking, with reference to reported Japanese plans to attack his plane: "There is more danger of my being killed by the kindness of the Chinese than by enemy bullets."[133] Here also, the next morning, he heard privately from the governor of the province, General Sheng, wild tales of Russian intrigue which led him to ponder the future of Russian-Chinese relations.[134]

On September 29 they were in Lanchow, the capital of Kansu province, on the Yellow River. The next day they flew south to Chengtu, where Willkie addressed an audience of university students and saw an impressive training maneuver at the Chengtu Military Academy, where officers were being trained for "the new Chinese Army."[135] (Here a day's delay was caused by the presence of Japanese planes near the route of flight. Willkie remarked, "I feel very much complimented.")[136] He arrived in Chungking on Friday, October 2.

Willkie was prepared to be even more enthusiastic about China than about Russia. "Ever since I was a boy," he had said in speaking for United China Relief, "I have had a sentimental feeling about China."[137] His approach by air, across the vast spaces of Central Asia, over desert expanses and between towering mountain ranges, had had a quality of high adventure. The sight of mule trains plodding patiently back and forth on the months-long trip from the Sinkiang-Kansu border, where Russian trucks unloaded the military supplies that the Soviet Union somehow managed to spare, to the nearest Chinese railhead, dramatized China's wartime isolation. (This road, he wrote, was "a shoestring being used to support an enormous weight.")[138] The great crowds that lined the streets for miles to greet him in Lanchow, Chungking, and Sian stirred and humbled him—although, as he said, "any man who has run for President of the United States is used to crowds," and although he knew well enough that they had been officially assembled and had only the vaguest notion of who he was. To his ears there was friendly warmth in the shouts of "Wei Erh Chi! Wei Erh Chi!" ("as close as the Chinese language can come to Willkie"—meaning "Strengthen your inner self.")[139] And "there was nothing synthetic or fake about the faces I looked at. They were seeing, in me, a representative of America and a tangible hope of friendship and help."[140] "It is unfortunate," he wrote stingingly after his return, "that so many Americans still think of China in terms of great inert masses and not in terms of people, still think of the death of five million Chinese as something different from and less costly than the death of five million Westerners."[141]

As in other countries, Willkie's visit was a tremendous personal triumph. He may have baffled, a little, the university students at Chengtu by his prefatory wise-cracks about having a university president as his interpreter,[142] but his unmistakable enthusiasm and good will forbade any suspicion of disrespect. At other "refugee" universities and schools in the suburbs of Chungking, "he was loudly cheered by 1,000 Boy Scouts and Girl Guides when he kissed one tiny girl and exclaimed, 'You're a sweetheart,'" and by the university students to whom he said (in words less trite to them, one hopes, than to American students): "the hope of democracy, freedom and peace of the world is in your hands." Afterwards he talked with individual students, signed autograph books, and told the interpreter to tell the coeds, "I have traveled all over the world and seen many girls but think they are the best looking." Later a Chinese professor said: "Mr. Willkie made a great hit here. Truly great leaders never lose contact with the little people."[143]

And this was of course the secret of his success as a good-will ambassador: he assumed as a matter of course that people are people. He simply refused to recognize barriers of class, race, language, and nationality—and, suddenly, they were not there. The chorus of orphaned Chinese children who sang to him at a tea given him by Madame Chiang moved him no less deeply than if they had been English or American. "These orphaned children . . . challenge us to answer the question, 'Are we fighting this war to reestablish the world in which these children lost their parents, or are we fighting to eliminate imperialistic spheres of influence, mandates and the like, which only sow the seeds of future wars?'"[144]

Willkie's mission, however, here as elsewhere, was not merely to spread good will but to gather facts. Most of one day he spent inspecting factories —including a textile plant and a paper mill that had been moved from eastern China. In this, the Chinese had set an example for the Russians; but the latter had at least been able to use railroads, and there was no railroad to Chungking. Under such circumstances it would have been ungracious not to praise the operation of the factories, and Willkie did so; but in one plant that had obviously been prepared for his inspection, he remarked dryly that "he remembered that after regular inspections of his own establishments back home he always noted that the paint bill for the period was higher than usual."[145] He had no fault to find, however, with the morale of the workers—to whom, as in Russia, he continually stopped to talk.

This inspection tour involved a crossing of the Yangtse River, here flowing between steep, high banks; and Willkie showed his unabated energy by walking down 373 steps to the river and, after crossing it, climbing 365 steps, two at a time. He rejected with good-humored contempt the sedan chair that was waiting for him, remarking, "I am not that old."[146]

A large part of his six days in Chungking, however, was spent in discussion of China's position and problems in relation to the war as a whole. Some of the persons he talked to had been mentioned in a memorandum sent him by Russell Davenport before he left America, based on "a reliable source." Hollington Tong was described as "excellent"; H. H. Kung, Minister of Finance, as "charming, influential, reactionary, dishonest, intolerant; a profiteer and an appeaser; the best liar in China"; Ambassador Gauss as "prejudiced, uninformed, disliked, and can see only as far as the nearest length of red tape." "If you see one Soong sister, you should see them all—Madame Kung, like her husband, is extreme right; (a good friend, but terrible outside private life). Madame Sun [widow of Sun Yat-sen, founder of the Chinese Republic] is extreme left and infinitely more honest; Madame Chiang is halfway between." "Colonel Chennault would probably be wonderful to see."[147]

Of the Kungs, Willkie recorded only that in a conversation about "the revolution of ideas that is sweeping the East," they "knew their facts" and "held strong opinions."[148] His only comment on Madame Sun was that he had "a great time" at a dinner where he sat between her and Madame Chiang, and found "both ladies . . . full of information and wit."[149]

With some of the estimates—those of Tong, Gauss, and Chennault—Willkie found himself in complete agreement. Tong, of course, was a minor official, important only as he may have influenced Willkie's opinions of others. Gauss was in much the same position as Standley: he did not have the confidence of Chiang, was always by-passed in important negotiations, and was not invited to be present at the talks between Willkie and Chiang.

Willkie insisted on seeing Chennault, and was accompanied to his headquarters by General Joseph W. Stilwell, American commander in the China-Burma-India theater. There, characteristically, Willkie talked to the pilots and ground crews, discussing the war in Russia and the National League pennant race; and when one humorist queried, "Is there any chance of getting some women's auxiliaries over here?" he retorted in kind, "I thought you boys came over here to fight!"[150]

The talk with Chennault was long and frank. Stilwell gave his subordinate permission to tell Willkie anything he chose, and sat in the outer office for two hours while Chennault sold Willkie completely on a policy exactly the opposite of Stilwell's.[151] The airman was already a legendary figure, both in America and China, where, Willkie found, he had "no rival in popularity."[152] Before the Japanese attack on Pearl Harbor, he had organized an American Volunteer Group of pilots to fight against the Japanese, and had shown himself a genius at tactical air warfare. Now he believed that even with a limited air force—"105 fighter aircraft of modern design, 30 medium bombers and in the last phase, some months from now, 12 heavy bombers"—"constantly maintained at all times"—he could "accomplish the downfall of Japan."[153] Stilwell, on the other hand, felt that these hopes were chimerical; doubted that even such a limited force could be maintained by the only available supply route, the fearfully difficult and costly flight "over the Hump"; and feared that an air base near enough the coast to be effective for bombing could not be defended. His plan called first for the reconquest of Burma, the opening of the Burma Road, and the creation of an effective Chinese army.

The fact was that at the time the issue was almost academic, except in regard to future planning. In the overall strategy, victory in Europe had been put first; Japan had been challenged in the South Pacific and the challenge had to be made good. The China-Burma-India theater was the end of the line. Robert E. Sherwood records that when Willkie, after urging a second front in Europe, called for all-out aid to China, Roosevelt remarked, "You can't have it both ways." And Sherwood adds that "at this stage of the war it couldn't be had either way."[154]

But these difficulties only made Chennault's dream, which promised so much for so little, seem even more alluring,[155] and Willkie asked Chennault to put his plan into a letter to Roosevelt, which he promised personally to deliver. This was done.[156] Stilwell did not try to present his case. He was no salesman. And Willkie, probably influenced by the hostility of the Chiangs and the antagonism of Chennault, made no effort to draw him out. Two brief, bitter entries in Stilwell's diary tell the story. "October 5. . . . Saw Willkie at 2:30. Nothin'. He didn't ask a question. Completely sold on Chiang Kai-Shek and Madam. Advised me to put it on with a trowel. To hell with that stuff. . . . Willkie is being thoroughly immersed in soft soap, adulation and flattery." "October 7. Willkie off, thank God. On Pai Shi Yi trip he hardly spoke to me. Utterly indifferent."[157] For once, Willkie completely failed to recognize ability and integrity of the highest order.

So Chennault—who also had ability and integrity—won. But it was to a great extent an empty victory, for he was never given as much as he was promised, his accomplishments with what he did get were disappointing, and in the end the decisive attack upon Japan was made from the Pacific islands. In retrospect the whole affair seems almost a symbol of the futility to which any American policy toward China would have been doomed.[158]

But Willkie was optimistic, in the long conversations with the Chiangs, as well as sympathetic. Their story was, indeed, one that would have moved a far less responsive hearer: generations of exploitation by the West, which even at this date maintained "extraterritorial rights"; five years of war, bringing incalculable material and human losses, against a ruthless invader whom the United States and Britain had sought to appease—the former by selling gasoline and scrap iron, the latter by closing the Burma Road; the Allied decision to win in Europe first and the consequent pathetic trickle of supplies; the tendency in many quarters—including Churchill's government—to regard China as a second-rate power.

And those who told the story were no common narrators. The inglorious close of Chiang's career—due mainly, beyond reasonable doubt, to his own inadequacy in coping with admittedly colossal difficulties—need not obscure his real achievements nor his impressive, if puzzling, personality. Shrewd, stubborn, loyal to personal friends, and dedicated (unlike some of those friends) to China's welfare as he saw it, he made the most of the opportunity that Willkie's visit provided. As for Madame Chiang, extraordinarily gifted and totally unscrupulous, she was the one person who, in Willkie's mature life, completely anesthetized his critical judgment. After his return to America, a columnist wrote: "His praise of her and her work in a war-torn world transcends any paeans heard around these parts in a long time."[159] It was at Willkie's suggestion that Madame Chiang, a few weeks later, went to the United States to tell China's story to the people of America—and to try her charm on the President.[160] The results justified the suggestion—although nothing could change the basic facts of the war.

How Madame Chiang handled Roosevelt is revealed by Frances Perkins, who tells a story that the President himself enjoyed repeating. When he asked Madame Chiang what she thought of Willkie, she replied, "Well, Mr. President, he is really an adolescent, after all." And when he asked the same question concerning himself, her answer was, "Oh, Mr. President, you are sophisticated." Miss Perkins comments dryly, "As Roosevelt told this story . . . his obvious pleasure belied its point."[161] One hopes, in the interest of truth, that the story eventually got back to Willkie.

Nevertheless, the praise which Willkie in *One World* offers China and its leaders is, like his praise of Russia, not unqualified. In discussing Chinese inflation ("Much of the cargo flown over the Himalayas, I learned from pilots on the run, is paper money"), he lays part of the blame on "the failure of the government itself to adopt a sound fiscal policy," including price control and an adequate tax system, or to prevent "speculation in basic commodities. Some of the independent editors in China insisted to me that speculation was indulged in even by government officials themselves."[162]

Willkie also suggested that Chiang's personal loyalty "both to the extraordinary family into which he married and to the associates of his early years of struggle is . . . sometimes unreasonable"; and he noted "a sort of 'old school tie' . . . which automatically keeps some men in high position."[163] He reported further that the present government was in effect a dictatorship (though he did not use the term); and although in theory the masses were being educated for democratic citizenship, he noted "the feeling of impatience . . . especially in foreign circles not unsympathetic with China, at the centralized control of Chinese life which is exercised in Chungking."[164]

Reading between the lines, one can discover evidence of the autocracy, the incompetence, the corruption in high places, that eventually destroyed all popular support of Chiang's regime and made inevitable the triumph of the Communists.[165]

But to Willkie in October, 1942—as to other observers at the time—it seemed that China was on the way up and not on the way down. He had great hopes, in particular, of the "aggressive spirit" that he had found in "the great wealthy provinces to the West."[166] He looked forward, after victory, to "close economic and industrial cooperation between America and China for the benefit of each nation."[167] He saw—again like other observers—a difficult but not insoluble problem in the antagonism between Chiang's Kuomintang party and the Communists. He talked at length with Chou En-lai (present in Chungking because of a nominal truce) who impressed him as an "excellent, sober, sincere man . . . of obvious ability," and who "admitted impatience with what he regarded as the slowness of domestic reform in China" and "frankly was not willing to make predictions" about what would happen after the war. Still, Willkie decided, "if all Chinese Communists" were like him, "their movement [was] more a national and agrarian awakening than an international or proletarian conspiracy."[168] This judgment now seems naive; but at least he had the wisdom, almost unique among prophets concerning Communism, to make his judgment tentative.

6

On leaving Chungking, as on leaving Moscow, Willkie issued a formal statement, addressed to his countrymen but intended for the rest of the world as well. This one was no less blunt than the previous one, although it dealt mainly with a different subject. (When Chinese newspapermen, on his arrival in Chungking, asked him about his second-front statement, he replied, "I have the bad habit of saying what I think." But when asked his opinion about a second front in Asia, his answer was, "No more second front talk, either here or there.")[169]

Some of the items in his statement would be repeated in his "Report to the People": the need to shift from a defensive to an offensive posture; the need to increase the pitifully small flow of military goods to most of our allies; the need to make clear America's determination "to find some way of helping the colonial peoples who join the United Nations' cause to become free and independent nations."

It was the last item that was most important, and in some passages he dealt with it even more incisively than in later statements. The war, he insisted, was "not merely a technical problem for task forces" but "also a war for men's minds." The Western democracies must try to enlist not merely the passive sympathy but the active support of "nearly three fourths of the people of the world who live in South America, Africa, Eastern Europe and Asia. We have not done this and at present we are not doing this. We have got to do it."

In doing so, we must be both realistic and imaginative. "Most of the people in Asia have never known democracy. They may or may not want our type of democracy. Obviously, not all of them are ready to have democracy handed to them next Tuesday on a silver platter. But they are determined to work out their own destiny under governments selected by themselves." ("No foot of Chinese soil, for example, should be or can be ruled from now on except by the people who live in it.") Hence, "we must set up firm timetables under which they can work out and train governments of their own choosing and we must establish ironclad guarantees administered by all the United Nations jointly that they shall not slip back into colonial status."

And the time was *now*. "Some say these subjects should be hushed until victory is won. Exactly the reverse is true. Sincere efforts to find progressive solutions now will bring strength to our cause. Remember that opponents of social change always urge delay because of some present crisis. After the war, changes may be too little and too late."[170]

What was really explosive was Willkie's pronouncement that (as he put it in a broadcast to the Chinese themselves) "mankind is on the march. The old colonial times are past."[171] This was not so much a challenge to Allied leadership as a challenge to a way of thinking, a state of mind, a view of the world, that had dominated Western Europe for more than four centuries and that even in the United States was more or less taken for granted. This challenge was of course not new; but no man of Willkie's prominence had ever stated it in such absolute terms, nor to so wide an audience, nor in such a time of stress.

And of course no unique insight was necessary to grasp the fact that he was asserting. Other people might be *talking* about a world-wide revolution; Willkie was seeing it. "He has discovered the East," wrote Anne O'Hare McCormick, "and the overtone of surprise, indignation and urgency to do something about it . . . is the reaction of the sensitive and open-minded American who sees for the first time a strange, awakening world."[172] Even in the brief span of years between that day and this, the confirmation of his prophecy has been written by events across the world—in Viet Nam, Indonesia, Burma, India, the Middle East and Africa; and where this prophecy was unheeded by the ruling powers the confirmation has been written in blood.

But Willkie's vision—reaffirmed in his "Report to the People"—was beyond the grasp, even in imagination, of many of his countrymen. Ex-isolationists and Anglophobes like Nye and Rankin now rose in Congress to defend the British Empire and to charge Willkie, in scurrilous terms, with undermining Allied unity.[173] The columnist Mark Sullivan attacked both Willkie and Roosevelt for their concern with "a post-war vision" ("an opiate to our people") while neglecting the only important fact: "that we are not winning the war."[174]

Even some of his friends deplored his attack on colonialism with its implied criticism of Britain. Walter Lippmann took him to task publicly.[175] Joseph Alsop (to whom he had written on July 3, 1941 with a rare surrender to sentiment: "I am sorry they are sending you as far as Bombay, but I suppose it is all for the best. God bless you, old man, and any time I can be of help to you in any way, I am at your call")[176] sent him a long and critical letter, depreciating the importance of Burma and India to the Allied cause and arguing that the only alternative to British rule was Communist rule. In New York business and financial circles, many acquaintances who had applauded his plea for aid to Britain were now chilled by his insistence that colonialism must end.[177]

There was of course some editorial approval, as in the *New York Times;* and Henry Luce in *Life* improved the occasion by reading the British a lecture (as Willkie had carefully refrained from doing). As for popular sentiment, a reasonable guess would be that most Americans regarded colonialism as a side issue, best left alone for the duration of the war.[178]

Among those who generally approved was, probably, the President. Roosevelt was no admirer of colonialism,[179] although at the moment, friendship with Britain came before all else, and he had no intention of rousing Churchill's Tory temper. In this situation, as so often before, Willkie said what Roosevelt thought but found it inexpedient to say.

Accordingly it was to Willkie that Churchill—recognizing that "no foot of Chinese soil" meant Hongkong and that other phrases meant India—replied when, denying that the North African invasion had any but a military motive, he added: "Let me, however, make this clear lest there be any mistake about it in any quarter: we mean to hold our own. I did not become the King's First Minister to preside over the liquidation of the British Empire."[180]

On the whole, however, the British took Willkie's statement calmly. Probably the "man in the street" knew little and cared less about the colonies, even India. The Labor Party was officially anti-colonial. And most of the newspapers gave his speech editorial praise, with only minor reservations. The *Times* approved (and later reproved Churchill for his reply).[181] The *Daily Herald* commended him for calling attention to "the crippling lack of a master strategic plan." The *Daily Telegraph* called him a "Candid Friend." The Manchester *Guardian* of course agreed with him, and also noted that he "was careful not to blame the British directly."[182] There was also much support from members of the Commonwealth. When Willkie spoke at Toronto on November 25, although there had been early rumors of hostility, he received a rousing ovation from a crowd of nearly 18,000 that "jammed the Maple Leaf Garden."[183] Neither there nor in Britain were the people inclined to repudiate a friendship that had been freely offered when friends were few.

No other man, in fact, could have said so forcefully, and with so little offense, what needed to be said to the Western democracies.

There was one tangible and immediate result. On October 9 the State Department announced that the United States and Britain were beginning negotiations for the ending of extraterritorial rights in China.

7

Willkie left Chungking on October 7, the sixth day after his arrival, to visit the war front along the Yellow River. He flew to Chengtu, and then to Sian, the capital of Shensi province, where "a band was at the gate to greet him. For five miles Sian's main street was a solid mass of people,"[184] although the crowd had "waited hours in the rain" because his plane was late.[185] From Sian, after "a festive duck dinner," the party proceeded by train as far as was considered safe; and at dawn transferred to handcars, which in turn were abandoned several miles from the front, when Japanese artillery had begun shelling the line. The rest of the journey was made on foot. (The Japanese intelligence system was evidently working well. Twenty-three Japanese bombers attacked four cities along the rail line, and destroyed "a special blue coach" identical with the one in which Willkie traveled.)

At the front he looked across the river through a telescope into the muzzles of Japanese guns; was impressed by the Chinese defenses; reviewed, and then addressed, a division of troops, "calling them front-line 'blood-brothers' "; and was treated to beer and wine by the Generalissimo's son, a captain of artillery, who told him it had been captured in one of the frequent raids across the river.[186]

He returned to Sian and flew on to Chengtu the same day, arriving after dark.[187] At dawn on October 9 the *Gulliver* took off and headed northward on a 1600-mile flight over the Gobi Desert and the Mongolian Plateau to Chita, in southern Siberia; then onward another thousand miles to Yakutsk, only a few hundred miles from the Arctic Circle. Here the weather caused a brief delay and gave Willkie a chance to inspect the former Czarist penal colony, now a bustling, forward-looking outpost of Soviet civilization, run by a 37-year-old Communist official named Muratov, who "talked like a California real estate salesman" about the prospects of the "republic" that he ruled;[188] but who, Willkie felt, would make good his boasts. Then, after one more landing in Siberia at Seincham, the *Gulliver* reached Fairbanks, Alaska, on October 11. (The travelers had gained a day by crossing the international date line.)

On October 12 Willkie arrived in Edmonton, Alberta. Here he issued a press statement (which would appear on the day he reached the United States) that showed him still smarting from the slighting remarks attributed to Roosevelt by Chungking reports. He paid tribute to the other members of the party, briefly rehearsed the origin and aims of the trip, referred to "conclusions" "already reported . . . to the American people and . . . to the President," and promised to "report to my fellow citizens further and in full, and to the President, if he wishes, on such subjects as he desires to discuss with me." Then he added: "Incidentally, in regard to flippant statements made by certain public officials concerning the expression of my opinion in Russia on the question of a second front, I did not deem it appropriate or in good taste for me to reply to such personalities or flippancies while I was in other countries.

"I felt it my duty while abroad to uphold the hand of the President and all other United Nations officials, which I continued to do even after such remarks were made."[189]

The remark about "flippant statements" obviously referred to Roosevelt, as the latter immediately saw when he read it in the papers the next morning. Steve Early therefore called Sam Pryor (an air lines executive as well as a friend of Willkie, and hence in a position to get through a message) to say that the President was much "upset" by reports of Willkie's anger, and thought it very important that Willkie should see him before issuing any further statements. Pryor accordingly got in touch with Willkie by telephone as soon as he reached Minneapolis, and passed along the message. The recipient was reluctant. He was tired, he said, and wanted to go home and get some rest. But Pryor pointed out that he could not long avoid some sort of public statement; and in the end Willkie yielded, as he was bound to do, to what was practically a Presidential command.[190]

Accordingly, his comments to reporters in Minneapolis were limited to praise of the *Gulliver's* crew and comments on the geography of the *Gulliver's* flight. And when the subject of "flippant statements" was inevitably brought up, he tried to turn the barb away from Roosevelt: "I was gratified to find that the elements which criticized my trip were the same old die-hard Tory groups that still think America can live to itself."[191]

Willkie was angered again, however, when in a Columbus Day broadcast Roosevelt indulged in some sarcastic comments about "typewriter strategists." It seems clear from the context that the President was thinking mainly of professional journalists. But Willkie, still sensitive, took it as a personal attack.

At the airport, however, where he arrived at 4:30 p.m., he was his usual jovial self—although "ten pounds lighter than when he left . . . and shaggy-haired from lack of a haircut."[192] He hastened to greet the waiting reporters, many of them old friends from the 1940 campaign, asked them if they had been behaving themselves, and applauded their negative reply. "He then went before newsreel cameras and microphones to declare, 'I'm damned glad to be home.' "[193]

He reached the White House at 5:20, and talked with the President for ninety minutes. Vivid stories have been told (presumably based on his own account to friends) of what he said to Roosevelt. According to one, his first words were: "I know that you are the President and that you can throw me out, but until you do I am going to say a few things to you and you are going to listen."[194] Perhaps he did say exactly that. But probably the most accurate record of his side of the conversation is contained in a detailed memorandum "Draft notes for conversation with President Roosevelt. October 14, 1942."[195]

It began: "The main job you asked me to do was to talk to the leaders of the Middle East. This I did"—and he named them. He next stated the problems that had been discussed—the need for food, machines ("to keep their national economies going"), and trained personnel.

In the next section Willkie came to what he really wanted to say. "It is my duty to report to you that all the countries of the Middle East are looking to us even more for leadership in ideas than they are for material help. Qualified observers in nearly all these countries told me—and I found no reason to doubt their evidence—that Nazi ideas have found fertile soil among large numbers of people. This is not a pleasant report to make—but the traditions of British rule in the Middle East have created a vacuum as far as the Arab peoples are concerned, a vacuum which we have not filled and which the Germans and Italians are in part filling through our default. It is my personal belief that we must work hard to preserve our military cooperation with the British in this whole area—and this applies especially to Syria and the problems raised by General De Gaulle, but that we must work no less hard to give these people a feeling that they do not have: that we are not committed to an indefinite perpetuation of British imperialism in this area, but rather to the establishment of political freedom and economic liberty."

Willkie's "notes" continue: "You did not ask me to make a special report of Russia or China. But I reached certain conclusions, and received certain information, which I should pass on to you if you are interested: Mr. Stalin spoke to me in great frankness of his disappointment at the inadequacy of British and American supplies. You undoubtedly have the figures on deliveries. He gave me no impression that our failure to supply the Red Army with what it needs is likely to lead him to a separate peace as long as his armies can hold out. But he gave me the very clear feeling that it will most seriously affect our chances of working out any cooperation in the peace." (This was clearly the decisive factor in determining the phrasing of Willkie's second-front statement.)

Willkie listed Stalin's specific requests, and went on: "At the request of the State Department, I also talked to Mr. Stalin about our hope that the Russians and the Poles might be able to adjust their differences. As instructed, I did not press him for any commitment in this regard."

His comments on China were as follows. "The problem of inflation in China, which I personally regard as of equal gravity with the Japanese invasion of that country, is one which only the Chinese themselves can solve, in my opinion. There are two other problems in that country, however, which directly involve the United States:

(a) An American air force, under General Chennault, has accomplished some minor miracles with wholly inadequate forces. I am informed on good authority that he has at present nine bombers at his disposal. I found difference of opinion among competent experts on the feasibility of a really big-scale air offensive against Japan based on China. But I found no difference of opinion in the statement that a modest force—say 70/80 bombers, 150 pursuit planes, and 60 transports—could work more effectively from bases in China then from anywhere else in the Far Eastern theater of war. I also found unanimity in thinking that General Chennault should be given a command independent of control from British India.

(b) An independent American foreign policy, in the eyes of the Chinese, would be another major help to us, especially in the essential process of maintaining an offensive spirit in a country already five years at war. The British position in India, diversion of American planes to British fronts, the complete absence of British aid to China, and the deep-rooted suspicion that America has given at least acquiescence to British plans for restoration of its earlier imperial position in Asia—these are all factors tending to deplete the reservoir of good will we started with in China."

The next item is labeled "(Questionable)": "The entire trip convinced me—and I intend so to report to the American people—that this war requires from us a different personnel abroad. I was very favorably impressed with the personal qualities and imagination of American army officers. I found wholly deplorable the position in their respective countries of Ambassador Gauss in China, Ambassador Standley in Russia, Minister Dreyfus in Iran."

The final paragraph is marked "(Possible but questionable)": "As you know, one of my personal reasons for wanting to make this trip was to continue my effort to show the world that this country is united on the war. I think myself I had some success. Now that I am back, naturally, I shall feel free to carry on the most effective criticism I can on domestic issues and also on the way in which we are prosecuting the war. Anything I may say or write outside this room will be naturally my own opinion and will be clearly stated to be such. You and other members of the administration will be equally free to attack those personal opinions. But I think I should tell you quite frankly and bluntly, that during the entire period of my trip, I uttered no single sentence of criticism of you or of your policies, in order to show to foreign peoples this national unity on the war of which I speak. On the other hand, your press reference to me was cabled to China the night before I left that country and a few hours before I was to make a statement in which I believed, and still believe, that I was speaking for very large numbers of Americans and in complete consistency with my special mission for you. Unless you have reports to the contrary about what I said or did on the trip, I think you should cooperate in an effort to make the trip a symbol of national unity on the war."

The President's response was evidently conciliatory, for Willkie told newsmen immediately afterwards, at a press conference in the White House Lobby (where he sat nonchalantly on the edge of a table), that Roosevelt had "volunteered the statement that any reports that he (the President) had 'criticized me or my activities abroad were entirely erroneous.'" He reasserted his independence by repeating his demand for a second front, although this time he refused to specify a location. He remarked that he had talked with many military leaders during his trip, and that what was involved in such a decision was not an opposition between military and civilian opinion, but a choice by civilian authority between conflicting recommendations of military leaders. He ended with a promise to make "careful, crystal-clear reports to the American people."[196]

8

That night Willkie went to New York, and the next day to Rushville, where Mrs. Willkie and Philip (on a brief leave) were waiting for him. There, with his own Indiana soil under his feet, he relaxed, tried to order and assimilate the fantastically varied experiences of the past seven weeks, and worked on his "Report to the People."

This was made on Monday, October 26, at 10:30 p.m. Eastern War Time, over all four major networks. It had an estimated 36,200,000 hearers, one of the greatest radio audiences ever assembled in the United States (the record was the 62,000,000 who listened to President Roosevelt on December 9, 1941, after the attack on Pearl Harbor), and they heard what was perhaps Willkie's greatest speech. He was always most effective on the radio when he spoke calmly, and in this instance he was determined above all to seek his effects by means of facts and logic rather than emotion and rhetoric. Yet no one could miss the intense conviction that underlay his measured words. To many who listened, these words had the quality of revelation. When he had finished, the world looked different—and it would never look the same again.[197]

He began by explaining again the background of his trip, and his relation to the President. "It was clearly understood between him and me that apart from the specific matters handled for him, I should go as a free agent. I was at liberty to express my opinion while abroad and equally so when I returned."

The first great fact on which he dwelt was the smallness of the world. In seven weeks he had traveled 31,000 miles; the actual flying time had been 160 hours. "There are no distant points in the world any longer. The myriad millions of the Far East are as close to us as Los Angeles is to New York by the fastest train. . . . Our thinking and planning in the future must be global."

Moreover, the peoples of the world had been brought nearer not merely in time but in ideas. "All around the world, there are some ideas that millions and millions of men hold in common." Some of these ideas were about the United States, and constituted a "gigantic reservoir of good will." This was due to American hospitals and schools; to American enterprise in the commerce of ideas as well as goods; to American motion pictures; to the "aspirations and accomplishments" of American labor on the one hand and American business and industry on the other. And this admiration for America was untainted by the fear of imperialism. The "dread of imperialism," indeed, he "found everywhere." But it was as yet directed only toward Western Europe.

The United States itself, however, was creating liabilities. The great "reservoir of good will" was "leaking dangerously . . . through a thousand holes"—"punched by us."

One of these was the failure to make good the promises of military aid to our allies. He had followed "the flow of war materials," he said, while it divided and subdivided into infinitesimal trickles—"and I stopped talking about American production." He gave credit where it was due—to the quality of American planes and tanks when finally delivered, to the achievements of American personnel. But he warned: "We cannot win this war

40 per cent mobilized. . . . Five million Russians and five million Chinese have given their lives in this struggle. . . . We owe them more than boasts and broken promises." (This was the really valid part of his criticism of the American arms program—not that the distribution was inefficient or unwisely directed, but that the American production effort was still half-hearted, American sacrifices almost non-existent compared to those of other nations.)

Another drain upon the good will of the Eastern Allies—"the 200,000,000 people of Russia and the 450,000,000 people of China—people like you and me"—was failure "to define clearly our war aims." "They know what they are fighting for. They are not so sure of us. Many of them have read the Atlantic Charter. Rightly or wrongly, they are not satisfied. They ask . . . Is freedom supposed to be priceless for the white man, for the Western World, but of no account to us in the East?"

The symbol of this doubt, throughout the East, was India. "People of the East who would like to count on us . . . cannot ascertain from our government's wishy-washy attitude towards India what we are likely to feel at the end of the war about all the other hundreds of millions of Eastern peoples." They knew, however, what freedom meant to *them*—"the orderly but scheduled abolition of the colonial system." And Willkie agreed: "the rule of people by other peoples is not freedom, and not what we must fight to preserve."

He distinguished painstakingly between the British Commonwealth and "the remnants of empire" represented by the colonies. "We must remember that throughout the commonwealth there are men and women numbered by millions who are working selflessly and with great skill toward reducing these remnants . . . As Americans we must also recognize that we share with these men and women of the British Commonwealth of Free Nations the responsibility of making the whole world a commonwealth of free nations."

A related failure, though less crucial, was "the half-ignorant, half-patronizing way in which we have grown accustomed to treating many of the people in Eastern Europe and Asia." "We must wipe out the distinction in our minds between 'first-class' and 'second-class' allies. We must send to represent us among all our allies really distinguished men who are important enough in their own right to dare to tell our President the truth."

The final failure was "the atrophy of intelligence which is produced by stupid, arbitrary or undemocratic censorship. It has been suggested much of late, for example, that private citizens . . . should refrain from making suggestions about the conduct of the war. . . . This position threatens, I believe, to become a tight wall which will keep the truth out and lock misrepresentation and false security within." Even in regard to military operations, it was right and wise that there should be unrestricted civilian criticism. "The record of this war to date," he observed with masterly understatement, "is not such as to inspire in us any sublime faith in the infallibility of our military and naval experts." And he concluded: "Let's have no more of this nonsense. Military experts, as well as our leaders, must be constantly exposed to democracy's greatest driving power—the whiplash of public opinion, developed from honest, free discussion." And having thus defended his right to speak, he reiterated: "We and our allies must establish a second fighting front in Europe."

Willkie's question at the end was, "What does it all add up to?" His answer was: "A military victory, as such, will not be enough. . . . We must win the peace." To do so, three things were necessary: "first, we must plan now for peace on a global basis; second, the world must be free, economically and politically, for nations and for men that peace may exist in it; third, America must play an active, constructive part in freeing it and keeping its peace."

It was the second of these that expressed the great lesson of his round-the-world flight. "Men and women all over the world are on the march, physically, intellectually and spiritually. After centuries of ignorance and dull compliance, hundreds of millions of people in Eastern Europe and Asia have opened the books. Old fears no longer frighten them. They are no longer willing to be Eastern slaves for Western profits. The big house on the hill surrounded by mud huts has lost its awesome charm.

"Our Western World and our presumed supremacy are now on trial. Our boasting and our big talk leave Asia cold. Men and women in Russia and China and in the Middle East are conscious now of their own potential strength. They are coming to know that many of the decisions about the future of the world lie in their hands. And they intend that these decisions shall leave the peoples of each nation free from foreign domination, free for economic, social, and spiritual growth."

From this great and irresistible awakening of hitherto submerged peoples, America had nothing to fear. They wished America, in fact, "to be one of their partners in this grand adventure. They want us to join them in creating a new society, global in scope, free alike of the economic injustices of the West and the political malpractices of the East. But as a partner in that great new combination they want us neither hesitant, incompetent nor afraid. They want a partner who will not hesitate to speak out against injustice anywhere in the world."

Such was Willkie's "Report to the People." If to our ears his hopeful words sound hollow, the hollowness is in us and not in them. To most of those who heard them—barring always the irreconcilable reactionaries who would rather embalm the past than embrace the future—they had the ring of prophecy. They also sounded different, spoken in Willkie's own voice in his own country, than they had sounded in dispatches from Moscow and Chungking. His friend and fellow tourist, Joseph Barnes, declares that "the broadcast brought him a heavier response, by mail and telegram, than any speech Willkie ever made in his life [and all his major speeches brought a tremendous response] and 98 per cent of the messages were favorable."[198] Most people seemed to like to be told the truth.

President Roosevelt in his next press conference maintained his approving attitude (in another, three days later, he seemed to be satirizing Willkie's pronunciation of "reservoir"), saying cheerfully that there was "not a controversy in a carload," and only becoming irritated when a reporter pressed the question of whether he "agreed" with what Willkie had said. He repeated his previous answer and said he "would sing it if necessary."[199] This was probably, on the whole, an honest answer. If some of Willkie's criticisms had touched him personally, he was still not disposed to quarrel with the main points in Willkie's plea: a greater effort at home, an aggressive spirit in military planning and action, the abolition of colonies, and international cooperation.[200]

To Americans twenty-odd years later, this bold and imaginative venture, conceived and carried out by Willkie and approved and supported by Roosevelt, must seem remote and unreal; the good will gained in the Middle East, the Far East and Russia seems to have been totally dissipated, long since, by cold-war insanity (not all on one side) and the nationalistic convulsions of peoples to whom Western domination had given the desire but not the capacity for self-government. Even in our own country, "One World" is rarely used, except as a term of contempt by advocates of the "narrow nationalism" which Willkie abhorred.

One may choose to believe, nevertheless, that the millions of Americans who so eagerly followed the news stories of his trip, listened to his broadcast report, and read *One World* could never again accept so complacently the myth of America's unique superiority and self-sufficiency or the doctrine that a people's duty is only to itself.

XVIII

The Home Front Once More

1

Until he had reported on his world tour, Willkie declined to comment on domestic politics. The speech itself, nevertheless, had political implications—which were for the most part unfavorable to the Administration. For once, Willkie emulated Roosevelt in gaining maximum political effect from a "non-political" speech—all the more so because this effect was unsought. Some Roosevelt supporters privately called it "the best political speech of the campaign," adding cynically but correctly that Willkie "probably was strengthening the very groups within the Republican party which oppose him and the 'international' foreign policy which he espouses."[1]

When Willkie did state his political position, in a formal press release on November 1, he made explicit the criticisms of the Administration that had been implied in the "Report to the People": that in its conduct of the war, it had been "confused," "inefficient," and lacking in "courageous leadership," and had tried to hide these faults "behind a gradually tightening wall of censorship."

But to be critical of the Administration was not enough: "As to the Congressional elections, I think the first test of a candidate . . . should be whether he is whole-heartedly and completely for placing the full resources of the nation behind the national effort to win the war; also, whether he understands that there can be no negotiated peace, and that in view of modern developments, economic, political, and otherwise, the United States must bear its full responsibility in world affairs both now and after the war is over." As an example of a "liberal and enlightened" Republican Congressman, he pointed to Joseph Clark Baldwin, for whom he said he would vote. "And I of course expect to vote the Republican State ticket, anticipating, from the State platform and their statements, that Mr. Dewey and his fellow candidates will give New York a liberal government."[2]

How far Willkie's specific views were shared by the voters can only be guessed at; but at any rate the election revealed a powerful Republican trend. It is true that Dewey's triumph over a weak and divided opposition was expected; but his plurality of 600,000 was impressive. And in Congress the Republicans gained ten seats in the Senate and forty-three in the House. Even Hamilton Fish was able to ride the wave of Republicanism back into office.

On the strength of this victory, the Old Guard decided to challenge

Willkie's influence by presenting its own candidate for the National Chairmanship. Martin was determined to resign at the meeting of the National Committee in St. Louis on December 7, and the anti-Willkie forces picked as their candidate Werner W. Schroeder of Illinois. The fact that he had been a notorious isolationist, whose views usually coincided with those of Colonel McCormick, would make his election a resounding slap in the face to Willkie.

The latter struck back by saying "that if Schroeder should be chosen, he (Willkie) would repudiate the Committee and all its works."[3] For a time it seemed that this threat would be sufficient, since nobody doubted that he would keep his word. But at the last minute, Willkie's enemies, led by Taft (present as proxy for David S. Ingalls, who was in the Armed Services), decided to back Schroeder. It was so clear "that the purpose of the Taft-Schroeder group was to rebuke Willkie that somebody suggested that the committee change its name to the S. P. O. W. W., the Society for the Punishment of Wendell Willkie."[4] At any rate, Schroeder announced just before midnight on December 6: "I have enough votes to win."[5] At this point, Martin, who had been working all day to prevent an open contest, remarked resignedly, "As long as there is going to be a fight, we might as well have a good one."[6]

The Willkie strategy, since he and his friends did not control a majority of the votes, was to go all out to defeat Schroeder, and then take the best compromise they could get. (Dewey, disclaiming any desire for the 1944 nomination, sat on the sidelines and alienated nobody.)[7]

For a short time it looked as if the compromise candidate might be a very good one—Fred Baker of the state of Washington, whom Willkie considered "just the man."[8] He was relatively young, and not well enough known to have made many enemies; he was vouched for by Willkie's loyal friend Ralph Cake, National Committeeman from Oregon, who placed him in nomination.

The vote on the first ballot was 40 for Baker, 40 for Schroeder, 15 for Harrison Spangler of Iowa, three for Frank Gannett of New York, and one for Barak Mattingly of Missouri. Those who voted for Spangler were also anti-Willkie, but judged that to override him at this time and on this issue would be ruinous to the party. They therefore sat tight during the second ballot to see what would happen.

What happened was a somewhat surprising defection from the Schroeder forces. This time Baker got 43 votes, Schroeder 38. (Spangler still had 15, Gannett had four, Mattingly had one. Apparently there were two votes more than on the first ballot.) Now the Schroeder faction, foreseeing a possible victory for the man who was obviously if not avowedly Willkie's candidate, was as eager for a compromise as it had previously been stubborn in rejecting one. Accordingly, a motion to recess was made by a

Schroeder supporter.[9] (When Martin, unable to decide from a voice vote, called for a rising vote, "Taft was the first man on his feet.")[10]

The Baker forces opposed the motion but lost, 58-38.[11] The recess permitted the Schroeder and Spangler groups to get together; and now it was Baker's supporters who obviously had to yield. When the meeting was called to order an hour and three-quarters later (the only surprising fact is that the arrangement took so long), Baker and Schroeder joined in moving the unanimous election of Spangler.[12]

The most surprising event of the meeting was yet to come. Although Martin had said the day before that "he did not think the committee would adopt any resolutions,"[13] the group took "this occasion to reaffirm the resolution passed by it at its meeting on April 20 last . . ."[14] This was the resolution on international cooperation which Willkie had at that time forced the Committee to accept, and which Taft had strongly opposed. The new resolution was offered by none other than Taft. He gave no explanation of his change of position.

The passage of the resolution, together with the defeat of Schroeder, was an apparent triumph for Willkie, whose comment in reply to a question was, "A person should not boast after a victory."[15] In a more serious mood, he explained: "My fight was to prevent the masthead of the Chicago *Tribune* from being imprinted on the Republican party. I am happy that the result prevented that calamity. Mr. Spangler has a great opportunity for progressive public service."[16]

To a certain extent, the outcome *was* a Willkie victory. It was indeed extraordinary that a defeated Presidential candidate, so unorthodox in opinions and tactics, without any organized support, should have acquired such a powerful following in the Republican National Committee. It probably marked the high point of his political strength.

But if the Old Guard had lost face, it had gained power; for whereas Martin had honestly tried to be impartial, Spangler only pretended to be. He was, after all, an elderly party hack, a 1940 supporter of Taft, who in his first press conference emphasized his intention to devote his energy to "party organization rather than policy making" (as if the two had no connection) and admitted that he was "not a student of foreign affairs." He was, to be sure, careful to reject the label of "isolationism," and he even professed a mild internationalism.[17] But it was clear enough that he was a follower and not a leader.

Another feature of the meeting was also ominous—the first public appearance within the party of organized hate-Willkie propaganda. "Members of the committee, on their arrival at the hotel, received airmail letters from the Associated Ex-Willkie Workers Against Willkie, with headquarters at 225 Thirty-fourth Street, New York." The letter read in part: "He delivers voluminous speeches on the remaking of the world before the war is won. He worries about India. He tries to influence military strategy. He abets the Red 'party-line' feud against General Eisenhower over Admiral Darlan. He assists the Communist-inspired attack on states' rights. . . . It would be hard to find anywhere in history an example of such a complete reversal as that committed by Mr. Willkie. . . . he is merely a selfish opportunist without defined purposes who is attempting to force himself upon the Republican party as its next Presidential nominee."[18]

These were the regular lies—that Willkie was anti-British, that he was pro-Communist, that he was a "selfish opportunist" who had deserted all the principles he had professed in 1940—which from now on were to be repeated day in and day out: in Congress; in a part of the press; in circular letters, postcards, and pamphlets; and in the public speeches and private gossip of many influential Republicans.

And at least some of the people who repeated them not only believed them, but believed them with passion; although clearly, as Roscoe Drummond later said: "The Republican Old Guard had no excuse for being misled about Wendell Willkie. . . . they either had not paid attention to what he said, or did not believe he meant it."[19] In their eagerness to find a candidate whose personal appeal could match Roosevelt's, they had created a visionary figure in their own image, and when they found the real man irreconcilable with their imaginings, they were at first bewildered, then felt betrayed, and finally settled into unrelenting hatred.

One line of attack was that he should have foregone his world tour, and instead have stayed at home to offer leadership to his party in legislative activity and in the elections. Expressive of the reckless malice of the Old Guard was an editorial on this topic by John S. Knight, editor and publisher of the Akron *Beacon Journal,* who was normally middle-of-the-road in his opinions, but who could on occasion, it seemed, make a noise like Colonel McCormick. Published during Willkie's absence, it imputed to him "such a voracious appetite for the headlines that no . . . fat job in Wall Street could possibly satisfy it. . . . Thus the greatest kibitzer in history continues his Cook's tour with a flourish and a political warm-up that irks the military leaders of the United Nations, bewilders his former supporters and leaves the Republican party hopefully trying to capitalize on administration mistakes and recapture a few seats in Congress without the aid of its titular leader. . . . these are days that call for unselfish men and women who believe that winning the war is more important than staying in the headlines. . . . unless Willkie comes on home and gets down to work with the rest of his countrymen, many in America will agree with the estimate given him by Congressman John Vorys, Republican of Columbus, who described our No. 1 world traveler recently as 'that man who is snooping and whooping in Russia and China.' "[20]

One of many Republicans who agreed was Representative Shafer of

Michigan, who in a speech in the House on May 27, 1943, climaxed a series of rhetorical questions with "Did he assist any of the hundreds of Republican candidates for Congress who were waging a life-and-death struggle for the preservation of true Americanism? No. . . . Where was our leader? Was he perhaps in China on a junket arranged by the New Deal? . . . In the 1940 elections, what was he, Republican or New Dealer?"[21]

The last question was of course the give-away. What the Old Guard really had against him was his support of Roosevelt, and they hated him all the more because events had proved him right. How could they have asked his aid in an election when they had rejected his leadership on every important issue? His absence was therefore doubly gratifying; it freed them from embarrassment and also gave them an excuse to brand him as disloyal to the party.

Other persons spread falsehoods about Willkie's off-the-record speeches, where there was no published text to contradict them. A week after the St. Louis meeting Gardner Cowles wrote to Lem Jones concerning a report "being bandied about among Republican Congressmen" that Willkie had said in a talk to the Newspaper Guild that if he disapproved of the Republican nominee in 1944, he would run on a third party ticket. Jones replied that he had been at the meeting and had checked with others who were present; that "the subject of a third party was not even mentioned in the Boss' talk" and that there was "no discussion of it before or after the meeting."[22]

A final comment on the St. Louis meeting is that it marked the beginning of the rift between Willkie and Stassen. Willkie wrote to Geoffrey Parsons on May 9, 1944:

"I am sorry. My friends Mike and John [Cowles] are wrong.

"Governor Stassen, a few days before the meeting in St. Louis, made a public declaration approving Werner Schroeder as the Chairman of the Republican National Committee. Walter Rosenberry, his campaign manager, was present in St. Louis actively working against Baker—your candidate and mine—in our fight against Schroeder.

"The story that Stassen couldn't control Mrs. Carlson is a phoney. Mrs. Carlson came to my office a short time after the meeting. She said she was sorry that she had to oppose my viewpoint, but had done so at the request of Governor Stassen.

"As you know it was impossible to get the votes to elect Baker because Russ Sprague and Ruth Pratt refused to go along, and cast their votes for Frank Gannett. Added to this were the four or five votes Stassen controlled which were against Baker from the start.

"If we had had six or seven votes, we would have elected Fred Baker. When we couldn't get them there was nothing to do but vote for the compromise candidate, Mr. Spangler.

"Mr. Spangler's election as Chairman is entirely due to the activities of Governor Stassen. Whether this is a commendation or a condemnation, it is a fact."[23]

Stassen's position, as given at a later date, was that Willkie was mistaken in thinking that Stassen could control the votes even of the two committee members from Minnesota, and was also mistaken in thinking that Baker, young and unknown, had any real chance of being elected. Willkie was still, Stassen felt, unable or unwilling to recognize the facts of political life.[24]

Whatever the rights and wrongs of this particular situation, it is clear that during the last two years of Willkie's life, while he was carrying on a desperate fight against the Old Guard, he was estranged from the two most prominent young Republican "professionals."

2

If Willkie *had* been engaged in a "political warm-up" during the last months of 1942, the contest over the National Chairmanship would have called for weeks of planning, organizing, and maneuvering. Instead, it was a minor episode in the program of activities with which his days were crowded. His "Report to the People" did not end his efforts to impart to the Western Allies the lessons he had learned in the East. When the election fever had subsided, he went back to the cause that he really cared about.

Besides his many public speeches, he gave a number of off-the-record talks, including two to the press. His first was to the New York Newspaper Guild on November 19, and, as already noted, provided an occasion for his enemies in the Republican party to spread lies about what he had said. The other talk was made, with no untoward results, "to about fifty newspaper men who were with him in his 1940 campaign, at the Carlton Hotel in Washington in December, 1942. It was [wrote James A. Hagerty] the most remarkable reporting job of which I have knowledge. I would not [have] thought it possible before that, that a man could hold fifty hard-boiled newspaper men, for the most part weary of talk by years of coverage of speeches, for nearly five hours and have them at the end of that time eager to hear more."[25] Much the same impression was carried away by another hearer, Marquis Childs, who remembered also the spirit in which Willkie spoke. "He was deadly serious"—and plainly showed his annoyance, though only by a look, when interrupted by the drunken attempts at humor of one unappreciative guest.[26]

His public statements were naturally less reportorial (since many of his most interesting facts could not be published) and more controversial. Like his statements from China and his "Report to the People," they drew the fire of persons who could not or would not distinguish between being anti-colonial and being anti-British, in spite of his reaffirmation of his long-standing conviction concerning the urgent need for mutual understanding and friendship between the two nations. Willkie's answer to his critics was to stress the additional need for completely honest and uncensored interchange of opinion.

On the whole, his "One World" philosophy received a heartening reception. On November 6 he spoke in the Manhattan garment district at a noon-hour rally of the International Ladies Garment Workers Union on the occasion of the Union's gift to Russia of a hundred large hospital tents. He was greeted by "a roar . . . that swelled to tremendous proportions" as he moved through the packed street. From the platform he called for unity among the Allies. He praised Montgomery again, as a "fighting general"—and contrasted him with "some of the armchair generals in Washington [General McNarney, Deputy Chief of Staff, in a speech the day before had attacked "armchair strategists"] who take to the platform before they take to the battlefield." And of course he had praise for the Russians: "The battle of Stalingrad is as much our front as their front."[27]

He spoke the same evening to an invited audience in *New York Times* Hall; an audience which, if less boisterous, was no less attentive, and to which he spoke no less frankly. He decried "the attitude that this is an Anglo-American war" and the implication of this attitude "that those of us who are seeking in fact to make its strategy, its military command, its purposes both now and after the war common to all the United Nations must speak softly for fear that free discussion will disturb our British allies." He ridiculed such fear as baseless; and putting his confidence to the test, he called the "emphasis on an Anglo-American world" "essentially the old white man's burden philosophy . . . a philosophy resented by three-quarters of the world. . . . One of the most significant facts in the world today is the renaissance of the East. Not to recognize the possibilities of that awakened East is to accept Hitler's philosophy of a superior race." And the same was true of "the kind of imperialism we still practice within our own frontiers toward racial and economic groups. For once you draw the line which cuts people into different categories, into first class or free peoples and second class or unfree peoples, you have taken an irretrievable step toward the eventual full acceptance of Hitler's doctrine."[28]

Ten days later Willkie stated the same ideas, and others, even more eloquently, at the New York *Herald Tribune* Forum on Current Problems: "everyone of us has the obligation to speak out, to exchange ideas freely and frankly, across the Pacific, across the Atlantic, here at home. For unless the British people know what we are thinking here in America, and unless we have a similar idea of what they are thinking in England and in the Commonwealths, there can be no hope of agreement. We must know what the people of Russia and China aim for, and we must let them know our aims." And this policy must not be limited to nations formally allied in the war. "We must try to find out and openly express the desires and hopes of hundreds of millions of other peoples—in the torn heart of Europe, in India, on the embattled shores of the Mediterranean, in Africa, on the southern shores of Asia, and in our own hemisphere."

From this prologue he proceeded, once more, to tell the world what *his* opinions were on the over-riding issue of international relations—especially those between America and Western Europe on the one hand and, on the other, nations or areas that were politically and economically undeveloped and were non-European in culture.

"Now let's take a specific and difficult example of what lies before us if we are to give reality to those freedoms we have proclaimed. The Malay Peninsula and the islands of the South East Pacific are areas containing, among other things, the principal source of the rubber supply of the world. They are inhabited in part, at least by unlettered and, in some instances, perhaps savage people. Those who sneer when it is suggested that freedom and self-government can be brought to all men, feel that such areas must be ruled perpetually by some nation's colonial imperialism.

"Now assume that the Allies reconquer those areas—shall we return them to their previous status, where their defense was courageous but inadequate and their peoples undeveloped under the governmental custody of some one nation? Or shall they be wards of the United Nations, their basic commodities made freely available to the world, their safety protected by an international police force; the full yield of their resources used for their own health, their own education and development, and their own training—no matter how long it takes—in the practices of self-government?"[29]

To balance this implied criticism of Britain, Willkie spoke on November 20 at a British War Relief luncheon, and paid tribute to the British war effort in North Africa "that made possible everything that my country is doing there today," and also to British generosity in "deliberately playing down their own contribution in order to give an extra lift to America." He also recalled the banquet in the Kremlin, his defense of Britain against Stalin's charge, and his toast to the four great Allies, "who for peace and economic security must remain united after the war."[30]

On November 25 he addressed an immense "Aid-to-Russia" rally in Toronto. In a press conference on his arrival, taking note of adverse criticism of his view on colonialism, he declared: "we are in this war together and we should discuss it together. . . . I am talking these days to provoke discussion about post-war conditions and solutions." Those who would silence such a discussion must be either doubtful of the validity of their own ideas or fearful of those that they would suppress.[31] The speech itself was largely a powerful restatement of the substance of his *Herald Tribune* Forum address.

The forgotten nations amid all this controversy were those of Latin America. And to whom but Willkie—the spokesman for all good causes otherwise unheard—should they turn to gain a hearing? Interviewed on December 1 by a group of Mexican and Bolivian newspaper men, he remarked that "the 'Good Neighbor' policy appears to be based on pretty adjectives rather than practical realities," declared that "foreign policy should not be based solely on eulogies between countries but should develop an economic and social plan to raise the standard of living in each," and suggested "the elimination of trade barriers and a more equitable distribution of raw materials." In answer to a question, he asserted: "I oppose one country entering another through economic power in order to dominate it politically."[32]

The most sensitive point, however, in the discussion of colonialism-imperialism was the imagined injury to British-American relations; but Willkie was determined that the discussion should go on. "I am not against the British," he wrote to Drew Pearson on January 3 with reference to some item in Pearson's column, ". . . but I do think we must establish proper relations with Russia and China. In this sinister purpose, I have no known allies. Likewise, I do not believe the Colonial System, whether British, French, German, Portuguese or Dutch, is a thing which those fighting for freedom can be particularly proud of."[33] He continued the discussion on December 16, at a dinner of the Sons of Indiana where he was honored for the most distinguished service to the nation by an Indianan during the year, and where he engaged in a friendly debate with a Conservative Member of Parliament, Captain Gammons, who welcomed Willkie's "fearless and completely frank views about Britain and her policies." He then eloquently defended Britain's colonial system as "a sort of ladder on which many peoples of widely divergent attainments are climbing toward the same goal, that of complete self-government," and presented a challenge to America. "We are prepared to share the responsibility with you if you in turn are willing to accept any part of it." Willkie replied: "I pray that your ideas be adopted by those in authority."[34]

At least one of "those in authority" in Britain was not permanently offended by what Willkie had been saying—though he was perhaps a little worried. Winston Churchill wrote to him, in a note dated December 5, 1942: "I was very pleased to read your comments on my latest broadcast. Considering how much we value over here the help you gave us and the common cause in the dark days of 1940 [sic], it would always be a great sorrow to me if our lines of thought became opposed or even drifted apart. The future of the world largely depends on the honorable and fraternal relationship between our two countries."[35]

Although Willkie's pleas for free discussion were addressed chiefly to his own countrymen, by whom they were most needed, one of his most eloquent and incisive statements was printed in Lord Beaverbrook's London *Evening Standard*. He began with a brilliant, brief analysis of "the elements in America which may cause it again to turn inward": "A belief, whether right or wrong, that America in the past has contributed greatly to world struggles with no corresponding benefit either to herself or to her way of life. That she is always outwitted in international diplomacy and that she fights to preserve the imperialism of other nations. There are, of course, other causes which include racial and historic biases, war weariness, confidence in the strength of her own economic and political institutions and the belief that her great prosperity was created from her own internal resources and development." On the other hand, the British were justifiably critical of "our excessively high tariffs," "suspicious of our commercial self-seeking," and repelled by "the violations within our own life of our boasted traditions of freedom and equality."

But "surely the people of our two great nations, so long seasoned in the uses of democratic discussion, can face such questions without disturbance to our present war effort." And without such discussion, leading to "a common accord of purposes . . . while we fight, we will inevitably fall apart when the fighting is over.

"It is for this reason that I have been deliberately trying to provoke and, if you will, to 'prod' the leaders of both nations into frank statements of their post-war purposes. And it is for this reason that I fight for the right of your people and mine to express themselves freely to each other, unhampered by unnecessary censorship. . . . I believe that the American and British people can in good temper . . . through the methods by which they have always functioned so successfully within themselves reach conclusions as to purpose that are sounder than the wisest pronouncements of temporary leaders. . . . Let's get on with the discussion."[36]

3

While the discussion was going on, it was given a sharper point and a deeper intensity by the "Darlan Deal" in North Africa. No other event of the war aroused Willkie to such a pitch of anger and disgust, and on no other issue did he stand, in his own country, so nearly alone.

Certain facts are not in dispute. On November 8, 1942, British and American forces under the Command of General Eisenhower invaded French North Africa, hitherto controlled by the Vichy government nominally headed by Petain. De Gaulle and the Fighting French were not told of the plan. Bitter resistance, especially from the French Navy, was met at Casablanca and Oran, but was quickly crushed. The last resistance, at Casablanca, ended on Wednesday, November 11. Total casualties suffered by the American forces (who encountered the stiffest resistance) were 360 dead, 500 missing, 1,050 wounded.[37]

The Allies had planned to set up a French government, with complete authority over civilian affairs, but ruled out both Vichy and de Gaulle, and decided that the man to head it was General Giraud, a war hero who had recently escaped from a German prison and who was whole-heartedly opposed to any kind of collaboration with Germany. This choice, however, revealed a fantastic degree of ignorance on the part of the planners. For one thing, they could not have found a Frenchman anywhere who had less interest in, understanding of, and aptitude for, politics. And in the second place, the Vichyites who occupied the positions of military and political power in North Africa refused absolutely and unanimously to recognize Giraud's authority.

Eisenhower, who had been given supreme political as well as military authority, was in a quandary. Having found that "existing French sentiment in North Africa does not even remotely resemble prior calculations," and having concluded that "complete military occupation, the cost of which in time and resources would be tremendous, will be necessary unless we can deal with a strong French government of some kind in North Africa,"[38] he saw nothing to do but accept the solution that offered itself in the person of Admiral Jean Francois Darlan.

From this point on, the facts begin to be colored by the attitude of the person who states them, no matter who he is. But perhaps most informed persons would agree with a characterization of Darlan, the number two man in the Vichy government, as an unprotesting collaborator with the Nazis, an Anglophobe, an anti-Semite, a hater of democracy—but willing to deal even with the Allies in order to advance his personal fortunes. By chance he was in Algiers, visiting a son who had been stricken with polio, when the Allies landed. After blowing hot and cold until it was clear that the invasion had succeeded, he yielded to an ultimatum from Eisenhower and on Wednesday, November 11, ordered an end to resistance. His authority was recognized. But the fact was that resistance had already ended except at Casablanca, and even there "the decision to surrender dated from Monday."[39] One wonders why Eisenhower could not have simply brushed aside the Vichy generals, who had first fought senselessly and then surrendered without conditions. "As far as French leadership was concerned, the levers of power were unattended. Anyone could grasp them who could persuade the Americans to let him do so and to back up his pretense of power with their real power."[40] But apparently Eisenhower lacked the imagination to envision such a possibility, or else the boldness to test it.

Accordingly, he accepted Darlan, with the approval of his State Department adviser, Robert Murphy, as the political boss of North Africa. The enemies of the Allies remained in power; friends of the Allies went to prison; and although Eisenhower a little later professed satisfaction with the arrangement, he showed his private uneasiness by approving a rigid censorship to prevent correspondents from giving the American and British public any but the official version of what had happened. ("During November and early December there was a complete 'stop' on political writing.")[41] The outside world first learned of Darlan's new status on November 14 through a story from Vichy concerning his proclamation "that he had assumed full responsibility for French interests in North Africa."[42] On November 16 a United Press story from Allied Headquarters in North Africa read: "General Eisenhower revealed today that he had placed the stamp of approval on the civil and military organization set up in North Africa by Admiral Francois Darlan."[43]

By this time the British were getting worried, but in the United States, elation at the first spectacular conquest of territory by the Western Allies, and by a force predominantly American and under American command, left no inclination to criticize any aspect of the situation. The only protest was by a few weak voices from the Left—and by Willkie. On November 16 he was to speak at the *Herald Tribune* Forum, and the text of his speech, as released to the press, contained a vehement protest against the Darlan Deal. After the attack on political censorship already quoted, he went on: "Shall we in America be quiet, for instance, when our leaders after promising freedom to the French people, put into control over them the very man who has helped to enslave them? Shall we be quiet when we see our government's long appeasement of Vichy find its logical conclusion in our collaboration with Darlan, Hitler's tool? Such collaboration outrages the spirit of free people everywhere, whatever expediency dictated it. I tell you we cannot fight this war in silence, whatever our experts say. Because if we fight in silence, those same experts will, in the end, even winning the war, win nothing but blood and ashes."

This statement was not made on impulse. The manuscript texts[44] show that Willkie wrote and rewrote the passage with painstaking care, seeking the strongest possible effect. It is easy, therefore, to imagine his feelings when Secretary of War Stimson telephoned him, three quarters of an hour before he was to speak, and asked him to delete the passage.[45] According to Stimson's own account, "I . . . told him flatly that, if he criticized the Darlan agreement at this juncture, he would run the risk of jeopardizing the success of the United States Army in North Africa."[46] He also told Willkie "that his speech might cost 60,000 American lives."[47]

Willkie exploded. His wife had never seen him so angry nor heard him so profane. "The air was blue"—and her attempt to restrain him by a half-humorous, half matter-of-fact warning, "Wendell, they'll take out the telephone!" went unheeded. But when he had exhausted his vocabulary of swear-words, he partially yielded—as he was bound to do, although he considered Stimson's statements fantastic—and agreed to omit most of the first three sentences quoted above, leaving only the question: "For instance, shall we be quiet when we see our State Department's long appeasement of Vichy?"

But he was still seething with such fury that Mrs. Willkie decided to go with him, and as he prepared to leave for the Forum, she also put on her coat. To his savage question, "Where are *you* going?" she replied, "Wherever *you* go." And she did.[48]

Willkie already knew that United States censors had refused to allow the transmission to Britain of the released text.[49] He learned later that even the revised text was held up for twelve hours[50]—until Roosevelt had made a statement of his own. In it he said: "I thoroughly understand and approve the feeling in the United States and Great Britain and among all the other United Nations that, in view of the history of the past two years, no permanent arrangement can be made with Admiral Darlan. . . . The present temporary arrangement in North and West Africa is only a temporary expedient dictated only by the stress of battle." He listed the presumed benefits, and assured the country: "I have requested the liberation of all persons in North Africa who had been imprisoned because they opposed the efforts of the Nazis to dominate the world and I have asked for the abrogation of all laws and decrees inspired by Nazi governments or Nazi ideologists."[51]

This statement (another instance of Roosevelt's cutting the ground from under Willkie's feet) seemed to reassure almost all Americans except Willkie, who remained unmoved. In his Toronto speech on November 25, after referring to Stalin's 1939 "alliance of expediency with Germany," he declared: "I believe the moral losses of expediency far outweigh the temporary gains. And I believe that every drop of blood saved by expediency will be paid for by twenty drawn with the sword."[52]

In England he had plenty of support. A motion was introduced in the House of Commons by twelve Labor members to the effect that continued dealings with Darlan would "undermine faith in us among our friends in the oppressed and invaded lands and impair military, social and political prospects of the complete triumph of the United Nations." This, according to the *New York Times* correspondent, "expressed the private feelings of most members of the House."[53] Nevertheless, the motion was not debated. The government had agreed to give Eisenhower final authority, and its hands—and tongue—were tied.

But Willkie's were not. Moreover, the passing days confirmed his misgivings that the "temporary expedient" would become permanent. Eisenhower had wanted a "strong French government," and as long as Darlan gave it to him, why worry about principles? Almost three months after the invasion—when Darlan was dead and the censorship had been eased—

Drew Middleton wrote from Morocco: "As in Algeria, there is not the slightest sign of any other policy than improvisation."[54] And while "authoritative quarters" in Washington continued to insist, "We are working under a purely military understanding without political implications," and Hull was telling a press conference that "in view of the war effort, there is no time for the consideration of politics,"[55] Darlan was pressing his luck. He proclaimed himself "Chief of State in French Africa," "set up an imperial council to advise him" (composed exclusively of Vichyites) and appointed a commission to negotiate for Lend-Lease aid.[56] Emboldened by Eisenhower's broadcast to the French in North Africa praising their cooperation and observing that "all Frenchmen worthy of their country's great past have forgotten *their small differences of ideas,*"[57] he wrote to Eisenhower on the anniversary of Pearl Harbor to "convey the best wishes of French Africa for the Allied cause"; and the American commander acknowledged the message with "the greatest pleasure."[58]

He was so pleased with Darlan, indeed, that he permitted him to keep control of all the radio stations in North Africa and—incredibly—to forbid their use to the Office of War Information and the British Broadcasting Corporation.[59] Eisenhower also evidently failed to inquire whether his order of November 20 for the release of "all pro-Allied prisoners in French North Africa"[60] had been carried out; and when Roosevelt at a press conference on December 11 was asked about a report "that 25,000 foes of Vichy in North African prisons had not been released," he replied airily that "it should be taken with a grain of salt."[61] (On February 4, 1943, Giraud announced that 903 political prisoners had been freed since the Allied landings and that a study was being made of the remaining 5,500.[62] A decree freeing the latter was finally issued on May 15, after the Allied conquest of North Africa was complete.)[63]

Repeated protests from de Gaulle were of course ignored; perhaps they merely strengthened the Hull-Roosevelt bias against him. So was the sharp and widespread criticism by the British press and public. On November 21 a report from London stated: "Without exception the influential weeklies express concern over the repercussions of the bargain General Eisenhower has made and see a stain on the United Nations banner";[64] "unfortunate," "ugly," "an awful hazard" were some of the phrases used. And this feeling grew rather than diminished as time passed. On December 12 the *New Statesman and Nation* asked the pertinent question, "Who is the boss in North Africa, Darlan or the Allies?"[65]

In the United States, however, most persons were satisfied or silenced—except Willkie. In an interview published early in December in the *Christian Advocate* (the official publication of the Methodist Church) he asserted that "some of our leaders seem to forget that how we win the war may determine whether we win the peace." "With all my soul I hate this false finagling with expediency, temporary or permanent. . . . The peoples of the world must be given again the conviction that the banners Americans fight under bear bright clean colors."[66]

The result was a deluge of self-righteous condemnation. In Congress, House Majority Leader John W. MacCormack spoke of "unfair utterances" and "cheap sniping" at "the diplomatic work done before the entry of our troops into Africa. . . . It is unpatriotic to attempt to divide our people."[67] Senator Vandenberg was even more extreme and explicit: "The General [Eisenhower] may be guilty of 'false finagling with expediency,' but he is also guilty of 'saving American lives' and of saving months of time and of amazing bloodless victories. . . . He should not be shot at from the rear—and especially from the sanctuary of the home front." The Senator viewed with alarm the "anti-Darlan resentments" and "post-war ideologies" of "some of our unofficial strategists at home who by their current criticisms of the Darlan arrangement might succeed in upsetting it."[68]

Willkie responded as was to be expected. Intercepted by newsmen as he was leaving a luncheon of the National Conference of Christians and Jews, where he had received an award for "distinguished service to American unity and earnest efforts in the promotion of universal fellowship and good will," he hastily scribbled the following: "The Administration policy of expedience is defended by Senator Vandenberg, and the Chicago *Tribune* gives front-page commendatory prominence to the Senator's remarks. Such defenses give me reassurance of the rightness of my position.

"My belief is that the strongest force on our side in this war is not our armies but our moral position in the world. I fear the effect of our compromises and expediences on the millions of conquered peoples in Europe. Whether they ultimately rise against their oppressors and fight on our side will determine the number of lives that will be lost in this war.

"Temporary expedience will not reduce the number of American boys who must die. Such temporary expedience may well increase the number who will never come back."[69]

He put the same sentiment more tersely in a letter to William Agar dated December 21: "I think the route we are pursuing is a prostitute's route. It looks glamorous in the beginning but ends one way."[70] And to his old friend of Commonwealth & Southern days, Thomas W. Martin, who had sent him some editorials condemning his stand on Darlan, he replied on December 23, "I hope I am always as right as I was and will be proven to be about the Darlan matter."[71]

In the meantime, Roosevelt as well as Eisenhower seemed to be forgetting that the Darlan Deal was "only a temporary expedient." Five weeks after the invasion, the Admiral announced that his "sole purpose" was "to save French Africa, help free France and then retire to private life," and that he had "granted full and complete amnesty to all against whom any action had been taken because of sympathy to the Allies"; and the President showed his approval by issuing it from the White House.[72] (The last part of this statement—if not the first—was a lie, and if Roosevelt did not know it, something was wrong.)

On December 24, however, Darlan's luck ran out. He was fatally shot by a young French student, Fernand Bonnier de la Chapelle (an "ardent follower" of de Gaulle, whose "idealism . . . was used by older men").[73] Roosevelt's comment was: "The cowardly assassination of Admiral Darlan is murder in the first degree. . . . I hope that speedy justice will overtake the murderer or murderers."[74] Two days later the slayer was executed.

Giraud was immediately appointed in Darlan's place, without opposition from Darlan's henchmen. The Admiral, it appeared, had not been indispensable. To be sure, there was no reason for opposition from the Vichyites, who still remained in power—except that one, Yves Chatel, was replaced by another, imported from Argentina, as Governor of Algeria. This was Marcel Peyrouton, who promptly expressed his determination to "keep order in the minds and in the streets."[75] Drew Middleton reported from Morocco that all the trappings of a fascist state—secret police, concentration camps, anti-democratic propaganda, anti-Semitism, and general thuggery—still flourished without any sign of Allied disapproval.[76] In Algeria, meanwhile, "Jews and Frenchmen who had publicly expressed satisfaction at our landing were now serving jail sentences for their bad taste . . . those belonging to the uniformed fascist groups were being given more responsible jobs than ever. . . . The slogan of the occupation was, 'Keep the rascals in.'"[77] In late December, French officials arrested fifteen persons on the absurd charge of plotting to assassinate Giraud. All had worked for the Allies before the landings, and one of them, Dr. Aboulkar, had lent Murphy his apartment as a headquarters to plot the uprisings in support of the invasion.[78] But now Murphy "minimized the importance of the arrests, regretted that the strict censorship of political dispatches would have to stay on, intimated that Darlan had not been such a bad fellow after all, and in general tried to pour gin on troubled waters."[79]

Of all the Allied officials, only the British diplomatic representative, Harold Macmillan (later Prime Minister) showed any repugnance to these shameful facts. In mid-January he urged a meeting between Giraud and de Gaulle and "made it clear that the British and American people would not accept a continuance of present abuses under the French 'provisional government.'"[80] (This caused displeasure in "official circles" in Washington.)[81]

Macmillan was right. The situation could not last. It finally became clear even to the State Department that even in North Africa the men of Vichy had no popular support; and that the man who *did* have the support of ordinary Frenchmen everywhere was de Gaulle. The latter was given a degree of informal recognition by being invited to appear at the Casablanca conference of Roosevelt and Churchill and their staffs, where he and Giraud were persuaded to let themselves be photographed shaking hands; and from this time on, there was a gradual removal of fascist elements from the French administration in North Africa. Willkie's comment on the uninformative official communiqué issued at the close of the conference exactly fitted the situation. "Perhaps the French collaborators were reduced in status and the men who have risked their lives for freedom have now come into their own in North Africa. Anyway, we will hope that such is the case."[82] In answer, Secretary Hull at a press conference made a bitter attack on "critics from up on Mt. Olympus" who had condemned the policy in North Africa, accused them of "vicious, venomous vituperation," and charged that they did "not want information" about the true state of affairs.[83] Even the *New York Times* in an editorial (whose writer apparently did not read the dispatches of his paper's correspondents) sharply censured Willkie for his comment.[84]

In the light of the foregoing account, we may now assess Willkie's judgment on the Darlan Deal. Its apologists insisted, first, that it had saved American lives; second, that it was necessary if the Allies were to make a swift and successful invasion of Tunisia; third, that there was a good chance that it would bring over to the Allied side the powerful French naval forces at Toulon and also the government of French West Africa (which was not invaded); and finally, that there was no alternative except rule by force of arms over a rebellious population, which would have been a severe hindrance to the military campaign against the Axis.

But if expediency is the defense, it must also be the test. Those who sacrifice a moral principle to gain a material advantage ought at least to show that the advantage did in fact accrue. And the facts are these: first, that the fighting between Allied invaders and French defenders was over before Darlan's order to end resistance was issued; second, that the attack on Tunisia bogged down in the face of bad weather and swift German reaction, and that initial operations had no effect on the final battles five months later; and third, that the French naval units at Toulon did not join the Allies but were sunk, and that French West Africa, isolated by the Allied action, must soon have capitulated in any event.

The question of a possible alternative to Darlan must be given a less absolute answer, since even the most positive statements about the attitude of the French in North Africa were only guesses; and not merely the accuracy but even the honesty of some of these statements is in doubt. Waverley Root asserts that "when correspondents in Africa were being officially informed that the population was 90 per cent anti-de Gaulle, a high official connected with the services engaged in putting out this misinformation told me privately that the figure was right but that the attribution had been switched. American officials actually estimated the population to be 90 per cent pro-de Gaulle."[85] And Root is at least partially supported by Harold Macmillan in his estimate that 90 per cent of the French in North Africa wanted *some kind* of democratic government.[86] And if this is true, it is hard to see why there would have been any difficulty in throwing out the Vichyites, including Darlan, and establishing an effective French government without them. But most American leaders, including Eisenhower and Hull, seemed to see no moral obstacle to doing business with Darlan.

To Willkie, however, the moral issue was primary; and he also held that in the end the right course would prove the most "expedient." "It is impossible to tell," he declared immediately after the Casablanca conference, "in view of the elaborate censorship and propaganda,[87] whether the appointment of Darlans, Peyroutons and other Vichyites do [sic] or do not bring temporary gains. There is one thing, however, that we do know absolutely, namely, that such collaboration brings loss of faith to millions of sincere lovers of freedom everywhere, and to my mind such loss of faith will cost more, even in practical results, than can possibly be gained by some temporary expedient."[88]

This may stand as Willkie's last word on the Darlan Deal. And even in America it was not unechoed. A month later, the veteran foreign correspondent Edgar Ansel Mowrer, resigning in protest from the Office of War Information, spoke of the "muddled thinking and childlike gullibility" which led to "the fantastic blunder of utilizing the North African Fascists on their terms rather than on ours . . . putting them in political control as the price of their aid—in considering them not as our instruments but as our Allies. The terrible effects of our official policy are now patent."[89]

The conclusion is that Willkie was right about the Darlan Deal. That deal was a disgrace to America from first to last. It arose out of ignorance, stupidity and accident; it was continued through timidity, inertia and moral insensibility. It was sold to the American people by a steady stream of propaganda; it was shielded by rigid censorship from adverse criticism by on-the-spot reporters. It saved no lives and gained no military advantage. (Despite the failure of the initial drive on Tunis, which gave the Germans nearly five months to prepare their defenses, the total number of American fighting men killed, missing, or captured in the entire North African campaign, including the landings, was about 9,000.[90] So much for the 60,000 lives that Stimson said he was saving by censoring Willkie's speech, and the 18,000 that Arthur Krock assured his readers had been saved by the Darlan Deal."[91]

On the other hand, it damaged America's standing with her Allies and with the conquered peoples of Europe to a great though indeterminate degree. That the damage was not greater was due to the assassination of Darlan—an immense and undeserved stroke of luck for America. ("How lucky F.D.R. was in his assassination!" was a later comment by the eminent British writer D. W. Brogan.)[92] Had he lived, the French would have convicted him of treason, as they did Petain and Laval; but America could not have surrendered him; and how such a bitter conflict could have been resolved is hard to imagine. Yet the youth who had thus absolved America's leaders from the consequences of their folly was, with their hearty approval and with indecent haste, sent to the gallows.

The Darlan Deal is a dirty chapter in American history. The one clean page is Willkie's lonely protest.

4

There can be no doubt that Willkie's stand on Darlan, even more than his anti-colonialism, permanently alienated many Americans who had hitherto supported him. There can be as little doubt that by another action during the same brief period he lost still more potential votes. This was his defense before the Supreme Court of William Schneiderman, whose citizenship the Department of Justice was trying to revoke on the ground that he had been a Communist at the time he was naturalized in 1927. If one wonders why no action was taken until 1940, the answer is simple. The Stalin-Hitler pact was now in effect, and the Administration was anxious to show that it was not "soft" on Communism.

The case was taken to the Supreme Court, which on October 13, 1941 agreed to hear an appeal. Schneiderman's lawyer, Carol King, asked Willkie to take the case. She had no personal acquaintance or connection with him; she simply wrote to him like thousands of other persons who hoped for help of one kind or another. And on its face, the request was fantastic. Whether or not Willkie wished to get the Presidential nomination again, he was fighting for control of the Republican party; and according to all precepts and precedents, to defend a Communist under any circumstances could be nothing less than political suicide.

Nevertheless, Mrs. King's venture paid off. She enclosed the brief [presumably the one prepared for the Court of Appeals], and when Willkie found time to read it, about a week later (this was in the midst of his fight for the repeal of the Neutrality Act), he saw at once what he had to do. "I could not with my beliefs have remained satisfied with myself if I refused to accept the case if two conditions were true—(1) that Schneiderman was a decent fellow personally, and (2) that the record sustained the brief."[93] Having satisfied himself on these two points, he took the case—without compensation, and "against the advice of his close friends."[94]

He made public his decision on November 29. Arthur Garfield Hays, veteran liberal lawyer who was general counsel of the American Civil Liberties Union, immediately offered the Union's aid, and also made public a personal letter which began: "Seldom have I had a greater thrill than when I read in this morning's paper that you are going to argue the Schneiderman case in the Supreme Court."[95] It may be assumed, however, that such enthusiasm was rare.

One young associate "asked him point blank why he had agreed to argue the case." This was Willkie's answer: "When I was asked to handle this case I said no. There were too many other problems before me, my time was limited and my health taxed. I was asked to read the record of the case before giving my final decision. I agreed. I read the record and decided without further consideration to argue the case. Why? Because I saw myself as the man involved in the case. Here was a radical who had followed in [sic] his ideal and toward his objective. While I did not agree with his views, he was entitled to them and to a fair trial under our system and to the safeguards of our constitution. He had arrived in this predicament by a series of accidents of life. I had started as he had from pretty much the same point of thinking. My series of personal accidents had taken me down an opposite road. They might well have been different, and if they had I might now be in his predicament and in such event I would have wanted the type of representation and advocacy that satisfied me. These are things that we must understand—I took the case."[96]

It is to be noted that Willkie accepted the case before the declaration of war by Germany, following the attack on Pearl Harbor, which made the United States an ally of Russia.

Willkie submitted his brief to the Supreme Court on January 16, 1942 (three days after his meeting with Roosevelt and Churchill in the White House). He began with a sketch of Schneiderman's personal history, telling how he had been brought to the United States when about two years old; had spent his childhood and youth in poverty; had joined the Workers' Party, later named the Communist Party of America, in 1924 or 1925 (and still belonged to it); and had become a citizen in 1927, soon after his twenty-first birthday.

Willkie then presented three lines of argument. First, "Congress alone has the power to specify the prerequisites of naturalization and to date it has not specified membership in the Communist party . . . as grounds for denial of citizenship." Second, an oath to support the Constitution does not preclude an attempt to change it, even in "fundamental" ways, by the method prescribed for amending it. Third, Schneiderman had specifically denied that he had ever believed in or advocated the use of force or violence to change the form of the American government, and this denial could not be judged dishonest on the basis of "official" Communist pronouncements —"the conflicting writings largely of foreigners dealing with foreign conditions." "If Schneiderman can be deprived of his citizenship on the basis of these imputed views, the citizenship of every naturalized citizen in the United States is in danger."[97]

The case was not argued, however, until November 9 (the day after the invasion of North Africa); "it was an open secret that the government wished to have the issue delayed because of possible friction with Russia."[98] (The government brief, prepared by Solicitor General Charles Fahey, was not filed until November 4.) The session was attended by "an almost record crowd."[99]

Willkie spoke extemporaneously, having with him only "a much tracked-up record, a sheaf of quotations, and a page of notes scrawled in pencil."[100] And he was unabashed by the august presence of the Justices. Making the point, as in his brief, that Congress had not outlawed the Communist Party, he demanded bluntly: "Is this court going to substitute itself for Congress? If Congress wants to outlaw Communism, it can do so, but I don't want to see it done by judicial interpretation."[101] (It is fair to add that he would not have wanted it done by Congress, either!)

Unaccustomed though the Justices might be to such informality, their solemnity yielded to Willkie's wise-cracks. Regarding the social theories that Schneiderman had studied in his youth, he remarked, "If he can understand them, he's a better man than I am."[102] And at any rate, it was unfair to impute to him the views of other Communists: "You might as well try to show my beliefs by showing those of Ham Fish."[103] On the other hand, not everything in Communist writings was to be condemned. Referring to a document that he did not at the moment name, "he got a laugh from several of [the Justices] when he asked what were the terrible things imputed to the document and went on to note that one of them called for heavy or progressive income tax and another for education for all." "Why . . . every member of this court probably read that when he was sixteen to twenty-one and had his social thinking affected by it. Whether one believes in it or disbelieves in it, the Communist Manifesto is a tremendously important historical document." (Schneiderman had sworn, Willkie pointed out, that he subscribed to it "only as it pertained to the period when it was written.")[104]

These remarks all added up to the argument that a man could be a Communist without being bound to accept every doctrine advanced by Communist theorists—specifically, that "force and violence" were always legitimate means of overthrowing a non-Communist government. But were the Communists the only ones who in their writings apparently advocated or sanctioned "force and violence"? Again Willkie referred to an unidentified document, and quoted: "This country, with its institutions, belongs to the people who inhabit it. Whenever they grow weary of the existing government, they can exercise their constitutional right of amending it, or they can exercise their revolutionary right to overthrow it." "That,"

Willkie announced with relish, "is from the founder of my party." (It was from Lincoln's *Second Inaugural Address.*) Next he read a still more inflammatory passage: "God forbid we should ever be twenty years without such a rebellion. . . . The tree of liberty must be refreshed from time to time by the blood of patriots and tyrants." "That," he declared triumphantly, "is from Thomas Jefferson, the founder of the Democratic party."[105] Thus he dramatically illustrated, first, the injustice of condemning a person for alleged adherence to an abstract principle, however radical, and second, the American tradition of freedom of thought and speech, even in criticizing the government.

Willkie also dwelt on the fact that a decision against Schneiderman would set up a double standard of citizenship—one standard for those who were native born and another standard for those who had been naturalized. "When I read a review of a book by Henry Hazlitt [an economist then on the staff of the *New York Times*] . . . advocating revolutionary changes after this war, I thought how lucky Mr. Hazlitt was to be born in this country and couldn't be deported because he had some ideas."[106]

The government's case, as presented by Solicitor General Fahey, boiled down to the allegation that membership in the Communist Party simply precludes "true faith and allegiance to the United States."[107]

On February 16, 1943, the Court ordered a rehearing of the arguments in the case—presumably because on that date a new Justice, Wiley Rutledge, was sworn in to replace Justice Byrnes, who had resigned at Roosevelt's request to become Director of Economic Stabilization. The second hearing took place on March 12. This time it was noted that Willkie was "much more restrained in manner"—although there was still no lack of aggressiveness. He declared concerning Schneiderman's application for citizenship: "He was never asked if he was a member of the Communist Party. I don't think it ever occurred to anyone to ask him." He praised his client as a "young man of inquiring mind," and then went to the heart of the matter by asserting (what the government did not deny) that there was "never any overt act" of disloyalty. He called it "preposterous" to convict Schneiderman on the basis of certain selected passages from Communist literature: "To my mind, guilt in America is personal." Fahey again took the most limited and easily defended position: that the only significant points were that "Schneiderman believed in the principles of the Communist Party," and that these principles were "inimical to the Constitution."[108]

On June 21 the Court handed down its decision. Five of the Justices—Black, Douglas, Murphy, Reed, and Rutledge—approved Willkie's argument. Three—Frankfurter, Roberts, and Stone—dissented. Jackson disqualified himself because of his connection with the case as Attorney General.

The Court's opinions followed the arguments. Murphy, speaking for the majority, specifically declined to decide whether the Communist Party did or did not advocate the violent overthrow of the United States government, but concluded that differing views were possible and that Schneiderman should be given the benefit of the doubt. Rutledge, concurring, emphasized that if a person's citizenship could be revoked after so many years by overturning the findings as to fact of the court which originally granted him citizenship, the same thing "can be done after thirty years or fifty years. If it can be done for Schneiderman, it can be done for thousands or tens of thousands of others." Stone, dissenting vigorously and often sarcastically, insisted that there were no two ways of interpreting Communist literature, and that it was simply impossible for a person to be a member of the Communist Party and at the same time honestly affirm his loyalty to the Constitution.[109]

Willkie's comment on the decision was as uncompromising as usual. "I have always felt confident as to how the Supreme Court would decide a case involving such fundamental American rights. My bafflement has been as to why the Administration started and prosecuted a case in which, if they had prevailed, a thoroughly illiberal precedent would have been established."[110]

To what extent Willkie's advocacy influenced the Court's decision is hard to say. Perhaps the issue was so clear and fundamental that the decision would have been the same no matter who pleaded the case. But perhaps it did not seem so clear and fundamental before Willkie, with his sure grasp of great issues, dramatized and humanized the principle that was at stake. Even Supreme Court Justices are human. And another fact of which, being human, they would not have been unaware, was that Willkie was really pleading his case before the bar of public opinion, and that before that bar there was no one else, except the President himself, who was so powerful a pleader.

The effect of the decision can be stated more confidently. While Russia's immense contribution to the common cause was diminishing American enmity, the Court decision raised a new barricade against the professional Red-baiters, and helped Americans to think sanely about Russia and Communism. This in turn not only removed, for at least a few years, the fear of legal reprisal against individual citizens who chose to think and speak like free men but also aided the rapprochement with Russia which made possible the birth of the United Nations.

It is true that the first of these gains was later thrown away by the timid or conservative majority of the "Vinson Court," which—reflecting and sanctioning the national hysteria engendered by the Korean War, the Hiss case, and the atom-spy sensation and fomented by religious fanaticism and political ambition—upheld the principal anti-Communist provision of the Smith Act and also gave to Congressional committees unlimited inquisitorial powers. But theirs was not the last word, either; for later a new majority, braver and wiser, reaffirmed the liberties for which Willkie fought.

And in the meantime, the United Nations still exists—an instrument that the fumbling hands of humanity may sometime learn to use with saving skill.

As for Willkie himself, the effect on his political future could only be of one kind, whether he won or lost. Henceforth there would always be, in the view of many persons, some scrap of seeming substance in the recurrent charge that he was a Communist sympathizer. The acid comment of Harry Bridges (the West Coast labor leader that the government tried for a dozen years to deport as a Communist) at the time of Willkie's death—"Wendell Willkie was the only man in America who has proved that he would rather be right than be President"[111]—was true. The hatred of the Old Guard could hardly be increased, but a new weapon to use against him was always welcome. Representative Shafer, in the same speech in which he condemned Willkie's world tour, spoke for many Republicans in condemning him also for defending Schneiderman. Misquoting Willkie's remark about the *Communist Manifesto*—"Believe it or not, it is one of the greatest historical documents"—and complaining with unconscious humor, "He has never said as much for the Republican platform," Shafer concluded: "To the alien-born Schneiderman, advocate of those anti-religious, anti-marriage, anti-constitutional doctrines advocating a forcible overthrow of the American way of life, the titular head of the Republican party gave his services in the Supreme Court without fee."[112] (Would it have been more respectable if he had done it for money?)

And eight years after Willkie's death, when Schneiderman was convicted under the Smith Act,[113] the Chicago *Tribune* exultantly headed its leading editorial "Willkie's Wasted Labor"; and the editorial concluded, in the *Tribune's* inimitable manner: "The Republican nominee of 1940 has been exposed by events once more as a prize chump."

If Willkie's main aim in life had been in fact, as in the view of many of his critics, personal political advancement, the *Tribune's* epithet would have been deserved.

XIX

The Triumph of an Idea

1

"There are two methods of operating in politics," Willkie told reporters toward the end of 1943. "I am interested in principles, and if I can get them adopted, that's what I'm working for. Another method is this: A man just wants public office. That's legitimate, but what I'm working for is the adoption of certain beliefs I have. . . . Naturally," he added, with a candor that only the man who puts principles first can afford, "like any man who believes deeply in things, I would like to be the man who put these principles into execution."[1]

This statement explains Willkie's activities during 1943. His first concern was to impress his own beliefs on the public; his second, as the year drew to a close, was to lay the groundwork for a successful drive for the Republican Presidential nomination in 1944.

Still, while he wrestled with vast impersonal issues and forces, he did not allow his concern for humanity in general to make him casual in his contacts with human beings in particular. That this warmth of sympathy was reciprocated by many ordinary people is evident in a little anecdote given in a letter to Willkie in 1944 from his friend Rush Sturges, following a meeting between the two. "Do you remember the infernal racket going on in the street causing me to close the windows? Well, I stopped to say hello to the Italian foreman and he said, 'Ain't you the little guy that went with the big guy into that building over there and wasn't the big guy Mr. Willkie?' I replied that he was correct. 'Well,' he said, 'we thought it was Mr. Willkie and when we saw someone close the windows, we thought we were making too much damned noise, so we waited until Mr. Willkie came out.' "[2]

The natural magnanimity to which such actions were a natural response showed itself when he introduced Elmer Davis, Director of the Office of War Information, as the main speaker at a meeting of publishers and booksellers in honor of a group of visiting British publishers. Despite a sharp exchange with Davis over the censorship of his attack on the Darlan Deal, Willkie praised "the sincerity with which he has carried out his proclaimed purpose of giving the people the information they should have."[3]

Earlier in the year he had assumed a still more congenial obligation when he introduced Mme. Chiang Kai-shek (who had recently been a guest of the President and who had addressed Congress with brilliantly calculated effect) as the main speaker at a great aid-to-China rally in New York. Some who listened to the fervid eloquence with which he led up to the introduction of "my friend, Madam Chiang," may have felt that greater restraint might have been more effective. But there could be no doubt that he reflected the temper of the audience.

In early April, for a moment, Willkie abandoned himself to fun when he appeared for the second time on "Information, Please," and again made a hit with his radio audience. But the human interest story that won the widest attention concerned his friend Eddy Gilmore, Associated Press correspondent in Moscow. The story in the *Times* told (without the names) of Gilmore's falling in love with a Russian girl and of how, after the friendship was noted, "the girl was quietly removed from Moscow and if it hadn't been for the timely plea of Mr. Willkie she would have been sent to Siberia. The correspondent returned to America and went at once to Mr. Willkie, as an old friend, to ask him to intervene in his behalf.

"We read a brief report of these facts in a gossip column and asked Mr. Willkie if the story was true. He hesitated and reluctantly answered, 'Yes.'

"On June 14 he sent a cable to Marshal Stalin which said: 'Anything you can do to facilitate this union I will personally appreciate, for I have absolute confidence and am willing to vouch for Blank completely.'

"Five days later Marshal Stalin's reply was in the hands of Mr. Willkie. It read: 'I am glad to inform you that your request regarding Blank will be fulfilled. The decision was made as a special exception on your recommendation and vouching.' "[4]

Willkie commented in a letter: "I don't know when I have gotten more response to a brief story than I did to the one about the love affair. I never thought of myself as a cupid before, but, on reflection, I don't see why I am not qualified."[5]

Not all his undertakings as a "self-appointed trouble-shooter in a troubled world" (as the *Nation* called him with approval)[6] had happy endings. In another and still grimmer situation in Russia he interceded without effect. This was the case of two Polish Socialists, Alter and Ehrlick, who had been imprisoned for no other crime, as most American liberals believed, than being loyal to their own country rather than to Russia. Willkie had discussed their case with Molotov during his Moscow visit; and in March he added his appeal in their behalf to those of a number of other noted Americans. But the men had already been sentenced to death, and the sentence was carried out.[7]

Willkie was equally willing to protest an equally arbitrary and unjust, though less brutal, action by Congress. Robert Morss Lovett, long a noted teacher and scholar at the University of Chicago, now held a post in the government of the Virgin Islands; and by his record as a fighter for liberal causes, he had earned the enmity of Congressional Red-baiters. Unable to procure his dismissal, they persuaded their colleagues to join them in attaching a rider to an appropriation bill, in which it was stipulated that none of the money was to be used to pay the salaries of Lovett and two other persons similarly slandered as "subversive." The House of Representatives passed this measure on May 18 by a vote of 317-62.

On May 21 Willkie wrote an obviously hasty note to Senator Wallace H. White of Maine: "The vote of the house of Representatives which through legislative act determined the propriety of certain persons remaining on the Federal payroll because of their presumed political opinions, was to me a very disturbing procedure. . . . I am . . . alarmed when the guilt or innocence of anyone is determined not by orderly procedure but by Legislative enactment. . . . I write to urge you to so vote as to reverse the action of the House."[8] (The measure was nevertheless passed by the Senate; but the Supreme Court later held it to be unconstitutional.)

In the field of civil liberties Willkie also continued his crusade against racial discrimination. His previous warnings were given frightening point by the Detroit race riots of June 21, when thirty-four persons were killed and more than seven hundred injured. On July 24 Willkie was invited to present a "postscript" to a CBS radio broadcast entitled "Open Letter to the American People," which was a re-enactment of the Detroit catastrophe. He delivered an impartial indictment of the two major parties for their failure to satisfy the "human needs" of Negroes: "One party has the tendency to ask the Negro for his vote as a recompense for a simple act of justice done eighty years ago. The other retains political power by, in effect, depriving the Negro of his right to vote in one part of the country while seeking his vote in another on the plea of great friendship for his race. . . . One party cannot go on feeling that it has no further obligation to the Negro citizen because Abraham Lincoln freed the slaves. And the other is not entitled to power if it sanctions and practices one set of principles in Atlanta and another in Harlem."

And the issue, as he had said before, was not merely a domestic one; America's international standing was at stake. "Two thirds of the people who are allied with us do not have white skins. . . . Today the white man is professing friendship and a desire to co-operate and is promising opportunity in the world to come when the war is over. They wonder. When the necessities of war cease to make co-operation valuable to the white man, will his promises mean anything? Race riots in Detroit, Los Angeles and Beaumont, Texas, do not reassure them."

What *would* reassure them was a "practical, direct and positive" program to secure for American Negroes their rights as citizens and as human beings: "legal equality, equal opportunity for education, equality of expenditure of public money for health and hospitalization, equal economic opportunity and equal rights to serve in the armed forces." And of course they must have "adequate and decent housing," supplied by the government if private enterprise was unable or unwilling to do the job. Opposition to such a program was, he insisted, "fascism"—which it was one main purpose of the United Nations to destroy. And "all the forces of fascism are not with our enemies. . . . It is essential that we eliminate it at home as well as abroad."[9]

A different appeal to the national conscience had been made on May 2, at the Mt. Rushmore Memorial.[10] With the final victory in North Africa only a few days distant, many persons began dreaming of a relatively swift and easy path to total victory over the Axis. On the other hand, with John L. Lewis's Mine Workers engaged in another of a seemingly endless series of strikes, with war production still being slowed by private feuds among government officials, with dissension among members of the Cabinet being widely publicized, and with many persons grumbling over the pinch of rationing and price controls, there was a rising tide of cynicism and of bitterness against the government.

To this situation Willkie addressed himself. "Are you engaged in delusion and wishful thinking that the war will end shortly when we have not yet even entered Europe and have reconquered only one of the multitude of islands in the South Pacific? Are you one of those who understand the destructive forces of inflation, yet join pressure groups whose demands, if met, involve inflation inevitably?

"Are you one of those who, because others are seeking special advantages, adopt the philosophy that I might as well get my share, because everyone else is getting his? Does the failure of your government to stand firmly . . . against the arbitrary demands of arrogant men within our own society cause you to live and work less resolutely? Do you find excuses for your own inaction in the other manifest and manifold errors of our government? . . .

"If you do, then you are merely parrying the blows that weaken your country. You are not beating them."[11]

The last item in this brief kaleidoscopic survey of Willkie's personal and public activities during early 1943 (aside from the main task of getting the country to accept his "One World" philosophy) is his defense of liberal education in a world where mastery seemed to lie in the manipulation of physical forces by mechanical devices. Even the international organization of which he urged the establishment before the war was over, was a mechanism that must be run by *men*. "Governmental forms or world councils," no matter how painstakingly set up, would never automatically produce a better world.[12] Their success would depend on the wisdom of those who guided them. "The final victory will be won on the battlefields of men's minds."[13]

Yet the study of liberal arts, which supplied the weapons and trained the men for *this* battle, was being neglected because of the pressure to produce the tools of physical warfare and the men trained to use them. As the country approached total mobilization, the male population of colleges and universities dwindled toward zero, except for various specialized training programs sponsored by the Armed Forces.

The danger from this neglect of the liberal arts was the theme of a speech by Willkie at Duke University on January 14, 1943. Wartime pressures, he warned, might make habitual "the worship of leaders, willingness to be told what to think and the acceptance of unnecessary restrictions on freedom of speech." To prevent this evil we must keep in view the end for which the war was being fought. "This is a war for freedom—freedom here and freedom elsewhere. But if we are going to risk our lives for freedom we must at the same time do all we can to preserve the deep springs from which it flows."

To do so we must understand the true nature and source of freedom. "Recently, we have been prone to think of freedom in purely economic terms. It is true that a man cannot be free unless he has a job and a decent income.

"But this job and this income are not the source of his freedom. They only implement it. Freedom is of the mind. Freedom is in that library of yours, around which this campus is built."

Willkie drove home his point by an analysis of the German conception of education, with its glorification of knowledge in the abstract and its dehumanizing of the educational process. The result of thus divorcing education from life was manifest in recent German history. "We have seen the exaltation of government, the abasement of culture, and the resulting violation of all that civilization cherishes. . . . It is a tragedy as great as men have ever witnessed. And it is our task, a task in which we shall be engaged for the rest of our lives, first to stop it and then to repair it."

The wisdom and the will to achieve this goal must be developed by the study of the liberal arts. But liberal education as a cure for totalitarianism could not be imposed from without. "I have shuddered to hear a member of our government planning, after the war is over, to police the education of our late enemies, after the traditional manner of conquerors." The alternative was the attitude inculcated by the study of liberal arts—to place one's faith in truth, derived from the free dissemination of facts and opinion; not to sanction the suppression of these by censorship or the distortion of them by propaganda. "Spread the facts, analyze them, make them available to all the world. There is no other form of political warfare that can possibly win the great political struggle in which we are engaged. Truth alone can win it."[14]

Willkie had one more proposal to make. If the final battle was to be fought for men's minds, with ideas for weapons, and if the preparation for this battle was the study of the liberal arts, then "there should be some provision in the manpower program for leaving a nucleus in the colleges of men whose aptitudes qualify them as definitely for our long-range needs as other men are obviously qualified for, let us say, medicine.

"The men and women who are devoting their lives to such studies should not be made to feel inferior or apologetic in the face of a PT-boat commander or the driver of a tank. They and all their fellow citizens should know that the preservation of our cultural heritage is not superfluous."[15]

There was nothing illogical in this proposal; the organization necessary to fight a modern war allows the individual little choice as to how or where he will serve. But editorial writers (for instance, in the *New York Times* and the *Nation*) were probably right in calling it impracticable. Anybody could see why students of medicine or physics should be withheld from combat. But that the same privilege or compulsion should be extended to students of philosophy, history, literature, or art was an idea that the whole national tradition and attitude made impossible of acceptance, either by the public or the students themselves.

There can, however, be no dissent by civilized persons from Willkie's thesis that "the final victory will be won"—if it is won at all, in an age where no victory is possible except by foregoing the use of nuclear weapons —"on the battlefield of men's minds."

2

Upon this battlefield, if one may judge by the sales of *One World,* Willkie achieved during 1943 a spectacular success. This little book of perhaps 60,000 words was his final "report to the people" on his world tour. Despite its relative brevity, one wonders how he found time to write it at all. (On January 2 he sent a regretful note to Mrs. Raymond Clapper, of which the substance is repeated again and again in his correspondence: "With all the commitments I have, I just can't see how I can make the talk for you. I have got so much writing to do in the next few weeks that every time I think of writing something more I get nauseated.")[16]

But somehow he *did* write it—and he wrote it *himself.* The rumor that it was "ghosted" is another of the lies that his enemies were so assiduous in spreading. He naturally made use of the recollections and opinions of his traveling companions, Gardner Cowles and Joseph Barnes, who were personal friends and professional journalists; and in matters of style, he had the advice of Irita Van Doren.[17] But no one who has any ear for style can doubt that the language of *One World* is his own.

This judgment is confirmed by the manuscripts.[18] The earliest version has a note saying that it was completed on February 8, 1943. (The "Introduction" in this collection is dated in Willkie's hand "March 2, 1943"—as it is in the book.) It is a carbon copy on thin paper, much worked over—in pencil and in Willkie's own handwriting. Many passages are crossed out, many are added, many have the original language drastically revised. All these revisions are incorporated in another typewritten draft; and this again has been revised by the alteration of an average of three or four words on each page. Even the galley proofs contain occasional changes.

The revisions are as a rule in the direction of greater exactness and restraint, of an appeal to reason more than to emotion. Sweeping assertions are qualified; words highly charged with emotion are replaced by words that are emotionally neutral; the tone in general becomes more dispassionate and judicial.

One World was published by Simon and Schuster on Thursday, April 8, 1943, in a paperbound edition priced at $1.00 and a clothbound edition at $2.00. No one connected with the project foresaw the extent of the book's popularity. There was no unusual pre-publication advertising; there was no arrangement for distribution by any book club. The highest guess as to probable sales was 250,000, and Willkie himself "said privately he would be most pleased if the book reached 150,000 people."[19] Even the advance sales of 53,000 (in round numbers) did not prepare the firm for the avalanche of orders: 43,000 on Thursday, 18,000 on Friday, 48,000 on Monday, 61,000 on Tuesday.[20] To meet the demand, five sets of plates were made, and the printers ran their presses twenty-four hours a day for three weeks before the publishers caught up with their orders.[21] By August 4 it had sold, in various editions, a total of about 1,550,000 copies.[22] It topped the *New York Times Book Review* best seller list from May 9 to September 5. In October, 1944, the publishers stated that it had been "translated into virtually every foreign language. . . . During the past year alone, close to 3,000,000 copies were printed and distributed. Even in nations living under the Nazi yoke —in Denmark, in France, and elsewhere—editions were printed and widely distributed by the Underground."[23] (At his death one of the memorial tributes received by Mrs. Willkie was from "the Corporation of the Citizens of Karachi." And on the same occasion an American soldier in France heard from every radio the announcement: "Weelkie est mort!" "Weelkie est mort!"[24] No need to tell any citizen of freed France who Willkie was!)

The motion picture rights were sold to his own company, 20th Century-Fox, and a screen play was written by Lamar Trotti. It takes the members of an ordinary Indiana farm family, and their friends, and brings them dramatically to an understanding and acceptance of the fact that their destiny is inextricably interwoven with that of all the people of the seemingly remote lands that Willkie had visited. If it could have been produced and shown in 1943, it might well have shared the popularity of the book, even though one feels in reading the script that the unique distinction of the original work has been lost.

In 1943, however, when each passing month made it clearer that Willkie was aiming for the Republican Presidential nomination in 1944, the making and showing of the picture would have brought clamorous charges that it was campaign propaganda. Even after he dropped out of the race in April, 1944, his political position would have made the picture controversial. His death in October would seem to have removed this obstacle, and might even, one would think, have made the picture more poignant in its appeal. But the fact was, strangely, that with his death Willkie's hold on the popular imagination seemingly ceased to exist. The picture was never made.

The reported price of the motion picture rights was $100,000;[25] and Willkie boasted in a political speech in October of 1943 that the book had "made $350,000."[26] (But, as noted above, all the money was put into a trust fund to be used for worthy purposes.)

Willkie's real reward was less tangible. Like many other men, he took particular pleasure in an achievement outside his usual sphere of activity. "My life has been unbelievably full of satisfaction," he told a meeting of the Council on Books in Wartime, which had listed *One World* as an "imperative" for wartime reading, but the recognition accorded to his book was "the richest satisfaction of all."[27]

This recognition was deserved. The simplicity and directness of the style produced an absolute clarity that left the ordinary reader unaware of the medium, completely absorbed in the content; and this was a technical triumph of the highest order. But this effect was not merely a matter of technique; it sprang in part from the way in which Willkie *saw* things—simply, without personal or national prejudice, as innocent of convention and therefore as honest in observation and report as the child in the fable who saw and said that the Emperor had no clothes on.

The work appealed also because there was no suggestion of the air of omniscience that professional reporters, commentators, and diplomats find it next to impossible to avoid; no suspicion of condescension either to the people that he wrote about or to the people that he wrote *for*. The details of geography, of society, of personality, that he recorded were those that would have caught the eye of any perceptive and intelligent American traveler to unfamiliar lands. And the eagerness with which he satisfied his immense and unflagging curiosity could hardly be resisted by the most passive reader.

The heat, the dirt, the disease, the inequalities, the antagonisms, the social fragmentation, of the Middle East, except for the contrast supplied by Turkey; the drab and comfortless desperation of life in Russia, transcended by a fanatical unity of determination not to be beaten by the Nazis; the pathos of the uncomprehending endurance of China's masses and of the still unrewarded hopes of the awakened few; and everywhere an overtone of change, a deep vibration more felt than heard, as old foundations began to sink and slide, old walls began to crack and sway—all these he pictured for his fellow Americans and for the people of the West.

And after he had drawn the picture, he drew the moral, with the same clean strokes and the same clear colors. In the concluding chapters of *One World* he restated (often in words that he had used before and evidently felt he could not better) his basic beliefs concerning the relations between persons and between states.

His initial premise was that people are people—that race, language, religion, nationality are accidents that may modify but do not destroy certain desires and needs that all human beings have in common; for a certain measure of material comfort, a certain degree of participation in the government of their own group, a certain amount of individual freedom. And these needs and desires are also rights, which those who already enjoy them have a duty to help their less fortunate neighbors to attain. "Today we are called on [Willkie said a few months later] to affirm the equality of men and nations—all men and all nations. The starting point for that affirmation must be our own faith—our belief that such equality is not something of our own devising; that it is, instead, an equality bestowed by God."[28]

This was what Willkie believed—without cant, without dialectical evasion, simply as a concept validated, for him, both by intuition and experience. From it stemmed his condemnation of American isolationism ("we must have faith that men and women like ourselves in other lands are fit to be free . . . that if they are helped to freedom, they will govern themselves wisely and well. Fundamentally, the isolationist lacks this faith");[29] of European imperialism, with its other face of Asian and African colonialism; of totalitarianism in every form, whether Fascist, Communist, or monarchic; of the domination of the world by the great powers, even granting their benevolent intentions; and of the assumption of superiority by some groups over others on the basis of party, class, religion, race or nationality.

The effect of *One World* on American public opinion (not to go farther) is of course impossible to gauge objectively. Yet the enormous sales reveal, at the very least, an awakening of concern for the rest of the world that had no previous parallel in American history. It is natural to infer, also, that they reflect a large measure of agreement with Willkie's point of view. It is permissible to think, finally, that some of this agreement was due to his personal influence.

But this agreement, according to the regular pattern of his career, would not be translated into votes, although he did his best to make the book bring him some political profit: following the suggestion of Gardner Cowles and "sending autographed copies with many special messages to practically every Republican Congressman and Senator and some Democrats. The only ones I am omitting from the Republican list are fellows like Ham Fish, etc., whom [sic] I know would only use it for ill purposes."[30]

Even if the party leaders had been more friendly, however, many rank and file Republicans who were not hostile to either Willkie or his ideas, would shy away from the idea of putting into the White House so dramatic a personality. It might be true that Willkie sitting on his porch in Indiana, talking comfortably with people who would drive by, hesitate, stop their cars and come back to shake his hand,[31] was as solid and reassuring a figure as the country could have furnished. But most people's picture was of the New York lawyer, the world traveler, the defender of Communists, the challenger of long accepted precedents and persons.

These reservations were reflected to some extent in the reviews of *One World,* which often had political overtones. One such piece was written by Harold Stassen for the *New York Times Book Review;*[32] and whatever the writer's intention, the result was one of studied depreciation. He praised the "reporting" as "picturesque," but discovered "a tendency to be dogmatic and belligerent" in the discussion of international problems, along with a lack of "concrete suggestions" for solving them. Some of Willkie's arresting statements might be tolerated as "forgivable exaggerations." Still, "there would seem to be an over-emphasis on the evils of the British colonial system and an understatement of the evils of Communism." And the reviewer found "very little appraisal . . . of the religious backgrounds of the peoples and of the value placed upon the fundamental dignity of man in the respective countries." None of the statements were supported by analysis or quotation.

Arthur Hays Sulzberger, publisher of the *Times,* sent a shocked letter of apology.[33] But apparently the editor of the *Book Review* had already got in touch with Willkie, who wrote to Gardner Cowles on April 6: "Stassen was asked to write a review for the 'Times' on the assumption that he was a friend of mine. The 'Times' offered to let me write a reply to it, but I decided otherwise. His review is quite critical."[34] Despite this restrained comment, and despite the doubts raised by Stassen's part in the choice of a National Chairman, there can be no doubt that the unexplained hostility of the review, by a man whom he had once thought of as a personal friend and a sharer of his political philosophy, came as a painful surprise.

3

With *One World* safely in print, Willkie was considering another trip, the long delayed one to Australia and New Zealand. Rumors of such an intention appeared in the press, and on April 9 he issued a formal statement: "The reports are true that today I received an invitation from the Australian-American Association of Queensland, New South Wales, Victoria and South Australia. . . .

"Of course, if I can be helpful and if our government will consent, I shall be more than glad to go . . ."[35] But for some reason which the records do not reveal, the journey was never made. Perhaps there were objections from the State Department or the military or both.

There was, however, as has been seen, no lack of causes to fight for at home, even though the country seemed to be coming around to Willkie's view that it was not too soon to begin planning for some sort of world organization. On January 4 Representative Everett Dirksen of Illinois (not yet a convert to "Modern Republicanism") introduced a resolution to establish a "Congressional Joint Committee on Peace and Peace Preparation."[36] Three days later Representative Mundt of South Dakota (another "regular" Republican) introduced a bill calling for a 32-member commission to plan the peace—eight members to be appointed by Hoover, eight by Hull, eight jointly by the majority and minority leaders in the House, and eight by the corresponding officers in the Senate. On the same day Stassen was in the news as urging a "World Parliament."[37] On February 12 Under Secretary of State Sumner Welles urged "the United Nations to draw up a post-war program now for policing the world against new aggression and for bringing about economic reconstruction through international cooperation."[38] On March 5 the United States Chamber of Commerce called for some post-war plan.[39]

More significant than any of these was a resolution proposed in mid-March by Senators Ball of Minnesota and Burton of Ohio, Republicans, and Hatch of New Mexico and Hill of Alabama, Democrats. (This resolution was sometimes referred to in the numerous discussions to which it gave rise as "B2H2.") The crucial part, Paragraphs 4 and 5, provided for "the establishment of procedures and machinery for the settlement of peacetime disputes and disagreements among nations and for the assembly and maintenance of a United Nations military force available for immediate use against any future attempt at military aggression by any nation."[40] Willkie promptly wired his congratulations and added: "Let me know if there is anything I can do to help"—a gesture which may not have strengthened the authors' standing with their colleagues.[41] But they could welcome wholeheartedly the support of Senator Truman, who declared of the resolution: "I am proud that I played a part in its inception."[42]

On March 21 the world learned that Winston Churchill's opposition to any detailed discussion of the shape of the post-war world had yielded to the general pressure. He prefaced a long analysis of specific possibilities by expressing the "hope that the United Nations, headed by the three great victorious powers, the British Commonwealth of Nations, the United States and Soviet Russia, should immediately begin to confer upon the future world organization."[43]

The wave of sentiment eventually touched even Ohio Republicans. Governor Bricker, a prominent candidate for the 1944 Republican Presidential nomination, found it expedient in early April to declare that "America is not, never has been, and never will be an isolationist nation."[44] And in May Senator Taft avowed his willingness to approve something "along the general lines suggested in the League of Nations."[45] This, for Taft, was almost revolutionary. But in June he went even farther: "I believe that our people must commit themselves to use military force under certain conditions where aggression has been found by an international body to exist." Thus he tacitly admitted—while insisting that "we are not ready to make our decision now as to the kind of permanent organization we should have"[46]—that the decision-making process was already under way.

At the beginning of July Senator Vandenberg took the first decisive step toward the position for which he will be remembered in American history—that of Republican spokesman for a bipartisan foreign policy based on recognition of America's dependence on and obligations to other democratic countries. He joined with Senator White of Maine in offering a substitute for "B2H2," holding that the latter would give rise to debate that would do more harm than good. His own resolution, however, though wordy, seemed to cover the essential points. The authors of "B2H2," nevertheless, expressed their determination to fight for the original resolution.[47] The next day sixteen Senators and Representatives announced that they would spend the summer touring the country and speaking in favor of post-war cooperation with other nations.[48]

This awakening of the American people to their responsibilities as members of a world community was hastened by the turning, at last, of the tide of war. The Nazis were crushed in North Africa; Sicily was conquered; the advance in the Southwest Pacific, though still slow, was gathering momentum. In Russia it was clear that Germany's offensive power was spent. And if the fighting men themselves were strangely indifferent to the idea of trying to prevent the repetition of their painful experience,[49] their families and friends at home were not.

It is true that the country, particularly its politicians, was far from unanimity. "B2H2" was not merely attacked, as expected, by old-line isolationists like Senators Wheeler and Bennett Clark, and viewed with suspicion by Chairman Spangler (who predicted that "the American people will hesitate about agreeing to any limitation of their sovereignty at the peace conference");[50] but had a chilly reception from the Administration. (Senator Connally told the Senate that the White House and the State Department were opposed to the resolution in its present form.)[51] Nevertheless, the trend of opinion that "B2H2" represented was clearly and increasingly dominant.

Willkie's contribution to this trend was not limited to the writing of *One World*. In speech after speech and article after article (too numerous even to list) he pleaded with his countrymen not to reenact the catastrophic retreat into isolation that had followed World War I; but to go to work, without a moment's delay, to remove the possible causes of a second such retreat. "We will have no United Nations after the war," he warned a Metropolitan Opera radio audience on January 2, "unless we make the United Nations now a fact and not a mere euphonious phrase. . . . Successful instruments of either national or international government . . . cannot be created in a day. Nor is there much hope of their being created among the reawakened national impulses, the self-seeking, the moral degenerations and the economic and social dislocations that are always incident to a postwar period."[52]

Willkie repeated this warning, in a wider and more hopeful context, in an Independence Day broadcast sponsored by the War Writers' Board and the Columbia Broadcasting System. He repeated the familiar theme of the three choices—"narrow nationalism," "international imperialism," and a policy based on recognition of the equality in rights of nations and individuals—confronting the American people, and his confidence that an "overwhelming majority" would choose the last; would recognize "that this world is one world, that all parts of it for their own well-being are interdependent," and that the present need was for "a declaration of interdependence among the nations of this one world."[53]

The "narrow nationalism" to which this concept is opposed perhaps requires some further explanation. Willkie did not deny the need for some point of reference or attachment intermediate between the necessarily unique integrity of the individual and the necessarily abstract ideal of universal brotherhood. But this mean must not be destructive of the extremes —as was the nationalistic fervor of Nazi Germany. This need for the right kind of national loyalty was the subject of some impromptu remarks by Willkie in a Jefferson Bicentennial Symposium sponsored by the Library of Congress early in 1944:

"One of the problems—and it is a very delicate problem to suggest: I hesitate because it is so difficult to say it except clumsily and I have tried to write it several times but I have never written it yet to my satisfaction—somewhere in the democratic society, in addition to the preservation of individual liberties, which I agree is an affirmative thing, you have to develop something that gives to men in groups, or in the whole nation, some sort of joint aspiration."[54]

It was to some such incipient joint aspiration that Willkie tried to appeal in the latter part of his Independence Day broadcast, in a rare set piece of studied eloquence:

"It is you in the green hills of Vermont doing the chores of a son in Africa; you cutting your oats on the rolling prairies of Iowa; it is you in the dark earth of West Virginia, mining the coal that will put weapons in the hands of fighting men around the world; it is you rolling the tanks off the assembly lines in Michigan; it is you herding cattle on the flat plains of Texas; you riveting plates that will be ships in the yards of Oregon and California; yes, it is you in all this spreading land, rearing and educating the children who will be citizens of tomorrow; it is you who will shape the world."[55]

At the moment, this faith seemed justified. It was popular pressure now that was pushing a reluctant Congress and a strangely passive Administration into an immediate effort to establish some basis for a post-war world organization. (On April 19, the Associated Press reported a poll of the Senate on the question of committing the United States, now, to participation in a post-war "international police force." It found 24 Senators in favor, 32 opposed, and 32 undecided.[56] The Gallup Poll, putting the same question to the public, found 74 per cent in favor, 14 per cent opposed, and 12 per cent undecided.)[57]

In response to this surge of public sentiment, even the Republican Old Guard found it expedient to take some action. On June 1 Chairman Spangler announced that the National Committee had appointed a Republican Post-War Advisory Council of forty-nine party leaders to develop "a realistic peacetime program for American progress."[58] The Council consisted of the twenty-four Republican Governors, six Senators, thirteen Representatives, and six members of the National Committee.[59] Willkie was not included; and to justify this ommission it was somewhat lamely pointed out that Hoover and Landon, the two other former Presidential nominees, had also been omitted. That the Old Guard should have been willing to exclude Hoover, in order to be able to exclude Willkie also, showed their deadly fear of the latter's influence.

For nearly two months the Council remained quiescent. On July 24, however, Spangler announced that it would meet on Mackinac Island on September 6 and 7. Internationalist sentiment was rising at such a rate that the party must make some concession to it or be swept into oblivion.

There would be, however, no concession to Willkie. "The council here assembled," declared Jay G. Haydon of the Detroit *News* as the meeting opened, "was very apparently framed with a deliberate purpose of preventing Willkie from getting even one foot inside the door." Nevertheless, he reported, "the name of Willkie is heard . . . more than that of any other Republican." He explained this seeming paradox by the fact that Willkie possessed "a fanatically loyal following of voters, which the party must hold if it is to win next year's elections. For this reason [the party leaders] are anxious . . . to achieve a formula of words that will not leave Willkie any peg on which to base a critical blast."[60]

With Willkie not present in person, there was a chance for some other leader to hold the spotlight, but none did so. Dewey made a gesture of friendliness toward the internationalists by remarking that "he was not disturbed about United States surrender of any of its sovereignty by joining in an international arrangement for the preservation of peace."[61] But he did not join the group headed by Governor Baldwin of Connecticut who were working for a vigorous and forthright declaration. He apparently agreed with the majority that party unanimity was paramount; and this could be achieved only by an essentially evasive statement—one in which the specific content was reduced to the absolute minimum demanded by public opinion. It called for "responsible participation by the United States in a post-war cooperative organization among sovereign nations to prevent military aggression and to attain permanent peace with organized justice in a free world."[62]

Nobody could be offended by this resounding vote in favor of virtue and against sin. Willkie's comment was that it was "a very distinct step in the right direction";[63] and considering the past record of the party, this was true. The internationalist group at the conference, as they left, professed satisfaction. "They conceded privately, however, that their job of obliterating isolationism as a Republican label had just begun" and admitted that in their fight for "a simpler, more direct and more specific foreign policy statement," "they had given ground under the pressure of greater numbers."[64]

The Mackinac conference, nevertheless, made it safe for Congressional Republicans to follow a mildly internationalist line; and the House of Representatives on September 21, by a vote of 360-29, passed the "Fulbright Resolution," putting itself on record as favoring "the creation of appropriate international machinery with power adequate to establish and maintain a just and lasting peace among the nations of the world, and as favoring the participation of the United States therein, through its constitutional processes."[65]

The Senate still lagged. From causes that were not apparent, most of the older and more influential Senators seemed in no hurry to act, and there was no pressure from the President. In the meantime, however, the Big Three Foreign Ministers met in Moscow, and the communiqué issued at the end of the meeting included a statement on post-war policy (concurred in by China) which recognized "the necessity of establishing at the earliest practicable date a general international organization based on the principle of the sovereign equality of all peace-loving states, and open membership by all such states, large and small, for the maintenance of peace and security."[66]

There was now no excuse for further dawdling by the Senate, and on November 5, after much seemingly pointless wrangling and maneuvering, that body passed a modified form of the so-called "Connally Resolution." It incorporated the statement just quoted from the Foreign Ministers' communiqué; and this was preceded by the recommendation "That the United States, acting through its Constitutional processes, join with free and sovereign nations in the establishment and maintenance of international authority with power to prevent aggression and maintain the peace of the world." The vote was 85-5.[67]

This was a less definite commitment than "B2H2." But if it meant anything, it meant that the Administration was now not merely free but actually obligated to take immediate and definite steps toward setting up a post-war organization. And it was a commitment by the members of both parties in both Houses of Congress which seemed to preclude an isolationist reaction like that which followed World War I. This was what Willkie had been fighting for.

XX

The Fight for the 1944 Nomination: the Lines Are Drawn

1

Presidential politics in America never ceases. The moment the outcome of one election is known, speculation begins about the next, and possible candidates can hardly help beginning to weigh their chances and plan their strategy. Nevertheless, Willkie was certainly sincere in various statements made between the 1940 election and the end of 1942 that he had no political plans. The successive crises in world affairs involved him in activities that left little time for domestic politics, and at the same time made next to impossible any predictions about conditions and issues in 1944.

During 1943, however, the situation began to be clarified. America was on the way to victory in the war and to some kind of international cooperation after the war. Events had vindicated Willkie's stand, the country had accepted his ideas, why should it not accept *him*?

Moreover, the field of possible candidates seemed to be thinning out. Taft had withdrawn in favor of his fellow Ohioan, Governor Bricker, but the Governor seemed to have even less power than the Senator to capture the imagination of the public outside his own state. Stassen was apparently willing to wait; for in May he resigned as Governor of Minnesota and entered the Navy. And Dewey kept repeating that he would not be a candidate, while devoting himself strictly to giving New York an efficient and moderately liberal government.

It was clear that Willkie's chances depended on Dewey's sticking to this line. His sweeping victory in the contest for Governor had proved his vote-getting ability; he was not handicapped by an isolationist record; and though he was disliked by many of the Old Guard, he had not publicly affronted them. There could be hardly a doubt that if he wanted the Republican Presidential nomination in 1944, he could have it.

The Gallup Poll supported this assumption. In June, 1942, it found Willkie leading Dewey as the Republican favorite for the 1944 nomination, 52 per cent to 48 per cent.[1] But in March, 1943, it estimated that 69 per cent of Republican voters were "favorable" to Dewey's candidacy, while only 49 per cent were "favorable" to Willkie's. On the other hand, while only 13 per cent were opposed to Dewey as a candidate, 43 per cent were against Willkie.[2] In June another survey led to the same conclusion. A question as to the voters' preference among all possible candidates gave the following percentages: Dewey, 37; Willkie, 28; MacArthur, 15; Bricker, 10; Stassen, 7.[3] And again Dewey's advantage was greater than appeared at first glance because in a showdown between him and Willkie, the latter would get few votes from the supporters of MacArthur and Bricker. Still another comparison, equally to Willkie's disadvantage, was present in two more reports at the end of July, which showed Willkie losing a presumptive contest with Roosevelt (expected by everybody to be once more the Democratic nominee in 1944) by a margin of 59 per cent to 41 per cent,[4] while Dewey would now get 45 per cent—almost the same as Willkie got in 1940.[5] And finally, there was an ominous note in another Gallup survey a little later indicating that 58 per cent of the public wanted the country, after the war, "to remain pretty much the way it was," while only 28 per cent wanted "many changes and reforms."[6] The former group would obviously not want Willkie.

Dewey, however, gave no sign of being impressed. He took note of the sentiment in his favor only by having his secretary, Paul Lockwood, declare in a letter to party workers on February 26, "He is not and will not become a candidate for any other nomination during his term,"[7] which would not end until 1946. This remained his stated position until he was actually nominated.

He did not, however, silence his lieutenants, and on April 24 New York Secretary of State Thomas J. Curran, in a speech at the National Republican Club, took a slap at Willkie by predicting that the voters would defeat the New Deal in 1944, and that they would "see no advantage in shifting from a Democrat who knows that he is bigger than his party to a Republican who thinks he is bigger than his party."[8] This brought an answering blast from the loyal Rollie Marvin, in the form of a public letter to Ham Fish, who had sent out (under his Congressional frank) 5,000 copies of an article in the Fort Wayne *News-Sentinel* about a survey purporting to show that Willkie was in almost universal disfavor with Indiana Republicans. Correctly characterizing the *News-Sentinel* as "one of the most bitter-end, reactionary, isolationist newspapers in the United States," he noted that "Tom Curran . . . apparently fell for your line . . . indicating he thought the Republican party should nominate somebody smaller than the party, and consequently not Mr. Willkie. Undoubtedly a few will pursue this doctrine to its logical conclusion and search for midgets."[9]

Early in May (as victory in North Africa approached) there were reports of "a sudden upsurge of Dewey talk in many parts of the country," and charges by Dewey "opponents" that "at this moment his forces are more active in the search for delegates, especially in the South, than either Governor Bricker or Mr. Willkie."[10] The generally accepted explanation was that Dewey's original denial of interest in the 1944 nomination, made during his campaign for Governor, had been dictated by the belief that Roosevelt would be the Democratic candidate and that, with the war still going on, he would be unbeatable. This view, however, had been modified by the surprisingly strong Republican trend in the 1942 elections and by the more hopeful military situation. Accordingly, his friends were "working, with his knowledge, to prevent an early foreclosure of the Republican Presidential nomination for 1944 so that Mr. Dewey himself can be 'drafted' if the prospects look good."[11]

If Dewey's tactics provided almost a classic example in Presidential politics of the technique of watchful waiting, Willkie's were almost unique in the directness of his attack, the early date at which it was launched, and his determination to make success contingent on the unequivocal acceptance by the party of a set of specific principles.

The contrast was highlighted in the *Bulletin* of the New York Young Republican Club, printed for distribution to "young Republicans" in the Armed Forces, to which both Dewey and Willkie had been invited to contribute. Dewey promised that "the State government would not forget the sacrifices made by those in service" and also included a speech calling for the post-war return to the states and local communities of the powers assumed during the emergency by the Federal government. But Willkie, disdaining such prudent statements, threw down the gauntlet to the Old Guard: "More and more progressive, farsighted and internationally minded men and women are moving into the places of leadership in our party. These men and women are determined that the last taint of narrow nationalism shall be removed from the party. . . . We will not permit the stragglers, the compromisers or appeasers to retard or destroy the one instrumentality that exists to oppose the present Administration."[12]

2

This was in August, 1943. But if one were to set a starting point for Willkie's campaign for the 1944 nomination, it would perhaps be his ten-day visit to Indiana the preceding February. The occasion was an invitation by the Indiana Women's Republican Club to deliver a Lincoln's Birthday address; and he probably accepted it with the intention of feeling out the sentiment in his native state, which he had carried in 1940, but where most of the "organization" leaders had been alienated—"enraged" was the word used independently by two reporters[13]—during the following year by his support of Roosevelt's foreign policy. He gave no sign, however, of wishing to appease his opponents. He spoke briefly to the Indiana Legislature, where he was introduced by Democratic Governor Schricker and where he urged all-out support of the President in the prosecution of the war; was a guest, with Mrs. Willkie, at a luncheon sponsored by the Republican State Committee, at which they "shook hands with thousands who called to greet them";[14] attended a tea for Russian War Relief; and followed his formal evening address (which was "applauded mildly") with an impromptu speech "which brought the entire audience to its feet, cheering wildly."[15]

That his main address was applauded at all is surprising, for it was nothing less than an attempt to redefine the aims of the Republican party and to destroy the widely accepted stereotype of a Republican as "a socially unconscious, hidebound conservative." There was, of course, nothing new in his attack on "narrow nationalism"; but his audience would hardly be prepared for the vigor with which he supported—and even went beyond—the domestic policies of the New Deal. "There must never again be any question of the right of workers to bargain collectively through representatives of their own choosing, or of the fundamental right of our citizens to be free of racial discrimination. . . .

"And we must recognize that we, through our government, have a duty toward every citizen in this land to protect him or her . . . against the hazards of unemployment, old age, accident or ill health." (In Omaha, at the same time, Landon was attacking "Nazi New Dealers who hope to establish here what Hitler described in his early days as the National Socialist State.")[16]

His hearers must have liked as little his conclusion that these aims could only be accomplished by a program of economic expansion involving, necessarily, international cooperation; especially with the "overwhelming majority" of the earth's two billion people, who had recently "awakened," and who "fervently desire education, political emancipation and the opportunity to raise their standard of living." "This should be a challenge to Republicans."[17]

Willkie knew, of course, even without the lukewarm reception, that this was not the kind of challenge that his audience wished to hear. So at the end—as he had done on previous occasions—he tossed aside his manuscript and launched into an impromptu exhortation. "I call you now to the crusade of 1944 to save America. We are the vital, thinking party of this country. Let's go on the affirmative. Let's do something besides criticize. Let's throw off the lethargy and take the leadership.

"I am honestly convinced that everything we hold priceless rests in the hands of the Republican party between now and the day after election in 1944. Why should we be on the defensive always against a party that is a combination of Northern political machines of the worst type and Southern oligarchies that don't even allow Negroes to vote?"[18]

This *was,* it seemed, what the audience wanted. Yet it was apparently not so much the words as the manner of their delivery that inspired his hearers. "'By golly, that guy has become a Republican since Elwood, and I'm for him,' shouted a G. O. P. leader long opposed to Mr. Willkie."[19]

This reception would have encouraged a person who had far less self-confidence than Willkie. It did not, however, lead him to ignore other means of gaining political support. He wrote to John Cowles on March 25: "Things are developing. One of the things, however, as you have pointed out to me that I have to do is to break down the Congressional resistance but I have a difficult time figuring out how to go about that system[at]ically. When I come down to Washington, I find it so difficult to develop a natural way of doing this. Think it over. We have to do something about it."[20]

But the fact was that there was nothing Willkie could do about the antagonism of Congressional Republicans. He could not descend to professions of friendship that he did not feel, nor would he bargain for support on any other terms than agreement on basic principles. And with a majority of Republicans in Congress, who on the whole represented the most conservative elements in the party, such agreement was simply impossible.

Willkie's next widely publicized political foray was a trip to Michigan and Ohio at the end of May. On May 30 he addressed the General Assembly of the Presbyterian Church, meeting at Detroit, and while this address was of course non-political, his plea for a "One World" philosophy had clear political implications. Afterward he was the guest at a reception arranged by Mrs. Dudley Hay, Michigan's National Committeewoman, where he shook hands with a thousand Republican party leaders and workers. Most of them, wrote a reporter for the Detroit *News,* were "Willkie fans"—but not all. "Many, and they would be best known if named, were not; but in the game of politics, as in others, it is wise for a man to copper his bets."[21]

Outside the hotel, meanwhile, the followers of the native fascist Gerald L. K. Smith, who after Pearl Harbor had appropriated the name "America First," were parading with placards and passing out handbills applying to Willkie such epithets as "New Deal stooge," "Communist bootlicker," "fake, phoney and hypocrite," and "hired spokesman of 'Wall Street, Hollywood and the Whiskey Trust.'" Willkie's response was a message of thanks: "I doubt if anyone was ever so fortunate in the nature of his opposition."[22]

He made a somewhat similar comment a few days later at Oberlin, where he received an honorary LL. D. degree. Asked by newsmen whether he would enter the Ohio primary in 1944, he replied that he had not yet decided whether he would be a candidate, and then added: "Ham Fish is against me, Gerald L. K. Smith is against me, and I understand Landon is against me. If this keeps up, I may be nominated in spite of myself." Then, as an afterthought: "Say, add Colonel McCormick of the Chicago *Tribune* to that list."[23]

This brought a mild reproof from Landon's fellow Kansan, William Allen White. "I am unhappy about the recent Landon crack. He did not deserve to be put in the class with the Rev. G. K. Smith and Gerald Nye and that outfit."[24] To this Willkie replied: "I stand corrected. I offer in extenuation, however, that my friends should not expect me to be a Christian always—the turning of the other cheek gets to be a little tiresome. . . . Landon came east and at every port told newspapermen off the record that my standing in the mid-west was such that I would be hung if I even appeared in that section. . . .

"I know I should let all this float by. I made the remark in Ohio, half jocularly. I admit that in cold print it didn't sound that way. I am resolved to be a good boy. . . . I took your letter much to heart."[25]

This drew a long and friendly answer from White, dwelling on the duty of one in so high a position of leadership to resist such impulsive utterances. And again Willkie acquiesced, though again with reservations. "I naturally accept all the kindly things you have to say, without argument. I also agree with you that I should be very careful in extemporaneous speech and that I do owe a serious duty. I think you will permit me, however, to add to your kindly advice, 'But don't take yourself too seriously.' "[26]

Nevertheless, the responsibility that he had assumed could not be laid down. "You are the only American of either party," White told him, "who can step out and take the moral, intellectual and political leadership of this country. It must be done with dignity, but at the same time without a mealy-mouthed humility. You are quite right in saying, 'Don't take yourself too seriously.' But after all, you are what you are and the situation is what it is . . ."[27]

Many Republicans, however, had a different estimate of what the situation called for. In early June the veteran Republican Representative Leo Allen of Illinois released a statement that he had polled 180 of the 207 House Republicans and found 51 for Dewey, 33 for MacArthur, 32 for Bricker, and only 13 for Willkie; and the point that he obviously wished to make most strongly was not that the result was a victory for Dewey but that it was a defeat for Willkie.[28]

Outside of Congress, however, another observer reported that the Willkie forces were making gains. "Plans and programs of pickers of prospective Republican nominees are confused and slowed down. Wendell L. Willkie and an aggressive and growing organization of 'non-professionals' are blamed for the tossing of the grit into the gears. The Republican National Committee, appointed and anointed harmonizer and arranger in matters of this sort, has been put on the defensive, it appears, and with the fight of its life on its hands."[29] The reluctance of even the extremists to challenge Willkie except with words was shown when a group of Chicagoans urged Colonel McCormick to run against him in the Illinois primary in April, 1944. Willkie delightedly accepted, while Midwest political circles buzzed with anticipation. But the Colonel prudently declined: "Anybody can beat Willkie in Illinois, so I won't have to take the trouble." (Pressed for comment by newsmen, Willkie told them cheerfully, "Just say I had a good laugh.")[30]

It was true that Willkie was getting set for a drive for the 1944 nomination. Among other preparations, he asked Oren Root if it would be possible to get a list of the chairmen of the 1940 Willkie Clubs. Root's affirmative answer, dated July 30, found him in Rushville, "trying to get a little rest and also get caught up on some writing which I have agreed to do. I intend to spend the entire month out here. It will be the first real rest I have had in several years." As a part of this "rest" he had already "had a number of national committeemen out here and we had some good talks. I really think things are moving in good shape."[31]

On the same day that he wrote to Root, Willkie met with leaders of Indiana's Eighth Congressional District. The previous day he had declared in an interview "that he could not again run for the Presidency on any platform except one based on 'liberal, progressive ideas,'"[32] and after this conference he stated the kind of platform that he *would* run on. It was essentially the same that he had presented at Indianapolis in February. As usual, he tried to make his program more palatable by an attack on the Administration—also as usual, however, not for its professed principles but for its frequent abandonment of any principle except expediency.

But he also had a warning, as always, for his own party. It "must completely forsake the tempting notion that it can win by the amalgamation of the dissident groups in America; the ultra-nationalists, the economically selfish . . .; the people who are . . . unwilling to sacrifice the unnecessary luxuries and who refuse to endure in wartime without complaint the restrictions necessary for the common good. Above all, it must repudiate completely the religious and racial bigots." He concluded: "No party was ever presented with such an exciting challenge . . . nor with such an opportunity. . . . As one devoted to the Republican party, I ask to join you in this the most stirring cause of our time."[33]

The last sentence was tactful but unrealistic; the platform was Willkie's and not the party's, and *it* must join *him.* His statement was, in fact, a challenge to the impending Mackinac conference. The party leaders had excluded *him;* now he was daring them to exclude his ideas. But, though some of them must have been angered, they refused his dare; the resolutions adopted by the conference involved a verbal submission to his demands.

Willkie pressed his attack with an article in *Look,* in the issue dated October 5 but summarized in the *Times* of September 21. The editors asked him four questions and printed his answers. The first was, "Will you be available for the Republican nomination for President in 1944?" He answered: "If the Republican party intends to drive heart and soul for liberal objectives, such as I seek to outline below, I shall give it my complete and undeviating service, whether as the convention's nominee or as a worker in the ranks."

To the second question: "What kind of platform would be needed to re-establish the liberal leadership of the Republican party?" he answered that there were "five indispensable planks." The first two were simple and nobody would challenge them, at least in theory: "protection of minorities" and "efficient . . . administration." But the third was not simple, and the clearer Willkie made his meaning, the more fury it was bound to arouse. Heretofore the chief area of conflict between him and the Old Guard had been foreign policy; it had been assumed that in general they could get together on "a rebirth . . .of real enterprise" as an alternative to the New Deal's domestic program. But this assumption, never soundly based, simply vanished when Willkie spelled out what he meant—and what he did not mean—by *"real enterprise."* "Some of the talk we hear about 'free enterprise' or 'private enterprise' is just propaganda on the part of powerful groups who have not practiced real enterprise in a generation, and have no intention of doing so.

"We must distinguish between enterprise and private ownership. A corporation may be privately owned and still be the worst enemy of free enterprise. . . . We must prevent the further misuse of the word 'enterprise' . . . Workers on a production line are also enterprisers—or should have the opportunity to be. But this can only be brought about by making available to them a fair share of the profits derived from their efforts. A free enterprise system does not belong to a few at the top. That is a vested interest system. A free enterprise system belongs to everybody in it." (This was worse than defending a Communist. This was *being* a Communist.)

The fourth and fifth planks, like the first and second, were relatively brief: *"absolute guarantees must be provided by our society against unemployment*—and against want because of old age, injury or incapacity"; and the party must "crystallize its thinking on . . . an American policy toward conquered and liberated peoples and *toward the nations of the future."* (International commitments were taken for granted; the question was, "What kind?")

The third question was, "It is contended that, while the Republicans can surely improve our domestic affairs, the New Deal is most adept in the field of foreign relations. Is this true?" "The answer is no. . . . The New Deal foreign policy did not face the Hitler facts. . . . Defeatists will say that nothing could have been done; apologists will contend that domestic opposition, much of it Republican, made a constructive course impossible. Still, the stakes were worth a major effort; and such an effort was never made."

The fourth question was, "Can the Republican party win the election in 1944 and, if so, what should be its first step?" In Willkie's answer lies the key to the course he followed during the next six months. The Republican party, he declared, "like any human institution that wields power for long . . . became corrupted by vested interests within its own ranks and by reactionary forces. . . . It ceased to look ahead and plan for the interests of ordinary Americans. And so the people . . . lost confidence in the Republican party—and have never quite regained it. . . . That is why I say the *first* step toward victory in 1944 must be a victory of the liberal forces within the Republican party." And this was why he could never heed the well meant advice of friends to confine his attacks to the Democrats. Unless he could defeat the Old Guard first, the nomination would be worthless.

A final question was asked by Willkie himself: "What is the most important question before the American people today?" His answer was, "The war." "We are not heroes back here, but we have tremendous obligations to meet. It is a duty of our leadership—which has not been fulfilled—to see that no one uses the war as an instrument of profit . . ." And beyond this, "we must look ahead and make our victory mean something"; "free men, to stay free, must stand together."[34]

So here was the line on which Willkie was prepared to fight for the 1944 nomination. And this time there would be no shift of position.

3

There had already been several skirmishes between Willkie and his opponents; but the first full-scale engagement, in which the sound of the bombardment echoed from coast to coast, was the Battle of St. Louis on October 15. It was initiated by the Republican organization in Missouri, under the command of Edgar Monsanto Queeny, multimillionaire boss of the Monsanto Chemical Company. As a big business man with his eye on the main chance, he had chosen to do business with TVA rather than the Tennessee Electric Power Company. But when principles did not conflict with profits, he was a vehement opponent of the New Deal—both its domestic policy and its foreign policy. In 1940, believing that Willkie was the man who could end it, he had worked unstintingly for his nomination and election, but his disillusionment had been swift and complete—though it is evident that he never lost a grudging admiration for Willkie's courage. The two had met in March, 1943, when Willkie made a trip to Missouri following his Indiana visit, and Queeny remarked later: "I don't know of anyone who could have handled himself better in a rough and tumble debate than Wendell did with the organization Saturday night."[35] But he himself was not converted.

Willkie likewise refused to give ground. "If Ed does not believe in my political principles there is no reason in the world why he should support me and by the same token, I cannot change my political principles to satisfy him or any other man."[36]

This truce continued until September 12, when the press carried a letter signed by "Missouri State and national party officers"[37] and by "the entire Missouri delegation to the 1940 Republican national convention"[38] demanding that Willkie answer nine questions. Although the signers assured him, "We are not unfriendly," the questions speak for themselves.

"1. Do you believe that the United States should become a member of a world supra-national state? Would it place the United States armed forces under control of the world state?

2. If you favor a world state, what would you do about nations that refuse to come in? Would you force them in by military means?

3. Do you believe in absolute freedom of international trade without restrictions to protect the American standard of living?

4. Do you believe a world monetary system should be established, and if so, what relation would it have to the American dollar?

5. Do you believe in the free and unrestricted movement of peoples? If so, how do you propose to prevent peoples from Asia from overrunning the United States?

6. Do you believe that it is desirable to permit flooding our country with alien individuals and alien ideas?

7. In what other respects do you envision the political and economic organization of 'One World'?

8. Newspapers report you to have said that if the Republicans adopt a liberal platform they can win. What do you mean by a liberal platform? Be specific, please.

9. If you are not the Presidential nominee of the Republican party in 1944, will you actively support the nominee chosen by the convention?"[39]

Willkie's first response was temperate. "Most of the questions bear no relation to reality, but I'll be glad to sit down with Chairman Dalton and his group and discuss them."[40] This, however, was not what the questioners wanted. They wanted, instead, to put him on the spot publicly with a list of loaded questions. But if they thought they could thus trap or intimidate him, they still did not know the man they were dealing with. At the end of September Willkie announced that he would come to St. Louis on October 15 and answer the questions in a public speech.

The Republican State Committee promptly demonstrated its belief in "enterprise" of a sort by selling box seats for the speech at $50 apiece to pay off its $10,000 deficit—until Willkie put a stop to it by telegraphing, "As I am anxious that all citizens who wish to attend may do so without charge of any kind, I shall be glad personally to pay the cost of renting a hall, as I previously suggested, and I shall appreciate your refunding any payments already collected."[41] This was done, somewhat grudgingly. (The *Post-Dispatch* editorialized: "The Stop Willkie movement has got off to a magnificent fizzle.")[42]

On his arrival, Willkie commented good-humoredly to reporters that he had been planning to make a speech in the Middle West, anyway, and "this little controversy about the questionnaire gave me so much advertising I decided to make the speech in St. Louis. . . . I couldn't pay for all that advertising if I had to buy it at so much a line, and I am very grateful for it."[43]

Despite the advertising, Willkie's main speech was less well attended than he had hoped. Preparations had been made for an overflow crowd, which did not show up. "He drew something under 3,500 people, while a wrestling match next door drew more than 9,000."[44] It was broadcast, however, over NBC; but this arrangement, some hearers felt, had an unfortunate result, in that the speaker raced through his address, passing quickly from one point to the next and checking applause in an effort to finish in the allotted half hour—which, after all, he failed to do, so that the last part of his speech was cut off the air. Still, when he had finished, there was something like the old enthusiasm. "The crowd refused to leave the auditorium and began to cheer: 'We want Willkie.' There were also cries of 'You're the next President' and 'Speak some more.' Mr. Willkie, after nearly ten minutes of this ovation, climbed on a chair and signaled for quiet.

" 'These things I have said [,] I believe in as much as life itself and for these things I intend to fight to the very end.' "[45]

In the speech itself he quickly dismissed the questionnaire. "I assume that you want me to discuss these problems not in the manner of a schoolboy answering questions, but with the calm reason you are entitled to expect from a man whom the party has signally honored." Instead, he stated (as he had done many times before, most recently in *Look*) his views on the country's social and economic problems; ending, again, on the theme of war and peace. Some of the topics under the last heading were familiar, too: the necessity of avoiding "the old game of power politics"; of working "exclusively with the forces that are neither Nazi-tainted nor Fascist-stained" (the Allies had followed up the Darlan Deal with another, after Mussolini's overthrow in Italy, whereby the government of the liberated part of that country was placed in the hands of Marshal Badoglio, the former commander of Mussolini's armies); and of persuading Britain, Russia, and China to join with the United States in a "Declaration of Intention"—too definite ever to be repudiated—to make the United Nations a permanent organization.

And now he showed what he really thought of the resolution adopted at the Mackinac Conference, by placing beside it the resolution approved by the Republican convention in 1920, which was repudiated without audible protest immediately after Harding's election. The similarity was startling and ominous, and Willkie asserted: "The American people have the example fully in mind. . . . They will never elect as President a candidate who hedges or qualifies or whose record is ambiguous or one concerning whose position they have the slightest doubt on this basic issue of our day. . . . If the party selects from its many able men, as its candidate for President in 1944, a man whose record leaves no doubt that he is qualified for the leadership of such a cause, I shall, of course, support him.

"And it is unthinkable that the party will select any other kind."[46]

But how many Republicans, among those widely enough known to be considered for the nomination, had such a record?

Some of those who listened to this earnest but restrained discussion had, earlier in the day, seen the speaker in a different mood. At a luncheon arranged for him by Robert L. Lund, a former president of the National Association of Manufacturers, and attended by local business men and party leaders, Willkie told his hearers what he thought of the Old Guard mentality. Reporters were excluded, but through the closed doors they could hear "a terrible row" within, and later they noted the tight lips and "livid faces" of some of the departing guests. Willkie, however, emerged exuberant, and called out to the waiting newsmen, "Come on up to the room, boys, and I'll tell you what happened."[47]

What had happened, according to some accounts, was that Queeny, in introducing the guest, had continued his apparent attempt to prod Willkie into an explosion. "Our guest today is America's leading ingrate. In 1940, I raised two hundred thousand dollars and never got a thank you. Several times I have asked for an interview and have never even gotten a reply."[48] Whether or not these were Queeny's exact words, he achieved his purpose. There is remarkable agreement on Willkie's answer. "I don't know whether you're going to support me or not," he told the men who controlled the state's political machinery, "and I don't give a damn. You're a bunch of political liabilities, anyway." He added that "the days . . . when they could walk through their plants and cause their employes to tremble in their presence for fear of losing their jobs—when they could fire a man because they didn't like the color of his necktie—were gone forever and good riddance."[49] He went on to declare that "he was not accountable to them for what he thought, or to anybody else, except the people." In fact, "much of Willkie's discourse was devoted to the attempt to convince his hearers that the people, all over the world, had come to a new appreciation of their powers and had new demands to make of their governments. And he said flatly that when the interest of the people conflicted with the interest of business, the people must prevail."[50]

Yet these heresies, apparently, offended only the irreconcilables. On those less hardened, the Willkie magic still worked. Writers for two different newspapers described many of his hearers as "in a dazed condition" when they left the meeting.[51] "'If you hadn't heard him say it,' said one man, with the emphasis on the last three words, 'you would think it was dynamite—political suicide.'"[52]

Two other meetings found him discussing the Schneiderman case with "a group of Republican lawyers" who were members of the John Marshall Club, and making an impassioned defense of civil liberties; and, to "members of Republican women's organizations," denying "rumors" "that he was basically opposed to party organization,"[53] and warning them against seeking votes through "little complaints" and "crabbing" at the Administration.[54]

After a day and a half Willkie departed, leaving "Missouri politics in a stew and ferment."[55] He himself was confident that "a very large number . . . of the men and women active in the Republican organization in Missouri will go along with me" and "the rank and file . . . are overwhelmingly for me."[56] "Even Queeny admitted grudgingly that 'Willkie had done himself a lot of good here'"—adding a sarcastic comment on the main speech: "The Federal Unionists who want to replace American independence with the United States of the World should be especially satisfied . . ." Willkie received the remark with cheerful derision. "Just say Mr. Willkie laughed," he told reporters who sought a formal comment as he was leaving. And when they tried to bait him with a story of Hoover's having had a hand in the questionnaire ("Willkie's aides . . . have long felt," one reporter wrote, "that much of the opposition to their man has been inspired by Hoover"),[57] he simply answered, suiting the action to the words, "Just say he laughed harder."[58]

As Willkie passed through the station to his train, "soldiers and civilians addressed [him] by name, and groups gathered around him when he paused."[59] Clearly, to countless ordinary Americans he was still a hero.

One place where Willkie knew he was *not* a hero was the Republican side of the United States House of Representatives. Nevertheless, he went to Washington three days later to address a meeting of the "78 Club," composed of first-year Republican Representatives, and their guests. And again he carried the fight to his opponents, especially in the question period following the formal address. This address he himself described as "a scholarly analysis of the terms of service of men in power throughout history," leading to the conclusion that sixteen years was too long and that this should be made the main issue in the 1944 campaign. At the same time, "he deplored political sniping and mud-slinging against Mrs. Franklin D. Roosevelt [he had said the same thing to a San Francisco audience of Republicans a week earlier, adding, "Mrs. Roosevelt is one of the most intelligent women in America"],[60] the Office of Price Administration [on January 2, 1942 he had written the head of that agency, Leon Henderson: "I have an increasing respect for the job you are doing and just wanted to tell you so"],[61] the War Food Administration and other agencies."[62]

Then the fireworks started, with an attempt by Representative Miller of Missouri (a close ally of Queeny) to get specific answers to some of the items on the questionnaire. Willkie retorted that "he had been warned that he was to be put on the spot,"[63] asserted "that at this moment he had enough strength to win the nomination" if he wanted it,[64] treated the particular questions as their dishonesty deserved, and answered the last of them (Would he support the nominee if he failed to be nominated himself?): "I will, but I must reserve the right to name exceptions. Three I will name right now. I will not support Ham Fish, John L. Lewis, or Colonel McCormick."[65] At the end of three hours, Willkie emerged "with his hair tousled and his necktie out of place," to comment that he had had "a wonderful, enjoyable evening."[66] It was "the consensus of those who heard him that he had neither gained nor lost converts."[67]

4

Two days later, however, Willkie offered evidence of party loyalty by a speech in support of Joe R. Hanley, the Republican candidate, handpicked by Dewey, in a special election to choose a Lieutenant Governor of New York. A Hanley victory would of course be a Dewey victory, but there was no positive objection to the candidate, and so Willkie spoke for him (in Rollie Marvin's home city of Syracuse, to a crowd of 3,000) without reservation; praising his record in the State Senate, where he had been majority leader, as indicative of "intelligent respect for the needs of his fellow citizens." "Recently," he continued, "the people of this State elected a young and aggressive Republican governor. In the few months since his inauguration Governor Dewey has given ample proof of the sound, clean and able administration of New York's affairs that the people of this State may expect from him during the coming years. . . . Let us elect a Lieutenant Governor who will work with him rather than against him."[68]

Dewey, of course, played his part—though he would have noted the implication of the phrase "during the coming years." He telegraphed Willkie: "Have just heard your fine speech for Joe Hanley. It was great. Many thanks." To this Willkie replied: "Many thanks for your gracious wire. Joe Hanley, Rollie Marvin and I join in sending our kindest regards and respects."[69]

Hanley won by 345,000 votes, and a subhead in the *Times* read "Dewey to the Fore."[70] And elsewhere across the country similar victories suggested that the Republican resurgence of 1942 was continuing. But Dewey was still sticking to his line: "I am not and shall not become a candidate for the

Republican nomination in 1944. Nothing has happened to change anything I've said on the subject."[71] And a few days later he declined an invitation to enter the California primary.[72] At the same time Governor Warren of California stated unequivocally that he was "not a candidate for either position on the Republican ticket in 1944."[73] More and more, it seemed, the field was being left to Willkie. Furthermore, the Gallup Poll for October showed, for the first time in many months, a gain in favor among Republican voters; Willkie was now preferred by 29 per cent against 32 per cent for Dewey. (The corresponding figures in September had been 28 and 35.)[74]

This favorable situation was one that Willkie strove tirelessly to exploit. The St. Louis encounter had been preceded by a visit of several days in California, where he held a number of off-the-record conferences with Republican groups, as well as a meeting with West Coast labor leaders representing the AFL, the CIO and the Railway Brotherhoods, and had an hour-long talk with Governor Warren in Sacramento. Before flying East he also stopped in Reno, where he addressed "a meeting of the Council of State Governments, representing eleven Western States," spoke at a rally to sell war bonds, and met with local Republican leaders. (Many other Republicans were disappointed that his visit was "not properly published in advance" so that they could have given him a "real Nevada welcome.")[75]

On November 11 Willkie began a four-day visit to Wisconsin, where again (at least once) he challenged the party's conservatives by telling Milwaukee Republicans, "The Republican party is not going to become the anti-labor party and I'm going to see to it that it doesn't." And he added, "The Republican party must take stock and make itself worthy of winning in 1944."[76] On his next political outing, however—a two-week swing through Louisiana, Texas, Colorado and Wyoming, which began on November 18—he stayed out of the headlines, devoting most of his time to private conferences with local party leaders. (More than a month earlier, Turner Catledge had written: "He contends that even now he knows more of the down-to-the-precinct Republican leaders than any other man in the party, and that when convention time rolls around he will know twice as many as anybody else.")[77]

In the meantime, his enemies were not idle. On November 5 the *Times* reported that John Hamilton was on a stop-Willkie trip to the Pacific Coast. "Mr. Hamilton, who has already had conferences with Republicans in Illinois, Wisconsin, Minnesota, and North and South Dakota, is known to have arranged similar conferences in Washington, Oregon, California, New Mexico, Missouri and Indiana before his return . . ."[78] His procedure in each state was first to tell Republican leaders that Willkie was unpopular everywhere else and then to persuade them, if possible, to set up a favorite son candidate to block Willkie's bid for the state's votes at the convention.

Time and *Life* quickly picked up the story, with the latter declaring that Hamilton's "immediate backers" were Pew and Queeny.[79]

Willkie in Wisconsin commented: "I have been told that Hamilton and Pew are seeking to create enough favorite son candidates to prevent anyone else from securing a majority of the delegates before the convention . . . so that a dark horse could be pulled out of the hat," and recalled the "disastrous consequences" of the 1920 nomination of Harding through similar procedures.[80] This drew from Landon the question: "Who is Wendell Willkie to tell the Republican party where to head in?"[81] And shortly thereafter the 1936 candidate set out for the East Coast, to do there (apparently) what Hamilton was doing in the West. From New York on December 6 he predicted, on the basis of talks with "Republican party leaders" that Dewey would be nominated at the 1944 convention not later than the second ballot, and that Willkie was "likely to slip almost entirely out of the running" before the convention began.[82] Willkie's retort was: "If Governor Landon's recent speeches . . . represent the thinking of the Republican party, then certainly someone other than myself should lead the party in 1944."[83]

Dewey's response, when reporters told him of Landon's prediction, was "Thank you" and "No comment." Nor did he have anything to say about his own meeting with Landon.[84] When the latter met with Hoover on the following day, however, both issued statements: the ex-President urging caution in regard to foreign policy commitments, the ex-Governor (still in a prophetic mood) anticipating a sweeping Republican victory in 1944.[85] This was a regular line of Willkie's opponents. The implied question was, "If any Republican can win, why not pick one that is 'safe'?" So it was no surprise the next day when Hamilton, back from his six-weeks mission of setting up roadblocks in front of Willkie, chimed in with "I never saw Republicans so hopeful and enthusiastic as they are today." Under such circumstances it had been his duty (he implied) "to tell the leaders that any attempt to stampede the 1944 convention eight months in advance was bad politics." On the other hand, there was (he again implied) really no danger; Willkie was "not nearly as strong as has been represented."[86]

It is hard to say how deeply and widely based, at this date, the stop-Willkie movement was. Did Hamilton find anti-Willkie sentiment, did he create it, or did he invent it? Mainly, perhaps, he found it. William L. White gave him too much credit when he wrote, "Of course the 'stop Willkie' movement is largely Joe Pew's money and John Hamilton's mouth, both of which are relatively inexhaustible."[87] The Gallup Poll showed Willkie steadily losing strength after the November elections had revealed an unmistakable Republican trend. This trend not only worked against him in general, as noted above, but it strengthened Dewey—both directly and by making many persons think that he could now be persuaded to run.

It is doubtful that Hamilton's personal influence counted for much. But what he could and did do was to strengthen and bring together the different anti-Willkie attitudes—the outright antipathy of the Old Guard, the uneasiness of the temperamental conformists, the notion of the opportunists that he could now be dispensed with safely—and direct them toward a definite goal, that of keeping convention delegates uncommitted to Willkie.

There is evidence that in his stop-Willkie activities Hamilton had the hearty if unobtrusive cooperation of Harrison Spangler. On December 21, Jack Steele of the *Herald Tribune* wrote to his editor, Geoffrey Parsons: "Spangler and the Republican headquarters force are continuing to work night and day against Willkie and are doing him a lot of harm. I'm afraid he fails to appreciate the importance of the National Committee and the line-up of politicians against his nomination."[88]

Angered by the tactics of Willkie's opponents, some of his friends struck back. Governor William H. Wills of Vermont in a radio broadcast on January 8, 1944 flayed "the four-year locusts of Republican politics." These persons "had nothing constructive to say. They agreed on no candidate. They simply agreed in their hatred of the outstanding Republican of our time—Wendell Willkie." And he declared that should Willkie become "the victim of smart political manipulation in a stop-Willkie drive, with a handful of bosses dominating the Republican convention in 1944 as they did in 1920, I fear for our survival."[89]

Vermont, however, had few delegates; and the speech by Wills gave Hamilton an excuse for an answering blast against Willkie in which venom and self-righteousness vied with each other for the upper hand. He accused Willkie's managers of bringing "undue pressure on party leaders in every section of the country to pledge themselves to his cause . . . The intensity of this propaganda is such that it is called the 'Willkie blitz.' It is a deliberate attempt to foreclose the Republican Presidential nomination many months before the National Convention even assembles, to the exclusion of every other possible choice. Should such a plan succeed, it would make a farce out of our American way of selecting Presidential candidates."[90]

This, of course, was claptrap. There are no open or closed seasons in American Presidential politics. It is entirely ethical for any candidate to start his campaign at any time, and to make any claims that he wishes about the strength of his support. And it is impossible to "foreclose" the nomination before the delegates are chosen—a process that is not complete until a month or so before the convention. It was Hamilton himself who was working to frustrate the popular will—to postpone the decision, to set up favorite sons, to lay the groundwork for deals in smoke-filled rooms.

It may be argued that, politics being what they are, the activities of Willkie's opponents were as legitimate as his own. But it is fair to point out that Willkie was acting openly, that he was spending his own money, that he was fighting for principles and not against persons, and that while he might publicly express unflattering opinions of his opponents, he did not tell lies about them behind their backs. (Willkie wrote to Henry Luce in 1944: "I shall not believe the stories about you. I ask of you that you do not believe those circulated about me. For instance, Joe Pew and John Hamilton have said to a great many responsible people of late, including Congressman Chris Herter of Massachusetts, in apparent sympathy, that 'it's too bad Wendell is drinking himself to death.' As you know, I like a drink—I never take more than two—that is in one sitting."[91]—He was apparently forgetting the Kremlin banquet!)

The truth is that Willkie's integrity in his last years was so unbending as to raise a real question as to whether it did not unfit him for a career in politics. To the instances already given of his hatred of every kind of political deal, one more may be added. On one of his Western trips during this period he stayed for a day or two at the same hotel as Walter White, who tells the story. "That evening Wendell returned to his hotel in a more dejected spirit than I had ever seen him," to tell of a "brazen proposal" that he had received from the favorite son Governor of the state (which had "a sizable block of electoral votes"): that if Willkie "would promise him a certain post in the cabinet if elected," he would deliver to Willkie the state's votes in the convention.[92]

"'What did you tell him?' I asked.

"'I told him to go to hell,' Wendell replied, his anger mounting again. 'I have never made a deal yet and I'll be God-damned if I'll make one now, even to be President of the United States.'"[93]

Practical persons—and not only those who are politicians—will say that a man does not gain the Presidency or other high elective office by insulting influential persons when they propose routine political arrangements, and that he thereby deprives himself of the chance that he would have, if elected, to achieve by specific action a less imperfect social order. This is true. But when, by making the necessary compromises, a generally right-minded person *does* get elected, then those compromises will have been fewer and less important, and his chance of achievement will be greater, because there have been men like Wendell Willkie, who, when offered power at the price of principle, responded simply: "Go to hell!"

5

This was the man who was subjected to the most virulent hate campaign ever directed from within a major party toward a man who had been that party's Presidential nominee. And the question here is not of editorial attacks and slanted news stories in papers owned by right-wing Republicans. Such abuse is part of the game of politics and can be shrugged off as a minor annoyance (though in the long run it is doubtless not without effect). The poison somehow evaporates in the open air. But there is a kind of political underworld which manufactures and distributes malicious lies, which are hard to counteract because the exact origin and the exact audience are often unknown.

One document of this kind, already mentioned, is *One Man—Wendell Willkie,* a colossal smear purportedly written by C. Nelson Sparks (although the real sponsors were and remain unknown) and published at the beginning of December, 1943, in the midst of Willkie's pre-primary campaign for the 1944 nomination. Although quickly and irrefutably exposed as fraudulent in most if not all its charges,[94] it undoubtedly helped to undermine Willkie's standing. Even a Willkie admirer, confronted by it without warning, might well have been staggered by the wealth of circumstantial detail with which the writer bolstered his sensational assertions. To Willkie's enemies, eager to believe the worst and to broadcast any story that might discredit him whether they believed it or not, the appearance of the book can hardly have seemed less than providential; and afterward they were naturally in no hurry to confess that they had been taken in. (When Marquis Childs asked Ernest Weir, Republican Finance Chairman in 1940, about a story that he had helped distribute the book, Weir replied that he "hadn't sent many—only 20-50.")[95]

How much unpublished hate-Willkie literature was circulated during these months, one can only guess; but three items which came to William Evjue, crusading editor of the Madison, Wisconsin, *Capitol Times,* and a staunch Willkie supporter, suggest that the quantity was considerable.[96]

One item is a reproduction of that part of Representative Shafer's attack in the House of Representatives, in which Willkie is condemned as "the leader who did not lead." It is mimeographed on the letterhead of the "Wisconsin Office" of a New York insurance company and dated October 26, 1943; it begins "Dear Republican Leader" and is signed "Lester Bradshaw."

The second item is a printed postcard, unsigned, containing a denunciatory editorial from the LeMars, Iowa, *Globe-Post,* of which the tenor can be inferred from the concluding warning: "IF THE G.O.P. INSISTS ON WILTING WITH WILLKIE AGAIN, THIS TIME THEY CAN WILT ALONE!" It is postmarked "LeMars, Iowa, Feb. 5, 1944"—just after Willkie had announced that he would enter the Wisconsin primary.

The third item is dated "February 7, 1944," and is the longest and bitterest. It resembles *One Man—Wendell Willkie* in the scope and tone of its indictment, though it lacks the fictitious supporting evidence; and also in its dubious antecedents, though the purported author is named. It is an elegantly printed folder of some 3,000 words, entitled "OPEN LETTER to Honorable Wendell Willkie by Republican County Chairman." It is signed with the improbable name "Sherman Grindstaff," which nevertheless belonged to a real person, a delegate to the 1940 convention from Carter County, Tennessee. Some of the charges are these: "you were blitzed through the convention, Hitler style, by huge sums of money furnished by the international bankers"; "during those hard New Deal years" when real Republicans were trying to prevent the New Deal from breaking down "the principles that have made America great," "you were working against us on their side" (though the alleged writer came from Tennessee, he was apparently not familiar with the history of the Tennessee Valley Authority); "you did thrill the mothers of the country by your emphatic statement that if you were elected you would see to it that their sons would not be sent into a foreign war. . . . You admitted after the campaign . . . that you were merely indulging in campaign oratory. Shame! Shame!" "Your hired political travelers are going about the country falsely claiming the support of delegations from many states." In addition, Willkie is attacked for saying "mean things" about Landon, Hoover and Dewey; for urging a second front; for wanting to "use" the Republican party for his own ends; for being absent through most of the 1942 election period and then making speeches that "helped the enemy more than they did our party"; and for writing *One World* with the "paramount objective" of convincing the world that he was "an indispensable expert in the field of thaumaturgy."

Is this, one wonders, really the work of a Tennessee Republican who does not know much about the facts but knows what he does not like in politics? Or is it the work of a professional writer who is feigning naivete? And who paid, one wonders also, for the printing and distribution?

A final instance of hate-Willkie literature, which touches the absolute limit of moral squalor, appeared in the syndicated column of Dr. George W. Crane on February 22, 1944. This column, which probably had millions of readers, presented popular applications of what purported to be valid principles of psychology. This particular column was headed "Case Records of a Psychologist" and began: "Geometry says that with two points you can draw a straight line. Psychology states that by similarly taking a point in a boy's childhood and then connecting it with one from his manhood, you can usually extend a line on which his character may be charted." This statement was illustrated by "Case C-292," a "true drama" beginning with "Alex W." ("now . . . a famous American newspaperman"), who as a boy of ten, in 1904, lived near Elwood, Indiana, to which he was taken by his grandfather on the occasion of a Civil War veterans' reunion. Here he met "a pretty boy, aged 12" with "a shiny new bicycle" who offered to show him the town, took him to a drug store, ordered two sodas, told the clerk (after the sodas had been consumed) that Alex was paying for them, and then, after promising that next time he would treat Alex, remembered an errand and disappeared—permanently, despite a pledge that "he would be right back." The second "moral point" was located in a Senate committee hearing "after the presidential campaign of 1940. Pretty Boy is being questioned about some of his statements in that campaign. He blandly disclaims any intention of living up to those solemnly uttered promises, glibly stating that they were just campaign talk."[97]

This is the old lie based on Willkie's "campaign oratory" remark, with a new lie added. (Nobody could ever conceivably have called him a "pretty boy," and nobody remembers his having had "a shiny new bicycle" at the age of twelve.) This use of defamation disguised as science typifies the true character of those Republicans who were determined to destroy him.

How effective such measures were is a matter of conjecture. But what *was* effective in stopping Willkie was the widespread adoption of Hamilton's plan—though not necessarily at his suggestion—of "foreclosing" the nomination against Willkie by setting up favorite son candidates in key states. First, there was New York. Though Dewey was still denying that he was a candidate, he would have a solid grip, this time, on the entire delegation, and there was no reason to think that he would allow any part of it to stray into the Willkie camp. Second, there was Ohio, where on November 16 Governor Bricker formally announced his candidacy. This of course was no surprise; but it meant that here was another big state that Willkie could not enter. (He wanted to make the fight, anyway; but his friends "advised [him] very strongly"—and no doubt wisely—not to do so.)[98] Next, there was Illinois, where Colonel McCormick would not run but where the popular Representative Everett Dirksen announced his candidacy in early December, though nobody imagined that he would be nominated.[99] A fourth populous state where Willkie would have liked to enter the primary was Pennsylvania,[100] but in mid-February Governor Edward Martin announced that he would insist on an uninstructed delegation.[101]

The hardest blow, however, came from California, and, ironically, from a man whose views on both foreign and domestic issues seemed to be nearly identical with Willkie's. This was Governor Earl Warren, who on January 9 announced that he would enter the California primary. A statement addressed to his supporters read: "Since you who are carrying the responsibilities for Republican activities in this State, with knowledge that I do not seek the nomination for either the Presidency or the Vice Presidency, believe that I can best serve in this manner, I consider it my duty to do so."[102] This statement is entirely inadequate as an explanation of Warren's action, and it was natural that two of Willkie's lieutenants, Bartley Crum and Bruce Johnstone, should question his motives. On January 18 Johnstone wired an urgent plea that he give up his efforts to reach an agreement with Warren and enter the primary against him. "I am convinced and Bart concurs that we cannot afford longer delay in effort to secure compromise."[103] But Willkie's answering telegram to Crum indicates that he had decided against such a course. "Bart, you know my full mind. Won't you please talk to Johnstone and Herb Hanley?"[104]

Six days later Willkie made his decision public. "Many Californians have urged me to run in the California Presidential primary. They expressed the opinion that if I did I would win, while if I did not, the California delegation, with Governor Warren as its nominal candidate, would, in fact, be a part of the stop-Willkie movement.

"In the last few days I have discussed the situation fully by telephone with Governor Warren. He assures me that he is not and will not become a candidate for the Presidential nomination and that he has no agreement, arrangement or understanding with any candidate or potential candidate, that he is not and will not become associated with any stop-Willkie movement, that he is solely desirous of permitting the Republicans of California under his leadership to select delegates of their own choosing, reflective of the sentiments of their respective districts.

"I believe Governor Warren. In view of his assurances I have decided not to enter the California preference primary.

"I am particularly grateful to my California supporters and advisers who had urged that I enter the primary but who now join me in this decision while continuing to work in my behalf."[105]

This makes Warren's position still more mystifying. By preventing Willkie from entering the California primary, which was the one above all others that he wished to enter and in which he was most confident of making an impressive showing, Warren was, whether he admitted it or not, lending powerful support to the stop-Willkie movement. But why he chose to do so remains unclear.[106]

So Willkie was excluded from the five states having the largest number of convention delegates—322 out of a total of 1057—although he certainly had strong popular support in California, New York and Pennsylvania. If to these states were added Minnesota, whose 25 votes were committed to Stassen, and the Solid South (with 155 delegates), where his stand on equal rights for Negroes must have left him with little support, despite his visits to Louisiana and Texas, he would have nearly half the delegates against him from the start.

What made his position still more precarious was that the polls had shown a steady decline in strength since October. At the end of January the Gallup Poll credited him with the support of only 23 per cent of Republican voters, against 42 per cent for Dewey.[107] Only a spectacular demonstration of popular strength, proving that the polls were wrong and giving him a chance to win over some of the delegates from the "big five" states, would put him back in the running.

This was the background of the Wisconsin primary.

XXI

The Wisconsin Primary

1

The election year opened with a meeting of the Republican National Committee in Chicago on January 10, from which Willkie was able to derive at least some slight encouragement. A poll of the members as to their personal preference among the candidates showed that of the 59 willing to answer, 21 were for Willkie and 21 for Dewey.[1] And the Dewey sentiment among the Committee members only resulted in another Dewey denial that he wanted the nomination. When New York Committeeman Sprague spoke of his "impression" that Dewey would accept, and reporters asked the Governor if this meant that he had changed his mind, he replied, "Not in the slightest." It was true that he dodged the next query: "Are you willing or ready to use General Sherman's remark that 'if nominated I will not run, and if elected I will not serve'?" The answer was: "I am wholly and exclusively occupied with the administration of the affairs of the State of New York." But, after all, there has been only one Sherman. Finally, asked if he would accept a "draft," he commented: "I haven't had to meet that problem yet," and added after a brief pause: "I don't expect to have to meet it."[2]

Another event at this time, however, left Willkie profoundly depressed. In the *New York Times Magazine* of January 2 he had published an article entitled "Don't Stir Distrust of Russia," which was a blunt warning to politicians of both parties who might seek votes by such a method. The issue was "what Russia intends to do about the political integrity of the small states around her borders—Finland, Poland, the Baltic and the Balkan states." The view of many Republicans, he charged, was that "Stalin . . . will make ruthless territorial demands on the smaller states, and these demands will produce a violent anti-Russian reaction among those Americans who emigrated, or whose forebears emigrated, from those states"; and that this situation "will inevitably react against Mr. Roosevelt to the advantage of the Republican party.

"This kind of approach seems to me dangerously irresponsible and almost totally destructive."

On the other hand, the Administration's "signal failure to assume leadership of the new forces in the world" had left it with no policy at all. "With every mile the Red Army advances toward the Polish frontier, the United Nations are driven nearer a crisis. With every passing day the issues leading to actual or potential civil war in Greece, in Yugoslavia and in other Balkan states press in upon us. Are we to repeat in these regions the political errors of North Africa, of Sicily and of Italy? . . .

"On the other hand, do those who engage in domestic political manipulation of such delicate questions for their own purposes, who talk so freely of forcing Stalin to recognize the complete integrity of Poland and the Baltic states—do such pretended friends of the smaller nations have any method to offer by which 'to force Stalin'?" The decisive factor was "Russia's attitude"; and "it would be quite natural for [Stalin] in the face of such a lack of desire to co-operate on our part, to take whatever measures might seem necessary to establish Russian national security on a unilateral basis."

"Our principal objective," therefore, "must now be to persuade Russia to accept and give the guarantees of a general organization, in which we and she are both members, rather than to seek her own protection by political and military control over adjoining territories." And in lieu of Administration leadership, Willkie urged that public opinion "assert itself in favor of a new, rational, friendly, *common sense* attitude toward probably the most powerful ally that we have ever had."[3]

This analysis went to the heart of the matter. Almost alone among American political leaders Willkie was trying to talk sense to the American people on the most crucial issue that faced them. And of course he was prepared for criticism and abuse from extremists among his countrymen. But he was not prepared for the furious diatribe that the article provoked from *Pravda*. After angrily asserting that "with respect to Poland and Finland . . . the Soviet Union will be able to get an agreement with them itself and does not need the help of Mr. Willkie," the writer heaped invective on Willkie personally; labeling him, among other things, "an obedient speaking trumpet . . . reproducing the suspicious cries of those reactionary groups which are afraid of the victorious movement forward of the Red Army and the Allied Armies."[4]

This masterpiece of malice and perversion not only hurt Willkie personally, coming from the government of a people for whom he felt friendship and admiration, and whom he had done his best to help, even at the cost of losing friends at home; it also hurt him politically. The many Americans who wished to live on peaceful terms with Russia would naturally have felt that if any American could produce this result, Willkie was the man. But this outburst of hostility seemed to indicate that any other leader would do as well, if not better. On the other side, those who had previously damned Willkie as a Communist stooge could now deride him as a Communist dupe.

What hit Willkie hardest, however, was the evident threat to his hope for a peaceful post-war world, which he clearly saw was dependent on friendly relations between America and Russia. Yet Russia was now apparently saying to her Allies: "Don't meddle with affairs in Eastern Europe." And the principle on which she was acting was the rule, not of reason or justice, but of force. Still, Willkie did not give up hope. "Of course it was irritating," he remarked a month later to reporters who questioned him. ". . . But if we don't find the way to international cooperation, we are going to see another war the like of which the world has never known. And so let's not give way to hating."[5]

Privately, however, he confessed his depression. To Robert Kintner on January 19 he wrote: "As to . . . the post-war international organization—I am very blue. I don't like what is happening about the Polish boundary line. Assuming that Russia is correct in her demands, I still worry about those kind of problems being settled by force. Can it be possible that we will come out of this war no better than the last one?"[6]

Willkie's depression must have been increased by a more personal loss —the death on January 29 of William Allen White, one of the most loyal of all his friends, whose native generosity and irrepressible independence had made him recognize in Willkie a kindred spirit, and to whom the younger man, always responsive to well-wishers, accorded a special degree of affection and deference. On the night before his death (which was unexpected, although he had been seriously ill), White had told his son: "I wish you would write Wendell Willkie and tell him that for the last month I have been not only house-bound but bed-ridden and have been unable to help him in the matter of the Kansas delegation, and also please tell him how sorry I am."[7]

White was too free in thought and speech to have much in common with "regular" Republicans or perhaps to exercise much influence over them. But Willkie would have welcomed his moral support in the last-ditch fight for the nomination that was about to begin.

2

The hindsight born of Willkie's catastrophic defeat in the Wisconsin primary has led many persons to wonder why he chose to make it the test by which his candidacy would stand or fall. The arguments against such a decision were obvious. Wisconsin was probably the most isolationist state in the Union. Robert M. LaFollette, Sr., the most revered figure in Wisconsin's history, had been a bitter-end opponent of American participation in World War I and in the League of Nations, and his views dominated the Progressive Party, which in turn dominated Wisconsin politics for almost two decades. That its domination was now at an end was no help to Willkie, for its liberal domestic policies had been taken over by the New Deal and its isolationist foreign policy had been inherited by the Republicans.

These facts were evident in the voting record of Wisconsin Republicans in Congress. On every measure aimed at aiding the Allies or preparing the United States for war—the original Selective Service Act, Lend-Lease, extension of Selective Service, repeal of the Neutrality Act—Wisconsin Republicans had solidly voted "No."

It is not quite clear how their position on these issues squared with their support of Dewey in 1940. Nevertheless, the delegates to the Philadelphia convention had stuck with him, as a unit, through five ballots—although no other delegation did so. If Willkie had no support from the state in 1940, how could he expect any in 1944?

But the arguments on the other side were also strong. Many states where he would have liked to run, including several of the largest, were in effect closed to him. And he had to run somewhere. Moreover, he needed a dramatic victory. On December 14, 1943 he sent a brief note to William T. Evjue and enclosed a clipping from a column by Raymond Clapper which read: "Mr. Willkie's chief chance now is to demonstrate strength . . . by going into primaries, especially the Wisconsin primary in April, where he must make an outstanding showing. Organization politicians, if they are free to make the decision, will nominate Governor Dewey."[8]

On the other hand, if Willkie could win in Wisconsin, it would be assumed that he could win anywhere, and his opponents, foreseeing a repetition of 1940, would begin climbing on his bandwagon. Moreover, despite the expected strength of the opposition, Willkie had devoted and influential friends in the state, and he was able to line up a slate of highly respected delegates, headed by Vernon Thomson, Speaker of the State Assembly. Thomson, who was later to be Attorney General and Governor, had been a supporter of Dewey; but, failing in a personal attempt to learn whether the New York Governor was a candidate or not, he came out for Willkie.[9]

Finally, no Willkie ever ran from a fight; and in this one, as in all his political battles, Wendell was fortified by two beliefs: belief in his personal power to sway people to his own point of view, if he could only talk to them face to face, and belief in the good sense and right-mindedness of ordinary men and women.

He was to state and restate this second belief, with all the eloquence at his command, in the campaign itself. But now his comment to the press was factual and in a low key: "Here is a Midwestern State with an established leadership that holds views opposite to the views that I have on domestic and international affairs. I look upon this as a good State to make a test and I am anxious to make it. . . . I have no illusions as to the difficulty of that test."[10]

Four days earlier, he had displayed an even more striking degree of political courage in discussing the need for higher taxes—to which Congress, despite sharp prodding from Roosevelt, was making its customary reluctant and gingerly approach. With the nation's income soaring, while consumer goods were in short supply, the President doubted the government's ability to hold the line against inflation. In mid-January, therefore, he proposed a Federal tax increase of $10.5 billion a year, of which $2.7 billion would be returnable after the war.

Republican leaders promptly condemned the proposal as needlessly drastic, and Congress began to whittle it down. Then, on February 2, in one of a series of discussions sponsored by the *New York Times* on the topic "America Plans and Dreams," Willkie had his say. Stressing once more the need for American leadership in the post-war world, he pointed out that this depended on "domestic economic health," which in turn depended on a "realistic fiscal policy." Roosevelt's proposal, he asserted, was *not* realistic; its primary aim was to prevent inflation, while the real need was to keep down the national debt. Taxes must go up during the war so that they could come down afterward; we must "tax ourselves now beyond any limit that we have hitherto imagined possible" up to the limit set by the need for enough energy and enough capital to expand the economy after the war. He proposed to double Roosevelt's figure and add $16 billion in new taxes.

Willkie admitted that some "so-called experts will tell you that the American people will never stand for a tough tax program. I do not agree . . . Give the people an understanding of the issues involved, and they will do their duty to their country, however incredibly painful it may be."

But while he had faith in "the people," Willkie clearly had no faith in the nation's political leaders, especially in Congress; and if he could not persuade them, he would try to shame them into acting as he believed they should. If they wished to preserve the American system, they "must pay for it, and pay for it now. . . . Of course, this will mean hardship. Of course, this will mean discomfort. But the long future is worth the sacrifice.

"There is not much comfort in a fox-hole. There's little comfort waist-deep in mud on Guadalcanal. It is not comfortable to crash-land a flaming plane. There is small comfort in the cold sea; there is no comfort as a prisoner of the Japs. Why should we be comfortable?"[11]

Willkie's eloquence, however, was wasted; it did not change an item in the tax bill that Congress finally produced. Neither Congress nor the public was in the mood to be heroic. In Washington the only praise for his stand came from Roosevelt, who commented admiringly to his news conference that he himself "did not have the nerve to ask for $16,000,000,000. He added . . . that Mr. Willkie, like himself, was thinking a little about the next generation and not just about this one."[12] And on this issue even Roosevelt could not control Congress. It finally passed a bill adding an estimated $2.3 billion; and when Roosevelt vetoed it on February 22, in a message that Willkie rather unfairly called "violent and ill-tempered," Congress promptly overrode the veto. The Republican vote to override was 199-3 in the House, 32-1 in the Senate.[13]

In the meantime, two days after his speech on taxes, Willkie took off by plane for a three-week political tour of the West, beginning with a preliminary visit to Wisconsin. Thence, after he had announced that he would enter the Nebraska primary, his route took him to Utah; north through Idaho to Washington; south through Oregon (where he announced his entry in that state's primary, and expressed pleasure that Dewey's name was also to be entered)[14] to California (where he had a "social visit" with Governor Warren—which lasted four hours!);[15] north to Washington again; east through Montana, Wyoming and the Dakotas to Minneapolis; then south to Iowa and back to New York.

The contrast with 1940 is inevitable. Then he had had no time for the West, save for one brief early trip to California; concentrating instead on the great population centers of the East and Midwest. Now no state was too small, in terms of convention delegates, to be worth a visit. Then, when many Americans were dispirited because of the lingering depression and the shattering news from Europe, he was hearty and hopeful; when they were confused, he was confident; when they sought a leader, he stepped forward with revivalist fervor to lead a not too clearly defined crusade. Now, with ultimate victory certain, they were complacent, while he urged them to sterner efforts; now, under the strain of war, they wanted to get "back to normalcy," while he warned them of new dangers and new trials when the Axis was defeated. "For you and I will never in our time see a placid hour."[16]

And now he was harder and sharper in thought and speech; vagueness and sentimentalism had vanished. And now there were no shifts in position, either from expediency or through inadvertence. For in the first place, he had decided that, in terms of the goals he was seeking, they did not pay; and in the second place, he knew exactly where he stood.

These qualities were apparent in Milwaukee, where he began the current phase of his campaign by meeting his delegates and holding a press conference ("off the record" in that he asked not to be quoted directly), where one reporter was impressed by "listening to him answer questions for an hour with not the slightest attempt at evasiveness." He confessed, for instance, that he was "deeply disturbed" over Russian-Polish relations and suggested (without histrionics) "that if the administration had taken a firmer stand at the outset, it might have had considerable effect on the views of Joseph Stalin." And on the subject of taxes he was equally frank; "a group of well meaning friends had prepared a harmless, meaningless tax speech for him, but . . . he had discarded it for a speech of his own, wise or unwise"; "the public is entitled to the truth" and "must carry its share of the war burden."[17]

Two days later, in Utah, Willkie reiterated this stand. "Someone must tell the people the truth. That's just the kind of a fellow I am." And this time "the people" included the party's leaders. "The Republican party has been talking about unsound financial practices for eleven years. . . . It has been talking about excessive deficits. What is it now going to do about them?"[18]

In the same mood at Twin Falls, Idaho, the next day he stated with merciless clarity the most damaging argument against his candidacy by the independent liberals whose support he must have to defeat Roosevelt. "Can we afford to turn the country over to the Republican party—will we be sure, if we do so, that it will not return to narrow nationalism, economic Toryism and to a disregard of the advancing social obligations of our times? And even if the leader selected and the platform adopted give assurances, can that leader lead his party to forward-looking thinking? Or will he be constantly subjected to defeat and frustration by recalcitrants within his own party?"[19]

These questions were easier to ask than answer, and he could only point out that the Democratic party also had a powerful reactionary wing and assert that the Republican party had lately been altered by an infusion of new men and new ideas. And he was not vague as to the ideas that *he* was trying to infuse. He warned in Tacoma against allowing the party to be taken over by "a rabble of malcontents";[20] in Sheridan, Wyoming, against excessive emphasis on states' rights ("we can't adopt a formula that goes back before the Civil War and didn't work very well then");[21] in California, against "regional, social, economic and religious prejudices" and against letting "free enterprise" be made "a cloak for predatory practices, or the frenzied pursuit of quick and easy profits."[22]

In spite of his deadly seriousness, however, Willkie had not lost his sense of humor. It might, indeed, have seemed so when in Montana he allowed himself to be initiated into the Blackfeet Indian tribe; but he retrieved the situation by remarking, when told that the name of the master of ceremonies was Chief Bull, "I had thought that Chief Bull lived a considerable distance south and east of here."[23]

On his return, after a two-week breathing spell, Willkie paid a two-day visit to New Hampshire, where the first Presidential primary was to be held on March 15. Here he hoped for a sweeping victory, but the results were indecisive. Of the eleven delegates elected, six were Willkie supporters, although not officially pledged to him; two were pledged to Dewey; and three were uncommitted.

3

Wisconsin had an "open" primary, in which anyone could vote in the primary of either party, regardless of past affiliations; and some Willkie supporters hoped that many Progressives and liberal Democrats might enter the Republican primary to vote for Willkie. But this hope was delusive; the liberals already had Roosevelt, and what they would naturally want, to assure his reelection, was a conservative Republican nominee.

Moreover, many liberals (like Senator Norris, for instance, and unlike Roosevelt) never overcame their early aversion. While Willkie fought—more unreservedly than any member of the Administration, including the President himself—for civil rights, social justice, a reasonably regulated economy, acceptance of international obligations, and thereby earned the enmity of the reactionaries in both parties, he met with only grudging approval or cynical distrust from many spokesmen for liberalism.

This perverse antipathy is most glaringly displayed in an article written by Fred Rodell of the Yale Law School and published in *Harper's Magazine* for March, 1944, under the title "Wendell Willkie: Man of Words." That such an article should have been written by a professor of law in one of America's great universities and published in one of America's most widely respected periodicals remains incredible. False in many key statements of fact, fallacious in most of its inferences, it sought to convince its readers that Willkie was (in his own words prefacing his answer) "as a lawyer, most ordinary; as a businessman, naive; as a public figure, insincere."

He had, Rodell charged, begun a career as a teacher but had deserted the academic profession because, though he had "a quick superficial grasp" of what he read, he lacked "the scholar's patience to dig deep. So he switched to the talker's profession . . . the law." But he was "never, even in embryo, a great lawyer." "Though he argued court cases from time to time, he was more at home" in "a conference room or a committee hearing than in . . . a courtroom." "Typically, he left behind in Ohio no tangible accomplishments." He was made president of Commonwealth & Southern not because of his ability but because it was thought that, as "a financial district Democrat" with "a winning way," he would make a good front man in dealing with the Roosevelt administration; and he "never . . . mastered the intricacies of corporation finance." Yet, after all, it was to his credit "that he did not really run C & S," which was "never . . . a financial success," even after "New Deal competition . . . taught C & S the highly lucrative lesson that lower electric rates mean . . . bigger net profits."

In politics, it was his skill in talking that won him the nomination in 1940 (here the author ignored the usual charge of fraud to make his point about a "man of words"); and thereafter his speeches were "just campaign oratory." When he subsequently joined a law firm, "he was never expected to carry his share of the legal work—nor has he done so. From a front man he has graduated into a figurehead." In the Schneiderman case, to be sure, "though others had done all the legal dirty work of preparing the case . . . there is little doubt that his forensic contribution played some part in the result." He did not, however, deserve any moral credit, for in "the field of civil liberties" "only a conservative who is stupid will be illiberal."

Finally, just as "he was Wall Street's spokesman in 1940, he is no less Wall Street's spokesman in 1944. Yet it would be absurd to assume that Wendell Willkie is working for Wall Street today. He is working single-mindedly, consecrated as on a crusade, for Wendell Willkie for President."[24]

The article was published at a time when it was calculated to be most damaging to Willkie's chances in the primaries and was naturally given wide circulation by his enemies. How would ordinary people know that it was almost all a lie?

The schedule of the Wisconsin campaign was announced on March 17.[25] Willkie would arrive on Saturday, March 18, at Madison; go to Richland Center for a speech that evening; return to Madison to spend the night and Sunday morning with Governor Walter S. Goodland in the Executive Mansion; go to Neenah Sunday afternoon as the guest of John R. Kimberly; on Monday visit Oshkosh, Fond du Lac and Ripon (sometimes regarded as the birthplace of the Republican party); Tuesday, Appleton and Green Bay; Wednesday, Manitowoc and Sheboygan; Thursday, Kenosha and Racine; Friday, Beloit and Janesville; Saturday, Waukesha; Monday (after the usual Sunday lay-off), Milwaukee; Tuesday, LaCrosse and Wisconsin Rapids; Wednesday, Chippewa Falls, Menomonie and Eau Claire. On Thursday he would close his campaign at Superior and then move on to Nebraska.

In the meantime, his rivals were far away, pretending indifference to the outcome. Dewey was quietly at work in the Governor's Mansion in Albany; MacArthur and Stassen were in the South Pacific.

It was at all times clear that Dewey, had he wished, could have won without a contest. He had won in 1940; as Governor of New York he was now immensely stronger; by his moderate liberalism in that office, his non-commitment on national issues (except for conventional attacks on the Roosevelt administration), and his cautious internationalism, he had won the favor of middle-of-the-road Republicans without offending the Old Guard; and though he had enemies, his persistent assertions that he was not a candidate left them without a point of attack. No aspirant for the Presidency had ever played his cards more skillfully. In its own way his performance was almost as masterly as Willkie's in 1940.

The time came, however, when he had to commit himself in regard to Wisconsin. A slate of delegates, including some of the state's most prominent Republicans, had been entered in his name. Did they have his approval or not? When this question had to be answered, he acted decisively. On February 25 he sent identical telegrams to all his delegates:

"I understand that petitions for your election as a delegate running in my name have been filed at Madison. The use of my name meets my strongest disapproval and I earnestly hope you will withdraw the petition filed for you. I appreciate the interest you have evidenced and I am sure I can rely on your friendship in acceding to my request."[26]

On the face of it, the issue was now settled. But was it? On February 25 his delegates met in Milwaukee, and though the meeting was behind closed doors, persons outside could plainly hear the irrascible Old Guarder who was the real leader of the delegation, Fred R. Zimmerman, dominating the discussion: "Dewey knew six months ago that this delegation would be pledged to him. Why did he wait until this last week to make up his mind? I think Dewey is hoping we boys will stick." "Zimmerman seemed to be implying," wrote one of the listening reporters, "that Dewey would be able to say to the convention that he had told Wisconsin delegates he did not want his name used 'but in spite of it they sent me 24 delegates.'"[27] Most of the boys decided to stick.[28]

Stassen was also playing his cards carefully. His enlistment in the Navy seemed to have taken him out of the race, but at the beginning of 1944 it became evident that his supporters thought otherwise. Early in January Governor Goodland publicly announced his support of Stassen;[29] in due course a slate of delegates was selected; and on March 13 Senator Joseph H. Ball, the moving spirit in the Stassen drive, began an active campaign, with a luncheon talk at Madison, a reception in the Governor's office, a press conference and an evening radio speech.[30]

It was now Stassen's turn to be heard from, and on March 21 Secretary of the Navy Knox made public a message from Stassen which read in part: "I do not seek and will do nothing personally to secure the nomination. If, notwithstanding this position, I were nominated, I would consider it my plain duty to accept and would do so."[31]

Willkie was quick to comment: "It is difficult to know from the announcement whether Governor Stassen is a candidate or not. . . . Obviously those who seek the preference of the voters of Wisconsin should discuss the issues with them, or if they have rendered themselves unable to do so, they should decisively and not ambiguously withdraw from the contest."[32]

Behind the brusqueness of this statement lay Stassen's responsibility (as Willkie believed) for the election of Spangler as National Chairman in 1942; his slighting review of *One World;* and a promise (as Willkie understood it) not to enter the Wisconsin primary. To his friend Milton Polland, Willkie explained his anger by telling of a meeting in the Willkie apartment in New York shortly before the Minnesota Governor left for duty in the Pacific, where some such dialogue as the following took place. Stassen said, "I'm going to be in the Navy and won't be available in 1944, and I'm instructing my friends to support you. I want to see you nominated."

"I didn't get you up here to embarrass you," Willkie replied. "If you want to go into the Wisconsin primary, I'll stay out."

"No," was the answer, "I'm young enough to try later on. I'm saying this because I really feel this way. Your thinking and mine are very much alike. I think the hope of the party in 1944 lies with you."[33]

What seems to have happened by early 1944 was that Stassen's friends had concluded (with reason, as the sequel showed) that Willkie had no chance to be nominated; that therefore, if Dewey stayed out, Stassen *did* have a chance; and that, when informed of their opinion, he told them to use their own judgment.[34] There is nothing reprehensible about this; yet it is easy to understand Willkie's feeling—that Stassen had no chance (this also was correct) and was acting only to get his name before the public in preparation for 1948, and that he must have known that whatever success he had would be at Willkie's expense, since in the public mind they stood for much the same things. After the Wisconsin campaign was over, however, Willkie resumed his customary magnanimity. On the way to Nebraska, where Stassen was also entered, he told reporters: "I have no personal battle with Governor Stassen. I think he is a fine man. But I am here to discuss issues."[35]

The third candidate who was not running was MacArthur. A popular hero of the war in the Pacific, whose standing with many of his admirers was strengthened by the belief that he and his forces were being slighted in favor of the European theater of operations, he had indicated, though not publicly, that he was available. Since he was a military leader, whose political views were little known, his candidacy naturally—though as yet with no encouragement from him—became a rallying point for advocates of the "narrow nationalism and economic Toryism" that Willkie so often denounced; and also, of course, for many well-meaning Americans who were attracted by the glamor of MacArthur's personality and military achievements.[36]

4

Only one thing was predictable about the Wisconsin primary—that Willkie, even without visible opponents, would make it a good fight. (He remarked in his first speech: "I don't intend in this campaign to do any mumbling in a barrel.")[37] It was in fact, as Willard Shelton wrote when it was over, in an admirable summing up for the *Nation,* "one of the most fantastic Presidential campaigns in American history. . . . With terrible earnestness—and the phrase is used advisedly—he has at once attempted the almost irreconcilable task of reforming the Republican party and of asking rank-and-file voters to entrust him, in spite of all the venomous opposition to him, with the party's leadership. . . . His deliberate defiance of his enemies, his determination to speak his mind plainly on delicate issues, were almost incredible."[38]

The explanation is simple—though to some persons it will also be incredible. Willkie desired the Presidency only as an instrument for putting into practice the policies in which he believed. If the Republican party could not be persuaded to accept these policies, he did not wish to be its nominee. Now at last the war declared against him by the Old Guard for his support of Lend-Lease would be fought to a finish. The party was not big enough to hold both him and them, and Wisconsin Republicans must choose.

"I firmly believe," he told a crowd in an impromptu speech at Oshkosh on his second day of campaigning, "that it is my duty to bring the Republican party to a viewpoint on international and domestic policies where it will . . . be entitled to power . . . I am asking you to vote for my [delegates] . . . so that I can fight for those things for which the Republican party must stand if it is to deserve victory in 1944."

And he was determined that if he was defeated, the whole nation should know why. "The eyes of the nation," he told the same audience, "are focused upon the Wisconsin Presidential primary. If the voters of this great Midwestern state say in the election that they want the Republican party to pursue a policy of ultra economic conservatism and narrow nationalism then . . . the leaders of that type of thinking will move into greater control of the party.

"By the same token, if the voters of Wisconsin say they want the Republican party to ignore the issues of the day in the fallacy that they can outmatch the master politician, then all of these men will take courage from the results of the vote.

"On the other hand, if you believe that the issues must be met and determined by a sovereign people; if you agree with me that we must restore the things that made America great by providing an opportunity for the individual to get ahead and live their own lives [sic] uncontrolled by government; if you believe as I do that America must come to understand other nations or face the certainty of another war, then vote for the delegates pledged to my candidacy.

"If you do that, . . . the Republican party will attract thousands and thousands of independent voters without which the Republican party has no chance of winning in 1944."[39]

And as the campaign proceeded, Willkie hit harder and harder. Mercilessly he flayed the Old Guard—for their unreasoning hatred of Roosevelt; for their disdainful dismissal, in the name of patriotism, of responsibility for the freedom and social advancement of other peoples; for their willingness to trade the nation's welfare for a party advantage. "Some people hate the administration so much that whatever the administration is for, they are against. They don't think, they react. They are pathological."[40] Through hatred of Roosevelt they "opposed every effort to prepare this nation prior to Pearl Harbor, and since Pearl Harbor they have stood in equally blind opposition to acts designed to make us stronger. That's the issue in Wisconsin. I am proposing a set of principles with which the Republican party would deserve to win in 1944, not policies and principles that are blind, not principles of negation, not principles of hate."[41] "I have fought desperately," he said earlier, "to liberalize the party, so that it represents modern thinking, so that men could rally around it . . . so that it could be entitled to win."[42] "The Republican party must become something that you don't have to enter by a crooked passkey."[43]

In the same spirit he justified his break with the party leadership over Lend-Lease: "I shall never be prouder of anything I ever did in my life."[44] Conceding that "80 to 85 per cent of his party opposed him on his lend-lease policy," he demanded: "Where was the Republican voice? What would have been today the position of the Republican party? We would have been the party with little foresight, and with little courage, the party that welched, the party that failed the cause of liberty."[45] "I was criticized for backing lend-lease," he reminded another audience. "I did that for my country and my party, so that in 1944 no man could say the Republican party could not see the inevitable. Who will now stand up publicly and say that we should not have helped Great Britain so that the British could fight and hold off our enemies until we were ready?"[46]

And while thus reopening old wounds he inflicted new ones by identifying the pre-war isolationists with those persons who in 1944 wished to base the Republican campaign on the inconveniences and discontents of war. Saying that he had been urged to "speak against the war," he declared: "If that is the price of the election of my delegates in Wisconsin, then I want none of them elected."[47] "Any party," he told a later audience, "that seeks to get back into power by appeasement, by narrow nationalism and by capitalizing on the discontents of war doesn't deserve to win."[48] "There are certain people who are opposing me because I won't do the things they want me to do. Some of them want me to base my campaign on discontent—the fact that you have had to give up gasoline. They want to make that a national issue. They want to make food rationing a national issue, and the fact that many of us are working harder and that we have sons overseas fighting in the armed forces. . . . Those are the same people, who advocate these things, who were in favor of strict neutrality in 1940, who opposed arming Guam, who were opposed to giving 50 destroyers to Great Britain, who were against lend-lease . . . That was my greatest handicap in the last campaign. Those cowardly, yielding people who didn't want to fight for what is right—and now they are at it again.

"Today in Wisconsin I seek to defeat those same forces."[49]

There is a touch of campaign oratory here. What was wrong with the isolationists was not cowardice or weakness of will, but the "narrow nationalism" that forbade them to see the meaning of what was happening in Europe and Asia or to let their sympathies be swayed by the massive human misery that resulted. But he was right in holding that the behavior of the Old Guard was all of a piece—that narrow nationalism, economic Toryism and a pathological hatred of Roosevelt all went together, and that together they produced a state of mind in which anything that hurt the Administration was good for the country, any means of replacing the Administration was legitimate, and any Republican who supported the Administration on any issue was a traitor to his party. "I have," Willkie boasted, "the greatest and best list of enemies of any man in public life in America."[50]

In some ways the natural candidate of Willkie's enemies was MacArthur. But as practicing politicians they inclined toward a "regular" Republican, and this, as things stood, meant Dewey. What to do about Dewey was therefore one of Willkie's main problems. His behavior in asking his candidates to withdraw had been impeccable. But most of his delegates were running, nevertheless—which meant that Dewey was running. And though Willkie had once admitted that this way of playing the political game was "legitimate," he really felt that it was not—that a man should or should not be a candidate, and that if he was, he should discuss the issues. In his Ripon speech, Willkie asserted: "There is an even better way to destroy a party than by adopting tactics of negative partisanship, and that is, to take no stand on the issues at all." This had been the policy of the Whigs in the years before the Civil War, and it had proved suicidal. "One of the major functions of a political party is to give men of conviction a platform from which to argue their cause, both within the party and outside it. . . . a political leader with convictions has, not only a public duty, but a party duty, to state his convictions openly and argue them to the best of his ability."[51]

This was in a prepared speech, but in impromptu talks he was less restrained. "I almost despise those who remain silent more than those who speak out in open opposition."[52] And part of the reason for Dewey's silence, he charged, was the desire to find out the trend of public opinion and then go along with it, instead of trying to guide it as a leader should. Such was the practice of "the trend boys, who view things not in terms of ideas, or principles and platforms, but of charts and graphs."[53]

Willkie took one last fling at Dewey (and at the backers of Stassen and MacArthur) in a farewell message as he left the state: "I don't want the people of Wisconsin to have to buy a pig in a poke . . . I wanted them to know the beliefs and purposes of at least one candidate . . ."[54]

Assailing his rivals, however, would not by itself win Willkie delegates; he had also to erase the widespread notion that he and Roosevelt held identical views. To Willkie himself the differences were clear. "I would like to point out," he said in a speech at Green Bay, "that there is no man in public life in America who has disagreed with the President on so many phases of foreign policy."[55] In fact, he declared, he had been "the only important Republican who had spoken out against the Roosevelt administration's policy on Vichy, on the Italian fascists, on Darlan in North Africa, and on 'Mr. Roosevelt's acquiescence in the violation of the Polish boundary.' "[56] "What the people want to know," he asserted in another speech, "is: 'Is or is not the United States going to urge that the boundary line of Poland be determined by some method of international arbitration, or are we going to continue on a policy of expediency? Are we going to recognize a lot of puppet kings and Fascists, or are we going to deal with democratic elements?' "[57]

And as the Administration had apparently lost faith in its professed democratic principles, so it seemed also to have lost faith in the people—in the democratic process itself. In an informal speech to newsmen at the very beginning of the campaign, Willkie commented: "Some of the most momentous discussions in the history of mankind have taken place the last few months at Teheran and elsewhere, yet not one of us has sufficient information about any of these discussions or about the conclusions reached to be able to talk about them. The party in power has shown a total disregard of the processes by which a free people arrive at their conclusions."[58] Evidently "the present Administration has been in power too long . . . is tired and cynical."[59]

In this view he received unexpected support from Bernard De Voto, noted historian, literary critic, and crusader for liberal causes, who acknowledged a copy of Willkie's speech at Concord, New Hampshire, with a letter calling himself "a tired New Dealer." He had "voted for the New Deal three times," but "over the years I have come to feel that the administration—I do not mean Mr. Roosevelt alone but rather the whole complex of power—does not truly accept the democratic postulates on which it is supposed to be based. I have come to believe there is a New Deal assumption that they (the people) are too damn dumb to know what is best for them and so must be cozened, deceived and tricked for their own good."[60] This was exactly Willkie's view, and he quoted the letter with zest, adding, "There are literally millions of tired New Dealers in the United States and the Republican party can have them for the asking if it pursues the right policies."[61]

The "right policies" were implicit in his criticisms of his rivals and of Roosevelt. The first was total victory in the war. "In 1944," he said in his first speech, at Richland Center, "we, all of us, must loyally support the war cause and the peace cause and our government itself in so far as it devotes itself single-mindedly to those purposes."[62] Especially, America must brace itself to accept the fact that in the coming invasion of Western Europe, "the casualty lists will be long—heartbreakingly long."[63] "Don't let us make political capital," he pleaded on another occasion, "out of forthcoming invasion losses; don't capitalize on the worries and weariness of war."[64]

Concerning the second "right policy," support of an international organization to maintain peace, Willkie made three points. First, it would be to the advantage of the great powers. "As an individual supports the police and fire departments," he said, "so I assume it is to the national self-interest of the United States, Great Britain, Russia and other countries to put out the fires of aggression and to destroy the bandits before they destroy civilization."[65]

Second, it would give small countries their only hope of survival. "Small nations . . . do not have the power to stand up against a neighbor two or three times as high, and their salvation is in settlement of a dispute by adjudication rather than force."[66]

And finally, it would help prevent a war in which the United States would be on one side and Russia on the other. He condemned those who "are willing to divide the world into two groups and then prepare for the next war." To the charge that he was a Communist, he retorted: "I know how powerful Communism is and how powerful Russia has become under that system. All I want is to prevent that country and my country from coming into conflict."[67] "If that war comes," he warned, "it will make this war look like a toy war."[68]

The third "right policy" concerned domestic affairs, and here Willkie selected with sure judgment what has been since the depression the great issue of our time: "the relationship of government to the economic life and social well being of its citizens." With admirable clarity he sketched the development since the Civil War of two schools of thought on the best economic system for America. "The material accomplishments were so great and the development so incredibly rapid that many men became sincerely convinced that any limitation of accomplishment or development by way of regulation or taxes or even social protection was an inevitable deterrent and eventual destroyer of the very yeast of the system.

"On the other hand, the abuses were so glaring, the greed so obvious and the disregard of human values so frequent and so flagrant that many men with equal sincerity came to believe that the very system was in conflict with human well being. . . .

"One group stubbornly and doggedly fought every social advance and the other turned more and more to the philosophy that government control was the cure for every ill."

The Roosevelt administration had "largely adopted and exploited" the second view: "that there is an irrepressible and inevitable conflict between a society built upon economic incentive and a society of human welfare.

. . . Do you want security, or initiative? Do you want protection, or adventure? This is a factitious issue. We need both. . . . For if we truly understand the potentialities of modern science, industrial development and international comity, we must know that we can develop here in America a society in which the rewards will be ample to unleash the myriad energies of our people, a society which will at the same time give human protection far beyond anything heretofore envisioned."[69]

Such was Willkie's message, and he preached it to everyone: internationalism to farmers, social responsibility to labor unions, government regulation to business men. Recognizing that each group had special problems, he denied that any group should be given special privileges, or that there could be a genuine conflict of interest. What was good for the country would be good for the farmers and for the unions and for business.

5

These issues, Willkie declared again and again, should guide the citizen in casting his vote—not the personalities of the candidates. But the fact is, as he had insisted four years earlier in "We the People," that "the American people do not give their vote to policies; they give their vote to *men*." Was he, in fact, in his intensive campaign throughout Wisconsin—covering 1400 miles and making 40 speeches in 22 cities[70]—placing his faith in the reasonableness of the public? Or was he, instead, trusting them to respond to honesty, courage and idealism?

So the question is (though of course the man and his beliefs cannot be separated), "What kind of personal image of Willkie did Wisconsin voters finally get, and whence was it derived? That is, apart from the doctrines that he preached, what was his campaign like?"

The most conspicuous feature of it, according to after-the-fact accounts, was its disorganization. It has been said that the campaign was "amazing for its confusion, intrigue, inefficiency and stupid blundering."[71] The day-by-day stories in the local newspapers, however, give a totally different impression. All these papers, or nearly all, told their readers well in advance the time and place of Willkie's scheduled speeches in the area. Furthermore, there are no suggestions that the facilities secured in each community were not the best available, or that as a rule the attendance did not meet or surpass expectations. At his first speech at Richland Center, a community of less than 5,000, he drew an audience of 2,200; the high school band played; and members of the Kiwanis and Lions Clubs, the American Legion and the Chamber of Commerce, served as ushers.[72] It is true that this was the home town of Vernon Thomson. But in Sheboygan the following Wednesday, though the Republican county chairman refused to sponsor the meeting and it was "arranged by young political amateurs," he drew "the largest meeting ever seen in the Armory,"[73] and the local paper complimented the committee.[74]

This was the only overt rebuff that Willkie received from a local party leader. "In other counties," said the Milwaukee *Journal* story, "Republican chairmen have taken care of the meetings regardless of whether they personally are for Willkie"; and the chairman of the State Committee, Thomas E. Coleman, though he personally considered Willkie to be an egotist and an opportunist,[75] maintained complete neutrality.[76]

In some places, in fact, the interest was astounding. On Friday at Elkhorn (population under 2,000) Willkie drew more than 1,000 persons to a 15-minute speech at 11 o'clock in the morning,[77] and he also did well with a similar speech at 10:30 Saturday morning in Evansville (population 2,500), where 600 persons turned out.[78] Friday, in fact, was almost like 1940, with people waving to him along the road and "large groups" gathering at crossroads hamlets to catch a glimpse of him.[79] And nearly every day there were luncheon and dinner meetings attended by several hundred prominent local citizens; while evening speeches in cities of moderate size (20,000 to 50,000) regularly drew audiences of 1,500 to 2,000. When it is remembered that there was a war going on, with many persons working overtime and gasoline being strictly rationed; and that March in Wisconsin can be (and this year *was*) a wintry month, Willkie's reception was surprisingly good. (The only disappointing turnout was at Milwaukee, where the auditorium was set up for 6,500 persons and the audience was generally estimated at between 4,000 and 5,000.)[80]

Also encouraging was the friendly treatment that Willkie got from the local newspapers. Not only was the coverage and commentary detailed and factual, but most editorial writers, if they did not support his candidacy, nevertheless praised his sincerity and frankness. Only a handful followed the hate-Willkie line of Hearst's Milwaukee *Sentinel* and McCormick's Chicago *Tribune* (and even the *Sentinel* carried a good deal of straight reporting).

With the *Tribune,* however, Willkie carried on a running battle. The *Tribune* story (March 19) on the Richland Center speech began: "Wendell L. Willkie, the defeated 1940 Republican Presidential candidate, and a favorite son of Wall Street banking interests tonight assumed the role of farm expert . . ." The March 20 story on Willkie began: "Wendell L. Willkie, defeated 1940 Republican Presidential candidate, today left Madison for Neenah to confer with John R. Kimberly, millionaire paper manufacturer and socialite." The March 21 account began: "Wendell L. Willkie tonight delivered a homily on 'political morals' and 'party unity.' The defeated 1940 G. O. P. candidate read his printed essay on 'The function of political party' [sic] into a radio microphone in the gymnasium of Ripon College.

The attendance was estimated at 1,150, about two-thirds of them Ripon College students or persons of high school age who can't vote."

Willkie of course hit back. On March 21 he told a luncheon meeting at Appleton: "If the Tribune's candidates win in the primary, Franklin Roosevelt will for four years longer be President of the United States."[81] At Racine on March 23 he thanked his audience for coming to hear him when "morning after morning you have read distortions of my motives, misrepresentations of what I have been doing and defamation of me for three and a half years."[82] It is more than doubtful that these exchanges cost Willkie any votes.

There is no evidence, either, that his attempt to reach the public was greatly hampered by lack of funds, though clearing up the indebtedness afterwards was a troublesome process.[83] What worried his managers more was that, as in 1940 (though Marquis Childs commented on the "tremendous improvement" in his speaking technique),[84] his voice threatened to give out after the first day and he remained hoarse throughout the rest of the campaign. This not only lessened the effectiveness of his speaking, but the medical attention that he required helped put his party behind schedule.[85]

And at best it was hard to keep Willkie on time for engagements. At the Borg Plant in Delavan on Friday morning (March 24), it took strenuous efforts to drag him away from conversations with workers.[86] When he passed an auction on his way to Madison Saturday morning, he stopped the party, climbed on an old farm wagon, held up a horse-collar while he made appropriate wise-cracks, and ended with a serious speech. (Speaking outdoors did not help his throat.)[87]

In retrospect, some of those involved remembered these frequent delays (on Wednesday, March 29, as a result of a heavy snowstorm, it took the party five hours to cover the hundred miles from Wisconsin Rapids to Eau Claire)[88] as the salient feature of the campaign, which turned it into a "nightmare."[89] But it is in the nature of things that political campaigns should be disorganized.

On the whole, it is clear that in its general aim—to bring Willkie into personal contact with as many people as possible—the campaign was a success. Wisconsin voters saw and heard and read about him in situations that clearly revealed the many facets of his character: scholarly and philosophical in his prepared speeches at Richland Center and Ripon; "shaking his unruly locks and roaring his defy at his calumniators" at Appleton;[90] familiar and sarcastic at Racine ("How do you think that I—who came from the mud-flats of Indiana—got where I am? By being a nut?") while "the crowd howled its approval";[91] ragging his friends the correspondents when they had to sit in the choir loft in the chapel at Beloit College ("I have seen some strange sights in my travels, but perhaps the strangest is the group of eminent correspondents who have never heretofore sat in a choir");[92] turning to account, with the same kind of humor, a misadventure at Milwaukee, where a locally eminent but ancient Republican devoted a preliminary speech to a eulogy of MacArthur and then presented Mrs. Willkie as "one who bears the aroma of her native Hoosier state"—"I've heard Indiana described in many ways, but I have not heretofore thought of the sweet smells that come from there";[93] stopping to console the small owner of a dog which had been run over by one of the cars in the Willkie motorcade and stopping again at the nearest city to buy the boy a black cocker spaniel;[94] but always returning, day after day, doggedly, passionately, with "terrible earnestness," to the theme of building a Republican party that would deserve the people's trust. "The whole country is looking to the decision in Wisconsin."[95]

And with him always was Mrs. Willkie, trim, unflustered, smiling or serious as the occasion asked, gracious to the public, attentive to her husband's needs, winning the praise of everybody.[96]

What Willkie's hearers were thinking, nobody could be sure. Despite occasional outbursts of enthusiasm, the audiences were, like the speaker, serious. It was widely remarked that the speeches at Richland Center and Ripon were more like lectures than campaign talks. What the candidate had to say called for reflection rather than applause. But did the silence of his hearers indicate "avid attention" or merely that they were "unreceptive"?[97] Willkie himself professed to be pleased: "They are listening to me, trying to understand what I am trying to tell them."[98] But some of his party found the response—or lack of it—"disquieting."[99] Even when more informal speeches produced a more evident reaction ("when he throws away the manuscript and speaks off the cuff he is terrific"),[100] the dominant mood remained serious. "Laughs were few"[101] was a typical comment.

Still, most observers judged that the audiences were friendly. An article in the Janesville *Gazette* assured Willkie that "he had found a host of new friends and supporters here. . . . big audiences at his five speeches in the county were attentive, sober and thoughtful if they were not demonstrative."[102] The Milwaukee *Journal* also spoke of the "large audiences . . . warm and enthusiastic"; not "tumultuous" but "unusually attentive."[103] In fact, Willkie's reception seemed so favorable that, as James A. Hagerty reported in the *New York Times,* "in some instances county chairmen, who at first refused to have any part in arranging Willkie meetings . . . have become cooperative."[104]

Yet at the end of the campaign several observers commented on the prevailing apathy of the public: "there isn't a great deal of interest aroused."[105] This was especially true of younger persons: almost no men in uniform were present, even at the evening meetings. "Instead," wrote

Marquis Childs, "they crowd the movie theaters, recreation centers . . . the taverns and the cocktail lounges."[106]

Willkie himself was pessimistic as to the outcome, betting against himself with the newsmen and intimating that they were betting on him in order to keep his spirits up.[107] (Despite his killing schedule, he would regularly join them after his last speech to have a drink and talk over the way things were going.)[108] But most observers, while stressing the uncertainty of the result, thought he would get a majority of the delegates. The sympathetic *Wisconsin State Journal* forecast that sixteen to eighteen would be for Willkie.[109] The Hearst Milwaukee *Sentinel,* in a violent editorial attack, showed that it was worried by urging all his opponents to get together and vote for Dewey.[110] Even some anti-Willkie politicians conceded him an edge. Bernhard Gettelman, leader of the Dewey delegation until he complied with Dewey's request to withdraw, thought that Dewey would get five and Willkie the rest. Lester Bradshaw, signer of an anti-Willkie letter circulated in the fall of 1943 and an announced supporter of Bricker, judged that Willkie was certain of fifteen delegates.[111]

Some of these predictions were made before a last-minute speed-up of activity by Willkie's opponents. On April 2 the Chicago *Sun* reported: "Almost coincident with Willkie's leaving the state . . . the Dewey forces swung into action with broadcasts over a state-wide hook-up," to be "continued every night" until the election. "Billboards urging the election of Dewey delegates have sprung up throughout the state . . ." The *Wisconsin State Journal* of the same date noted that the Dewey organization had sent out 220,000 pieces of mail. The Racine *Journal-Times* on March 30 stated that individual Dewey delegates planned week-end broadcasts from local stations; that "pamphlets boosting MacArthur" were "being distributed by his eleven delegates"; that Stassen's supporters were bringing the popular Representative Walter Judd to campaign for their candidate, that they had mailed "an eight-page tabloid paper" filled with praises of Stassen to 300,000 rural boxholders and were now distributing it in the cities, that each of his nineteen delegates was sending out 1,000 postcards, and that at least three of them were going on the air.

6

With the nation watching, Wisconsin voters went to the polls on April 4. Those voting in the Republican primary elected seventeen of Dewey's delegates (all who had not withdrawn), four of Stassen's, three of MacArthur's, and none of Willkie's.

The figures are not easy to interpret, since the vote was not for the candidates themselves but for their delegates. But, accepting as a basis of comparison the average vote cast for the delegates at large of each candidate,[112] it appears that Dewey got 40 per cent of the total, MacArthur 24, Stassen 20, and Willkie 16.

The first question concerning this overwhelming and unforeseen defeat was "Why? What happened?" Willkie himself blamed it principally on Wisconsin's isolationist tradition and illustrated his belief by a story told him by Willard Smith; of a wealthy Wisconsin farmer who during World War II entered a bank and asked for a $500 war bond, then, when he saw it, said he would take a $1,000 one. When the banker, curious, asked why he had changed his mind, he pointed to the first one and said: "That one has Woodrow Wilson's picture on it."[113]

There is no doubt that he was partly right. Willkie was the most uncompromising internationalist in American public life, and Wisconsin was the most isolationist state. "The ghost of Old Bob La Follette," some of his advisers told him, "still stands beside the polling booths in the Wisconsin hinterlands."[114] And the younger generation, which might have looked at the world with other eyes, was not voting.

It is fair to assume, also, that Willkie's insistence on the total defeat of Germany injured him in the minds of many persons of German descent.[115] In fact, a German Lutheran minister followed Willkie around Wisconsin attacking him for allegedly wanting to punish Germany after the war.[116]

This, however, was a minor matter. Willkie's rejection by Wisconsin Republicans was only an extreme case of his rejection by Republicans in general. A comment in a local paper before the election summed up the situation precisely: "Now Willkie . . . asks for repudiation of Wisconsin Republican Congressmen, who were reelected in 1942 on their record of opposition to the administration foreign policy before Pearl Harbor. In the nation Willkie asks Republicans to repudiate their members of Congress . . ."[117] (How little inclination Wisconsin Republicans had to comply with Willkie's plea was shown when they chose Joseph R. McCarthy as their candidate for the Senate two years later, and when he was elected and reelected.)

Willkie's domestic program had as little appeal as his foreign policy. He was asking Republicans to take over the program of the New Deal—only to run it in more efficient and less partisan fashion. But the fact was that opposition to the New Deal was almost the definition of Republicanism—was what gave Republicans their identity and in their own eyes justified their existence. Even after four years of struggle Willkie did not yet fully comprehend what a writer in the Chicago *Sun* aptly called "the enormous capacity of the GOP to resist reform."[118]

And its resistance was getting stronger. Gardner Cowles, after "traveling around Iowa a lot" in January, 1944, "talking with Republican county chairmen, other Republican leaders, and with small town business men and bankers," reported to Willkie that he was "amazed at their conservatism. They have shifted to the right substantially in the last twelve months."

Cowles's next comment—"The vast majority of them favor Dewey because they think he is 'safe' and you are not"[119]—points toward the final and most decisive cause of Willkie's defeat: the habit of party regularity. This was what gave Dewey and Stassen their immense advantage—they had always been Republicans. Moreover, their advocacy of internationalism or domestic reform was never based on principle, but on what they asserted were practical needs. The Old Guard might disapprove, but there was no threat to their existence. The innovators could always be held in check, since as "regulars" they would never wreck the party for the sake of a principle.

There was also another way in which party loyalty worked against Willkie. Many Republicans who were themselves friendly to Willkie recognized that "the Old Guard . . . would rather see Roosevelt win a fourth term than see Willkie win the nomination"; "would fight Willkie to the last ditch and spend millions doing it"; and even if he were nominated would still work to defeat him, and would undoubtedly succeed. Dewey, on the other hand, had made no political enemies; he could unite the party.[120]

So there is really no mystery about Willkie's defeat. He was simply not a Republican, and Wisconsin Republicans knew it. [121] They might respect his sincerity and admire his courage and give him a friendly reception (though probably many who came to hear his public speeches were Democrats); but they would not vote for him as their party's leader.

So in a way it *was* "issues" that decided the election—as Willkie wished. It did not matter whether his campaign was disorganized or not; whether it was well financed or not; whether Stassen entered or stayed out. The question was, "Should the Republican party be reformed?" and the answer of Wisconsin Republicans was a decisive "No!"

To many persons, both friends and enemies, Willkie's Wisconsin campaign seemed to lead to a dead end of futility. (The Chicago *Tribune,* almost choking on its glutted malice, editorialized: "From today on, Mr. Willkie can be dismissed as a minor nuisance.")[122] But in fact the campaign determined the outcome of the 1944 Presidential election. It won Dewey the nomination and lost him the election.

If he could win without effort against such strenuous opposition, it was clear to Republican leaders that all opposition would henceforth be futile. And although he had not asked for the nomination, they were willing to give it to him—on his own terms, and without any promises or commitments.

But to non-Republicans it looked as if he had not *dared* to commit himself. If he had been silent on issues before the nomination in order not to offend powerful factions in the party, was he likely to take a strong stand afterwards? If the Old Guard was willing to accept *him,* was it not a logical inference that he would be willing to accept the Old Guard? Willkie had forced Wisconsin Republicans to make a choice and had focused the eyes of the nation upon it. And the choice they made showed millions of independent voters that the party did not desire or intend to reform, and so left them with no alternative but Roosevelt.

Willkie got the bad news in Nebraska, where he was again waging a strenuous campaign. It was probably the hardest blow that he ever had to take. In other battles that he had lost, there had always been some partial triumph to sweeten the bitterness of defeat. Even in losing the Presidency in 1940 he had been able to find satisfaction in his immense popular vote. But the outcome of the Wisconsin primary was empty of encouragement or solace.

It was not merely that he had suffered a personal defeat; he could still say, as he had said in 1940, "I don't have to be President." It was not even that the principles he believed in had seemingly been rejected; public opinion might change. What he had been testing, as he saw it, was the democratic process itself; and he was now forced to question whether his faith in that process ("I have come into Wisconsin to campaign because I believe deeply in the right of the people to make . . . conclusions and because I believe in their infinite wisdom")[123] was soundly based.

For no candidate in a major campaign had ever trusted the people so fully or spoken to them so unreservedly as Willkie had in Wisconsin. Nobody had ever appealed to the electorate so unashamedly on behalf of reason against unreason, idealism against expediency, altruism against selfishness. Nobody had ever told them with such clarity and passion that the welfare of the individual, of the nation, and of mankind were henceforth inseparably united. Yet no candidate in any election where the circumstances were at all comparable had ever been so overwhelmingly defeated.

Yet in this darkest hour he did not lose the human touch, the considerateness for other persons, without respect to status, which proves the genuineness of his equalitarian principles. In a news conference the next morning, "after the newsmen of his own party had asked their questions"—in answer to one of which he had said, "Off the record, it looks like Dewey on the first ballot"—he looked at "the only stranger present" (Arthur Thomas, the manager of Radio Station WJAG in the small city of Norfolk, Nebraska) as if inviting him to speak, and the latter did so: "Still, off the record, a lot of your friends and supporters will wonder what your attitude will be if Dewey gets the nomination."

Willkie's reply was brusque: "Certainly you don't expect me to answer that." And the meeting broke up. But later, when one of the Willkie party phoned to cancel the radio time that had been reserved on WJAG, he told Thomas "that Willkie had asked him to apologize to 'that Norfolk radio man' for his curt reply and explain that his mind was burdened with turning over the decision to retire."[124]

Willkie gave a hint of his feelings in a luncheon speech at Fremont: "When I think of what I have seen around the world and think of crowds that cheer wildly for petty criticism of minor groups, I feel a bit heartbroken because I know how much my party could do and how much my country needs it. . . . Perhaps the conscience of America is dulled. Perhaps the people are not willing to bear sacrifices . . ."

And he prefaced his evening speech at Omaha by saying: "I wish I could speak to you from my heart tonight. I cannot, because there are too many factors that prevent it. If I spoke what's on my mind, I would make too great a castigation of American politics."[125] Instead, he delivered his speech as planned. Only the newsmen knew what he was going to do at the end of it.

The speech itself was the most powerful indictment ever delivered of Roosevelt's foreign policy since the beginning of the war. "The Roosevelt administration," he insisted, had "not dealt squarely with the rest of the world in this war" or "with the American people." It had acted with secrecy and it had acted without principle. It had "used the excuse of military expediency to cover up the letting down of people who are our friends and dealings with the Fascists who are our enemies," and it had "discouraged the efforts of the American press to inform us candidly of the facts of the international situation." And by not taking the lead in setting up "a continuously functioning Council of the United Nations," it had suggested to other countries that "we have something to hide," and thus had given the Russians (for example) some reason for inferring a "hidden hostility and suspicion" toward them, and hence a reason for sometimes acting "with what seems to be a disregard of our common interests."

And they and others might find further grounds for distrust when they looked at our "political record" in North Africa and Italy. "Darlan, Peyrouton, Badoglio and the King of Italy were not conjured up by Nazi propaganda to fool the people of Europe about United States policy. They were, as far as we know, the tokens of our sincerity in dealing with two nations that had lost their freedom." While the President was refusing to recognize De Gaulle's National Liberation Committee and was joining Churchill "to prop up the senile monarchy in Italy," French and Italian patriots were fighting and dying to defeat the Germans. "While the President supports tired old Fascists in the areas our armies control, millions of Europeans are preparing to help our invasion of the Continent."[126] In short, the Administration seemed not to know what the nation was fighting for.

Yet "the losses in young American lives which we have already taken and are now facing in even greater numbers can only be justified if this becomes truly a war for liberation. For if we deny those fighting for free-lom in France, as this administration is denying them, we shall face not only civil war in that country but the repudiation here of all we thought we were fighting for.

"If we deny the democratic elements in Italy, as this administration is denying them, we shall slow up our armies and make still more terrible the tasks that lie ahead of us.

"If, in our foreign policy, we deny anywhere the aspirations of those who want to be free, as secret policies inevitably tend to deny them, we shall be laying the groundwork for a third world war."

Willkie concluded: "The American people have faith in the processes of democracy. They want a foreign policy that will affirm that faith."[127] These were brave words after what had happened in Wisconsin.

Whether attacks on deals with fascists was a good way to win Republican votes in Nebraska was a question that no longer needed to be asked. For when Willkie had finished his main speech, he read a personal statement.

"It has been my conviction that no Republican could be nominated for President unless he received at the convention the votes of some of the major Midwestern states. For it is in this section of the country that the Republican party has had its greatest resurgence.

"Therefore I quite deliberately entered the Wisconsin primary to test whether the Republican voters in that state would support me in the advocacy of every sacrifice and cost necessary to winning and shortening the war and in the advocacy of tangible, effective economic and political cooperation among the nations of the world for the preservation of peace and the rebuilding of humanity.

"The result of the primary is naturally disappointing to me and doubly so since the candidate who led at the polls is known as one active in such organizations as America First, opposed to the beliefs which I entertain.

"As I have said many times, the country desperately needs new leadership. It is obvious now that I cannot be nominated. I therefore am asking my friends to desist from any activity toward that end and not to present my name at the convention.

"I earnestly hope that the Republican convention will nominate a candidate and write a platform which really represents the views which I have advocated and which I believe are shared by millions of Americans. I shall continue to work for those principles and policies for which I have fought during the last five years."[128]

The battle was ended, but the war would go on.

XXII

"Nothing Is Here for Tears"

1

It is tempting to surmise, and has often been said, even by those who knew him well, that Willkie died of a broken heart. But other friends deny it, and his own words bear them out. Even on the day after the primary he commented, with a kind of boyish pride: "I went down just the way I'd like to go down, fighting for a principle."[1] And his letters to his friends, after the first shock was over, show a swift revival of his buoyant spirit. Sending a note of thanks to Milton Polland—"I will always feel myself much in your debt"—he added: "It was a good fight. There are many battles yet ahead. Don't get discouraged."[2] Answering a letter from Don Anderson he declared: "I am feeling wonderful. As a matter of fact, I haven't felt better for many a day."[3] And to Madison's other editor, William Evjue, he wrote: "It was a great satisfaction to have you in this fight with me, and I want you to know that I intend to continue my efforts to see the principles we believe in realized within the Republican party." (Evjue in answer commented on the rarity of such thanks from a defeated candidate, spoke of Willkie's world-wide fame and added: "Yet you take time out to write a letter to an obscure editor out in the hinterlands with the assurance that you are going to continue the fight for the principles to which you are committed.")[4] Finally, he told Josephine Pinckney, acknowledging a "sweet but sassy note" which "moved me much": "I know most people assume that one situated as I am must be depressed. As a matter of fact, I am on top of the wave. And I didn't dip my colors in falling. You probably don't realize how much satisfaction there is in that. For you have not had to live under the crushing pressures of political expediency."[5]

The last phrase gives one key to his state of mind. For months, as events forced upon him the conclusion that to achieve his aims he must win the nomination, he had of necessity never spoken or acted without having to consider how his candidacy would be affected. In the blessed sense of release from this unrelenting inward stress, he must have found, after all, some sweetness at the bottom of the bitter cup. To one friend he "appeared happier, and more determined to fight for his ideals, now that he was free of the suspicion of doing and saying things solely for political reasons."[6]

He must have found pleasure, also, in the nation-wide response to his courageous fight and his forthright withdrawal.

There were, of course, some comments besides the Chicago *Tribune's* that were less than gracious. Taft was characteristically chilly and pontifical: "Mr. Willkie has apparently recognized the inevitable. It is unfortunate that he has allowed his natural disappointment to lead him to attack Republicans who disagree with him on foreign policy. Nevertheless, his withdrawal will produce a greater unity of all Republicans behind the principles declared at Mackinac." Bricker, still a candidate, had friendly words for "an unselfish and patriotic act."[7] Dewey declined comment on "political questions."[8]

But from many of the rank and file there was unalloyed praise. Don Anderson of the *Wisconsin State Journal* wrote to Willkie a week after the election: "We are getting the strongest mail we have ever had in my newspaper experience commending us for our fight, and expressing the hope that in some way you will be able to make your voice effectively heard."[9] His own mail was similar. The mood of most of it was summed up in a telegram from William Lowe Bryan, President Emeritus of Indiana University: "Hail but not farewell."[10]

The same note was dominant in the editorial praise, some of it eloquent. The Buffalo *Courier-Express* commented: "When historians get American history of the last few years in proper perspective, they will see Willkie as the man who was right . . . at what the so-called practical politicians would call the wrong time. . . . Now the man who was right bows himself out of the Presidential race—but he can't bow himself out of the American scene, where his figure looms larger than before."[11]

There was, to be sure, one sour note in the chorus: the expectation that he would now support Dewey. The Wisconsin primary—so ran the thought—had been a family quarrel, in which personalities rather than principles were involved, and the important thing now was to get together and beat the Democrats.

This attempt to blur the issues in Wisconsin was most blatantly evident in *Time,* whose account made Willkie look like the "prize chump" that the Chicago *Tribune* later called him. "Wisconsin had clearly voted no confidence in global goodwill and a foreign policy of generalities. They had voted against the 'crusade' kind of internationalism—a crusade which had never been clearly defined, which was hopelessly confused with New Dealism. . . . No one could doubt the Wisconsin voters' willingness to participate internationally, but they want to do it on a realistic basis—and as Republicans. . . . Wisconsin isolationists, according to Wisconsin, formed only one part of the vote for one candidate. Wisconsin, it would seem, had voted out of the way a massive road-block on the way to internationalism."[12]

Such a muddling of fact and logic could only be deliberate. And Willkie, to whom it seemed that Wisconsin voters had only shown their confidence that Dewey would never do anything that they did not want him to, showed remarkable restraint in a letter to Henry Luce. "I thought the article misstated the facts about the Wisconsin primary and therefore drew erroneous conclusions. Naturally, being human and in view of your many expressions of friendship for me, I thought it appropriate to call your attention to what I, at least, thought an undeserved blow when the blows were falling rather thick. . . . But forget it. I am the first to recognize your complete right to express any opinion you have in publications which you own.

"I do hope you have more luck in shaping the Republican Party than I have had. Perhaps after some experience in your new endeavor you will decide that your field is journalism . . ."[13]

The hurt went deep, however; and in conversation he was apparently less restrained, for he wrote to Luce again on May 9: "Let me apologize for having been so argumentative at Beth's dinner about the Time article. You must excuse some things for depth of feeling. I don't think anyone can know how much of my being I gave in an effort to make the Republican party worthy of leadership. The temporary defeat moved me much. And perhaps, like Hamlet, I was over-anxious for my cause to be reported as I understood it to be."[14]

2

After his withdrawal from the contest for the nomination, Willkie also withdrew temporarily from public life. For a longer time than at any period since the beginning of 1940, he failed to make a public speech or issue a statement to the press. Not until May 25 did he again make a public appearance, and then a non-political one, at a dinner in honor of his friend Walter White of the NAACP, to which he gave $5,000 from the Willkie Trust Fund.[15]

Two weeks before the opening of the Republican National Convention, however, Willkie returned to the political arena. A group of friendly newspaper publishers invited him to write a series of brief articles discussing the issues that would confront the parties in their conventions and campaigns.[16] In response, Willkie produced seven articles, which appeared daily beginning June 12, and which he later summarized in a "Proposed Platform" for the Republican party.

The first piece, on "Federal Power and States' Rights," exposed the folly of those Republicans who wished the party to embrace the latter doctrine. Agreeing that "the present Administration's arbitrary use of vast authority"[17] was rightly to be opposed, he dismissed as irrelevant "the worn-out issue of states' rights versus strong federal government. That is not an issue; that is a relic."[18] The Republican party had had its birth in the need for a central government strong enough to compel national unity, and similar needs were still present. "We cannot, for instance, have forty-eight different minimum wage laws; nor can we have a variety of state policies if we hope to protect the farmer against the precipitate downward spiral of post-war agricultural prices. . . . The number of such problems increases steadily with every step in our industrial growth and expansion. And the more we move, as we must move, into the affairs of the world, the more this will be true. For we will be living and functioning and trading in a world where other peoples have granted to their governments the power and authority to act for them."

What was needed, then, was not a weaker central government; but first, "local administration of federal functions in their local applications"; and second, "the substitution of government by law for government by caprice and unlimited discretion." These were the policies that Republicans should espouse—instead of fighting "behind an outmoded mask of states' rights . . . to prevent social and political advance, or . . . to weaken the federal government to such an extent that the United States will be unable to play its appropriate role in the world today."

From states' rights it was a short step to Negroes' rights, since Republicans in effect now used the first to deny the second, and opposed Federal anti-poll tax and anti-lynching laws. This party policy must be reversed; thirteen million Negroes—"one tenth of the nation"—would not, after the war, be willing to wait indefinitely for the freedoms that the war was supposedly being fought to protect; nor would they be won back to the Republican party by "vague assurances of future actions expressed in pious platitudes." And it was not merely a matter of votes but of justice. "The Constitution does not provide for first and second class citizens." Negro Americans were entitled to the same opportunities as white Americans: in education, in jobs, and in the Armed Services.

Willkie's third topic was "Social Security," and here his comments could only be described as revolutionary. Whereas the Old Guard had now grudgingly accepted, as the price of self-preservation, the initial New Deal program, Willkie declared that it did not go far enough. "Need knows no rules of eligibility or coverage. Protection against old age, illness and economic misfortune must be a *right* for everyone . . . regardless of a man's previous earnings." And children as well as the aged must be protected. As at one time "our society left the education of children to the parents' ability to pay," and then "changed civilization" by deciding that "all children should be educated regardless of their parents' income," so now we must cease to leave "the feeding, clothing, shelter and medical care of our children to be determined by their parents' income alone. . . . We must begin the moment the war is over to see that every child in America grows up with the basic necessities of good food, adequate clothing, medical care and a decent home."

If this sounded like "socialism," Willkie had an answer: "We whose faith is in a freely competitive society have the special obligation of seeing that all 'start fair' . . ."

In discussing the "Economy of Demobilization," he declared bluntly: "We are not going to *return* to anything." And with equal bluntness he added: "Already, looking to the future, men are asking: Must we have war to have jobs?" His answer was "No"—if government spending was used to prevent the previous "wide fluctuations of our economic cycle," if tax laws were revised "to encourage risk capital," and if "new and effective methods" could be found to control monopoly—"the Trojan horse of the free enterprise system . . ."

These were conventional views, but in his piece on "Labor" he once more showed himself to be in his social thinking far ahead of most Democrats as well as most Republicans; although he acknowledged that the former in general had understood, as the latter in general had *not,* "that for labor the essential content of freedom is different in today's industrial society from what it was in the agricultural society of an earlier age. Men no longer able to own, or to aspire to own, small businesses and farms have sought new solutions for a need that all Americans must respect—the need to control for themselves the circumstances which dictate their working lives." "The essential content of freedom" now involved the right to strike, the right to bargain collectively, and "an annual wage to those who work in plants with long seasonal or periodic shut-downs." The means to this end was "labor-management cooperation": "It is time for both labor and management to grow up . . ." As part of this growing-up process, labor must become responsible, "must drive from its midst its racketeers, adopt democratic procedures, and account for its funds and activities both to the public and to its own membership." Government regulation should be a last resort. And the desired changes would be speeded by "a real labor representative in the Cabinet."

In the article on "Tariff and International Trade" Willkie warned again of the evils of trade wars with "state-controlled economies" and urged, instead, "revision of our tariff and cooperation in a policy of international currency stabilization," through the instrumentality of the United Nations. And beyond this, the need must be recognized for long-term investments in under-developed areas. "The startling contrast in the level of comfort in our modern industrial countries and the hard struggle for bare subsistence in technically undeveloped countries is one of the most painful—and dangerous—aspects of international relations." And both private investment and government aid must be accompanied by "full recognition that the day of economic imperialism is over."

In the final piece, on "Foreign Policy," Willkie again reprehended deals with fascists, and also any plans that might exist for a world organization dominated by the great powers. The small nations must have a voice in shaping their fate; the great ones must surrender some measure of their supposed autonomy. And the Republican platform must recognize the latter fact, rejecting "quibbling words" like "integrity" and "sovereignty." And above all, the American people must recognize the necessity of adhering to America's professed ideals: "we must encourage men's just aspirations for freedom not only at home but everywhere in the world."

These little essays have a prophetic quality. And once again the American public responded to Willkie's inspired common sense. Two days after the first article appeared, Willkie wrote a characteristic note of appreciation to Gardner Cowles: "It is apparent now that the series of articles, from the distribution standpoint, have proven to be an amazing success. They are being run in full in literally thousands of newspapers.

"The suggestion of the method that made this possible was entirely yours. As you know, it is a little difficult for me to express appreciation because I am always afraid I'll slop over and be too sentimental."[19]

And the articles were evidently successful from more than "the distribution standpoint." On June 15 Lem Jones wrote to Fred Baker: "The mail has been almost unbelievable, running 1300 to 1500 a week."[20]

Once again, however, Willkie was unable to translate personal popularity into political power. Nothing could have been less appealing to the Old Guard—now, in harmonious conjunction with Dewey, in full control of the party—than Willkie's "Proposed Platform." They must, in fact, have congratulated themselves once more on the outcome of the Wisconsin primary.

And having once got rid of Willkie they were taking no chances. Normally, a former Presidential candidate would have been made a member of his state's delegation. At the very least, he would have been invited to present his views to the platform committee. But Willkie was ignored.

On Dewey's side the motive was simply to avoid discord; personal vindictiveness was not among his faults. But the Old Guard welcomed the opportunity for revenge. The interloper who for four years had been trying to take over the party, who had told them to go to hell, who did not give a damn whether they supported him or not, who called them narrow and pathological, who boasted that they were his enemies, who was a standing reproach to the isolationism that many of them still secretly cherished—this man was now in a position where (they thought) they could humiliate him as he had humiliated them. Spangler justified the snub on the grounds that "Willkie had practically seceded from the party," since he refused to commit himself beforehand to support the convention's choice for President.[21]

The National Chairman did, however, preserve the proprieties. On May 17 he wrote to Willkie: "The Committee on Arrangements for the National Convention has assigned a seat on the platform for you with the other honored guests and we have also set aside for your use six box seats, five seats in the arena and five seats in the mezzanine section of the Stadium."[22] Willkie must have sat and looked at the letter a long time, for in the margin are many doodles. But for the time being he kept silent. Not until Spangler announced on June 16 that "Mr. Willkie and other prominent personalities in the party have been invited to attend the convention,"[23] did he hint in public how he felt. His comment was brief and caustic: "Mr. Spangler very kindly offered me a ticket so that I could listen to the proceedings of the convention."[24]

He did not use the ticket, but friends kept him posted on what was going on. Most of them were nominally supporting Dewey. Sam Pryor, however, found so much latent opposition to Dewey that he thought a deal could be made with the Bricker forces to give the Ohio Governor the Vice Presidential nomination and put Willkie once more at the head of the ticket. But when he telephoned the proposition to Willkie, he got the inevitable answer: "Sam, I can't do it."[25]

With Dewey's nomination certain, the chief interest and activity now centered on the writing of the platform, especially the foreign policy plank. It might have been thought that this had been settled by the Mackinac Island declaration of the year before, but now the battle must be fought again. Taft had been appointed chairman of the committee in an obvious attempt to hold the internationalists in check, and the outcome was bound to be an elastic verbal formula that the candidate—as well as others—could interpret as he chose.

On June 23 the *Times* published the text of such a formula, reportedly worked out by Taft and Vandenberg;[26] but the final official statement was to have been kept secret until presented on the floor of the convention. Willkie later asserted that it was so "closely guarded, except from the leading candidate, that even Republican governors who were delegates could not get copies of the proposed platform to study."[27] He himself, however, secured a copy,[28] called a news conference and delivered a blistering criticism.

He began by quoting in part the proposed foreign policy statement.

"[We seek] peace and freedom based on justice and security.

"We shall achieve such aims by international cooperation and not by joining a world state.

"We favor responsible participation by the United States in (a)[29] postwar cooperative organization among sovereign nations to prevent military aggression and to attain permanent peace with organized justice in a free world. Such organization should develop effective cooperative aims to develop peace forces to prevent or repel military aggression. Pending this we pledge continued collaboration with the (principal) United Nations to assure these ultimate objectives.

"It should promote world opinion to influence the nations to right conduct, develop international law and create an international tribunal to deal with justiceable disputes.

"Pursuant to the Constitution of the United States, any treaty made on behalf of the United States with any other nation or any association of nations shall be made only by and with the advice and consent of the Senate of the United States provided two-thirds of the Senators present concur."

Willkie's comment was: "In 1920 the Republican Convention adopted a foreign relations plank which provided as follows: 'The Republican party stands for agreement among the nations to preserve the peace of the world. We believe that such an international association must be based upon international justice, and must provide methods which shall maintain the rule of public right by the development of law and the decision of impartial courts, and which shall secure instant and general international conference whenever peace shall be threatened by political action so that the nations pledged to do and insist upon what is just and fair may exercise their influence and power for the prevention of war.'

"Thirty-one leading Republicans, interpreting this language, assured the American electorate that a Republican victory was the surest road to an effective world organization. The Republicans won the election of 1920. A Republican President, claiming that he in no way repudiated his party's platform, immediately after the election announced that the League of Nations was dead.

"A Republican President elected under the proposed platform of 1944 could, with equal integrity, announce that the United States would not enter any world organization in which the nations agreed jointly to use their 'sovereign' power for the suppression of aggression.

"And every effective world organization proposed could be rejected as a world state. And all proposed joint forces for the suppression of aggression could be called armed forces and not 'peace forces.' And each proposed step taken by any world organization in which we might participate could be called a treaty and, as such, would be subject to ratification by two-thirds of the Senate.

"The net result would be no international organization. No effective international force for the suppression of aggression. No peaceful world. Another world war fought in vain. And the youth of America once more betrayed."[30]

No one could deny the deadly parallel. But no Republican could admit it without disrupting the semblance of harmony so arduously achieved. So even the Republican internationalists (Austin, Ball, Burton, Edge and others) defended the statement and by implication condemned Willkie.

Taft took forty-five minutes to read the platform to the Convention, staying awake with difficulty while he did so. The delegates present (more than three-quarters of them were absent and the galleries were almost empty) took twenty seconds to adopt it.[31]

The nomination of Dewey was equally perfunctory. The only real enthusiasm shown during the entire convention was aroused by a speech by Hoover, when he said, "I am sure that if the Republican party comes into power it will not be to liquidate either the economic welfare or the independence of the United States."[32]

Willkie's message to Dewey—"Hearty congratulations on your nomination. You have one of the great opportunities of history"—contained, as was noted in the press, no promise of support. (To a worried wire from Bartley Crum one of Willkie's secretaries responded: "Telegram dictated by common courtesy. No change in sentiment. Period of watchful waiting to continue some time longer.")[33]

3

It would seem that Willkie had more friends at the Democratic National Convention than at the Republican, and that some of them wished to make him Roosevelt's running mate. Their efforts are apparently referred to in a cryptic note from Roosevelt to Senator Norris, dated July 17, just before the convention: "I don't think there is any possible danger of Willkie, though feelers were put out about a week ago."[34]

A circumstantial account of what happened at the convention was given Willkie by Drew Pearson (whom Willkie liked and trusted) in a letter dated August 1. "You would have been surprised," he wrote, "at the number of friends you had there and the number of people who spontaneously expressed the hope and the wish that you might be on the ticket, even though . . . you might not even have considered such a proposition." Among them were "Ed Laughlin, new head of Tammany Hall" and Senator Wagner, who seriously considered proposing Willkie's name to the convention. But by the time they got an audience with Leo Crowley, who was apparently Roosevelt's principal agent at the convention, the decision for Truman had been already made—although Crowley "admitted that he had talked to the President about it and the President had said that if there should be a spontaneous move in the convention, he, F. D. R., would be favorably disposed."[35]

Probably Crowley is correct in saying: "I am sure Mr. Roosevelt had never seriously considered Wendell Willkie for his running-mate in 1944."[36] The President (though he had "once told his son James to tease the party regulars that, come the next election, he and Willkie would run together")[37] must have recognized that, as Crowley said, "from the viewpoint of the convention delegates his nomination would have been impossible."[38] He must have known, also, in view of Willkie's biting criticism of Administration foreign policy, that Willkie would never let himself be put in a position where, as in the Vice Presidency, he would have to share responsibility for that policy but would have no power to change it.

The question would seem to be settled by a letter that Willkie wrote on June 13, 1944, to Charles Davis, who had been publicizing the idea that Willkie should be elected Vice President on a ticket with Roosevelt, who would then resign to become head of a world state: "I would not accept the nomination if it were offered me and I would not serve if elected, and it will embarrass me very much if any mention or activity is carried on advocating any such proposal."[39]

Yet Roosevelt, even for Willkie, had a fascination. And during the casual byplay concerning the Vice Presidential nomination, the two men were pondering a future alliance that, if fate had permitted its formation, might have changed the shape of American politics.

The initiative came from Roosevelt. He and Willkie had not met since Willkie's White House visit following his round-the-world trip, but the President's liking and respect for his former rival had not lessened. They had survived Willkie's blunt statements during the trip, his sharp criticisms of the Administration in the "Report to the People," and even his unsparing condemnation of the Darlan Deal. On December 18, 1942, for instance, when Willkie received *The American Hebrew* medal for "promotion of better understanding between Christians and Jews in America," the news stories carried a statement by the President, who had been one of the judges, that he had voted for Willkie "because he is working so consistently throughout this war and with other nations for tolerance and better understanding."[40]

Still stronger evidence is supplied by a letter from Roosevelt to Willkie three months later. In this the President took pains to refute Marquis Childs' contention in an article in *Look* that there was "a desire on the part of Washington to shut [Willkie] up or discredit him."[41]

"Dear Wendell:

"Somebody called my attention to an article about you by an old friend of mine in the Saturday Evening Post. [This was a slip.]

"In view of certain allegations made by Brother Childs, I want to tell you one or two things with the utmost simplicity.

"First, I certainly did not give you any hint of the North African invasion plans. Nor, did I to anyone else except the top Army and Navy people who knew about them anyway. Even the Vice President and Cabinet were given no hint.

"Secondly, the record will show that I did not say I was too busy to read what you had to say in the 'second front' statement from Moscow. What I did say was that I had been too busy to read the papers that morning and therefore did not know what you had said.

"Third, I have in no way 'seemed determined to belittle Willkie.' The contrary is true. I have on many occasions done just the opposite.

"Childs' article was a bit puerile. In regard to the press conference, I did not make a crack at your pronunciation of 'reservahr.' I used the word in my own way which happens to be very close to your own way. But it was the press and not me who created the whole thing as a grand joke and made an episode out of nothing.

"It is true, of course, that Stimson called you up in regard to what you were going to say about the Darlan matter. That, however, is water over the dam and things in North Africa seem to be fairly quiet for the American forces behind the lines.

"I guess Childs was trying to make trouble between us because I honestly think you are doing your best to help all of us, from top to bottom, win the war.

Always sincerely,"[42]

Willkie sent a noncommittal reply on March 19: "Thank you very much for your letter of last week. I apologize for not having answered heretofore but I have been out of the city. I appreciate very much the things you had to say."[43]

There is no reason to think that there was any enmity between the two men or that their failure to meet again was due to anything except circumstances. First, the war was in general going well on both the production front and the fighting fronts. The President no longer needed Willkie's help. Second, his current crusades were within the Republican party: to force it to take a firm internationalist stand and to persuade it to make him its nominee. Success in either enterprise would have been made far harder by any public association with Roosevelt. But after the Wisconsin primary it seemed that though Willkie had partially succeeded in the first endeavor, he had definitely failed in the second; and that therefore there was no obstacle, after the election was over, to their joining forces.

The fullest account of how the project originated is given by Samuel Rosenman in *Working with Roosevelt.*[44] "During the last week in June, 1944, the President called me into his office and said: 'Governor Pinchot has just been in to see me. He has had a meeting recently with Willkie. They talked about the possibility of a new setup in American politics. It was Willkie's idea.'" It was an idea, however, that must often have occurred to Roosevelt, and now there was no limit to his enthusiasm. "I think the time has come for the Democratic party to get rid of its reactionary elements in the South and to attract to it the liberals in the Republican party. Willkie is the leader of those liberals. He talked to Pinchot about a coalition of the liberals in both parties, leaving the conservatives in both parties to join together as they see fit. I agree with him one hundred per cent and the time is now—right after election."

But it turned out that "after election" was not soon enough; Roosevelt wanted Rosenman to go to New York to see Willkie at once, and when Rosenman suggested that Willkie might think they were trying to get his support in the coming campaign, Roosevelt told him to "explain . . . in advance that what you want to see him about has nothing to do with the election."

Willkie agreed, on condition that the meeting should be secret. Should it become known that he had met Roosevelt's representative, it would be widely reported and believed that he was making a deal to support the President in the election; and whatever influence he might have on liberal Republican or independent voters would be destroyed. Accordingly, on July 5 they met secretly for lunch at the St. Regis Hotel.

Willkie was quite as receptive as Roosevelt had hoped. "Both parties are hybrids," he commented. He wanted a new political lineup after the war and a fight on clean-cut issues "between all the liberal forces on the one hand and all the conservative forces on the other." In foreign policy, especially, he was hopeful of great benefits from a liberal triumph. "You tell the President," he said to Rosenman, "that I'm willing to devote almost full time to this. A sound liberal government in the United States is absolutely essential to continued cooperation with the other nations of the world. I know some of these reactionaries—especially those in my own party. They'll run out on the other nations when the going gets tough—just as soon as they can."

Willkie's eagerness is not hard to understand. For four years he had fought the Old Guard from inside the party, and had finally lost. Perhaps he would have more success in fighting them from the outside. He and Rosenman even got to the point of discussing what groups and individuals they could count on to join a "liberal" party. And Willkie was more than willing to discuss the same topic with Roosevelt—after the election.

The President—"the master politician of his day"—was the last man to question the need to wait. But when he learned the outcome of Rosenman's mission, he was apparently swept away by his enthusiasm. Without consulting Rosenman, he sent Willkie the following letter, dated July 11.

"Dear Wendell:

"I will not be able to sign this because I am dictating it just as I leave on a trip to the westward.

"What I want to tell you is that I want to see you when I come back, but not on anything in relationship to the present campaign. I want to talk to you about the future, even the somewhat distant future, and in regard to the foreign relations problems of the immediate future.

"When you see in the papers that I am back, will you get in touch with

General Watson? We can arrange a meeting either here in Washington or, if you prefer, at Hyde Park—wholly off the record or otherwise, just as you think best.

Always sincerely yours,"

Some readers will still think that Roosevelt was being disingenous; but the tone of Willkie's answer suggests that he accepted the President's letter as having been written in good faith, although he again stressed his desire for delay.

"My dear Mr. President:

"I have your gracious note of the thirteenth. The subjects concerning which you suggest we have a talk on your return from the West are, as you know, subjects in which I am intensely interested. I am fearful, however, that any talk between us before the campaign is over might well be the subject of misinterpretation and misunderstanding. And I do not believe, however much you or I might wish or plan otherwise, that we could possibly have such a talk without the fact becoming known.

"Therefore, if it is agreeable to you, I would prefer postponement of any such talk until after the November elections.

"I hope you will understand that I make this suggestion because you in a great way, and I in a small one, have the trust and confidence of people who might see in the most innocent meeting between us at this time, some betrayal of the principles which each of us hold so deeply.

Believe me with great respect
Sincerely yours,"[45]

One cannot help regretting that a letter so deeply felt and finely phrased was never sent. Still more to be regretted are the events that caused Willkie to leave it in his files. He did not send it immediately, of course, because he knew the President was not in Washington. He did not send it later because in the meantime the letter to which it was an answer had become public property.

Willkie never accused Roosevelt personally of being responsible for the "leak." And, in fact, he is apparently cleared by a note attached to a copy of the letter in the Roosevelt Library: "No one must see this. A. C. T."[46] Nevertheless the letter got out. On July 24 Willkie wrote to Henry Luce: "Early this morning Len Lyons called me and said he had an item that the President had written me a letter before leaving Washington, asking me to see him on his return. As you and one intimate friend were the only ones who had seen the letter, I was naturally surprised. On my stalling, he said, 'Well, Mr. Willkie, I might as well be frank. A White House source gave me the item and I was merely calling you for confirmation or denial.' I then, of course, told him I could do neither. I assume he will run it. It indicates, however, just what I was saying to you that I could have no conversation as proposed in the letter without its exploitation."[47]

Whether Lyons printed the item or not, it soon became common knowledge. By August 11 the gossip was so widespread that the *Times* took notice of it in a front page article, which spoke of "all those who had seen the note."[48] How far those responsible for the publicity were motivated by the wish to compromise Willkie is unclear, for the "sources of unimpeachable integrity, who said they had seen the note," stated that the President had made it clear that he was not concerned with the present campaign. Willkie continued to decline comment, but perhaps his feeling can be inferred from a passage in a letter to Gardner Cowles on August 15: "You need have no fears about my accepting any position from either Franklin Roosevelt or Thomas Dewey. I am so fed up on pragmatic politicians that there is no inducement that would prompt me to serve under either of them in any capacity."[49] And when Roosevelt on August 18, the day after his return, denied in his press conference that he had sent the letter, it was another turn of the screw.[50]

It may well be that the President, caught off guard and unaware of how widespread and well authenticated the story was, denied it with the idea of protecting Willkie. But under the circumstances his denial could only serve to strengthen suspicion. Perhaps it was on this occasion that Willkie said: "I've been lied to for the last time."[51]

Or perhaps it was when he read the letter, dated August 21, in which Roosevelt tried to smooth things over.

"Dear Wendell:

"A most unfortunate thing happened at my Press Conference on Friday. I had written you on July thirteenth, just as I was leaving for Hawaii and Alaska, a purely personal note telling you I hoped much to see you on a non-campaign subject sometime after I got back. Quite frankly when I was asked—in a series of questions about foreign affairs—whether I had written to you to invite you to Washington, I said 'No.' That afternoon Steve Early said to me 'Are you sure that you did not write to Wendell Willkie?' And it flashed into my mind that I had written you before I left.

"The interesting thing is how my note to you got to the press. I have been trying to find where the leak was down here, as I regarded it as a purely personal note between you and me. As far as I can remember I said nothing about it to anybody, though it is possible that I told Leo Crowley that I was going to ask you if we could talk the subject over. I am awfully sorry that there was a leak on a silly thing like this—but I still hope that at your convenience—there is no immediate hurry—you will stop in and see me in Washington or run up to Hyde Park if you prefer.

"I hope you have had a good summer. My trip in the Pacific was extraordinarily interesting. I hope to be able to tell you about it and about how I am trying to keep China going. Our friend, Madame Chiang, is in Brazil with her sister, Madame Kung, and I hope they will both come here before they return home.

Always sincerely,"

If Willkie composed an answer to this letter, it is not in the files. Despite the President's obvious eagerness to retain his friendship, two items must have sharpened his sense of betrayal: first, the evident untruth (implied if not explicitly stated) that Roosevelt had forgotten about the first letter; and second, his attempt to depreciate, by the phrase "a silly thing like this," a matter that Willkie regarded as deeply serious.

Willkie's feelings after the August 18 press conference are revealed in a letter that he wrote on that day to former Governor James M. Cox of Ohio, a friend of his Akron years. At the beginning of August, in the hope of protecting himself to some extent in his dealings with the White House, Willkie had asked Cox, who was Roosevelt's friend as well as his, to act as an intermediary; and Cox attempted, just before Roosevelt's return, to establish lines of communication. But he acted with such caution that Roosevelt's assistants did not understand his mission, and before matters could be straightened out, Willkie called the whole thing off.[52]

"My dear Governor:

"In view of the events of the last few days, particularly in view of the President's denial of his invitation to me to discuss certain matters with him, I am quite reluctant for you to discuss with the President the matters you and I discussed.

"So you may know the details. I did receive a letter from the President. I guarded it very carefully, but Jonathan Daniels, one of the Presidential assistants, and others, passed out the fact of the invitation to several gossip columnists and others, with the result that I had to take some protective measures of my own.[53]

"As the President has now denied even the existence of the invitation, I would much prefer not to have any discussion with him, either direct or indirect. For it is evident to me now that even if he would wish such discussion to be in good faith and on the right plane, some of his associates would violate the understanding.

"It has been a great joy to renew our old acquaintance and I hope to see you many times in the coming days.

Cordially yours,"[54]

It says much for both men—for Roosevelt's appreciation of Willkie's ability and character and for Willkie's willingness, in spite of the evidence, to accept the President's assurances of good faith—that except for Willkie's illness they might still have got together. Roosevelt on his return straightened out the confusion in regard to Cox's mission and at once sought his aid in communicating with Willkie. But for the time being, apparently, the latter's decision remained firm, and Cox did not enter the picture again.[55]

Willkie's desire to have no more dealings with the President was strengthened when the latter's letter of August 21 also got into the public press[56] and when on August 25 Roosevelt admitted at a press conference that he *had* been in communication with Willkie. This time the latter permitted himself a brief public statement: "It is true that Mr. Roosevelt has written to me asking that I confer with him. I would much prefer that no such conference occur until after the election, but if the President of the United States wishes to see me sooner, I shall of course comply.

"I have had no contact or communication with the President other than the two letters which he wrote to me."[57]

The President *did* wish to see him sooner, and for a good reason. Roosevelt was considering making Willkie the chief American representative in whatever body was established, after the defeat of Germany, to guide the political reconstruction of Europe, and giving him wide authority in regard to civil and political affairs—even over Eisenhower and the supreme military command.[58]

And this was a matter that seemingly could not wait. At the end of July the Allies broke out of the Normandy beachhead. During the last week of August Paris and Marseille were liberated, Allied forces reached the Rhine and crossed the Belgian border, while in Italy they drove onward north of Rome. In the East the Nazi puppet governments of Rumania and Bulgaria surrendered as the Russian juggernaut swept forward; and the Red Army was on the outskirts of Warsaw. The whole Hitler regime seemed on the verge of collapse. And no plans had been agreed on by the Allies, or even by America's leaders among themselves, for the period following that collapse. The situation called for a leader whose imagination was unfettered by outworn formulas, who was resourceful and resolute, who could command the respect of those with whom he had to deal. Roosevelt had evidently decided that Willkie was the man.

So the President kept trying—this time through David Niles, a Presidential assistant who was a friend of Bartley Crum. Crum passed on to Willkie the President's request that he would come to Hyde Park for a talk during or soon after the Labor Day weekend. Willkie agreed to the meeting, but no date was set, and he went to Rushville for the weekend. But he apparently intended to return to New York immediately afterwards; although he had been trying for weeks to schedule a trip to San Francisco in connection with a legal case in which his law firm was engaged. He made an appointment with Bartley Crum for the following Wednesday to discuss further his meeting with the President; [59] and he had a luncheon date with the British Ambassador the day after.[60] It is also said that Roosevelt "asked for his private telephone number in Indiana . . . and sent word that he would want to see him before he went on to California . . ."[61]

But the meeting was not to be. When Willkie returned to New York after Labor Day, it was to enter the hospital. A month later he was dead.

There is no evidence as to whether Willkie would have accepted the European post. As to whether he and Roosevelt could have redrawn the traditional boundaries between American political parties, the answer is doubtful. To a majority of political partisans, names mean more than principles. One may question, also, whether a sharp ideological division between the major parties would really serve the cause of democracy better than the traditional system. But Willkie and Roosevelt fighting together against the Republican Old Guard and the Democratic "Southern Bourbons" would have been something to see.

4

While Willkie and Roosevelt were projecting a realignment of American political parties, a campaign was being fought between the parties as they then were.

From the time when he learned the outcome of the Wisconsin primary, Willkie had known that sometime he would have to answer the question that a reporter had then annoyed him by asking: "Would he support Dewey if Dewey was the nominee?" The answer was simple—though baffling to the party regulars. He would support Dewey—if Dewey would commit himself to American membership in a post-war international organization with genuine power, and commit himself so clearly and irrevocably as to make impossible a repetition of Harding's surrender to the isolationists in 1921.

Willkie had arrived at this answer even before the Wisconsin primary. On March 16 he wrote confidentially to New Orleans newspaper publisher Ralph Nicholson:

"My interest in politics is entirely because of certain deep convictions I entertain. If I could be President under the stipulation that I was to carry out other and different principles, I would not even consider seeking the Presidency.

"As you know, among the questions on which I feel deeply is the problem of the relationship of our country with the rest of the world. I don't know Governor Dewey's views on this subject except in a most general and sketchy way. I have carefully read everything he has said on the subject from 1940 on. With my convictions, it would be quite difficult to advocate the election of one concerning whose views on this subject I entertain any doubts. Perhaps if Mr. Dewey begins to discuss issues, he will completely clarify his position . . ." Willkie insisted that he had no personal quarrel with Dewey. "I never entertain personal animosities in regard to individuals except in those rare instances where I think their character entitles them to condemnation."[62]

It is clear that he doubted whether Dewey would meet the test and that he was therefore prepared to withhold his support regardless of the consequences. On May 1 he wrote Dorothy Thompson: "Please present my resignation as a Director of Freedom House to the Board at the next meeting. There is an oncoming political campaign close at hand. I may take some very determined and perhaps unexpected positions according to accepted political standards. I am, therefore, resigning from all connections which may in any way embarrass either myself or those with whom I would otherwise be associated."[63]

The strength of his determination is shown by a letter to Marquis Childs written on May 10, and printed by Childs in his column two months after Willkie's death.[64] The occasion was the rumor that Willkie was to be offered the Cabinet post of Secretary of the Navy (Secretary Knox had died suddenly on April 28).

"I, of course, have no way of measuring how many, or if any, people believe in me. If, however, I have only one follower, I certainly owe it to him not to use the faith of that relationship for purely political purposes or permit the administration or the Republican party to use it for such purposes.

"As I have said to you, I happen to believe that this is the most critical moment in the history of liberty.

"All I personally believe in is at stake—free government, civil liberty, economic justice and real accord, not alone among the nations, but among the peoples of the world.

"Let us assume, as is asserted by Mr. [Elmo] Roper and is said by many others, that millions of people believe in me and are turning to me for leadership.

"Should I use that faith merely for place, or permit others to use that faith for political ends? . . .

"I am going to do my duty at this time as my conscience permits me to see my duty, no matter what the price in criticism or in personal denial. Nor will I be deflected by present or anticipated praise.

"Now do not get the notion that I am taking myself too seriously or have lost my sense of humor.

"Everything that I am saying is upon the assumption that people do have faith in me.

"Otherwise, the suggestions made to me by both Republicans and Democrats about high positions would have no meaning."

In the same letter he enclosed a story by Turner Catledge suggesting that Senator La Follette was in effect "joining the Republicans," and that if he did so he might become chairman of the Senate Foreign Relations Committee. "All these things," Willkie added, "I took into account in my fight in Wisconsin. . . . Naturally, as a Republican, I would prefer to work within the Republican party, but I will be damned if I am going to sit by while the peace of the world is wrecked as it was in the 20's."

In the same mood he wrote on May 19 to a friend who had urged him *not* to support Dewey: "You of course have a notion that the tremendous pressures which are being brought to bear on me will not affect me, though they are, at times, annoying. . . . Frankly, I have not decided what I am going to do. I am terribly troubled."[65] And after the convention, of course, the efforts to draw or push him into the Dewey camp were redoubled. He told Judge Rosenman at their meeting on July 5 that "he had been subjected to terrific pressure to come out for Dewey—pressure from Dewey himself, and from others who were house guests with him over the holiday."[66]

At the same time, his distrust of Dewey had been intensified by the events preceding and following the convention. The implications of his own exclusion from the convention were seemingly confirmed when, immediately after it, Dewey appointed Werner Schroeder Vice Chairman of the National Committee, and made James S. Kemper of Chicago, another reactionary and isolationist ally of Colonel McCormick, chairman of the Finance Committee.

Meanwhile, the stress placed upon Willkie by the conflicting loyalties of his friends is sharply revealed in a letter that he wrote to John Cowles on July 8. Cowles had written on July 4 that he intended to support Dewey and hoped Willkie would see his way clear to do the same at a later date. He went on to say that he was "deeply distressed by the apparent rift between you and Johnnie Hanes. In my opinion, none of your friends did more for you in the last year than Johnnie, and none was more completely loyal to you and your interests." Willkie answered:

"I have nothing but the kindliest feelings toward Johnnie Hanes, which feelings, of course, I also have towards Ralph Cake, Fred Baker and Sinclair Weeks. As a matter of fact, I feel much indebted to each of them. You and Mike and I were engaged in a joint enterprise with those fellows. That enterprise did not turn out as we hoped. . . .

"After it was dissolved differing members of the group made differing alignments which, of course, was their complete privilege and right. And I never suggested to any of them that there could possibly be any limitation on their right to do so by reason of our previous joint operation. . . .

"May I say I fully appreciate and understand the strong party tugs on the hearts of Ralph, Sinclair and Fred . . . As for Johnnie—he is one of the finest and most effective fellows I ever knew. In the last month he has turned his great effectiveness into a sustained drive to secure my support for Governor Dewey. After he had my clients, business and personal friends and friendly publishers, etc., etc., all join in the drive, I did what you would have done—took measures to try to stop it. This does not cause me to think less of him; it merely means that I want to live as you do, free of pressures."[67]

As the summer passed, Willkie wrote other letters to those who tried in friendly fashion to win his support for the Republican ticket. Each one deepens without changing the lines of the self-portrait that emerges from the passages already quoted. It is the portrait of a man beyond the reach of partisan appeals, of praise or blame, of threats or bribes; soberly hopeful of a brighter future beyond the somber present; eager for friendship but not at a price; offering to all who trusted him the support of an integrity that was absolute.

Thus, to one friend who argued that "in order to succeed in politics it was necessary to 'play the game' " and support the party nominee, he replied:

"The fact that some people look upon politics as a game in which victor and loser should jump across nets and shake hands with each other, is a matter that concerns me not at all. Nor does the fact that somebody may think me a sorehead or not a good loser affect me in the slightest. . . .

"Frankly, I have not as yet determined what to do in the fall elections. What I will do, however, is determine my course entirely upon the basis of what is entirely right. And I should count myself of little value to my country in its critical hour if my course was deflected by criticism or resentment which I have not at all."[68]

The same even-tempered resolution is evident in a letter to a friend of one of his law partners, who was also a friend of Dewey.

"I hear from a great many people. These days they quickly divide themselves sharply into two groups—[one of which is composed of] those who intend to support the President or Governor Dewey. Such people believe I owe a duty of public leadership to support their respective choice. And most of them just can't understand how it is possible to do otherwise. They have little effect on my thinking.

"The other group—and it is a very large one—is confused. They want help and guidance in determining which of the two candidates they should support. And literally thousands of them write to me asking me to help them. These people represent the independent vote that will determine the election. And they are a [sic] very thoughtful, earnest people. I am watching the evidence as it comes in in order later to be able to help them. That is my conception of the best service I can render at this time. And I at least, am resolved to do it disinterestedly and dispassionately."[69]

To many Republican friends, Willkie's stand seemed unreasonable. Dewey had, indeed, been making speeches that made him sound like a confirmed internationalist. But nothing would have satisfied Willkie at this point short of the outright denunciation of Old Guard isolationists that he himself had delivered in the Wisconsin primary; whereas Dewey's whole plan of campaign was built on a truce with the Old Guard. Willkie's ineradicable distrust of Dewey appears again in a letter to Robert Bradford, one of his young Republican admirers who was later Governor of Massachusetts —a letter which may stand as the final word on Willkie's political position during the summer of 1944. Bradford, too, had urged him, though with obvious reluctance and understanding, to come out for Dewey. Willkie replied:

"There is a great body of Americans around which you and I and Mayo [Shattuck] and fellows like us—and I mean this quite literally—must build a party fit to govern this country. You are in active politics and naturally your emphasis is from and for those whose values are affected by party regularity. There is a very large body of Americans who are very sick of party regularity, and unfortunately, or fortunately, they are the people who fundamentally agree with the policies which you and I believe in. The real problem is how to hold their belief in one's sincerity and at the same time support a candidate who they instinctively know (no matter what he says) does not represent the same viewpoint and who in fact, in many ways, represents just the opposite viewpoint. . . . I give you my assurance that I am not going to do anything definite until after Labor Day. . . . I do want you to know how deeply I appreciate your friendship and advice."[70]

That the man who wrote these letters would let himself be used, knowingly or unknowingly, to further the fortunes of either candidate, is a notion that is almost ludicrous. Nevertheless, Dewey made the attempt.

The occasion was the Dumbarton Oaks conference (so-called from the mansion in Georgetown, a suburb of Washington, in which it met), which opened on August 21 to lay the ground work for a permanent United Nations organization, and which must have buoyed Willkie's spirits after so many discouragements. Now, as he had wished, before the fighting was over, the great powers were coming together to plan a world organization —and one in which the small powers would have a voice. (A hopeful augury had been supplied by the Bretton Woods conference, which during July had worked out agreements for the establishment of an International Monetary Fund and a World Bank.)

Coming in the midst of a Presidential campaign, an event of such immense significance for the future was bound to give rise to political maneuverings. Dewey's problem, like Willkie's in 1940, was how to keep the Administration from stealing the show. His first move was a statement on August 16 vigorously attacking the alleged intention of the Big Four (the United States, Great Britain, Russia and China) to dominate the world organization. This drew from Secretary Hull a denial of any such intention on the part of the United States and an invitation to Dewey to cooperate in the forthcoming negotiations. The New York Governor responded by appointing John Foster Dulles to serve as his representative in conferences with Hull.

The stage was now set for a master-stroke by Dewey—an invitation to Willkie to come to Albany and discuss foreign policy issues with him and Dulles. This would seem to the public a natural as well as a generous move—to invite Willkie's cooperation in the area where he had been most concerned and most critical, that of the party's foreign policy. A refusal would seem indicative of personal resentment, while an acceptance would give the impression that he was, at last, supporting Dewey in the campaign. It was a strategem worthy of Roosevelt himself.

But Willkie was also a master of the game of politics—when he was forced to play. When Elliott Bell, in Dewey's presence, tried to telephone Willkie about midnight Saturday, August 19, he was told that he had gone to bed and could not be disturbed. (Willkie was notorious for keeping late hours and getting along with little sleep.) Dewey then sent a telegram (thus leaving a record of his exact words), which read: "I tried to reach you by telephone tonight but was told you had retired. I am sorry to have missed you. Foster Dulles and I have conferred extensively today and I should like to have the benefit of your views if you could join us at any time on Sunday or Sunday evening before Mr. Dulles goes to Washington."

Dewey had better luck with the telegram than with the phone call. Willkie's answering telegram is marked "A M 1 05." But the content can scarcely have been wholly gratifying to the recipient.

"I shall be glad to meet Mr. Dulles on his way to the conference. . . . I wish I had known your desire for my views prior to your original statement." He himself, he said, had worried about whether the rights and interests of the small states were to be protected; but he had "made inquiry . . . of the Washington authorities" and had been "given strong affirmative assurances. Therefore I had determined to await results before entering into any public discussion. However since . . . both you and Secretary Hull have agreed that the discussions between the Secretary and Mr. Dulles are to be of a non-partisan character I shall be glad to give your representative Mr. Dulles freely of my views."[71]

This exchange left a clear picture of Dewey as a politician and Willkie as a statesman. Moreover, the meeting with Dulles on Monday was so arranged that reporters and photographers did not learn of it until it was over.

The two men talked for an hour and a half, and issued a joint statement which was generally noncommittal but sounded like Willkie. "We have conferred extensively about international problems bearing on world organization to insure lasting peace. There was a full exchange of views not animated by partisan considerations nor having to do with any candidacy, but by the desire of both of us that the United States should play a constructive and responsible part in assuring world order."[72]

If it seems that in this encounter Willkie himself was treating politics as a game, one need only remember that two months earlier he would have welcomed a chance to share with Dewey his views on American foreign policy, and that then Dewey had closed every channel of communication that was within his control. In attempting now to reopen a channel, did he really want Willkie's opinions, or did he want the votes of Willkie's followers? The answer seemed obvious.

5

Despite the energy, resoluteness and confidence with which Willkie confronted every issue and event during the months following the Wisconsin primary, one cannot read his letters written toward the end of the summer without becoming aware of a subtle change of mood—a loss of buoyancy, a lessening of the old eagerness for a good fight, an edge of grimness in his discussion of issues, a somber note in his avowals of faith. And even less than before his withdrawal from the contest for office did he find time for relaxation; not once during the summer did he return to the Indiana farms that he loved so much.

Yet there were moments when his former zest reasserted itself. When Hamilton Fish threatened a suit for libel against playwright Maxwell Anderson because of a political advertisement, Willkie was quick to say "Yes" to a request that he serve as counsel for the defense, and he made public the telegram in which he did so. "I shall count it a public service to represent you in any libel action which Hamilton Fish may bring against you, growing out of his Congressional campaign."[73] In the end Fish decided not to sue.[74] (In the election, though Willkie did not live to see it, he was finally defeated.)

Another reminder of past battles, which must have given Willkie a wry amusement, was an invitation from Bruce Bliven, immediately after Dewey's nomination, to do a piece on Dewey for the *New Republic*. Presumably what was wanted was the same kind of hatchet job that had been done on *him* in 1940, and he might have been excused for resenting the effrontery of such an offer—though from a certain point of view it might be looked on as an apology. At any rate, his refusal was amiable: "I would have a lot of fun doing what you suggest, but I am not the one to do it."[75]

One event during the summer that gave him particular pleasure and a few hours of relaxation was the première on August 1 of a motion picture on the career of Woodrow Wilson, produced by his own company, Twentieth Century-Fox. In a way, *Wilson* was a substitute for the *One World* movie that was never made. It was written by the same script writer,

Lamar Trotti; it dealt with the same general theme; and Willkie must have been more than pleased by the brilliant performance—not easily forgotten by anyone who saw it—of Alexander Knox in the title role. Willkie took an ingenuous delight in playing the role of patron of the arts, and on this occasion he gave a dinner to a number of friends.[76]

In the academic world, perhaps even more than in that of the arts, Willkie admired distinction; and accordingly he must have been deeply gratified when, in the same month of August, he was invited to become a member of the editorial board of *The American Scholar,* monthly publication of Phi Beta Kappa (of which he had been elected an honorary member by the Indiana University chapter in November, 1943). Formal election was to have taken place on October 28.[77]

Another line of activity toward which Willkie was drawn from time to time was that of newspaper publishing. Now that a political career was at least temporarily closed to him, he may have thought that a newspaper would be the most effective means of placing his ideas before the public. Even before the Wisconsin primary, in fact, he had been seriously considering the offer of a well-to-do admirer, W. S. Woodfill, to finance the purchase of the Indianapolis *Star* following the death of the owner, John C. Shaffer, in the fall of 1943. But it was sold to other persons before a final decision was made.[78]

The day after the announcement of the sale, however, came the sudden death of Colonel Frank Knox, who still owned the Chicago *Daily News,* although the management had been in other hands since he had become Secretary of the Navy. Woodfill again approached Willkie, this time concerning the purchase of the *Daily News,* and again found him enthusiastic. (His friend Ernest Klein also wrote to say that the paper was for sale and suggested that Willkie form an organization to buy it.)[79] This time a definite offer was made; but final agreement waited while Willkie tried to find time to get to Chicago to deal in person with the trustees of the Knox estate. His visit was first set for July, then postponed until September. But by then it was too late.

While the deal for the *Daily News* was hanging fire, Willkie remained alert to other possibilities. On August 1, 1944 he wrote to his old friend Joseph Daniels of Indianapolis: "I see where Dick Fairbanks has died. Naturally I don't know anything about the status of his estate or his family, but if the [Indianapolis] *News* is for sale, why don't we get a group together and buy it?"[80]

It is tempting to speculate on what Willkie's career as editor and publisher would have been like, for it is obvious that in many ways he was supremely equipped to achieve success. Especially enticing to the imagination is what he would have done with the Chicago *Daily News* by way of challenge to Colonel McCormick and the *Tribune.*

But this is the stuff of dreams.

The first suggestion of a heart attack came while Willkie was on the train to Indiana for his long postponed visit; although perhaps there had been earlier inklings of something wrong. His brother Fred, who had recently seen him, thought he looked unhealthy and overweight.[81] And his wife surmised from his unwonted irritability that he was not feeling well, although he said nothing about it.[82]

After he reached Rushville, the pain became intense and Mary Sleeth finally broke down his characteristic resistance to calling a doctor. He accepted the doctor's diagnosis but not his prescription—that he immediately enter an Indianapolis hospital. If he could get back to New York, he reasoned, he could perhaps conceal the nature of his illness. "Nobody listens to a man with a bad heart," he told Miss Sleeth. "I still have a lot of things I want to say."[83]

A brief and partial recovery let him put the plan into effect. But on the train he had another attack; it was a haggard and almost helpless Willkie to whom Lem Jones, after anxious moments of waiting while all the other passengers left the train, was finally led by a porter. (Willkie's message to Jones had stipulated that Mrs. Willkie and Philip were not to be told; but Mary Sleeth had telephoned them and they also were at the station.) But still he rejected Jones's suggestion that he call an ambulance and, supported by Jones and the porter, managed to reach a taxi which took him to his apartment. Thence he was taken by ambulance to Lenox Hill Hospital.[84]

The secret was kept. It was announced publicly that he was suffering from colitis, and needed rest. Walter Winchell, indeed, heard a rumor of a heart attack; but when he telephoned an inquiry, Jones lied loyally.[85]

And, after the first few days, it seemed in fact that rest was all he needed. Gradually his strength returned and his spirits rose. He began to write letters, to see friends, to follow the news with his former avidity. It is true that there were up and downs; and during one of the latter, on September 19, he wrote to Governor Saltonstall of Massachusetts a letter containing a rare confession of weakness and a still rarer note of reproach.

"Lying in the hospital this evening, I was frankly a little hurt to read in the evening newspapers that you should say the Dewey ticket would do 'a doggone sight better' in Massachusetts than the Willkie ticket did in 1940, and that Governor Dewey was a man in whom the people could have confidence. The inference, as the papers play it, was plain. I, of course, am experienced enough to know that the papers play a thing as they wish to. But it came to me, perhaps because I am not feeling well, as something of a shock that, in view of our long friendship and also in view of the fact that on every occasion I have done everything I could to advance your cause, you would make any remarks from which such an inference could arise.

"I am a frank person. I never let the sun set on any possible feeling between myself and one of my friends. So I am dropping you this note."

Saltonstall replied that by his remark he "was trying to emphasize a trend . . . and in no way meant to reflect personalities." And on September 27 Willkie was writing to the same correspondent with all his old vigor and assurance.

"I want you to know that I don't think Governor Dewey's Louisville speech clarified the situation. On the contrary, it further muddied the problem. . . . I hope you do not get yourself so closely tied up with the recent nonsense Dewey has been talking that you sink with him if he sinks. Of course as a Republican Governor, you will want to support him formally but . . . the only way that fellows like you and me can really contribute to our party's welfare at this time is by a certain aloofness which may force the candidate to take the right course, if anything can do so."[86]

In this mood Willkie must have taken a grim pleasure in the appearance in *Collier's Magazine* of two articles that he had been asked to write after the Democratic convention had approved a platform which, like that of the Republicans, dealt evasively with the two great issues: international cooperation and racial equality.[87]

In the first article, called "Cowardice at Chicago," Willkie accused both parties of conscious inconsistency in their formulas approving an international organization. "Both parties and both candidates used the term 'sovereign' to indicate something that must be securely guarded, lest we lose our independence as a nation. And in so doing they were deliberately trying to soothe the fears of those people who do not want us to give up a single selfish advantage for the sake of a common good. We are presented with an extraordinary proposition: We are jealously to guard our sovereignty; other nations are likewise to guard their sovereignty; but somehow all nations are to be welded together into an international organization with the *power* to prevent aggression and preserve peace." "What we shall create is at best a consultative pact of the 'peace-loving' nations."

It is of course true that Willkie's proposed limitation of sovereignty would have been as unacceptable to the Soviet Union as to the United States Senate, and that the United Nations as it stands embodies all that the great powers could agree on. But it is possible that the American people, had they understood the alternatives, would have been willing to support the proposition "that in helping to create an organization which will *limit the sovereign power of all nations to make war,* we shall be using, not sacrificing America's sovereignty for the end for which it was intended: the security and peace of the American people." And acceptance of this principle by the American government would have exerted a powerful influence against the "narrow nationalism" that is the greatest force, and the greatest curse, in the world today.

No less vigorous was Willkie's condemnation of the provision in the Republican platform that "any treaty or *agreement*" (Willkie added the italics) must be approved by a two-thirds vote of the Senate. This provision gave a minority of Senators, who might represent "less than eight per cent of the country," the power to prevent effective international cooperation of any kind. With devastating documentation from American history, he showed that most of the significant agreements between the United States and other countries had been effected by executive action, and that attempts to put such agreements in the form of treaties, subject to approval by two-thirds of the Senate, showed an almost unbroken record of frustration. As Willkie saw it, the Republican party was mortgaging America's future for the sake of isolationist votes.

The second article, "Citizens of Negro Blood," was Willkie's final public utterance. In it he listed the ways in which Negro Americans were being deprived of equitable treatment.

"Not only is the Negro in many parts of the country denied his legal rights in violation of the Constitution, but he is denied the freedom and substance of opportunity in such matters as equal education, equal chance for economic advancement, and his just share of such public services as playgrounds, hospitals and community provisions for health and welfare of all kinds. He is systematically housed in the worst sections of our large cities, and for his poor housing frequently charged exorbitant rents. He is traditionally the 'last hired' and the 'first fired.' He is too often denied protection under the law. But of all the indignities and injustices Negro men and women suffer today, the most bitter and ironic is the discrimination and mistreatment they have received in the armed forces of their country—the country for which they are being asked to give their lives."

These glaring wrongs the party platforms ought to have acknowledged and promised to correct. Instead, the Democratic platform plank on minority rights merely affirmed a general belief in the relevant parts of the Constitution. "In the name of party harmony the small but powerful group of reactionary party hacks—and they were not all from the South—were deferred to." And the Republican plank, while it acknowledged the existence of certain evils, made no specific proposals for correcting them, with one exception—a permanent Federal Fair Employment Practices Commission.

Willkie himself proposed three other measures: an anti-poll tax law, an anti-lynching law, and an executive order ending discrimination in the Armed Forces. With crushing logic he abolished the common objection to the first two as being unconstitutional; and he pointed out that the Selective Service Act specifically provided that: "In the selection and training of men under this act, there shall be no discrimination against any person on account of race or color." "All that was necessary," he concluded, "was for the Republicans in their platform to call upon the Commander-in-Chief to enforce the law he is sworn to uphold, and to pledge that if the present Commander-in-Chief did not do so, their candidate—if elected—would."

He himself, had he been elected President, would have gone farther. In an interview with Samuel Grafton in the summer of 1943, "He said his approach to the Negro would be the same [as to labor], that if he were elected President he would put a Negro either in his cabinet or on the Supreme Court. Then he spoke a sentence that I cannot forget. He said: 'If I am elected, and if I do not do this, I want you to write a piece saying that on such and such a day, in Rushville, Indiana, Wendell Willkie made such and such a statement to you, and that Wendell Willkie is a liar.' "[88]

Willkie did not have to be elected President to prove that he was not a liar. His public record from the end of 1940 until his death was one of absolute integrity. He closed it with these words: "I write this article with the deliberate intent of helping to arouse a public opinion that will require these candidates ["Presidential, gubernatorial, Congressional"] to put aside generalities, evasions and pious platitudes and deal in concise, concrete terms with this human, this national, this world problem."

6

Neither Willkie nor his public had reason to think, when these words appeared in print, that they would be his last. He had, in fact, made a remarkable recovery. At the end of September his doctors told him that if he were an ordinary patient, they would release him immediately, but that since he was the kind of man he was—that is, so heedless of his physical health—they would keep him in the hospital a little longer. Then he was to take a good rest of two or three months—which, after considering various possibilities, he decided to spend in Rushville.[89]

The few intimate friends who got to see him had the same impression as his doctors—that he was his old self, on the road to complete recovery. Roscoe Drummond, for instance, saw him on September 30. "He had telephoned me at my hotel to come and see him and conspiratorially told me how to get to his room by a side elevator so I wouldn't run into objecting nurses.

"He was looking rested, robust, and buoyant. He was eager to talk of everything and his energy filled the little hospital room to overflowing. All the New York Sunday newspapers were strewn on the floor where he had tossed them after reading and a dozen of the latest books were piled helter-skelter on a little table beside his elbow."[90] He had resumed his habit of chain smoking.[91]

Altogether, the situation seemed to justify the conclusion of a letter dated October 5 from Raymond Baldwin, another friend whose loyalty was unflagging, to whom Willkie had apparently written in a moment of discouragement. "So cheer up, old man, there's plenty of the wine of life left in the cup yet. Your work isn't done."[92]

There was only one note of sadness during these days—the death of Al Smith on October 3. The next day Willkie paid him tribute in a telegram to his daughter, which read in part: "His whole approach to government was human and sympathetic and . . . his personal integrity was inviolate."[93]

On Saturday, October 7, the public learned that Willkie himself had been close to death: that he had been "stricken by a streptococcic throat infection three days ago," that on Thursday night he had had a temperature of 104 (according to the next day's story, "doctors despaired of saving his life"), but that large doses of penicillin had saved him. He was now, in the judgment of his physician, Dr. Benjamin Salzer, "out of [the] critical category."[94]

But the strain on his heart had been too great. On Saturday night he suffered another severe heart attack.

From this also, however, he rallied. "Shortly after 1:00 A.M. Dr. Salzer walked into Mr. Willkie's room as a nurse was swabbing his infected throat. 'How does your throat feel?' he asked.

"'How can I talk with my mouth full of that stuff?' he joked.

"'Maybe you'd like a scotch and water as a stimulant—you could use one,' the doctor suggested.

"'Okay, if you make it warm.' He had his scotch and water warm."[95]

Moments later he suffered another attack. At 2:20 a. m. on Sunday, October 8, he died of a coronary thrombosis. Mrs. Willkie, who had herself been in another hospital with a minor illness, reached him five minutes before the end. His son Philip was at sea.

Lem Jones broke the news to the waiting reporters. "An hour before Jones had brought out words of hope. Now he came out with hands extended, palms upraised." He was crying. "It's all over. He went very fast."[96]

It was too late for the morning papers. Radio carried the news to the public. Many who had never seen him nevertheless experienced, after the first stunned instant of unbelief, a sense of overwhelming personal loss. They had not known how intimate a part of the American scene he had become, how closely entwined his life had been with all their hopes of a better society, when the war had ended, within and beyond America's borders.

Then came the tributes—from every part of the world whose oneness he had affirmed, and from the high and low in his own country. Even some of the statements from public figures triumphed over convention and rang true. Senator Wagner called him "the most influential private citizen in the United States. . . . He died a gallant fighter in the battle he loved and at the very peak of his powers." Ambassador to Britain John G. Winant sought to express a different and perhaps a deeper truth: "When I thought of Willkie I often thought of the West. . . . In his own way this man from Indiana was a pioneer. . . . He had a magnificent obsession. If he had cared less he might have lived longer; but we don't think so much of long life these days but of intensity of caring."

One message that would have pleased Willkie more than the eulogies of the great came from representatives of one of the minority groups about whose acceptance as human beings he had cared most intensely. The Red-caps of the Pennsylvania Terminal expressed their sorrow at the death of "the most courageous champion in recent times of all minority groups, particularly members of the Negro race."

In London, in the pub that he had visited (decorated with pictures of the visit, now draped in black), his darts partner led the gathering in "a solemn toast": "We're sorry he's gone. He was a proper gent—very easy to know."[97]

On Monday his body lay in state in the Fifth Avenue Presbyterian Church ("I wisht I knew where they were taking the body," a cab driver had remarked at the first news of Willkie's death; "I sure would like to look at that man again")[98] while 60,000 persons filed past the coffin. And on Tuesday at his funeral 35,000 gathered in the streets, besides 2,500 inside the church. "Among those without cards of admission a Harlem woman . . . was first in line. She arrived at 11:00 A.M. The funeral was at 3:00. She said: 'I admire him for what he did for my people.'"[99]

The memorial address was given by Dr. John Sutherland Bonnell, pastor of the church and a personal friend, to whom it evidently did not matter that for years Willkie had not been, in any meaningful sense, a member of any church. No exclusive creed could win the allegiance of that free spirit.

Secretary Stimson offered burial in Arlington National Cemetery, but Mrs. Willkie was right in feeling that as far as any particular place could be associated with one whose vision had embraced the earth, that place was Indiana. His grave is on a pleasant slope in Rushville's cemetery, his monument an open volume carved in stone. On the pages are some of the sentences with which he stirred the minds and hearts of men—and of which the echoes do not die.

7

How wide and deep Willkie's influence was thought to be is shown by the clamor that arose, when he himself could no longer speak, over whether his support would have gone to Dewey or Roosevelt. Drew Pearson quoted in his column and his broadcast a statement by Willkie that clearly implied a leaning toward Roosevelt.[100] This drew a sharp rejoinder from Henry Luce: "He completely distrusted Franklin Roosevelt's statesmanship and had no intention of voting for him or supporting him."[101] Both Luce and Sinclair Weeks expressed the opinion that in the end he would have supported Dewey.[102] At the same time Roscoe Drummond insisted that Willkie had not made up his mind: "I should like to put into the record that as of eight days before his passing, when on Saturday morning, September 30, I talked with him for an hour in his room at the Lenox Hill Hospital, he had not decided which candidate he would support."[103]

The controversy continued, until Mrs. Willkie felt obliged to issue a public statement: "I am distressed because many people are saying that they knew how Wendell Willkie was going to vote in the coming election. I am sure he had not made his decision. No one could speak for him while he was living; and I ask, out of respect for his memory, that no one should attempt to speak for him now."[104]

It is certainly true that he had not made a decision to support either Dewey or Roosevelt. He had said so repeatedly in letters written during the summer and up to the time of his death; he had said so to Lem Jones only three days before the end.[105]

What he would have done if he had lived is another question. But the evidence leads to certain conclusions about which there is no reasonable doubt.

First, it must be clear from the preceding account that Willkie would never have supported Dewey. If his opinion had not been changed by anything that Dewey said before October 8, it would not have been changed by anything that he said—or could have said—later.

It is also reasonably—if not quite absolutely—clear that he would never have endorsed Roosevelt. The only direct evidence that he might have done so is a comment to Henry Luce on the latter's statement that "a Fourth Term . . . would be the unhappiest thing that could happen to America politically." After saying "I reciprocate your thoughts about Franklin Roosevelt," Willkie qualified the statement by adding: "The question of the type of leadership by which he might be succeeded is almost determinative from my point of thinking. In other words, there is something to Hamlet's notion to bear those ills we have rather than fly to others that we know not of."[106] On the other hand, he told Raymond Baldwin at the time of Dewey's nomination that he would never support Roosevelt for a fourth term,[107] and his harsh attacks in the Wisconsin primary would have been hard to unsay. Moreover, in his letters, even at the last, he spoke of himself as a Republican and repeatedly expressed his concern for the future of the party.

What he *would* have done, it seems clear, was to continue his silence until shortly before the election and then issue a statement summing up, objectively but incisively, the case for and against each candidate. Then he would have told his hearers that each should be guided by his conscience. As a matter of fact, this was essentially what he did in *An American Program,* the preface of which is dated September 25 and which was published on the day before he died.[108]

The same issue of the *New York Times* that told of Willkie's death carried the headline "Four Powers Agree on a New League Charter": and the following day it published the text of the Dumbarton Oaks agreement. The foundation had been laid for the United Nations, and however far that organization might fall short of Willkie's ideal, it nevertheless represented the longest step that the United States had yet taken toward membership in a world community. No further statement is needed as to how far Willkie was responsible for this result. The preceding record speaks for itself.

There is likewise no need for another analysis of Willkie's influence on the policies of the Republican party since 1940.[109] One person's opinion, for what it is worth, is this: that if to one man more than any other may be attributed whatever liberal tendencies exist in the Republican party today—whatever acceptance may have been granted to the principles that American responsibility for the welfare of other nations is necessary and is right; that the Federal government's responsibility for the health, education and welfare of all its citizens is inevitable and is desirable; and that equal rights and opportunities must not be denied to any human being because of the color of his skin, the shape of his beliefs, or the place and conditions of his birth—that man is Wendell Willkie.

Still more in the realm of conjecture is a third question that nevertheless comes inevitably to the mind: How would American policy have been altered abroad and at home if Willkie had lived?

In foreign policy it seems clear, first, that the course of the cold war with the Soviet Union has been essentially independent of the influence of individuals; that the long-standing tradition of Russian imperialism, along with an unshakable commitment to a Communist ideology, has made continuing rivalry inevitable. But, second, the State Department's chronic inability—alike under Roosevelt, Truman, Eisenhower, Kennedy and Johnson—to find any means of opposing Communism in politically backward countries except by supporting anti-democratic regimes would have remained the object of Willkie's relentless attack; and it seems possible that he could have commanded a following strong enough to exert significant influence. And, finally, his conviction that colonialism was done for, expressed over the years with the same persistence, eloquence and evenness of temper as when he was alive, would have strengthened and guided America's efforts to hasten and smooth the transition of non-European countries from servitude to political independence.

Even more on the home front, one may think, his voice would have been heard and heeded; especially, his presence would have helped to resolve the two great moral crises of the fifties (one of which still confronts us with unabated urgency), namely, McCarthyism and segregation. For the long and agonizing strife arising from these issues could have been mitigated and shortened if only one voice, strong enough to be heard throughout the nation, had been raised in behalf of democracy and decency against the tyrannous and obscene forces which were unleashed and intensified by the Senator from Wisconsin and the white supremacists of the South.

And if Willkie had lived, there would have been one man with the sensitivity to perceive, the courage to say, and the power to compel attention while saying, not merely that McCarthy was a liar but that his activities were no less subversive, no less un-American, and far more destructive of the nation's strength than were the activities of the Communists themselves; and not merely that segregation was unconstitutional, or that it forced America to fight in chains the battle against Communism for the minds of men, but that it was a total denial of the central doctrines of democracy and Christianity. There would have been one man to organize the opposition to McCarthy's political gangsterism; there would have been one man to organize support for the Supreme Court's 1954 decision outlawing segregation in the schools.

But Willkie did not live. The war between the United States and Russia that he saw as the ultimate human disaster is something that some Americans are still more than willing to risk. The United Nations, to which he looked forward as the ultimate human hope, is still struggling for existence. State Department policy is still muddled. The Republican Old Guard, though repeatedly rebuffed by the voters, still dominates the party. McCarthyism is resurgent in a hundred hate groups. Segregation still persists, despite the Civil Rights Act of 1964—blatant and brutal in much of the South, covert and sullen in much of the North. Wendell Willkie is seemingly forgotten, and the battles that he fought are still to be won.

What meaning, therefore, has his life?

"We have no logic for luck. There is no calculus of expediency. But we do know how to do that which is right, and that is the only rule we need to follow if we want to win and deserve to win in politics."[110] These words of Willkie's early idol, Newton D. Baker, which Willkie recalled a month before his death, are the key to his career. Not a profound philosopher, he knew intuitively the fallacy of directing or judging a line of conduct according to the immediate consequences; for the consequences of every action are infinite. And therefore one acts, as he said so often in his homely accent, according to "principles," with a faith defiant of all appearances; the faith of all who fight—it may be, obscure, alone, and in mortal danger—for causes that more prudent men call "lost"; not only without the hope of personal reward, but without visible grounds for belief that their efforts will ever have effect; making the tremendous assumption that the universe is on the side of what they call right.

To the objection that Willkie's enemies also thought that they were right, and in fact that the greatest crimes in history have been perpetrated by those who also believed that the universe was on their side, the answer is evident. What saved his passionate faith from sinking into fanaticism was his innate, unstudied, almost unconscious feeling of fellowship with other human beings. And it was this bond of fellowship that inspired the fervent response from so many of those he met; above all from the great company of the dispossessed—dispossessed of their human birthright of freedom—whose voice he was.

And therefore, if Wendell Willkie should be no longer remembered and his words remain unread, his influence will continue—unceasing, increasing and incalculable—in the thoughts and words and acts of those who loved him; from whom in turn the impulse passes on to men and women of other generations.

The fight for freedom never ends.

Notes

A NOTE ON GENERAL SOURCES

Particular sources are acknowledged in individual notes. Also, at the beginning of the notes on each chapter, I have listed the principal sources for that chapter. Here I will deal more generally with the materials on which this biography is based.

One indispensable source has been the files of the *New York Times*. It is not quite true that the *Times* contains *all* the news that is fit to print, but it certainly gives fuller coverage than any other newspaper. Often, for instance, where other papers give only a summary of an address by some public figure, the *Times* will give the full text. It is a unique and invaluable institution, and I have made an exhaustive examination of everything in it about Willkie between 1933, when he is first mentioned, and the end of 1944, several months after his death.

For additional details concerning events of particular importance, such as the 1940 Republican National Convention, I have consulted the files of other newspapers that are in my opinion especially reliable and representative. Among these may be mentioned the *Christian Science Monitor*, the New York *Herald Tribune*, the Washington *Post*, the Louisville *Courier-Journal*, and the St. Louis *Post-Dispatch*. In the same way I have used the weekly magazines of news and opinion, such as *Time* and the *Nation*. I have also read all (I think) of the articles by or about Willkie in periodicals of general interest and national circulation, such as the *Atlantic* and the *Saturday Evening Post*, as well as many in other magazines. But I do not claim to have made an exhaustive survey of periodical literature.

Seven books about Willkie have been published. They are listed here in the order of their appearance.

(1) Herman O. Makey, *Wendell Willkie of Elwood*. Elwood, Indiana: National Book Company, 1940. This is a campaign biography, chiefly important for its generally reliable and partially documented account of Elwood and of Willkie's family and early life.

(2) C. Nelson Sparks, *One Man: Wendell Willkie*. New York: Raynor Publishing Company, 1943. This is an extensive compilation of the lies that were circulated about Willkie by his enemies among the Republican Old Guard, the isolationists, and assorted "liberals," with some added fabrications that I have encountered nowhere else.

(3) Alden Hatch, *Young Willkie*. New York: Harcourt, Brace, 1944. This is a sort of "boy's life of Willkie," bringing the story down to his enlistment in the Army in 1917. It is based on original research, was read and approved by Willkie before publication, and in early chapters undoubtedly recreates much of the atmosphere of the Willkie home. The form is fictional, however; and so, according to some of Willkie's early associates, are many of the details. Though a number of sources are listed, there is no systematic documentation.

(4) Mary Earhart Dillon, *Wendell Willkie*. New York: Lippincott, 1952.

This is a full scale account of Willkie's career after becoming president of Commonwealth & Southern in 1933. About forty pages are given to the preceding forty-one years of his life. There is a list of sources, but no detailed documentation. This is unfortunate because much of the book is based on personal interviews, which are obviously the source of many statements which my own sources contradict.

(5) Joseph Barnes, *Wendell Willkie: The Events He Was Part Of, The Ideals He Fought For.* New York: Simon and Schuster, 1952. This volume is exactly described by the subtitle. Like the volume last mentioned, it gives only a summary treatment of Willkie's early life, and it is only partially documented. Unlike that volume, however, it is thoroughly reliable.

(6) Muriel Rukeyser, *One Life.* New York: Simon and Schuster, 1957. This book by a distinguished contemporary poet is a poet's treatment of the subject, an attempt to reveal and dramatize the inner life of the hero. The interpretation, though clearly based on wide knowledge, is necessarily highly subjective, and the reader's response is likely to be the same.

(7) Donald B. Johnson, *The Republican Party and Wendell Willkie.* University of Illinois Press, 1960. The title accurately describes this book, which is thorough, fair-minded, and scrupulously documented. My own research on this central phase of Willkie's career was completed before Dr. Johnson's book appeared, and our findings on most significant questions coincide.

Another important general source of material about Willkie is the many biographies of Franklin Roosevelt and the many volumes of memoirs, letters, and diaries by persons connected with Roosevelt or with his administration.

There is at present no outstanding collection of unpublished Willkie material in any library. Perhaps the most important is at the Franklin D. Roosevelt Library in Hyde Park. This contains much material on the relations between the Commonwealth & Southern Corporation and the Tennessee Valley Authority, on the 1940 campaign, and on the personal relations between Willkie and Roosevelt.

One very important source not generally available to scholars is Willkie's private papers, which have been preserved by Mrs. Wendell Willkie and Philip H. Willkie. Most of this material is related to the period from 1940 on, although there is some correspondence, mostly with relatives and early friends, dating from the thirties.

Probably the most important part of this collection is two four-drawer filing cabinets of personal correspondence with other important public figures, some of whom were close friends. Most of this is unpublished. I have examined it carefully, and while it contains no sensational revelations, it provides a wealth of background material. There are also nine cabinets of general correspondence, apparently including all the hundreds of thousands of letters, arranged in straight alphabetical ("telephone directory") order, which Willkie received from the public, together with the acknowledgements. A very casual sampling indicates that in at least some instances correspondence with the same person is divided between these files and the files of special correspondence already mentioned. In addition, there are three boxes of correspondence belonging to 1940 and 1941, dealing mostly with the campaign and with Lend-Lease. These I have not examined. The collection should also contain, according to the inventory compiled after Willkie's death, two drawers of Commonwealth & Southern correspondence; but this is missing.

Another important part of the collection is three cabinets of "speeches, writings, articles, reprints from editorial comments, with pertinent correspondence interfiled" (inventory description). This is a nearly (not quite) complete collection of Willkie's public utterances, including even the impromptu whistle-stop speeches of the 1940 campaign (of which stenographic transcripts were made).

A valuable item not now a part of this collection is a file of letters written after Willkie's death by friends and associates in response to a solicitation for reminiscences.

It is to be hoped that these materials will soon be placed in a suitable library and made accessible to researchers. The same comment applies to a collection of recordings now in the possession of Samuel F. Pryor, who states that it contains recordings of the entire 1940 Republican National Convention and of all Willkie's speeches during the campaign. Through Mr. Pryor's kindness I was able to listen to as many of the campaign speeches as I had time for!

A final source is personal interviews with Willkie's relatives, friends and associates, or those connected in some way with important events in which he also was involved. I have interviewed some sixty persons and corresponded with others whom I was unable to see. Their names are given in the appropriate places.

CHAPTER 1

The chief printed sources are Makey and Hatch, together with the files of the local newspapers—the *Daily Record*, the *Daily Press*, and the weekly *Free Press*—for the period 1892-1904. These are in the Elwood Public Library. My most important source has been Robert T. Willkie, Wendell's oldest brother, who has supplied me in interviews and letters with full and vivid reminiscences, and who read the chapter (and a number of other chapters). I also had helpful interviews with the other brothers, Fred and Edward, before their deaths. The following persons also shared their recollections of the Elwood background, the Willkie family, and Wendell during his early years: Eric Cox, Mrs. Ralph Donaldson, Mrs. Earl Guisinger, Paul Harmon (who also read this and the following chapter in manuscript), Katherine Henze, Abe Levi, Earl McCarel, Lepha McCurdy, Roscoe Proctor, and Calvin Sizelove. A few details have come from letters in the Correspondence.

[1] The facts in this and the preceding paragraph are taken from Herman O. Makey, *Wendell Willkie of Elwood* (Elwood, Ind.: National Book Company 1940), pp. 16-43.

[2] This letter is in the private correspondence, which will be referred to hereafter as "Correspondence."

[3] Makey, p. 86; Alden Hatch, in *Young Willkie* (New York: Harcourt, Brace, 1944), p. 49, says he "died in 1873, when he was forty years old." He gives the name of Lewis's father as Johan Ludwig Treusch; Makey gives the first name as Louis. He lived in Erbach in Hessen-Darmstadt.

[4] Ibid.

[5] Hatch tells a romantic story of their escape from Hamburg minutes ahead of the police.

[6] Robert T. Willkie to the writer. This source will be referred to as "R. W."

[7] Makey, p. 86.

[8] Hatch, pp. 17-18, represents them as having been in danger of being lynched because of their anti-slavery sentiments, and as having walked all the way back to Indiana. Robert Willkie thinks the first statement is "probably true," but never heard about their walking all the way back.

[9] R. W.

[10] Hatch, p. 19.

[11] R. W. gives the date of his death as 1870.

[12] Makey, p. 87. Hatch gives the last two dates as 1859 and 1862.

[13] R. W.

[14] All these details were supplied by R. W.

[15] Makey, p. 88; and R. W.

[16] Amos E. Long of Denver, Indiana, in a letter to Willkie dated June 14, 1940. (Correspondence.)

[17] From the first school report (and apparently the last for some years), written by Herman Willkie and entitled "Manual of the Public Schools of Elwood: 1890-91: And Rules and Regulations." It is dated 1890, and was shown me by Elwood's historian, Joseph De Hority.

[18] The details in the two preceding paragraphs, except where otherwise noted, are from Makey, pp. 37-38, 88-89.

[19] Record of "General Orders," Madison County Court, Anderson, Indiana. I could find no record of his resignation as superintendent, but assume that, as Hatch says, it occurred in 1890. Records now in the office of the superintendent of schools show several payments to Herman Willkie (evidently in addition to his salary), for such items as "janitor services," up to July 1, 1890, but none after that date.

[20] Edward Willkie to the writer.

[21] This trait was also stressed by Eric Cox of Elwood in an interview with the writer.

[22] Fred Willkie to the writer.

[23] Cox.

[24] R. W.

[25] I cannot locate the source of this detail.

[26] R. W.

[27] Ibid.

[28] Akron *Beacon Journal*, April 1, 1925, p. 15.

[29] Makey, pp. 106-07.

[30] Edward Willkie to the writer. He remembered the name as Pat Brady, but Paul Harmon thinks it was Pat Bradley.

[31] R. W.

[32] Elwood *Free Press*, May 26, 1893.

[33] Calvin Sizelove to the writer.

[34] R. W.

[35] R. W. thinks it more likely that the first speaker was Andrew Jackson (Jack) Behymer, a political spell-binder with some success in local politics until it began to be suspected that his votes in the State Legislature were governed by something more substantial than principles.

[36] R. W.

[37] Ibid. It has also been stated that the break came when he joined a Masonic Lodge. (*Indiana Freemason*, March, 1958, p. 7.) But R. W. states, "My father was not a Mason."

[38] Ibid.
[39] Miss Katherine Henze, of Elwood, to the writer.
[40] Miss Lepha McCurdy, of Elwood, to the writer.
[41] R. W. Miss McCurdy has a similar impression.
[42] Ibid.
[43] Ibid.
[44] Makey, p. 110.
[45] Paul Harmon in a letter to the writer.
[46] Makey, p. 106. R. W. says three hundred.
[47] R. W.
[48] Makey, p. 89. The other two houses where the Willkie family lived were at 19th and South A Streets (October, 1891, to June, 1894) and at the corner of 23rd and North A.
[49] R. W.
[50] Ibid.
[51] Hatch, p. 78; Makey, p. 125.
[52] Edward Willkie to the writer.
[53] R. W.
[54] I am not at liberty to name my informant, who only said that such an accusation was made.
[55] That this was a frequent charge, I heard from several sources, whom I prefer not to name; and one person asserted with some vehemence that the charge was true.
[56] This quotation comes from Frank Martindale of Plymouth, Indiana, who was present. The rest of the quotation is from the Indiana *Daily Student*, June 9, 1912, p. 1. Another student, George Henley, of Bloomington, Indiana, wrote to Willkie on January 15, 1940: "I remember your father and recall one, and possibly two, of his talks to the law school, in which he discussed the practice of law from the realistic standpoint. To me he epitomized the loyal, able, and hardworking Indiana lawyer." (Correspondence.)
[57] Makey, p. 101.
[58] Ibid., pp. 102-03.
[59] Ibid., p. 99.
[60] Edward Willkie to the writer.
[61] Makey, p. 99.
[62] Edward Willkie to the writer.
[63] Mrs. Wendell Willkie, and others, to the writer.
[64] R. W.
[65] Paul Harmon commented on an early version of this paragraph: "Certainly she inspired affection in my case. She was kind to me."
[66] This account, given by Robert and confirmed by Earl McCarel, differs considerably from that of Mr. Hatch, presumably obtained from Wendell. Since Robert was four years older, he is more likely to have remembered it correctly. Hatch also gives an expanded account of the boat trip mentioned in the next paragraph.
[67] Robert and Edward Willkie and Earl McCarel to the writer.
[68] R. W.
[69] Ibid.
[70] Eric Cox and George De Hority, of Elwood, recall this detail.
[71] Paul Harmon in a letter to the writer.
[72] R. W.

[73] Eric Cox.
[74] R. W.
[75] Fred Willkie to the writer.
[76] R. W.
[77] Fred Willkie.
[78] R. W.
[79] Mrs. Ralph Donaldson.
[80] Mr. Hatch represents the visit as lasting till midnight, and recreates the conversation. Obviously, however, a Presidential candidate in the last month of a campaign such as Bryan conducted does not devote an entire evening to casual conversation with a private individual, even if that individual is a much closer personal friend and a much more powerful political figure than Herman Willkie was. Robert vouches for the visit, but not for the length, which may have been an hour or so. The available files of the local papers mention Bryan's visit to Elwood but give no details. The date was October 9.—Leaving aside the fictional ornaments, however, Robert thinks that Hatch's account of the Willkie household in Chapters 3 and 4 captures a good deal of the prevailing spirit and of his father's part in creating it.—The Willkie habit of holding family debates is remembered by many people in Elwood.
[81] Letter from Mrs. Margaret Sprong, dated October 30, 1940. (Correspondence.)
[82] R. W.
[83] Abe Levi to the writer. The other details in this paragraph, unless otherwise specified, are from Makey, pp. 124-25.
[84] This story was relayed to the writer by Mrs. Ralph Donaldson.
[85] This quotation comes from R. W., via his wife and Mrs. Donaldson.
[86] Fred Willkie to the writer.
[87] Paul Harmon remembers Mr. Willkie's saying this to him and Wendell on several occasions.
[88] R. W.
[89] Fred Willkie to the writer.
[90] R. W., quoted in the Louisville *Courier-Journal,* June 30, 1940, Sec. 1, p. 11.
[91] Letter to William A. De Hority, dated May 30, 1939. (Correspondence.)
[92] Paul Harmon to the writer.
[93] Both expressed this feeling in interviews with the writer.

CHAPTER 2

The sources are in general the same as for Chapter 1, with the following additions: the files of the Indiana *Daily Student;* the official transcript of Willkie's academic record at Indiana University; and interviews (sometimes supplemented by letters) with Lillian Gay Berry, Maurice Bluhm, Mrs. Ralph Campbell, George De Hority, Wilbur Gruber, Kenneth Kunkel, Frank Martindale, Mrs. Elmer Meyer (Gwyneth Harry), and Ben Scifres.
[1] According to the official transcript of Willkie's high school record, reproduced by Makey, p. 119.
[2] Earl McCarel to the writer. His account is confirmed by a letter to Willkie from Leonard Spach, dated December 26, 1939: "Do you remember the club L. T. O. M.—you, McCarel, Jacobs and myself & use to meet in your basement and gym?" (Correspondence.) Hatch (p. 84) gives the name of the club as

"K. O. R. T."—"Knights of the Round Table." This, however, according to R. W., was a social club made up of older boys and young men "who had rather good jobs, enough position to wish to give dances and enough money to pay for them." Makey (p. 122) tells of Willkie's forming a club "K. O. B." ("King of the Beasts") after leaving the high school fraternity because "the members put on airs with his friends." No other source mentions this club.

[3] This phrase was used to the writer, independently, by Calvin Sizelove, a high school classmate, and George Henley, a college classmate.

[4] Makey, p. 123.

[5] This and the following details, unless otherwise specified, were given to the writer by George De Hority.

[6] Letter dated October 28, 1936, answering one from Brig. Gen. L. R. Gignilliat. (Correspondence.)

[7] Makey, p. 117.

[8] Ibid., p. 116.

[9] Hatch (pp. 76-78) represents Wendell as the leader and the one who did the painting. According to Earl McCarel, however, Wendell was only one of the group, and the actual painting was done by Leonard Spach while Wendell and McCarel held his legs.

[10] Earl McCarel to the writer. Hatch (pp. 78-79) gives a somewhat different account, ending with the statement that Wendell got an "epic paddling." But R. W. and McCarel doubt that "paddling" was ever a punishment at the high school. Another account, substantially the same as McCarel's, appeared in the Louisville *Courier-Journal's* Sunday Magazine, June 16, 1940, pp. 1-2.

[11] See Hatch, p. 85.

[12] Later Mrs. Earl Guisinger, who told the episode to the writer.

[13] Mrs. Ralph Campbell (Hazel Smith) to the writer.

[14] R. W.—Hatch (pp. 98-99) elaborates on the bakery episode, which occurred during the severe, though brief, depression of 1907, when money was scarce.

[15] Katherine Henze to the writer, summing up what was suggested by many others.

[16] Miss Henze, among others, remembers this episode. And see Hatch, p. 91.

[17] Makey, p. 119. A normal program included four courses, but during his abbreviated last semester (he entered Indiana University about three weeks before the normal end of the semester in January, 1910) Wendell took only three.

[18] Eric Cox to the writer.

[19] Letter from Mrs. R. E. Hartman (Frances Swihart) dated Oct. 26, 1942. (Correspondence.) According to Paul Harmon, Bing's phrase was the more familiar "calling a spade a spade."

[20] I have this version from Earl McCarel. Hatch (p. 90) gives the misquotation as "inside the nurse."

[21] Makey, p. 120; Hatch, p. 101; and interviews with Katherine Henze and Mrs. Earl Guisinger (Eunice Carter). Miss Henze remembers the topic as government ownership of the railroads, and this is Hatch's version. I have followed Makey and Mrs. Guisinger—not that it matters.

[22] Louisville *Courier-Journal,* June 16, 1940, Sunday Magazine, p. 1.

[23] Calvin Sizelove to the author.

[24] The foregoing details were given to the writer by R. W. and George De Hority.

[25] The preceding paragraphs are based on statements of Mrs. Meyer to the writer. A story concerning himself and Gwyneth which Willkie evidently told on more than one occasion (see Hatch, pp. 112-14, and Janet Flanner, "Rushville's Renowned Son-in-Law," the *New Yorker*, 16:29 [October 12, 1940]) was that Gwyneth failed to get a bid to join the high school sorority, the Deltas, because of the snobbishness of some members who looked down upon her family, that he consequently resigned from the Betas, and that it was this that gave rise to his anti-fraternity attitude at the University. Mrs. Meyer, however, denies the story, insisting that neither she nor her family ever suffered from social discrimination; Katherine Henze, her close friend, remembers nothing about it and was "surprised" to read about it in Hatch; George De Hority (whom Hatch represents as having a dramatic argument with Wendell on the subject) and Earl McCarel have no recollection of it; and Robert (who was at the University but would almost certainly have been told of such a momentous happening in his brother's life) never heard of it. (All in interviews with the writer.) Without accusing Willkie of deliberate invention, I suggest that, thirty-odd years later, his memory played him false and magnified some minor episode into this more striking account.

[26] Fred Willkie to the writer.

[27] R. W.

[28] These details are from Hatch, pp. 106-07; Makey, pp. 49-50; and R. W.

[29] Makey, p. 54.

[30] These details are from R. W. and Paul Harmon.

[31] This account is based, except for a few details added from Hatch, on the account given to the writer by Paul Harmon, who is also quite definite that Wendell's job was *not* ended, as in Hatch's narrative, by a storm which blew down and ruined the circus tent: Wendell simply got tired of the job. For what follows, the only authority is Willkie's account, as given by Hatch.

[32] The following account, unless otherwise specified, is based on the Elwood *Daily Record* for the period in question.

[33] This is Robert Willkie's view of the strike.

[34] Hatch (pp. 134-37) tells of the attempt of two local toughs to beat up Wendell and his father. But there is no mention of such an event in the newspapers, although lesser incidents are reported; and Robert doubts that anything more was involved than possibly some pushing and shoving. Edward Willkie, however, thought that some such episode actually occurred.

[35] See Hatch, pp. 138-40. R. W. confirms the story in general.

[36] Hatch (pp. 137-41) gives a considerably different version, which he got from Willkie and his brother Fred. (Letter to the writer, dated July 1, 1959.) "At the hearing on September 21 the injunction was indefinitely postponed"—presumably by the judge's rejection of the company's application. Herman Willkie, however, persuaded the union "to force it to a decision . . . and the revived injunction was scheduled to be heard before Judge Anderson of the Federal Court in Indianapolis"; where, "after a hearing lasting over a month, during which hundreds of witnesses were examined, Edward M. Daniels, Master in Chancery . . . recommended to Judge Anderson that the injunction be denied." This account, despite the circumstantial details, presents certain difficulties. It is not clear how the union, as defendant, could "revive" a suit that the company, as plaintiff, had withdrawn. Furthermore, I could find in the Elwood newspapers no record of any further action. Robert's recollection is that "there was a hearing in

Judge Anderson's U. S. District Court, Indianapolis, in which some temporary restraining order was issued and the Judge threatened Father with contempt of court for some advice he gave the strikers." When I attempted to check the court record at the Federal Records Center in Chicago, I found that the volume which *might* have contained an account of the case (though court records of that date seem to have been sketchy and haphazard) was missing when the records were turned over to the Center. I incline to rely on the newspapers.

[37] The date of matriculation, as given in the official transcript of Willkie's record, is January 4, 1910. The University was then on the "quarter system," with three terms during the regular college year, the summer session being regarded as the fourth quarter. (It changed to the semester system beginning with the year 1915-16, when Willkie took his final year in Law School.) Willkie therefore entered at the beginning of the second term. R. W. points out that he must have been excused from his final month of study at Elwood High School, which was on the semester system, with the first half year running until about the end of January. In the transcript of his high school record there is the notation "Graduated Jan. 29, '10."

[38] George De Hority and others have mentioned the poker games, which seem to have raised eyebrows in some circles. Perhaps this is the source of later unfounded stories of Willkie's prowess as a poker player.

[39] Letter dated March 8, 1937. (Correspondence.)

[40] These details were given by Miss Berry to the writer.

[41] E. g., Frank Martindale, Ben Scifres, and George De Hority.

[42] See the *New York Times*, June 30, 1940, p. 2.

[43] This account is based on information given to the writer by R. W., Wilbur Gruber, and Paul Harmon, as well as on Hatch (pp. 151-54) and Makey (pp. 134-35).

[44] See the *Times*, June 30, 1940, p. 2; *Time*, July 8, 1940, p. 15. None of his fellow students that I have interviewed remember it or think it likely.

[45] See Makey, p. 135.

[46] See Hatch, p. 163, and Makey, p. 129.

[47] These details are taken from an article in the *Indiana Alumni Magazine*, October, 1940, p. 4; Hatch, pp. 164-65; Makey, pp. 129-30; and an interview with George De Hority. There is some difficulty about dates. The Union records show that McNutt was elected in the spring of his sophomore year. Since this seems to have been a genuinely popular election, the reforms must already have taken place, although the *Alumni Magazine* article implies that they were the result of repeated efforts—and Wendell had been at the University only a little over a year. Paul Harmon does not credit the story about McNutt; he "was never in our political camp, and we would never have thought of such a thing." In this connection, Frank Martindale told the writer that he thought Willkie's share in this and other campus movements had been overstated.

[48] This account is based on the *Daily Student* of April 18, 20, and 23, and an interview with Frank Martindale.

[49] It has been said (by Hatch, p. 167, and by the writer of the *Alumni Magazine* article mentioned above) that Willkie was in charge of arranging this convention, which was never held because the date he set was that of a baseball game with Purdue that would decide the conference championship. This event occurred in 1916; a correct account of it is given below.

[50] Kenneth Kunkel to the writer.

[51] Makey, p. 134. He gives no source for the quotation stating the qualifications for the office.

[52] Ibid., pp. 133-34; Hatch, pp. 170-71. The latter lets the reader infer that the tournament was sponsored by the Boosters' Club for the first time during Willkie's presidency, but it had been instituted two years before. He gives thirty-nine as the number of teams competing.

[53] These are quarter credits. The semester credits of his final year in Law School have been changed to quarter credits in the ratio of 2 to 3. In all, Willkie attended the University for 11 regular quarters (there would be 12 in a normal four-year course), beginnnig in January, 1910 and ending in June, 1913; 3 summer sessions, in 1910, 1912, and 1914; and 2 semesters in 1915-16. His credits in each subject were as follows: Law, 69½; History, 32½; English, 23; Economics, 17; Chemistry, 15; Greek, 15; Mathematics, 15; Latin, 10; Philosophy, 8; Education, 4; Hygiene, 3.

[54] These details come specifically from Ben Scifres, although often stated or implied by others of Willkie's friends.

[55] Letter dated January 31, 1940. (Correspondence.)

[56] Hatch, p. 156.

[57] E. K. Lindley to the writer.

[58] *New York Times,* June 19, 1941, p. 18.

[59] Hatch, p. 160.

[60] Some of these details are from Hatch, pp. 161-62, but the quotation is from Stanley Walker's Introduction to *This is Wendell Willkie: A Collection of Speeches and Writings on Present-Day Issues* (New York: Dodd, Mead, 1940), p. 17. Hatch says he got twelve students; while in an account by a young acquaintance of Willkie in later years, the number is put at fifteen. (Letter from David A. Morse to Mrs. Willkie, dated December 4, 1944. This is one of a number of such letters written after Willkie's death, some by request. They will be referred to hereafter as "Memorial Tributes.")

[61] Hatch, p. 168.

[62] *Times,* July 31, 1940, p. 12.

[63] The many picturesque accounts published during the 1940 campaign of adventurous vacation jobs during his years at the University may be dismissed as campaign literature. There is no evidence that the 1909 experience was repeated. Parts of three summers (1910, 1912, and 1914) he spent in summer school at the University. The rest of the time he doubtless had unglamorous local jobs.

[64] R. W.

[65] This quotation and the material that follows, unless otherwise specified, are from Mrs. Meyer to the writer in a letter and an interview. She denies any recollection of Hatch's story (pp. 157-58) about trying to get Wendell to dance at a cabaret.

[66] Letter to the writer dated April 26, 1953.

[67] Maurice Bluhm to the writer. I have discussed this episode with Maurice Bluhm, George De Hority, Paul Harmon, Frank Martindale, Ben Scifres, and Wilbur Gruber, as well as Mrs. Meyer.

[68] Mrs. Meyer to the writer.

CHAPTER 3

For the Coffeyville experience I have relied mainly on correspondence between Willkie and his former students; for the months in Puerto Rico on

Hatch and Fred Willkie; for the relations between Willkie and Gwyneth Harry, on their correspondence and on information supplied by her, by Robert and Edward Willkie, and by Paul Harmon; for the last year in law school, on sources already cited, along with interviews with Harry Shackleford and Kenneth Kunkel; for his courtship and marriage, on Hatch and Makey, and interviews with Mrs. Willkie, Mrs. Ralph Donaldson, and Donald Thornburgh. The account of his Army experiences is based particularly on interviews with Frank Cantwell, Shackleford Miller, and Donald Thornburgh; others who contributed were Robert Willkie, Stephen Noland, Harlan Hadley, Dr. F. W. Bratten, Henry Sherrard, Harris Musgrave, and Percy Ruch; Daniel M. Phillipe, secretary of the 325th Artillery Association, was also helpful.

[1] Hatch, p. 180.

[2] Makey, p. 139.

[3] From the "Memoir" (apparently the school annual) of Coffeyville High School, dated 1915, quoted in a letter from H. B. Austin to Willkie, dated April 27, 1939. (Correspondence.)

[4] *Newsweek,* 16:16 (July 8, 1940).

[5] Letter dated May 16, 1937. (Correspondence.)

[6] Letter from Virginia Childress, undated but answered September 28, 1936. (Correspondence.)

[7] Letter from Blanche McNulty, undated but acknowledged July 20, 1942. (Correspondence.)

[8] Letter from Lois Fenn, dated January 27, 1938. (Correspondence.)

[9] Letter from Gladys Conkling Watson, dated November 4, 1934. (Correspondence.)

[10] Letter from Leona Misch Love, written in 1939. (Correspondence.)

[11] Letter from Arthur W. Levan, acknowledged by Willkie January 5, 1937. (Correspondence.)

[12] Letter from Dr. R. E. Prather, acknowledged by Willkie April 3, 1940. (Correspondence.)

[13] Letter from Pat Allen, dated January 28, 1936. (Correspondence.)

[14] Letter in answer to the preceding, dated February 3, 1936. (Correspondence.)

[15] Letter to Virginia Childress, dated September 28, 1936. (Correspondence.)

[16] Letter to Dr. R. E. Prather, dated April 3, 1940. (Correspondence.)

[17] Letter to Lois Fenn, dated February 1, 1938. (Correspondence.)

[18] Hatch, p. 187. Walker (p. 17) says his salary at Coffeyville was $90 a month.

[19] See Note 3 above.

[20] Hatch, p. 188.

[21] New York *Herald Tribune,* June 25, 1940, p. 13.

[22] Hatch, p. 192.

[23] Fred Willkie to the writer.

[24] See Hatch, pp. 194-95. His chapter on Willkie's Puerto Rican experience strikes me as being reliable as well as readable.

[25] Barnes, p. 28.

[26] Mrs. Meyer to the writer. Hatch (p. 198) gives a similar account, which he presumably got from Willkie—although he also talked to Mrs. Meyer. At any rate, Willkie approved his version.

[27] According to R. W., Gwyneth sometimes confided in his wife (an Elwood girl) her unhappiness at Wendell's growing indifference.

[28] This is the opinion of Paul Harmon and Robert Willkie, though the latter is in general a partisan of Gwyneth.
[29] R. W.
[30] Edward Willkie to the writer.
[31] Mrs. Meyer to the writer.
[32] Letter to Willkie dated July 9, 1941. (Correspondence.)
[33] Maurice Bluhm to the writer.
[34] Mrs. Meyer to the writer.
[35] Correspondence.
[36] Letters dated July 9 and July 16, 1941. (Correspondence.)
[37] Letter dated September 16, 1945. (Correspondence.)
[38] Letter dated September 26, 1943. (Correspondence.)
[39] Harry Shackleford to the writer.
[40] See Makey, p. 133, and the *Times*, June 30, 1940, p. 2.
[41] These facts are from the files of the *Daily Student*. They differ considerably from previous accounts.
[42] Letter to the writer. The impression has often been given that Willkie was active in debating throughout his university career, but there is no record of his having engaged in it as an organized activity until his final year in Law School.
[43] *Daily Student*, June 3, 1916. Hatch (p. 206) describes the prize as "the twenty volumes of the Encyclopedia of Law and Procedure" (R. W. says this is correct), and quotes Dean Hogate (p. 203) as introducing Willkie at the graduation exercises as "the winner of the prize, not alone as the best student in this year's senior class, but also as the best student in each year of his three years' attendance at the Law School." No source for the quotation is given.
[44] Makey, p. 127. He gives the number of graduates as eighteen, but the program lists twenty-two, five of whom were expected to complete their work during the summer.
[45] The only detailed account of what Willkie said is in Hatch (pp. 204-05) and is here summarized. Concerning its accuracy, one can only say that it sounds plausible. The last sentence takes note of Makey's statement (p. 127) that the speech was "a strong criticism of the law school and its methods" and Dillon's assertion that it was "a diatribe against the conservatism of the Law School, its faculty and the state supreme court" (p. 25). (In his application for a job with Firestone in 1919 Willkie did not mention any of his law school professors as references.) The published accounts also vary in other respects. Dillon says his fellow students "helped prepare" the speech and "egged him on to give it." (Mrs. Willkie told the writer that she vaguely recalled Wendell's having said that he did it partly "on a dare.") On the other hand, Hatch says (p. 202) that those friends who knew of his intention were "worried" and tried to persuade him to say something else.
[46] *Times*, June 30, 1940, p. 2. Ernest K. Lindley told the writer that President Bryan used the same words—"the most radical speech you ever heard"—in describing the speech to him. All accounts agree that some official notice was taken of his temerity, but do not agree on all details. Hatch (pp. 205-06) pictures him as being left empty-handed "when his class filed up to the platform" to get their diplomas, and then being made to wait three days before being "summoned before authority and unceremoniously handed the sheepskin." Dillon says (p. 25): "Immediately after the exercises he was

summoned to the President's office and told never again to attempt to be 'amusing.' When the class on Commencement Day arose to receive their diplomas he was the only one to be passed over. His diploma was privately awarded to him several days later." Makey says (p. 127) that "when the diplomas were distributed, he did not receive his," but got it *two* days later, with "a strong private lecture." (Of course nobody bothers to give sources.) To anyone who has been connected with a college or university, such accounts are rather hard to credit. Mrs. Willkie is sure that he was not publicly humiliated by failing to get his diploma, but that the faculty and administration "teased" him (her word) by suggesting that his degree might be withheld. The program, dated "Friday, June Ninth, Nineteen Sixteen, Eight P. M.," gives the title of Willkie's speech, does not mention any awarding of diplomas, but *does* list "Admission of the Candidates to the Bar," which was apparently automatic at graduation. According to the official transcript of his record, he received his LL. B. degree on June 14.

[47] An item in the *Indiana Alumni Quarterly* of April, 1916, mentions him as the Democratic candidate for prosecuting attorney in the 15th Judicial District, Madison County, but R. W. says this is incorrect.

[48] Hatch, pp. 208-09.

[49] Makey, p. 144. Confirmed by R. W.

[50] Calvin Sizelove to the writer, confirming Hatch (p. 211). The date, however, must have been 1919, after Wendell's discharge from the Army, for the records show that John Lewis was mayor from 1918 to 1922. It should be understood that the episodes related in this section do not necessarily belong to the period of eleven months between his graduation from law school and his joining the Army.

[51] Hatch, pp. 211-12. Confirmed by Paul Harmon. This episode, too, actually belongs to a different period. The date was Nov. 14, 1914, just after Wendell had resigned his position at Coffeyville.

[52] Letter dated March 29, 1929. (Correspondence.)

[53] Abe Levi to the writer.

[54] Mrs. Willkie to the writer.

[55] R. W. to the writer. Edward's memory, understandably, was not so clear, but he confirmed the story in substance.

[56] Mrs Willkie to the writer.

[57] See Hatch, pp. 199-201.

[58] Makey, p. 143.

[59] This is according to the records of the University. Makey and Hatch are mistaken as to the dates.

[60] Makey, p. 142.

[61] See Hatch, p. 214.

[62] Mrs. Ralph Donaldson to the writer.

[63] See Hatch, p. 215; Makey, p. 143. Confirmed by Mrs. Willkie.

[64] Hatch, p. 217.

[65] New York *Herald Tribune*, June 28, 1940, p. 2.

[66] R. W.

[67] Hatch's story (pp. 223-24) of Herman Willkie's waking Robert and Wendell with news of the war and of their rushing off to enlist immediately is dramatic but fictional. Robert had been married and living away from home for more than a year.

[68] R. W.—The date of Wendell's departure is confirmed by an item in the Elwood *Call-Leader,* May 11, 1917, p. 5.
[69] Letter to Arthur W. Levan dated January 5, 1937. (Correspondence.)
[70] R. W.
[71] Donald Thornburgh to the writer.
[72] This and the following dates connected with Willkie's military career, unless otherwise specified, are from a 1940 campaign leaflet entitled "Wendell Willkie: World War Veteran." A copy is in the Franklin D. Roosevelt Library at Hyde Park.
[73] I have combined Thornburgh's account with Willkie's, as repeated by Robert, of what is clearly the same episode, although details differ.
[74] Mrs. Willkie to the writer.
[75] The quotation is from Mrs. Charlotte Farrar, sister of Mary Sleeth, in the *Herald Tribune,* August 19, 1940, p. 14.
[76] Makey, p. 146.
[77] Mrs. Willkie to the writer.
[78] Letter from A. C. Blinn to the writer dated November 28, 1958.
[79] This date is from Makey, p. 146.
[80] This phrase was used by Mrs. Meyer in a letter to the writer, and (according to Dr. F. W. Bratten, veterinarian in Willkie's unit) by the commanding officer of Willkie's regiment, Colonel Bundell.
[81] These details were supplied by Henry Sherrard, Dr. Bratten, and Donald Thornburgh.
[82] Frank Cantwell, second lieutenant of Battery F, to the writer.
[83] Harris Musgrave, of Battery F, to the writer. The other details in this paragraph are from Makey, pp. 149-50.
[84] Henry Sherrard to the writer. Makey (p. 150) gives a slightly different version. The soldier who overheard the exchange was O. W. Robbins of Twelve Mile, Indiana.
[85] Harris Musgrave to the writer.
[86] Henry Sherrard to the writer.
[87] Shackleford Miller to the writer.
[88] Percy Ruch to the writer.
[89] Donald Thornburgh to the writer. Miller recalls the period as lasting only five days, but Thornburgh has the impression that it was longer.
[90] The preceding details were recalled by Shackleford Miller.
[91] Letter from Dr. Paul R. Fletcher, surgeon, with rank of major, in the 325th Artillery, dated February 24, 1939. (Correspondence.)
[92] Stephen Noland to the writer.
[93] Recollections vary as to the reason. As Shackleford Miller remembers it, the order to fill the vacancies came just as the regiment was ready to leave for the front. Miller, as regimental adjutant, went over the list with Colonel Bundell. There was one vacant captaincy, as battalion adjutant, and Miller suggested Willkie. The Colonel approved, but questioned whether he would want to be taken out of the line and given a headquarters assignment; and Miller was commissioned to find out. Somewhat to his surprise, Willkie wanted the promotion, and he was recommended for it. But on the day when the order was expected putting the promotions into effect for the 325th (the 326th and 327th had received theirs a few days before), the Armistice was signed, and all ranks frozen. Willkie was deeply disappointed. Donald Thornburgh's recollection is somewhat different: that the promotions were

ordered *after* the Armistice, but were then for some reason held up, although the officers scheduled to receive them were assured that they would get the promotions if they remained in France, and were given an opportunity to do so; but Willkie was anxious to get home and did not wait. (Thornburgh himself had been recommended for promotion to major.) Miller agrees that officers were given a choice of remaining in France for some time after the Armistice, and thinks some of these may have been promoted; but he is quite clear that the general order for promotions preceded the Armistice. Clinton M. Harbison, the battalion commander, wrote in answer to a query: "I remember the fact that he failed to receive the promotion, and that he was quite bitter about it, and so expressed himself at the time: but I never knew why the promotion was denied him. . . . my recollection is that it was after the Armistice." Possibly the answer is buried somewhere in the Pentagon; but in 1940, when the Akron American Legion Post received many inquiries about Willkie's war record, it apparently obtained a statement from the Adjutant General's Office which not only made no mention of the captaincy, but put him in the wrong regiment (saying he was transferred to the 159th Field Artillery and went to France with that unit). (From a letter by Charles F. Nutter of Akron to James E. Van Zandt, National Commander of the Veterans of Foreign Wars, in Mr. Nutter's files.)—Here I am willing to let the matter rest.

[94] Letter from Charles F. Nutter referred to in previous note.

[95] Makey, p. 149.

[96] Frank Cantwell to the writer.

[97] Donald Thornburgh to the writer.

[98] Stephen Noland to the writer.

[99] Ibid.

[100] Percy Ruch to the writer.

[101] Shackleford Miller to the writer. Frank Cantwell also recalled Willkie's serious study of military law; and Stephen Noland remarked that "he used every legal method to win his cases, regardless of the evidence."

[102] Stephen Noland to the writer. Frank Cantwell also remembered the case.

[103] Makey, p. 149.

[104] This account was given by Shackleford Miller to the writer. R. W. says Willkie visited Italy after the Armistice but has no details. Charles F. Nutter says, also, that Willkie told him about a trip through southern France and northern Italy. Possibly he and Miller crossed the border briefly on the trip just described.

[105] Letter from Dr. Fletcher, as above.

[106] "Wendell Willkie: World War Veteran."

[107] Shackleford Miller to the writer. Makey (p. 151) says the discharge was at Camp Sherman.

[108] Letter to Dr. Fletcher, dated February 27, 1939. (Correspondence.)

CHAPTER 4

The chief printed sources for this chapter are stories in the Akron *Beacon Journal* from 1919 to 1929 which I was able to trace with the aid of the *Beacon Journal's* Research Department and the Akron Public Library. Other information was received largely through interviews (sometimes supplemented by correspondence) with Charles F. Nutter, Edson A. Oberlin, Jr., Ray

Sutliff, Joseph Thomas, Aldrich Underwood, and, of course, Mrs. Wendell Willkie and Philip Willkie; through briefer interviews with E. H. Hauenstein, William H. Kroeger, and Cletus Roetzel; and through correspondence with A. C. Blinn, Harvey Firestone, Jr., and William F. O'Neil.

[1] Ernest K. Lindley to the writer. Mr. Lindley did not have a chance to check the story with his father, but it was confirmed by his mother.

[2] See Dillon, pp. 27-28 and Barnes, pp. 31-32. These accounts were generally confirmed by Mr. Dailey in an interview with the writer.

[3] See Dillon, p. 27. Her account has been largely confirmed, and extended, by Mrs. Willkie, as well as by Robert and Edward and various acquaintances of the family, in interviews with the writer.

[4] The letter of application and other data are from the records of the Firestone Company and were shown me by Mr. Joseph Thomas. Other dates and salaries have often been given.

[5] *Beacon Journal,* July 3, 1940. This was one of six articles written by Floyd Taylor of the New York *World Telegram,* which appeared daily beginning June 30. They will be referred to hereafter as "Taylor."

[6] Ibid., October 25, 1940 (speech at the Firestone Clubhouse).

[7] Stanley Walker, Introduction to *This Is Wendell Willkie,* p. 20. Barnes gives the same figure (p. 33). Company records show that his salary was increased to $3000 on July 1, 1919; to $3600 on September 1; and to $5400 on January 1, 1920. These raises show the value placed upon his services by the Company, and an offer of $10,000 if he would stay seems entirely probable.

[8] Mrs. Willkie to the writer.

[9] Philip Willkie to the writer.

[10] These details are from an address by Joseph Thomas at the dedication of the Willkie Plaque on December 10, 1953. Mr. Thomas supplied me with the full text. Unless otherwise specified, later references to "Thomas" are to this source.

[11] *Beacon Journal,* October 25, 1940.

[12] Karl H. Grismer, *Akron and Summit County* (Akron: Summit County Historical Society, n. d.—but the account goes to 1952), p. 409.

[13] *Beacon Journal,* May 3, 1921.

[14] From an account in the files of Charles F. Nutter of Akron. Some of the following details are also taken from this source; others are from an interview with Mr. Nutter, an article by Craig Wilson in the *Beacon Journal,* December 6, 1953, and a letter from Summit Post (now Wendell Willkie Post) of the American Legion to Mrs. Willkie following her husband's death.

[15] These and the following facts and quotations are from the columns of the *Beacon Journal.* I assume that a speech was given on the day before the account was printed, unless otherwise specified, and it is the earlier date that I have given in each case.

[16] The reader will perhaps be jarred, allowing for some reportorial inaccuracy, by the rhetorical and grammatical imprecision in this characteristic example of Willkie's oral style. But the force of his emotional appeal evidently made his hearers oblivious to such defects.

[17] Reprinted in the *Times,* September 2, 1944, p. 13.

[18] This and the preceding details were supplied by Edson Oberlin to the writer.

[19] Ray Sutliff told the writer that Willkie explained his desire for an early news story on his impending departure for New York by saying that it would

give him an excuse for refusing speaking engagements.

[20] Aldrich Underwood to the writer.

[21] *Beacon Journal,* November 27, 1953. Guinther added: "I was sorry to see him later reading from printed pages during his campaign. His forte was just talking."

[22] Philip Willkie to the writer.

[23] See Note 17 above.

[24] *Beacon Journal,* July 2 and July 11, 1924.

[25] Ibid., July 17, 1924.

[26] Dillon, p. 33.

[27] In the *Beacon Journal* story of Willkie's Kiwanis Club speech, Willkie is said to have "introduced the resolution that took the support of James Cox away from the delegation." Presumably what is meant is that Willkie's resolution freed the delegates from supporting Cox.

[28] *Beacon Journal,* July 17, 1924. Joe Seiber was an Akron attorney reputed to be among the leaders of the local Ku Klux Klan.

[29] There are typed copies of these two items in the Willkie file in the *Beacon Journal* Research Department, dated July 8 and July 9; but I could not locate them in the issues of those dates.

[30] Ibid., July 11.

[31] Ibid., July 3 (Clinton W. Gilbert).

[32] Barnes, p. 37.

[33] R. W.

[34] *Beacon Journal,* June 20, 1925.

[35] Ibid., August 13.

[36] Ibid., November 4.

[37] Thomas.

[38] Charles F. Nutter to the writer.

[39] Edson Oberlin to the writer.

[40] Joseph Thomas to the writer.

[41] E. H. Hauenstein, Secretary of the Court of Appeals, Akron, to the writer.

[42] Edson Oberlin to the writer.

[43] Ray Sutliff and Cletus Roetzel, among others, have a vivid memory of this gesture.

[44] Joseph Thomas to the writer.

[45] *Beacon Journal,* June 28, 1940. Barnes tells of another case that Willkie won in similar fashion, by noting that three witnesses for the other side, none of them especially well educated, all used the word "profile"—a word much more natural to the Harvard trained lawyer who had called them (p. 54). Weitzel also tells how "a little old lady remembered Willkie's last lawsuit in Akron . . . remembered how she went to Willkie and told him of the trouble her son was in . . . and how the great lawyer went into a criminal court and freed her son with the tremendous power of his eloquence . . . and charged her no fee at all." This is doubtless a legend, but that such legends should have been attached to him tells something of what he was. One cannot imagine their being told of Taft or Dewey.

[46] Edson Oberlin to the writer.

[47] *Beacon Journal,* March 7, 1925.

[48] Thomas.

[49] These details are from an interview with Philip Willkie, supplemented by Mrs. Dillon's account (pp. 31-32). Mr. Kroeger himself, in talking with the

writer, said that the case arose simply from a "misunderstanding," and that he preferred not to discuss it.

[50] Mrs. Dillon's account of the case is highly colored. A Firestone official has stated to the writer with reference to her picture (p. 32) of Willkie facing "the ten opposing lawyers," "I can assure you that there were not ten lawyers representing Firestone in this case or anywhere near it."

[51] This point of view was stressed by Thomas to the writer.

[52] August 9, 1929.

[53] Philip Willkie to the writer.

[54] Mrs. Willkie to the writer.

[55] Janet Flanner, "Rushville's Renowned Son-in-Law," *New Yorker,* 16:34 (October 12, 1940).

[56] Ibid.

[57] Paul Harmon and Edward Willkie to the writer.

[58] *Christian Science Monitor,* August 8, 1940, p. 1.

[59] Robert and Edward Willkie to the writer.

[60] Paul Harmon to the writer.

[61] Correspondence.

[62] Letters dated April 5 and May 18, 1937. (Correspondence.)

[63] Mrs. Willkie to the writer.

[64] Louisville *Courier-Journal,* June 20, 1940, Sec. 1, p. 5 (Inez Robb).

[65] Letter to Charles T. Carpenter. (Correspondence.)

[66] *Christian Science Monitor,* June 12, 1940, p. 7 (Barbara E. Scott Fisher).

[67] Virginia Irwin, "Mrs. Willkie," *Everyday Magazine,* p. 3D in the St. Louis *Post-Dispatch,* June 25, 1940.

[68] Letter to Mrs. Robert Hall. (Correspondence.)

[69] Irwin.

[70] New York *Herald Tribune,* June 28, 1940, p. 5.

[71] "I Am Not Nominating Him," *Saturday Evening Post,* 212:113 (June 22, 1940).

[72] *Beacon Journal,* Centennial Issue, July 21, 1925, Sec. C, p. 5.

[73] Thomas to the writer.

[74] Taylor.

[75] Charles F. Nutter and Ray Sutliff to the writer.

[76] Lem Jones to the writer.

[77] Louisville *Courier-Journal,* June 20, Sec. 1, p. 14 (Inez Robb).

[78] "We the People," *Fortune,* 21:64 (March, 1940).

[79] Flanner, p. 31. Miss Flanner says the club was in Ontario, but the *Beacon Journal,* August 8, 1929, gives the location as Quebec.

[80] From a story by D. M. Wilson in the file of Charles F. Nutter. The account adds that Willkie told the story to Al Blinn, the general manager of the Company, who wished to complete the joke by introducing Willkie to the clerk; but Willkie, considerate of the young man's feelings, declined.

[81] Taylor. Mr. O'Neil commented in a letter to the writer: "While I have no specific recollection of the Taylor quote . . . it sounds as though it could very well have happened."

[82] Mrs. Willkie to the writer.

[83] Ibid.

[84] Gardner Cowles to the writer.

[85] Mrs. Joseph Barnes to the writer.

[86] Taylor.

[87] Charles Nutter to the writer.
[88] Barnes, p. 42. Makey (p. 159) refers to a "story" that Cobb told Willkie to "figure up his earnings in the last year," and "promised to double that figure." Mrs. Dillon says (p. 34) that he was offered "three times his Akron salary." But in a letter to Wilbur F. Pell, Jr., dated January 28, 1935, we find him writing "when I made $3,000 a year practicing law in Elwood" and "when I had an income of $25,000 in Akron."
[89] Johnson, p. 114.
[90] Barnes, p. 36.
[91] *Beacon Journal*, February 18—a special article occasioned by Willkie's birthday—and May 24, 1928.
[92] Aldrich Underwood to the writer.
[93] Maurice Bluhm to the writer.
[94] Taylor.
[95] Letter shown to the writer by Mr. Lang.
[96] *Beacon Journal*, September 24, 1929.
[97] Mrs. Willkie to the writer. She denies that he ever voiced the exclamation sometimes attributed to him, and indicative of a different mood, "Hell, Mother, we'll take this town."

CHAPTER 5

Basic sources for this and all the following chapters include Barnes, Dillon, and the *New York Times*. In addition, this and the chapter immediately following are based on numerous periodical articles by and about Willkie which appeared between 1933 and 1939 and which are mentioned in particular notes, and on the text of a number of his speches not given in full in the newspapers but reprinted in pamphlet form and distributed by the utility industry. A considerable number of these articles and speeches were collected in *Wendell Lewis Willkie: Occasional Addresses and Articles* (Stamford, Conn., 1940). A third important group of sources consists of the following reports of hearings by Congressional committees (in parentheses are abbreviated titles used in notes):

Muscle Shoals. Hearings Before the Committee on Military Affairs, House of Representatives, Seventy-third Congress, First Session, on H. R. 4859. Washington, D. C., 1933 ("Muscle Shoals Hearings").

Tennessee Valley Authority. Hearings Before the Committee on Military Affairs, House of Representatives, Seventy-fourth Congress, First Session, on H. R. 6793. Washington, D. C., 1935 ("TVA Hearings").

Public Utilities Holding Companies. Hearings Before the Committee on Interstate and Foreign Commerce, House of Representatives, Seventy-fourth Congress, First Session, on H. R. 5423. Washington, D. C., 1935. Part 2 ("House Hearings on Holding Company Act").

Public Utility Holding Company Act of 1935. Hearings Before the Committee on Interstate Commerce, United States Senate, Seventy-fourth Congress, First Session, on S. 1725. Washington, D. C., 1935 ("Senate Hearings on Holding Company Act").

Investigation of the Tennessee Valley Authority. Hearings Before the Joint Committee on the Investigation of the Tennessee Valley Authority, Congress of the United States, Seventy-fifth Congress, Third Session, Pursuant to Public Resolution No. 83. Washington, D. C., 1939. Parts 2, 6, 7, 10 ("TVA Investigation").

A fourth group of sources includes an 89-page pamphlet entitled *The Commonwealth & Southern Corporation and Its Subsidiary Companies: A Public Utility Holding Company Group: Outline of History and Development,* dated February 26, 1935 *(History and Development)*; the annual reports to the stockholders of Commonwealth & Southern from 1931 through 1939 (both this and the preceding item were made available to the writer by Mr. Granville Bourne); and *Moody's Manual of Investments: Public Utilities,* from 1930 to 1940.

The most important unpublished sources are in the Roosevelt Library, especially P[ersonal] P[residential] F[iles] 3111 and O[fficial] F[iles] 42, 3030, and 4040. (Willkie's correspondence as president of Commonwealth & Southern, which, according to the inventory, should be among his private papers, is missing.)

A final source is interviews with Philip H. Willkie, George Roberts, and Granville Bourne, and correspondence with Mr. Bourne, A. C. Blinn, and David E. Lilienthal.

[1] The figures are from the *New York Times.*

[2] "House Hearings on Holding Company Act," Part 2, p. 604.

[3] *Times,* January 22, 1935, p. 20.

[4] "Pyramiding" can be clarified by a simple example. A corporation, A, has assets of $100 million. Of this capital value, $40 million is in bonds, carrying a relatively low interest rate because they have first claim on corporation earnings and are therefore ordinarily a safe investment; $30 million in preferred stock, with guaranteed dividends somewhat higher than the interest rate on bonds, since they involve a greater risk in that no dividends are paid until interest charges on the bonds have been met; and $30 million in common stock, on which dividends are paid after meeting the claims of bondholders and preferred stockholders. The holders of the common stock (sometimes referred to as the "equity") obviously take a greater risk and are therefore considered to be entitled to a higher return on their investment (if they can get it) than the holders of the "senior securities." Presumably it was because of this greater risk that in the twenties and thirties only the common stock, as a rule, carried the right to vote for a board of directors, who determine corporation policy. (In practice, the voting stock would often represent far less than 30 per cent of the total assets.)

In the corporation described, therefore, an investment of $15 million plus (representing ownership of more than half of the common stock) would ensure control of a hundred million dollar corporation.

Now a holding company, X, is set up which buys this $15 million of common stock in Corporation A, against which it issues securities of its own to the value of $15 million, divided in the same ratio as before: 40 per cent in bonds, 30 per cent in preferred stock, and 30 per cent in common stock. Control of the whole company is now vested in the owners of 15 per cent plus of the capital of Corporation X, so that an investment of $2.25 million now controls the original investment of $100 million.

Next, Corporation X (the holding company) may gain control of three other operating companies (B, C, and D) each with a total capital of $100 million. Now an investment of $9 million controls a total of $400 million.

In the same way another holding company, Y, may be set up, controlling four operating companies (E, F, G, H) having a total capital of $400 million. And now a super holding company is set up which with $18 million buys the controlling shares of the common stock of X and Y, and issues new securities of its own in the same ratio. Now $2.7 million controls $800 million.

These dizzy operations could in theory be continued indefinitely. And the ratio between the controlling and the total investment becomes still more fantastic because, in practice, ownership of 50 per cent of the common stock is not necessary for control. A small solid block can often exercise control because the owners of the rest are scattered, unorganized, and uninformed.

The catch in the whole system is that only the operating companies earn any genuine income; and eventually this income becomes unable to sustain the interest and dividends on the securities of the holding companies.

[5] For an account of the situation in 1931, see James C. Bonbright and Gardner C. Means, *The Public Utility Holding Company* (New York: McGraw-Hill, 1932). In fairness to Insull it should be said that it was never proved to the satisfaction of a jury that he had *intended* to swindle investors. The truth may be that he himself got lost in the maze he had created.

[6] *Times*, March 13, 1935, p. 4.

[7] Ibid., May 24, p. 4.

[8] *History and Development*, p. 4.

[9] *Times*, May 30, p. 28. It was first listed on the Stock Exchange on October 10, 1929, opening at 23⅞ and closing at 24.

[10] Ibid., May 30, p. 28; June 26, p. 40; July 3, p. 29.

[11] Cobb's career is summarized by Dillon, pp. 35-36.

[12] George Roberts to the writer.

[13] *Times*, June 29, 1932, p. 31.

[14] Ibid., January 8, 1930, p. 6; June 11, p. 38; August 7, p. 33. The *Times* account of the January merger stated that more than 50 per cent of C & S common stock was owned by four other holding companies: American Superpower Corporation, United Corporation, Electric Bond and Share Company, and United Gas Improvement Company. (According to Barnes, p. 49, the first two were controlled by J. P. Morgan and Company and Bonbright and Company, respectively.) At the end of 1934 the Corporation reported that 644,125 shares of preferred stock were owned by 18,230 individuals; 225,615 by 1,918 "trustees, estates, and institutions"; and 629,376 by 834 "firms, corporations, banks and trust companies." Of the common stock, 13,513,373 shares were owned by 171,039 individuals; 823,239 by "trustees" etc.; and 19,311,437 by "firms, corporations" etc. (*History and Development*, p. 21.)

[15] As a matter of financial convenience, some of the 165 were given a continued nominal existence for varying lengths of time.

[16] The remaining 5 per cent came from the Transportation Securities Corporation, which was "in effect an asset realization company for transportation properties" (the brief day of the electric street car and interurban line was passing), and the General Corporation, "a similar company for coal, ice, water and other property and securities." C & S owned "all the capital stock" of these two companies. (*History and Development*, p. 3.)

[17] Five of the companies (Consumers, Ohio Edison, Alabama, Georgia, and Tennessee) were much larger than the others.

[18] *Times*, May 25, 1930, Sec. 2, p. 9; see also *History and Development*, pp. 13-14.

[19] Ibid., January 11, 1939, p. 37.

[20] These and the following figures, unless otherwise specified, are from the *Times*.

[21] For the year ending May 31, 1930, about 70 per cent of C & S gross earnings came from the sale of electricity; for the calendar year 1938 about 82 per cent came from this source. The remainder was mainly from transportation and gas.

[22] *Times,* July 24, 1938, p. 3.

[23] According to *History and Development* (p. 47), at the end of 1934 the properties of the operating companies of C & S were valued at $1,040 million. Of this, $436 million (about 42 per cent) was in bonds and debentures (defined by Willkie to a Senate committee as "a debt due at a fixed time and bearing a fixed rate of interest"; bonds and debentures are sometimes referred to as the "funded debt"); $225 million (22 per cent) was in preferred stocks; and the remainder, $378 million (36 per cent), was credited as the value of the common stock, all (except a minute percentage of TEPCO's) owned by the holding company. Against this last, C & S had the following securities outstanding: a "funded debt" of $52 million; preferred stocks listed at $150 million (1,500,000 shares at $100); and common stock listed at $168 million (33,600,000 shares at $5). (There is a discrepancy of a few million here which I am not enough of an accountant to account for.) The holding company and the operating companies also maintained about $70 million in liquid assets (such as cash and government bonds) to meet any sudden needs of the operating companies which could not be met in the usual way, that is, by selling securities.

[24] See *History and Development,* p. 17.

[25] George Roberts to the writer.

[26] *Fortune,* 15:202 (May, 1937).

[27] A. C. Blinn in a letter to the writer.

[28] *Times,* January 25, p. 23. It is odd that, less than three months later, he told a Congressional committee, in answer to a question as to how long he had been president of C & S, "Since January 1, I believe." ("Muscle Shoals Hearings," p. 233.)

[29] A proxy notice of the 1939 annual meeting of C & S stockholders gives this figure, plus $815 in director's fees. (*Times,* June 3, 1939, p. 28.) Willkie told a Congressional committee that it was much less than Cobb had received; that no officers of C & S received bonuses; and in answer to the question, "Could you figure out what the percentage of the gross expenditure is that is represented by the salaries of the executives?" said, "It is not half of one per cent." ("House Hearings on Holding Company Act," Part 2, pp. 639ff.)

[30] Makey, p. 161.

[31] Walker, p. 23.

[32] Gordon Hamilton, "Wendell Willkie of C & S," *Current History,* 51:21 (February, 1940).

[33] "Muscle Shoals Hearings," pp. 223-30.

[34] *Times,* May 29, 1933, p. 3.

[35] Ibid., pp. 1, 3.

[36] "House Hearings on Holding Company Act," Part 2, p. 578.

[37] *TVA: Democracy on the March* (New York: Harper, 1944), p. 6.

[38] Ibid., p. 39.

[39] *Times,* August 25, p. 23.

[40] Ibid., September 14, p. 33.

[41] Ibid., September 15, p. 1.

[42] The complete scale for these companies, as given by Willkie to a Senate

committee, was: $1.00 for the first 15 KWH; 4½ cents for each of the next 50; 2 cents for each of the next 135; 1¼ cents for each of the next 500; and 1 cent for all over 700. ("Senate Hearings on Holding Company Act," p. 546.) The *Times* account listed some comparable rates: New York City, $4.50 and $10.85; Chicago, $2.94 and $7.44; St. Louis, $2.05 and $5.80.

[43] Lilienthal thought that Willkie was going on "the assumption that the New Deal would prove to be a one-term aberration and that the country would soon return to normal." (Barnes, p. 69.)

[44] Letter dated May 21, 1936, in the Roosevelt Library (PPF-3111).

[45] See, for instance, C. Nelson Sparks, *One Man: Wendell Willkie* (New York: Raynor Publishing Company, 1943), p. 25, and the *New Republic,* 103: 321-22 (September 2, 1940).

[46] Telegram in the Roosevelt Library (OF-3030). Bernard F. Weadock, vice president of the Edison Electric Institute, testified before a Congressional committee that Willkie was absent from the meeting at which the action was voted (because, ironically, he was conferring with Lilienthal), but that he was opposed to the action; Weadock produced a copy of the minutes to confirm his testimony. ("TVA Investigation," Part 10, pp. 4223-24.)

[47] *Supreme Court Reporter,* 56:470.

[48] *Times,* November 19, p. 3.

[49] "Political Power," *Atlantic Monthly,* 160: 215 (August, 1937).

[50] These details are from a reprint of the speech. It is not reported in the *Times.*

[51] *Times,* November 1, p. 38.

[52] Ibid., November 18, Sec. 3, p. 7. Willkie's speeches were now being widely reported.

[53] See Barnes, p. 84. Willkie's speech is reprinted in *Addresses and Articles,* pp. 213-36.

[54] *Times,* November 26, pp. 1, 2.

[55] Ibid., February 23, p. 6.

[56] The act is summarized in the *Times,* August 27, 1935, p. 11.

[57] "House Hearings on TVA," pp. 243-50.

[58] This was Willkie's statement as quoted in the *Times,* July 14, Sec. 3, p. 7.

[59] *Times,* February 19, p. 1.

[60] Dillon says (p. 77) that "Willkie had directed the legal strategy" of the case. She gives no authority, and I know of no evidence that Willkie had any part in anti-TVA litigation prior to the "Nineteen Companies Suit."

[61] Official transcript of Roosevelt's press conference, January 14, 1938, in the Roosevelt Library.

[62] Letter to Clement Wood, May 24, 1939. (Correspondence.) The Act is summarized in the *Times,* August 27, pp. 1, 8.

[63] Roosevelt in his message to Congress urging the Holding Company Act declared that thirteen holding companies controlled three-fourths of the nation's utility business. (*Times,* March 13, 1935, p. 4.) According to Bonbright and Means (p. 95), the subsidiaries of "pure holding companies" in 1931 produced 72 per cent of the country's total output of electric power.

[64] *Times,* May 29, 1933, p. 17.

[65] "Muscle Shoals Hearings," p. 295.

[66] The bankers who retired were C. E. Groesbeck, A. L. Loomis, Ray P. Stevens and Landon Thorne. Those added to the board were Preston Arkwright (Georgia Power), Jo Conn Guild (Tennessee Electric Power), A. C. Blinn

(Ohio Edison), D. E. Karn (Consumers Power), and R. S. Wallace (Central Illinois Light). (*Times*, June 21, 1934, p. 31.) There is no suggestion in this story that the resignations were forced or that the persons resigning differed with Willkie on policy, but it was widely believed that such was the case—that he disapproved of some features of the organization and financing of C & S. Joseph Barnes states in a letter to the writer: "I have often heard WLW say that his own housecleaning in C & S had turned up and eliminated more corruption than Washington had ever heard of, and that it was the reason why the rightwing utility interests always feared and hated him." But Willkie did not go into detail.

[67] *Times*, June 21, 1934, p. 31.

[68] *History and Development*, pp. 69-70.

[69] Ibid., pp. 18-19.

[70] According to a statement filed by C & S with the SEC in 1935, the Georgia Power Company adopted the plan on January 1, 1934, and TEPCO on February 1, the latter as part of the January 4 contract with TVA.

[71] *Times*, January 22, 1935, p. 20. C & S derived most of its income from dividends on the common stocks of the operating companies. It also, in 1938, owned some bonds and preferred stocks of the Southern companies. ("TVA Investigation," Part 10, pp. 4233-34.)

[72] "Senate Hearings on Holding Company Act," p. 616.

[73] Ibid., p. 584.

[74] *History and Development*, p. 20.

[75] Alva Johnston, "The Man Who Talked Back," *Saturday Evening Post*, 211:31 (February 25, 1939).

[76] "Government and the Public Utilities," *Addresses and Articles*, p. 230.

[77] *Fortune*, 15:190 (May, 1937).

[78] *History and Development*, p. 17. (Some of the arithmetic is mine.) The same trend continued throughout the decade. For 1939 the average annual use of residential customers was 1,196 KWH at an average rate of 3.09 cents. And residential customers were supplying 27.5 per cent of the system's gross earnings. ("Annual Report to Stockholders, 1939.")

[79] "Senate Hearings on Holding Company Act," p. 622. Willkie told a House committee that a similar comment had been made by a Federal Trade Commission investigator ("the methods of your supervision, arrangement, and your complete elimination of intermediate holding companies is a matter of commendation"), but when Willkie suggested that he put this in his report, he answered, "Oh, Mr. Willkie, if I put anything in my report favorable to a public-utility holding company, I will be criticized." ("House Hearings on Holding Company Act," Part 2, p. 580.)

[80] Johnston, p. 44.

[81] Letter from W. K. Turner, dated August 28, 1939. (Correspondence.)

[82] This clipping is in the Correspondence and apparently appeared shortly before August 30, 1939.

[83] Washington *Post*, June 28, 1940, p. 4 (Henry Paynter).

[84] See "House Hearings on Holding Company Act," Part 2, pp. 1334-53.

[85] "Senate Hearings on Holding Company Act," p. 606.

[86] Ibid., p. 578.

[87] *Times*, February 27, p. 51.

[88] Ibid., March 15, p. 2.

[89] Speech to the Bond Club of New York, December 19, 1935, in *Addresses and Articles,* pp. 259-60.
[90] This list is taken from a bibliography of Willkie's speeches and writings which is among his private papers. It seems unnecessary to give the exact titles and dates. All are from 1934 and 1935.
[91] These quotations are from the text as reprinted in *Addresses and Articles,* pp. 239-50.
[92] See Barnes, p. 68. A 1940 campaign memorandum in the Roosevelt Library (OF-4040), written by Roosevelt's press secretary, Steve Early, calls Willkie's "role of a high-minded crusader . . . so obviously hypocritical that other utility leaders dubbed Willkie 'Jesus Christ.' "
[93] *Wendell L. Willkie, 1892-1944: Courageous Pioneer of the Utility Industry* ("Address . . . delivered at a National Newcomen Society Luncheon of the Newcomen Society of England . . . at New York . . . on December 20, 1950"), pp. 19-20.
[94] *Addresses and Articles,* p. 267.
[95] This is not mentioned in the *Times,* but is listed in the bibliography referred to above. It is referred to in a letter dated August 17, 1936, from Willkie to his brother Robert, who had recently seen it. Wendell says: "This, my first venture in the movies, has brought me considerable fan mail." (Correspondence.)
[96] *Times,* April 16, p. 6.
[97] Ibid., May 11, 1938, p. 10.
[98] Ibid., December 4, p. 33.
[99] Ibid., August 18, p. 29; December 23, p. 37.

CHAPTER 6

General sources are the same as for Chapter 5.
[1] "Political Power," *Atlantic Monthly,* 160:212 (August, 1937).
[2] *TVA: Democracy on the March,* p. 22.
[3] "Who Pays the Bills for TVA?" *Addresses and Articles,* p. 276.
[4] *Times,* June 17, 1938, p. 31.
[5] "Who Pays the Bills for TVA?" p. 275.
[6] "Political Power," p. 212.
[7] See, for example, an article by Harold L. Ickes, "In Defense of the New Deal Power Program," *New York Times Magazine,* November 7, 1937, p. 22.
[8] *Times,* July 24, 1938, p. 5.
[9] "TVA Hearings," p. 236.
[10] "TVA Investigation," Part 2, p. 946.
[11] For the whole C & S system, the annual gross earnings varied from less than 10 per cent of the stated capitalization in 1933, the worst year, to slightly less than 15 per cent in 1937, the best year.
[12] Taxes and depreciation are other factors frequently mentioned as favoring the government, but these are too complicated to go into.
[13] *Times,* April 5, 1935, p. 39.
[14] Ibid., November 17, 1937, p. 14.
[15] *Fortune,* 15:188 (May, 1937). (In a letter to his mother dated April 26, 1937, commenting on the article, Willkie said that he had been given a chance "to correct any errors of fact" but not "any of the inferences or conclusions or impressions."—Correspondence.) The last statement quoted from

Fortune seems to contradict Willkie's testimony in the Senate Hearings on the Holding Company Act (p. 548) that uniform rates were in effect throughout Alabama, Georgia, and Tennessee. But apparently rates were uniform only for customers in a certain class, and rural residential customers were in a different class from urban residential customers.

[16] See, for instance, the *New Republic*, 103:322-25 (September 2, 1940).

[17] "TVA Investigation," Part 7, pp. 2857-2918.

[18] See Barnes, p. 106.

[19] This testimony was included in "an Offer of Proof to the Federal Power Commission on November 23, 1959 in Docket No. E-6836." A copy was given me by Granville H, Bourne. Mr. Bourne also gave me a copy of a letter from Harlee Branch, Jr., president of the Southern Company (which replaced C & S as the holding company for the Southern group of operating companies), dated October 18, 1960, in answer to a request on my behalf, and one passage deserves quotation: "As a young lawyer, I was assigned the task of obtaining affidavits in Northwest Georgia regarding the construction of 'spite-lines' and the removal of private utility service facilities by TVA partisans and supporters. A large number of affidavits and photographs were obtained but these were rejected by the three-judge court which heard the TVA case. I assume that this material was published as a part of the record of that trial and included in the appeal documents when the case was taken to the Supreme Court." See also Wade H. Wright, *History of Georgia Power Company, 1805-1956* (Atlanta, 1957), pp. 277-78.

[20] In 1951, the Alabama Power Company was serving 98 per cent of all the farms in its service area. See Thomas W. Martin, *The History of Electricity in Alabama* (Birmingham, 1953), p. 76. The record of the Georgia Power Company is also good. See Wright, p. 295.

[21] Letter to the writer dated June 30, 1960.

[22] *Times*, December 18, 1933, p. 35.

[23] Ibid., August 16, 1938, p. 1.

[24] The average rate for residential customers throughout the system, of whom there were more than a million, and the per cent by which this was lower than the national average were: 1932—5.19 cents per KWH, 7 per cent; 1935—3.81 cents, 21.3 per cent; 1936—3.53 cents, 25 per cent; 1937—3.28 cents, 25.3 per cent; 1938—3.15 cents, 26 per cent; 1940 (first quarter)—2.95 cents, no figure available for comparison. These figures are from the Corporation's annual reports to the stockholders.

[25] *Times*, July 23, p. 24.

[26] Ibid., April 16, p. 33.

[27] Ibid., October 4, 1937, Sec. 4, p. 7 (Rufus Terral).

[28] "House Hearings on TVA," p. 254.

[29] Press conference, January 14, 1938; official transcript in Roosevelt Library.

[30] "TVA Investigation," Part 10, p. 4245.

[31] Ibid., Part 7, pp. 2703-04.

[32] Ibid., pp. 2709-10, 2765.

[33] *Times*, March 13, 1935, p. 4.

[34] "TVA Investigation," Part 7, pp. 2709-88.

[35] It was denied by the Supreme Court on April 25, 1938. (*Times*, April 26, 1938, p. 1.)

[36] "TVA Investigation," Part 6, pp. 2620-27.

[37] The *News* suspended publication in December, 1939, and Milton laid the blame on persons who had been angered by his campaign for public power. (*Times*, December 17, 1939, p. 6.)

[38] "TVA Investigation," Part 7, pp. 2815-54. See also the *Times*, February 11, 1939, p. 13.

[39] *Times*, December 8, 1938, p. 12; January 26, 1939, p. 11.

[40] "TVA Investigation," Part 10, p. 4226.

[41] *Times*, August 2, p. 24.

[42] A telegram from Willkie to Louis Howe confirms an appointment for September 24, 1934, and states that he will bring Arkwright (Roosevelt Library, OF-3030), but there is no other reference to an appointment on this date, and it is not in the Kanee copy of Roosevelt's appointment diary. (Although considered the fullest and most reliable of several informal records of Roosevelt's appointments, this diary is surprisingly casual and haphazard.)

[43] *Times*, December 14, p. 5.

[44] Mrs. Willkie confirmed this story to the writer.

[45] This and the following letters between Willkie and Roosevelt, unless otherwise specified, are in the Roosevelt Library (PPF-3111).

[46] Roosevelt wrote a "Memo for Mac" dated May 23: "I would like to see Wendell Willkie sometime in July." (In Roosevelt Library—PPF-3111.) But apparently he did not.

[47] Letter dated May 21 in Roosevelt Library (PPF-3111).

[48] *Addresses and Articles*, pp. 273-78.

[49] See for instance his speech to the Bond Club of New York on December 19, 1935, entitled "The Public Utility Problem," reprinted in *Addresses and Articles*, p. 267.

[50] *Times*, December 2, p. 39.

[51] See, for instance, the *Times* summary of part of his testimony before the Congressional committee investigating TVA, May 27, 1938, p. 4.

[52] Entry in appointment diary.

[53] *Times*, September 9, p. 2.

[54] The full text of the statement is in the Roosevelt Library (OF-42). It is summarized in the *Times*, September 20, p. 1.

[55] *Times*, September 22, p. 26.

[56] Ibid., October 1, p. 1.

[57] Ibid., October 11, Sec. 3, p. 4.

[58] Roosevelt Library (OF-42).

[59] *Times*, December 20, Sec. 4, p. 3.

[60] This letter and the documents related to it which are quoted below are in the Roosevelt Library (OF-42).

[61] *Times*, January 19, 1937, pp. 1, 4.

[62] Ibid., January 27, p. 5.

[63] A summary of the early stages of the case is given in the *Times*, November 14, 1937, Sec. 3, p. 1.

[64] Official transcript in Roosevelt Library. Senator Norris charged that as part of the agreement to extend the C & S-TVA contract on October 7 Willkie had agreed to call off the suit. Willkie denied this, and was vigorously supported by Louis Wehle, the President's own representative at the meetings: "during the negotiations . . . the idea of Commonwealth and Southern's

discontinuing or delaying its litigation against TVA was not discussed." (*Times,* January 20, p. 11.)

[65] Roosevelt Library (OF-42).

[66] Philip Willkie to the writer.

[67] These letters are in the Roosevelt Library (OF-42), along with a tentative press statement prepared *before* the conference for release afterwards, and a letter from Lilienthal dated September 19 urging that TVA hang on to its present customers and try to get more—a view clearly implying his opposition to power pooling.

[68] Letter dated February 6, in Roosevelt Library (OF-42). Reported in the *Times,* February 16, p. 37.

[69] *Times,* November 10, p. 11.

[70] Letter in Roosevelt Library (PPF-3111).

[71] *Times,* November 14, Sec. 3. p. 1.

[72] Official transcript in Roosevelt Library. Summarized in the *Times,* November 24, p. 1.

[73] *Times,* December 1, p. 18.

[74] Ibid., November 14, 1937, Sec. 3, p. 1.

[75] Ibid., December 11, p. 6.

[76] Ibid.

[77] Ibid., January 2, 1938, Sec. 4, p. 7.

[78] Ibid., November 24, 1937, p. 6.

[79] Ibid., January 22, 1938, p. 1.

[80] Ibid., January 16, p. 2.

[81] Ibid., January 19, p. 2.

[82] Ibid., March 6, p. 4.

[83] Ibid., March 11, p. 2.

[84] Ibid., May 11, pp. 1, 10.

[85] Ibid., December 13, 1938, p. 37, summarizing testimony of Julius Krug to the TVA investigating committee. See also Willkie's testimony, Part 10, pp. 4256-66 of the record of the investigation itself. A story in the *Times* when terms were finally agreed on (February 3, 1939, p. 25) says that the accounting firm set a value of $86 million on TEPCO's electrical properties, exclusive of the retirement reserve; and that Willkie offered to sell at this price and then went down to $81 million.

[86] Ibid., March 3, p. 1; March 5, p. 1; March 7, p. 6; March 9, p. 1; March 23, p. 1.

[87] Ibid., May 26, p. 2.

[88] Ibid., May 28, p. 1.

[89] "TVA Investigation," Part 10, pp. 4225ff.; and for a summary see the *Times,* November 24, 1938, pp. 1, 43.

[90] *Times,* December 8, p. 13; December 13, p. 37.

[91] Ibid., January 31, p. 1.

[92] Ibid., February 1, p. 35.

[93] Ibid., February 2, p. 27.

[94] Ibid.

[95] Ibid., February 3, pp. 1, 25.

[96] Ibid.

[97] Ibid., February 12, Sec. 4, p. 8 (Turner Catledge).

[98] Ibid., February 25, p. 2.

[99] The writer raised with Mr. Lilienthal the reasons for the seemingly sudden

settlement, and his answering letter, dated October 3, 1960, is quoted in full.

"I'm afraid you have made the problem more complicated than it actually was.

"Willkie insisted that T. V. A. buy the 'TEPC in its entirety' by having the T. V. A., a Federal agency, *buy the common stock.* This was nonsense, a propaganda position, and he knew it. So of course it was turned down, for he would have had us in court in a minute, via some of his stockholders, and the old rat race of litigation would have begun all over again.

"We said that T. V. A. would buy *property,* and the municipalities would be prepared to buy *property,* each taking that part of the TEP *physical* assets that fitted our respective functions, i. e., generating and transmission for T. V. A., distribution for the municipalities. When the lawsuit went against Willkie, we then were ready to do just that; the ultimate transaction was a sale of physical assets, not of common stock.

"We both knew we could reach an agreement about price; the effort to have the Federal Government buy common stock, illegally, was the stumbling block all along."

If I understand Mr. Lilienthal, he is saying that the common stock did not represent any part of the value of the physical properties. In the end, however, TVA and the municipalities *did,* in effect, pay $7 million for the common stock. It does not appear to me that Mr. Lilienthal's explanation is adequate.

[100] *Times,* June 14, p. 1.

[101] Ibid., June 18, Sec. 3, pp. 1, 5.

[102] Ibid., June 27, p. 6.

[103] Ibid., July 11, p. 39.

[104] Ibid., August 16, pp. 1, 33.

[105] Ibid., p. 33.

[106] Ibid., August 18, p. 35.

[107] An anticlimatic note is necessary to complete the story of Willkie's career as a utility executive. In 1940 his opponents pointed out as a reflection on his ability (perhaps even on his honesty) that no dividends were paid on C & S common stock after 1932, and that at the beginning of 1935 dividends on preferred stock were cut from $6 to $3, and by the beginning of 1940 were about $22.5 million in arrears.

The facts are correct but the inference is not. First, it should be made clear that the bondholders and preferred stockholders of the subsidiary companies were paid in full throughout the depression. Second, people forget how long the depression was. (They had not forgotten in 1940; but then he was being blamed for the depression itself!) In 1938 the amount of electricity sold by C & S for other than residential use (more than three-fourths of the total) was still lower than it had been in 1929, after rising higher during the 1937 economic upswing. Finally, C & S could by 1939 have paid all the arrears in dividends on the preferred stock, except that the policies of TVA made it impossible for the Southern companies either to refinance or to obtain capital for needed expansion, and therefore part of the profit of these subsidiaries that would have gone to C & S stockholders as dividends on their common stock was withheld to meet this need. (See "Report to the Stockholders for the Year Ended December 31, 1935," p. 3.)

The sale of TEPCO and changes in methods of accounting demanded by the SEC make comparisons difficult during the forties. But in 1948, the last full year of its existence, C & S had total gross earnings of more than $279 million; gross electric earnings of more than $235 million; a tax bill of $45 million; and a net income of nearly $29 million—equal to 60 cents a share on the common stock after paying the regular $6 dividend on the preferred. (*Moody's Manual of Investments: Public Utilies*, 1949, pp. 1278-79.) And some of the arrears on the preferred stock had been paid. In the end, the Southern group of companies became a separate "integrated" system called the Southern Company. In the North, Consumers, Ohio Edison, and Central Illinois Light became separate companies. C & S ended as it had begun, with an exchange of its stock for the stock of the Southern Company or one of the Northern companies. It was estimated in 1951 that holders of the preferred stock were now getting the equivalent of an annual dividend of $6.81 a share, and the common stockholders the equivalent of 40 cents a share. (*Times*, June 24, 1951, Sec. 3, pp. 1, 4.) The stockholders who stuck with C & S did not do so badly after all.

CHAPTER 7

The sources of this chapter are in general the same as those of preceding chapters, except that I have made more extensive use of the Correspondence.

[1] Granville Bourne to the writer.

[2] Mrs. Van Doren to the writer.

[3] Johnston, "The Man Who Talked Back," p. 34.

[4] Barnes, pp. 71-72.

[5] Letter from A. C. Blinn to the writer.

[6] Letter to the editors of *Harper's Magazine*, answering a defamatory article by Fred Rodell, called "Wendell Willkie: Man of Words," in the March, 1944 issue. It was printed in the unnumbered end pages of the May issue.

[7] Kenneth Kunkel to the writer.

[8] George Roberts to the writer.

[9] Flanner, "Rushville's Renowned Son-in-Law," p. 34.

[10] Granville Bourne to the writer.

[11] Edward Willkie to the writer. Other details in this paragraph were supplied by Philip Willkie.

[12] Philip Willkie to the writer.

[13] Ibid.

[14] Miss Sleeth to the writer. The story has appeared in print several times, with very slight variations.

[15] Philip Willkie to the writer. Mrs. Willkie's recollection (stated to the writer) is that this liability amounted to several hundred thousand dollars.

[16] Miss Sleeth to the writer. Willkie did buy 17 percent of the stock of the Rushville National Bank in 1936, but he did not buy any more (Philip Willkie to the writer); and perhaps his buying this much was mainly a matter of local loyalty.

[17] Miss Sleeth and Philip Willkie to the writer.

[18] May 13, 1940, p. 100.

[19] Philip Willkie to the writer.

[20] Letter to Wilbur F. Pell, Jr., dated January 28, 1935. (Correspondence.)

[21] In 1952 the fund totaled about $190,000 (Barnes, p. 316). At first Gardner Cowles was sole trustee, but some years after Willkie's death the trusteeship was transferred to Philip Willkie.

[22] Letter dated February 28, 1941. (Correspondence.)
[23] *Times*, October 12, 1943, p. 22.
[24] Mrs. Van Doren to the writer.
[25] Correspondence.
[26] Akron *Beacon Journal*, December 27, 1946.
[27] Letter to Mrs. Robert Hall, of Indianapolis, dated December 17, 1937. (Correspondence.)
[28] Flanner, p. 34.
[29] Lem Jones to the writer.
[30] This quotation is not for attribution.
[31] Barnes, p. 156.
[32] R. W.
[33] Ibid.
[34] Paul Harmon to the writer.
[35] Mrs. Dudley Hay to the writer, repeating a story told her by Ralph Cake, who was in the party. The date would have been February, 1944, when Willkie was sounding out political sentiment in the West, preparatory to his try for the 1944 nomination.
[36] Samuel Pryor to the writer.
[37] Mrs. Hay to the writer.
[38] Mrs. Van Doren to the writer.
[39] Other clubs which Willkie listed at one time or another in his *Who's Who in America* write-up were the Recess, Manhattan, Blind Brook, and the Downtown Association.
[40] Their application was endorsed by C. E. Groesbeck, an associate in the utility industry, on October 9, 1935. (Correspondence.)
[41] R. W.
[42] Mrs. Willkie to the writer.
[43] *This Week* (in the New York *Herald Tribune*), August 18, 1940, p. 7.
[44] Philip Willkie to the writer.
[45] Correspondence.
[46] Correspondence.
[47] Johnston, p. 11. Some of the details are from Barnes, p. 140.
[48] Quoted by Barnes, p. 141.
[49] Hamilton, "Wendell Willkie of C & S," p. 21.
[50] Mrs. Van Doren to the writer.
[51] Flanner, p. 31.
[52] Memorial Tributes.
[53] August 29, 1939. Later (May 12, 1940) he reviewed for the same publication John C. Long's *Mr. Pitt and America's Birthright.*
[54] George Roberts to the writer.
[55] Letter dated August 22, 1939. (Correspondence.)
[56] Barnes, p. 316; Flanner, p. 34: "Willkie's only real snobbery is a sincere hankering for literary society."
[57] Correspondence.
[58] The Correspondence contains a telegram from W. W. Ball setting the date as February 23, 1939.
[59] Telegram dated May 4. (Correspondence.)
[60] Flanner, p. 34.
[61] Mrs. Van Doren to the writer.
[62] Letter dated January 8, 1941. (Correspondence.)

[63] Letter dated March 27, 1941. (Correspondence.)
[64] Philip Willkie to the writer.
[65] This observation was made by the writer. Other items of interest were the *Encyclopedia Britannica*, the *Dictionary of American Biography*, the "American Statesman" series, the *Harvard Classics*, Macaulay's works, Woodrow Wilson's *History of the American People*, biographies of Lincoln by Albert J. Beveredge and Carl Sandburg, along with Lincoln's own writings, Winston Churchill's *Life and Times of Marlborough*, and many other works of British and American history and biography.
[66] Mrs. Van Doren to the writer.
[67] R. W.
[68] Mrs. Van Doren to the writer.
[69] *A Front Row Seat* (University of Oklahoma Press, 1953), p. 243.
[70] R. W.
[71] Correspondence.
[72] Correspondence.
[73] Mrs. Willkie to the writer.
[74] Correspondence.
[75] Letter to L. L. Engelking of the *Herald Tribune*, dated June 20, 1944. (Correspondence.)
[76] Letter to Marylois Purdy, dated June 23, 1944. (Correspondence.)
[77] Letter dated July 29, 1943. (Correspondence.)
[78] *A Front Row Seat*, p. 244.
[79] Ibid., p. 245.
[80] Letter dated October 23, 1944. (Memorial Tributes.)
[81] Letter dated June 5, 1944. (Correspondence.)
[82] Letter dated April 21, 1943. (Correspondence.) It would appear that this affection was imperfectly reciprocated.
[83] Letter to National Council of Bar Examiners, dated August 29, 1944. (Correspondence.)
[84] Letter dated October 14, 1941. (Correspondence.)
[85] Letter dated July 12, 1944. (Correspondence.)
[86] "Wendell Willkie: A Study in Courage," in *The Aspirin Age*, ed. Isabel Leighton (New York: Simon and Schuster, 1949), p. 450.
[87] "Breadth, depth, and elevation" have been called by Van Wyck Brooks the three dimensions of literature. It appears to me that they may equally well be taken as the three dimensions of human character.

CHAPTER 8

Among printed materials, the most important special sources for this chapter are several speeches by Willkie printed in *Addresses and Articles;* articles written by him which appeared in the *Atlantic*, the *Saturday Evening Post*, the *New Republic*, *Readers Digest*, *Fortune;* and two articles about him in the *Saturday Evening Post* by Alva Johnston and Hugh Johnson. (All these are specified in the notes.) Persons who supplied material in interviews included Mrs. Willkie, Philip Willkie, Edward Willkie, Harold E. Stassen, John and Gardner Cowles, M. E. Halloran (reporter for the Cowles newspapers), Russell Davenport and Oren Root.
[1] Letter from Whiting to Willkie at some time after the 1940 convention. (Correspondence.)

[2] *Times*, February 23, 1939, p. 22.
[3] Mary Sleeth to the writer.
[4] Barnes, p. 152. Mrs. Willkie does not remember that they were very active.
[5] All the details in this paragraph were supplied by Philip Willkie.
[6] To an audience of 200 women at a meeting of the Round Table Forum of the Town Hall Association. See the *Times*, December 4, p. 28. His correspondence reveals that in 1934 he gave another $100, at the request of James W. Gerard, to help make up the deficit incurred in the 1932 campaign.
[7] Many newspapers reported the story, with slight variations in the text, on December 6. The names of his friends were Murray Parker, Frank Enright, and George Carson.
[8] Correspondence.
[9] *Addresses and Articles*, p. 320. James A. Farley has stated that on December 1, 1938 he had lunch with Willkie, who "expressed great admiration for the President and his program. He said he disagreed with him only on the power question, where Willkie felt Roosevelt was being led astray by Thomas G. Corcoran and Frank McNinch. . . . Willkie told me he was a firm Democrat and had cast his vote for Governor Lehman and the rest of the Democratic ticket." *Jim Farley's Story* (New York: Whittlesey House, 1948), p. 157. I know of no other record of Willkie's expressing "admiration" for Roosevelt—though of course he always approved of the general aims of the New Deal.
[10] Philip Willkie and Mrs. Willkie to the writer. Mrs. Willkie asked her husband, while they were on their way to register, "Why don't you change your registration to Republican?" and though he did not commit himself at the time, he told her when he came out, "Well, I've done it!"
[11] Letter to Edwin C. Heinke of the Indianapolis *Times*, dated February 19, 1940. (Correspondence.)
[12] Undated letter in Correspondence. Further light is thrown on the topic by a letter written March 26, 1936, to Blair Coan of Chicago, in answer to a letter violently attacking Roosevelt.

"I have your letter of March 9, which disturbs me a little bit.

"If I had any contact with anyone who was either writing an article against the Administration or . . . had worked with the Republican Committee, the Black Committee [which had investigated the lobbying against the Holding Company Act] would attempt to paint the picture that I was attempting to control the politics of the nation.

"I should therefore appreciate it if you would not write to me with regard to such matters. I must leave your letter in the file and when my files are next searched, some committee similar to the Black Committee will draw misleading inferences." (Correspondence.)

[13] *Addresses and Articles*, p. 312.
[14] Ibid., p. 314. The reference is to Frank Hague, who expressed his philosophy of government in the celebrated comment: "I am the law."
[15] Ibid., pp. 315-16.
[16] "Brace Up, America!" p. 749.
[17] Ibid.
[18] Ibid., p. 751.
[19] Ibid., p. 756.
[20] P. 71.
[21] P. 74.

[22] *Addresses and Articles,* pp. 335-37.
[23] *Times,* November 2, p. 14.
[24] This was an article contracted for by *Readers Digest* and "planted" in the *North American Review,* where it had the title "Why I Believe in America." (This also gave an excuse for "condensing" it.) In a letter dated July 19, 1944, Willkie wrote in answer to an inquiry by John Bainbridge of the *New Yorker:* "The Reader's Digest asked me to write and paid for the article . . . I was greatly surprised when it appeared in the North American Review . . . If my recollection is correct, the Readers Digest had been after me for some time to write an article for them." (Correspondence.)
[25] *Readers Digest,* 35:4 (December, 1939).
[26] Ibid., p. 2.
[27] *Addresses and Articles,* p. 348.
[28] "I Am Not Nominating Him," *Saturday Evening Post,* 212:9 (June 22, 1940).
[29] *Times,* November 22, p. 13.
[30] Ibid.
[31] "I Am Not Nominating Him," p. 9.
[32] *Times,* June 2, 1939, p. 16.
[33] The program is reprinted in full in *Addresses and Articles,* pp. 281-302, from the *Bulletin of America's Town Meeting of the Air.*
[34] Johnston, "The Man Who Talked Back," p. 11.
[35] Barnes, p. 157.
[36] P. 52. Moley did not mention Willkie again until May 20, 1940.
[37] Quoted by Barnes, p. 157.
[38] P. 45. The letters mentioned do not seem to have been preserved.
[39] *Times,* November 29, p. 22.
[40] Ibid., January 17, p. 39.
[41] Ibid., January 31, p. 5.
[42] Ibid., February 1, p. 20.
[43] Letter dated February 13, 1940. (Correspondence.) Enclosed was a newspaper clipping summarizing a speech in which Wilhoite had defended public power, criticized the propaganda of the private companies, and then added, "I would like to vote for Wendell Willkie for President if Mr. Roosevelt does not run."
[44] Russell Davenport to the writer.
[45] *Times,* January 31, p. 5.
[46] Taylor. (See Chapter 4, Note 5.)
[47] 102:371.
[48] Ibid.
[49] Ibid.
[50] Ibid.
[51] Ibid., p. 372.
[52] Ibid.
[53] 21:64.
[54] Ibid., p. 168.
[55] Ibid., pp. 64-65.
[56] Ibid., p. 171.
[57] Ibid., p. 172.
[58] Ibid., p. 173.
[59] *Addresses and Articles,* p. 365.

[60] "I Am Not Nominating Him," p. 116.
[61] "Wendell Willkie's Hat Is on His Head," *Nation,* 150:469 (April 15, 1940).
[62] *Life,* 8:80 (April 22, 1940). The other details are from the same source. Dillon (pp. 128-29) adds a few not given in *Life.* The writer remembers the program in general but not in detail.
[63] Letter dated April 9, 1940. (Correspondence.) The names were chosen from alumni directories of a number of colleges and universities, according to Mr. Root—whose general attitude deserves a further note. Robert Willkie has written: "I saw Root [at the convention] and told him I could get a half dozen genuine fine signature telegrams in four different states by simply saying I wanted them. . . . He said, 'No, we do not want telegrams engineered from the top.'" (R. W. to the writer.)
[64] Russell Davenport to the writer.
[65] *Times,* April 15, p. 7.
[66] See the *Herald Tribune,* June 29, p. 4.
[67] *Time,* 35:17 (June 24, 1940).
[68] According to Mrs. Willkie's statement to the writer, Willkie "could not understand why the government seemed to favor Franco."
[69] "House Hearings on TVA," p. 256.
[70] *Readers Digest,* 35:2 (December, 1939).
[71] *Times,* April 11, p. 14.
[72] Ibid., April 17, p. 1.
[73] Ibid., April 5, p. 15.
[74] Ibid., April 6, p. 18.
[75] Ibid., April 16, p. 38.
[76] Ibid., April 17, pp. 1, 20.
[77] Ibid., April 8, p. 4.
[78] Information about many of these persons, together with anecdotes of how they got interested in Willkie and what part they played, are given by Dillon, Chapter IX.
[79] Barnes, p. 163.
[80] *Times,* May 3, p. 12.
[81] Ibid., May 5, p. 3.
[82] Ibid., May 1, p. 1.
[83] Ibid., May 5, p. 3.
[84] John and Gardner Cowles to the writer.
[85] *Herald Tribune,* June 29, p. 2.
[86] Edward Willkie to the writer. Dillon says (p. 127) that at the funeral of his mother, who had died on March 10, Willkie told his three brothers "that he had decided to seek the Presidential nomination at Philadelphia in the coming June." This is contradicted by Edward's statement as well as by many of Willkie's own in the following weeks. What he said was perhaps that he was *thinking* about it. One other item has a bearing on the date of his decision. His correspondence contains a 5-page biographical sketch, described as having been approved by Willkie himself, with a covering letter to William G. Irwin of Columbus, Indiana, suggesting that it be released through some Indiana newspaper. The letter, which refers to two earlier drafts that had been sent, is dated May 8.
[87] Gardner Cowles to the writer.
[88] M. E. Halloran, reporter for the Cowles newspapers, to the writer.
[89] *Time,* 35:18 (May 20, 1940).

[90] *Times,* June 11, p. 31.
[91] Ibid., May 26, p. 16.
[92] Ibid., June 15, p. 11.
[93] Ibid., June 19, p. 1.
[94] Ibid., May 26, p. 16.
[95] Ibid., June 21, p. 17. The final Gallup Poll, taken during the week of the Convention but not announced until ten days later, showed 44 per cent for Willkie, 29 per cent for Dewey, and 13 per cent for Taft. (Ibid., July 7, p. 2.)

CHAPTER 9

In this and the following four chapters, I have drawn on the following newspapers, especially, besides the *Times:* the New York *Herald Tribune,* the *Christian Science Monitor,* the Louisville *Courier-Journal,* the St. Louis *Post-Dispatch,* the Washington *Post,* the Akron *Beacon Journal,* and the Chicago *Tribune.* Among books, a basic source from this point on is Donald B. Johnson, *The Republican Party and Wendell Willkie* (University of Illinois Press, 1960). Material has also been drawn from *The Secret Diaries of Harold Ickes,* Vol. III (New York: Simon and Schuster, 1954); Raymond Clapper, *Watching the World* (New York: McGraw-Hill, 1944); Roscoe Drummond, "A Study in Courage," in *The Aspirin Age,* ed. Isabel Leighton (New York: Simon and Schuster, 1949); Joseph W. Martin, Jr., *My First Fifty Years in Politics* (New York: McGraw-Hill, 1960); and *Official Proceedings of the 22nd Republican National Convention* (Washington, D. C., 1940). Persons interviewed, in addition to those mentioned in the notes to the preceding chapters, include Turner Catledge, Harold Gallagher, Guy Lemmon, Joseph W. Martin, Jr., Rolland Marvin, Samuel Pryor, and Harry Shackleford. Information has also been obtained through correspondence with Frank McKay of Grand Rapids, Michigan; John S. Powers of Buffalo, New York; and Basil Walters of the Chicago *Daily News.*
[1] Barnes, p. 163.
[2] Donald B. Johnson, *The Republican Party and Wendell Willkie,* p. 65.
[3] The foregoing account was given the writer by Harry Shackleford and Guy Lemmon.
[4] *Times,* June 7, p. 16.
[5] *Time,* 35:23 (June 10).
[6] Ibid., 35:18 (May 6).
[7] *Newsweek,* 15:20 (April 15).
[8] *Christian Science Monitor,* June 7, p. 16.
[9] *Times,* April 20, p. 17. This should not be confused with his speech to the American Newspaper Publishers Association in New York on April 25. Also taking part were Senator Pepper of Florida and Glenn Frank, chairman of the Republican Program Committee, which had recently issued an elaborate report on the policies that the party should follow.
[10] *Herald Tribune,* June 29, p. 2.
[11] *Secret Diaries,* III, 165.
[12] Basil Walters of the Chicago *Daily News* in a letter to the writer.
[13] *Times,* May 21, p. 17.
[14] Letter from James L. Wright of the Buffalo *Evening News,* dated December 7, 1944. (Memorial Tributes.) Not all the comment on Willkie's speech was favorable. The *Nation* printed a frantic tirade calling it "blantant, in-

temporate demagoguery" and Willkie "the closest thing to a native American fascist yet to receive serious consideration as Presidential timber" (150:748 [June 22]). What really happened was that "in stressing the need for greater business efficiency in government . . . he juxtaposed a reference to the efficiency of the Hitler government— merely to show that it was something to realize and combat." (*Christian Science Monitor,* September 10, p. 1.)

[15] *Time,* 35:18-19 (June 24).
[16] *Life,* 8:104 (May 13).
[17] *Times,* May 6, p. 7.
[18] Ibid., May 20, p. 6.
[19] Ibid., p. 1.
[20] Quoted in *Time,* 35:18 (May 27).
[21] *Times,* June 10, p. 10.
[22] Ibid., May 20, p. 11.
[23] Ibid., May 26, p. 16.
[24] Ibid., May 17, p. 15.
[25] Ibid., May 21, p. 16.
[26] Ibid., May 19, p. 4.
[27] Ibid., June 10, p. 7.
[28] P. 22.
[29] See, e. g., *Newsweek,* 15:31 (June 24).
[30] *Herald Tribune,* June 25, p. 19.
[31] *Times,* June 11, p. 1.
[32] As noted in the last chapter, Willkie in his speeches at Boston and Brooklyn took a less clear line, and seemed by implication to be criticizing Roosevelt's speech, which he had declined to comment on directly. (*Times,* June 13, p. 10.) But he had also said, two days after the speech, "As to foreign affairs . . . I am in accord with the administration." (Ibid., June 13, p. 10.)
[33] Turner Catledge to the writer.
[34] *Times,* June 23, p. 2. The following quotation is from June 24, p. 10.
[35] Ibid., June 21, p. 1.
[36] Dillon, p. 167. Harold Talbott tried unsuccessfully to move Willkie to "a beautiful suite of rooms in the Warwick Hotel."
[37] *Times,* June 16, p. 4. *Time* also took notice (35:18 [June 24]).
[38] *Times,* June 20, p. 20; June 23, p. 4.
[39] Harold Gallagher to the writer.
[40] *Times,* June 25, p. 18. A later story suggests that this was the number he had seen since he arrived.
[41] St. Louis *Post-Dispatch,* June 26, p. 10A (Marquis Childs).
[42] Akron *Beacon Journal,* June 25, p. 2; *Times,* June 26, p. 13.
[43] *Times,* June 26, p. 13.
[44] Ibid.
[45] Ibid., p. 12.
[46] St. Louis *Post-Dispatch,* June 30, p. 8A.
[47] *Times,* June 24, p. 12.
[48] Ibid., June 25, p. 17.
[49] Ibid., June 27, p. 4.
[50] Rolland Marvin to the writer.
[51] Akron *Beacon Journal,* June 24, p. 6.
[52] Ibid., June 23.
[53] Ibid., June 18.

[54] *Herald Tribune*, June 27, p. 17.

[55] *Times*, June 27, p. 6.

[56] Ibid., June 24, p. 10.

[57] *Post-Dispatch*, June 28, p. 4A.

[58] *Times*, June 21, p. 17.

[59] Ibid., June 22, p. 10. Joseph Martin, in *My First Fifty Years in Politics*, written twenty years later, used language identical with Simpson's: "I have never seen anything like the flood" of telegrams to the delegates (p. 155).

[60] Jonathan Mitchell, "How They Won with Willkie," *New Republic*, 103:49 (July 8, 1940).

[61] *Herald Tribune*, June 26, p. 16. Dillon (pp. 149-50) gives Harold Talbott credit for suggesting that the Willkie Clubs should have their members send telegrams to the delegates; it seems not impossible, however, that some of the more brilliant might eventually have thought of this idea themselves. She also says that Harold Gallagher, whose standing in the American Bar Association was high, telephoned many state and local bar associations asking them to have their members send telegrams. Mr. Gallagher told the writer that this was completely untrue.

[62] Ibid., June 27, p. 14.

[63] *Post-Dispatch*, June 27, p. 4A.

[64] *Herald Tribune*, June 28, p. 5.

[65] *Times*, June 22, p. 10.

[66] Mitchell, p. 48.

[67] *Times*, July 12, p. 16.

[68] John S. Powers of Buffalo in a letter to the writer. The only open on-the-spot allegation of improprieties was in the "Washington Merry-Go-Round," where Drew Pearson and Robert Allen stated that delegates "found that many of the wires [urging Willkie's nomination] had the same spelling and grammatical mistakes. Also that batches of the signatures [presumably on the "declarations"] appeared to be in alphabetical order—indicating a common source." (Washington *Times-Herald*, June 27.) Obviously the authors are simply repeating, without checking, what was told them by anti-Willkie delegates.

[69] *Secret Diaries*, III, 234.

[70] June 28, p. 2 (Harlan Miller).

[71] Quoted in the *Times*, June 20, p. 20.

[72] Ibid., May 31, p. 38.

[73] Ibid., June 16, p. 4.

[74] Ibid., June 24, p. 1.

[75] Ibid., June 13, p. 10.

[76] See Krock's column in the *Times*, October 10, 1944, p. 22. Johnson in a long note (pp. 78-79) discusses the matter in detail and concludes firmly that Willkie was "being facetious." I agree, but must record that Turner Catledge is convinced that Willkie was sincere.

[77] Dillon, who here as elsewhere clearly reflects the picture as Hamilton wished it to be seen, assigns him a leading part in the Willkie drive at the convention, including the responsibility for the Sunday night meeting. On the last point she is supported by Johnson, who does not give his source. If this is correct, I suggest that the idea of the meeting came originally from Samuel Pryor, about whose support of Willkie there is no question, and who (as I gathered from an interview) was on very friendly terms with

Hamilton. The latter's political views were at all times very different from Willkie's, and I know of no other evidence that he played the decisive part described by Dillon, and doubt that he did. He later had a special motive in playing up his contribution, namely, to magnify his grievance in not being retained by Willkie as National Chairman; and, as the reader will have occasion to note, he is not a reliable witness. Probably Davenport's comment to the writer, in answer to a question, accurately describes Hamilton's attitude: "He could have done a lot to hurt us and he didn't."

[78] Dillon, p. 149. Johnson (p. 79) adds the names of Stassen, Gardner Cowles, Senator Styles Bridges of New Hampshire, James Allen of Kansas, James Douglas of Illinois, Frank Horton of Wyoming, and Edgar Queeny of Missouri. Stassen is unlikely to have been present, as the following account will show; and most news reports of the convention indicate that Bridges was active mostly in his own behalf. Barnes (p. 177) lists Halleck, Barton, and Horton as the only professionals on Willkie's "original team" at Philadelphia and says that "not until June 22 did his strategy committee include professionals like" Baldwin, Bridges, Marvin, Simpson, Pryor, Hallanan, and Weeks. Except in regard to Marvin and Hallanan, this is definitely misleading.

[79] This account was given the writer by Gardner Cowles, and is substantially the same as that given by Barnes. As Mr. Stassen remembered the events, in talking with the writer, Willkie asked him to be floor manager only after he had made his public announcement of support. He asked if it wasn't late to be changing floor managers, and Willkie answered that he didn't have one. Stassen agreed, after talking with some other Willkie supporters, including Baldwin, Halleck, and Carr. It is understandable that after so many years different persons should have different recollections of such a hectic period.

[80] Harold Stassen to the writer. I am not clear as to why the announcement was delayed for almost twenty-four hours after Stassen completed his task as temporary chairman and turned the gavel over to Martin. Perhaps it was felt that the announcement would have the greatest psychological effect at this time.

[81] *Times*, June 25, p. 18. The eight signers were Representatives Woodruff of Michigan, Knutson of Minnesota, Keefe and Bolles of Wisconsin, Clevenger and Lewis of Ohio, Mundt of South Dakota, and Gillie of Indiana.

[82] Ibid., June 26, p. 18.

[83] Ibid., June 25, p. 19. Presumably the same advertisement appeared in all New York and Philadelphia papers, and possibly others, though I have not checked.

[84] Ibid., June 26, p. 17.

[85] Ibid., June 27, p. 5.

[86] *Official Proceedings of the 22nd Republican National Convention* (Washington, D. C., 1940), pp. 154-55.

[87] See the Washington *Post*, June 27, Sec. 1, p. 5.

[88] *Official Proceedings*, p. 158.

[89] As Russell Davenport recalled the events of the evening, Indiana passed initially because of confusion resulting from the fact that Halleck had not yet arrived. The reason for his lateness was that the cab in which he and Davenport were riding got caught in a traffic jam. Dillon says (p. 159) that Halleck rode to the convention hall with John B. Hollister (Taft's law partner);

but perhaps Davenport was in the same cab. Incidentally, Davenport had no recollection of the fright and indecision on Halleck's part of which Dillon gives such a melodramatic account (derived possibly from Hamilton); although Halleck had worked with him on the nominating speech, which was largely written by Davenport. Halleck himself described the Dillon account of his indecision as "a lot of nonsense!" (Johnson, p. 69n.) I am inclined to agree. Halleck did ask Martin's advice before accepting, and Martin advised him to do it. Martin himself had originally been asked by Pryor and Weeks to nominate Willkie; but this would have meant resigning as permanent chairman of the convention, and besides, as he told them, "I don't think your man Willkie has a chance." (Martin, p. 151.)

[90] *Times*, June 27, p. 3.

[91] *Herald Tribune*, June 27, p. 1.

[92] Russell Davenport to the writer.

[93] The writer listened to the nominating speeches on Wednesday night and to the balloting on Thursday, but recalls only a few vivid details and a general impression of the irresistible dramatic appeal of the proceedings, which no subsequent convention of either party has approached.

[94] Martin, p. 153.

[95] The preceding details are from the *Times*, June 27, p. 2 (Charles W. Hurd) and p. 3 (Sidney Shalett).

[96] *Herald Tribune*, June 27, p. 16 (Bert Andrews). Among the many misstatements in Dillon's account, perhaps the most extraordinary is that Halleck's speech "fell flat" (p. 159). It is supported to some extent by Marquis Childs: "If you take at their transparent and obvious value the faces of the amateurs who created the Willkie boom, it is over, finished." (*Post-Dispatch*, June 27, pp. 1A, 8A.) What does one do with such a statement besides putting it dutifully in a footnote?

[97] *Monitor*, June 27, p. 7 (Richard L. Strout). Willkie himself had said the same thing on his arrival in Philadelphia: "If I don't get the nomination, it won't be worth anything anyhow." (*Time*, 36:14 [July 8].)

[98] Martin, p. 155.

[99] These details are from various accounts in the *Times* and *Herald Tribune*.

[100] *Herald Tribune*, June 27, p. 1.

[101] *Times*, June 27, p. 3. Each item is on a separate line.

[102] Washington *Post*, June 27, p. 1.

[103] Martin, p. 154.

[104] *Times*, June 27, p. 3.

[105] Johnson, p. 92, quoting Pryor's statement in an interview.

[106] Washington *Post*, June 28, p. 3 (Edward T. Folliard). An article in the *Herald Tribune*, June 26, p. 17, discusses the ticket shortage. Each of the 2,000 delegates and alternates got one ticket besides his own. In addition, one ticket each was allotted to about 300 party workers and to the 200-odd Republican members of Congress. Aside from these, each state got an allotment "based on the size of the delegation and its proximity to the convention city," with Pennsylvania getting about 6,000, besides the 1,500 for Philadelphia business men who raised $250,000 to bring the convention to the city. Ohio got 600 and Illinois 400. This accounts for 11,000 of the 15,000 seats available, with allotments for forty-five states, including New York and New Jersey, not included. Since it is estimated that 20,000 persons were present during the balloting, there cannot have been more than 5,000 standees.

[107] Oren Root, entering the galleries Wednesday night, was depressed because everybody around him seemed to be wearing a Dewey button or a Taft feather; but most of them turned out to be for Willkie. Robert Willkie sat beside the wife of an alternate delegate supporting Taft, but she was shouting "We want Willkie," too. Harold Gallagher, who had some tickets that he never got time to dispose of, was told by a Dewey delegate from New Jersey that he heard his own family shouting down to him to vote for Willkie. (All in interviews or letters to the writer.)
[108] *Newsweek,* 16:16 (July 8).
[109] *Times,* June 25, p. 16.
[110] Ibid., June 27, p. 3.
[111] Barnes, p. 185.
[112] Martin, p. 155.
[113] *Monitor,* July 2, p. 20 (Erwin D. Canham).
[114] *Official Proceedings,* p. 283.
[115] *Newsweek,* 15:31-32 (June 24); *Times,* June 24, p. 10.
[116] *Times,* June 26, p. 18.
[117] Dorothy Dunbar Bromley, "The Education of Wendell Willkie," *Harper's Magazine,* 181:485 (October, 1940).
[118] Dillon, p. 163. She also says (p. 165) that Pew would have liked to switch to Willkie if James had been willing to release him. This is possible but doubtful.
[119] Stassen had advised against the poll on the ground that it would be a lengthy affair that might annoy the other delegates, but Mack insisted that the vote was not correct, and Marvin supported him. (Johnson, p. 96n.; and Rolland Marvin to the writer.)
[120] *Herald Tribune,* June 28, p. 2 (Emmett Crozier).
[121] *Times,* June 28, p. 3.
[122] *Herald Tribune,* June 28, p. 2 (Emmett Crozier).
[123] *Official Proceedings,* pp. 304-05.
[124] Martin, p. 157. Landon also urged him to recess the convention until the next day, holding out the hope that then the convention would turn to him (Martin) as the compromise candidate. But Martin could not be moved.
[125] According to Dillon (pp. 165-66), the switch to Willkie was engineered by the leader of the Michigan state Republican organization, Frank McKay; partly in payment of a personal debt to Hamilton, partly because of Willkie's promise that McKay could name the Federal district judges in the state. McKay denied the first of these allegations in a letter to Johnson (see p. 99n.) and the second in a letter to the writer. They sound like more Hamiltonian fiction; especially as he is represented as being "shocked that any candidate would bargain with the federal judgeships." This gives a touching picture of Hamilton's sensibilities, since it is common knowledge that Federal district judges are named by local party leaders. One remembers two judges nominated by President Truman to Illinois districts whom the Senate refused to confirm because Senator Douglas had not been consulted. But of course the episode never happened. John Cowles told the writer that on two occasions at Philadelphia he was commissioned by important Republicans to approach Willkie with offers to swing some votes his way in return for certain commitments. One was to support a prospective Vice Presidential candidate who was completely unfitted for the office. The other was simply a request that if Willkie was elected, he would consult the person (not necessarily take

his advice) if he was considering making a cabinet appointment from that state. But Willkie turned this down as well as the other.

[126] From the *Official Proceedings*. At one point during the sixth ballot when the chant of "We want Willkie!" threatened to become more than Martin could cope with, he shouted, "Well, if you'll keep quiet long enough, maybe you'll get him." (Martin, p. 158.)

[127] The Pennsylvania delegation had been caucusing in a room outside the convention hall, and were still arguing (with James fatuously insisting that he still had a chance) when former Senator Reed returned to the hall, discovered that Willkie was practically nominated (he did not realize that he *was*) and on his own authority announced the votes for Willkie. See the *Monitor*, July 2, p. 20 (Erwin D. Canham). See also Johnson, p. 100.

[128] It has been pointed out that this was not correct. Nebraska first passed, and later announced 6 for Taft and 8 for Willkie. It was never changed. See Johnson, p. 100. Apparently nobody has previously noticed that Alaska cast 1 vote for Taft, which was not changed. However, nobody voted against Bricker's motion to make the vote unanimous.

[129] *Times*, June 25, p. 18.

[130] *Post-Dispatch*, July 1, p. 3.

[131] *Newsweek*, 16:15 (July 8, 1940).

[132] Martin, p. 160.

[133] Washington *Post*, June 29, p. 1. Dillon says (p. 147) that Baldwin had been promised the Vice Presidential nomination in return for giving Willkie the Connecticut vote on the first ballot, and this is confirmed by Martin (p. 159). Both Willkie and Baldwin must have known, however, that to choose candidates from adjoining states would have been a departure from the invariable practice of having different parts of the country represented by the two leaders of the national ticket, and can hardly have been surprised that other party leaders desired a different arrangement. Dillon also says (p. 171), in contradiction not only of Martin but of the newspaper accounts, that McNary was eager to accept.

[134] *Times*, July 1, p. 1.

[135] June 29, p. 14. Dillon (p. 171) calls the choice of McNary the "first blunder of the campaign."

[136] Ickes, *Secret Diaries*, III, 223. This is confirmed in *Jim Farley's Story*, p. 244: "We all agreed that . . . McNary added strength to the Republican ticket."

[137] *Newsweek*, 16:17 (July 8, 1940).

[138] *Times*, June 24, p. 10. Obviously there was no way of telling exactly how much was spent by groups and individuals for local advertising. But this kind of advertising was not expensive.

[139] Ibid., p. 12.

[140] *Herald Tribune*, June 27, p. 23. Here perhaps may be inserted Senator Bridges' answer to Senator Norris' allegation that Willkie was nominated by the "Power Trust": "I have personal knowledge of efforts by his own business associates to prevent him from running, on the ground that his nomination would make the utility industry a political football in this campaign. I have personal knowledge of strong influence brought to bear by interests closely identified with the utility industry to stop his nomination. Furthermore, there were within the industry powerful individuals who heartily disliked, envied, and feared Mr. Willkie because of his progressive and liberal

policies as to rate reduction, as to labor policies, and his refusal to be a part of back-door political arrangements. . . . Wendell Willkie was nominated in spite of and not because of the power interests." (*Congressional Record*, October 2, 1940, p. 19644.) In view of Senator Bridges' later career he may not be considered a reliable witness, but this statement sounds convincing.

[141] Many of Sparks' charges are refuted in detail by Bill Cunningham in an article in the Boston *Herald*, December 19, 1943. One monstrous story—that Willkie's nomination was dictated by Ogden Reid, publisher of the *Herald Tribune*, and Thomas W. Lamont because Willkie had promised support to Britain—has a small kernel of truth in that at a party given by Mrs. Reid in the spring of 1940, those present included Lamont, Willkie, Taft, and the British ambassador, Lord Lothian, and that in a discussion of aid to Britain, Willkie expressed himself in favor, and Taft in opposition. The story is mentioned here because, as Johnson notes (pp. 105-06 and n.) it has been supported by Harry Elmer Barnes, who has had some standing as a serious historian. He can have none hereafter. As for the Sparks book, this writer suspects that it was part of a *real* conspiracy to discredit Willkie. The *Beacon Journal* reported at the time it was published (December 7, 1943) that many persons who knew Sparks doubted that he was the author; and much other anti-Willkie literature was circulated between this date and Willkie's withdrawal from the contest for the Presidential nomination in early April, 1944; though no doubt some of this was done by individuals.

[142] "Getting Nominated Is an Intricate Business," *New York Times Magazine*, April 20, 1952, p. 67.

[143] "Who Controls the Conventions?" *New York Times Magazine*, August 12, 1956, p. 38.

[144] In a letter to Mr. Stokes, I asked if he would give me the evidence for his statement, but received no reply; it is a legitimate inference that he had no evidence to give. The phrase "revealed later" presumably refers to the Sparks book. It may be mentioned that during the 1940 campaign Willkie accused Stokes of unfair treatment, an unusual episode in his career since his relations with reporters were usually good. See the Washington *Post*, August 26, 1940, p. 2 (Harlan Miller). I had a similar experience with Fulton Lewis, Jr., who made a similar charge in a radio broadcast in (I believe) early 1952.

[145] Such a denial has been explicit or implied in the statements of all the persons with whom I have discussed the nomination. A list of their names is given at the beginning of the notes to Chapter 6.

[146] *Times*, June 24, pp. 1, 12.

[147] 16:14 (July 8, 1940).

[148] 151:6 (July 6, 1940).

[149] June 30, 1940, Sec. 3, p. 1.

[150] *Herald Tribune*, June 26, 1940, p. 21.

[151] "Wendell Willkie: A Study in Courage," in *The Aspirin Age*, p. 459.

[152] *Watching the World* (New York: McGraw-Hill, 1944), p. 158. The list of witnesses could be extended indefinitely.

CHAPTER 10

New sources for this and the following three chapters include the following volumes of memoirs and letters: Marquis Childs, *I Write from Washington* (New York: Harper, 1942); Edward J. Flynn, *You're the Boss*

(New York: Viking, 1947); Lord Halifax, *Fullness of Days* (London: Collins, 1957); Charles Michelson, *The Ghost Talks* (New York: Putnam, 1944); Frances Perkins, *The Roosevelt I Knew* (New York: Viking, 1947); *F. D. R., His Personal Letters, 1928-1945,* edited by Elliott Roosevelt and Joseph Lash. 2 vols. (New York: Duell, Sloan and Pearce, 1950); Samual I. Rosenman, *Working with Roosevelt* (New York: Harper, 1952); Robert E. Sherwood, *Roosevelt and Hopkins* (New York: Harper, 1948); Grace Tully, *F. D. R., My Boss* (New York: Scribner, 1949); William Allen White, *Autobiography* (New York: Macmillan, 1946).

For the background of the foreign policy issues in the campaign, the following have been used: Walter Johnson, *The Battle Against Isolation* (University of Chicago Press, 1944); William L. Langer and C. Everett Gleason, *The Challenge to Isolation, 1937-1940* (New York: Harper, 1952); *The United States in World Affairs, 1933,* and *The United States in World Affairs, 1934-1935* (New York: Published for the Council on Foreign Relations by Harper & Brothers, 1934 and 1935). For analysis of the election results two volumes may be mentioned: Samuel Lubell, *The Future of American Politics* (New York: Harper, 1952); and *The Political Almanac, 1952.*

Besides the persons previously mentioned, the following contributed information in interviews or correspondence: Elliott V. Bell, Pierce Butler, Jr., Pierce Butler, III, Bartley Crum, and Mrs. Dudley Hay.

Two unpublished sources which I have not examined but which ought to be used in any attempt at a definitive account of the 1940 Presidential campaign are (1) two files in the Franklin D. Roosevelt Library on the Republican and Democratic campaigns respectively; and (2) two cartons of correspondence among the Willkie papers, labeled in the "Inventory": "Box of 1940 correspondence turned over by Mr. Gallagher, in order" and "Box of 1940 correspondence with special big shots, separated."

[1] *Times,* June 29, p. 1.

[2] Akron *Beacon Journal,* June 29.

[3] Washington *Post,* July 2, p. 1.

[4] See the *Herald Tribune,* June 28, p. 4.

[5] Ibid., July 2, p. 16; July 5, p. 16.

[6] *Times,* July 3, p. 1. The other members were Martin, Baldwin, David Ingalls (Taft's campaign manager), Halleck, Carr, Mrs. Ruth Hanna McCormick Simms (a Taft supporter), Paul Krusi (chairman of the Tennessee convention delegation), Oren Root, Mrs. Ruth de Young Kohler ("wife of Herbert V. Kohler, president of the Kohler Company, Kohler, Wis. and special writer for the Chicago Tribune"), Representative J. William Ditter of Pennsylvania and Senator John G. Townsend of Delaware. A very full account of the organization of the campaign is given by Johnson, Chapter 4.

[7] Dillon, p. 177. She accuses Willkie of ingratitude as well as dishonesty, declaring that Hamilton was "the one man above all others responsible" for Willkie's getting the nomination. This is not true, but if it were, it would raise some question as to Hamilton's own integrity in accepting a pledge from all the candidates that he would keep his job and then working actively for Willkie.

[8] John Cowles to the writer. Hamilton talked with Cowles about the matter several times after Willkie's death. Cowles is quite sure that Willkie himself never made such a promise, but thinks it likely that someone else made it

without authority. (Incidentally, Willkie tentatively offered the post of National Chairman to Cowles, who declined.) Russell Davenport told the writer that Willkie specifically denied making the promise, but that Charlton MacVeagh insisted that he did make it. It is perhaps not hard to see how an honest misunderstanding could arise.

[9] Russell Davenport to the writer.

[10] In a letter to Henry Luce dated June 9, 1944, Willkie wrote: "John's stories about why I didn't reappoint him National Chairman, has [sic] no relation to the facts. I didn't appoint him because fifteen advisers unanimously agreed that to do so might produce a national scandal under the facts then existent." (Correspondence.) The reader may compare this with a letter from Hamilton to Dr. Henry Evjen, printed in "The Willkie Campaign: An Unfortunate Chapter in Republican Leadership," *Journal of Politics*, 14:246 (May, 1952), and reprinted by Johnson, p. 112: "I have in my files letters from many of Mr. Willkie's personal friends written during the Fall of 1943 and the Spring of 1944 to the effect that Mr. Willkie had told them his failure to appoint me was the greatest political mistake he ever made. Added to that I have a letter from Mr. Willkie himself making that direct statement." It is my considered judgment that no such letter was ever written.

[11] Martin, pp. 103-06.

[12] *Times*, July 11, p. 10.

[13] Ibid., July 18, p. 4.

[14] Ibid., July 17, p. 1.

[15] Ibid., July 18, p. 3.

[16] *Working with Roosevelt*, pp. 216-18.

[17] *Times*, July 19, p. 2.

[18] *Christian Science Monitor*, October 24, p. 7 (Roscoe Drummond).

[19] *Times*, July 17, p. 6.

[20] Ibid., July 28, p. 7 (James A. Hagerty).

[21] Ibid., July 25, p. 12.

[22] *Life*, 9:78 (August 12, 1940).

[23] *Times*, July 9, p. 13.

[24] Ibid., August 1, p. 16.

[25] Ibid., August 6, p. 14.

[26] Chicago *Tribune*, June 28, p. 4. This shows that Dillon's account (pp. 191-92) of Elwood's hostility to Willkie is grossly exaggerated. Some ill feeling *resulted* from some aspects of the acceptance ceremonies, and some local Democrats resented Willkie's turning Republican. But these were a minority.

[27] *Times*, August 20, p. 14. In his *Secret Diaries* (III, 396), Ickes reveals that he got the phrase from columnist Jay Franklin (John Carter).

[28] Chicago *Tribune*, August 29, p. 15.

[29] *Herald Tribune*, August 29, p. 1.

[30] Taylor. (See Chapter 4, Note 5.)

[31] *Herald Tribune*, August 19, p. 14.

[32] Makey, p. 280.

[33] The foregoing details are from a number of newspapers, especially the *Herald Tribune*.

[34] Chicago *Tribune*, August 17, p. 8.

[35] *Herald Tribune*, August 18, p. 22.

[36] Ibid., August 18, p. 29. At the last minute, Martin had asked to be shown around Rushville, and on returning they rushed to get on the train, forgetting

the luggage, including the speech, which had been left in another automobile.
[37] Mrs. Dudley Hay, who was sitting just in front of the platform, noticed this detail.
[38] A poll by Elmo Roper, reported in *Life,* July 29, p. 20, showed 70.7 per cent of the public in favor "of compulsory military training for all young men," and only 22.6 per cent opposed.
[39] *F. D. R., His Personal Letters,* II, 1055. Roosevelt is referring specifically to the proposed sale of destroyers to Britain but undoubtedly had Selective Service in mind as well.
[40] *Times,* August 18, p. 8.
[41] It is printed in full in the *Times,* August 18, p. 33.
[42] Letter of J. D. Ferguson of the Milwaukee *Journal* to Mrs. Willkie, dated January 10, 1945 (Memorial Tributes).
[43] This and the quotations from Hoover and Vandenberg are from the *Herald Tribune,* August 18, p. 30.
[44] Philip Willkie to the writer.
[45] *Times,* August 18, p. 35.
[46] 103:262 (August 26, 1940).
[47] Russell Davenport to the writer.

CHAPTER 11.

[1] Dillon says (p. 188): "It was generally conceded that up to the time of the acceptance speech, Willkie was elected." I know of no evidence to support this statement. On the contrary, the Gallup Poll reported after the election that even before the acceptance speech, 60 per cent of the population thought Roosevelt would win. (*Times,* November 13, p. 16.)
[2] According to Philip Willkie, the Democrats for Willkie group was organized on Willkie's initiatitive to give an impression of wide and varied backing and so to forestall the accusation that his Democratic support was simply a revival of the Liberty League of 1936.
[3] P. 20.
[4] September 8, Sec. 4, p. 8 (Turner Catledge).
[5] Washington *Post,* September 11, p. 11.
[6] Quoted in the Washington *Post,* August 18, p. 15.
[7] *Times,* August 29, p. 10.
[8] Ibid., September 8, p. 48.
[9] Ibid., August 20, p. 14.
[10] Ibid., September 8, p. 1.
[11] Ibid., September 11, p. 1.
[12] Washington *Post,* August 19, p. 7.
[13] The amendment as originally passed provided that "whenever the Secretary of War or the Secretary of the Navy determines that any existing manufacturing plant or facility is necessary for the national defense and is unable to arrive at an agreement with the owner of such plant or facility for its use or operation by the War Department or the Navy Department, as the case may be, the Secretary, under the direction of the President . . . may take immediate possession of such plant or facility and operate it either by government personnel or by contract with private firms pending determination of the issue."
[14] *Times,* August 30, p. 10.

[15] Ibid., September 1, p. 3.
[16] Ibid., August 31, p. 6.
[17] Ibid., July 3, p. 1.
[18] *Monitor,* July 6, p. 1. The House actually passed the bill on July 10.
[19] Dillon, p. 178.
[20] *Times,* January 18, 1941, p. 1. In 1940 they gave only $276,725. Though the family clans were large, the $5,000 limit apparently had some effect.
[21] Ibid., August 4, p. 1.
[22] Ibid., August 12, p. 8.
[23] After the 1940 defeat, many wealthy contributors to the Republican party withdrew their support, leaving the National Committee practically bankrupt. One of them, Ernest Weir (whom Willkie during the campaign had wished to fire as chairman of the Finance Committee), tried to force Martin to resign either from Congress or from the National Chairmanship, and asserted "that the men who put up the cash in the party should have the decisive influence in its councils." Martin refused and *he* resigned. Willkie's comment was: "The thing I like about Joe Martin is that he has the guts to tell those fat cats to go to hell." (An exception to the general conduct of the "fat cats" was Joseph Pew, who gave generously without asking favors or attempting to dictate policy.) (*My First Fifty Years in Politics,* pp. 124-26.)
[24] *Monitor,* July 25, 1940, p. 1 (Drummond).
[25] August 4, p. 4.
[26] These points were stressed by Edward Willkie to the writer.
[27] *Times,* July 30, p. 1.
[28] P. 10.
[29] Sec. 4, p. 8 (Luther Huston).
[30] Dillon, p. 200.
[31] August 29, p. 9 (Frederick W. Carr).
[32] August 30, p. 20 (Erwin D. Canham).
[33] *The Aspirin Age,* p. 459.
[34] Canham, as above.
[35] The origin of this meeting has been told by former Governor Nathan L. Miller of New York. Willkie telephoned him and "said he sensed that all was not well between him and the Republican leaders—would I find out the cause if I could." At the same time, some of these leaders had "discussed the same thing" with him and asked him if he "could do anything about it." He went to Rushville, suggested the conference, and Willkie at once sent out the telegrams of invitation. (From "Remarks" made at memorial exercises at the National Republican Club, October 24, 1944.—Memorial Tributes.)
[36] *Monitor,* September 6, p. 2.
[37] *Times,* September 6, p. 1.
[38] Gardner Cowles, who visited Willkie at Colorado Springs, has told the writer of his impression that Willkie *was* slighting visiting Republicans because of the strenous effort (which he was certainly making) to round up Democratic votes. Harold Gallagher and other friends have agreed that he *was* inclined to take for granted the support of "regular" Republicans and party workers, as well as personal friends, while he tried to win over those who were against him (and usually remained so).

At the same time, this attitude can be easily exaggerated, as in Dillon's account of Hoover's visit to Colorado Springs: "Hoover was kept waiting while Willkie chatted amicably with Elliott Roosevelt about his vacation, although Hoover had flown in from a fishing trip upon the request of the candidate. It was an unthinking slight to the former President, but resented by all Republicans" (p. 186). The facts appear to be as follows. According to Russell Davenport, Hoover had been seeking an interview with Willkie, although for some reason he did not want to ask for one directly; and Willkie, not overjoyed at the prospect, was induced to extend the invitation. General Hugh Johnson showed up at the same time (here I follow the newspaper accounts), and Willkie told newsmen that he was entertaining his noted guests at dinner. A waggish reporter inquired whether Elliott Roosevelt, who also happened to be at the hotel, was to be included; whereupon Willkie said, "Is Elliott Roosevelt here?" and then, reaching for the telephone, "Sure, why not?" At this, Hoover "showed annoyance" and said, "I wouldn't urge that too strongly." But Willkie said again, "Why not? Why not? I would like to meet him." When the call got through, however, he merely asked Elliott to drop in for a chat, and they talked for about twenty minutes, mostly about fair allotment of radio time during the campaign—a natural subject, since Elliott owned a radio station and since there had recently been much public discussion of whether the President's "fireside chats," for which he normally received free radio time, should be regarded, during the campaign, as "non-political." Hoover, meanwhile, had refused to see Elliott and sulked in another room. (This account is from the *Times*, August 12, p. 8.)

39 Washington *Post*, August 27, p. 7.

40 *Times*, July 19, p. 8; August 29, p. 12; September 10, p. 1.

41 Madison (Wis). *Capitol Times*, March 25, 1944.

42 *Times*, September 5, p. 18.

43 Ibid., August 31, p. 28.

44 Ibid., September 19, p. 1.

45 Some labor leaders, notably in the CIO, were strongly isolationist. But, despite vehement Republican assertions to the contrary, labor leaders exercise little influence on the general attitude of the rank and file, as any study of election results will show.

46 *Times*, June 29, p. 1.

47 *Jim Farley's Story*, p. 243.

48 *Times*, June 29, p. 3.

49 Ibid., July 2, p. 1.

50 Ibid., July 1, p. 1.

51 *F. D. R., My Boss*, p. 239.

52 *Times*, Aug. 20, p. 14. Not everybody agreed with Ickes. The Roosevelt Library (OF-4040—Box 5) has about a hundred letters to the President concerning Willkie's challenge. They are from enemies as well as friends, and express all points of view. But many friends urge him to accept.

53 Ibid., August 21, p. 1.

54 *You're the Boss*, p. 168.

55 *Times*, August 21, p. 14.

56 Ibid., August 25, p. 34.

57 Ibid., August 30, p. 15.

58 Ibid., September 1, p. 1.

59 Ibid., July 6, p. 1.

60 Ibid., August 24, p. 8.

61 Ibid., August 28, p. 1.

62 Ibid., August. 6, p. 14.

[63] 103: 314-32.
[64] Joseph Barnes commented in a letter to the writer that the actual author of the *New Republic* article was reputed to be Professor Fred Rodell of the Yale Law School, who authored an equally unscrupulous attack on Willkie in the March, 1944 issue of *Harper's Magazine.*
[65] *Labor Relations Reference Manual,* Vol. VI (March 1, 1940 - August 31, 1940), pp. 849-56.
[66] Letter to Willkie from James F. Barrett, dated October 24, 1940. (Correspondence.)
[67] *Times,* September 3, p. 13; September 4, p. 20; September 5, p. 19; September 7, p. 8. A circumstantial refutation of the charges in the *New Republic* article was inserted in the *Congressional Record* (October 2, 1940, pp. 19639-19644) by Senator Bridges. Under the circumstances, a skeptical approach to this account is also proper; but to me it seems generally convincing.
[68] Ibid., August 28, p. 10.
[69] Ibid., August 27, p. 1.
[70] Ibid., July 30, p. 1.
[71] Ibid., August 17, p. 1.
[72] Ibid., August 18, p. 2.
[73] Ibid., p. 1.
[74] Ibid., August 19, p. 1.
[75] Ibid., August 20, p. 1.
[76] Ibid., August 3, p. 1. Apparently a very round-about approach had been made through Archibald MacLeish and Russell Davenport. (Ickes, *Secret Diaries,* III, 292.)
[77] Ibid., August 10, p. 1.
[78] See "Memorandum" by F. D. R. dated August 2, 1940, in *F. D. R., His Personal Letters,* II, 1050.
[79] See William L. Langer and C. Everett Gleason, *The Challenge to Isolation,* p. 754.
[80] Louisville *Courier-Journal,* September 1, Sec. 1, p. 6 (Alsop and Kintner). This is confirmed by Ickes, III, 313.
[81] III, 293.
[82] *Monitor,* September 4, p. 6 (Richard L. Strout).
[83] *Times,* September 4, p. 1.
[84] Ibid., September 5, p. 19.
[85] *Monitor,* September 6, p. 3.
[86] *Times,* September 7, p. 8.
[87] Ibid., September 22, Sec. 4, p. 3.

CHAPTER 12

[1] *Monitor,* September 19, p. 1 (Drummond).
[2] The details are from the *Times,* September 14. The reporter for the Chicago *Daily News* estimated 3,000 persons at the Union Station, 3,000 at the Stockyards, 30,000 at Cicero, and 10,000 at the Carnegie-Illinois plant; also 1,000 at the Wilson Packing Company plant and 2,000 at the Crane Company plant.
[3] *Daily News,* September 13, p. 1.
[4] *Times,* September 15, p. 2.
[5] Ibid., September 14, p. 1.

[6] Ibid., September 15, p. 2.
[7] Ibid., September 14, p. 1.
[8] *Daily News,* September 14, p. 4.
[9] *Times,* September 14, p. 1.
[10] Ibid., September 15, p. 2.
[11] Ibid. Secretary Hull and others triumphantly attacked the statement that Roosevelt had telephoned Hitler and Mussolini, whereas in fact he had cabled them. Russell Davenport, in talking with the writer, took the blame for this error, saying that in discussions with the research staff the word "call" had been used, and he had assumed, in preparing the material for Willkie, that this meant "telephoned." The detail, of course, had no relevance to the real issue.
[12] Ibid., September 23, p. 2.
[13] *The United States in World Affairs, 1933* (New York: Harper, 1934), p. 134.
[14] *Times,* September 22, p. 43.
[15] Ibid.
[16] Ibid., September 28, 1938, p. 4.
[17] *Fullness of Days,* p. 195.
[18] Hull himself quoted it in replying to Willkie. *Times,* September 17, 1940, p. 12.
[19] Ibid., October 31, 1938, p. 14.
[20] In Coffeyville on September 16, in San Francisco on September 21, in St. Louis on October 17, and elsewhere.
[21] *Times,* August 1, p. 16.
[22] *Watching the World,* p. 160.
[23] Lem Jones to the writer.
[24] Marquis Childs attributes the story to Mrs. Willkie, in his column appearing in the Eau Claire, Wisconsin, *Leader,* March 26, 1944, during the Wisconsin primary campaign.
[25] Edward Willkie to the writer.
[26] R. W.
[27] The details in these paragraphs were given by Lem Jones to the writer.
[28] Geoffrey Parsons reported a few days after the campaign began that "because of his lack of experience" Gallagher was "the object of some criticism" (*Herald Tribune,* September 16, p. 8). But if he was permanently unpopular, it was because, according to Edward Willkie, he was "one of the few people on the train who would say 'No.'"
[29] Harold Gallagher to the writer.
[30] Stephen Noland, Indianapolis newspaperman who had known Willkie since his Army days, told the writer that Willkie simply did not want to be bothered by having to see local party leaders. Edward Willkie, however, said it was impossible for the candidate to see everybody, although he wanted to, and that a committee, including John Hollister, decided whom he should see. Perhaps his attitude varied with his mood and his physical condition.
[31] This account is based on interviews with Davenport and Crum, and letters from Bell and Butler. It is in sharp contrast with the picture of chaos and dissension, with Davenport the villain, painted by Dillon (doubtless reflecting Hamilton's view). Several of her statements were specifically denied by Bell.
[32] *Herald Tribune,* September 15, p. 14 (Parsons).
[33] Letter to Mrs. Willkie dated December 14, 1944. (Memorial Tributes.)

[34] *Herald Tribune,* September 16, p. 8 (Parsons).
[35] Ibid.
[36] Ibid., September 29, p. 32 (Crozier).
[37] Washington *Post,* September 23, p. 2 (Folliard). Willkie's microphone technique might have improved still more if he had been able, as he wished, to have his old friend Donald Thornburgh go with him and take charge of all broadcasting arrangements. As Guy Lemmon remarked to the writer, Willkie would have listened to him, and he would not listen to anybody else. But the Columbia Broadcasting System, with which he had a position, would not give him a leave of absence; and though he offered to resign, Willkie would not let him. (Donald Thornburgh to the writer.)
[38] *Herald Tribune,* September 16, p. 8.
[39] Barnes, p. 197. Drummond in the *Monitor* (October 3, p. 1) puts the number at 50 to 60.
[40] Harold Gallagher to the writer.
[41] Quoted by Wright in a letter to Mrs. Willkie dated December 7, 1944. (Memorial Tributes.)
[42] Chicago *Tribune,* September 16, p. 1.
[43] *Herald Tribune,* September 17, p. 18.
[44] Ibid.
[45] *Times,* September 17, p. 1.
[46] Ibid., p. 10.
[47] Ibid.
[48] Ibid., September 18, p. 1.
[49] Ibid., September 19, p. 19.
[50] It was rumored that Hoover wished to introduce Willkie in San Francisco and "had an intermediary approach a friend of Willkie's. The answer was a polite 'No.'" Hoover then "made it a point to be out of California" during Willkie's visit. (Washington *Post,* September 23, pp. 1-2. [Folliard].)
[51] *I Write from Washington,* p. 211.
[52] Ibid., p. 210.
[53] Ibid., p. 212.
[54] Ibid.
[55] *Times,* September 21, p. 1.
[56] *Herald Tribune,* September 29, p. 32 (Crozier).
[57] Letter to Alfred P. Sloan, Jr., dated March 30, 1942. (Correspondence.)
[58] *Herald Tribune,* September 20, p. 14.
[59] *Times,* September 20, p. 16.
[60] Ibid.
[61] Ibid., September 21, pp. 1, 10; *Herald Tribune,* September 21, pp. 1, 8.
[62] *Times,* September 22, p. 43.
[63] *Herald Tribune,* September 23, p. 1 (Crozier). The memorandum given him by the local committee at Klamath Falls is worth a footnote: "Reference should be made to the famous Klamath potatoes. Possible reference to the fact that E. H. Harriman built a home on Upper Klamath Lake, calling the scene there the most beautiful in western America. Mention should also be made of Crater Lake. He could say that, God being willing, he would return some time to see the most beautiful lake in the world. Don't forget the pelicans and other wild fowl which cover the lake." To the committee it must certainly have seemed like ingratitude that he "found it impossible to touch these subjects in his brief greeting." (Ibid.)

[64] *Times*, September 24, p. 14.
[65] Ibid.
[66] Ibid., September 25, pp. 1, 18.
[67] *Herald Tribune*, September 26, p. 1.
[68] Washington *Post*, September 28, p. 3.
[69] *Times*, September 27, p. 13.
[70] The writer was in Madison at the time, but could not summon the energy to try to fight his way into the University Field House. Plenty of accounts were available, however.
[71] Stephen Noland, then of the Indianapolis *News*, to the writer. Another member of the group was James A. Hagerty of the *New York Times*.
[72] Dillon's charge (pp. 206, 221) that Davenport (contemptuously referred to as "the poet") produced speeches that were too "literary" and hence not natural on Willkie's lips is in my judgment unfounded.
[73] Dillon has a story that Willkie called Hamilton at this time and asked him to take over the National Chairmanship, alleging that Martin "had double-crossed him" (p. 211). This is incredible. Edward Willkie, far closer to his brother than was Hamilton, has told the writer in a letter: "I am sure that there was no thought of replacing Martin with Hamilton"; and this has been orally confirmed by Mr. Pryor. Mr. Martin, also, in a interview with the writer, denied that he ever heard of such a proposal; and, as evidence of Willkie's continuing good will, cited a statement by Willkie when he was seeking the 1944 nomination. "I want you on my side more than anything else." Bartley Crum, also, declared in an interview with the writer that Martin offered to resign on the night of the election and Willkie would not let him.

CHAPTER 13

[1] *Times*, September 29, p. 40.
[2] Dillon, p. 213. News of the meeting became public a week later, after he had met (more openly) with William Green. But what had been said on either occasion remained unknown (*Times*, October 7, p. 1).
[3] *Times*, October 1, p. 16.
[4] Ibid., p. 17.
[5] *Herald Tribune*, October 3, p. 13; October 4, p. 12.
[6] *Times*, October 3, p. 1.
[7] Ibid., p. 18.
[8] Frances Perkins, *The Roosevelt I Knew*, p. 117.
[9] *Times*, October 5, p. 8.
[10] Ibid., October 8, p. 17.
[11] Ibid., October 9, p. 19.
[12] Ibid., p. 18.
[13] Ibid., October 10, p. 16.
[14] Ibid., October 11, p. 14.
[15] Ibid., October 12, p. 9.
[16] Ibid.
[17] See the Chicago *Tribune*, August 17, p. 8 (in a story about the acceptance speech): "Elwood has no colored residents, but sleeping quarters have been provided for 1,500 Negroes in the National Guard Armory."
[18] *Times*, October 14, pp. 1, 10.
[19] Ibid., October 15, p. 11.

[20] Ibid., October 18, p. 15.
[21] Ibid., October 16, p. 18.
[22] Ibid.
[23] Russell B. Porter, *Times,* October 27, p. 35.
[24] See, for example, Turner Catledge, *Times,* October 15, p. 11; and Alsop and Kintner in the Louisville *Courier-Journal,* September 24, Sec. 1, p. 4.
[25] *Times,* October 25, p. 13.
[26] Letter to Willkie from his boyhood friend Edgar Ball, dated December 6, 1942. (Correspondence.)
[27] Letter to Willkie from Edwin L. Pillsbury dated March 15, 1941. (Correspondence.)
[28] *Times,* October 20, p. 7.
[29] October 30, p. 17. It was answered (November 2, p. 12) by a similar piece of propaganda, signed by Robert E. Sherwood, Sinclair Lewis, Dorothy Thompson, Franklin P. Adams, Stuart Chase, Carl Van Doren, Wolcott Gibbs, Elmer Rice, John Gunther, John Chamberlain, Henry Seidel Canby, Louis Bromfield, Herbert Agar, Marc Connelly, Edna Ferber, George S. Kaufman, Roger Burlinghame, James Thurber, Thornton Wilder, and Lewis Gannett.
[30] *Monitor,* October 11, p. 12. This may be contrasted with Dillon's account (pp. 219-220) of the trip as "something of a riot." Here, perhaps, it is appropriate to give the proper tone to Pierce Butler's celebrated characterization of the campaign train. According to Dillon it was J. Wells Farley, a Boston attorney, who visited the train on the morning of its arrival in Massachusetts, and, exasperated by Willkie's impulsive changes of plan (another detail that only she seems to have heard of) and by finding the candidate not yet up, irritably inquired of Butler what was going on, and got an answer in keeping with his mood. As Bartley Crum recalled the episode in an interview with the writer, however, it was Governor Saltonstall (this certainly makes a better story) who was the early visitor and inquired where he could find someone in authority. Butler in his turn inquired: "Governor, have you ever been in a whorehouse when the madam was out and all the girls were running around putting nickels in the jukeboxes?" Saltonstall admitted that he had not. "Then," said Butler, "you can't understand the operation of this campaign train." But in this version (which is certainly true in spirit if not in the identity of the questioner) the remark appears not as a bitter outburst but as a good-humored quip.
[31] *Times,* October 18, p. 1.
[32] Ibid., October 23, p. 16.
[33] Samuel I. Rosenman, *Working with Roosevelt,* p. 222. Rosenman places these developments in "midsummer" and "late summer," but the use of these terms in their ordinary sense would seem to put the change too early. In the Gallup Poll, which in this campaign was remarkably in harmony with private estimates, Willkie's low point was reached in the results announced on October 6 (there was a lag of about two weeks between the polling and the report), when he had 44 per cent of the major party vote and 32 electoral votes. On October 18 the corresponding figures were 45 and 117; on October 27, 45.5 and 117; and on November 4, 48 and 196. The difference between the last figures and the actual outcome could be attributed to Roosevelt's last-minute campaigning.
[34] P. 224. Rosenman and the President's secretaries, "Missy" Le Hand and Grace Tully, used to joke in Roosevelt's presence about his "non-political"

speeches and always drew a "pleased laugh . . . followed by a mock-indignant protestation of innocence."

35 Ickes, *Secret Diaries*, III, 35.

36 *Times*, October 24, p. 14.

37 Ibid., October 30, p. 18.

38 Ibid., October 29, p. 17.

39 Robert E. Sherwood, *Roosevelt and Hopkins*, pp. 189-90. Sherwood adds generously, and truthfully, that Willkie did himself an injustice—that in fact he never knew when he was licked.

40 *Times*, October 24, p. 14

41 Ibid., October 29, p. 17.

42 Willkie did not *always* say that Roosevelt *intended* to get America into the war. At times he merely accused him of being reckless; but at other times he implied that the President *wanted* war.

43 *Roosevelt and Hopkins*, p. 187.

44 October 31, p. 22.

45 Edward Willkie to the writer.

46 See the Gallup Poll report on September 22 (*Times*, p. 34). In May, 1940, only 36 per cent of the persons polled considered it more important to aid Britain than to stay out of war; each month the figure rose until in September it was 52 per cent.

47 Willkie never admitted that he had been disingenuous in 1940 in asserting his belief that America could stay out of the war. He wrote to Westbrook Pegler on July 28, 1942: "When you say that I was stalling during the campaign, there is nothing that I can do about it except to say that you are mistaken.

"The facts are that I was convinced at that time that the United States did not necessarily have to become involved in war. I personally thought, and I advocated and have never been convinced otherwise—although it is not susceptible to proof—that if America had become strong and productive and provided all the armaments that the democracies required, we would not have become involved in this war. When I became convinced to the contrary [i. e., that because of America's belated start in the production of armaments, involvement *was* inevitable], I said so frankly. The matter of the possibilities of my election did not determine my beliefs or what I advocated in the slightest." (Correspondence.) He made a similar statement in a letter to Roy Howard on July 14, 1942.

On the other hand, there is testimony that even in 1940 Willkie predicted with astounding accuracy the outbreak of war in the Pacific. Dr. Harold Barnard has recorded that during the campaign "I asked him on the evening of October 22, 1940, just how we would be drawn into a shooting war. His answer was the Japs would attack us at Pearl Harbor, of course; they would do it on a Sunday morning, because the Fleet would be in port, the attack would come out of a clear sky, as this was the Jap way of doing things with complete surprise. I then asked when. His answer [was,] 'Thirteen months.' I then said, 'That is a funny number to pick out,' and he replied he thought it was but he would stick to it. . . . I asked if he thought they—the Japs—would then attack the West Coast and why they would dare do such a sneaky attack? His reply was they were betting on the ineptitude in Washington and the increase in our strength in the Pacific; they did not want the West Coast but would strike south at all of the islands clear thru and including Australia." (Letter from Dr. Barnard to the writer, February 18, 1965.)

[48] *Times*, October 1, p. 18. Lehman did, however, almost alone among Willkie's critics, make an effort to avoid personalities.

[49] Ibid., October 26, pp. 1, 8.

[50] He was also the man whom Willkie saved from national ridicule by refusing to sanction the publication of a number of innocent but silly letters which he had allegedly written and which had fallen into the hands of certain Republicans, who were eager to publish them. But Willkie said, when the question was raised: "We're not running that kind of campaign." (Barnes, p. 207.) These letters are referred to by Charles Michelson, *The Ghost Talks*, p. 197; by Dwight MacDonald, *Henry Wallace, the Man and the Myth* (New York: Vanguard, 1947), pp. 120-24; and by John T. Flynn, *The Roosevelt Myth* (New York: Devin-Adair, 1948), pp. 226-29. (Flynn's account is apparently based on a series of articles by Westbrook Pegler.) Wallace had an interest in theosophy and other occult beliefs, and some comments in the letters would seem to most readers expressive of a mild form of lunacy. There is some confusion in the accounts of these letters. Apparently there were two sets: one, described by Flynn, to an off-beat character named Nicholas Roerich, who is addressed as "Dear Guru" (a "guru" being a sort of teacher of the mysteries of theosophy); and another, discussed by MacDonald, to "a female astrologer" named "Zenda," who was connected with Roerich. Michelson does not specify which set of letters was involved. MacDonald concludes that the Zenda "letters—the damaging ones, at least—were *probably* forgeries." But at any rate the consternation aroused in the Democratic high command by the threat of publication was genuine and intense.

[51] Dillon, p. 216.

[52] *Times*, October 25, p. 37.

[53] Ibid., October 25, p. 17; October 26, p. 8.

[54] Ibid., November 1, p. 17.

[55] Ibid., October 26, p. 12.

[56] Ibid., October 27, p. 41. Almost the whole page is devoted to comments by labor leaders on Lewis's speech.

[57] Sherwood, *Roosevelt and Hopkins*, p. 193. Lewis's speech would have hurt Willkie more if the story of how it was financed had been known to the Democrats. Marquis Childs has told the story (*I Write from Washington*, pp. 206-07) of how the cost of the broadcast over all the major networks ($45,000 according to Dillon) was borne by William Rhodes Davis, an oil millionaire with a shady background including connections with the Nazi government. In order to "get around" the Hatch Act, "the oil man and his associates set up a kind of political black bourse, exchanging checks at a furious rate to insure that no individual would be listed as giving more than five thousand dollars. . . . Willkie told me after it was all over that he had never heard of Davis before Sam Pryor told him of the oil man's willingness to pay for the Lewis broadcast." Willkie ought, Childs suggests, to have been more curious about Davis and his motives; and certainly his casual acceptance of it is hard to reconcile with his early public insistence that the Hatch Act be adhered to in spirit as well as letter. But here again the furious pace and pressure of the campaign seems to have led him into positions that in more sober moments he would never have thought of taking. —Incidentally, his correspondence contains an exchange of letters with Davis

in the spring of 1941, in which he inquired whether it was true, as he had heard, that Davis was circulating the story that before his trip to England, Willkie had been told by Thomas Lamont, Helen Rogers Reid, and Henry Stimson what line he was to take. Davis's answer was a contemptuous brush-off, and aroused Willkie to one of the rare outbursts of anger that got onto paper: "I have your very impertinent letter. I had written as one gentleman to another concerning a statement that had been attributed to you. Your replies are merely cheap inferences."

[58] *Times*, November 1, p. 14.

[59] Ibid., November 2, p. 7.

[60] Ibid., November 5, p. 29.

[61] Ibid., October 26, p. 9.

[62] Ibid., November 5, pp. 1, 15.

[63] Edward Willkie to the writer. An unpublished portion of Ickes' diary records that there was indeed a story that Willkie was sexually impotent and that high Democratic officials discussed the possibility of making use of it in the campaign. Such is the stuff of Presidential election politics.

[64] *Times*, November 5, p. 22.

[65] Reminiscences of Charles C. Barry of the American Broadcasting Company enclosed in a letter to Mrs. Willkie, dated November 20, 1945. (Memorial Tributes.)

[66] Lem Jones to the writer.

[67] *Times*, November 6, p. 5.

[68] James L. Wright of the Buffalo *Evening News* in a letter to Mrs. Willkie, dated December 7, 1944. (Memorial Tributes.)

[69] Nicholas Roosevelt, *A Front Row Seat*, p. 244.

[70] Pierce Butler, III, to the writer. Others present were Elliott Bell and Paul Smith, who had also been on the campaign train.

[71] *Times*, November 9, p. 8 (Anne O'Hare McCormick).

[72] Ibid., November 7, pp. 1, 12.

[73] The figures in this paragraph are taken from *The Political Almanac, 1952*.

[74] *Times*, November 8, p. 2.

[75] *The Future of American Politics*, pp. 51, 132, 136.

[76] *Times*, November 10, p. 2.

[77] Dillon, p. 196.

[78] *My First Fifty Year in Politics*, pp. 108-109.

[79] Ibid., p. 108.

[80] *Secret Diaries*, III, 361.

[81] E. g., in his speech at Louisville on October 28: "Compared to the issues at stake, I am unimportant and so is Franklin Roosevelt."

[82] For what it is worth, I include the Gallup Poll estimate of the sources of the votes of the two candidates with reference to the preceding election (*Times*, December 8, p. 2).

	Sources of Roosevelt's Votes	*Sources of Willkie's Votes*
1936 Roosevelt voters	19,400,000	4,700,000
1936 Landon voters	900,000	13,300,000
1936 third party voters	300,000	400,000
First voters (too young to vote in 1936)	3,000,000	1,900,000
Didn't vote in 1936	3,500,000	1,900,000
Total	27,100,000	22,200,000

An estimated 2,500,000 Landon voters and 3,500,000 Roosevelt voters in 1936 did not vote in 1940 because of death and other causes.

[83] This conclusion is borne out by the results of a *Fortune* poll reported in October, 1940 (22:66-67). Only 29.9 per cent of those interviewed were unalterably opposed to a third term, and it may safely be assumed that almost all of these normally voted Republican.

[84] See, for example, in the *Times*, Turner Catledge's reports from the West Coast (October 14, p. 12; October 15, p. 11), Warren Moscow's report on New York State (October 25, p. 17), and Russell B. Porter's report on New Jersey (October 25, p. 13).

CHAPTER 14

Besides the usual sources, four London newspapers supplied information about Willkie's English visit: the *Times*, the *Daily Herald*, the *Daily Express*, and the *News Chronicle*. Concerning the relations between Willkie and Roosevelt, additional sources include: Eleanor Roosevelt, *This I Remember* (New York: Harper, 1949); Ross T. McIntire and George Creel, *White House Physician* (New York: Putnam, 1946); and John Gunther, *Roosevelt in Retrospect* (New York: Harper, 1950).

[1] *Times*, November 11, p. 1.

[2] Ibid., November 17, p. 3.

[3] Ibid., November 18, p. 14.

[4] Ibid., November 30, p. 1.

[5] Ibid., April 6, p. 24.

[6] Letter dated January 4, 1941. He made a similar comment in a letter to Arthur Hays Sulzberger on March 28. (Correspondence).

[7] The full text is given in the *Times*, November 12, p. 12.

[8] Ibid., December 16, p. 1.

[9] Letter from Oren Root to Russell Davenport, dated December 12, 1941. (Correspondence).

[10] *Times*, November 8, p. 8 (James A. Hagerty).

[11] Correspondence.

[12] Correspondence. Willkie's reply shows why he was liked and trusted by most newspapermen: "If any questions arise in connnection with my position on any subject, if you will let me hear from you, I will be glad to give you the information directly and without reservation."

[13] *Times*, December 19, p. 37.

[14] Ibid., December 18, p. 31.

[15] Ibid., November 21, p. 39.

[16] Ibid., November 30, pp. 1, 8.

[17] Correspondence.

[18] *Times*, December 15, Sec. 4, p. 2.

[19] P. 145 (New York: Harper, 1952).

[20] *Times*, December 31, p. 1.

[21] Ibid., December 28, p. 3.

[22] Ibid., January 3, p. 4.

[23] I cannot locate the source of this comment.

[24] *Times*, November 12, p. 18.

[25] Ibid., December 30, p. 6.

[26] Ibid., December 5, p. 12.

[27] Ibid., December 8, p. 43.
[28] Ibid., December 24, Sec. 4, p. 6 ("Topics of the Times").
[29] Ibid., January 7, p. 4.
[30] Ibid., January 11, pp. 1, 3.
[31] Ibid., pp. 1, 5.
[32] Ibid., p. 4.
[33] Ibid.
[34] Ibid., January 12, p. 1.
[35] Ibid., January 11, p. 4.
[36] Correspondence.
[37] *Times*, January 19, p. 34.
[38] Ibid., January 13, p. 4.
[39] Ibid., January 18, p. 7.
[40] Ibid., January 13, p. 1.
[41] Ibid.
[42] Ibid., January 14, p. 1.
[43] Letter to Robert P. Allen, as above. Among those who exerted the pressure were Roy Howard and Bruce Barton, who at a dinner party on January 11 tried by every possible means to persuade him to silence. The primary authority for this statement must remain unnamed; but it is confirmed in part by a story written by John Neville for the NANA after Willkie's death, of which a copy is in Memorial Tributes.
[44] *Times*, January 17, pp. 1, 8. Thomas's vote was 99,557—two-tenths of 1%.
[45] Ibid., January 20, p. 6. He had made essentially the same statement on January 14 (*Times*, January 15, p. 12), and in a letter to Robert P. Allen dated January 17, in which he also states that before making definite plans he had asked the advice of Goeffrey Parsons, Helen Rogers Reid, and John Cowles, all of whom approved. He invited Cowles to go with him. (Correspondence).
[46] *Times*, January 16, p. 13.
[47] Ibid., January 19, p. 34. Hull had already—presumbly not without Roosevelt's approval—invited Willkie to "come to see him any time he had any question to ask about the foreign situation." (Ibid., January 20, p. 6).
[48] Ibid.
[49] There had been one other—on November 23, 1937.
[50] *Times*, January 20, p. 6.
[51] *The Roosevelt I Knew*, p. 117. Miss Perkins does not specify the date or occasion, but since it was after the election, it can only have been this one.
[52] *Times*, January 20, p. 6.
[53] *Roosevelt and Hopkins*, pp. 2-3.
[54] This text of the note is from the facsimile on p. 27 of Churchill's *The Grand Alliance* (Boston: Houghton Mifflin, 1950; Vol. III of *The Second World War*). A different version, presumably dictated from memory, is given in *F. D. R.: His Personal Letters*, II, 1109. On his return Willkie told his brother Edward of Churchill's reception of the note. Not being able to spot the quotation, he asked Willkie the source, and when told that it was from Longfellow's *The Building of the Ship*, insisted on getting a volume of Longfellow and reading the whole piece. At the end he remarked, "God, that's lousy poetry!" (One is not quite sure whether "lousy" is one of Churchill's occasional ventures into American slang or whether it expresses Willkie's sense of Churchill's reaction.)

[55] *Times*, January 26, p. 7.
[56] London *Times*, January 28, p. 4.
[57] *New York Times*, January 30, p. 8.
[58] Ibid., January 27, p. 1.
[59] Ibid.
[60] London *News Chronicle*, January 28, p. 1.
[61] London *Daily Herald*, January 28, p. 3.
[62] *New York Times*, January 31, p. 5.
[63] *News Chronicle*, January 28, p. 6.
[64] *New York Times*, January 27, p. 1.
[65] *News Chronicle*, January 28, p. 1.
[66] Laski's comment on the meeting, in a letter to Roosevelt, is worth quoting: "I had a couple of hours with your late rival, at his request.—I think he wanted to see an English socialist 'in the flesh.' I thought him shrewd, very agreeable and warm-hearted; but incredibly inexperienced in political argument and unaccustomed to the exploration of what Holmes used to call his 'inarticulate major premises.' . . . But his gesture of sympathy did good here and, as I suspect, ruled him out of the Republican nomination in 1944." (Letter dated February 18, 1941 in Roosevelt Library, OF-4040.)
[67] Most of the foregoing details are from the *New York Times*, January 28-31.
[68] Mrs . Van Doren to the writer.
[69] London *Times*, February 6, p. 4.
[70] John Cowles in a letter to the writer. Mr. Cowles explained that the trip was the result, initially, of cables from "several Irish-American organizations . . . criticizing him for making statements that they regarded as too British. Almost simultaneously, one of Willkie's close political advisers cabled from the U. S. that Willkie's pro-British statements were alienating the German and the Irish elements in the Republican party, and suggesting that Willkie might be wise to go to Dublin before returning to the U. S. to indicate that he was not ignoring the Irish." Once the idea had been suggested, however, Willkie immediately took a larger view.
[71] London *Times*, February 5, p. 4.
[72] This is Harold Ickes' version of what Willkie had told Robert Kintner. (*Secret Diaries*, III, 439-440.)
[73] John Cowles, as above.
[74] Edward Willkie to the writer.
[75] The quotations are from Willkie's speech at Montreal on March 25, 1941.
[76] *New York Times*, January 28, p. 1.
[77] Ibid., January 29, p. 5.
[78] London *Times*, January 28, p. 4.
[79] *New York Times*, January 30, p. 8.
[80] *Daily Herald*, January 30, p. 5.
[81] London *Times*, February 5, p. 4.
[82] Ibid., February 4,, p 4.
[83] *Daily Herald*, February 4, p. 3.
[84] London *Times*, February 6, p. 4.
[85] *New York Times*, February 2, p. 21.
[86] London *Times*, February 5, p. 5.
[87] *New York Times*, January 30, p. 8.
[88] *News Chronicle*, January 30, p. 1.
[89] Marquis Childs, who had the story from Eden, to the writer.

[90] London *Times,* January 31, p. 4.
[91] *Daily Herald,* January 31, p. 3
[92] *New York Times,* February 2, p. 21.
[93] *Daily Herald,* February 3, p. 6.
[94] Ibid., February 4, p. 3.
[95] London *Times,* February 4, p. 4.
[96] Ibid.
[97] *New York Times,* February 4, p. 7.
[98] Edward Weeks, repeating Willkie's own account.
[99] Correspondence.
[100] Ibid.
[101] *Daily Herald,* February 3, p. 6.
[102] Dillon, pp. 239-40. Samuel Pryor told the writer that he had the same story, in even fuller detail, from Juan Trippe, president of Pan American.
[103] Willkie's answer to Fred Rodell, *Harper's Magazine,* April, 1944 (end pages).
[104] According to a report in the *Times,* February 7, pp. 1, 8.
[105] Ibid., January 15, p. 1.
[106] Ibid., January 23, p. 1 (indirect quotation).
[107] Ibid., January 24, p. 7.
[108] Ibid., p. 5.
[109] Ibid., Feb. 5, p. 10.
[110] Ibid., February 6, p. 8.
[111] *Herald Tribune,* February 12, p. 12.
[112] *Times,* February 12, p. 10.
[113] *Herald Tribune,* February 13, p. 3 (Alsop and Kintner).
[114] Washington *Post,* February 12, p. 2.
[115] Ibid. The *Times* account says the delay was due to his having left the statement at his hotel.
[116] All the quotations are from the verbatim report of the hearings in the *Times,* February 12, pp. 4-6.
[117] Ibid., p. 6.
[118] Ibid., February 13, p. 8. According to the *Herald Tribune* (February 13, p. 1), the speech was delivered without manuscript or notes.
[119] Chicago *Tribune,* February 13, p. 2.
[120] February 13, p. 14.
[121] *Times,* February 13, p. 1. According to Secretary Stimson's MS diary, Willkie stated privately that the "high authority" *was* Roosevelt. (Langer and Gleason, *The Undeclared War,* p. 280.
[122] Ibid., February 14, p. 1.
[123] Ibid., February 12, pp. 1, 6.
[124] P. 635. For a brief period following Willkie's English visit, he and Hopkins were apparently on more friendly terms; for when Hopkins returned from England a few days after Willkie, he said in answer to a reporter's question: "Willkie's all right." (*Times,* February, 16, p. 5.) But later they were again alienated, perhaps by Willkie's persistent criticism of the Administration for what he considered its incompetence.
[125] *Herald Tribune,* October 19, 1944.
[126] *My First Fifty Years in Politics,* p. 129.
[127] Elizabeth R. Valentine, "A Defeated Candidate Remains a Leader," *New York Times Magazine,* June 1, 1941, p. 24.
[128] *Times,* February 1, p. 20. On February 14, Drew Pearson and Robert Allen

reported a rumor that "certain G. O. P. big shots inspired a clique of Young Republicans to oppose Wendell Willkie at the recent convention in Des Moines." Pew, Weir, and Hoover were named. (Louisville *Courier-Journal*, February 14, p. 7.)

[129] *Times*, February 2, p. 30.

[130] Ibid.

[131] Ibid., February 3, p. 5.

[132] Ibid., January 31, p. 13.

[133] Ibid., March 12, p. 1. After the election Dean Alfange, the Democratic candidate, wrote Willkie a "generous letter," to which he replied: "In supporting your opponent, I was not opposing you as a person. . . . I took part in the Congressional campaign to aid in the elimination of isolationism in the Republican party and to promote national unity in our foreign policy." (Letter dated March 20, 1941. Correspondence.)

[134] *Times*, March 24, p. 1; March 25, p. 18.

[135] *Watching the World*, p. 166.

[136] *Autobiography*, p. 645.

[137] The most Rev. Gerald Shaughnessey, Bishop of Seattle. Willkie asked for an apology, stating the facts, but got only a repetition of the charge (*Times*, April 19, 1941, p. 32).

[138] Fred Rodell, in *Harper's Magazine*, March, 1944.

[139] George W. Crane, in a column published in the Green Bay (Wisconsin) *Press Gazette*, February 22, 1944 (and presumably in hundreds of other newspapers).

[140] Letter to John Haynes Holmes, April 6, 1943. (Correspondence.) He is explaining, in declining to become a member of the National Committee of the American Civil Liberties Union that his reason is simply that "I have so many obligations now that I find I cannot take on any more." "It is not a matter whether it would help or harm me."—To Russell Davenport, also, he stated that his charges that Roosevelt was leading the country into war were the one thing that he regretted in the conduct of the campaign and the one thing he would do differently if he were doing it over. (Russell Davenport to the writer.) That this was Willkie's feeling is further confirmed by Gardner Cowles.

CHAPTER 15

Important new sources for this chapter are three articles in *Collier's Magazine* by Lindbergh, Willkie, and Roosevelt, which appeared respectively in the issues dated March 29, May 10, and October 4, 1941; an interview with Adlai Stevenson; and William L. Langer and C. Everett Gleason, *The Undeclared War, 1940-41* (New York: Harper, 1953). For background material the reader may refer to Wayne S. Cole, *America First: The Battle Against Intervention, 1940-41* (Madison, Wisconsin: University of Wisconsin Press, 1953); Herbert Feis, *Road to Pearl Harbor: The Coming of War Between the United States and Japan* (New York: Creative Age Press, 1950); and Basil Rauch, *Roosevelt: From Munich to Pearl Harbor* (Princeton, N. J.: Princeton University Press, 1950).

[1] It should perhaps be pointed out at the beginning that the present account naturally magnifies Willkie's share in the battle and necessarily omits many details having no direct connection with his career.

[2] *Times*, November 8, p. 1.
[3] Ibid., May 4, p. 4.
[4] Ibid., April 20, p. 21.
[5] April 20, p. 19.
[6] Reproduced by Barnes, p. 387.
[7] Harold Gallagher to the writer.
[8] Letter dated Aug. 18, 1942. (Correspondence.)
[9] See for instance the letter to Eugene Stetson quoted in Chapter 7.
[10] Harold Gallagher in a letter to the writer.
[11] *Times*, March 25, pp. 1, 12; March 26, p. 18.
[12] Ibid., March 27, p. 12.
[13] *Watching the World*, p. 25.
[14] *Times*, April 24, p. 1.
[15] Ibid., April 28, p. 10.
[16] Ibid., June 25, p. 6.
[17] Adlai Stevenson to the writer.
[18] *Times*, May 4, p. 4.
[19] Ibid., April 26, p. 1.
[20] Ibid., July 18, p. 6.
[21] Ibid., October 5, p. 4.
[22] Ibid., May 11, p. 21.
[23] Ibid., May 24, p. 7.
[24] Ibid., September 12, p. 2.
[25] Ibid., September 14, p. 20.
[26] Ibid., April 18, p. 8.
[27] Ibid., May 11, p. 31.
[28] Ibid., August 6, p. 6.
[29] Telegram to Maxwell Anderson, July 29, 1944. (Correspondence.)
[30] *Times*, April 11, p. 1.
[31] *F. D. R.: His Personal Letters*, II, 1116.
[32] *Times*, April 26, p. 1.
[33] Ibid., p. 5.
[34] Ibid., May 11, p. 31.
[35] Ibid., May 8, p. 1. The text of Willkie's speech is given on p. 10.
[36] The text is given in the *Times*, June 7, p. 6.
[37] Ibid., March 25, p. 12.
[38] Ibid., May 28, p. 28. The text of the speech is on p. 2.
[39] Ibid., June 1, p. 23.
[40] Ibid., May 29, p. 3. Roosevelt telegraphed Willkie on May 29: "I am grateful to you for what you did and said yesterday. It helps a lot." (Roosevelt Library, OF-4040.)
[41] Ibid., June 8, p. 46.
[42] Ibid., June 27, p. 11.
[43] *Secret Diaries*, III, 509, 511.
[44] Correspondence.
[45] Ibid.
[46] *Times*, July 5, p. 9.
[47] Ibid., July 10, p. 1.
[48] Ibid., July 24, p. 1.
[49] Ibid., July 23, p. 20.
[50] Ibid., July 24, p. 1.

[51] Ibid., p. 9.
[52] Ibid., July 25, p. 9.
[53] Ibid., August 8, p. 1.
[54] Ibid., October 31, p. 4.
[55] Ibid., August 6, p. 6. Statement by fifteen eminent Republicans, referred to above.
[56] Ibid., July 27, p. 32.
[57] Ibid., August 1, p. 8.
[58] Ibid., September 2, p. 19.
[59] Ibid., September 9, p. 25.
[60] Ibid., September 10, p. 26.
[61] Ibid., September 11, p. 29.
[62] Ibid., September 12, p. 24.
[63] Ibid., September 16, p. 18.
[64] Ibid., September 21, p. 13.
[65] Ibid., September 26, p. 1.
[66] Ibid., September 12, p. 1.
[67] *Collier's Magazine,* 108:42 (October 4, 1941). Summary in *Times,* September 26, p. 8.
[68] *Times,* October 12, Sec. 4, p. 3.
[69] Ibid., October 7, p. 1.
[70] P. 114.
[71] P. 115.
[72] *Times,* October 22, p. 8.
[73] Ibid., October 24, p. 3.
[74] Ibid., November 7, p. 41.
[75] Ibid.
[76] All from the *New York Times* between October 3 and October 23. These are only a small fraction of the stories. The figures are usually from official German announcements.
[77] Ibid., October 19, p. 3.
[78] Ibid., November 14, p. 3.
[79] Ibid., December 8, p. 6.
[80] Ibid., December 12, p. 26.
[81] Ibid., December 8, p. 6.
[82] Ibid., December 9, p. 44.
[83] Ibid.
[84] Among works by the "revisionist" school may be mentioned Charles A. Beard, *President Roosevelt and the Coming of War: A Study in Appearances and Realities* (New Haven: Yale University Press, 1948); William H. Chamberlain, *America's Second Crusade* (Chicago: Regnery, 1950); and Charles C. Tansill, *The Back Door To War: The Roosevelt Foreign Policy, 1933-1941* (Chicago: Regnery, 1952).

CHAPTER 16

The only important new sources for this chapter are two volumes of reminiscences: Merriman Smith, *Thank You, Mr. President* (New York: Harper, 1946); and Walter White, *A Man Called White* (New York: Viking, 1948).

[1] *Times,* March 20, p. 15. There had been a previous report (February 17, p. 1) of a contemplated trip to China.

[2] *F. D. R.: His Personal Letters,* II, 1249-50
[3] Merriman Smith, *Thank You, Mr. President,* p. 269.
[4] Frances Brown, "National Unity: A Willkie Formula," *New York Times Magazine,* December 14, 1941, p. 23.
[5] *F. D. R.: His Personal Letters,* II, 1251.
[6] Irita Van Doren to the writer. Mrs. Van Doren worked with Willkie on the letter, which they had difficulty in phrasing to his satisfaction.
[7] *Times,* December 16, p. 5.
[8] *The Roosevelt I Knew,* pp. 117-18.
[9] *F. D. R.: His Personal Letters,* II, 1227. Note on memorandum to General Watson dated October 28, 1941: "Speak to me about seeing Wendell Willkie next week."
[10] In the Roosevelt Library, OF-4040. They were especially numerous after Willkie's support of Lend-Lease in a Town Hall speech on January 16 and after his Chicago speech on June 6. There were also many letters suggesting that he be given a cabinet post.
[11] *Roosevelt and Hopkins,* p. 475. Merriman Smith says: "Friends of the President were dubious about giving Willkie a high . . . post in the war government . . . because of his flighty antics." (*Thank You, Mr. President,* p. 269.) It is evident that most of Roosevelt's political associates were, unlike their chief, never able to think of Willkie except in partisan terms.
[12] *Roosevelt and Hopkins,* p. 475. Sherwood quotes an account by Hopkins "written January 14, 1942": "On Tuesday morning (January 13), when I saw the President in his bedroom, I urged him to appoint Nelson that day." The President agreed.
[13] Arthur Krock, in the *Times,* January 18, Sec. 4, p. 3—evidently on the authority of Willkie himself.
[14] *Times,* January 16, p. 1 (Frank L. Kluckhohn).
[15] *Roosevelt and Hopkins,* p. 475.
[16] *Thank You, Mr. President,* p. 270. Probably another motive for Roosevelt's action was that the Truman Committee was about to publish a scathing report (which Nelson had tried vainly to suppress) on the confusion and inefficiency of the production program (Krock, as above). The prospect of all this criticism finally overcame the President's indecision.
[17] *Times,* January 14, p. 1.
[18] Ibid., January 15, pp. 1, 10.
[19] *F. D. R.: His Personal Letters,* II, 1287.
[20] Correspondence. One would like to know more about this party, but I have found no other reference to it unless it is the one described by Grace Tully: "Willkie came and remained well on toward midnight, and from the sounds of laughter in the Study, where dinner was served, it was clear to me that the two men enjoyed being together." (*F. D. R., My Boss,* p. 58.) She puts this meeting "shortly after the 1940 elections," but it could not have taken place before Willkie's return from England, and a mistake of a year or so in the date is not hard to accept.
[21] Ibid.
[22] Letter from Willkie to Roosevelt dated June 2. (Correspondence.)
[23] Correspondence.
[24] Barnes puts this episode in June, during Churchill's second visit; but on June 30, after leaving, Churchill sent Willkie a telegram expressing regret at not having been able to arrange a meeting. (Correspondence.)

[25] The point of this story as told to the writer by Milton Polland, who had it from Willkie himself, was that Willkie was a "great joker." I prefer this account to the lurid imaginings of Louis Adamic in *Dinner at the White House* (pp. 182-83); and even Barnes, I think, treats the episode too solemnly (p. 279).
[26] Letter to Daniel Willard. (Correspondence.)
[27] "Let's Look Ahead," *New York Times Magazine*, February 15, 1942, p. 5.
[28] *Times*, February 25, p. 13. Speech at St. Vincent's Hospital dinner.
[29] "Let's Look Ahead," p. 1.
[30] *Times*, May 12, p. 13. Speech at Union College.
[31] "Let's Look Ahead," p. 33.
[32] *Times*, May 12, p. 13.
[33] Ibid., April 24, p. 5. Speech at the University of Rochester.
[34] Ibid., April 20, p. 11.
[35] Ibid.
[36] Ibid., April 21, p. 13.
[37] Ibid., April 24, Sec. 4, p. 10 (James A. Hagerty); see also April 22, p. 18.
[38] Ibid., April 21, p. 13.
[39] Ibid., August 4, p. 17.
[40] Memorial Tributes.
[41] *A Man Called White*, pp. 203-04.
[42] Joseph W. Martin to the writer.
[43] Ibid.
[44] Dillon, p. 311. Mrs. Dillon mentions Alan Valentine as one of the group, but Mr. Altschul told the writer that this is a mistake.
[45] *Times*, June 7, p. 36.
[46] Ibid., June 25, p. 1. Bartley Crum told the writer of a story that Roosevelt offered his support as a "private citizen" if Willkie ran for the Covernorship. None of Willkie's other friends seems to have heard the story; but Roosevelt would certainly have preferred him to Bennett, and might have found ways to help him.
[47] Ibid., July 1, p. 18.
[48] Ibid., July 2, p. 23.
[49] Lem Jones to the writer.
[50] Ibid.
[51] *Times*, April 9, p. 26.
[52] Correspondence.
[53] *Times*, April 5, p. 40 (James A. Hagerty).
[54] Ibid., April 21, p. 18.
[55] Ibid.
[56] Ibid.
[57] Ibid., May 10, p. 36.
[58] Ibid., May 23, p. 1.
[59] Ibid., May 24, p. 37.
[60] Ibid., June 7, p. 37.
[61] Ibid., June 14, p. 27.
[62] Ibid., June 16, p. 15.
[63] Ibid., June 19, p. 24.
[64] Ibid., June 23, p. 14.
[65] Letter to Benjamin Teitel, dated June 23. (Correspondence.)
[66] Dorothy Hays, in a letter to Lem Jones on June 21, following a meeting of

county leaders at Albany, reported hearing frequent and violent expressions of this view. She mentions J. Russel Sprague (Nassau County), Thomas J. Curran (Manhattan), and John Crews (Brooklyn). (Correspondence.)

[67] John Cowles narrated this episode to the writer.

[68] Correspondence.

[69] Letter to Drew Pearson, dated June 26, 1942. (Correspondence.)

[70] Letter dated January 29, 1942. (Correspondence.)

[71] *Times,* June 28, 1942, p. 31.

[72] Ibid., December 18, p. 18.

[73] Ibid., January 11, p. 29.

[74] Ibid., January 29, p. 23.

[75] Ibid., March 20, p. 1.

[76] Ibid., July 19, p. 10.

[77] *A Man Called White,* p. 201.

[78] *Times,* June 18, p. 42.

[79] *Saturday Evening Post,* 214:14, 50 (June 12, 1942).—He had used the last sentence (except with "justice" in place of "the liberties") in his article "Fair Trial" in the *New Republic,* March 18, 1940.

[80] *Times,* July 20, p. 28.

[81] Correspondence.

[82] *Times,* January 27, p. 19.

[83] Ibid., January 10, p. 19. The last clause is somewhat cryptic, but the obvious meaning seems to be that America will win the war and that the *principles* of "American democracy" will eventually prevail in other countries.

[84] Ibid.

[85] Ibid., January 25, p. 29.

[86] Ibid., August 8, p. 1.

[87] Ibid., December 21, p. 13.

[88] Ibid., January 7, p. 10.

[89] Ibib., January 14, p. 14.

[90] Ibid., February 13, p. 16.

[92] Ibid., January 18, p. 1.

[93] Ibid., February 13, p. 16.

[94] Ibid., February 27, p. 21.

[95] Ibid., July 19, p. 10.

[96] Ibid., June 9, p. 7.

[97] Ibid., July 1, p. 11.

[98] Ibid., August 8, p. 3.

[99] Correspondence.

[100] Ibid.

[101] Lem Jones to the writer.

CHAPTER 17

The most important new source for this chapter is Willkie's own *One World* (New York: Simon and Schuster, 1943; references are to the cloth-bound edition). Material has also been drawn from the following volumes of memoirs: Henry C. Cassidy, *Moscow Dateline* (Boston: Houghton Mifflin, 1943); Claire L. Chenneault, *Way of a Fighter* (New York: Putnam, 1949); Walter Graebner, "Wendell Willkie in the Kremlin," in *They Were There,* ed. Curt Reiss (New York: Putnam, 1944); William H. Standley and Arthur A. Ageton, *Admiral Ambassador to Russia* (Chicago: Regnery, 1955); *The Stilwell Papers*, ed. Theodore H. White (New York: William Sloane Associates, 1948); and Alexander Werth, *The Year of Stalingrad* (London: Hamish Hamilton, 1946). In addition to the regular news sources may be mentioned the files of the London *Times* and an article in *Look*, October 5, 1943, composed of statements about Willkie by a number of leading press and radio correspondents.

[1] *Times, October* 15, p. 7.

[2] Barnes, p. 289.

[3] Correspondence.

[4] *F. D. R.: His Personal Letters*, II, 1336.

[5] Correspondence.

[6] William H. Standley and Arthur A. Ageton, *Admiral Ambassador to Russia*, p. 266.

[7] *Times*, August 24, p. 5.

[8] *One World*, p. 103.

[9] Alexander Werth, *The Year of Stalingrad*, p. 261. (This is Willkie's account to Werth.)

[10] Roosevelt gave a fairly full account of the development of these plans in a press conference following the North American invasion. (*Times*, November 11, pp. 1, 7.)

[11] *Roosevelt and Hopkins*, p. 635.

[12] *Times*, October 18, Sec. 4, p. 3 (Arthur Krock).

[13] Ibid., August 22, p. 6.

[14] Washington *Post*, September 27, Sec. B, p. 7 (Ernest K. Lindley). This apparently contradicts Mrs. Dillon's statement: "He had been given no briefing as to his conduct, nor as to his personal relationship with the American embassies and legations in the countries which he visited" (p. 267). Since no authority for this statement is given, I prefer to believe Mr. Lindley. It is obvious that throughout her chapter on Willkie's tour, Mrs. Dillon relies almost solely on the oral accounts of a few disgruntled diplomats who were personally resentful of Willkie's activities, without checking these accounts against other available testimony. The result is a gross distortion of Willkie's words and actions, especially in the story of the Russian visit.

[15] *Times*, August 21, p. 14.

[16] Ibid., August 10, p. 9.

[17] Ibid., August 12, p. 12.

[18] *One World*, pp. 2-5.

[19] *Times*, September 4, p. 3.

[20] *One World*, p. 7.

[21] Ibid., p. 11.

[22] Ibid., p. 12.

[23] *Times*, September 7, p. 3.

[24] Frank Gervasi, "Willkie at the Front," *Collier's Magazine*, 110:61 (October 24, 1942). See also the Washington *Post*, October 16, p. 6. The Gervasi piece is a rare instance of unfriendliness to Willkie by a news reporter. It is generally smart-alec in tone, full of snide remarks about Willkie's naiveté and tactlessness. Churchill found the article "most offensive" and apologized to Willkie for its having been passed by the censor, whom he reprimanded. (Correspondence.)

[25] See the preceding note.
[26] *One World,* p. 13.
[27] Ibid., p. 15.
[28] *Times,* September 9, p. 3.
[29] London *Times,* September 9, p. 5.
[30] *New York Times,* September 12, p. 4.
[31] Ibid., September 15, p. 3.
[32] Ibid., September 13, p. 4.
[33] Ibid., September 17, p. 6.
[34] *Time,* 40:26 (September 28, 1942).
[35] *One World,* p. 20.
[36] De Gaulle later wrote that Willkie already had his mind made up that the situation in Syria was merely a struggle between two imperialisms, both equally detestable; and he calls Willkie's comments on him in *One World* a caricature. See *The War Memoirs of Charles De Gaulle: Unity, 1942-1944* (New York: Simon and Schuster, 1959), p. 31. The fact is that Willkie's comments (pp. 23-24) are completely objective, and one wonders whether the General had actually read them or had been given a distorted account by someone else.
[37] *One World,* p. 23.
[38] Ibid., p. 25.
[39] Barnes, p. 298.
[40] *One World,* p. 26.
[41] *Times,* September 13, p. 6.
[42] London *Times,* September 14, p. 3.
[43] Washington *Post,* September 27, Sec. B, p. 7.
[44] *Times,* September 11, p. 4. Willkie gives a slightly different version of the remark in *One World,* p. 45.
[45] *Times,* September 9, p. 3.
[46] Ibid., September 15, p. 3.
[47] Ibid., September 11, p. 4.
[48] Ibid., September 13, p. 6.
[49] London *Times,* September 14, p. 3.
[50] *Look,* 7:32 (October 5, 1943).
[51] *One World,* p. 21.
[52] Ibid., p. 22.
[53] Ibid.
[54] Ibid., p. 29.
[55] Ibid., p. 30.
[56] Ibid., p. 34.
[57] Ibid., p. 35.
[58] Willkie says in *One World* "Thursday, September 18"; but Thursday was the 17th.
[59] Standley, p. 268.
[60] Ibid., p. 292. This bias colors his long account of Willkie's visit and his comments to other persons. He told Admiral Leahy, for instance, that Willkie "had made a poor impression on all classes of Russians" and that his visit "had been definitely detrimental to Allied prestige." (William H. Leahy, *I Was There* (New York: Whittlesey House, 1950), p. 124.) Dillon does not mention Standley as a source, but she uses much of the same material and follows the same line.

[61] Ibid., p. 270.
[62] *Times*, September 19, p. 3.
[63] Ibid.
[64] Standley, p. 271.
[65] Ibid., p. 272.
[66] Ibid., p. 274.
[67] Ibid., p. 283.
[68] *Times*, September 26, p. 4.
[69] Ibid.
[70] Standley, p. 291.
[71] *Times*, September 25, pp. 1, 3.
[72] London *Times*, September 21, p. 5.
[73] Henry C. Cassidy, *Moscow Dateline*, p. 258.
[74] *One World*, pp. 64-69.
[75] See Standley, p. 273, and Dillon, p. 272. Their accounts should be taken with more than a grain of salt.
[76] Standley, p. 273.
[77] *One World*, pp. 73-74.
[78] Ibid., pp. 52-53.
[79] Standley, p. 272.
[80] *Times*, Sept. 20, p. 2.
[81] Standley, p. 272.
[82] *Look*, 7:34 (October 5, 1943). Dillon calls this "the most distressing episode of the entire flight." According to her account, Willkie "suddenly decided" to present the bouquet, harassed an embassy aide into going to a park and picking a "tawdry bunch of flowers," and "stunned" the audience and alarmed the Secret Police (who "tensed for action") when he presented them (pp. 273-274). According to Henry C. Cassidy, however, "the idea was conceived by Edward Page, third secretary of the American Embassy, who recalled the hit Ribbentrop had made in 1939 by presenting flowers to Olga Lepeshinskaya at a performance of the same ballet. It was prepared by Maurice Seltzar, Soviet handyman for the embassy, who obtained the flowers by climbing over the wall into the Intourist garden and picking them." (*Moscow Dateline*, p. 257.) Again, I choose to believe a known and reputable source rather Dillon's anonymous informant.
[83] Standley and Dillon give similar incredible accounts of what Willkie said at Vishinsky's dinner. They allege, first, that he "lost the confidence" of the Russians by promising not to report to the outside world anything unfavorable to Russia; and second, that he incurred the resentment of the British by disparaging Britain's ability and will to fight, and declaring "that only two countries can be depended on to see us through the war—the Soviet Union and the United States." (Standley, pp. 275-77; Dillon, pp. 271-72.) Both statements would have been so totally out of character, so absolutely in contradiction of everything he said and did during the last years of his life, so irreconcilable with his continuing friendship with a number of British leaders (including Sir Archibald Clark-Kerr, the British Ambassador to Russia) and the uniformly friendly treatment which he continued to receive from the British press, that they can be dismissed out of hand. (Standley was deaf and admits that he could not hear clearly what Willkie was saying.) Moreover, Joseph Barnes, who was present, says flatly that Willkie made no such statements.

[84] Cassidy, p. 258.
[85] *Times*, September 22, p. 6.
[86] Standley, pp. 280-84.
[87] Cassidy, p. 263.
[88] These details are from the *New York Times*, September 26, p. 4; the *Herald Tribune*, September 26, pp. 1. 2; and *One World*, pp. 55-58.
[89] Cassidy, p. 263.
[90] Somewhere I have read or been told that Willkie was offered a thoroughgoing inspection of the front, but did not feel equal to the demand on his time and energy, and so asked that American military men (General Bradley; General Philip Faymonville, in charge of Lend-Lease; and Colonel Joseph A. Michella, the American military attaché) accompany him; knowing that the Russians would then arrange only the "routine" visit.
[91] Standley, p. 286.
[92] Ibid., p. 312.
[93] *One World*, p. 77.
[94] Werth, pp. 260-61.
[95] *Herald Tribune*, September 27, p. 2. (He was, in fact, only fifty.)
[96] Barnes, p. 301.
[97] Standley, p. 286.
[98] Charles G. Barry (Memorial Tributes).
[99] Cassidy, p. 265.
[100] Barnes, p. 301.
[101] Cassidy, p. 266; Graebner, p. 330; Standley, p. 289; *New York Times*, Sept. 28, pp. 1, 2; Dillon, pp. 274-75; Barnes, pp. 301-02.
[102] Cassidy, p. 266.
[103] Barnes, pp. 301-02. Dillon gives as the translation of Stalin's last statement, "I think you are the kind of fellow who would steal airplanes yourself" (p. 275). Since Barnes was present and understood Russian, it is reasonable to assume that his version is correct. Incidentally, this episode disposes of the nonsense written by Standley and Dillon about the effect of Willkie's alleged statements at Vishinsky's dinner.
[104] *Times*, September 27, p. 3.
[105] Ibid., November 11, p. 1.
[106] Ibid., June 22, p. 3.
[107] Ibid., July 23, p. 4.
[108] Ibid., July 27, p. 2.
[109] Ibid., October 7, p. 12.
[110] Ibid., October 8, p. 3.
[111] Ibid., October 10, p. 4.
[112] Ibid., September 28, p. 2.
[113] Ibid., September 29, p. 5.
[114] Ibid., September 30, p. 11.
[115] Ibid., September 20, p. 12.
[116] Ibid., October 5, pp. 1, 6.
[117] Ibid., October 6, p. 9.
[118] September 27, p. 3.
[119] *Life*, 13:35 (October 5, 1942).
[120] *One World*, pp. 81-83.
[121] *Times*, September 29, p. 5.
[122] *One World*, p. 81.

[123] This last topic, Willkie told his brother Edward, was, along with "women," what Stalin seemed to be most interested in talking about.

[124] *One World*, p. 83. Two years later Eric Johnston reported a similar impression of Stalin: "He has a merry twinkle in his eye. . . . He is a very friendly man. He likes a joke." (*Times*, July 14, 1944, p. 6.)

[125] *Life*, 13:35 (October 5, 1942).

[126] *Times*, September 29, p. 5.

[127] *One World*, p. 53.

[128] Ibid., p. 101.

[129] See "Draft Notes for Conversation with President Roosevelt, October 14, 1942," summarized below.

[130] *One World*, p. 86.

[131] London *Times*, September 28, p. 4.

[132] *One World*, p. 75.

[133] *Times*, October 3, p. 1.

[134] *One Word*, p. 114.

[135] Ibid., pp. 146-47.

[136] *Times*, October 3, p. 3.

[137] Ibid., June 12, 1942, p. 18.

[138] *One World*, p. 123.

[139] *Times*, October 4, p. 6. Another account says he was "given an official Chinese name, 'Yweierchi,' which means 'powerful foundation,' and in all official communications during his visit he will be known as 'Mr. Powerful Foundation.' " (September 24, p. 1.)

[140] *One World*, p. 128.

[141] Ibid., pp. 109-10.

[142] Dillon, p. 279. No source is given, but the remarks attributed to Willkie sound completely authentic.

[143] *Times*, October 6, p. 9.

[144] Ibid., October 5, p. 3.

[145] Ibid.

[146] Ibid.

[147] Correspondence.

[148] *One World*, p. 140.

[149] Ibid., p. 139.

[150] *Times*, October 8, p. 3.

[151] See *One World*, pp. 141-44; also Chennault's *Way of a Fighter*, p. 212.

[152] *One World*, p. 142.

[153] Chennault, p. 212.

[154] *Roosevelt and Hopkins*, p. 635.

[155] Harry Hopkins was also an ardent supporter of Chennault.

[156] Chennault, p. 212.

[157] *The Stilwell Papers*, ed. Theodore H. White, pp. 156-57, 159.

[158] To get an idea of the incredible complexities of the whole situation, one need only look into Herbert Feis's *The China Tangle* (Princeton University Press, 1953); or *The United States Army in World War II * * China-Burma-India * * Stilwell's Mission to China* (Washington: Department of the Army, 1955).

[159] Washington *Post*, October 16, 1942, p. 10B (Hope Ridings Miller).

[160] *One World*, pp. 140-41.

[161] *The Roosevelt I Knew*, p. 74. Admiral Leahy has another version of the

story: "President Roosevelt in talking with Madame Chiang accused her of being a 'vamp,' because she had so deeply impressed Wendell Willkie on his recent visit to China as to obtain from him promises to do for China everything she asked.

"Madame Chiang answered with a smile, 'Mr. President, that does not qualify me as a "vamp" because Mr. Willkie has all the emotional reactions of an adolescent.'" (*I Was There,* p. 154.)

[162] *One World,* p. 152.

[163] Ibid., p. 135.

[164] Ibid.

[165] For a detailed and appalling picture (which I believe to be accurate) of China in the last years of the war, see Theodore H. White and Annalee Jacoby, *Thunder Out of China* (New York: William Sloane Associates, 1947).

[166] *Times,* October 4, p. 6.

[167] Ibid., October 5, p. 3.

[168] *One World,* pp. 137-38.

[169] *Times,* October 3, p. 1.

[170] Ibid., October 7, p. 10. Most of the statement is repeated in *One World,* pp. 181-83.

[171] Ibid., October 7, p. 10.

[172] Ibid., October 30, p. 22.

[173] Ibid., October 24, p. 4; October 8, p. 5.

[174] Washington *Post,* October 30, p. 9.

[175] Ibid., November 3, p. 7.

[176] Correspondence.

[177] This attitude was expressed to the writer by Frank Altschul.

[178] On this point my impression is different from that of Barnes, who says: "For the most part, Americans liked what he said about the end of colonies" (p. 307).

[179] Although on January 20, 1942, Roosevelt asked Leahy to tell Petain of his desire to see France, including "the French Colonial Empire," "reconstituted in the post-war period" (*F. D. R.: His Personal Letters,* II, 1275), he said in a memorandum to Hull on January 24, 1944: "I saw Halifax last week and told him frankly . . . that I had, for over a year, expressed the opinion that Indo-China should not go back to France, but that it should be administered by an international trusteeship. France has had the country—thirty million inhabitants for nearly one hundred years, and the people are worse off than at the beginning" (ibid., p. 1489). Other memoranda (pp. 1490, 1493) indicate disapproval of permanent French control of Morocco.

[180] *Times,* November 11, p. 4.

[181] Barnes, p. 308.

[182] *New York Times,* October 28, p. 4.

[183] Ibid., November 26, p. 7.

[184] *Time,* 40:35 (October 19, 1942).

[185] *One World,* p. 128. The account in *Time* puts this episode after his return from the front the next day. But the trip to the front was made by train.

[186] These details are from *Time,* pp. 35, 37; *New York Times,* October 10, p. 4; and *One World,* pp. 148-49.

[187] *Times,* October 11, p. 11.

[188] *One World,* p. 98.

[189] *Times,* October 13, pp. 1, 6.

[190] Samuel Pryor to the writer.
[191] *Times,* October 14, p. 1.
[192] Ibid., October 15, p. 7.
[193] Ibid.
[194] Dillon, p. 288.
[195] Correspondence.
[196] *Times,* October 15, p. 7
[197] The complete text is given in the *Times,* October 27, p. 8.
[198] P. 311.
[199] *Times,* October 30, p. 4.
[200] W. H. Lawrence, however, writing on November 1, says: "It was reported reliably that the President was angered privately by Mr. Willkie's renewed demand for public pressure on the military leaders" and by his comment on "the record of this war." (Ibid., November 1, Sec. 4, p. 8.)

CHAPTER 18

New sources have been used only in regard to the Darlan episode. They include the following: Dwight D. Eisenhower, *Crusade in Europe* (New York: Doubleday, 1948); William L. Langer, *Our Vichy Gamble* (New York: Knopf, 1947); A. J. Liebling, *The Road Back to Paris* (Garden City, N. Y.: Doubleday, 1944); Waverley Root, *Secret History of the War* (New York: Scribner, 1945); Henry L. Stimson and McGeorge Bundy, *On Active Service in Peace and War* (New York: Harper, 1949).
[1] *Times,* November 1, Sec. 4, p. 8 (W. H. Lawrence).
[2] Ibid., November 1, p. 1.
[3] St. Louis *Post-Dispatch,* December 6, p. 3A (Charles G. Ross).
[4] Louisville *Courier-Journal,* December 8, p. 10 (Robert L. Riggs).
[5] *Times,* December 7, p. 1 (W. L. Lawrence).
[6] *Post-Dispatch,* December 7, p. 1A (Curtis Betts).
[7] *Times,* November 13, p. 24
[8] Letter to Geoffrey Parsons, dated December 4. (Correspondence.)
[9] *Post-Dispatch,* December 8, p. 6A (Betts).
[10] *Herald Tribune,* December 8, p. 1 (Bert Andrews).
[11] Dillon says (p. 264) that Martin made the motion to recess, and that the motion was carried because of a misunderstanding which led some Baker supporters to vote for it. But the vote was a fairly accurate reflection of the Willkie and anti-Willkie sentiment among the Committee members.
[12] *Times,* December 8, p. 1. According to Curtis Betts and Charles Ross, in the St Louis *Post-Dispatch,* the build-up for Baker was engineered by Martin and other "insiders" in order to "knock off Schroeder" and open the way for a compromise. (December 8, pp. 1A, 3A). But Mr. Martin denied this to the writer; and Willkie's letter to Parsons, together with the 38 votes against the motion to recess, shows that Baker's support at all times came exclusively from the Willkie camp.
[13] *Post-Dispatch,* December 7, p. 1A (Betts).
[14] *Times,* December 8, p. 1.
[15] Ibid., December 8, p. 28.
[16] Washington *Post,* December 8, p. 1.
[17] *Times,* December 9, p. 29 (W. L. Lawrence).
[18] *Post-Dispatch,* December 6, p. 3A. One of the signers was the novelist Ayn Rand.

[19] *The Aspirin Age*, p. 459.
[20] Akron *Beacon Journal*, October 11,1942.
[21] *Congressional Record*, 89: A2616.
[22] Letters dated December 14 and December 18, 1942. (Correspondence).
[23] Correspondence. The letter is marked "Not mailed." There is no indication of the exact context of events in which it was written, nor of why it was never sent. That it was left in the files, however, indicates that Willkie wished to save it "for the record."
[24] Harold Stassen to the writer.
[25] Memorial Tributes.
[26] Marquis Childs to the writer.
[27] *Times*, November 7, p. 7.
[28] Ibid.
[29] Ibid., November 17, p. 20.
[30] Ibid., November 21, p. 4.
[31] Ibid., November 26, p. 7.
[32] Ibid., December 2, p. 2.
[33] Correspondence.
[34] *Times*, December 17, p. 17.
[35] Correspondence. The speech referred to was Churchill's broadcast on November 29, in which he first discussed specifically the problems of post-war organization. (*Times*, November 30, p. 5.) Willkie's comment (in answer to a request by newsmen) was: "Mr. Churchill's report on what Great Britain and the Commonwealth have accomplished was masterly. I was also glad to hear him speak of post-war problems even though his references applied only to Europe and were brief. Nevertheless, the very fact that he mentioned the subject was encouraging. For there are those who believe that the answer to these problems as they concern not only Europe but the Middle East and Asia must be well under discussion and formulation before the war is over." (Ibid.)
[36] *Herald Tribune*, December 8, p. 15.
[36] *Times*, November 24, p. 1.
[38] Letter dated November 14, quoted by William L. Langer, *Our Vichy Gamble*, pp. 357-58. See also Eisenhower's *Crusade in Europe*, p. 109.
[39] Waverley Root, *Secret History of the War*, III, 518. Root is anti-Darlan, and makes a powerful case. Other details are from Langer, who considers the "Vichy gamble," including the Darlan Deal, to have been justified, although his conclusion is stronger than his evidence. Eisenhower's own defense is given in *Crusade in Europe*, Chapter 6. This is a plausible statement, which makes clear that the initial blame belongs to the State Department, which was totally wrong in imagining that the French leaders would welcome the Allied landings. The question is, Did these leaders, as Eisenhower states, continue to possess such power that they had to be accepted on their own terms? And were his sources of information in this respect more reliable than those of the reporters whom he would not allow to tell their stories and whom he casually disparages (p. 128)? The wider moral issues are of course ignored.
[40] Root, III, 521-22.
[41] *Times*, January 28, 1943, p. 4 (AP). Eisenhower later admitted that this was an error (*Crusade in Europe*, pp. 131-32), at the same time defending it at some length.

[42] Ibid., November 14, pp. 1, 4.
[43] Ibid., November 16, p. 6.
[44] Correspondence. The above quotation is taken from what appears to be the final draft.
[45] According to an exchange of letters with Elmer Davis (Correspondence), it was Davis who initiated the request; he got in touch with Stimson via Archibald MacLeish and John J. McCloy. Willkie thought from what McCloy told him that the request had originated with MacLeish, and made such a statement in public in McCloy's presence. Davis wrote an angry letter taking Willkie to task for this statement and assuming full responsibility for Stimson's act. Willkie wrote a note of apology to MacLeish, while vigorously defending himself in an answering letter to Davis.
[46] Henry L. Stimson, *On Active Service in Peace and War,* p. 593.
[47] Barnes, p. 312.
[48] These details were given to the writer by Mrs. Willkie.
[49] The Correspondence contains a telegram from British correspondent Don Iddon, dated Nov. 16, 6:30 a.m., telling him of this fact.
[50] Barnes, p. 312.
[51] *Times,* November 18, p. 4. The same day Roosevelt also spoke at the *Herald Tribune* Forum, and vigorously attacked those who criticized the conduct of the war while necessarily ignorant of the facts. Barnes implies that this attack was aimed at Willkie, but it is more likely that Roosevelt was thinking chiefly of Representative Melvin Mass of Minnesota, who had returned recently from a trip through the Pacific area and had attacked the Administration violently for allegedly neglecting the Pacific war and concealing naval losses.
[52] Ibid., November 26, p. 6.
[53] Ibid., November 27, p. 4 (James MacDonald).
[54] Ibid., January 28, 1943, p. 6.
[55] Ibid., December 3, p. 6 (Harold Callender).
[56] Ibid., December 2, p. 1 (AP).
[57] Ibid. December 4, p. 6 (italics added).
[58] Ibid., December 7, p. 4.
[59] Ibid., December 8, p. 13 (Harold Callender).
[60] Ibid., November 21, p. 5.
[61] Ibid., December 12, p. 3.
[62] Ibid., February 5, 1943, p. 5.
[63] Ibid., May 16, p. 27.
[64] Ibid., November 21, 1942, p. 5.
[65] Ibid., December 13, p. 15.
[66] Ibid., December 6, p. 57.
[67] Ibid., December 16, p. 15.
[68] Ibid.
[69] Ibid., December 17, p. 60.
[70] Correspondence.
[71] Ibid.
[72] *Times,* December 17, p. 7.
[73] Ibid., December 23, 1943, p. 2. At the time it was suggested that the assassin was a Nazi sympathizer seeking revenge on Darlan for having sold out to the Allies. As far as the writer knows, the full story of the assassination has never been told.
[74] Ibid., December 25, 1942, p. 1.

[75] Ibid., January 26, 1943, p. 5.
[76] See his accounts in the *Times* on January 28 and 29 and those of C. L. Sulzberger on March 31 and April 1.
[77] A. J. Liebling, *The Road Back to Paris*, p. 220.
[78] Ibid., pp. 227-29.
[79] Ibid., p. 235.
[80] *Times*, January 15, p. 4.
[81] Ibid., January 16, p. 3.
[82] Ibid., January 27, p. 5.
[83] Ibid., January 28, p. 3.
[84] Ibid., p. 18.
[85] III, 524.
[68] *Times*, January 15, p. 4. Drew Middloton agreed (January 16, p. 3). Raymond Daniel, however, judged that 90 per cent of the French in North Africa *were* anti-De Gaulle. (*Times*, January 31, p. 5.)
[87] He wrote to Palmer Hoyt about this time (the letter is undated): "Every correspondent that returns tells me that they are permitted to write articles that support the Administration's policy in North Africa, while articles critical of it are repressed." (Correspondence.)
[88] *Times*, January 25, p. 4.
[89] Ibid., February 26, p. 7.
[90] Ibid., May 26, p. 9.
[91] Ibid., December 9, 1942, p. 3.
[92] *New York Times Book Review*, February 28, 1960, p. 10. Brogan speaks of Darlan as "that truly detestable man" and quotes a resistance leader as saying that "Darlan was malignant" and hence worse than Laval.
[39] Letter to Mrs. King, dated December 18, 1942. (Correspondence).
[94] Barnes, p. 321.
[35] *Times*, November 30, p. 1.
[96] David A. Morse in Memorial Tributes. There are some seeming slight discrepancies between this account and the statement made to Mrs. King.
[97] This summary is based on the *Times*, January 17, p. 9, and the St. Louis *Post-Dispatch*, January 16, p. 14.
[98] *Times*, June 22, 1943, p. 6.
[99] Ibid., November 10, p. 1.
[100] Carol King, quoted by Barnes, p. 323.
[101] *Herald Tribune*, November 10, p. 14 (Bert Andrews). Willkie wrote to Helen Rogers Reid, owner of the *Herald Tribune*, on June 12, that Andrews' account was "the best article I have ever read on any court proceeding." (Correspondence).
[102] *Times*, November 10, p. 20.
[103] Ibid.
[104] *Herald Tribune*, November 10, p. 14.
[105] Ibid.
[106] *Times*, November 10, p. 20. If the *Times* reporter is quoting correctly, Willkie's grammar—like that of many public figures when speaking extemporaneously—is somewhat unorthodox.
[107] *Herald Tribune*, November 10, p. 15.
[108] All these quotations, of which the last is indirect, are from the *New*
[111] Ibid., October 9, 1944, p. 15.
[109] The opinions are printed in *The Supreme Court Reporter*, 63:1333-1375.

[110] *Times*, June 22, p. 6.
[111] Ibid., October 9, 1944, p. 15.
[112] *Congressional Record*, 89:A2617.
[113] On August 6, 1952.

CHAPTER 19

No new sources are used in this chapter.
[1] *Times*, October 2, p. 28.
[2] Correspondence.
[3] *Times*, May 19, p. 22.
[4] Ibid., July 14, p. 5.
[5] To John N. Wheeler, dated July 17, 1943. (Correspondence.)
[6] 156:111 (January 23, 1943).
[7] *Times*, March 6, p. 36.
[8] Correspondence.
[9] *Times*, July 25, p. 5.
[10] Roosevelt's first invitation to speak there had been issued in August, 1941, but Willkie had pleaded that he had too many other speaking engagements. (*F. D. R.: His Personal Letters*, II, 1199-1200.)
[11] *Times*, May 3, p. 19.
[12] Ibid., June 1, p. 24. Speech at Detroit to the General Assembly of the Presbyterian Church.
[13] Ibid., October 14, p. 5. Speech at Union College, Schenectady.
[14] All quotations to this point are from the *Times*, January 15, p. 13.
[15] *Herald Tribune*, January 15, p. 5.
[16] Correspondence.
[17] These statements are based on interviews by the writer with Mr. Cowles, Mr. Barnes, and Mrs. Van Doren; a statement in an advertisement by the publishers in the *New York Times* (May 24, 1943, p. 32); and Barnes's account in his biography, pp. 313-14.
[18] These are in the Library of Congress, and were personally examined by the writer.
[19] Publisher's advertisement in the *Times*, May 24, p. 32.
[20] Advertisement, ibid., April 16, p. 19.
[21] Advertisement, ibid., May 24, p. 32.
[22] *New York Times Book Review*, August 15, p. 8.
[23] "Publisher's Note" in *An American Program*.
[24] Russell Langworthy to the writer.
[25] *Times*, July 21, p. 17.
[26] St. Louis *Post-Dispatch*, October 16, p. 1.
[27] *Times*, May 7, p. 17.
[28] Ibid., December 12, 1943, p. 30. Radio speech for United Church Canvass.
[29] Ibid., March 27, 1943, p. 12. Speech for United China Relief.
[30] Correspondence. In this connection an anecdote told the writer by Lem Jones is too delightful not to repeat. The writing of some hundreds of "special messages" was obviously too time-consuming a task for a man so desperately pressed as Willkie; and accordingly a skilled penman was employed to inscribe the messages and sign Willkie's name. (This does not imply that the words were not sincere.) When the task was done, and the person had been paid, Willkie felt, apparently, that such an unusual service

called for a special reward, and inquired if there were not some favor that he could do. "Yes," was the reply, "will you autograph a copy of the book for me?"

[31] Louisville *Courier-Journal,* August 24, 1943, Sec. 1, p. 7 (Samuel Grafton).
[32] April 11, p. 1.
[33] Dated April 13, 1943. (Correspondence.)
[34] Correspondence.
[35] *Times,* April 10, p. 30.
[36] Ibid., January 5, p. 11.
[37] Ibid., January 8, pp. 10, 40.
[38] Ibid., February 13, p. 24 (indirect quotation).
[39] Ibid., March 6, p. 34.
[40] Ibid., March 16, p. 1 (summary).
[41] Ibid., March 17, p. 4.
[42] Ibid., March 20, p. 5.
[43] Ibid., March 22, p. 4.
[44] Ibid., April 8, p. 1.
[45] Ibid., May 26, p. 20.
[46] Ibid., June 20, p. 12.
[47] Ibid., July 3, p. 6.
[48] Ibid., July 4, p. 10.
[49] All reporters agreed that they *were* indifferent. See, for instance, Drew Middleton in the *New York Times Magazine,* May 2, 1943, p. 3.
[50] *Times,* March 16, p. 5 (indirect quotation).
[51] Ibid., March 17, p. 1.
[52] Ibid., January 3, p. 39.
[53] Ibid., July 5, p. 6.
[54] Correspondence. Archibald MacLeish, then Librarian, wished Willkie to edit his remarks for publication, and Willkie tried, but gave it up. MacLeish replied on June 24, 1944: "You are the doctor and that must be the answer. We will tuck the account of the Seminar away in our files where, perhaps, some future scholar will stumble on it and marvel, as I did at the time, at the hopefulness and directness of that long statement of yours."
[55] *Times,* July 3, p. 6.
[56] Ibid., April 19, p. 1.
[57] Ibid., May 2, p. 25.
[58] Ibid., June 1, p. 1.
[59] Ibid., p. 21.
[60] Detroit *News,* September 5, p. 4.
[61] *Times,* September 6, p. 1.
[62] Ibid., September 8, p. 1.
[63] Ibid., September 9, p. 29.
[64] Ibid. (Turner Catledge.)
[65] Ibid., September 22, p. 1.
[66] Ibid., November 2, p. 14.
[67] Ibid., November 6, p. 1.

CHAPTER 20

Among sources of this chapter not previously mentioned may be specified the following: James L. Wick, *How Not to Run for President* (New York: Vantage Press, 1952; an important article by Willkie in *Look,* October 5, 1943;

and several items from the files of William T. Evjue, editor of the Madison, Wisconsin *Capitol Times*.

[1] *Times*, June 20, p. 11.
[2] Ibid., March 7, p. 8.
[3] Ibid., June 27, p. 9.
[4] Ibid., July 31, p. 7.
[5] Ibid., August 8, p. 29.
[6] Ibid., August 22, p. 33.
[7] Ibid., February 26, p. 38.
[8] Ibid., April 25, p. 25.
[9] Ibid., May 3, pp. 1, 11.
[10] Ibid., May 9, Sec. 4, p. 10.
[11] Ibid., May 4, p. 25 (Warren Moscow).
[12] Ibid., August 4, p. 38.
[13] Herbert R. Hill, ibid., February 21, p. 27 and W. H. Lawrence, ibid., February 28, Sec. 4, p. 8.
[14] Ibid., February 12, p. 11.
[15] Ibid., February 21, p. 27.
[16] Ibid., February 13, p. 1.
[17] Ibid., February 12, p. 11.
[18] Ibid., February 21, p. 27.
[19] Ibid.
[20] Correspondence.
[21] May 31, p. 1 (W. A. Markland).
[22] *Times*, May 31, p. 20.
[23] Ibid., June 2, p. 22.
[24] Letter dated June 8, 1943. (Correspondence.)
[25] Letter dated June 14, 1943. (Correspondence.)
[26] Letter dated July 8, 1943. (Correspondence.)
[27] Letter dated July 20, 1943. (*Selected Letters of William Allen White*, ed. Walter Johnson [New York: Holt, 1847], p. 449.
[28] *Times*, June 12, p. 14.
[29] Ibid., July 25, Sec. 4, p. 12 (C. P. Trussell).
[30] Ibid., July 2, p. 11; July 3, p. 14; July 17, p. 1.
[31] Letter dated August 12, 1943. (Correspondence).
[32] *Times*, August 12, p. 10.
[33] Ibid., August 13, p. 11.
[34] *Look*, 7:25-27 (October 5, 1943). Italics Willkie's.
[35] Letter to Charles J. Graham of Pittsburgh dated March 5, 1943. A copy is in the file of Willkie's correspondence with Graham.
[36] Letter to Charles J. Graham dated April 29, 1943. (Correspondence.)
[37] *Times*, September 12, p. 20.
[38] Ibid., September 15, p. 17.
[39] Ibid., September 12, p. 20.
[40] Ibid.
[41] Ibid., October 7, p. 19.
[42] St. Louis *Post-Dispatch*, October 8, p. 20.
[43] Ibid., October 15, p. 1.
[44] Des Moines *Register*, October 17, Sec. 3, p. 1.
[45] *Herald Tribune*, October 16, p. 1.
[46] *Times*, October 16, p. 8.

[47] Turner Catledge to the writer.

[48] James L. Wick, *How Not to Run for President,* p. 31. This is a compendium of typical Old Guard propaganda against Willkie, and cannot be trusted, but this comment by Queeny sounds in character.

[49] The quotation between dashes is from a comment by Turner Catledge to the writer. The rest is from his account in the *Times,* October 17, p. 4.

[50] *Post-Dispatch,* October 16, p. 1.

[51] Ibid., Des Moines *Register,* October 17, Sec. 3, p. 3.

[52] *Post-Dispatch,* October 16, p. 5.

[53] Ibid., October 16, p. 5A.

[54] Louisville *Courier-Journal,* October 17, Sec. 1, p. 6.

[55] Des Moines *Register,* October 17, Sec. 3, p. 1.

[56] *Times,* October 17, p. 10.

[57] *Post-Dispatch,* October 17, p. 11A.

[58] *Herald Tribune,* October 17, p. 10.

[59] Post-Dispatch, October 17, p. 1.

[60] Louisville *Courier-Journal,* October 16, Sec. 1, p. 7 (Drew Pearson).

[61] Correspondence.

[62] *Herald Tribune,* October 21, p. 14 (Don Cook).

[63] Detroit *News,* October 21, p. 21.

[64] *Herald Tribune,* October 21, p. 14. According to this reporter, all those present who were interviewed "agreed that Mr. Willkie did not commit himself as to whether he would seek the nomination." This contradicts the story by Wick (p. 32) and Dillon (p. 320) that Willkie told his hearers, "Whether you like it or not, I am going to be nominated."

[65] Ibid.

[66] *Post-Dispatch,* October 20, p. 10C.

[67] Detroit *News,* October 21, 21. See also the *Post-Dispatch* story.

[68] *Times,* October 22, p. 36.

[69] Ibid., p. 1.

[70] November 3, p. 1.

[71] Ibid., November 4, p. 1.

[72] Ibid., November 6, p. 8.

[73] Ibid., November 7, p. 20.

[74] Ibid., October 24, p. 12.

[75] Telegram from William M. Kearney to Basil Brewer dated January 3, 1944. (Correspondence). Other details are from the *Times,* October 3, p. 17. Dillon characteristically remarks (p. 318) that the trip was "replete with political blunders," including the claim to one group of Republicans that he would have 400 votes (which he specified) on the first ballot at the 1944 convention. She says that these "rash statements" appeared "in the press," but does not say where. They are not in the *Times,* in which it is simply said that he "was forthright in presenting his views and asked his conferees' opinions in return." Apparently Johnson did not meet the statements, either, since he gives her work as his source. I suggest that they were never made. A final comment is that Willkie's "blunders" must have been committed after leaving Los Angeles, from which *Time's* correspondent wrote: "If he has not completed the capture of California by the time he leaves San Francisco . . . this is my last flyer in political prognostication." (*Time,* 42:19 [October 11, 1943.])

[76] *Times,* November 14, p. 48.

[77] Ibid., October 24, Sec. 4, p. 3.
[78] P. 11.
[79] *Life*, 15:30 (November 15, 1943). Dillon says (p. 313) that in the spring of 1943 Willkie asked Hamilton to manage his campaign for the 1944 nomination. This is poppycock.
[80] *Times*, November 12, p. 43.
[81] Ibid., November 13, p. 28.
[82] Ibid., December 6, p. 1.
[83] Ibid., December 7, p. 29.
[84] Ibid., December 8, p. 1.
[85] Ibid., December 9, p. 17.
[86] Ibid., December 10, p. 19.
[87] Editorial in the Emporia *Gazette*, reprinted in the *Wisconsin State Journal*, January 21, 1944.
[88] Correspondence. Steele declared that at the meeting of the National Committee on January 10 Willkie supporters should demand Spangler's resignation.
[89] *Times*, January 9, p. 14.
[90] Ibid., January 15, p. 5.
[91] Letter dated June 9, 1944. (Correspondence.)
[92] White says "deliver the state's electoral votes," but this must be a slip.
[93] *A Man Called White*, p. 204. The governor may have been Ralph Carr of Colorado, a Willkie supporter in 1940 who strongly opposed him in 1944.
[94] See Chapter 9, n. 170.
[95] Letter from Childs to Willkie dated January 22, 1944. Childs added: "I am carrying a story on it tomorrow."
[96] These items were shown to the writer by Mr. Evjue.
[97] Green Bay, Wisconsin, *Press Gazette*, February 22.
[98] Letter from Willkie to Paul Bellamy of the Cleveland *Plain Dealer*, dated March 2, 1944. (Correspondence.)
[99] He said he did so at the request of 36 fellow Congressmen from thirteen states, and denied that he was joining Hamilton's stop-Willkie movement. But it was noted that 35 of the 36 were anti-Willkie. See *Time*, 42:18-19 (December 13, 1943).
[100] Letter to Walter Annenberg of the Philadelphia *Inquirer*, dated January 20, 1944: "Confidentially, I am thinking of entering the Pennsylvania primaries. . . . If for any reason you think I should not, let me know." (Correspondence.)
[101] *Times*, February 16, p. 2.
[102] Ibid., January 9, p. 15. Johnson (p. 259) and Barnes (p. 355) say that Warren had told Willkie of his intention when Willkie visited California in October. (They met on October 1.) Later events make this seem doubtful. On November 17, however, Bartley Crum, one of his supporters in California, sent him a telegram urging him to enter the primary and make a strong fight (the inference is, against Warren). (Correspondence.)
[103] Correspondence.
[104] Ibid.
[105] *Times*, January 24, p. 1.
[106] Bartley Crum, in an interview with the writer, stated that Warren had agreed that if Willkie withdrew, a substantial number of the delegates would be chosen from among Willkie's supporters, but this was not done. When the writer sought information from Mr. Warren himself, who had become Chief Justice, he replied: "As you can well understand, my present position does

not leave me free to discuss political matters, particularly when they might get into the field of controversy. . . . I am sure you know, however, that I had great admiration for Mr. Willkie and was in accord, generally speaking, with his views." Here the mattter must rest.

[107] *Times*, January 30, p. 32.

CHAPTER 21

An invaluable source for this chapter was three large scrapbooks of clippings from Wisconsin newspapers covering the primary campaign, lent me by Don Anderson, editor and publisher of the *Wisconsin State Journal*. Mr. Anderson was also among those who supplied information in interviews. Others were Thomas E. Coleman, William T. Evjue, Milton Polland, and Willard Smith.

[1] *Times*, January 13, p. 6.

[2] Ibid., January 12, pp. 1, 10.

[3] Pp. 3, 4.

[4] *Times*, January 6, p. 1. Stalin's relation to the episode is not clear. According to Edward R. Stettinius, Under Secretary of State, Stalin was "greatly upset" by the *Pravda* article, and Stettinius expected him to make amends, either in "a public statement" or a private "note of apology." (Letter from Gardner Cowles to Willkie, dated February 18, 1944, summarizing a letter from Stettinius, in Correspondence). Barnes prints a letter to Willkie from the British Ambassador in Moscow, Sir Archibald Clark-Kerr (later Lord Inverchapel), who had happened to be in New York when the *Pravda* attack was published, telling of Stalin's reception of a message that Willkie had asked the Ambassador to give him: "that a few more attacks like this would elect him to the White House." "It clearly shook him a bit," Clark-Kerr reported. At the same time Stalin said that Willkie's article had been generally disliked; but after jokingly suggesting that he send a message saying he did not want Willkie to be the next President, he said that he had nothing against Willkie personally and that he was willing to send a message of regret and to see that no more attacks were made on Willkie in the Soviet press. Later, however, he told Clark-Kerr that some more remarks by Willkie had made him change his mind about the personal message, although he would keep his promise about the press. (Barnes, pp. 351-52.)

[5] *Times*, February 5, p. 15.

[6] Correspondence. Russia had made clear her intention to annex much of eastern Poland, justifying her action on the ground that the new boundary would approximate the so-called "Curzon Line," which had been recommended as Poland's eastern border after World War I, but which had been replaced by a boundary much farther east as a result of a military victory by Poland over a then almost helpless Russia.

[7] Letter to Willkie from William L. White dated January 29, 1944. (Correspondence.)

[8] Note and clipping in Mr. Evjue's files.

[9] Thomson's statement was reprinted in the *Wisconsin State Journal* on January 20.

[10] *Times*, February 6, p. 34. Johnson states (p. 254) that Willkie himself did not want to enter the Wisconsin primary, and only did so "because of demands by his financial backers in New York that he prove his strength in the Midwest." This "decision was made at a meeting in February at the

Ambassador Hotel." Undoubtedly such pressure from his financial supporters was one factor in Willkie's decision, but it was only one. Lem Jones, one of Johnson's sources, gave a similar account to the writer; but he did not say that Willkie was reluctant—only that he recognized the odds against him. Jones himself, along with John Cowles, Bartley Crum and Milton Polland, advised strongly against it. (Interviews with these persons by the writer.) But Willkie was making his own decisions, as always.

Furthermore, if Jones's recollection of the date is correct, there is evidence that the decision had already been made. On January 4, for instance, the *Wisconsin State Journal* announced that Willard R. Smith, associate editor, was taking a three months leave of absence (that is, until the date of the primary) to help with Willkie's campaign. On January 20, Vernon Thomson announced his support of Willkie. And on February 5 Willkie met with his entire slate of delegates in Wisconsin. (*Times*, February 6, p. 34). They must have been selected before any meeting held in February.

Also relevant is the fact, stated by Milton Polland to the writer, that in late 1943, State Chairman Thomas E. Coleman and other organization leaders met him, as Willkie's representative, and tried to get him to agree to have an uninstructed delegation. When he declined, they proposed an arrangement to give six delegates each to Willkie, Dewey, Bricker, and Stassen. Polland objected that Dewey and Stassen were not candidates; but he did propose to Willkie that the delegation should be divided evenly among Willkie, Dewey and Bricker. Willkie, however, preferred to fight it out.

[11] *Times*, February 3, p. 14.
[12] Ibid., February 5, p. 16.
[13] Ibid., February 28, p. 11.
[14] Ibid., February 13, p. 36.
[15] Ibid., February 14, p. 34.
[16] Ibid., February 19, p. 11. He repeated the statement during the Wisconsin campaign. See the Beloit *News*, March 25.
[17] Sheboygan *Press*, February 7. According to Johnson (p. 264n.) it was John W. Hanes who drafted an outline for the innocuous speech, telling Willkie that a tough speech on taxes would kill him politically. Johnson discusses the reception of Willkie's speech in some detail.
[18] *Times*, February 8, p. 34.
[19] Ibid., February 9, p. 11.
[20] Ibid., February 12, p. 9.
[21] Ibid., February 18, p. 32.
[22] Ibid., February 14, p. 34.
[23] Ibid., February 17, p. 24.
[24] The article includes pp. 305-12, in Volume 188. Willkie's answer, together with a rejoinder from Rodell, is in the unnumbered end pages of the April number.
[25] In the Milwaukee *Journal*, among other papers.
[26] Fond du Lac *Commonwealth-Reporter*, February 24. Dewey sent a slightly different telegram to Bernhard Gettelman, the head of the delegation (see the *Times*, February 24, p. 1) and Johnson quotes the latter as having been sent to the delegates.
[27] Madison *Capitol Times*, February 25 (Aldric Revell).
[28] Gettelman and six others withdrew.

[29] *Wisconsin State Journal,* January 14. According to Willard Smith, Willkie's supporters had been hoping to get Goodland's endorsement and were much disappointed when it went to Stassen.

[30] I believe this story was in one of the Madison papers on March 14.

[31] *Times,* March 22, p. 36.

[32] Ibid.

[33] Milton Polland to the writer.

[34] These statements are based on interviews with Mr. Stassen, Gardner Cowles, and Alfred B. Connable, Jr., of Kalamazoo, Michigan, and correspondence with Mr. Ball. Willkie told Cowles the same story that he told Polland. And Stassen later gave Cowles the same explanation that he gave the writer. He also told Connable, according to the latter's recollection, that he had not intended to enter the Wisconsin primary but yielded to the urging of his friends. Mr. Ball in a letter to the writer dated October 13, 1960, comments: "I frankly cannot remember definitely whether we discussed the Wisconsin primary plans with Stassen by mail or otherwise. . . . I do recall at the time the primary was on and shortly before we entered it, our feeling was very definitely that Willkie did not stand much chance there and that it was therefore important for our group in the party to get into that primary. I do remember discussing it with Willkie himself at one time and expressing that viewpoint." That the Stassen organization was formed well before the primary, with or without Stassen's knowledge, is shown by a letter to Willkie from John Cowles dated October 8, 1943: "The Stassen people are planning to make an aggressive fight in many states." (Correspondence.)

[35] Superior *Telegram,* April 1; Racine *Journal-Times,* April 1. But the outcome of the primary seems to have rekindled his anger, for he commented in a letter to Rush Sturges dated May 8: "I don't have much respect for the Stassen people. They are substantially responsible both for the election of Chairman Harrison Spangler and also for the results in Wisconsin. I pled with them earnestly not to produce both results." (Correspondence.)

[36] The MacArthur boom burst at the end of April, after Representative Miller of Nebraska published an exchange of letters with MacArthur, in which he himself violently attacked the Administration and MacArthur expressed approval. The resulting uproar caused MacArthur to withdraw publicly and definitely.

[37] *Wisconsin State Journal,* March 19.

[38] "Willkie Against the Gods," *Nation,* 159:412 (April 8, 1944).

[39] Oshkosh *Northwestern,* March 20.

[40] *Wisconsin State Journal,* March 22.

[41] Green Bay *Press Gazette,* March 30.

[42] Appleton *Post-Crescent,* March 22.

[43] *Wisconsin State Journal,* March 23.

[44] Milwaukee *Journal,* March 22.

[45] Green Bay *Press Gazette,* March 22.

[46] Milwaukee *Journal,* March 21.

[47] Fond du Lac *Commonwealth-Reporter,* March 20.

[48] Janesville *Gazette,* March 25(?).

[49] Sheboygan *Press,* March 23. The *Times* on March 24 quoted Willkie as saying in this or another speech: "The reason I was not elected President in 1940 was that I had to lug the load of leaders in my party who opposed Selective Service and aid to Britain."

[50] Racine *Journal-Times*, March 28.
[51] *Wisconsin State Journal*, March 21.
[52] Kenosha *News*, March 23.
[53] Superior *Telegram*, March 30.
[54] Janesville *Gazette*, March 31.
[55] Ibid., March 22.
[56] Green Bay *Press Gazette*, March 22.
[57] Janesville *Gazette*, March 28. Perhaps his comments on the Polish boundary issue were not quite fair, since he had himself had experience of the difficulty of dealing with Russia. But he was after all only a private citizen. Roosevelt was President of the United States.
[58] Milwaukee *Journal*, March 19.
[59] *Capitol Times*, March 23.
[60] *Wisconsin State Journal*, March 26.
[61] La Crosse *Tribune and Leader-Press*, March 26.
[62] *Wisconsin State Journal*, March 19.
[63] Ibid., March 26.
[64] Wisconsin Rapids *Tribune*, March 29.
[65] Wausau *Record-Herald*, March 24.
[66] Ibid.
[67] *Wisconsin State Journal*, March 22.
[68] Green Bay *Press Gazette*, March 22.
[69] *Wisconsin State Journal*, March 21.
[70] Janesville *Gazette*, March 31.
[71] Dillon, p. 329.
[72] Milwaukee *Journal*, March 19.
[73] Ibid., March 23.
[74] Sheboygan *Press*, March 23.
[75] Thomas Coleman to the writer.
[76] Green Bay *Press Gazette*, March 20.
[77] Ibid.
[78] Ibid., March 25.
[79] Ibid., March 24.
[80] Sheboygan *Press*, Eau Claire *Leader*, and Milwaukee *Journal*, March 28; Wisconsin Rapids *Tribune*, March 29.
[81] *Wisconsin State Journal*, March 22.
[82] Wausau *Record-Herald*, March 24.
[83] The facts about the financing of the campaign are a little difficult to ascertain. The *Wisconsin State Journal* on March 27 printed the reports on expenses which had been officially filed by Willkie and Stassen. The figure for the former was $14,195, for the latter $7,930. Apparently no reports had been filed for the Dewey and MacArthur organizations. At the same time Willkie reported having received $18,674. This does not agree with Dillon's statement (p. 330) that "about $17,000 was spent, and all of it raised in Wisconsin except $1,800 which came from the New York office. After the campaign was over, unpaid bills amounted to $7,500, which Willkie and Polland personally split." Mr. Polland told the writer that the last statement was correct according to his recollection, but that it was not correct that so little money came from New York. Willard Smith, who in his own words "was given charge of the checkbook" of the local Willkie organization, told the writer he thought total expenditures were about $27,000, that there was a

deficit too large for Willkie personally to settle under the Wisconsin corrupt practices law, and that John R. Kimberly lent money which he never got back in full. A final item is that on August 9, John W. Hanes, treasurer of the entire campaign organization, wrote to Willkie that about $13,000 was still owing (evidently for the expenses of the New Hampshire visit and the few days of campaigning in Nebraska as well as for the Wisconsin campaign). In a recent letter, however, Mr. Hanes assured the writer: "it is my recollection that . . . no one suffered any loss other than his close friends who were glad to undertake the obligation in his behalf."

[84] Eau Claire *Leader*, March 26.

[85] Janesville *Gazette*, March 25.

[86] Ibid., March 24.

[87] Ibid., March 25. Don Anderson also commented to the writer on this episode.

[88] Wisconsin Rapids *Tribune*, March 29. During most of the campaign the Willkie party, including the correspondents, traveled in a motorcade, the cars being supplied by the Friede Rent-a-Car Company of Madison. (Milwaukee *Journal*, March 22.)

[89] Willard Smith to the writer.

[90] Chicago *Daily News*, March 22.

[91] *Wisconsin State Journal*, March 24.

[92] Janesville *Gazette*, March 24.

[93] Milwaukee *Journal*, March 28.

[94] Green Bay *Press Gazette*, March 25.

[95] *Wisconsin State Journal*, April 2.

[96] See the Green Bay *Press Gazette*, March 22; Sheboygan *Press*, March 23; Janesville *Gazette*, March 25.

[97] *Wisconsin State Journal*, March 19; *Capitol Times*, March 27.

[98] *Wisconsin State Journal*, March 19.

[99] Appleton *Post-Crescent*, March 21.

[100] Milwaukee *Journal*, March 26.

[101] Eau Claire *Leader*, March 31.

[102] March 25.

[103] March 25.

[104] March 27, p. 13.

[105] Viroqua *Broadcaster*, March 30; see also the Wisconsin Rapids *Tribune*, March 31.

[106] *Wisconsin State Journal*, March 23.

[107] Philip Willkie, who spent a three-day leave in Wisconsin during the campaign, to the writer.

[108] Willard Smith to the writer.

[109] March 29.

[110] March 28.

[111] *Newsweek*, 23:24 (April 17, 1944).

[112] E. g., an incomplete tabulation showed that Dewey's three candidates polled, respectively, 110,813; 96,503; and 94,244; the average being 97,187. Willkie's four polled 41,722; 40,139; 39,700; and 38,720, for an average of 40,070. The figures (and other data in this paragraph) are from the *Capitol Times* of April 5 and include 2,306 of 3,076 precincts. The *New York Times* on April 20 (p. 36) gave a limited number of final figures.

[113] Willard Smith to the writer.

[114] Milwaukee *Sentinel*, March 19.

[115] In a letter to Helen Rogers Reid dated April 10, 1944, Willkie spoke of "Joe Ball's speeches for Stassen in Wisconsin and Nebraska," in which "he demanded a United Nations declaration against dismemberment of Germany or violation of her territorial rights. I do not happen to be wise enough to know what should be done about Germany, but I am smart enough to know the effects on German American voters in Wisconsin and Nebraska of such chatter." (Correspondence.)

[116] Don Anderson to the writer. He added: "I can't prove that he was hired by the opposition." William T. Evjue agreed that the German descent of many voters was one cause of Willkie's defeat.

[117] Juneau *Independent*, March 31.

[118] March 23, 1944.

[119] Letter dated January 21. (Correspondence.) Also relevant at this point is a letter from Oren Root to John W. Hanes, dated March 28, 1944, expressing the strong opinion that the funds of the Independent Clubs, originally contributed to the Associated Willkie Clubs, should not be used to finance Willkie's primary campaign. "It is a regrettable but I think a conservative assumption that a minority of all our contributors, and not much more than a majority of the Committee, are today still friendly to Willkie." (Correspondence.) It should be made clear that Root in this letter is speaking only in his capacity as trustee of the funds of the Independent Clubs. Personally, he was no less in sympathy with Willkie now than he had been in 1940.

[120] *Capitol Times*, January 6, 1944 (Aldric Revell).

[121] Turner Catledge, who was sent to Wisconsin by the *Times* after the election to find out what had happened, told the writer that this was essentially his conclusion.

[122] Quoted in the *Times*, April 6, p. 18.

[123] Milwaukee *Journal*, March 19.

[124] Letter from Arthur Thomas to John M. Henry of the Des Moines *Register* and *Tribune*, dated December 19, 1944. (Correspondence). Thomas added: "I never met a man who impressed me so much in such a short time as Willkie."

[125] *Times*, April 6, p. 15.

[126] He had earlier recognized by implication the existence of Fascist elements in the Chinese Nationalist Government, in speaking of post-war aid to China and "the need to see that this assistance is rendered in such a way that it is beneficial to the healthy elements in Chinese political life."

[127] *Times*, April 6, p. 16.

[128] Ibid., pp. 1, 15. The "candidate who led at the polls"—by a large margin —was Fred R. Zimmerman, who was Willkie's most violent and vindictive critic. (At the February 25 meeting of Dewey delegates referred to above, Zimmerman was heard to say of Willkie: "I'll follow him from county to county and district to district," telling labor audiences, "Willkie's labor record is lousy. He ground his men into the dust," and telling Republicans, "If you want Rooevelt elected, vote for Willkie."—*Capitol Times*, February 25). He immediately denied that he had ever been connected with America First. But he could not deny that he shared its essential views.

CHAPTER 22

Sources for this chapter not previously referred to include Willkie's *An American Program* (New York: Simon and Schuster, 1944); an interview with Samuel Rosenman; and a letter to the writer from Leo Crowley.

[1] *Times,* April 6, p. 15.
[2] Letter dated April 18, shown to the writer by Milton Polland.
[3] Letter dated April 17. (Correspondence.)
[4] These letters are in Mr. Evjue's files. Willkie's is dated April 14.
[5] Letter dated May 1. (Correspondence.)
[6] Walter White, *A Man Called White,* p. 204.
[7] *Times,* April 6, p. 18.
[8] Ibid., April 7, p. 1.
[9] Letter dated April 14. (Correspondence.)
[10] Telegram dated April 6. (Correspondence.)
[11] *Times,* April 6, p. 18.
[12] *Time,* 43:18 (April 17, 1944).
[13] Letter dated April 18. (Correspondence.)
[14] Correspondence.
[15] *Times,* May 26, p. 11.
[16] The papers were the New York *Herald Tribune,* the Boston *Herald,* the Minneapolis *Star Journal* and *Tribune,* the Des Moines *Register* and *Tribune,* the Portland *Oregonian,* and the San Francisco *Chronicle.* The articles were collected, along with a "Proposed Platform" and two articles which Willkie wrote for *Collier's Magazine* after the conventions, in a little volume called *An American Program,* published early in October.
[17] All quotations are from *An American Program.*
[18] On June 19, 1944, Willkie wrote to Mrs. Eugene Meyer: "Obviously we should keep the state governments as effective and in control of as large areas as possible. I do, however, become completely sick and fed up with all this talk about states' rights." (Correspondence.)
[19] Letter dated June 14. (Correspondence.)
[20] Correspondence. Willkie prepared a synthesis of the seven articles in a "Proposed Platform" "in the event" (he wrote in the Foreword to *An American Program*) "that I might have the opportunity to fight for the ideas I believed in at Chicago. The opportunity never came." The text of the "Proposed Platform," of which no news had previously been released to the press, appeared in the *Times,* July 11, 1944, p. 10.
[21] Johnson, p. 291 and n.
[22] Correspondence.
[23] *Times,* June 16, p. 32.
[24] Ibid., June 17, p. 8.
[25] Samuel Pryor to the writer.
[26] Pp. 1, 12.
[27] *An American Program,* p. 38.
[28] According to Dillon (p. 347), Willkie got it from a "distinguished newspaperman" (who had received it as a press release for future publication) on condition that he would not publish it until after it had been read to the convention, and that he either "misunderstood the agreement or wilfully broke his promise." One can only surmise whether this is true.
[29] Words in parentheses were deleted in the final draft.
[30] *Times,* June 28, p. 1. Willkie explained his action by saying that "as a Republican I am desperately anxious for my party to pursue a course that will entitle it to win the November elections. As I am not a delegate to the convention I take this method of presenting my views on the proposed foreign policy plank in the platform."

[31] Ibid., June 28, p. 11.
[32] Ibid.
[33] Telegram dated June 29. (Correspondence.)
[34] *F. D. R.: His Personal Letters,* II, 1522-23. The Roosevelt Library (OF-4040) has a copy of this letter and also of Norris's telegram: "For God's sake don't permit the Democratic convention to nominate Willkie for Vice President. It will drive millions of progressive voters away from the ticket headed by you if he is your running-mate."
[35] Correspondence.
[36] Letter to the writer dated July 9, 1956.
[37] John Gunther, *Roosevelt in Retrospect,* p. 115.
[38] See Note 36.
[39] Correspondence.
[40] *Times,* December 18, p. 16.
[41] *Look,* 7:32 (March 6, 1943).
[42] *F. D. R.: His Personal Letters,* II, 1404-05.
[43] Correspondence.
[44] Pp. 463-70.
[45] This letter, first printed by Barnes, is in the Correspondence. The preceding letter from Roosevelt, as well as the following one, are in *F. D. R.: His Personal Letters.*
[46] OF-4040. After the initials is penciled "Audrey C. Turner"—presumably a Presidential secretary.
[47] Correspondence. I have not checked to see whether, or when, Lyons did run the item.
[48] *Times,* August 11, pp. 1, 8.
[49] Correspondence.
[50] The official transcript of the relevant part of the conference, in the Roosevelt Library, reads as follows.
Q. "On this question of foreign policy, sir, considerable stories have been published in New York principally, that you had issued some sort of invitation to Mr. Willkie to come down and have a talk on foreign policy. Is there any basis of truth in that?"
The President. "Not that I know of."
Q. "Not that you know of?"
The President. "Sounds like New York stories."
Q. "Can't hear you, Mr. President."
The President (a little louder). "I don't know anything about it."
Q. "Would you like to have a talk with Mr. Willkie?"
The President. "Well, that's rather a personal matter. And the question is whether I should discuss it on—on or off the record with the press. And the answer is that it's a personal matter."
A week later the following exchange took place.
Q. "Have you been in touch with Mr. Willkie?"
The President. "Well, yes, privately."
Q. "Would privately, sir, preclude any—?"
The President. "Yes. Yes." (Much laughter.)
Q. "Can you tell us, sir, whether you are going to have a private meeting with him?"
The President. "Not that I know of. No date. I may."
[51] Philip Willkie to the writer.

[52] This information is from Barnes, who goes into the affair in some detail (pp. 374-76). In Cox's autobiography, *Journey Through My Years,* the author mentions some letters from Willkie which must "remain sealed" for the present. In 1954 I approached Governor Cox, through his son, James M. Cox, Jr., concerning these letters. The latter replied: "What facts do come to mind indicate that Governor Cox would not wish to reopen the subject. However, I will forward your correspondence to him and should he wish otherwise I shall be happy to advise you." Apparently Governor Cox confirmed his son's judgment. Willkie's Correspondence, which I had not then examined, contains no significant letters to Cox besides those here quoted.

[53] It is not clear what these "protective measures" were, nor what grounds Willkie had for blaming Daniels for spreading the news of Roosevelt's letter. Also, it is odd that during his three-hour talk with Cox on August 2 (Barnes, p. 375) he did not give his prospective emissary the full background.

[54] Hardly had Willkie mailed this when he dispatched a hasty postscript, stressing still more strongly his desire to end negotiations. (Correspondence.)

[55] A letter to Willkie from Albert Lasker (an intimate friend of both Willkie and Cox) read over the phone by Lasker's secretary on August 23 reads in part: "Governor Cox phoned me from Dayton last night saying he had heard from Hyde Park and they had asked him to get in touch with you." (Correspondence.)

[56] Barnes, p. 377.

[57] *Times,* August 26, p. 9.

[58] This and other facts in the following account, which differs in one or two minor details from that given by Barnes, were supplied to the writer by Bartley Crum.

[59] Barnes, p. 378.

[60] Lem Jones to the writer.

[61] Drew Pearson, Louisville *Courier-Journal,* October 12, 1944, p. 7. Pearson says the California client was the Gianninis—presumably the noted banking firm.

[62] Correspondence.

[63] Ibid.

[64] Detroit *Free Press,* December 14 and 15, 1944. Barnes says (p. 364) that he sent similar letters to twenty newspapermen who were his friends. A letter to Willard Smith, of the same date, is in parts identical and in parts different. The Correspondence contains similar letters to such non-journalistic friends as Thomas W. Lamont and George Roberts.

[65] Letter to Elmer Todd of Seattle. (Correspondence.)

[66] *Working with Roosevelt,* p. 465.

[67] Correspondence. Willkie's sincerity in professing his continued regard for Hanes is proved by a letter to the latter dated August 18: "It has been a matter of great distress to me that after our very intimate, wholesome and loyal associations we find ourselves in a new and different situation with differing political viewpoints. That phase is bound to pass at the latest in three months and it is my great desire when the tenseness of the moment has passed, that we may find ourselves in close collaboration in other endeavors." He signed himself "Loyally yours."

[68] Letter to Ernest White of Syracuse, dated July 28, 1944. (Correspondence.)

[69] Letter to Theodore Kiendl, dated August 23, 1944. (Correspondence.)

[70] Letter dated July 28. (Correspondence.)

[71] *Times,* August 21, p. 1. The time of Willkie's answering telegram is from the copy in the Correspondence. Dewey's choice of Dulles as his foreign policy adviser can hardly have increased Willkie's confidence. He must have remembered introducing Dulles as a speaker to the Economic Club on March 22, 1939, and he could hardly have forgotten the line that Dulles took. "Only hysteria entertains the idea that Germany, Italy or Japan contemplates war upon us. . . . I can see no justification for our participation in the senseless cyclical struggle which, under our present world system, always goes on between static and dynamic forces." (Ibid., September 3, 1944, Sec. 4, p. 3.)
[72] Ibid., August 22, pp. 1, 32. A later report in the *Times* (August 24, p. 1) gives in detail Willkie's views on what the Republican attitude toward the Dumbarton Oaks conference should be.
[73] Ibid., July 30, p. 1.
[74] Ibid., August 26, p. 13.
[75] The letter from Bliven is dated June 28; Willkie's answer, June 29. (Correspondence.)
[76] Barnes, p. 374.
[77] Correspondence ("Fraternities").
[78] Dillon (pp. 340-41) gives a full account of the project and also of the plans to buy the Chicago *Daily News.*
[79] Letter dated May 17, 1944. (Correspondence.)
[80] Correspondence.
[81] Fred Willkie to the writer.
[82] Mrs. Willkie to the writer.
[83] Mary Sleeth to the writer. The wording given by Barnes (p. 384) is slightly different but the substance is the same.
[84] These details were given to the writer by Lem Jones.
[85] Lem Jones to the writer.
[86] Correspondence. For Dewey's speech at Louisville, see the *Times,* September 9, p. 28. It does not in itself deserve Willkie's sweeping condemnation. Republican internationalists might well find in it a good deal of encouragement.
[87] They were printed in the issues dated September 16 and October 7, but actually appeared more than a week before those dates. They were reprinted in *An American Program,* from which the following passages are quoted.
[88] Louisville *Courier-Journal,* October 17, 1944, p. 8.
[89] Lem Jones to the writer.
[90] *The Aspirin Age,* p. 467.
[91] Roscoe Drummond to the writer.
[92] Correspondence.
[93] Telegram to Mrs. John A. Warner. (Correspondence.)
[94] *Times,* October 7, p. 15.
[95] Ibid., October 9, p. 15.
[96] Ibid.
[97] Ibid.
[98] Ibid.
[99] Ibid., October 11, p. 1.
[100] Louisville *Courier-Journal,* October 9, p. 8.
[101] Ibid.
[102] *Times,* October 10, p. 16.

[103] *Christian Science Monitor*, October 9. In *The Aspirin Age* (p. 467) Drummond prints a letter which he received from Willkie on Monday, October 2, confirming the latter's oral statement that he had not decided.

[104] *Times*, October 22, p. 1.

[105] Lem Jones to the writer.

[106] Letter dated June 9, 1944. (Correspondence.)

[107] *Times*, October 22, 1944, p. 40.

[108] "A total of 67,812 copies of the book were sold, almost all immediately on its appearance . . ." (Barnes, p. 384).

[109] A detailed and convincing analysis of this topic is given by Johnson in his final chapter: "Wendell Willkie and the New Republicanism."

[110] *Times*, September 2, 1944, p. 13.

Index

Note. References following Willkie's own name have been limited to events or facts which could not be conveniently listed under other headings.

INDEX